INTRODUCTORY
MATHEMATICAL ECONOMICS

INTRODUCTORY

MATHEMATICAL ECONOMICS

■ ■ ■

Second Edition

D. Wade Hands

University of Puget Sound

New York   Oxford

OXFORD UNIVERSITY PRESS

2004

Oxford University Press

Oxford   New York
Auckland   Bangkok   Buenos Aires   Cape Town   Chennai
Dar es Salaam   Delhi   Hong Kong   Istanbul   Karachi   Kolkata
Kuala Lumpur   Madrid   Melbourne   Mexico City   Mumbai
Nairobi   São Paulo   Shanghai   Taipei   Tokyo   Toronto

Library of Congress Cataloging-in-Publication Data

Hands, D. Wade.
    Introductory mathematical economics / D. Wade Hands.—2nd ed.
      p. cm.
    Includes bibliographical references and index.
    ISBN 0-19-513378-1
      1. Economics, Mathematical. I. Title.

HB135 .H358 2003
330'.01'51—dc21   2002192675

Printing number: 9 8 7 6 5 4 3 2 1

Printed in the United States of America
on acid-free paper

To Faye

CONTENTS

■ ■ ■

PREFACE

■ ■ ■

The first edition of *Introductory Mathematical Economics* was published in 1991. It was designed to serve as the primary textbook for undergraduate courses in mathematical economics. In preparing the second edition I have made numerous minor improvements—adding (and subtracting) a few problems, rewriting parts that seemed to be unclear, changing the mathematical review of the first edition to a new Chapter 0, and generally improving the readability (and thus teachability) of the text—but I did not make substantive changes in the subject matter. For the most part, the topics covered in this edition are the topics covered in the first edition. In particular, I have retained almost all of the economic applications from the first edition, and while many of these applications originally came from relatively recent economic theory, they seem less "recent" today; on the other hand, these applications have repeatedly proven to be effective for teaching introductory mathematical economics and may in fact be *more* appropriate for today's undergraduates than they were for those of a decade ago.

The book assumes that the student is familiar with calculus through partial differentiation and with basic matrix operations. In terms of the standard mathematical coursework in U.S. universities, this usually translates into one year of calculus and some exposure to linear algebra and matrix theory. Although these mathematical prerequisites are highly recommended, over the years many students have successfully completed my mathematical economics course armed with only one semester of (even business) calculus. For convenience, all of the prerequisite mathematics is summarized in Chapter 0. This initial chapter serves both as a precourse mathematics refresher and as a handy reference if needed later in the text. Regarding economics prerequisites, it is preferable that students have taken intermediate-level courses in both micro- and macroeconomics, although most of the economic material is accessible to a well-prepared introductory student.

The text's pedagogical approach—and in this respect it differs from other available texts, as it did when it was originally published—is that a first course in mathematical economics should be an *economics* course. The student should learn to *do* economics by actually applying the mathematical tools to problems in economic theory; the mathematics should not be disconnected from its economic applications. In the process of doing such applications, the student will also learn a good deal of mathematics and acquire a certain amount of mathematical sophistication. The student will learn by repeated application how mathematics and economics interanimate each other, how particular mathematical tools have developed to deal with problems of the types that frequently occur in economics, and how economic questions can be formulated to take advantage of existing mathematical tools. To this end I have not offered any mathematical results without an economic application, and all end-of-chapter problems are economics problems. These end-of-chapter problems should be considered to be an integral part of the text; many are quite detailed and require a substantial amount of economic interpretation in addition to the mathematical analysis. Of course, there are a few end-of-chapter problems that require only that a numerical answer be computed for a problem that is already set up in the proper form. In a world of quick and easy mathematical software, however, such computational problems should not be—and are not—the main emphasis. For the majority of the problems, the emphasis is not computation, but rather mathematical economics: conceptualization, interpretation, and proof.

Many, many people have contributed to this book in many, many ways; I am indebted to them all. First my teachers, in particular Robert Becker of Indiana University, who first inspired my interest in mathematical economics. Though our research interests have grown apart over the years, I remain forever indebted to Bob Becker, both as a teacher and as a model of professional integrity. Second, my students, who cheerfully endured draft after draft of this book: first as chapters, then as a completed manuscript, and finally as the first edition. They have served as motivators, proofreaders, and problem testers; I am indebted to each of them. Although it may be unfair to the rest, I would particularly like to mention Wayne Hickenbottom, who endured the manuscript not only as a student when it was only one chapter, but then again years later as a colleague when it was in its final stages. Third, I am indebted to all of the people I have worked with at Oxford University Press—particularly Kenneth MacLeod, who originally signed me, and Stephen McGroarty, my current editor. Finally, I gratefully acknowledge the contributions of the following academic reviewers of the manuscript. Their careful and conscientious work has made the text far better than it would have been without them: Richard Anderson, Texas A&M University; Ian Bain, University of Wisconsin—Milwaukee; Maxim Engers, University of Virginia; Luis Fernandez, Oberlin College; Roy Gardner, Indiana University; Jim Grant, Lewis & Clark College; Terry Heaps, Simon Frazer University; Michael B. Ormiston, Arizona State University; Sunil Sharma, University of California—Los Angeles; and Steven R. Williams, University of Illinois—Urbana-Champaign for the first edition, and John Baxley, Wake Forest University; Hsueh-Ling Huynh, Boston University; Paul Kadjo, Pennsylvania State University; and John C. Kane, SUNY—Oswego, for the second edition.

D. W. H.

MATHEMATICAL NOTATION

■ ■ ■

Mathematical Symbols

$\exists$	there exists
$\forall$	for all
lim	limit
ln	natural logarithm
max	maximum (or maximize)
min	minimum (or minimize)
∞	infinity
$\Re$	set of real numbers
$\Re_+$	set of nonnegative real numbers
$\Re_{++}$	set of positive real numbers
$\Re^n$	n-dimensional real space
$\Re^n_+$	nonnegative orthant of $\Re^n$
$\Re^n_{++}$	positive orthant of $\Re^n$
$[a, b]$	interval between a and b with both a and b included
$[a, b)$	interval between a and b with a included (b excluded)
$(a, b]$	interval between a and b with b included (a excluded)
(a, b)	interval between a and b with both a and b excluded
$x \in A$	x is contained in A (x is an element of the set A)
$x \notin A$	x is not contained in A (x is not an element of the set A)
$x \geq y$	x is greater than or equal to y when $x \in \Re$ and $y \in \Re$ $x_i \geq y_i \; \forall i = 1, 2, \ldots, n$ when $x \in \Re^n$ and $y \in \Re^n$
$x > y$	x is greater than y when $x \in \Re$ and $y \in \Re$ $x_i > y_i \; \forall i = 1, 2, \ldots, n$ when $x \in \Re^n$ and $y \in \Re^n$
$x \approx y$	x is approximately equal to y

$\emptyset$	the empty set
$A \times B$	Cartesian product of sets A and B
$A \cap B$	intersection of the sets A and B
$A \cup B$	union of the sets A and B
$A \subset B$	the set A is a subset of the set B (A is contained in B)
$A \equiv B$	A is identically equal to B (equal by definition)
$\displaystyle\sum_i$	summation over i $\left(\text{i.e., } \displaystyle\sum_{i=1}^{n} x_i = x_1 + x_2 + \cdots + x_n\right)$
$\displaystyle\prod_i$	multiplication over i $\left(\text{i.e., } \displaystyle\prod_{i=1}^{n} x_i = x_1 x_2 x_3 \cdots x_n\right)$
$a \Rightarrow b$	a implies b
	b if a (a is sufficient for b)
	a only if b (b is necessary for a)
$a \Leftrightarrow b$	a iff (if and only if) b
	a is necessary and sufficient for b
$|a|$	absolute value of $a \in \Re$
x^T	transpose of vector x
A^T	transpose of matrix A
$|A|$	determinant of square matrix A
$A \geq 0$	matrix A with each element $a_{ij} \geq 0$
$A > 0$	matrix A with each element $a_{ij} > 0$
adj A	adjoint of square matrix A
I	identity matrix
Δx	change in x
$f: A \rightarrow B$	function f from domain A to range B
$f(x)$	value of function f at x
$f'(x)$	derivative of function $f: \Re \rightarrow \Re$ at $x \in \Re$
$df(x)/dx$	same as $f'(x)$
$f''(x)$	second derivative of function $f: \Re \rightarrow \Re$ at $x \in \Re$
$d^2 f(x)/dx^2$	same as $f''(x)$
$\dot{x}(t)$	derivative of x with respect to time t $(dx(t)/dt)$
$\partial f(x)/\partial x_i$	partial derivative of $f: \Re^n \rightarrow \Re$ with respect to x_i at $x \in \Re^n$
$\nabla f(x)$	gradient vector of $f: \Re^n \rightarrow \Re$ at $x \in \Re^n$
$Jf(x)$	Jacobian matrix of $f: \Re^n \rightarrow \Re^n$ at $x \in \Re^n$
$Hf(x)$	Hessian matrix of $f: \Re^n \rightarrow \Re$ at $x \in \Re^n$
$\displaystyle\int$	integral

The Greek Alphabet

A	α	alpha
B	β	beta
Γ	γ	gamma
Δ	δ	delta
E	ε	epsilon
Z	ζ	zeta
H	η	eta
Θ	θ	theta
I	ι	iota
K	κ	kappa
Λ	λ	lambda
M	μ	mu
N	ν	nu
Ξ	ξ	xi
O	o	omicron
Π	π	pi
P	ρ	rho
Σ	σ	sigma
T	τ	tau
Y	υ	upsilon
Φ	φ	phi
X	χ	chi
Ψ	ψ	psi
Ω	ω	omega

C H A P T E R

REVIEW OF MATHEMATICS

■ ■ ■

This introductory chapter reviews the mathematics needed as background for the material in the text. Much of the chapter will be familiar to you. A few concepts will be new, depending on exactly which mathematics courses you have taken and what was covered, but most of the concepts should be familiar. There is no reason to try to memorize all (or even most) of the mathematical concepts in this chapter; simply read through it before starting Chapter 1 and then refer to it whenever you need a refresher later in the text.

0.1 Some Basic Mathematical Concepts

Sets

A **set** is any collection of distinct objects; these objects are called the **points** or **elements** of the set. The set of students in a classroom and the set of integers greater than 1 but less than 10 are examples of sets. A set S that contains the three elements x, y, and z is written

$$S = \{x, y, z\}.$$

Many sets contain an infinite number of elements; examples include the set of all positive integers $I = \{1, 2, 3, 4, \ldots\}$ and the set of all real numbers $\Re$.

To indicate that a particular element x belongs to a set S (is an element of S), we write

$$x \in S.$$

If r does not belong to the set S (is not an element of S), we write

$$r \notin S.$$

Sets are often characterized in terms of the properties of their elements. For instance,

$$S = \{x \mid x \text{ has property } s\}$$

1

is read, "S is the set of all x such that x has property s." For example, $\Re_+$, the set of all nonnegative real numbers, could be written as

$$\Re_+ = \{x \mid x \in \Re \text{ and } x \geq 0\}$$

or as

$$\Re_+ = \{x \mid x \geq 0\}.$$

Set A is a **subset** of set B, or A is contained in B, iff every element of A is also in B. If A is a subset of B, the relationship is written

$$A \subset B.$$

For example, if $C = \{1, 2\}$ and $D = \{1, 2, 3, 4\}$, then $C \subset D$. The **null set** or the **empty set,** denoted by $\varnothing$, is a set that contains no elements. The empty set is a subset of any set.

The **union** of two sets A and B, denoted $A \cup B$, is the set of elements contained in A, in B, or in both A and B. Thus,

$$A \cup B = \{x \mid x \in A \text{ or } x \in B\}.$$

For example, if $C = \{1, 2\}$ and $E = \{2, 3, 4\}$, then $C \cup E = \{1, 2, 3, 4\}$.

The **intersection** of two sets A and B, denoted by $A \cap B$, is the set of elements contained in both A and B. Thus,

$$A \cap B = \{x \mid x \in A \text{ and } x \in B\}.$$

For example, if $C = \{1, 2\}$ and $E = \{2, 3, 4\}$, then $C \cap E = \{2\}$. The symbol $/$ is often used to indicate exclusion from a set. Thus when $E = \{2, 3, 4\}$, the set $E/\{3\}$, read "the set E excluding the set $\{3\}$," is equal to $\{2, 4\}$.

If two sets have no elements in common, they are called **disjoint sets;** thus A and B are disjoint iff $A \cap B = \varnothing$. Two sets A and B are **equal,** denoted $A = B$, iff they have exactly the same elements. Thus $A = B$ iff $A \subset B$ and $B \subset A$ (or $A \cap B = A \cup B$).

In general, the order of the elements in a set does not matter; for example, if $C = \{1, 2\}$ and $F = \{2, 1\}$, then $C = F$. In sets of certain types, though, the order does matter. The most common type of these so-called **ordered sets** is the **ordered pair;** (a, b) is an ordered pair iff $(a, b) = (a', b')$ implies that $a = a'$ and $b = b'$.

The **Cartesian product** of two sets, denoted $A \times B$, is the set of all ordered pairs (a, b), where the first element comes from set A and the second element comes from set B. Thus the Cartesian product $A \times B$ is given by

$$A \times B = \{(a, b) \mid a \in A \text{ and } b \in B\}.$$

The Cartesian product of set A with itself is written $A \times A = A^2$. Thus the set of all points in the Euclidean plane, Euclidean 2-space, is $\Re \times \Re = \Re^2$. Similarly, the set of all ordered triples of real numbers, Euclidean 3-space, is $\Re \times \Re^2 = \Re^3$, and the set of all ordered n-tuples of real numbers, Euclidean n-space is

$$\Re^n = \{x \mid x = (x_1, x_2, \ldots, x_n), \text{ where } x_i \in \Re \; \forall \; i = 1, 2, \ldots, n\}.$$

Functions and Related Topics

Functions

A **function** is a particular relationship between the elements of two sets; it assigns a unique element in the **range** set to each element in the **domain** set. The function $f: X \to Y$ with domain X and range Y assigns a unique $y \in Y$ (the **dependent variable**) to each $x \in X$ (the **independent variable**). If both X and Y are the set of real numbers, then the function $f: \Re \to \Re$ is a real-valued function of a single real variable, and if $X = \Re^n$ and $Y = \Re$, then $f: \Re^n \to \Re$ is a real-valued function of n real variables. Often the domain of a multivariate function is divided into a set of parameters that are constant for the purposes of the analysis and a set of independent variables that are allowed to vary during the analysis. Thus a function $f: \Re^n \times \Re^m \to \Re$, written as $y = f(x; \alpha)$ with $y \in \Re$, $x \in \Re^n$, and $\alpha \in \Re^m$, may be reduced to $f: \Re^n \to \Re$, written as $y = f(x; \alpha)$ when the m independent variables $\alpha \in \Re^m$ are treated as parameters.

Limits and Continuity

If $x \in \Re^n$ and $y \in \Re^n$, then the **Euclidean distance** between $x = (x_1, x_2, \ldots, x_n)$ and $y = (y_1, y_2, \ldots, y_n)$, denoted $d(x, y)$, is given by

$$d(x, y) = \left[\sum_{i=1}^{n} (x_i - y_i)^2 \right]^{1/2}.$$

Given this definition of distance, for any $\varepsilon > 0$, we can define an ε **neighborhood** of a particular $x_0 \in \Re^n$, denoted $N_\varepsilon(x_0)$, as all the points in $\Re^n$ less than $\varepsilon > 0$ from x_0 in distance. Thus an ε neighborhood of $x_0 \in \Re^n$ is given by $N_\varepsilon(x_0) = \{x \in \Re^n \mid d(x_0, x) < \varepsilon\}$.

The **limit** of a function $y = f(x)$ as the variable x approaches a particular value x_0, written as $\lim_{x \to x_0} f(x)$, is the value that y approaches as x gets closer to x_0. More formally, y_0 is the limit of $f(x)$ as x approaches x_0 iff for any $\varepsilon > 0$, however small, there exists a $\delta > 0$ such that $x \in N_\delta(x_0)/\{x_0\}$ implies that $f(x) \in N_\varepsilon(y_0)$.

The function $f: \Re^n \to \Re$ is **continuous** at $x_0 \in \Re^n$ iff $\lim_{x \to x_0} f(x) = f(x_0)$. A function is continuous iff it is continuous at every point in its domain.

Exponential and Logarithmic Functions

In general, an **exponential function** of a single real variable x is a function of the form $y = f(x) = a^x$, where $a > 0$ is the base of the exponent. A common exponential function is $y = e^x$, the exponential function with base e, where e is the irrational number

$$e = \lim_{m \to \infty} \left(1 + \frac{1}{m} \right)^m = 2.71828 \cdots.$$

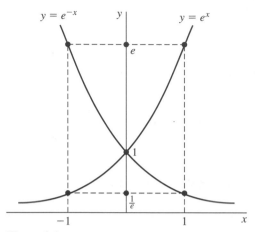

$y = e^{-x}$ y $y = e^x$

Figure 0.1

The functions $y = e^x$ and $y = e^{-x}$ are shown diagrammatically in Figure 0.1. The function $y = e^x$ also has a limit representation, given by

$$e^x = \lim_{n \to \infty} \left(1 + \frac{x}{n}\right)^n.$$

The irrational number e also forms the basis of the **natural logarithms.** The natural logarithm function $y = \ln x$ is defined as $e^y = x$ iff $y = \ln x$. The expression $y = \ln x$, read as "y is the natural log of x," is thus equivalent to the expression $e^y = x$, read as "the power to which you raise e in order to get x is y."

Probability Theory

The basic intuitive idea behind the notion of probability is the following. Suppose that there exists a finite set of possible cases or outcomes (the total number of cards in a deck, the number of sides on a die, etc.) and that a certain subset of these cases or outcomes has a particular property (being a spade, having three or fewer spots, etc.). Then the probability of this event θ, the chance of randomly selecting an outcome that has this particular property, is given by

$$\theta = \frac{\text{number of cases with the property}}{\text{total number of cases}}.$$

Thus the probability of a head appearing on a fair coin is $\frac{1}{2}$, the probability of a spade being drawn from a deck of cards is $\frac{1}{4}$, and so on.

If there are a total of n possible cases, $\theta_i = $ the probability of event i, and the probability of each event is independent, then the two most basic properties of probabilities are

$$\sum_{i=1}^{n} \theta_i = 1 \quad \text{and} \quad \theta_i \theta_j = \text{probability of both } i \text{ and } j.$$

Probabilities sum to 1, and the probabilities of the occurrence of two independent events is the product of the probabilities of their individual occurrences. For $x_i =$ the value (or payoff) of event i, two important definitions involving probabilities are

$$\text{Expected value } (EV) = \sum_{i=1}^{n} \theta_i x_i = \bar{x}$$

and

$$\text{Variance (var)} = \sum_{i=1}^{n} \theta_i (x_i - \bar{x})^2.$$

0.2 Calculus

Calculus of One Variable

The Derivative

If $f : \Re \rightarrow \Re$ is a function of one variable, then the **derivative** of the function, denoted df/dx or $f'(x)$, is defined as

$$f'(x) = \lim_{\Delta x \to 0} \frac{f(x + \Delta x) - f(x)}{\Delta x}.$$

If this limit exists at a particular $x_0 \in \Re$, then the function is **differentiable** at x_0 and $f'(x_0)$ is the derivative of the function evaluated at the point x_0. Geometrically the derivative is the slope of the tangent to the function at the point. A function is **continuously differentiable** on a certain domain if it is differentiable and if $f'(x)$ is continuous for all points in the domain.

Some Rules of Differentiation

$\dfrac{da}{dx} = 0$, where a is a constant

$\dfrac{d(ax^b)}{dx} = bax^{b-1}$, where a and b are constants $(b \neq 0)$

$\dfrac{d(\ln x)}{dx} = \dfrac{1}{x}$

$\dfrac{d(e^x)}{dx} = e^x$

$\dfrac{d\left(e^{f(x)}\right)}{dx} = e^{f(x)} f'(x)$

$\dfrac{d(a^x)}{dx} = a^x \ln a$, where a is a constant

$\dfrac{d[f(x) + g(x)]}{dx} = f'(x) + g'(x)$

$\dfrac{d[f(x)g(x)]}{dx} = f(x)g'(x) + g(x)f'(x)$ Product rule

$$\frac{d[f(x)/g(x)]}{dx} = \frac{g(x)f'(x) - f(x)g'(x)}{[g(x)]^2} \text{ with } g(x) \neq 0 \qquad \text{Quotient rule}$$

$$y = f(x) \text{ and } x = g(z) \text{ imply that } \frac{dy}{dz} = \frac{dy}{dx}\frac{dx}{dz} = f'(x)g'(z) \qquad \text{Chain rule}$$

Higher-Order Derivatives

The derivative of a function that is already a derivative is a **second derivative** (or a **second-order derivative**). If $y = f(x)$, then $f'(x)$ is the first derivative and $f''(x) = d[f'(x)]/dx$ is the second derivative, denoted either $f''(x)$ or $d^2 f(x)/dx^2$. Derivatives of a higher order (third, fourth, etc.) are computed in a similar manner.

Taylor Series

Let $f: \Re \to \Re$ be a one-variable function with continuous derivatives of all orders. The function $f(x)$ can always be written as the following Taylor polynomial expansion around any point $x_0 \in \Re$

$$f(x) = f(x_0) + \frac{f'(x_0)(x - x_0)}{1} + \frac{f''(x_0)(x - x_0)^2}{1 \cdot 2} + \frac{f'''(x_0)(x - x_0)^3}{1 \cdot 2 \cdot 3}$$

$$+ \cdots + \frac{f^n(x_0)(x - x_0)^n}{1 \cdot 2 \cdot 3 \cdots n} + R_n(x),$$

where $R_n(x)$ is the remainder of the series. The size of $R_n(x)$ will depend on the number of terms in the series n. This expression is sometimes called the **Taylor series with remainder.**

For certain functions, **analytic functions,** the remainder $R_n(x)$ approaches 0 as $n \to \infty$. If $f(x)$ is an analytic function, then it can be written as the following **Taylor series expansion** around x_0:

$$f(x) = f(x_0) + \frac{f'(x_0)(x - x_0)}{1} + \frac{f''(x_0)(x - x_0)^2}{1 \cdot 2} + \cdots.$$

Often the infinite power series of the Taylor series expansion is truncated at one of the early terms to form a **Taylor series approximation** of the function. For example, if the series is truncated after the second-derivative term, the result is a **second-order Taylor series approximation** of the function, given by

$$f(x) \cong f(x_0) + f'(x_0)(x - x_0) + \frac{f''(x_0)(x - x_0)^2}{2}.$$

Maxima and Minima

Throughout this section, function f is a one-variable function defined on a subset of the real numbers: that is, $f: D \to \Re$ with $D \subset \Re$. A point $x^* \in D$ is a **global maximum** of f if

$$f(x^*) \geq f(x) \qquad \text{for all } x \in D.$$

A point $x^* \in D$ is a **strict (or unique) global maximum** of f if

$$f(x^*) > f(x) \qquad \text{for all } x \in D, \, x \neq x^*.$$

A point $x^* \in D$ is a **local maximum** of f if it is a maximum for all x within some ε neighborhood of x^*, that is, if

$$f(x^*) \geq f(x) \qquad \text{for all } x \in N_\varepsilon(x^*).$$

A point $x^* \in D$ is a **strict (or unique) local maximum** of f if it is a strict maximum for all x within some ε neighborhood of x^*, $x \neq x^*$, that is, if

$$f(x^*) > f(x) \qquad \text{for all } x \in N_\varepsilon(x^*).$$

Global minima, strict global minima, local minima, and strict local minima are all defined by reversing the inequalities in the foregoing definitions.

If f is differentiable, the **first-order (necessary) condition** for x^* to be an interior optimum (maximum or minimum) is that x^* be a **critical point** of the function, that is, where $f'(x^*) = 0$. Note that this is only a necessary, not a sufficient, condition; it says that if x^* is a maximum or minimum (local or global), then $f'(x^*) = 0$.

Since this vanishing-derivative condition holds for a maximum, a minimum, or even an inflection point, an additional condition is required to distinguish between these three cases. From Figure 0.2 we see that if x^* is to be a strict maximum, then $f'(x^*) = 0$ and $f'(x)$ must be positive for all $x < x^*$, while $f'(x)$ must be negative for all $x > x^*$ (these properties must hold throughout the domain for a global maximum and within some ε neighborhood for a local one). These inequalities require the derivative $f'(x)$ to be decreasing as the function passes through x^*; locally this is guaranteed by a negative second derivative at x^*, that is, $f''(x) < 0$. This gives us the following result:

$$\text{If } f'(x^*) = 0 \qquad \text{and} \qquad f''(x^*) < 0,$$

$$\text{then } x^* \text{ is a strict local maximum of } f.$$

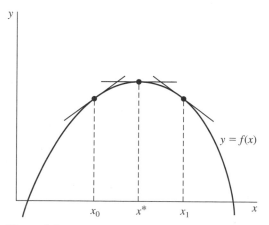

Figure 0.2

The condition $f'(x*) = 0$ is called a **first-order** (necessary) **condition,** while
the condition $f''(x) < 0$ is called a **second-order** (sufficient) **condition.** The
second-order condition is sufficient in the sense that when it is combined with
the first-order condition, the two jointly guarantee a maximum.

Similarly we have the following result for a minimization problem:

$$\text{If } f'(x*) = 0 \quad \text{and} \quad f''(x*) > 0,$$

then $x*$ is a strict local minimum of f.

Integration

The Indefinite Integral

If $F: \Re \to \Re$ is a differentiable function with $dF(x)/dx = F'(x) = f(x)$, then
$F(x)$ is the antiderivative, or integral, of $f(x)$:

$$\int f(x)\, dx = F(x) + c.$$

The function to be integrated, $f(x)$, is called the **integrand,** and c is the **constant
of integration.**

Some Rules for Integration

$$\int x^n\, dx = \frac{x^{n+1}}{n+1} + c, \qquad n \neq -1$$

$$\int \frac{dx}{x} = \int x^{-1} dx = \ln x + c \qquad x > 0$$

$$\int a^x\, dx = \frac{a^x}{\ln a} + c$$

$$\int e^x\, dx = e^x + c$$

$$\int [f(x) + g(x)]\, dx = \int f(x)\, dx + \int g(x)\, dx \qquad \qquad \text{Additivity}$$

$$\int kf(x)\, dx = k \int f(x)\, dx, \text{where } k \text{ is a constant}$$

$$\int f(x)g'(x)\, dx = f(x)g(x) - \int f'(x)g(x)\, dx \qquad \qquad \text{Integration by parts}$$

The Definite Integral

The **definite integral** of a continuous function of a single variable evaluated on
the interval $[a, b] \in \Re$ is equal to the area under the curve $f(x)$ between the values
a and b. Thus,

$$\int_a^b f(x)\, dx = A,$$

where A is the area shown in Figure 0.3.

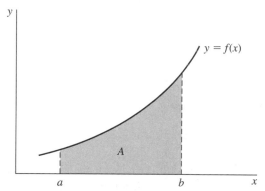

Figure 0.3

The First Fundamental Theorem of Calculus

If $f(x)$ is a continuous function of a single variable, then

$$\int_a^b f(x)\,dx = F(b) - F(a), \text{ where } F'(x) = f(x).$$

The definite integral of the derivative of a function over an interval is simply the difference in the values of the function at the ends of the interval.

The Second Fundamental Theorem of Calculus

If $f(x)$ is a continuous function on $\mathfrak{R}$ and

$$G(x) = \int_a^x f(t)\,dt,$$

then $G(x)$ is differentiable on $[a, b]$ and $G'(x) = f(x)$. *Note:* Some calculus texts reverse the labels on these two theorems.

Differential Equations

An equation in which the variables are derivatives is called a **differential equation.** If the differential equation is linear in its variables (the derivatives), then it is called a **linear differential equation;** if the nth derivative is the highest-order derivative in the equation, then it is called an ***n*-th-order differential equation.** Thus,

$$a_0 f + a_1 f'(x) + a_2 f''(x) + \cdots + a_n f^n(x) + a_{n+1} = 0$$

is the general form of an nth-order linear differential equation with constant coefficients. If the constant a_{n+1} is equal to zero, then the differential equation is **homogeneous.** For instance, if a, b, and c are constants, then $af + bf' + cf'' = 0$ is a second-order homogeneous linear differential equation.

A **general solution** to a differential equation is a function $y = f(x)$ that satisfies the equation. Often differential equations are restricted to satisfy particular initial conditions; in such a case the solution is a **particular solution.**

Multivariate Calculus

Partial Derivatives

If $f: \mathfrak{R}^n \to \mathfrak{R}$ is a real-valued function of n real variables

$$y = f(x_1, x_2, \ldots, x_n),$$

then the **partial derivative** with respect to variable x_i, denoted $\partial f/\partial x_i$ is given by

$$\frac{\partial f}{\partial x_i} = \lim_{\Delta x_i \to 0} \frac{f(x_1, x_2, \ldots, x_i + \Delta x_i, \ldots, x_n) - f(x_1, x_2, \ldots, x_n)}{\Delta x_i}.$$

Thus the partial derivative is the change in the function when variable x_i is changed and all other variables in the function are held constant. Geometrically the partial derivative is the slope of the tangent to the function parallel to the yx_i plane.

The same rules used in computing the derivatives of a one-variable function apply in computing partial derivatives: all the variables other than the one being differentiated with respect to are treated as constants. For example, if the function is

$$y = f(x_1, x_2) = 16x_1^2 + 10x_1x_2 + x_2^3,$$

then $\partial f/\partial x_1 = 32x_1 + 10x_2$ and $\partial f/\partial x_2 = 10x_1 + 3x_2$. Higher-order partial derivatives are computed similarly.

It is often useful to characterize the n partial derivatives of an n-variable function in vector notation. Such a vector of partial derivatives is called a **gradient** (or **gradient vector**) of the function, and it is denoted ∇f. Thus,

$$\nabla f = \left(\frac{\partial f}{\partial x_1}, \frac{\partial f}{\partial x_2}, \ldots, \frac{\partial f}{\partial x_n} \right)$$

is the gradient of the function $f: \mathfrak{R}^n \to \mathfrak{R}$. If the partial derivatives are to be evaluated at a particular point $x_0 \in \mathfrak{R}^n$, then we write

$$\nabla f(x_0) = \left(\frac{\partial f(x_0)}{\partial x_1}, \frac{\partial f(x_0)}{\partial x_2}, \ldots, \frac{\partial f(x_0)}{\partial x_n} \right).$$

First-order (necessary) conditions for the maximum or minimum of an n-variable function are perfectly analogous to the one-variable case: vanishing derivatives. If $x^* = (x_1^*, x_2^*, \ldots, x_n^*)$ is a maximum (local or global) of an n-variable differentiable function, then $\partial f(x^*)/\partial x_i = 0$ for all $i = 1, 2, \ldots, n$. Using the gradient notation just given, if $x^* \in \mathfrak{R}^n$ is a maximum of $f: \mathfrak{R}^n \to \mathfrak{R}$, then

$$\nabla f(x^*) = 0.$$

As in the one-variable case, this first-order condition applies to either a maximum or minimum.

The Total Differential

When $f(x)$ is a differentiable function of one variable, the *differential* or *total differential* is given by

$$dy = f'(x) \, dx.$$

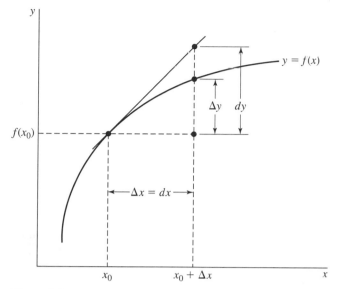

Figure 0.4

As depicted in Figure 0.4, this differential dy is the vertical change along the tangent to the function. The change in the independent variable $\Delta x = dx$ causes the value of the function to change by Δy, while dy is the estimate of this change along the tangent line. The smaller Δx is, the closer the approximation dy to Δy.

If f is a differentiable function of n variables, then the differential (or total differential) dy is

$$dy = \frac{\partial f}{\partial x_1} dx_1 + \frac{\partial f}{\partial x_2} dx_2 + \cdots + \frac{\partial f}{\partial x_n} dx_n = \sum_{i=1}^{n} \frac{\partial f}{\partial x_i} dx_i.$$

If gradient notation is used, then the total differential of an n-variable function is

$$dy = \nabla f(dx)^T,$$

where $dx = (dx_1, dx_2, \ldots, dx_n)$ and T indicates transpose (defined shortly).

0.3 Matrices and Related Topics

Matrices

Consider the following system of n linear equations in n unknowns $(x_1, x_2, \ldots, x_n)$:

$$a_{11}x_1 + a_{12}x_2 + \cdots + a_{1n}x_n = d_1$$
$$a_{21}x_1 + a_{22}x_2 + \cdots + a_{2n}x_n = d_2$$
$$\cdots\cdots\cdots\cdots\cdots\cdots\cdots\cdots\cdots\cdots\cdots$$
$$a_{n1}x_1 + a_{n2}x_2 + \cdots + a_{nn}x_n = d_n.$$

Notice that the system is square; the left side has n rows and n columns, the position of each variable is indexed by its coefficient: the coefficient of the variable in the ith row and jth column is a_{ij} (so a_{34} is the coefficient of the term in the third row and the fourth column).

The coefficients of the variables in the foregoing system can be written in the form of an $n \times n$ *matrix*—a rectangular, ordered array of elements that has n rows and n columns. The matrix that represents the coefficients of the variable in the foregoing system of equations is

$$
A = \begin{bmatrix}
a_{11} & a_{12} & \cdots & a_{1n} \\
a_{21} & a_{22} & \cdots & a_{2n} \\
\vdots & \vdots & & \vdots \\
a_{n1} & a_{n2} & \cdots & a_{nn}
\end{bmatrix}.
$$

Such a matrix, one with the same number of rows and columns, is called a **square matrix.** Often matrix A is written as $A = [a_{ij}]$, indicating that matrix A has a representative element a_{ij}. Matrices that are not square—for instance, a matrix having n rows and m columns (with $m \neq n$)—are termed $n \times m$ matrices. The convention is that the number of rows is cited first, then the number of columns.

One special class of matrices includes those that have only one row or one column; such matrices are called **vectors.** A matrix that is $n \times 1$ has n rows and 1 column and is called an n-dimensional **column vector,** while a matrix that is $1 \times n$ has 1 row and n columns and is called an n-dimensional **row vector.** In the following examples, x is a column vector and y is a row vector:

$$
x = \begin{bmatrix} x_1 \\ x_2 \\ \vdots \\ x_n \end{bmatrix} \qquad y = (y_1, y_2, \ldots, y_n).
$$

Vector operations are discussed in the next section as special cases of matrix operations.

Matrix Operations

Addition

Two matrices $A = [a_{ij}]$ and $B = [b_{ij}]$ can be added only if they have the same number of rows and columns. If A is $r_a \times c_a$ and B is $r_b \times c_b$, then the matrix sum $A + B$ exists only if $r_a = r_b$ and $c_a = c_b$. The sum is obtained by adding the matrices term by term. For instance, if both matrices are $n \times n$, then the matrix sum $A + B$ is given by

$$
\begin{bmatrix}
a_{11} & \cdots & a_{1n} \\
\vdots & & \vdots \\
a_{n1} & \cdots & a_{nn}
\end{bmatrix}
+
\begin{bmatrix}
b_{11} & \cdots & b_{1n} \\
\vdots & & \vdots \\
b_{n1} & \cdots & b_{nn}
\end{bmatrix}
=
\begin{bmatrix}
a_{11} + b_{11} & \cdots & a_{1n} + b_{1n} \\
\vdots & & \vdots \\
a_{n1} + b_{n1} & \cdots & a_{nn} + b_{nn}
\end{bmatrix},
$$

and the resulting sum is also an $n \times n$ matrix. The sum of two matrices does not depend on the order, and thus $A + B = B + A$.

Subtraction of two matrices A and B is also performed term by term. Thus when A and B are the $n \times n$ matrices just shown, the matrix difference $A - B$ is given by

$$
A - B = \begin{bmatrix} a_{11} - b_{11} & \cdots & a_{1n} - b_{1n} \\ \vdots & & \vdots \\ a_{n1} - b_{n1} & \cdots & a_{nn} - b_{nn} \end{bmatrix}.
$$

As in the case of addition, the matrices do not need to be square to be subtracted, but both must have the same number of rows and columns.

Scalar Multiplication

Multiplication of a matrix $A = [a_{ij}]$ by a scalar k is also executed term by term. Thus we have

$$
kA = \begin{bmatrix} ka_{11} & ka_{12} & \ldots & ka_{1n} \\ ka_{21} & ka_{22} & \ldots & ka_{2n} \\ \vdots & \vdots & & \vdots \\ ka_{n1} & ka_{n2} & \ldots & ka_{nn} \end{bmatrix} = Ak.
$$

Matrix Multiplication

Matrix multiplication is substantially more complex than either matrix addition or scalar multiplication. One reason is that matrices in general do not commute under multiplication; that is, AB need not be equal to BA.

I will begin by introducing some of the language of matrix multiplication. When the matrix product AB is formed, it is appropriate to say that matrix B was **premultiplied** by matrix A (or that A was **postmultiplied** by B); correspondingly, the product BA is formed by premultiplying matrix A by matrix B (or postmultiplying B by A). Two matrices can be multiplied only if they **conform,** and they conform only if the number of columns in the first matrix is the same as the number of rows in the second.

More formally, matrix A that is $n \times m$ and matrix B that is $p \times q$ can be multiplied to form the matrix product AB iff $m = p$. Alternatively, the matrix product BA can be formed iff $q = n$. In the former case, the product AB is a matrix that is $n \times q$, and in the latter case the product BA is a $p \times m$ matrix. The key point to remember is that multiplying an $n \times m$ matrix by a $p \times q$ matrix requires that $m = p$, and so the resulting product is $(n \times m)(p \times q) = n \times q$; it is as if the two inside dimensions (m and p) cancel when the product is formed. Likewise $(p \times q)(n \times m) = p \times m$ when $q = n$, as if the inside dimensions cancel.

Now consider the product $AB = C$ of two conformable matrices; matrix A is $n \times m$, and B is $m \times q$. Each (i, j)th term of the resulting $n \times q$ matrix C is given by

$$
C_{ij} = \sum_{k=1}^{m} a_{ik} b_{kj} \qquad \text{for } i = 1, 2, \ldots, n \qquad \text{and} \qquad j = 1, 2, \ldots, q.
$$

For example, let A be 2×2 and B be 2×3. Then the product $AB = C$ is given by

$$\begin{bmatrix} a_{11} & a_{12} \\ a_{21} & a_{22} \end{bmatrix} \begin{bmatrix} b_{11} & b_{12} & b_{13} \\ b_{21} & b_{22} & b_{23} \end{bmatrix} = \begin{bmatrix} c_{11} & c_{12} & c_{13} \\ c_{21} & c_{22} & c_{23} \end{bmatrix}$$

$$= \begin{bmatrix} a_{11}b_{11} + a_{12}b_{21} & a_{11}b_{12} + a_{12}b_{22} & a_{11}b_{13} + a_{12}b_{23} \\ a_{21}b_{11} + a_{22}b_{21} & a_{21}b_{12} + a_{22}b_{22} & a_{21}b_{13} + a_{22}b_{23} \end{bmatrix}.$$

To take another, perhaps simpler, example, let B be 2×3 and consider multiplication by the two-dimensional row vector $x = (x_1, x_2)$. First notice that xB is defined and the product is 1×3, while Bx is undefined. The product xB is given by

$$(x_1, x_2) \begin{bmatrix} b_{11} & b_{12} & b_{13} \\ b_{21} & b_{22} & b_{23} \end{bmatrix} = (x_1b_{11} + x_2b_{21}, x_1b_{12} + x_2b_{22}, x_1b_{13} + x_2b_{23}).$$

As yet another example, note that the system of linear equations in three unknowns, x_1, x_2, and x_3, given by

$$7x_1 + 5x_2 - x_3 = 5\alpha_1 + 2\alpha_2,$$
$$2x_1 - x_2 + 10x_3 = \alpha_1 - \alpha_2,$$
$$x_1 + 10x_2 + 4x_3 = 2\alpha_1 - \alpha_2/2$$

can be written as $Ax = B\alpha$, where

$$A = \begin{bmatrix} 7 & 5 & -1 \\ 2 & -1 & 10 \\ 1 & 10 & 4 \end{bmatrix}, \qquad x = \begin{bmatrix} x_1 \\ x_2 \\ x_3 \end{bmatrix},$$

$$B = \begin{bmatrix} 5 & 2 \\ 1 & -1 \\ 2 & -.5 \end{bmatrix}, \qquad \text{and} \qquad \alpha = \begin{bmatrix} \alpha_1 \\ \alpha_2 \end{bmatrix}.$$

The Transpose of a Matrix

An important matrix manipulation is transposition, which results in the **transpose** of a matrix (the transpose of A is usually written as A^T). The transpose A^T of a matrix A is formed by transforming the rows of A into the columns of A^T and the columns of A into the rows of A^T. Thus the transpose of A^T of the 3×2 matrix A is 2×3:

$$A = \begin{bmatrix} a_{11} & a_{12} \\ a_{21} & a_{22} \\ a_{31} & a_{32} \end{bmatrix} \qquad A^T = \begin{bmatrix} a_{11} & a_{21} & a_{31} \\ a_{12} & a_{22} & a_{32} \end{bmatrix}.$$

Similarly, a $1 \times n$ row vector $x = (x_1, x_2, \dots, x_n)$ can be transposed into the $n \times 1$ column vector x^T:

$$x^T = \begin{bmatrix} x_1 \\ x_2 \\ \vdots \\ x_n \end{bmatrix}.$$

In general, $A \neq A^T$, but certain special square matrices do have the property that $A = A^T$ and are called **symmetric matrices.**

Determinants

The Determinant of a Matrix

The **determinant** of a square matrix is a unique scalar value associated with the matrix. If matrix A is 2×2, then its determinant, denoted $|A|$, is

$$|A| = \begin{vmatrix} a_{11} & a_{12} \\ a_{21} & a_{22} \end{vmatrix} = a_{11}a_{22} - a_{21}a_{12}.$$

If A is 3×3 then the determinant is,

$$|A| = \begin{vmatrix} a_{11} & a_{12} & a_{13} \\ a_{21} & a_{22} & a_{23} \\ a_{31} & a_{32} & a_{33} \end{vmatrix} = a_{11} \begin{vmatrix} a_{22} & a_{23} \\ a_{32} & a_{33} \end{vmatrix} - a_{21} \begin{vmatrix} a_{12} & a_{13} \\ a_{32} & a_{33} \end{vmatrix} + a_{31} \begin{vmatrix} a_{12} & a_{13} \\ a_{22} & a_{23} \end{vmatrix}$$

$$= a_{11}(a_{22}a_{33} - a_{32}a_{23}) - a_{21}(a_{12}a_{33} - a_{32}a_{31}) + a_{31}(a_{12}a_{23} - a_{22}a_{13})$$

$$= a_{11}a_{22}a_{33} - a_{11}a_{32}a_{33} - a_{21}a_{12}a_{33} + a_{21}a_{32}a_{31} + a_{31}a_{12}a_{23} - a_{31}a_{22}a_{13}.$$

This 3×3 determinant could also be written as

$$|A| = \sum_{i=1}^{3} (-1)^{i+1} a_{i1} |A_{i1}|,$$

where $|A_{i1}|$ is the determinant formed by the matrix that remains after the ith row and the first column of A have been deleted. Frequently the expression is written as

$$|A| = \sum_{i=1}^{3} a_{i1} |C_{i1}|,$$

where $|C_{i1}| = (-1)^{i+1} |A_{i1}|$. The determinant $|C_{i1}|$ is called the **cofactor** of element a_{i1}, and this method of computing the determinant is called **expansion by cofactors.** The idea is to reduce the 3×3 problem to three separate 2×2 determinants. If the initial problem were 4×4, then by the same technique we would first reduce the problem to four 3×3 determinants and then reduce each of these to three 2×2 determinants, and so on. If the initial matrix is $n \times n$, the foregoing expression becomes

$$|A| = \sum_{i=1}^{n} a_{i1} |C_{i1}|.$$

The choice of the first column in these expansions was entirely arbitrary. The expansion-by-cofactor technique for computing determinants can be applied to any row or column. Thus in general we have the determinant of an $n \times n$ matrix A given by either

$$|A| = \sum_{i=1}^{n} a_{ij} |C_{ij}|, \qquad \text{for any column } j = 1, 2, \ldots, n$$

or

$$|A| = \sum_{j=1}^{n} a_{ij}|C_{ij}|, \qquad \text{for any row } i = 1, 2, \ldots, n.$$

Properties of Determinants

1. $|A| = |A^T|$. A matrix and its transpose have the same determinant.

2. $\begin{vmatrix} ka_{11} & ka_{12} \\ a_{21} & a_{22} \end{vmatrix} = \begin{vmatrix} ka_{11} & a_{12} \\ ka_{21} & a_{22} \end{vmatrix} = k\,|A| \qquad$ for any scalar k.

   Multiplication of any row (or column) of the determinant by a scalar multiplies the value of the determinant by that scalar.

3. $\begin{vmatrix} a_{11} & a_{12} \\ a_{21} + ka_{11} & a_{22} + ka_{12} \end{vmatrix} = \begin{vmatrix} a_{11} & a_{12} + ka_{11} \\ a_{21} & a_{22} + ka_{21} \end{vmatrix} = |A| \qquad$ for any scalar k.

   Adding (or subtracting) a scalar times any row (or column) of a matrix does not change the value of its determinant.

4. $\begin{vmatrix} a_{11} & a_{12} \\ ka_{11} & ka_{12} \end{vmatrix} = \begin{vmatrix} a_{11} & ka_{11} \\ a_{21} & ka_{21} \end{vmatrix} = 0 \qquad$ for any scalar k.

   If any rows (or columns) in a determinant are multiples of each other, then the determinant is zero.

5. A matrix with a zero determinant is called a **singular matrix,** and thus a matrix with $|A| \neq 0$ is a **nonsingular matrix.**

The Identity Matrix

One special matrix that plays an important role in matrix analysis is the **identity matrix,** denoted I. An identity matrix is a square matrix with ones on the main diagonal and zeros everywhere else. For instance, the 3×3 identity matrix I_3 is

$$I_3 = \begin{bmatrix} 1 & 0 & 0 \\ 0 & 1 & 0 \\ 0 & 0 & 1 \end{bmatrix}.$$

The identity matrix is important because it plays the same role in matrix multiplication that 1 plays in the multiplication of numbers: it returns that which it is multiplied by. Thus for an $n \times m$ matrix A, we have $I_n A = A$, where I_n is the $n \times n$ identity matrix and $AI_m = A$, where I_m is the $m \times m$ identity matrix. If A is square, then $IA = AI = A$.

The Inverse of a Matrix

For any matrix A the **inverse** of A, denoted A^{-1}, is a square matrix of the same dimension such that

$$AA^{-1} = A^{-1}A = I.$$

Such an inverse exists (uniquely) if the matrix A is nonsingular, that is, if $|A| \neq 0$.

The inverse of a nonsingular matrix can be computed by using the relationship $A^{-1} = \text{adj } A / |A|$, where adj A is the **adjoint** of the matrix A. The adjoint of a matrix is the transpose of its cofactor matrix, that is, the transpose of the matrix formed by replacing each element a_{ij} with its cofactor $|C_{ij}|$. In the $n \times n$ case, this means that the inverse A^{-1} is given by

$$A^{-1} = \begin{bmatrix} \dfrac{|C_{11}|}{|A|} & \dfrac{|C_{21}|}{|A|} & \cdots & \dfrac{|C_{n1}|}{|A|} \\[2ex] \dfrac{|C_{12}|}{|A|} & \dfrac{|C_{22}|}{|A|} & \cdots & \dfrac{|C_{n2}|}{|A|} \\[2ex] \vdots & \vdots & & \vdots \\[2ex] \dfrac{|C_{1n}|}{|A|} & \dfrac{|C_{2n}|}{|A|} & \cdots & \dfrac{|C_{nn}|}{|A|} \end{bmatrix}.$$

In the 2×2 case, this reduces to

$$A^{-1} = \begin{bmatrix} a_{11} & a_{12} \\ a_{21} & a_{22} \end{bmatrix}^{-1} = \begin{bmatrix} \dfrac{a_{22}}{|A|} & \dfrac{-a_{12}}{|A|} \\[2ex] \dfrac{-a_{21}}{|A|} & \dfrac{a_{11}}{|A|} \end{bmatrix}.$$

For example, when

$$A = \begin{bmatrix} 3 & 1 \\ 2 & 1 \end{bmatrix},$$

then the inverse A^{-1} is

$$A^{-1} = \begin{bmatrix} \dfrac{1}{|A|} & \dfrac{-1}{|A|} \\[2ex] \dfrac{-2}{|A|} & \dfrac{3}{|A|} \end{bmatrix} = \begin{bmatrix} 1 & -1 \\ -2 & 3 \end{bmatrix}.$$

ECONOMIC APPLICATIONS OF
ONE-VARIABLE CALCULUS

■ ■ ■

It is not a coincidence that marginal analysis in economics appeared after the development of differential calculus; the former is intimately related to the latter. The three authors who have traditionally been credited with initiating the marginal revolution in economics during the 1870s are Jevons, Menger, and Walras; of these three, Jevons and Walras explicitly used calculus in their presentation, and Walras went so far as to claim that calculus was essential to an understanding of economic theory. Many of the standard results in elementary economic theory (particularly microeconomics) are straightforward applications of theorems from differential calculus.

The exploitation of the intimate connection between marginal economic analysis and differential calculus begins in Chapters 1 and 2. Both chapters open by using calculus techniques to derive some standard results from elementary economic theory. The discussion in Chapter 1 is restricted to one-variable calculus, while Chapter 2 applies multivariate techniques. The point in both chapters is to derive familiar economic results by using familiar calculus techniques. While a few students may have seen some of these derivations in other economics courses, the material will be presented as if totally new. Neither the economics nor the mathematics will be new, but the particular combination of economics and calculus will be.

The first two chapters continue by introducing certain classes of functions that are extremely useful in economics. Chapter 1 introduces concave and convex functions and their economic applications, while Chapter 2 describes homogeneous functions. In both cases, the functions have particular mathematical properties that lend themselves to economic interpretation. Although these properties are purely mathematical, the functions themselves are often neglected in mathematics courses because interest in them stems primarily from their economic applications. The discussion of these functions is an example of the development of a particular mathematical topic being influenced at least in part by its usefulness in economics.

1.1 Applications of One-Variable Calculus from Introductory Economics

Demand and Marginal Revenue

Consider the following example of a linear demand curve

$$Q = -P + 5, \tag{1.1}$$

where P is the market price and Q is the quantity demanded. This demand curve is shown in the top half of Figure 1.1; the diagram in the bottom half shows the total revenue (TR) associated with each level of output along this demand curve. The total revenue is simply the price times the quantity $(TR = PQ)$. For instance, when the price is \$4, the quantity demanded is 1 unit and the total revenue is \$4. With a price of \$3, the quantity demanded is 2 units and the total revenue is \$6. The total revenue function can be found by simply substituting the demand relation (1.1) into the definition of total revenue. This substitution gives the total revenue function

$$TR = TR(Q) = PQ = (-Q + 5)Q = -Q^2 + 5Q. \tag{1.2}$$

This is the total revenue function depicted in the bottom of Figure 1.1.

In introductory economics courses, the marginal revenue (MR) is usually defined as the change in total revenue caused by one more unit of output. Given this (discrete change) definition, marginal revenue is given by

$$MR = TR(Q + 1) - TR(Q) = \frac{\Delta TR}{\Delta Q}\bigg|_{\Delta Q = 1}, \tag{1.3}$$

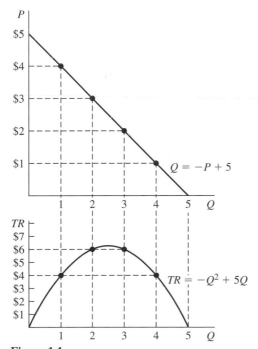

Figure 1.1

P	Q	TR	MR
5	0	0	
			) 4
4	1	4	
			) 2
3	2	6	
			) 0
2	3	6	
			)−2
1	4	4	
			)−4
0	5	0	

Figure 1.2

where the symbolism $|_{\Delta Q=1}$ on the right-hand side simply indicates that the changes in output should be taken 1 unit at a time. Based on (1.3), the marginal revenue associated with increasing output from 0 to 1 unit is $4, from 1 unit to 2 units is $2, and so on. Figure 1.2 provides a table of the marginal revenue associated with the demand curve (1.1) when marginal revenue is defined in terms of a 1-unit change in output.

Geometrically, the 1-more-unit definition makes marginal revenue the slope of the line connecting each successive pair of integer values along the total revenue curve. This relationship can be easily seen by examining Figure 1.3. Notice that in expanding output from 1 unit to 2 units the total revenue increases from $4 to $6. Thus, the marginal revenue is $2. Also notice that the slope of the line passing through points (1, 4) and (2, 6) on the total revenue curve is precisely 2. By construction, this same relationship will hold for any other two outputs Q and $Q + 1$. For example, the marginal revenue associated with increasing output from 4 units to 5 units is given by the slope of the line connecting (4, 4) and (5, 0), that is, $MR = -4$.

This 1-more-unit definition serves its purpose in introductory economics, but it is now time to consider a derivative definition. Instead of defining marginal revenue in terms of a discrete, 1-unit, change in output, let us define it for an infinitesimal change. In other words, let us define **marginal revenue** as the first derivative of the total revenue function:

$$MR = \frac{dTR(Q)}{dQ}. \tag{1.4}$$

The derivative in (1.4) is the proper definition of marginal revenue; the 1-more-unit version is used in introductory economics because most students lack the requisite background in differential calculus. This change from a 1-more-unit to a derivative definition is certainly not restricted to marginal revenue—it applies just as well to all the other marginal concepts employed in elementary economics (marginal cost, marginal product, marginal utility, etc.). One of the goals of

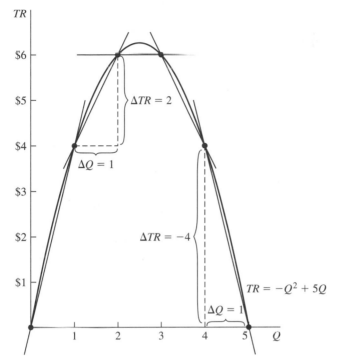

Figure 1.3

Chapters 1 and 2 is to systematically redefine all the marginal concepts from elementary economics in terms of derivatives.

For a geometric interpretation of the derivative definition of marginal revenue, examine Figure 1.4. This diagram is a blowup of the earlier total revenue function between the output levels of 1 and 2 units. When 1-unit increments are used, $\Delta TR / \Delta Q$ is given by the slope of line A. If we continue to decrease the size of the increment, then, in the limit, we have the slope of the tangent T. The slope of the tangent T is, of course, the derivative of the total revenue function evaluated at $Q = 1$. Thus, the marginal revenue at any particular level of output is merely the slope of the tangent to the total revenue function at that output.

For the specific demand function in (1.1) we have

$$MR = \frac{dTR}{dQ} = -2Q + 5, \tag{1.5}$$

since $TR = -Q^2 + 5Q$. For this particular demand function, the marginal revenue is equal to the price when $Q = 0$, but marginal revenue falls twice as fast as the demand curve, giving it a quantity intercept of $Q = 2.5$ and negative values thereafter. This MR function is shown in Figure 1.5.

Now that we have a derivative-based definition of marginal revenue, we can consider cases more general than the specific demand curve in (1.1). Let us consider a linear demand curve for which the specific numerical values of the parameters are

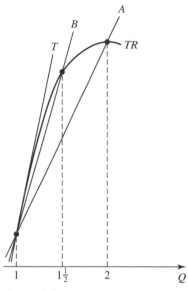

Figure 1.4

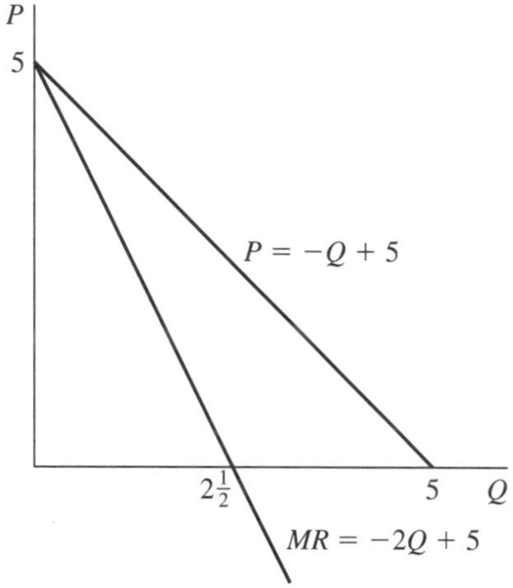

Figure 1.5

unknown. In other words, let

$$Q = -aP + b, \tag{1.6}$$

where a and b are unknown (but strictly positive) parameters. Equation (1.6) tells us that the demand curve is linear: it has a quantity intercept of b, a price intercept of b/a, and a slope of $-1/a$ (note it is dP/dQ, not dQ/dP, since price is on the vertical axis). Let us now determine the shape of the marginal revenue curve.

Since the marginal revenue is the derivative of the total revenue function, the first step is to find the total revenue function associated with (1.6). Remembering that we want TR as a function of Q and not of P, we have by substitution

$$TR = PQ = \left(-\frac{Q}{a} + \frac{b}{a}\right)Q = -\frac{Q^2}{a} + \frac{bQ}{a}. \tag{1.7}$$

We take the derivative of (1.7) to find the marginal revenue:

$$MR = \frac{dTR}{dQ} = -\frac{2Q}{a} + \frac{b}{a}. \tag{1.8}$$

The expression in (1.8) tells us that the particular shape of the MR function we found for the earlier case where $Q = -P + 5$ actually holds for all linear demand functions. When demand is linear, MR is also linear; MR has the same value as demand when $Q = 0$, but has a quantity intercept one-half that of the demand curve, since MR decreases twice as fast as demand. Thus, for any linear demand curve, the marginal revenue can be represented as in Figure 1.6, regardless of the specific numerical values of the parameters.

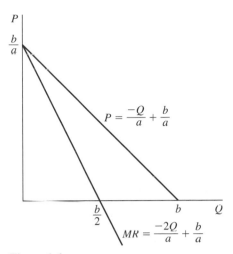

Figure 1.6

Both examples considered so far have been linear. Before we leave the topic of marginal revenue, let us consider a nonlinear example. Suppose the demand curve is given by

$$Q = -P^{1/2} + 10. \tag{1.9}$$

Notice that (1.9) is nonlinear, but otherwise it has the standard properties: it slopes downward, and it cuts both axes.[1] To find the *MR* function for this demand curve, we follow the same steps as for the linear case. Rewriting (1.9) so that quantity is the independent variable, we have

$$P = (-Q + 10)^2 = Q^2 - 20Q + 100. \tag{1.10}$$

Computing total revenue for this demand function, we have

$$TR = PQ = Q^3 - 20Q^2 + 100Q. \tag{1.11}$$

Taking the derivative of (1.11) to find marginal revenue gives

$$MR = \frac{dTR}{dQ} = 3Q^2 - 40Q + 100. \tag{1.12}$$

Compared with the *MR* functions computed earlier, the function in (1.12) has a rather peculiar shape. Besides being nonlinear, it crosses the horizontal axis twice, once at $Q = \frac{10}{3}$ and once at $Q = 10$. For all quantities less than $\frac{10}{3}$ or greater than 10, marginal revenue is positive; and for all quantities between $\frac{10}{3}$ and 10, it is negative with a minimum $Q = \frac{20}{3}$.

This example seems to suggest that the nice properties exhibited by the linear case, such as marginal revenue cutting the horizontal axis exactly halfway between the origin and the quantity intercept of the demand curve, are simply a result of the linearity and are not general properties of the marginal revenue function. They do not necessarily hold for nonlinear demand functions, even ones with other standard properties. Indeed, very little can be said regarding the shape of the marginal revenue function for the general nonlinear case. This may suggest why economics instructors and textbook authors always draw linear demand curves for models in which marginal revenue is important (such as monopoly).

One thing we know about marginal revenue, even in the nonlinear case, is that if the demand function crosses the vertical axis (if demand is defined for $Q = 0$), then P and MR are the same at that quantity. To derive this result, consider the total revenue function for the general case,

$$TR = PQ = P(Q)Q. \tag{1.13}$$

The demand function in (1.13), $P(Q)$, is written with quantity rather than price as the independent variable (sometimes called the **inverse demand function**). Let us assume this demand function is differentiable, but put no additional restrictions on its shape. Taking the derivative via the product rule, marginal revenue is given by

$$MR = \frac{dTR}{dQ} = P(Q) + Q\frac{dP}{dQ}.$$

Notice from this expression that $Q = 0$ implies that $MR = P(Q)$, the desired result. A second general feature of the marginal revenue function that can be derived from this expression is that marginal revenue is always less than price ($MR < P$) when the demand curve is downward sloping ($dP/dQ < 0$). Of course since demand almost always slopes downward, this means that the marginal revenue curve is normally below the demand curve at every level of output.

Elasticity

Let us now discuss elasticity in terms of derivatives, particularly, the price elasticity of demand. Recall that the price elasticity of demand is a measure of the relative price sensitivity of the demand curve: the sensitivity of the quantity demanded to a change in the (own) price of the good. It is often measured by using the elasticity coefficient ε', where

$$\varepsilon' = \frac{\%\Delta Q}{\%\Delta P}, \tag{1.14}$$

with P the price and Q the quantity demanded. Since most demand curves slope downward, the numerator and denominator of (1.14) will have opposite signs, making $\varepsilon' < 0$. Sometimes economists convert the elasticity coefficient to a positive value by defining it as $|\varepsilon'|$. With or without the absolute value restriction, the coefficient is used to classify demand (or the portion of the demand curve under consideration) as relatively price-sensitive (elastic) or not very price-sensitive (inelastic). The standard classification scheme is as follows:

Relatively elastic $\iff \varepsilon' < -1 \ (|\varepsilon'| > 1)$,

Relatively inelastic $\iff \varepsilon' > -1 \ (|\varepsilon'| < 1)$,

Unitary (unit) elastic $\iff \varepsilon' = -1 \ (|\varepsilon'| = 1)$.

Now for a particular demand curve, like the one given in (1.1), we can apply the definition of ε' from (1.14) to compute the elasticity for any particular price–quantity combination along the demand curve. Since the percentage change (%Δ) in any variable is computed by dividing the change in the variable by its initial value, the coefficient in (1.14) can be written as

$$\varepsilon' = \frac{\Delta Q / Q}{\Delta P / P}, \tag{1.15}$$

For the demand curve (1.1), if we start at the quantity–price combination (1, 4) and move down the demand curve to the quantity–price combination (2, 3), the elasticity of demand is

$$\varepsilon' = \frac{1/1}{-1/4} = -4,$$

since $\Delta Q = 1$, $\Delta P = -1$, $Q = 1$, and $P = 4$. Therefore, the demand curve (1.1) is relatively elastic in the region between $P = 4$ and $P = 3$. If, however, we start further down the demand curve at the quantity–price combination (3, 2) and move down to the combination (4, 1), the elasticity coefficient is $\varepsilon' = \left(\frac{1}{3}\right) / \left(\frac{-1}{2}\right) = \frac{-2}{3}$. This shows a region of relative inelasticity. The elasticity between any other two points along the demand curve could be computed in a similar way.

The first thing to notice about these computations is that even though the demand curve (1.1) is linear (and thus has constant slope), the elasticity is not constant as we move down the demand curve. The second thing to notice is that the definition given in (1.14) and (1.15) does not guarantee that the same numerical value will always be obtained between the same two points on the same demand curve; it depends on where one starts the computation. For instance, instead of going from point (1, 4) to point (2, 3), suppose that we start at (2, 3) and go to (1, 4). This latter computation gives us the coefficient $\varepsilon' = \left(\frac{-1}{2}\right) / \left(\frac{1}{3}\right) = \frac{-3}{2}$, while the former gave us $\varepsilon' = -4$. When the direction of the computation is changed, we obtain an entirely different numerical value for the coefficient. To avoid this problem, economists often compute elasticity by using the midpoint as the initial price–quantity combination rather than either end point.

Whether the midpoint is used as the initial price–quantity combination or whether the absolute value is taken, all the elasticity measures based on (1.14) are **arc** elasticity measures; the measure the elasticity over a finite interval (arc) of the demand curve. But what is the price elasticity of demand at a particular point on the demand curve? This question brings us to the derivative definition of the elasticity coefficient.

To derive a derivative-based elasticity coefficient, we begin with our arc elasticity measure and reduce the interval of change to a smaller and smaller limit. Rewriting the preceding definition in (1.15), we have

$$\varepsilon' = \frac{P}{Q} \frac{1}{(\Delta P / \Delta Q)}. \tag{1.16}$$

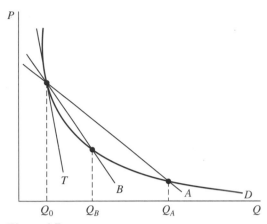

Figure 1.7

If the demand function is linear, then the $\Delta P/\Delta Q$ on the right-hand side of (1.16) is simply the slope of the line. On the other hand, if the demand function is nonlinear, then $\Delta P/\Delta Q$ represents the slope of the line passing through the two points on the demand curve along which ε' is being measured. For instance, if we measure ε' from Q_0 to Q_A along the nonlinear demand curve in Figure 1.7, then the $\Delta P/\Delta Q$ term in (1.16) is the slope of line A. If we reduce the size of ΔQ to the distance between Q_0 and Q_B, then the relevant $\Delta P/\Delta Q$ is the slope of line B. As $\Delta Q \to 0$, the relevant slope approaches the slope of the tangent T or the derivative of the demand function evaluated at point Q_0. This process of letting ΔQ approach 0 and taking the limit gives the **point elasticity coefficient** ε:

$$\varepsilon = \lim_{\Delta Q \to 0} \varepsilon' = \frac{P}{Q} \lim_{\Delta Q \to 0} \frac{1}{(\Delta P/\Delta Q)} = \frac{P}{Q} \frac{1}{(dP/dQ)} = \frac{P}{Q}\frac{dQ}{dP}, \qquad (1.17)$$

where the demand curve is $Q = D(P)$ with price as the independent variable.

Let us apply the definition of point elasticity of demand to the linear demand curve in (1.1). Since $Q = -P + 5$, we have $dQ/dP = -1$. Thus, for any (Q_0, P_0) combination that satisfies (1.1), the point elasticity of demand is given by $\varepsilon = -P_0/Q_0$, so for instance at $(4, 1)$, $\varepsilon = \frac{-1}{4}$ and at $(1, 4)$, $\varepsilon = -4$. In addition to being able to compute the point elasticity of demand for any particular quantity–price combination, we can write the point elasticity exclusively in terms of Q by simply substituting from (1.1). This substitution gives us the coefficient $\varepsilon(Q) = (Q - 5)/Q$.

Now let us examine the more general case of a linear demand curve. Recall that the demand curve (1.6) was linear, but the parameters in the function were the unknowns a and b. From (1.6) we have $dQ/dP = -a$. Thus, for any quantity–price combination that satisfies $Q = -aP + b$, we have $\varepsilon = -aP/Q$. Or, in terms of the quantity demanded alone,

$$\varepsilon(Q) = \frac{Q - b}{Q}. \qquad (1.18)$$

Since the parameters in this example are unknowns, the expression in (1.18) allows us to derive some very general information about the elasticity of a linear demand curve. First, we can substitute $\varepsilon = -1$ into (1.18) to determine the output when the demand is unit elastic. This substitution gives us $Q = b/2$. Thus, the linear demand curve is unit elastic at the output that is halfway between the origin and the quantity intercept of the demand curve. Recall that this is also the output where $MR = 0$; we will see shortly that this is not just a coincidence.

A similar analysis of (1.18) for the relatively elastic case ($\varepsilon < -1$) and the relatively inelastic case ($\varepsilon > -1$) gives us the following results:

$$\varepsilon < -1 \;\Leftrightarrow\; Q < \frac{b}{2},$$

$$\varepsilon > -1 \;\Leftrightarrow\; Q > \frac{b}{2}. \tag{1.19}$$

The linear demand curve $Q = -aP + b$ is elastic for all quantities between 0 and $b/2$, unit elastic only at $Q = b/2$, and elastic for all quantities between $b/2$ and b. Of course, this implies that the demand curve is elastic precisely when $MR > 0$ and inelastic when $MR < 0$. These results are shown in Figure 1.8.

In the preceding subsection, we argued that while the marginal revenue is relatively easy to compute for most nonlinear demand curves, it does not always have the same nice properties as the linear case. Is this also true for elasticity? In other words, what can be said about ε in the general case?

To answer this question, it is useful to determine the general relationship between marginal revenue and elasticity. We just determined the relationship for the linear case, but what about the general relationship? To this end, recall the general form of the demand function

$$P = P(Q). \tag{1.20}$$

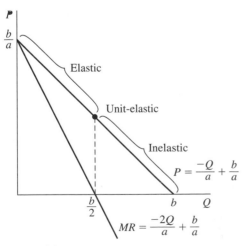

Figure 1.8

In (1.20) quantity rather than price is the independent variable, and we are assuming that the function is differentiable. We are not assuming anything particular about its shape, however. As shown previously for this general case we have

$$MR = \frac{dTR}{dQ} = P(Q) + Q\frac{dP}{dQ}. \tag{1.21}$$

Since $P = P(Q)$, we can write (1.21) as

$$MR = P\left(1 + \frac{Q}{P}\frac{dP}{dQ}\right). \tag{1.22}$$

Now, given that $\varepsilon = (P/Q)(dQ/dP)$, we have

$$MR = P\left(1 + \frac{1}{\varepsilon}\right) \tag{1.23}$$

for all points where dQ/dP is defined. Equation (1.23) gives the general relationship between marginal revenue and the elasticity coefficient ε. When $\varepsilon = -1$ then $MR = 0$; when $\varepsilon < -1$ then $MR > 0$; and when $\varepsilon > -1$ then $MR < 0$. Thus the relationship between MR and ε found in the linear case also holds for nonlinear demand functions. The bad part of this result is that since marginal revenue can have such a variety of shapes in the nonlinear case, almost nothing can be said about the elasticity in general. Some demand functions are relatively elastic, others are relatively inelastic, and still others, such as the linear case, have regions of both elasticity and inelasticity.

One interesting example that often appears in the literature is the demand function

$$Q = AP^a, \tag{1.24}$$

where $A > 0$ and $a < 0$. Computing the elasticity coefficient for this demand function, we have

$$\varepsilon = \frac{P}{Q}\frac{dQ}{dP} = \left(\frac{P}{Q}\right)(aAP^{a-1}).$$

Or, by (1.24),

$$\varepsilon = \left(\frac{P}{AP^a}\right)(aAP^{a-1}) = \left(\frac{1}{AP^{a-1}}\right)(aAP^{a-1}) = a.$$

This demand function has constant elasticity. If $a = -1$, then it is unit elastic; if $a = -3$, then it is relatively elastic; and so on. Exploration of the relationship between marginal revenue and the parameter a is left to the reader as an exercise.

The only type of elasticity we have discussed so far is the own-price elasticity of demand: the elasticity of demand with respect to the good's own price. Many other types of elasticity are used in economics. We briefly mention a few here. The concept of elasticity is actually so general that we can give a generic mathematical definition of elasticity for any functional relationship between two variables. If $y = f(x)$ is any differentiable function, the **elasticity of y with respect to x,** expressed $\varepsilon_{y,x}$, is defined as

$$\varepsilon_{y,x} = \frac{x}{y}\frac{dy}{dx}, \qquad (1.25)$$

The point elasticity just discussed is the own-price elasticity, so $\varepsilon = \varepsilon_{Q,P}$.

Common examples of elasticity measures used in consumer choice theory (other than the own-price elasticity) are the income elasticity and the cross-price elasticity of demand. Because the quantity demanded depends on the income M available, we can define the income elasticity of demand as

$$\varepsilon_{Q,M} = \frac{M}{Q}\frac{dQ}{dM}.$$

A positive income elasticity ($\varepsilon_{Q,M} > 0$) means that the good is normal, while a negative income elasticity ($\varepsilon_{Q,M} < 0$) indicates that it is inferior. Also, since goods are related in consumption by being either substitutes or complements, the quantity demanded of good 1, denoted Q_1, is often a function of the price of some other good, say good 2, denoted P_2. Under these conditions, we can discuss the cross-price elasticity of demand given by

$$\varepsilon_{Q_1,P_2} = \frac{P_2}{Q_1}\frac{dQ_1}{dP_2}.$$

In this case $\varepsilon_{Q_1,P_2} > 0$ means that the two goods are substitutes, while $\varepsilon_{Q_1,P_2} < 0$ indicates that they are complements.

There are also various elasticity measures that originate outside consumer choice theory. In production theory, economists often discuss the elasticity of supply or the elasticity of demand for a factor of production (input) such as labor. These definitions and the definitions of elasticities of all the other types used in economics follow naturally from the generic mathematical definition in (1.25).

Cost Functions

A firm's total cost function TC relates its total cost of production to various levels of output (y or Q). This cost function is normally divided into variable costs VC, which depend on (are a function of) the level of output, and fixed costs FC, which are independent of the level of output. According to the standard definition of short-run and long-run production, short-run costs involve both fixed and variable components, while all costs are variable in the long run. Given these definitions, the general form of the short-run total cost function is

$$TC(y) = VC(y) + FC, \qquad (1.26)$$

where y is the firm's output level. For the rest of this chapter, we simply start with cost functions given by an expression like (1.26): either (1.26) exactly, for the general case, or specific examples, where VC and FC are given explicitly. In later chapters, however, cost functions will be derived from the firm's underlying technology (production function), factor prices, and optimizing behavior.

Let us consider a specific example of a short-run total cost function. Suppose that variable costs are given by $VC(y) = 4y^2$ and that fixed costs are given by $FC = 100$. Under these conditions the total cost function is

$$TC(y) = 4y^2 + 100. \qquad (1.27)$$

This function tells us that the total cost of producing $y = 1$ is $TC(1) = \$104$, the total cost of producing $y = 5$ is $TC(5) = \$200$, and so on.

As the reader will realize from other economics courses, total costs are not the only cost concepts of interest to economists; average and marginal costs are equally important. Let us examine average cost first. In the short run, there are three average cost functions: average total cost (ATC), average variable cost (AVC), and average fixed cost (AFC). These functions are defined as follows:

$$ATC = \frac{TC(y)}{y}, \qquad AVC = \frac{VC(y)}{y}, \qquad \text{and} \qquad AFC = \frac{FC}{y}.$$

Notice that $ATC = AVC + AFC$, since $TC = VC + FC$. Intuitively, we see that average cost is simply the cost per unit of output: ATC is the total cost per unit of y, AVC is the variable cost per unit of y, and so on. For the specific numerical example in (1.27), these average functions become

$$ATC = 4y + \frac{100}{y}, \qquad AVC = 4y, \qquad \text{and} \qquad AFC = \frac{100}{y}. \qquad (1.28)$$

Now let us consider the marginal cost (MC). In introductory economics marginal cost is usually defined as the additional cost associated with one more unit of output, but we will move directly to a derivative definition. If we let the change in output go to the limit ($\Delta y \to 0$) the **marginal cost** becomes the first derivative of the total cost function:

$$MC = \frac{dTC(y)}{dy}. \qquad (1.29)$$

Since $TC(y) = VC(y) + FC$ and $dFC/dy = 0$, we can also write (1.29) as

$$MC = \frac{dVC(y)}{dy}. \qquad (1.30)$$

Applying this derivative definition of marginal cost to the specific numerical example in (1.27), we have

$$MC = 8y. \qquad (1.31)$$

Notice from (1.28) and (1.31) that the AVC and MC for this particular numerical example do not have the standard U shape from introductory textbooks. In fact, for this particular example AVC and MC are linear. A U shape would result if the marginal cost function were quadratic. Since marginal cost is the derivative of the total cost function, a quadratic marginal cost would result from a cubic total cost function. Thus a general form of the total cost function that yields a U-shaped marginal cost curve is

$$TC(y) = ay^3 + by^2 + cy + d, \tag{1.32}$$

where the parameters a, b, c, and d are suitably restricted to make economic sense. Examples of such cost functions are given later in this chapter as well as in the problems at the end.

Even though the relationship between the form of the cost function and its economic properties is significant, some important results in cost theory have nothing to do with this relationship. Because of the way in which average cost and marginal cost are defined, there are several purely mathematical relations between them. We close this brief introduction to cost theory by examining one of these mathematical relations.

Let us look at the relationship between average total cost and marginal cost. Since $ATC = TC/y$, the quotient rule gives us

$$\frac{dATC}{dy} = \frac{y\,(dTC/dy) - TC}{y^2}. \tag{1.33}$$

Or rewriting (1.33) in a more convenient way,

$$\frac{dATC}{dy} = \frac{dTC/dy - TC/y}{y} = \frac{MC - ATC}{y}. \tag{1.34}$$

From (1.34) we have the following relations between ATC and MC (for $y > 0$):

$$MC > ATC \iff \frac{dATC}{dy} > 0,$$

$$MC < ATC \iff \frac{dATC}{dy} < 0, \tag{1.35}$$

$$MC = ATC \iff \frac{dATC}{dy} = 0.$$

The relations in (1.35) are extremely useful. They tell us that when the average total cost is rising ($dATC/dy > 0$), then the marginal cost must be above the average total cost ($MC > ATC$); when the average total cost is falling ($dATC/dy < 0$), then the marginal cost must be below it ($MC < ATC$); and finally, when average total cost is at a critical point ($dAFC/dy = 0$), then $MC = ATC$. These relations hold purely because of the definitions of marginal and average total cost; they are independent of the economic properties of these cost functions. Although they are purely mathematical properties, they can be used to transfer economic restrictions from one cost function to another cost function. For instance, when ATC has the textbook U shape, then (1.35) tells that MC will slope upward as it cuts through the minimum point on the ATC. It is also important to note that because of the relation between total and variable cost, an identical relationship exists between MC and AVC. Confirmation of this is left to the reader.

Income–Expenditure (Keynesian) Multipliers

Thus far all our examples have come from microeconomics. We now discuss an example of one-variable calculus applied to a topic from elementary macroeconomics. The topic is the expenditure **multiplier** in a simple income–expenditure (Keynesian) macroeconomic model. Even though the model is linear—thus making the derivative (slope of the tangent) the same as the slope of the relevant line—this is a useful case to consider for a number of reasons. First, the simple income–expenditure model is often used as one of the building blocks for more complex macro models that involve various types of nonlinearity. Second, the multiplier is a topic that many introductory students memorize rather than really understand, and the derivative presentation often helps with intuition. Finally, discussing the multiplier allows us to introduce one of the two main types of comparative statics result that will be examined in detail in later chapters. This comparative statics technique will not be officially introduced (or formally defined) until Chapter 3, but the idea is sufficiently important that the sooner it can be introduced the better.

Consider the (very) simple income–expenditure macromodel

$$
\begin{aligned}
C(Y) &= mY_d + C_0, \\
Y_d &= Y - T, \\
T &= T_0, \\
I &= I_0, \\
G &= G_0,
\end{aligned}
\tag{1.36}
$$

where C = consumption, Y = national income, Y_d = disposable income, T = taxes, I = investment spending, G = government spending, and m = marginal propensity to consume, with $0 < m < 1$. A zero subscript on any variable indicates that it is **autonomous:** it is a parameter determined outside the model and in particular does not depend on Y.

The economy's aggregate **expenditure** (AE) is given by $AE = C + I + G$. The equilibrium level of income Y^* is the level of income at which aggregate expenditure is equal to national income. Verbally, we say that the equilibrium level of income is a level of income Y^* such that the amount of aggregate expenditure generated by that level of income, $AE(Y^*)$, is exactly equal to the level of income itself. Diagrammatically, the equilibrium is shown by Y^* in Figure 1.9 (where the AE curve crosses the 45° line), and algebraically it is the solution to the linear equation

$$
Y^* = C(Y^*) + I + G.
$$

Substituting from (1.36), this equilibrium condition becomes

$$
Y^* = m(Y^* - T_0) + C_0 + I_0 + G_0.
\tag{1.37}
$$

If we use $A = C_0 + I_0 + G_0$ to represent the sum of autonomous expenditures, we have the following simple expression for the equilibrium level of income in this model:

$$
Y^* = \frac{-mT_0}{1 - m} + \frac{A}{1 - m}.
\tag{1.38}
$$

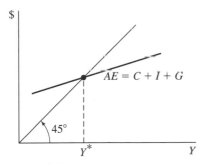

Figure 1.9

The **multiplier**—more accurately, the autonomous expenditure multiplier—answers the question of what happens to the equilibrium level of income Y^* when there is a change in autonomous expenditure A. That is, what is $\Delta Y^*/\Delta A$? Since the functions involved are linear, $dY^*/dA = \Delta Y^*/\Delta A$, and the multiplier relation can be obtained by simply differentiating the equilibrium condition in (1.38) with respect to A. Performing this differentiation we have

$$\frac{dY^*}{dA} = \frac{1}{1-m}. \tag{1.39}$$

Rewriting (1.39) in terms of finite (Δ) changes, we have the multiplier formula familiar from introductory macroeconomics:

$$\frac{\Delta Y^*}{\Delta A} = \frac{1}{1-m}. \tag{1.40}$$

From (1.40) we see that if $\Delta A = 500$ and $m = 0.75$, then $\Delta Y^* = 2000$, and so on. This is just the first of many cases we will examine in which the impact of a parameter change on an equilibrium value can be computed simply by taking the derivative of the equilibrium expression with respect to the relevant parameter. The equilibrium expression (1.38) can also be used to derive the autonomous tax multiplier ($\Delta Y^*/\Delta T_0$), but that is left as an exercise for the reader.

1.2 Optimization Examples from Introductory Economics

Profit-Maximizing Output: Perfect Competition

Consider a perfectly competitive firm that sells its output y at market price $p > 0$ and has the differentiable total cost function $TC(y)$. Since the firm is perfectly competitive, it has no control over the market price: so p is a parameter for the firm. The firm can sell all the output it desires at p, but it cannot change p. Under these circumstances, all the firm must decide on the right amount of output, that is, the profit-maximizing output. The profit function (π) for a perfectly competitive firm with price p and total cost $TC(y)$ is given by

$$\pi(y) = py - TC(y). \tag{1.41}$$

Equation (1.41) may define either short-run or long-run profit depending on whether $TC(y)$ is a short-run or a long-run cost function. We consider only the short-run case in this section.

Since the problem facing the perfectly competitive firm is constrained to one choice variable, y, it can be analyzed by using the standard calculus technique for the maximization of a one-variable differentiable function (reviewed in Chapter 0).

A bit more formally, the competitive firm's problem is

$$\text{Max}_{y} \ \pi(y), \tag{1.42}$$

where $\pi(y)$ is defined by (1.41). The first-order (necessary) condition for $y^* > 0$ to solve (1.42) is that y^* be a critical point of the profit function; that is, we must have[2]

$$\pi'(y^*) = p - \frac{dTC(y^*)}{dy} = 0. \tag{1.43}$$

Since we know from the earlier discussion that $dTC/dy = MC$, the first-order condition in (1.43) can be rewritten in a more familiar form as

$$p - MC(y^*) = 0 \quad \text{or} \quad p = MC(y^*). \tag{1.44}$$

Although the $p = MC$ condition for profit maximization by a perfectly competitive firm will be familiar to most readers from introductory microeconomics, we need to be very precise about what it does and does not say. It definitely does not say, as is often implied in introductory classes, that setting $p = MC$ will yield a profit-maximizing output for the perfectly competitive firm. What the condition does say is that **if** profit is being maximized at some y^*, then it must be the case that $p = MC(y^*)$. Condition (1.44) is only a first-order (necessary) condition, not a second-order condition. Remember that the second-order condition is a condition that, when combined with the first-order condition, guarantees that the point is a local optimum. The second-order condition for the problem (1.42) is

$$\pi''(y^*) < 0, \tag{1.45}$$

where $\pi''(y^*)$ is the second derivative of the profit function evaluated at the y^* that satisfies the first-order condition in (1.43) or (1.44). Taking the second derivative in (1.45) for the perfectly competitive firm, we have

$$-\frac{d^2TC(y^*)}{dy^2} < 0. \tag{1.46}$$

Since $d^2TC/dy^2 = dMC/dy$, the second-order condition in (1.46) can be rewritten more simply as

$$\frac{dMC(y^*)}{dy} > 0. \tag{1.47}$$

In summary, then, if $p = MC$ and MC slopes upward at a particular y^* [if both (1.44) and (1.47) hold at y^*], then y^* solves (1.42) and is the profit-maximizing output for the perfectly competitive firm. With these general results in mind, let us now examine a specific numerical example.

Suppose that the price of the firm's output is $21 ($p = 21$) and that the short-run total cost function is given by

$$TC(y) = \frac{y^3}{12} - 2.5y^2 + 30y + 100. \tag{1.48}$$

What is the profit-maximizing output $y*$ for this perfectly competitive firm?

We solve this problem in two ways. First, we solve it by using the MC function; this entails the first- and second-order conditions (1.44) and (1.47). Second, we solve the problem by using the profit function directly; this entails the first- and second-order conditions (1.43) and (1.45). These two approaches are of course mathematically equivalent, but since this is our first example of an optimization problem in economics, it is a good idea to go through both approaches.

For the first approach, let us compute MC by taking the derivative of the total cost function in (1.48). This calculation gives us

$$MC(y) = \frac{y^2}{4} - 5y + 30. \tag{1.49}$$

If maximum profit occurs at $y*$, then the first-order condition tells us that $p = MC$ or

$$21 = \frac{y^2}{4} - 5y + 30, \tag{1.50}$$

since $p = 21$. Rearranging (1.50), we have

$$y^2 - 20y + 36 = 0,$$

or

$$(y - 18)(y - 2) = 0. \tag{1.51}$$

Now, solving (1.51), we have two critical points that satisfy the first-order condition:

$$y* = 18 \quad \text{and} \quad y** = 2. \tag{1.52}$$

Which value in (1.52) is the profit-maximizing output? To answer this, we need to check the second-order condition.

Differentiation of the MC function gives

$$\frac{dMC(y)}{dy} = \frac{y}{2} - 5. \tag{1.53}$$

Thus for $y* = 18$ we have $dMC(18)/dy = 4 > 0$, and for $y** = 2$ we have $dMC(2)/dy = -4 < 0$. Since the second-order condition for a maximum (1.47) requires that MC slope upward, the profit-maximizing output is $y* = 18$. The critical point $y** = 2$ is actually a point of minimum profit, since it satisfies the second-order condition for the minimization of $\pi(y)$. Both critical points are depicted in Figure 1.10.

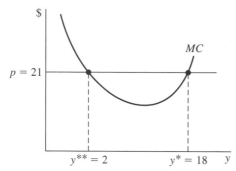

Figure 1.10

The second approach to the maximization problem is to find the critical points of the profit function directly. Given the total cost function in (1.48) and the fact that $p = 21$, the firm's profit function can be written as

$$\pi(y) = 21y - \left(\frac{y^3}{12} - 2.5y^2 + 30y + 100\right). \tag{1.54}$$

The first-order condition in (1.43) requires that

$$\pi'(y^*) = 21 - \frac{y^2}{4} + 5y - 30 = 0. \tag{1.55}$$

Rearranging (1.55) gives us the same equation that we had in (1.51), and so we can solve for the critical points $y^* = 18$ and $y^{**} = 2$ just as we did before. The second-order condition (1.45) is now

$$\pi''(y^*) = -\frac{y^*}{2} + 5 < 0,$$

which again implies that $y^* = 18$ is the profit-maximizing output for the firm. As stated earlier, the two approaches are mathematically equivalent; the algebra is just a little different. Also the first approach, using marginal cost, is often easier to interpret economically. For instance, the second-order condition (1.45), which says that the second derivative of the profit function should be negative, is not particularly easy to translate into economics. But the second-order condition (1.47), which says the *MC* should slope upward, can easily be given an economic interpretation, such as diminishing returns.

No matter which approach is used for the computation, it is important to remember that profit-maximizing output does not necessarily mean an output with a positive profit. It means the firm is doing the best that it can do, not that it is doing particularly well. It may still be true that $\pi(y^*) < 0$ even though y^* satisfies both the first- and second-order conditions. Such a situation is depicted in Figure 1.11. The particular numerical example we just examined does not have this difficulty, though; for the perfectly competitive firm with $p = 21$ and total cost given by (1.48), the maximum profit is $\pi(y^*) = \$62$.

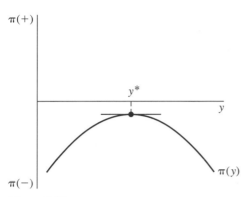

Figure 1.11

Profit-Maximizing Output: Monopoly

We now consider the case of a profit-maximizing firm that is a monopolist rather than a perfectly competitive firm. The profit for the monopolist, as for the competitive firm, is given by

$$\pi(y) = TR(y) - TC(y) = py - TC(y).$$

Profit is simply total revenue minus total cost regardless of how much market power the firm possesses. Given this, how does the profit-maximizing behavior of the monopolist differ from that of a perfectly competitive firm?

The key difference is that since the monopolist faces the entire market demand curve, price is not merely a parameter, as it was for the perfectly competitive firm. Assuming a downward-sloping demand curve (as we will throughout this section), the monopolist must choose between (1) charging a relatively high price and selling only a few units and (2) charging a relatively low price and selling a larger number of units. For the monopolist, price is a choice variable, not a parameter. Actually, saying that price is a choice variable is a bit too strong. The monopolist faces a demand curve for the product; that demand curve represents all possible price–quantity combinations available to the monopoly firm. The monopolist will find the profit-maximizing output, much as a perfectly competitive firm does, but then the monopolist must set the price in such a way that consumers will in fact demand that profit-maximizing output.

Since the price that can be charged depends on the demand relation, we will write the monopolist's demand function as $p = p(y)$ with output (quantity) as the independent variable. Combining this demand function with the definition of profit, we have the following objective function for the monopolist:

$$\pi(y) = TR(y) - TC(y) = p(y)y - TC(y). \tag{1.56}$$

Assuming that $p(y)$ and $TC(y)$ are differentiable, the monopolist's profit function will be a differentiable function of one variable. Of course, the first- and second-order conditions for the maximization of π at y^* remain

$$\pi'(y^*) = 0 \quad \text{and} \quad \pi''(y^*) < 0.$$

The difference between this case and the preceding competitive case is simply that the derivatives π' and π'' will involve more complex terms, since $p = p(y)$.

Applying the first-order condition $\pi'(y^*) = 0$ to the profit function in (1.56), we have

$$\pi'(y^*) = \frac{dTR(y^*)}{dy} - \frac{dTC(y^*)}{dy} = 0. \tag{1.57}$$

Since $dTR/dy = MR$ and $dTC/dy = MC$, this first-order condition can be rewritten in the more familiar form

$$MR(y^*) = MC(y^*). \tag{1.58}$$

Notice that the first-order condition for the competitive firm, $p = MC(y^*)$, is simply a special case of (1.58), where $TR(y) = py$.

The second-order condition for profit maximization on the part of a monopolist is

$$\pi''(y^*) = \frac{dMR(y^*)}{dy} - \frac{dMC(y^*)}{dy} < 0,$$

or

$$\frac{dMC(y^*)}{dy} > \frac{dMR(y^*)}{dy}. \tag{1.59}$$

The second-order condition requires that the marginal cost curve cut the marginal revenue curve from below at the profit-maximizing output. Again, note that for the second-order condition as well as the first-order condition, perfect competition is merely a special case. The second-order condition in (1.59) reduces to $dMC(y^*)/dy > 0$ in the competitive case, since $TR = py$ implies that $dMR/dy = 0$.

Once the profit-maximizing output y^* has been found, it needs to be substituted back into the demand function $p = p(y)$ to find the profit-maximizing price $p^* = p(y^*)$. Figure 1.12 depicts the profit-maximizing price and quantity for a monopolist with a linear demand curve and U-shaped marginal cost. As with perfect competition, of course, profit maximization does not mean positive profit. The actual amount of profit as the profit-maximizing output will be given by $\pi^* = p(y^*)y^* - TC(y^*)$; it could be positive, negative, or zero. Numerical examples for the monopoly case are left as problems for the reader.

Consumer Choice

The previous maximization examples came exclusively from the production side of the economy. It is now time to discuss consumer choice. The examination will be brief; a much more detailed discussion of consumer choice theory will be provided later, after the necessary mathematical tools have been developed. This section simply demonstrates how, with a little creativity, one-variable calculus can often be applied to economic problems that initially appear to be beyond its scope.

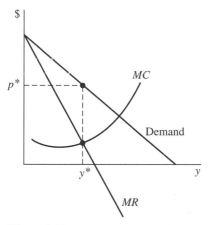

Figure 1.12

One variable maximization techniques seem to be a reasonable tool in pro duction theory. The firm, regardless of its market power, must find the profit maximizing level of output, a problem that is naturally amenable to the technique of one-variable unconstrained maximization. This is not the case for consumer choice theory. Consumers choose goods to maximize utility; but they do not choose only one good, and their choices are not completely unconstrained. For the consumer choice problem to be interesting at all, it must include at least two choice variables (goods), and it must explicitly take into account the consumer's budget constraint. Since the techniques for solving multivariate constrained opti mization problems are not discussed until Chapter 8, a proper treatment of con sumer choice theory must be postponed until that time. What we offer here is only a (often quite useful) one-variable shortcut approach to the problem.

Consider a consumer who is purchasing only two goods, x and y. This con sumer has a certain amount of money income (M) to spend on the goods, and the prices of the two goods are given by p_x and p_y. The consumer has a differentiable utility function that assigns a nonnegative real number to each possible bundle of goods x and y, or a bit more formally: $U: \Re^2_+ \to \Re_+$. Given this information, the consumer choice problem is

$$\text{Max}_{\{x,y\}} U(x, y)$$

$$\text{Subject to: } p_x x + p_y y = M.$$

(1.60)

Note that this is a two-variable constrained maximization problem. How are we to solve such a problem and find the utility-maximizing consumption of the two goods x^* and y^*?

The trick we use is to notice that the constraint essentially eliminates one degree of freedom in the problem. The budget constraint is a functional relation-ship between x and y: therefore we can solve the budget constraint for y in terms of x. Once we have y as a function of x, we can substitute this into the utility func-tion and thus eliminate y altogether. Once we have expressed utility as a function of only one variable, we can maximize utility precisely as we maximized profit in the production examples. The constraint allows us to eliminate one of the two variables, and this reduces the problem to a one-variable maximization problem, which we can handle with the tools in this chapter.

To see how this technique works, let us consider an example. The budget constraint is the same as in (1.60), but utility is given by the function $U(x, y) = xy$. Notice that this is a utility function with the standard microeconomic properties: the indifference curves (combinations of x and y that provide the same level of utility) have the standard "bowed-in" shape. With this particular utility function, the consumer choice problem becomes

$$\underset{\{x,y\}}{\text{Max }} U(x, y) = xy$$

$$\text{Subject to: } p_x x + p_y y = M.$$

(1.61)

The first step is to rearrange the budget constraint so that y is a function of x. Of course the choice of x as the final choice variable is arbitrary; we could just as well solve the budget constraint for x in terms of y, and then maximize with respect to y. Rearranging the budget constraint so y is a function of x, we have

$$y = g(x) = \frac{-p_x x}{p_y} + \frac{M}{p_y}.$$

(1.62)

Substituting y from the budget constraint (1.62) back into the utility function, we have utility as a function of x alone:

$$\bar{U}(x) = xg(x) = \frac{-p_x x^2}{p_y} + \frac{Mx}{p_y}.$$

(1.63)

Now the messy two-variable constrained maximization problem has been reduced to a more manageable one-variable unconstrained maximization problem. The consumer choice problem is now to maximize $\bar{U}(x)$ in (1.63) by choice of x. We know that any x^* that solves the problem must satisfy the first-order condition[3]

$$\bar{U}'(x^*) = 0.$$

Taking the derivative of (1.63) and setting it equal to zero, we have

$$\bar{U}'(x^*) = \frac{-2p_x x^*}{p_y} + \frac{M}{p_y} = 0,$$

or

$$x^* = \frac{M}{2p_x}.$$

(1.64)

The expression in (1.64) is the demand function for good x; it shows the utility-maximizing consumption of good x as a function of the parameters M and p_x (and implicitly p_y). For instance, if $p_x = \$2$, $p_y = \$1$, and $M = \$12$, then our consumer will purchase 3 units of good x because $x^* = 3$ for these values.

BOX 1.1

Time Inconsistency

Often new developments in economic theory can be conveyed by using relatively simple mathematical models. One such economic idea is the notion of **time inconsistency.** The problem arises in a number of different contexts, but most of the discussion has focused on rational expectations macro models. The time inconsistency problem arises in the context of such models when the monetary authority (in the United States, the Federal Reserve) is unable to follow a credible policy of zero inflation. The argument was first presented in Kydland and Prescott (1977), and related results can be found in Barro and Gordon (1983a, 1983b); our discussion follows Mankiw (1988).

In general, the monetary authority employs various policy instruments to control the rate of inflation π and the level of aggregate real output y in the economy. We simplify somewhat and assume that the monetary author ity can control π directly. The inflation–unemployment trade-off is given by the Phillips curve, and it represents a constraint on the choices of the monetary authority. Let us assume that this constraint is given by the expectations-augmented Phillips curve

$$y - y^* = \alpha(\pi - \pi^e), \tag{a}$$

where y^* is the full-employment real output (the natural rate), π^e is the expected rate of inflation, and α is a positive scalar. In such a model, output can only be greater than the natural rate ($y > y^*$) when there is an inflationary "surprise" ($\pi > \pi^e$). If economic agents in this economy form their expectations rationally, then $\pi - \pi^e$ and thus $y = y^*$; the level of output will be the natural rate.

Now the monetary authority desires high output and price-level stability. So if we characterize the preferences of the monetary authority by a utility function $U(y, \pi)$, a suitable function might be

$$U(y, \pi) = y - \beta\pi^2, \tag{b}$$

where β is a positive scalar. The problem for the monetary authority is thus to maximize the utility function in (b) subject to the constraint given by the Phillips curve in (a).

Since agents in the economy have rational expectations, an obvious **rule** for the monetary authority to follow is simply to set $\pi = 0$. Given this rule, the rational expectations of the agents in the economy imply that $\pi^e = \pi = 0$, and thus $U^* = y^*$ is the utility level of the optimal policy rule. Under rational expectations—and thus $y = y^*$—no other policy will achieve a more desirable result than $\pi = 0$.

Now consider a **discretionary policy,** in which is the monetary authority chooses π for a given level of expected inflation by maximizing (b) subject to the constraint (a). Using the substitution technique to maximize (b) subject to (a) we substitute the Phillips curve from (a) into the utility function (b) to reduce the problem to a single variable π. After this substitution the objective function becomes

$$U(\pi) = y^* + \alpha(\pi - \pi^e) - \beta\pi^2.$$

Taking the derivative $dU/d\pi$ and setting it equal to zero, we have the first-order condition

$$\alpha - 2\beta\pi^* = 0 \qquad \text{or} \qquad \pi^* = \frac{\alpha}{2\beta} > 0.$$

The optimal rate of inflation under discretion π^* is strictly positive. Combining this with rational expectations, we have $\pi^* = \pi^e > 0$ and $y = y^*$, which implies that the monetary authority achieves a lower level of utility under discretion than under a rule.

This result certainly seems contrary to our economic intuitions. How could the monetary authority (or any economic agent) be worse off with choice (discretion) than without choice (a rule)? After all, one of the choices available under discretion is $\pi = 0$. How could one be better off with a rule than with discretion when one of the discretionary choices is to follow the rule? The explanation lies in the problem of **time inconsistency.** If the discretionary authority were to announce a zero inflation rate (the optimal rule), the public would not find such an announcement credible. It would not be credible because once the public forms an expectation of zero inflation, there is, given (a) and (b), a built-in incentive for the monetary authority to cheat, that is, to increase inflation. Since such an increase is always present under discretion, the public will never believe a promise of zero inflation. The monetary authority could convince the public that it would not take advantage of the incentive to cheat only if no such opportunity to cheat existed: that is, only if the monetary authority was bound by a fixed rule and had no discretion. Thus we have time inconsistency: under discretion the optimal policy (zero inflation) is not consistent over time, while the only consistent policy ($\pi > 0$) is suboptimal. Kydland and Prescott (1977) apply this basic argument to other types of government–rational public interactions that are more microeconomic: cases such as flood control and patent policy. It is a quite general result that holds in a broad class of strategic models and has generated a substantial literature.

Sources
Barro, R. J., and D. B. Gordon. 1983a. A positive theory of monetary policy in a natural rate model. *Journal of Political Economy* 91: 589–619.

———. 1983b. Rules, discretion and reputation in a model of monetary policy. *Journal of Monetary Economics* 12: 101–12.

Kydland, F. E., and E. C. Prescott. 1977. Rules rather than discretion: The inconsistency of optimal plans. *Journal of Political Economy* 85: 473–91.

Mankiw, N. G. 1988. Recent developments in macroeconomics: A very quick refresher course. *Journal of Money, Credit, and Banking* 20: 436–49.

To find the quantity of good y consumed, we simply take the optimal consumption of good x from (1.64) and substitute it back into the budget constraint. When x^* is given by (1.64), we have from (1.62) that

$$y^* = -\frac{p_x}{p_y}\left(\frac{M}{2p_x}\right) + \frac{M}{p_y},$$

or

$$y^* = \frac{M}{2p_y}. \tag{1.65}$$

The expression in (1.65) is the demand function for good y; it shows the utility-maximizing consumption of good y as a function of the parameters M and p_y (and implicitly p_x). For the earlier numerical example, where $p_x = \$2$, $p_y = \$1$, and $M = \$12$, we have $y^* = 6$. Notice that once the demand for x had been obtained in (1.64), it was not really necessary to go through the algebraic substitution to obtain the demand for y. Since (1.64) implies that one-half of the available income is spent on x, the other half must be spent on y, as (1.65) indicates.

1.3 Introduction to Concavity and Convexity

Concave and Convex Functions

Certain classes of functions are very useful in economics because they provide a mathematical characterization of important economic properties. Concave and convex functions are two such classes. In this section, we define and discuss the mathematical properties of concave and convex functions. In the next section we briefly discuss some of their applications in economics.

A function of a single variable $y = f(x)$, $f: \Re \to \Re$, is **strictly concave**[4] iff for all $x_0, x_1 \in \Re$ with $x_0 \neq x_1$ and for all $0 < \theta < 1$,

$$f(\hat{x}) > \theta f(x_0) + (1 - \theta) f(x_1), \tag{1.66}$$

where $\hat{x} = \theta x_0 + (1 - \theta)x_1$. If the strict inequality in (1.66) is replaced by $\geq$, then the function is merely **concave** rather than strictly concave. Obviously all strictly concave functions are concave, but not vice versa. Although only the one-variable case is discussed here, the definitions of concave and strictly concave are identical for the multivariate case, where $f: \Re^n \to \Re$ and $x_0, x_1 \in \Re^n$.

The definition of strict concavity is easy to interpret when it is viewed geometrically. To this end, consider Figure 1.13. As $\hat{x}$ is defined, it lies along the x axis between x_0 and x_1; if $\theta = \frac{1}{2}$, then $\hat{x} = (x_0 + x_1)/2$; if $\theta \to 0$, then $\hat{x} \to x_1$; and if $\theta \to 1$, then $\hat{x} \to x_0$. Since the definition requires that (1.66) hold for all $x_0, x_1 \in \Re$ and for all $0 < \theta < 1$, it is equivalent to requiring the condition to hold for all $\hat{x}$ between two arbitrarily chosen values x_0 and x_1 in $\Re$. Figure 1.13 depicts one such $\hat{x}$. Note that the value of the function at this $\hat{x}$ is given by $f(\hat{x})$, while the value of the point on the line between $(x_0, f(x_0))$ and $(x_1, f(x_1))$ directly above $\hat{x}$ is given by $\theta f(x_0) + (1 - \theta) f(x_1)$. These two points give us a nice geometric interpretation of

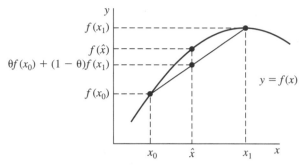

Figure 1.13

the strict-concavity condition (1.66); it requires the function to be "bowed upward" so that $f(\hat{x})$ is **above** $\theta f(x_0) + (1 - \theta) f(x_1)$. For concavity alone (rather than strict concavity), linear segments in which $f(\hat{x}) = \theta f(x_0) + (1 - \theta) f(x_1)$ are allowed. At least in the case of strict concavity, the formal definition is consistent with what our intuition would tell us something "concave" ought to look like.

This intuition also seems to carry over to the definition of a convex function. A function of a single variable $y = f(x)$, $f: \Re \to \Re$, is **strictly convex** iff for all $x_0, x_1 \in \Re$ with $x_0 \neq x_1$ and for all $0 < \theta < 1$,

$$f(\hat{x}) < \theta f(x_0) + (1 - \theta) f(x_1), \tag{1.67}$$

where $\hat{x} = \theta x_0 + (1 - \theta) x_1$. And as with concavity, weakening the strict inequality in (1.67) to $\leq$ defines a function that is **convex** rather than strictly convex. Geometrically, convex functions are "bowed downward" so that $f(\hat{x})$ is **below** $\theta f(x_0) + (1 - \theta) f(x_1)$ for all $x_0, x_1 \in \Re$ and $0 < \theta < 1$.

There are two important things to note about convex functions and their relationship to concave functions. First, a linear function is both concave and convex, although it is not strictly either. By the definition of $\hat{x}$, a linear function will always have $f(\hat{x}) = \theta f(x_0) + (1 - \theta) f(x_1)$, and thus it will satisfy both (1.66) and (1.67) with weak inequalities. Second, $-f(x)$ is convex (or strictly convex) iff $f(x)$ is concave (or strictly concave). This is very helpful in reducing our work in this section. Since anything that can be said about the concave function f can also be said about the convex function $-f$, there is no reason to discuss the properties of both types of function. We discuss the properties of concave functions, since those are more common in economics, and leave it to the reader to reverse all the inequalities for the convex case.

Thus far, derivatives have not entered into our discussion of concave (or convex) functions; in definitions (1.66) and (1.67) we did not even require the function f to be differentiable. Now we want to provide a way of characterizing a (differentiable) concave function in terms of its first derivative.

A differentiable function of a single variable, $y = f(x)$, $f: \Re \to \Re$, is **strictly concave** if for all $x_0, x_1 \in \Re$ with $x_0 \neq x_1$,

$$f'(x_0)(x_1 - x_0) + f(x_0) > f(x_1). \tag{1.68}$$

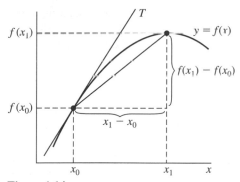

Figure 1.14

The relationship between (1.68) and the definition of concavity in (1.66) is easiest to see when (1.68) is rewritten as the following two conditions:

$$x_1 - x_0 > 0 \quad \text{implies } f'(x_0) > \frac{f(x_1) - f(x_0)}{x_1 - x_0}, \tag{1.69a}$$

$$x_1 - x_0 < 0 \quad \text{implies } f'(x_0) < \frac{f(x_1) - f(x_0)}{x_1 - x_0}. \tag{1.69b}$$

The case of $x_1 - x_0 > 0$ is drawn in Figure 1.14. The slope of the tangent T at x_0 is the derivative $f'(x_0)$. If the function is strictly concave, then the slope of the line between $(x_0, f(x_0))$ and $(x_1, f(x_1))$ will be less than the slope of the tangent T, or, in other words, the tangent will be everywhere above the function when the function is strictly concave. This is precisely what condition (1.69a) says. Condition (1.69b) gives the same restriction for the case of $x_1 - x_0 < 0$. For mere **concavity,** the inequality in (1.68) is weakened to $\geq$. The first-derivative definition of concavity will prove extremely useful in economic problems involving optimization. The inequalities are reversed for convex functions.

The third and final characterization of strict concavity involves the second derivative of the function. Suppose that a function $f: \Re \to \Re$ is at least twice differentiable and has a strictly negative second derivative ($f''(x) < 0$) for all $x \in \Re$. What does this negative second derivative say about the shape of the function? Well, since the first derivative is the rate of change in the function, the second derivative is the rate of change in the first derivative. Thus if $f''(x) < 0$ for all x, the slope of the function is always decreasing with respect to x. But if the slope is always decreasing, then the tangent is always above the function and so the function must be strictly concave. Likewise, if $f''(x) > 0$ for all $x \in \Re$, then the function is strictly convex. Finally, if weak inequalities are allowed on the second derivative ($\leq$ or $\geq$), the functions are concave or convex, respectively.[5]

There are many reasons for using the second-derivative characterization of concavity and convexity rather than those discussed earlier. One reason is that the second derivative often has a nice economic interpretation. Another reason is simply that the second derivative is usually much easier to check than the other conditions that characterize concavity and convexity.

Discussing this second-derivative characterization of concavity raises the issue of local versus global concavity. Both the nonderivative and first-derivative characterizations of concavity (and convexity) already discussed were global; that is, they were properties that held over the entire domain of the function. Either the function was strictly concave or it was not; we did not discuss a function that is strictly concave in one region of its domain and strictly convex in another part. We could have discussed such cases, but we did not.

Now the second-derivative characterization of concavity and convexity can be applied globally as well; we could say that a function is globally strictly concave because $f''(x) < 0$ for all $x \in \Re$. The problem is that the second-derivative test is rarely used this way in economics. Rather, the second-derivative test usually appears in the context of the second-order condition for an optimization problem. In such cases f'' is evaluated at only one point: the critical point x^* where $f(x^*) = 0$. Checking the second derivative at the critical point usually gives us only local information. This issue is examined further in the next section, in which we consider some economic examples.

Before we turn to these economic examples, let us briefly discuss the concept of quasi-concavity. Quasi-concavity is not just another way of checking for concavity or strict concavity; quasi-concavity is an entirely different mathematical property. Actually, it is not fair to say that it is entirely different; it is simply a much weaker concavity-like property.

A function of a single variable $y = f(x)$, $f : \Re \to \Re$, is **strictly quasi-concave** iff for all $x_0, x_1 \in \Re$ with $x_0 \neq x_1$ and for all $0 < \theta < 1$,

$$f(x_1) \geq f(x_0) \qquad \text{implies } f(\hat{x}) > f(x_0). \tag{1.70}$$

where $\hat{x} = \theta x_0 + (1 - \theta)x_1$, as before. As with the earlier concepts, for mere **quasi-concavity** we change the strict inequality on the right-hand side of (1.70) to $\geq$, and we merely reverse the inequalities for quasi-convexity and strict quasi-convexity.

Why do we need yet another concavity-like concept? The answer lies in the fact that quasi-concavity is a much weaker mathematical property than concavity. All concave functions are quasi-concave, but not vice versa. For example, return to the strictly concave function in Figure 1.13. Applying the inequality in (1.70), we can see that this function is also strictly quasi-concave. Now consider the function in Figure 1.15. This function is most certainly not concave; in fact, it is strictly convex. And yet by (1.70) the function in Figure 1.15 is strictly quasi-concave. Quasi-concavity and quasi-convexity are thus very weak notions of concavity and convexity.

Of course, we would not be interested in these weaker forms of concavity and convexity unless they occurred naturally in some economic context. We will see in Chapter 8 that this is, in fact, the case. The second-order conditions for certain constrained maximization problems can be reduced to the quasi-concavity of the

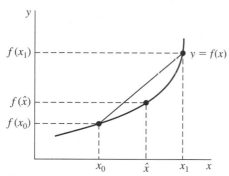

Figure 1.15

relevant objective function. But for now let us return to the more common notions of concavity and strict concavity and examine some of the economic contexts in which they arise.

Concavity and Convexity in Economics

Concavity and convexity (but more so concavity) surface repeatedly in upcoming chapters. Here we merely sketch some of the reasons for the frequency with which these properties of functions appear in formal economics. We discuss three such reasons, which is by no means an exhaustive survey.

The first reason for the importance of concavity and convexity is that these concepts can often be given an economic interpretation. For instance, consider a short-run production function $y = f(L)$ relating labor input L to output y. If this production function is differentiable, the derivative $f'(L)$ measures the marginal product of labor MP_L. If this function is twice differentiable, then the second derivative $f''(L)$ measures the rate of change in the marginal product with respect to labor (dMP_L/dL). If $f''(L) < 0$, then the function has the property that the marginal product decreases as labor is added. Economically, the property of decreasing marginal product is called **diminishing returns,** and it is a standard assumption on short-run production functions. Of course, if the property $f''(L) < 0$ holds over the entire domain of the function ($\Re_+$ here), then we can also say that the short-run production is strictly concave. Thus the economic property of diminishing returns is equivalent to the mathematical property of strict concavity. This is just one of many examples in which concavity and convexity lend themselves to easy economic interpretation; many others appear in the chapters that follow.

The second reason for the importance of concavity and convexity was already suggested; it is the intimate connection between these properties and the second-order conditions for optimization. In our earlier discussion of the profit-maximizing, perfectly competitive firm, the first- and second-order conditions for maximization at y^* were $\pi'(y^*) = 0$ and $\pi''(y^*) < 0$, respectively. The second-order condition is really a restriction on local strict concavity; it says that "close" (within some $\varepsilon > 0$) to y^* the function π must be strictly concave. Now, if

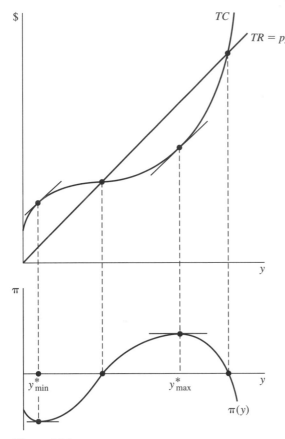

Figure 1.16

$\pi''(y^*) < 0$ for all y, then the second-order condition will surely hold, since global concavity always implies local concavity. For some models the economic structure will automatically guarantee such global structure, but often this is not true. Even in the relatively simple case of perfect competition, the cost function could be such that the profit function has the shape depicted in the bottom diagram of Figure 1.16. In fact, this was the case for our numerical example in which the price was $p = 21$ and the total cost function was given by the cubic expression in (1.48). For such cases the profit function is neither globally concave nor globally convex. The important thing is that the function is locally strictly concave around the profit-maximizing output y^*_{max} and locally strictly convex around the other critical point, the profit-minimizing output y^*_{min}. For some of the optimization problems we discuss in upcoming chapters, the economic structure will guarantee the global concavity and convexity of the functions involved; for others the properties will hold only locally, if at all. In any case, the second-order conditions are intimately connected to the properties of concavity and convexity.

BOX 1.2
Chaos in Economics

An economic model that involves only a one-variable function is not neces-sarily a simple economic model. Functions of one variable, even relatively well-behaved differentiable functions of one variable, often exhibit quite complex behavior. A relatively simple function of one variable can generate a series of values so complex that the function appears to be random. Such mathematical systems are fully deterministic but appear to be random (whether in one or more dimensions) are called **chaotic.** The study of such chaotic systems is the field of **chaos theory.** Seminal contributions to the mathematics of chaos theory were made by Li and Yorke (1975) and May (1974, 1976). Some of the early economic applications include those of Baumol and Quandt (1985), Benhabib and Day (1982), and Day (1983). Anderson, Arrow, and Pines (1988), Day (1994), and Kelsey (1988) provide a variety of different approaches to the general question of chaos in eco-nomics. Brock, Hsieh, and LeBaron (1991) discuss various tests that can be performed on time series to determine whether they are in fact chaotic.

The simplest system that exhibits chaotic behavior is a one-variable nonlinear difference equation. A difference equation is simply an equation in which the value of the variable at a particular time t (say x_t) determines the value of the variable in the next period (x_{t+1}) and time takes on integer values. Such difference equations generate a path of the variable x through time t. For example,

$$x_{t+1} = 5x_t$$

is a linear difference equation; if $x_0 = 1$, then $x_1 = 5$, $x_2 = 25$, $x_3 = 125$, and so on. Linear difference equations generate relatively simple time paths, but the same is not always the case for nonlinear difference equations. Difference equations of the general form

$$x_{t+1} = f(x_t)$$

with $f : \Re \to \Re$ and $t = 0, 1, 2, \ldots$ can exhibit quite complex (even **chaotic**) behavior.

An example of a one-variable nonlinear difference equation that exhibits such chaotic behavior is

$$x_{t+1} = ax_t(1 - x_t),$$

where a is a constant parameter between 3.83 and 4. When $a = 3.9$ and the initial value of x is given by $x_0 = 0.99$, the foregoing equation generates the following time path for the variable x: $x_1 = 0.0386$, $x_2 = 0.1448$, $x_3 = 0.4829$, $x_4 = 0.9735$, $x_5 = 0.1006$, $x_6 = 0.3528$, $x_7 = 0.8903$, $x_8 = 0.3808$, $x_9 = 0.9195$, $x_{10} = 0.2881, \ldots$ As t increases, this function continues to generate a series of values for variable x that appear to be random. The behavior is bounded—x does not systematically explode toward plus or minus infinity—but it also never reaches an equilibrium or a periodic orbit. An **equilibrium** (or **fixed point**) is a point x^* such that $x^* = f(x^*) = ax^*(1 - x^*)$; a **periodic orbit** (or **cycle**) is a value the system returns to after a finite number of periods (a 2-cycle is returned to after two periods; a 3-cycle is returned to after three periods, etc.). The paths generated by our difference equation and other equations like it are indistinguishable from a purely random process; they are thus aptly named chaotic systems.

In an important paper Li and Yorke (1975) proved that if a nonlinear difference equation has a point x_t such that $x_{t+3} < x_t < x_{t+1} < x_{t+2}$, then chaotic behavior will always result. This theorem by Li and Yorke, which provides a sufficient condition for the existence of chaos, has been the foundation for most economic applications of chaos theory. These economic applications have included classical economic growth models, monetary general equilibrium models, variations on the standard consumer choice problem, and many others.

Sources

Anderson, P. W., K. J. Arrow, and D. Pines, eds. 1988. *Complex economic dynamics.* Santa Fe, NM: Addison-Wesley.

Baumol, W. J., and R. E. Quandt. 1985. Chaos models and their implications for forecasting. *Eastern Economic Journal* 11: 3–15.

Benhabib, J., and R. H. Day. 1982. A characterization of erratic dynamics in the overlapping generations model. *Journal of Economic Dynamics and Control* 4: 37–55.

Brock, W. A., D. A. Hsieh, and B. LeBaron. 1991. *Nonlinear dynamics, chaos, and instability.* Cambridge, MA: MIT Press.

Day, R. H. 1983. The emergence of chaos from classical economic growth. *Quarterly Journal of Economics* 98: 201–13.

———. 1994. *Complex economic dynamics.* Vol. I. Cambridge, MA: MIT Press.

Kelsey, D. 1988. The economics of chaos or the chaos of economics. *Oxford Economic Papers* 40: 1–31.

Li, T., and J. A. Yorke. 1975. Period three implies chaos. *American Mathematical Monthly* 82: 985–92.

May, R. B. 1974. Biological populations with nonoverlapping generations: Stable points, stable cycles, and chaos. *Science* 186: 645–47.

———. 1976. Simple mathematical models with very complicated dynamics. *Nature* 261: 459–67.

The final reason we cite for the importance of concavity and convexity is actually a formalization of a mathematical argument that was implicit in the preceding discussion. We honor this result by making it the first (and only) theorem in this chapter. This theorem is called the **local–global theorem.**

> **THEOREM 1.1:** Point x^* is the global maximum of the differentiable concave function $f: \Re \to \Re$ iff $f'(x^*) = 0$. When f is strictly concave, the global maximum is also unique.
>
> **PROOF:** Since the "only if" part of the theorem holds for all differentiable functions, concave or not, we need consider only the "if" part of the theorem. Notice that since f is concave, from (1.68) we know that
>
> $$f'(x^*)(x - x^*) + f(x^*) \geq f(x)$$
>
> for all $x \in \Re$. Now if $f'(x^*) = 0$, this condition implies that $f(x^*) \geq f(x)$ for all $x \in \Re$, proving that x^* is global maximum of f. If f is strictly concave, the foregoing inequality is strict and $f(x^*) > f(x)$ for all $x \in \Re$, proving that x^* is a unique global maximum of f.

This is a very powerful theorem; it asserts that for concave functions the first-order conditions for a maximum are **both** necessary and sufficient. It is called the local–global theorem because it says that for concave functions any local maximum is global as well. By reversing some inequalities, the theorem asserts an equivalent relationship between convex functions and the global minimum. The theorem can also be extended[6] to functions of more than one variable where $f: \Re^n \to \Re$ with $n > 1$.

As important as this result is, it should not come as any real surprise, given the earlier discussion regarding the relationship between concavity and the second-order conditions. The strict concavity of a function basically means that the second-order condition holds throughout the domain; under these conditions it is no surprise that a vanishing first derivative is both necessary and sufficient for a maximum. If the function is concave but not strictly concave, it will have a linear region where $f'' = 0$ holds for all points within some interval, but all such points are still global maxima if $f' = 0$; it is simply that no point is unique.

PROBLEMS

1.1 Consider the demand function given by $Q = BP^{-1}$ with $B > 0$.
 (a) Find the marginal revenue for this demand function.
 (b) Explain why your result in (a) does not contradict the result that $P = MR$ when $Q = 0$.

1.2 Consider the upward-sloping linear demand curve $Q = aP + b$ with $a > 0$ and $b > 0$.
 (a) Find the marginal revenue for this demand function.
 (b) Sketch the relationship between this demand function and its marginal revenue function.

1.3 Consider the so-called constant elasticity demand curve $Q = AP^a$ with $a < 0$ and $A > 0$.
 (a) Find the marginal revenue for this demand function.
 (b) Find restrictions on the parameter a that will make $MR > 0, MR < 0$, and $MR = 0$.

1.4 The elasticity of supply (E_s) is given by

$$E_s = \frac{\%\Delta Q^s}{\%\Delta P} = \frac{\Delta Q^s / Q^s}{\Delta P / P},$$

where $Q^s =$ quantity supplied and $P =$ price. The supply curve is relatively elastic if $E_s > 1$, relatively inelastic if $E_s < 1$, and unit elastic if $E_s = 1$.

For an upward-sloping **linear** supply curve, it is a well-known result that if it cuts the price (vertical) axis it is relatively elastic; if it cuts the quantity (horizontal) axis it is relatively inelastic; and if it goes through the origin it is unit elastic. **Prove** this result.

1.5 In macroeconomic monetary theory, it has been suggested that the demand for real money balances m is given by

$$m = e^{-\alpha\pi},$$

where π is the expected rate of inflation and α is a strictly positive parameter.
(a) Find the elasticity of the demand for real money balances with respect to the expected rate of inflation $\varepsilon_{m,\pi}$.
(b) If the demand for real money balances is unit elastic, then what is the relationship between the parameter α and the expected rate of inflation π?

1.6 Suppose there are only two consumers in a particular market. Let the demand curve of consumer 1 be given by $q_1 = f(P)$ and the demand curve of consumer 2 be given by $q_2 = g(P)$, where $Q = q_1 + q_2$ and P is the market price of the good. Find the relationship between the price elasticity of the market demand curve ε and the price elasticities of the two individual demand curves ε_1 and ε_2.

1.7 The demand function $x^* = M/2p_x$ was derived in (1.64) of the text. Find the own-price elasticity of demand ε_{x,p_x} and the income elasticity of demand $\varepsilon_{x,M}$ for this demand function.

1.8 For the following short-run cost functions, find MC and AVC and (roughly) graph them (show their general shape, maximum or minimum points, etc.).
(a) $TC(y) = y^3 - 60y^2 + 1210y + 600.$
(b) $TC(y) = \dfrac{y^3}{3} - 50y^2 + 3500y + 50.$

1.9 If the short-run total cost is given by the general quadratic function

$$TC(y) = ay^3 + by^2 + cy + d,$$

where a, b, c, and d are scalars, find restrictions that make MC and AVC strictly positive and U shaped.

1.10 For the following short-run production function

$$y = 15L^2 - L^3,$$

$y =$ output and $L =$ labor input.
(a) Find the marginal product of labor $(MP_L = dy/dL)$.
(b) Graph the MP function for this production function.

APL
MPL
NPL

1.11 Find the following multipliers for the income–expenditure macromodel given in (1.36).
(a) The autonomous tax multiplier (ΔY^* caused by ΔT_0).
(b) The "balanced budget" multiplier (ΔY^* caused by ΔT_0 and ΔG_0 with $\Delta T_0 = \Delta G_0$).

1.12 The price–cost margin (sometimes called "markup") m for an imperfectly competitive firm is defined as

$$m = \frac{P - MC}{P}.$$

Find the relationship between the elasticity of the firm's demand curve ε and the profit-maximizing m.

1.13 If a perfectly competitive firm has a long-run total cost ($LRTC$) function $LRTC = 200Q - 24Q^2 + Q^3$, find the long-run equilibrium **price** in the market for this good.

1.14 Find the profit-maximizing output $Q*$ for monopolistic firms with each of the following demand–cost combinations.
(a) $P = 10 - 0.1Q$ $TC(Q) = 2Q + 0.025Q^2$.
(b) $P = 22 - 2Q$ $TC(Q) = Q^3/3 - 10Q^2 + 50Q + 45$.
(c) $Q = -P + 25$ $TC(Q) = Q^3/12 - 2.5Q^2 + 30Q + 100$.
(d) $Q + 2P - 90 = 0$ $ATC(Q) = Q^2/2 - 20Q + 82.5 + 125/Q$.

1.15 Find the profit-maximizing quantity $Q*$ and price $P*$ for a monopolist with the linear demand curve $P = -bQ + c$ and constant AVC given by $AVC = a$.

1.16 Suppose a monopolistic firm has the short-run production function $Q = L^{1/2}$, where $Q = $ output and $L = $ labor input. If the wage w per unit of labor is $4 and fixed cost is $100, find the following.
(a) Total cost (as a function of Q, not L).
(b) Average total cost.
(c) Marginal cost.
(d) The profit-maximizing output $Q*$ when demand is given by $P = -8Q + 96$.

1.17 A perfectly competitive firm in both the product and input markets can produce output y by using labor L according to the production function $y = -L^2 + 10L$. If the firm's output sells for $10 per unit ($P = 10$) and it pays a wage of $40 per unit of labor ($w = 40$), what is the profit-maximizing level of employment $L*$ for this firm?

1.18 A monopsonistic firm is the single buyer of a particular input. Suppose that the supply of labor to a monopsonist is given by $w = L^{1/2}$, where $w = $ wage and $L = $ labor supplied. Find the profit-maximizing quantity of labor employed ($L*$) and the wage ($w*$) paid by this monopsonist when the production function is $y = 2L^{1/2}$ and the output sells for a price of $p = $13.50.

1.19 Consider the consumer choice problem given in (1.60) for the case of $U(x, y) = x + \ln y$.
(a) Use the substitution technique discussed in the chapter to find the utility-maximizing consumption of the two goods ($x*$ and $y*$).
(b) From the expressions found in (a) find the own-price, cross-price, and income elasticities for both goods. That is, find ε_{x,p_x}, ε_{x,p_y}, $\varepsilon_{x,M}$, ε_{y,p_y}, ε_{y,p_x}, $\varepsilon_{y,M}$, and $\varepsilon_{y,M}$.
(c) At what price would the own-price elasticity of the demand for good x be unit elastic?

1.20 Suppose that a particular economy produces only two outputs, good x and good y. The only input in the economy is labor L, and the total labor supply is fixed at 1; so $L_x + L_y = 1$, where L_x is the labor used in the production of x and L_y is the labor used in the production of y. The production functions for goods x and y are given by $x = 2L_x^{1/2}$ and $y = 2L_y^{1/2}$, respectively. Find the equation for the **production possibilities curve** for this economy and graph it. Is this production possibilities curve a concave function?

1.21 Prove, by applying the definition in (1.66), that the linear consumption function $C = mY + C_0$ is both a concave and a convex function.

1.22 Prove that the average fixed cost function $AFC(y) = FC/y$ is strictly convex function by applying the second-derivative test **and** by directly applying the definitions of a strictly convex function.

1.23 The **Laffer curve** is the relationship between the tax rate t and tax revenue T; it is named after Arthur Laffer, the economist who popularized its use as a policy tool during the early 1980s. The **Laffer effect** occurs when the Laffer curve slopes downward, that is, when an increase in the tax rate causes such a substantial reduction in the amount of labor supplied that tax revenue falls. If the demand for labor is perfectly elastic at wage $\bar{w}$ and the supply of labor $S(w)$ is an upward-sloping function of the after-tax wage rate [so that $dS/dw > 0$ and $w = (1 - t)\bar{w}$], then the tax revenue received by the government is

$$T = tS(w)\bar{w}.$$

Given this tax revenue function, what must be true of the relationship between the elasticity of labor supply $(w/S)(dS/dw)$ and the tax rate t, for the Laffer effect to occur?

1.24 One of the earliest contributions to mathematical economics was J. H. von Thünen (1783–1850). He felt that his discovery of a formula for the "natural wage" was so significant that he had it inscribed on his tombstone:

$$w^* = (ap)^{1/2},$$

where w^* = aggregate natural labor (wage) income per year, a = aggregate consumption per year, and p = real aggregate output/income (real GDP) per year. In von Thünen's model, when the real wage income is w, the real rate of interest r is given by $r = (p - w)/w$ and aggregate savings S is $S = w - a$.
(a) Interpret von Thünen's definition of the real rate of interest r.
(b) Interpret his definition of savings S. What assumption did von Thünen make about who (which income group) did the saving in the economy?
(c) Show that von Thünen's formula for the natural wage w^* is the solution to the problem of maximizing the total return on savings. That is, show that w^* solves the problem

$$\underset{\{w\}}{\text{Max}} \ r(w)S(w).$$

1.25 The substitution technique developed in the chapter for solving the two-variable consumer choice problem can be used to solve other types of two-variable constrained optimization problems. For instance, the long-run total cost function of the firm is based on solving the following two-variable constrained minimization problem:

$$\underset{\{L,K\}}{\text{Min}} \ wL + rK$$

$$\text{Subject to: } y = f(L, K),$$

where $y = f(L, K)$ is the production function, L = labor, K = capital, w = wage, and r = price of capital. Answer the following questions for the particular case where $f(L, K) = LK/100$ and $w = r = \$1$.
(a) Use the substitution technique discussed in the chapter to find the cost-minimizing quantities of labor and capital L^* and K^*.

(b) The long-run total cost function $LRTC = wL^* + rK^*$, that is, the total cost of employing the cost-minimizing quantities of the two inputs. Use the information from (a) to find an expression for $LRTC$.

(c) Find expressions for the long-run average total cost $(LRATC)$ and the long-run marginal cost $(LRMC)$. Sketch the shape of these curves.

(d) Do the cost functions in (a) and (b) make economic sense given the production function? Explain.

1.26 Tee time. Certain goods require time to consume. In addition to the dollar price of good x_1 there is often a "time price" as well. If the individual is consuming two goods x_1 and x_2 then in addition to the standard budget constraint,

$$p_1 x_1 + p_2 x_2 = M,$$

there would also have to be a time constraint,

$$t_1 x_1 + t_2 x_2 + L = T.$$

The t_i terms represent the time required to consume each unit of good x_i, the L represents the time spent working (labor time), and T represents the total time available for working and consumption.

If the individual's only source of income is labor, then the M in the dollar budget constraint will be given by $M = wL$, where w represents the wage per unit of labor. If we combine the two constraints under the assumption that labor is the individual's only source of income, we obtain the single (combined) constraint

$$(p_1 + wt_1)x_1 + (p_2 + wt_2)x_2 = wT.$$

If the individual has the particular utility function $U(x_1, x_2) = x_1 x_2$, then his or her consumer choice problem will be given by

$$\text{Max}_{\{x_1, x_2\}} U(x_1, x_2) = x_1 x_2$$

$$\text{Subject to: } (p_1 + wt_1)x_1 + (p_2 + wt_2)x_2 = wT.$$

(a) Suppose x_1 is golf, a good that requires both time and money to consume, while x_2 is a composite consumption good that has no time price ($t_2 = 0$) and has a unit dollar price ($p_2 = 1$). Use the substitution technique to **solve** the maximization problem under these assumptions. In other words, find expressions for the utility-maximizing consumption of golf (x_1^*) and the composite consumption good (x_2^*) as a function of the parameters of the problem (p_1, t_1, w, T).

(b) Find the comparative statics impact of a change in the wage (w) on the demand for golf (x_1^*). That is, sign the derivative dx_1^*/dw.

NOTES

1. Actually the demand function has the standard properties only for quantities between 0 and 10 (inclusive). The discussion will be restricted to this well-behaved region.

2. Recall that the first-order condition is necessary only for an interior optimum (i. e., a maximum that occurs in the interior of the domain). Since $\Re_+$ is the natural domain for y, the restriction that $y^* > 0$ is actually an interiority restriction. In Chapter 9 we discuss noninterior (boundary) optima in detail, but until then we consider only interior

optima; all maximum and minimum values are assumed to be strictly positive and thus in the interior of their domain.

3. The second-order condition does hold for this problem, although we will not discuss it.

4. Concave (and convex) functions are defined only for domains that are convex sets. A set S is convex if $x_0 \in S$ and $x_1 \in S$ implies that $\theta x_0 + (1 - \theta)x_1 \in S$ for all $0 \le \theta \le 1$. Since $\Re$ is a convex set, the definition above is fine; but if the domain of the function were restricted to a subset D of $\Re$ ($f: D \to \Re$, $D \subset \Re$), then the definition of concave and would require that D be a convex set.

5. Actually f is strictly concave if $f''(x) < 0$ for all $x \in \Re$, but f is concave iff $f''(x) \le 0$ for all $x \in \Re$. Note that the latter is based on "iff" while the former is based simply on "if." The function $f(x) = -x^4$ provides a counterexample to extending "only if" to the former expression.

6. See Takayama (1985, p. 87).

CHAPTER 2

ECONOMIC APPLICATIONS OF
MULTIVARIATE CALCULUS

■ ■ ■

In Chapter 1 we applied one-variable calculus in at least two separate ways. First, we used one-variable calculus to derive some economic propositions that were already familiar from introductory and intermediate economic theory. Second, we introduced some economically important classes of functions (concave and convex) and examined a number of their properties. In this chapter we will discuss multivariate (multivariable) calculus in a similar manner. We redefine some familiar economic concepts in terms of partial derivatives and/or the total differential, and then introduce some additional classes of economically useful functions (homogeneous and homothetic). The main difference between the two chapters lies in the emphasis on optimization. In Chapter 1, we discussed some examples of one-variable optimization problems in economics, but we do not examine multivariate optimization in this chapter; that important subject is deferred until the introduction of comparative statics in Chapter 3.

2.1   Partial Derivatives and the Total
Differential in Economics

Consumer Choice Theory

In the most general form of the consumer choice problem, the consumer is maximizing utility by choice of n different commodities (n being an unspecified, but possibly large, finite number). The problem can be written as

$$\begin{aligned} &\operatorname*{Max}_{\{x\}}\ U(x)\\[2mm] &\text{Subject to}:\ \sum_{i=1}^{n} p_i x_i = M. \end{aligned} \tag{2.1}$$

In (2.1) x is an n-dimensional vector representing the quantities of the n commodities consumed by the individual. Since only nonnegative quantities are considered, we have $x = (x_1, \ldots, x_n) \in \Re_+^n$. And $U(x)$ is the utility function of the consumer with $U: \Re_+^n \to \Re_+$. For most applications U is assumed to be at least twice differentiable. The prices of the goods are given by the price vector $p = (p_1, \ldots, p_n) \in \Re_{++}^n$ and the money income is $M \in \Re_{++}$; prices and money income together determine the budget constraint $\sum_{i=1}^n p_i x_i = M$. These prices are competitive market prices, since they are simply parameters to the consumer. If the consumer had market power, the prices would actually be functions of the quantities consumed, rather than merely parameters.

In Chapter 1, the consumer choice problem was briefly examined for the specific $n = 2$ utility function $U(x, y) = xy$. The purpose of that brief examination was simply to show how a two-variable problem could be reduced to a much simpler one-variable problem. In this chapter we introduce the general n-good problem only to show how the economic concepts of consumer choice theory can be defined in terms of partial derivatives and/or the total differential. As stated in Chapter 1, the comprehensive discussion of consumer choice theory will be postponed until the formal techniques on n-variable constrained optimization have been developed (in Chapter 8).

The first concept that we discuss is marginal utility. For a consumer making choices over n goods, the **marginal utility** of good i, denoted MU_i, is the change in the consumer's total utility ΔU caused by a particular change in the consumption of the good Δx_i with the consumption of the other $n - 1$ goods unchanged ($\Delta x_j = 0$ for all $j \neq i$). Thus we have that $MU_i = \Delta U / \Delta x_i$ (or $MU_i = \Delta U / \Delta x_i|_{\Delta x_i = 1}$ if only 1-more-unit changes are being considered). If the change in x_i is made smaller and smaller, then in the limit as $\Delta x_i \to 0$, the marginal utility becomes the partial derivative of the utility function with respect to the quantity of the good consumed. Thus the marginal utility of good i is defined as

$$MU_i = \frac{\partial U}{\partial x_i}. \tag{2.2}$$

For example, if $n = 2$ and the utility function is of the Cobb–Douglas form

$$U(x_1, x_2) = x_1^{1/2} x_2^{1/2}, \tag{2.3}$$

then the marginal utility functions for good 1 and good 2 are, respectively,

$$MU_1 = \frac{\partial U}{\partial x_1} = \frac{x_2^{1/2}}{2x_1^{1/2}},$$

$$MU_2 = \frac{\partial U}{\partial x_2} = \frac{x_1^{1/2}}{2x_2^{1/2}}. \tag{2.4}$$

As another example, consider the n-variable form of the general Cobb–Douglas utility function

$$U(x) = \prod_{j=1}^n x_j^{a_j} = x_1^{a_1} x_2^{a_2} \cdots x_n^{a_n}, \tag{2.5}$$

where $a_j > 0$ for all $j = 1, 2, \ldots, n$ and $\sum_{j=1}^{n} a_j = 1$. In this case the marginal utility of any good i is given by

$$MU_i = \frac{\partial U}{\partial x_i} = a_i x_i^{a_i - 1} \left(\prod_{\substack{j=1 \\ j \neq i}}^{n} x_j^{a_j} \right). \tag{2.6}$$

A simple substitution reveals that (2.3) and (2.4) are merely special cases of (2.5) and (2.6) when $n = 2$ and $a_1 = a_2 = \frac{1}{2}$. Note that in both cases MU_i is undefined when $x_i = 0$, so for Cobb–Douglas utility functions, the choice space must be further restricted to $x \in \Re_{++}^n$.

One property that economists often attribute to economic agents is **diminishing marginal utility.** The utility function is said to have this property when additional units of any good decrease the marginal utility of that good. Given the partial derivative definition of marginal utility in (2.2), a utility function exhibits diminishing marginal utility if

$$U_{ii} = \frac{\partial MU_i}{\partial x_i} = \frac{\partial^2 U}{\partial x_i^2} < 0 \qquad \text{for all } i. \tag{2.7}$$

Direct computation reveals that both these Cobb–Douglas utility functions exhibit this property. For the $n = 2$ case given by (2.3), we have

$$U_{11} = \frac{-x_2^{1/2}}{4x_1^{3/2}} \qquad \text{and} \qquad U_{22} = \frac{-x_1^{1/2}}{4x_2^{3/2}},$$

expressions that are both strictly negative. For the general n-dimensional Cobb–Douglas case in (2.5) we have

$$U_{ii} = a_i(a_i - 1)x_i^{a_i - 2} \left(\prod_{\substack{j=1 \\ j \neq i}}^{n} x_j^{a_j} \right) \qquad \text{for all } i,$$

an expression that is also strictly negative since $(a_i - 1) < 0$. The condition $(a_i - 1) < 0$ is a result of the two restrictions $\sum_{j=1}^{n} a_j = 1$ and $a_j > 0$ for all j.

Although diminishing marginal utility is an important property with a long history in economics, it is not a property that is required for the consumer choice problem (2.1) to have a well-behaved solution. We will see shortly that diminishing marginal utility is not required for indifference curves to have the standard convex shape, and Chapter 8 reveals that diminishing marginal utility is neither necessary nor sufficient for the second-order conditions of the consumer choice problem to hold. Despite this, it remains a common assumption in economics that is worthy of careful examination.

Now diminishing marginal utility is an "own" effect; it is the relationship between the marginal utility of a particular good i and that of additional quantities of **that** good. What about the impact of the other $n - 1$ goods? What about the "cross" effects? The cross effect of good j on the marginal utility of good i is given by

$$U_{ij} = \frac{\partial MU_i}{\partial x_j} \qquad \text{for } i \neq j. \tag{2.8}$$

If the expression in (2.8) is strictly positive, then the goods are **complements with respect to the utility function,** since increased consumption of good j increases the marginal utility of good i. If the expression in (2.8) is strictly negative, then since increased consumption of good j decreases the marginal utility of good i, the goods are **substitutes with respect to the utility function.** Finally, if $U_{ij} = 0$ for $i \neq j$, the goods are said to be **unrelated with respect to the utility function.** The reader may verify by direct computation that both the previous Cobb–Douglas utility functions exhibit this type of complementarity between any two goods x_i and x_j with $i \neq j$.

Any one of these three cases—utility function substitutes, complements, or unrelated good—may hold; knowing that the individual has a well-behaved utility function that provides an economically reasonable solution to the consumer choice problem (2.1) does not rule out any of these three possibilities. In fact, since these are derivative, and therefore local, properties, it is possible for a particular utility function to exhibit complementarity for certain quantities consumed and substitutability for other quantities consumed. There are no general rules in this regard; it depends entirely on the particular utility function and therefore the underlying tastes and preferences of the individual consumer. It is important to note, though, that this type of substitutability and complementarity (substitutability and complementarity "with respect to the utility function") is not the only, or even the most common, way of defining these two concepts. Later we will discuss gross substitutes and gross complements, and much later (in Chapter 8) we discuss net substitutes and net complements. Both the gross and net conditions are restrictions on the relationship between the price of some good j and the demand for some other good i. Since these definitions are based on (observable) demand functions rather than utility functions, they often prove to be a more useful way of classifying the possible substitutabilities and complementarities between goods.

Next we discuss the indifference curve and the closely related concept of the marginal rate of substitution. Recall from microeconomic theory that an indifference curve is defined as the set of all combinations of the goods that give the same level of utility. Thus for the familiar $n = 2$ case, the indifference curve associated with any arbitrary utility level $\bar{U}$ is given by all $x = (x_1, x_2) \in \Re^2_+$ that satisfy

$$U(x_1, x_2) = \bar{U}. \tag{2.9}$$

For the n-variable case, (2.9) is simply the set of $x \in \Re^n_+$ that satisfies $U(x) = \bar{U}$.

As an example of (2.9), consider the $n = 2$ Cobb–Douglas utility function (2.3) for utility levels $\bar{U} = 1$ and $\bar{U} = 2$. These two indifference curves are given by

$$x_1^{1/2} x_2^{1/2} = 1 \qquad \text{and} \qquad x_1^{1/2} x_2^{1/2} = 2. \tag{2.10}$$

They are depicted in Figure 2.1

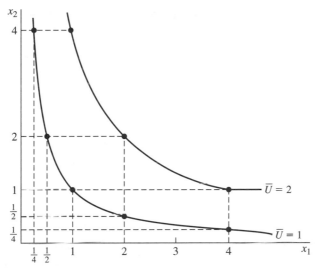

Figure 2.1

Also recall from microeconomic theory the definition of the marginal rate of substitution (*MRS*). The **marginal rate of substitution** is the rate at which the consumer can substitute one good for the other and still stay on the same indifference curve (keep the same level of utility). For the familiar $n = 2$ case, the *MRS* at a particular point $x = (x_1, x_2)$ is defined as the absolute value of the slope of the tangent to the indifference curve at that point, that is,

$$MRS = \frac{-dx_2}{dx_1}\bigg|_{U=\bar{U}}. \tag{2.11}$$

Since the numerator and the denominator have opposite signs, the negative on the right-hand side of (2.11) converts the expression to an absolute value and guarantees that the *MRS* is strictly positive. For the n-good case, the *MRS* is still defined two goods at a time; the *MRS* of any x_i for any x_j is simply $-dx_j/dx_i|_{U=\bar{U}}$. In both expressions the symbolism $|_{U=\bar{U}}$ merely indicates that the derivative is to be taken along an indifference curve, where $U(x) = \bar{U}$.

Let us return to the $n = 2$ Cobb–Douglas case in (2.3) and compute the *MRS* along the $\bar{U} = 1$ and $\bar{U} = 2$ indifference curves given in (2.10). Rewriting these indifference curves with x_2 as the dependent variable, we have

$$x_2^{1/2} = \frac{1}{x_1^{1/2}} \quad \text{or} \quad x_2 = \frac{1}{x_1} \quad \text{for } \bar{U} = 1$$

and

$$x_2^{1/2} = \frac{2}{x_1^{1/2}} \quad \text{or} \quad x_2 = \frac{4}{x_1} \quad \text{for } \bar{U} = 2.$$

Taking the required derivative, we have the marginal rate of substitution along $\bar{U} = 1$ given by

$$MRS_{\bar{U}=1} = -\frac{-1}{x_1^2} = \frac{1}{x_1^2}, \tag{2.12}$$

and for $\bar{U} = 2$ it is

$$MRS_{\bar{U}=2} = -\frac{-4}{x_1^2} = \frac{4}{x_1^2}. \tag{2.13}$$

From these two examples we can see that for this particular utility function and any arbitrary level $\bar{U}$, the MRS is given by

$$MRS = \frac{\bar{U}^2}{x_1^2}. \tag{2.14}$$

Since the arbitrary utility level must satisfy $x_1^{1/2}x_2^{1/2} = \bar{U}$ or $\bar{U}^2 = x_1 x_2$, we can write (2.14) in terms of any arbitrary point $x = (x_1, x_2)$ in the choice space as

$$MRS(x) = \frac{x_1 x_2}{x_1^2} = \frac{x_2}{x_1}. \tag{2.15}$$

The expression (2.15) allows us to easily compute the marginal rate of substitution for this particular utility function at any point $x = (x_1, x_2)$; at $x = (1, 1)$ $MRS = 1$ while at $x = (4, 1)$ $MRS = \frac{1}{4}$, and so on.

Thus far the MRS has been computed only for one specific utility function. What about the general case? What can we say about the MRS for an arbitrary utility function $U(x)$? We answer this question by taking two separate approaches. These approaches are mathematically equivalent, but we discuss both because both appear in the economics literature—not only for the MRS, but also in many other economic contexts. The first approach involves taking a total differential of the utility function, while the second approach involves differentiation of both sides of an identity.

For the first approach, let us take the total differential of the utility function $U(x)$ in the most general case where $x \in \Re_+^n$. This total differential is given by

$$dU = \sum_{i=1}^{n} U_i(x)\,dx_i, \tag{2.16}$$

where $U_i = \partial U / \partial x_i$ for all $i = 1, 2, \ldots, n$. If we are interested in the MRS of x_1 for x_2, then we simply let $dx_i = 0$ for all $i \neq 1, 2$ in (2.16). This means that we are considering the total differential only in the "directions" of x_1 and x_2, that is, only along the $x_1 x_2$ plane. With this restriction, (2.16) becomes

$$dU = U_1(x)\,dx_1 + U_2(x)\,dx_2. \tag{2.17}$$

Now the MRS is not defined for arbitrary changes within the choice space or even arbitrary changes in x_1 and x_2; it is defined **only** along an indifference curve $U(x) = \bar{U}$. If the changes in x_1 and x_2 occur along an indifference curve, then the level of utility does not change and therefore we must have $dU = 0$. Letting $dU = 0$ in (2.17) and rearranging gives us

$$\left.\frac{dx_2}{dx_1}\right|_{U-\bar{U}} = \frac{-U_1}{U_2}. \tag{2.18}$$

Given the definition of the MRS in (2.11), this expression implies that

$$MRS = \frac{U_1}{U_2}. \tag{2.19}$$

Thus for any arbitrary utility function, the MRS of x_1 for x_2 is given by the ratio of the marginal utility of x_1 to the marginal utility of x_2. If we had been interested in the MRS of x_i for x_j, the right-hand side of (2.19) would have been U_i/U_j. It is easy to check that (2.19) holds for the specific utility functions examined earlier. Notice that the MRS (2.19) is defined only when $U_2 \neq 0$. This is an additional restriction on the utility function, but it is easily satisfied: it simply means that the consumer is never completely satiated in x_2, that more of x_2 is always better than less. If $U_i > 0$ for all $i = 1, 2, \ldots, n$ (the relatively standard assumption of monotonic preferences), then the MRS will exist for every pair of goods.

For the second approach, we start not with the total differential but rather with the general form of the indifference curve. If we are concerned with goods x_1 and x_2, then the indifference curve is given by

$$U(x_1, x_2) = \bar{U}. \tag{2.20}$$

Since (2.20) is one equation in two unknowns (x_1 and x_2), it should be possible to solve (2.20) for x_2 as a function of x_1. Let us write $x_2 = x_2(x_1)$ as the general form of this solution.[1] Substitution of this solution back into (2.20) gives us an **identity** for the indifference curve (2.20) in terms of a single variable x_1:

$$U(x_1, x_2(x_1)) \equiv \bar{U}. \tag{2.21}$$

The expression (2.21) is an identity and not merely an equation because we have substituted the exact values that solve equation (2.20) back into it. For example, if we were to solve the equation $x + 4 = 10$ for $x = 6$ and then substitute $x = 6$ back into $x + 4 = 10$, we would have the identity $6 + 4 = 10$. The expression in (2.21) is the result of the same procedure.

Since differentiation across an identity (unlike a mere equation) is a valid mathematical operation, we can now differentiate both sides of (2.21) with respect to x_1. This differentiation gives us

$$U_1 + U_2 \frac{dx_2}{dx_1} = 0 \qquad \text{or} \qquad \left.\frac{dx_2}{dx_1}\right|_{U=\bar{U}} = \frac{-U_1}{U_2}. \tag{2.22}$$

Mathematicians often call the technique used in going from (2.20) to (2.22) **implicit differentiation,** but regardless of how it is labeled, the result is the same as that just obtained from the total differential approach:

$$MRS = \frac{U_1}{U_2}.$$

BOX 2.1
Pareto Efficiency and Competitive Equilibrium:
The First Fundamental Theorem of Welfare Economics

An allocation of resources is *Pareto efficient* (or *Pareto optimal*) if the only way in which a reallocation can make one person better off is to make someone else worse off. Consider the case of only two traders (A and B) and two goods (x and y) given by the Edgeworth box shown here. If $\bar{x}_i$ represents the initial endowment of good x and $\bar{y}_i$ represents the initial endowment of good y held by agent $i = A, B$, then the total endowment of good x will be $\bar{x} = \bar{x}_A + \bar{x}_B$ and the total endowment of good y will be $\bar{y} = \bar{y}_A + \bar{y}_B$. Since the dimensions of the Edgeworth box are $(\bar{x}, \bar{y})$, if A's holdings of the two goods are measured from the lower left-hand corner and B's from the upper right-hand corner, then each point in the box represents an allocation of the two goods to the two individuals.

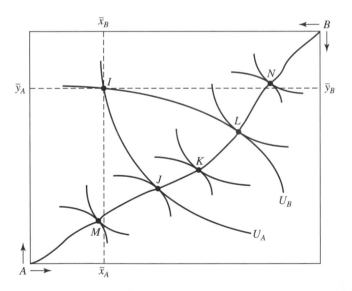

Notice that allocation I is **not** a Pareto-efficient allocation, since it is possible to reallocate the goods in such a way that one person is better off without making someone else worse off. Moving anywhere into the lens area defined by A's indifference curve through $I(U_a)$ and B's indifference curve through $I(U_B)$, would increase the level of utility of both individuals. However, if the initial allocation were given by J, K, or L (or M or N), then no reallocation would exist such that one individual could be made better off without making the other individual worse off. Thus points such as J,

K, L, M, and N, at which the indifference curves of the two individuals are just tangent, are Pareto-efficient allocations. The set of all such Pareto efficient allocations, shown by the curve running from one corner of the Edgeworth box to the other, is called the **contract curve.**

We are interested in relating these Pareto-efficient allocations to the allocations that might be achieved by competitive equilibrium prices. There is a long tradition in economics, going back to Adam Smith's "invisible hand" in 1776, which suggests that competitive equilibrium prices should achieve an efficient allocation of resources. Although this result, the **first fundamental theorem of welfare economics,** could be demonstrated diagrammatically for the case of two goods and two traders (in a way that may already be familiar to the student), we take a bit more formal approach. Let us define a **competitive** (or Walrasian) **equilibrium** as a set of prices $p = (p_1, p_2)$ and an allocation $x = x_A + x_B$ and $y = y_A + y_B$ such that the following two conditions hold:

1. The allocation (x, y) is feasible: $x = \bar{x}$ and $y = \bar{y}$.
2. If $U^i(x_i', y_i') > U^i(x_i, y_i)$ for some allocation $(x_i', y_i') \neq (x_i, y_i)$, then $p_x x_i' + p_y y_i' > p_x x_i + p_y y_i$ for $i = A, B$, where U^i is the utility function of agent i.

Condition 1 requires the supply to be equal to the demand for both goods, and condition 2 requires that equilibrium allocations be utility-maximizing for both individuals given their respective budget constraints. Another way to interpret condition 2 is to say that if either agent prefers another bundle over the competitive allocation, then the other bundle must be more expensive.

The first fundamental theorem of welfare economics states that every competitive equilibrium is Pareto efficient. To save space, we prove a slightly weaker version of the theorem, which states that there does not exist another feasible allocation that both individuals prefer to the competitive allocation. To prove this version, we suppose that it were not the case. We suppose that (x', y') with $(x_i', y_i') \neq (x_i, y_i)$, which has $U^i(x_i', y_i') > U^i(x_i, y_i)$ for $i = A, B$. Summing over the two agents and remembering that both bundles are feasible, we have $p_x \bar{x} + p_y \bar{y} > p_x \bar{x} + p_y \bar{y}$, which is a contradiction, so the theorem is proved. This relatively simple version of the first fundamental theorem is indicative of the type of argument used to prove more sophisticated versions, which include such things as many agents, many goods, and production. Standard references on the subject include works by Arrow and Hahn (1971) and Debreu (1959).

Sources

Arrow, K. J., and F. H. Hahn. 1971. *General competitive analysis.* San Francisco: Holden-Day.

Debreu, G. 1959. *Theory of value.* New Haven, CT: Yale University Press.

Both approaches are used in the economics literature and are employed in various contexts throughout this book. Since the two approaches are equivalent mathematically (although perhaps not aesthetically), the choice is a matter of technical convenience or ease of economic interpretation.

The final topic we discuss in this section is the issue of the shape, more particularly the convexity, of indifference curves. Recall from microeconomic theory that there are good economic reasons to believe that indifference curves are strictly convex to the origin. If this is the case, what restrictions does this strict convexity impose on the underlying utility function? Conversely, does diminishing marginal utility guarantee that indifference curves will have the proper shape?

To answer such questions, recall that the *MRS* is the absolute value of the slope of the tangent to the indifference curve. Given this, if the *MRS* is decreasing (getting flatter) as additional x_1 is consumed, then the indifference curve is strictly convex. Thus diminishing *MRS* (i.e., $dMRS/dx_1 < 0$) implies the strict convexity of the indifference curve $U(x_1, x_2) = \bar{U}$. This is shown by the slope of the tangents in Figure 2.2.

This argument can be stated more formally. Recall (2.21): that is, recall that an indifference curve can be written as a function of a single variable. If we solve $U(x_1, x_2) = \bar{U}$ for x_2 as a function of x_1, we can write $x_2 = x_2(x_1)$ as an expression for the indifference curve in explicit (rather than implicit) form. Since this is now a function of only one variable, we can apply the convexity results from the end of Chapter 1. There it was argued that if f is a function of one variable, then $f'' > 0$ implies that f is strictly convex. Applying this to the explicit form of the indifference curve, we have that the strict convexity of the indifference curve is implied by $d^2x_2/dx_1^2 > 0$. But this condition is just another way of writing $dMRS/dx_1 < 0$. Why? Because $MRS = -dx_2/dx_1$, and so $dMRS/dx_1 = -d^2x_2/dx_1^2$; thus $d^2x_2/dx_1^2 > 0$ is equivalent to $dMRS/dx_1 < 0$.

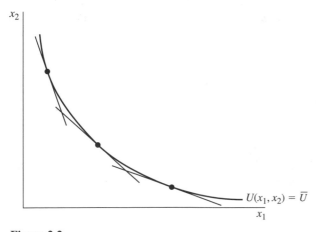

Figure 2.2

Given this relationship between diminishing *MRS* and the strict convexity of indifference curves, finding restrictions on the utility function that guarantee this convexity (that make $dMRS/dx_1 < 0$) would seem to be a relatively simple task. Unfortunately $dMRS/dx_1$ is a relatively messy derivative, since $MRS = U_1/U_2$ and both U_1 and U_2 depend on both variables x_1 and x_2. Not only do both marginal utilities depend on both variables, but variable x_2 is itself a function of x_1, since the derivative is being taken along an indifference curve. The *MRS* function to be differentiated is actually

$$MRS(x_1) = \frac{U_1(x_1, x_2(x_1))}{U_2(x_1, x_2(x_1))}.$$

Taking the derivative, we have

$$\frac{dMRS}{dx_1} = \frac{U_2[U_{11} + U_{12}(dx_2/dx_1)] - U_1[U_{21} + U_{22}(dx_2/dx_1)]}{U_2^2}, \quad (2.23)$$

where $U_{ij} = \partial^2 U/\partial x_i \partial x_j$. But we know that $dx_2/dx_1 = -U_1/U_2$, so substituting this into (2.23) eliminates all terms that are not derivatives of U. This substitution gives

$$\frac{dMRS}{dx_1} = \frac{U_2[U_{11} - U_{12}(U_1/U_2)] + U_1[U_{21} - U_{22}(U_1/U_2)]}{U_2^2}. \quad (2.24)$$

Since $U_{12} = U_{21}$, with some rearrangement the expression in (2.24) reduces to

$$\frac{dMRS}{dx_1} = \frac{U_2^2 U_{11} - 2U_1 U_2 U_{12} + U_1^2 U_{22}}{U_2^2}. \quad (2.25)$$

Now for diminishing *MRS*, the right-hand side of (2.25) must be strictly negative, and since $U_2^2 > 0$, we finally have the desired condition

$$U_2^2 U_{11} - 2U_1 U_2 U_{12} + U_1^2 U_{22} < 0. \quad (2.26)$$

Thus the utility function $U(x_1, x_2)$ exhibits a diminishing marginal rate of substitution and has strictly convex indifference curves if condition (2.26) holds. Notice that diminishing marginal utility ($U_{ii} < 0$) is neither necessary nor sufficient for condition (2.26). The results in Chapter 8 will demonstrate that condition (2.26) is equivalent to the second-order condition for the consumer choice problem in two variables and that such a condition must hold for any two goods x_i and x_j if the second-order conditions for the n-variable consumer choice problem are satisfied. At this time, though, we do not attempt to prove these assertions. Instead, we simply note that diminishing *MRS* imposes a rather elaborate restriction on the utility function and that this elaborate restriction does not depend in any obvious way on the assumption of diminishing marginal utility.

It is often easier to check a specific utility function for the property $dMRS/dx_1 < 0$ than the complexity of (2.26) might suggest. As an example, again consider the $n = 2$ Cobb–Douglas case given by (2.3). For this utility function, the explicit expression for an indifference curve is given by

$$x_2 = x_2(x_1) = \frac{\bar{U}^2}{x_1};$$ (2.27)

thus the slope of the indifference curve for this example is

$$\frac{dx_2}{dx_1} = \frac{-\bar{U}^2}{x_1^2}.$$

As argued earlier, strict concavity is implied by $d^2x_2/dx_1^2 > 0$, so taking this second derivative, we have

$$\frac{d^2x_2}{dx_1^2} = \frac{2\bar{U}^2}{x_1^3}.$$ (2.28)

Since $x_1x_2 = \bar{U}^2$, substitution of this expression into (2.28) gives us an expression for the second derivative along the indifference curve in terms of x_1 and x_2:

$$\frac{d^2x_2}{dx_1^2} = \frac{2x_2}{x_1^2}.$$ (2.29)

Since this expression is strictly positive, we have proved that the utility function $U(x_1, x_2) = x_1^{1/2}x_2^{1/2}$ has strictly convex indifference curves.

Production Theory

In this subsection we do for production theory what the preceding section did for consumer choice theory: we show how certain familiar economic concepts can be defined in terms of partial derivatives and/or the total differential. Although this discussion of production theory is much shorter than the discussion of consumer choice theory, it is not because production theory is any simpler or less important. The brevity is due to the fact that so much of production theory amounts to re-naming of the concepts from the discussion of consumer choice theory, and given the formal similarity of the concepts, a detailed discussion of either one greatly simplifies the presentation of the other. This similarity also allows us to refer the reader to the preceding subsection and the exercises for specific examples, further shortening the discussion.

Since the production side of the economy transforms inputs into outputs, it is no surprise that the fundamental production concept is the production function, a function relating inputs to outputs. More specifically, the production function $y = f(x)$ shows the maximum amount of output y that can be obtained from various combinations of inputs x. In the most general n-input case, x is the input vector $x = (x_1, \ldots, x_n) \in \Re_+^n$ and $f: \Re_+^n \to \Re_+$. For the two-input case, where $f: \Re_+^2 \to \Re_+$, the input vector x is sometimes represented by $x = (L, K)$, since labor L and capital K are the two production inputs already familiar to most readers.

Because we are interested in applying calculus techniques to production theory, the production functions we discuss are assumed to be (at least twice) differentiable and to exhibit smooth substitutability between the various inputs. But before proceeding with this "neoclassical" case, we digress a bit and warn the reader that in production theory (unlike utility theory) this case does not exhaust the interest of the economics profession. The motivation for an alternative non-neoclassical specification of production technology is often empirical: while some production processes undoubtedly exhibit differentiability and smooth substitutability between inputs, it is well known that not all do. Certain firms face technology with "fixed" coefficients: that is, inputs must be used in certain fixed proportions and cannot be freely substituted for one another. The prototype for many of these non-neoclassical production processes is the Leontief technology, discussed in Chapter 6. With the exception of the Leontief system, we focus exclusively on the neoclassical case of differentiability and the smooth substitutability of inputs.

The first production topic we discuss is the marginal product of an input (sometimes called the marginal physical product). For the differentiable production function $y = f(x)$ with $x \in \Re^n_+$, the **marginal product of input i,** denoted MP_i, is the partial derivative of the production function with respect to input x_i; thus $MP_i = f_i$, where $f_i = \partial f / \partial x_i$.

In the standard specification of a neoclassical production function, marginal products are strictly positive ($f_i > 0$ for all i), but each input exhibits diminishing marginal productivity. Diminishing marginal productivity (also called diminishing returns) is the property that the marginal product of an input decreases as more of the input is added to production. In terms of derivatives, diminishing returns to input i simply means that $f_{ii} < 0$, where $f_{ii} = \partial^2 f / \partial x_i^2$. Thus for a production function $y = f(x)$ with n inputs to have positive marginal products but diminishing returns to all inputs, we have $f_i > 0$ and $f_{ii} < 0$ for all $i = 1, 2, \ldots, n$.

As with utility functions, neither knowing that the own effect f_{ii} is strictly negative nor knowing that the function is economically "well behaved" necessarily restricts the signs of the cross effects $f_{ij} = \partial^2 f / \partial x_i \partial x_j$ for $i \neq j$. These cross terms may be positive, negative, or zero, depending on the specific production function and its properties. If the cross term f_{ij} is strictly positive, we say that the two inputs are **complements in production,** since an increase in the use of one input will increase the marginal product of the other. Factor complementarity is, in fact, a quite common, though by no means necessary, assumption in economic theory. Correspondingly, if f_{ij} is strictly negative for $i \neq j$, then the two inputs are considered to be **substitutes in production,** since increasing the quantity of one input decreases the marginal product of the other. Finally, $f_{ij} = 0$ for $i \neq j$ (sometimes called **unrelated inputs**) simply implies that neither of the two inputs directly affects the marginal product of the other. As in consumer choice theory, this complementarity and substitutability "on the production function" should not be confused with complementarity and substitutability on the input demand functions. The latter (discussed for $n = 2$ in Chapter 3 and $n > 2$ in Chapter 7) concerns the effect of a change in the price of one input on the profit-maximizing demand for another.

The production theory analogue of the indifference curve is the **isoquant,** a set of input combinations that give the same level of output. Thus for the $n = 2$ case, where the production function is $y = f(x_1, x_2)$, the isoquant associated with any arbitrary output level $\bar{y} \in \Re_{++}$ is given by

$$f(x_1, x_2) = \bar{y}. \tag{2.30}$$

For the n-input case, (2.30) would be the set of $x \in \Re^n_+$ such that $f(x) = \bar{y}$.

The **marginal rate of technical substitution** $(MRTS)$ is the rate at which two inputs can be substituted for each other and still leave the output unchanged (stay on the same isoquant). Thus the $MRTS$ of input x_1 for input x_2 is

$$MRTS = \frac{-dx_2}{dx_1}\bigg|_{y=\bar{y}}. \tag{2.31}$$

For the n-input case, we can define the $MRTS$ of any x_i for x_j in an analogous manner, that is, $-dx_j/dx_i|_{y=\bar{y}}$.

We can find the relationship between the $MRTS$ and the derivative of the production function in precisely the same way(s) used for (2.19). Taking the total differential of $y = f(x_1, x_2)$, we have

$$dy = f_1(x) \, dx_1 + f_2(x) \, dx_2. \tag{2.32}$$

Now along any isoquant we have $dy = 0$, so with some rearrangement (2.32) becomes

$$\frac{dx_2}{dx_1}\bigg|_{y=\bar{y}} = -\frac{f_1}{f_2}. \tag{2.33}$$

By substituting the definition of $MRTS$ from (2.31), this becomes

$$MRTS = \frac{f_1}{f_2}. \tag{2.34}$$

Thus the $MRTS$ of input x_i for input x_j is given by the ratio of the marginal products of the two inputs, that is, f_i/f_j.

Of course, just as diminishing MRS implies the convexity of indifference curves in utility theory, a diminishing $MRTS$ implies the convexity of isoquants in production theory. Rewriting the diminishing MRS condition (2.26) in terms of the production function $y = f(x_1, x_2)$, we have

$$f_2^2 f_{11} - 2 f_1 f_2 f_{12} + f_1^2 f_{22} < 0. \tag{2.35}$$

Now it is quite easy to see the mathematical similarities between utility theory and neoclassical production theory. Although these similarities certainly exist, and are in fact quite convenient, we want to stress in closing this section that it is only the mathematical and formal properties of these two theories that are the same. Marginal utilities are not "like" marginal products in any respect other than that both can be represented as partial derivatives of a single-valued function of many variables. The nice thing about calculus is precisely that it allows us to discuss these two very different things, the theory of production and the theory of consumption, within the confines of a single and relatively simple formal framework.

BOX 2.2
Superfairness

Most economic problems involve issues of both equity and efficiency. While economists have been relatively successful in providing a formal characterization of efficiency (see Box 2.1), the concept of equity or fairness has been much more resistant to formal analysis. The literature on superfairness represents one attempt to characterize fair allocations in a formal way analogous to the standard characterization of efficiency. Two general surveys of the topic are Thomson and Varian (1985) and Baumol (1986).

While it is possible to characterize superfairness in the general case of many agents, many goods, and production, we restrict our discussion to the simple case of two individuals and two goods where the relevant Edgeworth box (see Box 2.1) can be drawn. The fundamental notion in the analysis of superfairness is the concept of **envy.** We say that individual A is **envious** of individual B's allocation if A would rather have B's allocation than his or her own. Given this definition of envy, we can find the allocations in which A is not envious of B by finding allocations in which A would be indifferent to "trading places": that is, A would be indifferent between his or her own allocation and the allocation of B. In the first Edgeworth box shown here, in allocation I individual A is indifferent between A's allocation and what A would have if A traded places with B. The indifference curve for A drawn through allocation I is the standard indifference curve, but the mirror-image (concave) indifference curve through I is **not** the indifference curve for B; rather it is the indifference curve showing all the

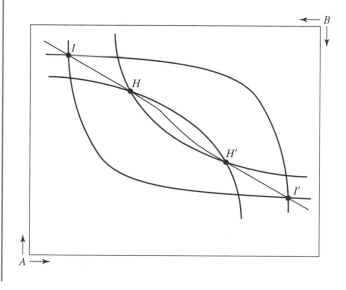

allocations A would consider indifferent to allocation I **if** A were given B's allocation. That is, the concave indifference curve through I shows all the allocations that A would find indifferent to allocation I if they traded places with B. Notice that since individual A is indifferent between their allocation and B's allocation at I, it must also be true that A is indifferent between their own allocation and B's allocation at I'. Thus we will say that allocations I and I' lie on A's **fairness boundary.** Notice that allocations H and H' lie on A's fairness boundary for the same reason, and by connecting all such allocations, we have the entire fairness boundary for A, shown by the curve through allocations I, H, I', and H'. Any allocation above this fairness boundary is considered to be more than fair (no envy) by A, while any allocation below this boundary is considered unfair (envious) by A.

A **superfair distribution** is an allocation that both individuals view as fair or more than fair, that is, an allocation in which neither individual is envious of the other's allocation. In the second Edgeworth box shown here, the fairness boundary for A is labeled FB_A and the fairness boundary for B is labeled FB_B; these boundaries cross at the midpoint where both individuals receive the same allocation of both goods. Both fairness boundaries must pass through this midpoint because both agents must be indifferent between their individual allocation and that of the other agent when both have exactly the same amounts of both goods. Since all the allocations that A considers to be more than fair are above FB_A and all those that B considers to be more than fair are to the left of FB_B, the two shaded areas are more than fair to both and thus, when the boundaries are included, constitute the superfair allocations. The midpoint (equal distribution) is a superfair allocation, but allocations on both sides of the midpoint may not be superfair.

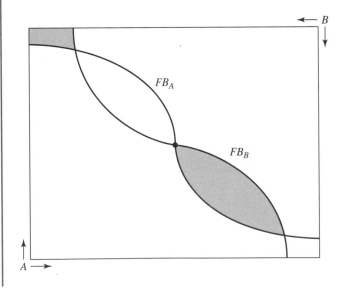

A number of interesting theorems have been proved for superfair allocations. One is that if both individuals have the same preferences, then the two fairness boundaries must coincide and no strictly superfair allocations (allocations that are more than fair to both individuals) exist. Another interesting theorem is that there always exists a Pareto-efficient allocation that is superfair. This theorem provides a nice connection between the standard results on economic efficiency and the equity notion of superfairness. Other such results are discussed in the references.

Sources

Baumol, W. J. 1986. *Superfairness: Applications and theory.* Cambridge, MA: MIT Press.

Thomson, W., and H. Varian. 1985. Theories of justice based on symmetry. In *Social goals and social organization: Essays in honor of Elisha Pazner,* edited by L. Hurwicz, D. Schmeidler, and H. Sonnenschein. New York: Oxford University Press.

The Equation of Exchange in Macroeconomics

We close this introductory discussion of multivariate calculus applications to familiar economic models with an example from macroeconomics. The macroeconomic example we consider is one of the fundamental propositions of classical macroeconomic theory: the quantity theory of money. This example allows us to introduce a total differential technique that is applicable in a number of other economic models.

The classical quantity theory of money (or inflation) is derived from a single fundamental equation, the equation of exchange. There are (at least) two ways of interpreting this fundamental equation. The first approach is to view it as the result of the manner in which certain economic concepts are defined, and the second way is to view it as an equilibrium condition for the aggregate money market. Although the latter is probably a better interpretation economically, we emphasize the former, since the latter, the aggregate money market approach, would push us prematurely into the realm of comparative statics, the main topic of the next chapter.

To begin, let p be the price level in the economy and let Q be the real output. In a one-good world, Q is the total output of the single good, and p is its price. In a more realistic case of many different goods, p is an index of the overall price level, and Q is an index of real output (such as deflated nominal income). In either case, the nominal gross domestic product (GDP) or nominal income Y, is given by $Y = pQ$. We restrict our discussion to the purest classical case of constant full employment. If supply and demand for labor are stationary and the labor market always clears, then Q is not a variable, but rather is a parameter Q_f, where Q_f represents the real output produced at full employment. Thus with the assumption of full employment, the nominal income is given by $Y_f = pQ_f$.

Now consider the money side of the economy. Let the economy's nominal money supply be given by M^s. Each year this nominal money supply must circulate sufficiently to purchase the nominal income (Y_f) of the economy. For instance, if the nominal income of the economy is \$400 billion ($Y_f = 400$) and the nominal money supply is \$100 billion ($M^s = 100$), then each dollar in the economy must, on average, "turn over" or "change hands" four times in a transaction involving final goods or services. This average turnover rate, called the **velocity of money** v, is simply the average number of times each dollar must turn over in order to purchase the economy's nominal income. Given this definition of velocity, the following equation must hold:

$$M^s v = Y_f \qquad \text{or} \qquad M^s v = p Q_f. \tag{2.36}$$

This equation is called the **equation of exchange**, and it is the fundamental equation for the classical quantity theory of money.

The most important result of the classical quantity theory of money is a one-to-one relationship between a percentage change in the money supply and the corresponding percentage change in the price level. All that is required to derive this result is to compute dp/dM^s from the equation of exchange (2.36) and the other assumptions of the classical macroeconomic model. This derivative can be obtained from (2.36) in several different (mathematically equivalent) ways; of these, we discuss two. The first is by far the simpler, but the second is much more general and applicable in a number of more complex models.

The first approach is simply to rewrite (2.36) so that p is the sole dependent variable and then to differentiate the expression for p to find the impact of a change in M^s. Rewriting (2.36), we have

$$p = \frac{v M^s}{Q_f}. \tag{2.37}$$

Now if Q_f and v are functions of M^s, the derivative of (2.37) with respect to M^s will depend on the exact form of these functions; but this difficulty does not arise in the purest form of the classical quantity theory. According to the assumptions of the classical model, both Q_f and v are parameters: Q_f is a parameter because the economy is always assumed to be at full employment; the velocity v is considered to be a parameter (less obviously) because it depends on the society's spending habits and available money substitutes—both things that are fixed in the short run. Given that both Q_f and v are parameters in (2.37), the desired derivative is simply $dp/dM^s = v/Q_f$. Substituting for v and Q_f from the equation of exchange, we can write this derivative in the more familiar form

$$\frac{dp}{dM^s} = \frac{p}{M^s}. \tag{2.38}$$

The derivative in (2.38) gives us two important economic implications of the classical quantity theory. First, since the right-hand side of (2.38) is strictly positive, (2.38) says that more money causes higher prices. Second, and more importantly, (2.38) actually provides a simple quantitative relationship between a given change in money supply and the corresponding change in price level. To see this quantitative relationship, recall the generic definition of elasticity from (1.25) in Chapter 1.

Applying this definition to money and prices, we see that the elasticity of the price level with respect to the money supply is given by $\varepsilon_{p,M} = (M^s/p)(dp/dM^s)$. Substituting (2.38) into this definition, we obtain a nice simple expression for the quantitative relationship between a change in M^s and the corresponding change in p:

$$\varepsilon_{p,M} = 1 \quad \text{or} \quad \%\Delta M^s = \%\Delta p. \tag{2.39}$$

Thus according to the purest form of the classical quantity theory, the price level is unit elastic with respect to the money supply: an x-percent increase in the money supply will generate an x-percent increase in the price level.

The foregoing approach is a very simple way of going from the equation of exchange to (2.38), but it is actually too simple to demonstrate much in the way a general technique. Since both Q_f and v are parameters, the equation of exchange (2.36) is merely a linear expression in two variables—hardly a great challenge when we want to find the derivative of one variable with respect to the other.

Let us now consider a more general case, in which the explicit form of the functional relationship among the four variables v, M^s, p, and Q_f is unknown. Of course, when this more general case is applied to (2.36), the result will be exactly the same as that already obtained; but much can be learned by going through the general case, since it is applicable in more complex models in which less information is available.

For the general case, suppose that all we know about velocity is that it is defined by a differentiable function G of the three variables M^s, p, and Q_f. Thus we have v given only as

$$v = G(M^s, p, Q_f). \tag{2.40}$$

How do we find dp/dM^s in such a general case?

We start by rewriting (2.40) as an implicit function of all four variables, that is,

$$F(v, M^s, p, Q_f) = 0, \tag{2.41}$$

where $F(\cdot) = v - G(\cdot)$. Since F is a function of four variables, the total differential of F is

$$dF = F_v \, dv + F_M \, dM^s + F_p \, dp + F_Q \, dQ_f, \tag{2.42}$$

where $F_x = \partial F/\partial x$. Since $F = 0$ for all values of the variables, we have $dF = 0$, and the total differential in (2.42) can be rewritten as

$$F_v \, dv + F_M \, dM^s + F_p \, dp + F_Q \, dQ_f = 0. \tag{2.43}$$

To find the desired relationship between dp and dM^s when v and Q_f are unchanged, simply set dv and dQ_f equal to zero in (2.43) and solve for dp/dM^s. After this substitution, a little rearrangement gives

$$\frac{dp}{dM^s} = \frac{-F_M}{F_p}. \tag{2.44}$$

The expression in (2.44) gives the general relationship between a change in M^s and the change in p when $dv = dQ_f = 0$ and the four variables are related by equation (2.41); it, of course, requires that $F_p \neq 0$.

Now if we have absolutely no additional information about the function $F(\cdot)$, then (2.44) exhausts what can be said about the relationship between ΔM^s and Δp. But such a complete absence of additional information would be very unusual in economic theory. Usually, as we will see many times in the coming chapters, economic models at least provide qualitative (sign) restrictions on the partial derivatives of functions like F, and often these can be used to sign expressions like (2.44).

Of course, in the special case of the classical quantity theory, not only do we have such qualitative information, but also we know the function F exactly. For the classical quantity theory, the function F is

$$F(v, M^s, p, Q_f) = M^s v - p Q_f = 0. \tag{2.45}$$

thus for this particular case, we have $F_M = v$ and $F_p = -Q_f$. Substitution of these specific values into the general expression (2.44) gives

$$\frac{dp}{dM^s} = \frac{v}{Q_f}.$$

Since $M^s v = p Q_f$, further substitution gives

$$\frac{dp}{dM^s} = \frac{p}{M^s},$$

precisely the result found in (2.38). Thus the total differential approach gives us exactly the same result as that found earlier by direct differentiation. Since the total differential approach is substantially more complicated than direct differentiation, it would not be used if we were interested only in a relatively simple model such as the classical quantity theory. It is important to go through the total differential approach because it can be used in more complex cases, where the exact form of function F is unknown.

2.2 Homogeneous Functions

In this section we discuss a very important class of functions, **homogeneous functions.** Like the convex and concave functions introduced at the end of Chapter 1, homogeneous functions are extremely useful because their mathematical properties can often be given a simple economic interpretation. First, we discuss the purely mathematical properties of homogeneous functions, and then we proceed to economic applications in both production and demand theory.

The Mathematics of Homogeneous Functions

A real-valued function of n variables $y = f(x)$, $f: \Re^n \to \Re$, is **homogeneous of degree r (h.d. r)** iff for all $x \in \Re^n$ and for all $\lambda \in \Re_{++}$

$$f(\lambda x) = \lambda^r f(x). \tag{2.46}$$

Note in this definition that x is a vector of n variables $x = (x_1, x_2, \ldots, x_n) \in \Re^n$, while λ is a strictly positive real scalar. Thus λx means that each variable x_i is being "scaled up" or "scaled down" by exactly the **same scalar** λ. Also it is important that the scalar λ not be confused with the degree of homogeneity r; if f is homogeneous of degree r, then (2.46) will hold for all $\lambda > 0$. For example, if a particular function f is h.d. 2, then $f(\lambda x) = \lambda^2 f(x)$ for all $\lambda > 0$; thus $f(2x) = 4f(x)$, $f(10x) = 100 f(x)$, and so on. Technically the function in the foregoing definition is "positively" homogeneous. There is a more general definition of homogeneity that allows $\lambda < 0$, but we will consider only the case of positive homogeneity because that is the version that appears most often in economics.

Our first theorem for homogeneous functions is called **Euler's theorem.** It relates the degree of homogeneity r to certain properties of the function's partial derivatives. It is an extremely useful theorem that has a wide variety of economic applications.

THEOREM 2.1: A differentiable function of n variables $f(x)$, $f: \Re^n \to \Re$, is homogeneous of degree r iff for all $x \in \Re^n$

$$r f(x) = \sum_{i=1}^{n} f_i(x) x_i, \text{ where } f_i(x) = \frac{\partial f(x)}{\partial x_i}.$$

PROOF: Define the function $g(\lambda) = f(\lambda x)$ for all $\lambda > 0$, and note that $g(1) = f(x)$. Differentiating $g(\lambda)$, we have

$$g'(\lambda) = \sum_{i=1}^{n} \frac{\partial f(\lambda x)}{\partial(\lambda x_i)} \frac{d(\lambda x_i)}{d\lambda} = \sum_{i=1}^{n} \frac{\partial f(\lambda x)}{\partial(\lambda x_i)} x_i,$$

so $g'(1) = \sum_i f_i(x) x_i$.

First, consider the "only if" part of the theorem. If f is homogeneous of degree r, then $g(\lambda) = \lambda^r f(x)$ and $g'(\lambda) = r\lambda^{r-1} f(x)$ for all $\lambda > 0$. In particular, $g'(1) = r f(x)$. This, combined with the preceding expression for $g'(1)$, implies that $r f(x) = \sum_i f_i(x) x_i$.

Now consider the "if" part of the theorem. If $r f(x) = \sum_i f_i(x) x_i$, then the foregoing expression for $g'(\lambda)$ implies that

$$r f(\lambda x) = \lambda g'(\lambda).$$

Now define $h(\lambda) = g(\lambda)/\lambda^r$ so that $h'(\lambda) = [\lambda g'(\lambda) - r g(\lambda)]/\lambda^{r+1}$. Since $r g(\lambda) = r f(\lambda x)$ by the definition of g, we have $r g(\lambda) = \lambda g'(\lambda)$ and thus $h'(\lambda) = 0$. But $h'(\lambda) = 0$ implies that $h(\lambda) = k$, where k is a constant, thus $g(\lambda) = \lambda^r k$ for all $\lambda > 0$. In particular, $g(1) = k$, but since $g(1) = f(x)$, this implies that $g(\lambda) = \lambda^r f(x)$ or $f(\lambda x) = \lambda^r f(x)$, which proves the theorem.

Our second theorem on homogeneous functions is presented as a corollary to Euler's theorem, but it can be proved directly from the definition of a homogeneous function.

THEOREM 2.2: If a twice-differentiable function of n variables $f(x)$, $f: \mathfrak{R}^n \to \mathfrak{R}$, is homogeneous of degree r, then its partial derivatives $f_j(x) = \partial f(x)/\partial x_j$ are homogeneous of degree $r - 1$ for all $j = 1, 2, \ldots, n$.

PROOF: From Euler's theorem we know that if f is h.d. r then $rf(x) = \sum_i f_i(x)x_i$. Differentiating this expression with respect to any arbitrary x_j, we have $r f_j = f_j + \sum_i f_{ij}(x)x_i$, where $f_{ij} = \partial^2 f/\partial x_i \partial x_j$. Now since $f_{ij} = f_{ji}$, this expression can be rearranged as

$$(r - 1) f_j = \sum_{i=1}^{n} f_{ji}(x)x_i,$$

which by Euler's theorem proves that any arbitrary $f_j(x)$ is homogeneous of degree $r - 1$.

Homogeneity and Production Theory

The language used to characterize the class of homogeneous functions seems to have a natural "production" sound to it. We speak of the impact of λx on the function as scaling up the variables when $\lambda > 1$ and scaling down the variables when $\lambda < 1$. Such language naturally seems to fit production theory, where the function is a production function and the variables are factor inputs; in this case $\lambda > 1$ is an increase in the scale of production and $\lambda < 1$ is a decrease in the scale of production. The degree of homogeneity determines how output will respond to such changes in the scale of production.

More formally, let $y = f(x)$, $f: \mathfrak{R}^n_+ \to \mathfrak{R}_+$ be a differentiable production function. First let us consider the case of f homogeneous of degree 1, so that $f(\lambda x) = \lambda f(x)$ for all $\lambda > 0$. This says that if all inputs are increased by exactly the same amount, the output will also be increased by that same amount; for instance, doubling all inputs will double output. In economics this property is called **constant returns to scale.** Thus the mathematical property of the production function being homogeneous of degree 1 corresponds exactly to the economic concept of the production process exhibiting constant returns to scale. For example, the Cobb–Douglas production function examined earlier, where $f(x_1, x_2) = x_1^{1/2} x_2^{1/2}$ exhibits constant returns to scale, since $f(\lambda x_1, \lambda x_2) = (\lambda x_1)^{1/2}(\lambda x_2)^{1/2} = \lambda f(x_1, x_2)$. Many other examples of constant returns to scale production functions appear in the economics literature. Often such production functions are called **linearly homogeneous,** but we do not use this term because it can be confused with linearity, a property that neither implies, nor is implied by, homogeneity of degree 1.[2]

Now suppose that f is homogeneous of degree r, where r is between 0 and 1 (sometimes called **subhomogeneous**). In this case scaling up all inputs by some $\lambda > 1$ will increase output by less than λ; we have $f(\lambda x) = \lambda^r f(x)$, but since $0 < r < 1$, this implies that $f(\lambda x) < \lambda f(x)$. In economics, such a property is referred to as **decreasing returns to scale:** doubling all inputs increases output by less than double. Note that the economic term, in this case decreasing returns, is defined on the basis of the impact of an **increase** in all the inputs (i.e., $\lambda > 1$); if $0 < r < 1$ and the inputs are scaled down (i.e., $\lambda < 1$), then $f(\lambda x) > \lambda f(x)$.

Also note that decreasing returns to scale have nothing whatsoever to do with diminishing marginal productivity (diminishing returns). Diminishing returns, as we have seen, is the property of negative second partial derivatives ($f_{ii} = \partial^2 f/\partial x_i^2 < 0$); it is a short-run concept based on varying one input and leaving all other inputs unchanged. Decreasing returns to scale is a long-run concept that has to do with the output response of an equal scale increase in all inputs. These two concepts are entirely independent. For instance, the Cobb–Douglas case $f(x_1, x_2) = x_1^{1/2} x_2^{1/2}$ has diminishing returns to both inputs and yet constant returns to scale, while $f(x_1, x_2) = (x_1^{3/2} - x_2^{3/2})/x_2$ does not have diminishing returns to either input and yet does have decreasing returns to scale.

Finally, and not surprisingly, the case of a production function that is homogeneous of degree $r > 1$ (sometimes called **superhomogeneous**) corresponds to the economic property of **increasing returns to scale.** In this case a scale increase in all inputs by $\lambda > 1$ causes output to increase by more than the scale increase, so $f(\lambda x) > \lambda f(x)$. Firms with production functions that have this property are often called **natural monopolies,** since their long-run per unit costs will fall as output expands.

The homogeneity of production functions has long been related to the so-called **marginal productivity theory** of factor income distribution. To see why this is so, consider the production function $y = f(L, K)$, where L and K are labor and capital inputs, respectively. Assume that f is differentiable and homogeneous of degree r. Given this homogeneity, Euler's theorem implies that

$$f_L(L, K)L + f_K(L, K)K = ry, \tag{2.47}$$

where $f_x = \partial f/\partial x$ = marginal product of input x. If the price of the firm's output is p, multiplication of both sides of (2.47) by p gives

$$pf_L(L, K)L + pf_K(L, K)K = rpy. \tag{2.48}$$

First, note that the right-hand side of (2.48) is the degree of homogeneity r multiplied by the total revenue of the firm py. Second, consider the coefficients on L and K in (2.48). In both cases the coefficients are the value of the marginal product of that input, that is, the price of the output times the marginal product of the input (pf_i). Now suppose that both factors are actually paid the value of their marginal product. Then (2.48) says that how these factor payments relate to the total revenue of the firm depends on the degree r of homogeneity of the production function. If the production function is h.d. 1 ($r = 1$), then paying each factor the value of its marginal product will totally "exhaust" the firm's revenue: total factor payments = total revenue. But if there are increasing returns to scale ($r > 1$), then we have

$$pf_L(L, K)L + pf_K(L, K)K > py, \tag{2.49}$$

and paying each factor the value of its marginal product will cause the firm to have more factor input expense than it receives in total revenue (overexhaustion). Finally, for decreasing returns to scale ($r < 1$), we have

$$pf_L(L, K)L + pf_K(L, K)K < py, \tag{2.50}$$

and factor input expense is less than total revenue (underexhaustion).

Because of this simple relationship between the degree of homogeneity and the distribution of factor income payments, certain economists have argued that a "marginal productivity theory of distribution" requires that production functions be homogeneous of degree 1, since it is only in the case of homogeneity of degree 1 that paying each input the value of its marginal product will exactly exhaust the firm's revenue. This argument confuses a sufficient condition for exhaustion (which homogeneity of degree 1 is) with a necessary condition for exhaustion (which homogeneity of degree 1 is not).

Finally, before moving on to demand theory applications of homogeneity, we want to emphasize that production functions need not be homogeneous of any degree. Because of their nice properties, homogeneous production functions appear quite frequently in economics. This leads some students to believe that all production functions must be homogeneous of some degree, something that is certainly not true. Homogeneity is simply a mathematical property that happens to correspond nicely with our economic intuitions regarding returns to scale. Production functions need not be homogeneous to be economically reasonable or (as we will see in later chapters) to satisfy the sufficient conditions for profit maximization. In fact, not only may production functions be nonhomogeneous, but they may be locally homogeneous but not globally homogeneous; they may be homogeneous of one degree for certain output levels and homogeneous of a different degree (or not at all) for other output levels. This is often how the U-shaped long-run average total cost (ATC) curve that appears in microeconomics textbooks is motivated: it is homogeneous of degree $r > 1$ for low outputs and homogeneous of degree $r < 1$ for high outputs.

One device that can be used to measure local homogeneity is the elasticity of scale ε_s. For a small-scale increase λ, where λ is positive but small, the corresponding change in output is $df(\lambda x)/d\lambda$. If we convert this derivative to an elasticity measure, we have

$$\varepsilon_s = \left. \frac{\lambda}{f(\lambda x)} \frac{df(\lambda x)}{d\lambda} \right|_{\lambda=1}, \tag{2.51}$$

where $\lambda = 1$ simply indicates that the coefficient is computed for $\lambda = 1$. This coefficient measures the local impact of the percentage change in output caused by the percentage change in scale. If $\varepsilon_s = 1$, the production function exhibits local constant returns to scale; if $\varepsilon_s > 1$, it exhibits locally increasing returns to scale; and if $\varepsilon_s < 1$, it exhibits locally decreasing returns to scale. Because this is a local measure, it can be used when the production functions is not (globally) homogeneous.

Homogeneity and Demand Theory

Although homogeneity plays as important a role in demand theory as it does in production theory, the emphasis is somewhat different. The direct demand theory analogue of the homogeneous production function, the homogeneous utility function, is useful in some specific applications, but it is not the most important use of homogeneity in the theory of consumer choice. The most important use of homogeneity in this context is the zero-degree homogeneity of consumer demand functions. To see why this property holds for consumer demand functions, recall the general form of the consumer choice problem given in (2.1):

$$\underset{\{x\}}{\text{Max }} U(x)$$

$$\text{Subject to: } \sum_{i=1}^{n} p_i x_i = M,$$

where $x \in \mathfrak{R}_+^n$, $U: \mathfrak{R}_+^n \to \mathfrak{R}_+$, and $U(x)$ is at least twice differentiable. Again, this problem is not given a complete treatment until Chapter 8; for now we simply assert that the general solution to the problem in (2.1) is a set of n consumer demand functions

$$x_i^* = x_i^*(p, M) \qquad \text{for } i = 1, 2, \ldots, n. \tag{2.52}$$

These demand functions indicate that the utility-maximizing consumption of each of the n goods is a function of all the prices $p = (p_1, p_2, \ldots, p_n)$ and the money income M.

Now consider the impact of increasing all the parameters (p and M) in the general consumer choice problem (2.1) by some scalar $\lambda > 0$. The impact of such scalar multiplication on the budget constraint is

$$\sum_{i=1}^{n} \lambda p_i x_i = \lambda M, \text{ which implies } \sum_{i=1}^{n} p_i x_i = M. \tag{2.53}$$

This demonstrates that the budget constraint is unaltered by a scale increase in all the parameters. But if the budget constraint remains unchanged and the utility function is the same, then the utility-maximizing demands in (2.52) must remain unchanged by a scale multiplication of prices and money income. Thus

$$x_i^*(\lambda p, \lambda M) = x_i^*(p, M) \qquad \text{for } i = 1, 2, \ldots, n \qquad \text{and} \qquad \lambda > 0. \tag{2.54}$$

That is, consumer demand functions are **homogeneous of degree zero** in prices and money income. For instance, doubling the prices of all goods and doubling the money income available to spend on the goods does not change the consumer's optimal choices. This important result has numerous implications for both micro- and macroeconomics. It is sometimes called the condition of **no money illusion.**

One important implication of the zero-degree homogeneity of consumer demand functions is the relationship between the various types of demand elasticity. Applying Euler's theorem to the ith demand function in (2.52), we have

$$\frac{\partial x_i^*}{\partial p_i} p_i + \sum_{\substack{j=1 \\ j \neq i}}^{n} \frac{\partial x_i^*}{\partial p_j} p_j + \frac{\partial x_i^*}{\partial M} M = 0. \tag{2.55}$$

Dividing this expression through by x_i^* gives

$$\frac{\partial x_i^*}{\partial p_i} \frac{p_i}{x_i^*} + \sum_{\substack{j=1 \\ j \neq i}}^{n} \frac{\partial x_i^*}{\partial p_j} \frac{p_j}{x_i^*} + \frac{\partial x_i^*}{\partial M} \frac{M}{x_i^*} = 0. \tag{2.56}$$

To see the relationship between the expression in (2.56) and the elasticity of demand, recall the various types of demand elasticity defined in Chapter 1: own price, cross price, and income. In Chapter 1, these definitions were given as if demand were a function of only a single variable. But here, where demand is explicitly a function of more than one variable (actually $n + 1$), these elasticities must be redefined in terms of partial derivatives. With these (partial) elasticities in mind, we closely examine each of the terms in (2.56). The term on the far left-hand side is the own-price elasticity of demand for good x_i, or ε_i, the $n - 1$ terms inside the summation sign are the cross elasticities $\varepsilon_{i,j}$, and the right-hand term is the income elasticity $\varepsilon_{i,M}$. Therefore (2.56) can be rewritten in the following sum-of-elasticities form:

$$\varepsilon_i + \sum_{\substack{j=1 \\ j \neq i}}^{n} \varepsilon_{i,j} + \varepsilon_{i,M} = 0. \tag{2.57}$$

This expression is extremely useful in a number of different contexts including econometric estimation of empirical demand functions. This expression and other homogeneity-based expressions will appear repeatedly in the chapters that follow.

Before leaving the topic of the zero-degree homogeneity of demand, we want to say a brief word about how it has influenced macroeconomics. It is an important implication (some would say the most important implication) of the zero-degree homogeneity of demand that a balanced inflation that scales up all prices and money income by the same amount will have no effect on economic behavior. In particular, the supply of labor (which we see in Chapter 8 is derived from the demand for leisure) will be unaffected by expansionary policies that raise all prices, including the price of labor, by the same amount. Such an argument led macroeconomists to the theory of the vertical Phillips curve relating inflation and unemployment. Unless workers have some form of "money illusion" about the impact of an increase in price level, behavior should be unchanged by inflation, and unemployment will remain close to the natural rate.

2.3   Homothetic Functions

In Chapter 1 after the discussion of concave functions, we introduced the notion of a quasi-concave function. We argued that quasi-concavity is useful in economics because it captures certain economically interesting properties of concave functions while being a much weaker restriction mathematically (all concave functions are quasi-concave, but not vice versa). Now, we introduce a class of functions, homothetic functions, that basically stand in the same relationship to homogeneous functions as quasi-concave stands to concave: homothetic functions share certain economically interesting properties but are mathematically less restrictive than homogeneous functions.

A function is homothetic if it can be written as a monotonic transformation of a homogeneous function. More formally,[3] the function $z = F(x)$, $F: \Re^n \to \Re$, is **homothetic** if there exist two functions f and G, where $f: \Re^n \to \Re$ is homogeneous of degree r and $G: \Re \to \Re$ with $G' > 0$, such that $F(x) = G[f(x)]$.

For examples of homotheticity, it is easier to start with a function and then examine the homothetic functions that can be derived from it via a monotonic transformation. The example we use is the two-variable Cobb–Douglas production function $y = x_1^{1/2} x_2^{1/2}$. Since f is h.d. 1, the most obvious homothetic function that can be derived from f is simply f itself. In terms of the foregoing definition, this amounts to letting $G(y) = y$ so that $F(x) = G[f(x)] = f(x) = x_1^{1/2} x_2^{1/2}$. Since any homogeneous function could be "transformed" to a homothetic function in precisely the same way, we have demonstrated that all homogeneous functions are homothetic: that is, that homogeneity is sufficient for homotheticity. Of course, homogeneity is not *necessary* for homotheticity; functions exist that are monotonic transformations of homogeneous functions that are not themselves homogeneous. Thus homotheticity is a weaker condition than homogeneity. As an example, let $y = f(x) = x_1^{1/2} x_2^{1/2}$ as before, but let $G(y) = \ln y$. Since $G'(y) = 1/y > 0$, the composite function $F(x) = G[f(x)]$ is homothetic for $y > 0$. But $F(x)$ defined in this way is not homogeneous. The function F is given by $F(x) = \ln(x_1^{1/2} x_2^{1/2}) = \left(\frac{1}{2}\right) \ln x_1 + \left(\frac{1}{2}\right) \ln x_2$, so for all $\lambda > 0$ we have $F(\lambda x) = \left(\frac{1}{2}\right) \ln(\lambda x_1) + \left(\frac{1}{2}\right) \ln(\lambda x_2) = \ln \lambda + F(x)$. Since there does not exist an r such that $\lambda^r F(x) = \ln \lambda + F(x)$ for all $\lambda > 0$, $F(x)$ is not homogeneous.

Probably the most important implication of homotheticity is that level sets (isoquants for production functions, indifference curves for utility functions) are radial blowups of each other. If a production function is homothetic, then the slope of the tangent to any isoquant at a point x_0, $MRTS(x_0)$, is the same as the slope of the tangent at λx_0, $MRTS(\lambda x_0)$, for all $\lambda > 0$; or equivalently, if a utility function is homothetic, then the slope of the tangent to any indifference curve at a point x_0, $MRS(x_0)$, is the same as the slope of the tangent at λx_0, $MRS(\lambda x_0)$, for all $\lambda > 0$. A utility function with this property is depicted in Figure 2.3. This property of homothetic functions is formalized in Theorem 2.3.

Verbally, Theorem 2.3 states that level sets of homothetic functions are radial blowups of each other, that each isoquant or indifference curve is simply a

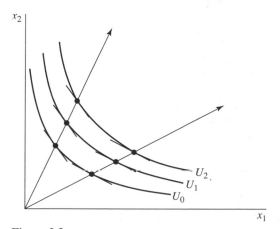

Figure 2.3

THEOREM 2.3: If $F(x)$ is a differentiable homothetic function of n variables and $\bar{F}$ is an arbitrary constant, then for all $\lambda > 0$ and for all i and j, $S_{ij}(x) = S_{ij}(\lambda x)$, where $S_{ij} = -dx_j/dx_i|_{F(x)=\bar{F}}$.

PROOF: Since $F(x) = \bar{F}$ implies that $dF = 0$, we have $S_{ij}(x) = F_i(x)/F_j(x)$ for all i and j, where $F_k = \partial F/\partial x_k$. Since F is homothetic, there exists a homogeneous function f such that $F(x) = G[f(x)]$ with $G' > 0$. Differentiating F with respect to any x_k, we have $F_k(x) = G'[f(x)]f_k(x)$, where $f_k = \partial f/\partial x_k$. Substituting this into S_{ij}, we get

$$S_{ij}(x) = \frac{G'f_i(x)}{G'f_j(x)} = \frac{f_i(x)}{f_j(x)}.$$

Since f is homogeneous of degree r, functions f_i and f_j are homogeneous of degree $r - 1$ by Theorem 2.2. Thus for all $\lambda > 0$,

$$S_{ij}(\lambda x) = \frac{f_i(\lambda x)}{f_j(\lambda x)} = \frac{\lambda^{r-1}f_i(x)}{\lambda^{r-1}f_j(x)} = \frac{f_i(x)}{f_j(x)} = S_{ij}(x).$$

magnification or a reduction of the unit isoquant ($\bar{y} = 1$) or the unit indifference curve ($\bar{U} = 1$).

Although the theorem refers to homothetic functions, it must apply to homogeneous functions also, since all homogeneous functions are homothetic. The real importance of Theorem 2.3, though, lies not in the fact that the radial blowup property, a property with important implications in both production and consumer choice theory, holds for homogeneous functions. Rather, the real importance of Theorem 2.3 lies in the fact that it holds for a much more general class of functions, those that are "merely" homothetic. Some of the demand theory implications of homotheticity are examined in Chapter 8. Examples of specific homothetic functions are found in the problems.

2.4   Concave Functions in n Variables

Chapter 1 provided a detailed discussion of concavity and convexity for the one-variable case of $f: \Re \to \Re$. At several points in that discussion we asserted that these one-dimensional results for concavity and convexity could be extended easily to the n-variable case in which $f: \Re^n \to \Re$. As the final topic in this chapter, we defend these assertions. Since the basic concepts have been introduced, we concentrate on strict concavity and leave it to the reader to weaken the inequalities for mere concavity and to reverse them for convexity.

Three conditions for the strict concavity of a one-variable function are given in Chapter 1. The first condition does not involve derivatives at all or even assume that the function was differentiable; the second condition is a restriction on the first derivative of the function; and the third condition is a restriction on the second derivative. Although all three can be generalized to n dimensions, we concentrate on the first two at this point. The n-dimensional generalization of the second-derivative condition is deferred until later, since it involves properties of matrices not introduced until Chapter 6.

First, we consider the most general of the three earlier definitions, the one that does not require differentiability. A function of n variables $y = f(x)$, $f: \Re^n \to \Re$, is **strictly concave** iff for all $x^0, x' \in \Re^n$ with $x^0 \neq x'$ and all $0 < \theta < 1$,

$$f(\hat{x}) > \theta f(x^0) + (1 - \theta) f(x'), \tag{2.58}$$

where $\hat{x} = \theta x^0 + (1 - \theta)x'$. This definition is identical to the one-variable case given in (1.66) except that $x^0, x' \in \Re^n$ rather than $x_0, x_1 \in \Re$. This is the most general definition of strict concavity; the earlier definition was simply a special case of (2.58) with $n = 1$. Although the definitions are identical, computation can be quite messy in higher dimensions. For instance, even in the relatively simple case of $n = 2$, where $x^0 = (x_1^0, x_2^0)$ and $x' = (x_1', x_2')$, the value $\hat{x}$ is given by

$$\hat{x} = (\hat{x}_1, \hat{x}_2) = \left[\theta x_1^0 + (1 - \theta)x_1', \theta x_2^0 + (1 - \theta)x_2' \right], \tag{2.59}$$

which can make the condition in (2.58) quite cumbersome to check.

Moving to the first-derivative characterization of strict concavity, we see that a differentiable function of n variables $y = f(x)$, $f: \Re^n \to \Re$, is **strictly concave** iff for all $x^0, x' \in \Re^n$ with $x^0 \neq x'$

$$\sum_{i=1}^{n} f_i(x^0) \left(x_i' - x_i^0 \right) + f(x^0) > f(x'), \tag{2.60}$$

where $f_i = \partial f / \partial x_i$. Again we see that the n-variable case is a straightforward generalization of the condition for the one-variable case. The expression in (2.60) may be quite messy to compute, but conceptually it is no different from expression (1.68). In vector notation (2.60) appears a bit simpler; it is

$$\nabla f(x^0)(x' - x^0)^T + f(x^0) > f(x'), \tag{2.61}$$

where ∇f is the gradient vector $\nabla f(x^0) = [f_1(x^0), f_2(x^0), \ldots, f_n(x^0)]$.

Unfortunately, the final characterization of strict concavity presented in Chapter 1, the second-derivative characterization, is not as simple to generalize to n-dimensions as the other two. In Chapter 1 we argued that $f''(x) < 0$ for all $x \in \Re$ was sufficient for the strict concavity of $f: \Re \to \Re$. But how are we to generalize such a condition to n dimensions? It seems unlikely that $f_{ii} = \partial^2 f / \partial x_i^2 < 0$ for all i would be sufficient, since there are $n(n-1)$ other second derivatives of the form $f_{ij} = \partial^2 f / \partial x_i \partial x_j$ for $i \neq j$ that can influence the behavior of the function in addition to the own effects f_{ii}. Because of this complexity, the second-derivative characterization of strict concavity is deferred until we have discussed matrix theory; the $n = 2$ case is discussed in context of a two-variable maximization problem in Chapter 3, but the main discussion is deferred until Chapter 7.

PROBLEMS

2.1 Find $U_1, U_2, U_{11}, U_{22}, U_{12}, U_{21}$, and MRS for each of the following utility functions. State whether the utility function exhibits diminishing marginal utility for each of the two goods, as well as utility function complementarity or substitutability.
(a) $U(x_1, x_2) = x_1 x_2$.
(b) $U(x_1, x_2) = x_1^{1/2} + x_2^{1/2}$.
(c) $U(x_1, x_2) = x_1^{1/3} x_2^{2/3}$.

2.2 Suppose that a particular good y is produced by using capital K and labor L according to the production function

$$y = f(K, L) = AL^2 K^2 - BL^3 K^3,$$

where $A > 0$, $B > 0$, and $f: D \to \mathfrak{R}_+$ with $D \subset \mathfrak{R}^2$.
(a) How should the domain of the function D be restricted to make economic sense?
(b) Find expressions for the following:

$$AP_L = \frac{y}{L}, \qquad MP_L = \frac{\partial f}{\partial L}, \qquad AP_K = \frac{y}{K}, \qquad MP_K = \frac{\partial f}{\partial K}.$$

(c) In most textbooks the MP curve cuts the AP curve at its minimum point. Is this true for the marginal and average products of labor and capital for this production function? (Show.)
(d) Find an expression for the marginal rate of technical substitution ($MRTS$) and **interpret it.**
(e) If K is fixed at some $\bar{K}$ in D, for what values of L does f exhibit diminishing returns to labor? Similarly, if L is fixed at some $\bar{L}$ in D, for what values of K does f exhibit diminishing returns to capital?

2.3 Show that the utility function $U(x_1, x_2) = x_1^{1/2} x_2^{1/2}$ exhibits a diminishing marginal rate of substitution (MRS) by **directly** verifying the inequality in (2.26).

2.4 It was argued in the text that diminishing marginal utility is neither necessary nor sufficient for diminishing marginal rates of substitution. Show that for the special case of a utility function that is **additively separable,** that is, $U(x) = \sum_{i=1}^{n} U^i(x_i)$ (the utility received from the consumption of each good is independent of the utility received from the consumption of the other goods), diminishing marginal utility for all goods is sufficient for diminishing marginal rates of substitution.

2.5 Does the production function $y = f(L, K) = L^{1/3} K^{2/3}$ exhibit a diminishing $MRTS$?

2.6 Show that if $x_i^*(p, M)$ is a demand function that solves the general consumer choice problem (2.1) for good i, then the following two conditions will hold, where $b_i = p_i x_i^*/M$, the budget share of the good i.

(a) $\sum_{i=1}^{n} b_i \varepsilon_{i,M} = 1$.

(b) $\sum_{i=1}^{n} b_i \varepsilon_{ij} = -b_j$ for any $j = 1, 2, \ldots, n$.

2.7 Are the following production functions homogeneous of any degree? If so, what degree and why? If not, why not?
(a) $y = f(L, K) = AL^a K^b$ with $A > 0$, $a > 0$, and $b > 0$.

(b) $y = f(K, L) = AL^2K^2 - BL^3K^3$ with $A > 0$ and $B > 0$.

(c) $y = f(L, K) = (AL^{1+a}K^{1+b})/(BL + CK)$ with $A > 0, B > 0, C > 0,$ $0 < a < 1$, and $0 < b < 1$.

2.8 Verify that Theorems 2.1 and 2.2 hold for the production function $y = f(x_1, x_2) = x_1^{1/2}x_2^{1/2}$.

2.9 Prove the following two results for a production function $y = f(x)$, $x \in \Re_+^n$, which is homogeneous of degree r.

(a) The function $\psi(x) = [f(x)]^{1/r}$ is homogeneous of degree 1.

(b) $f(0) = 0$.

2.10 For any production function $y = f(x_1, x_2)$ the **elasticity of technical substitution** σ is defined as

$$\sigma = \frac{MRTS}{(x_1/x_2)} \frac{d(x_1/x_2)}{dMRTS}.$$

(a) Show that σ can be written as

$$\sigma = \frac{f_1^2 x_1 + f_1 f_2 x_2}{f_2 x_1 x_2 \left[f_1 \dfrac{\partial MRTS}{\partial x_2} + f_2 \dfrac{\partial MRTS}{\partial x_1} \right]}.$$

(b) Show that the elasticity of technical substitution would be exactly the same if it were defined as

$$\sigma' = \frac{-MRTS}{(x_1/x_2)} \frac{d(x_1/x_2)}{dMRTS}.$$

In other words, show that $\sigma' = \sigma$.

2.11 Find the elasticity of technical substitution σ (defined in Problem 10) for the following production functions.

(a) Cobb–Douglas with $y = f(x_1, x_2) = x_1^{1/2}x_2^{1/2}$.

(b) Constant elasticity of substitution with $y = f(x_1, x_2) = [ax_1^p + (1-\alpha)x_2^p]^{1/p}$, where $0 < \alpha < 1$ and $p < 1$.

2.12 For the production function $y = f(x)$, $f: \Re_{++}^n \to \Re_+$, show that if f exhibits constant returns to scale and diminishing marginal productivity for all inputs, then each input has at least one complement in production.

2.13 Consider the general demand function for good i

$$x_i = x_i(p_1, p_2, \ldots, p_n, M),$$

where p_i = price of good i and M = money income. Suppose the following are true of this demand function: $\partial x_i/\partial p_j = 0$ for all $i \neq j$, and the Engel curve relating x_i to M is linear and goes through the origin. **Find** the own price elasticity of demand ε_{ii} under these conditions.

2.14 Prove that the elasticity of scale measure ε_s defined in (2.51) can be written as

$$\varepsilon_s(x) = \frac{\sum_i f_i(x)x_i}{f(x)}.$$

2.15 Let $y = f(x_1, x_2) = x_1^{1/2}x_2^{1/2}$ be a production function, and compute a new production function $F(x) = G[f(x)]$ for each of the following G functions. In each case explain whether the resulting $F(x)$ is homothetic or homogeneous.

(a) $G(y) = y^2$.

(b) $G(y) = y^{1/2}$.

(c) $G(y) = 1/y$.

2.16 Verify that Theorem 2.3 holds for the homothetic utility function $U(x_1, x_2) = \frac{1}{2} \ln x_1 + \left(\frac{1}{2}\right) \ln x_2$.

2.17 You are given the demand functions $x_1(p_1, p_2, M)$ and $x_2(p_1, p_2, M)$ that solve

$$\underset{\{x\}}{\text{Max}} \ U(x_1, x_2)$$

$$\text{Subject to: } p_1 x_1 + p_2 x_2 = M$$

for the case in which $U(x)$ is **homothetic.**

(a) What can be said regarding the shape of the Engel curves associated with x_1 and x_2?

(b) Find the income elasticity of demand for the two goods.

2.18 Consider the one-variable, short-run production function $y = f(x)$, where output $y > 0$, labor input $L > 0$, and $f' = df/dx > 0$. Show that for this one-variable case (unlike the multiple-input case) if f is homogeneous and exhibits decreasing returns to scale, then f has diminishing returns to labor.

2.19 Consider the following production relationships:

$$x_i^j = \text{output of firm } j \text{ in industry } i,$$

$$x_i = \sum_j x_i^j = \text{total output of industry } i,$$

$$L_i^j = \text{labor employed by firm } j \text{ in industry } i,$$

$$L_i = \sum_j L_i^j = \text{total labor employed in industry } i,$$

$$x_i^j = x_i^{a_i} L_i^j = \text{production function for firm } j \text{ in industry } i,$$
$$\text{where } a_i \text{ is a real constant.}$$

(a) Find the aggregate production function for each industry i [i.e., find $x_i = \sum_j x_i^j(L_i) = f(L_i)$].

(b) Find an expression for the marginal product of labor in each industry [i.e., find $f'(L_i)$].

(c) Prove that $0 < b_i < 1$ implies that industry i has diminishing returns to labor, where $b_i = 1/(1 - a_i)$.

(d) Assuming that there are only two industries $i = 1, 2$ and that the supply of labor is fixed $\bar{L} = L_1 + L_2$, find the equation for the **production possibilities curve (PPC)** for this economy in (x_1, x_2)-space.

(e) Find the **rate of product transformation** (slope of the PPC) for the two-industry case in (d).

2.20 Suppose that a consumer is purchasing two goods x_1 and x_2 and getting a quantity discount. That is, rather than facing parametric prices p_1 and p_2, the consumer faces prices that are functions of the quantities purchased, so $p_1 = p_1(x_1)$ and $p_2 = p_2(x_2)$ with $p_i' = dp_i/dx_i < 0$ for $i = 1, 2$. If this consumer has a fixed income (M) to spend on the two goods **and** the quantity discount functions $p_1(x_1)$ and $p_2(x_2)$ are linear (i.e., $p_i'' = d^2 p_i/dx_i^2 = 0$ for $i = 1, 2$), **find** the shape of the consumer's budget constraint (concave, convex, or linear).

2.21 Consider a simple trading economy with only two traders, A and B, trading two goods x and y. Suppose that the total available quantity of good x is fixed at $\bar{x}$ and total available quantity of good y is fixed at $\bar{y}$, so that $x_A + x_B = \bar{x}$ and $y_A + y_B = y$, where x_A is the quantity of good x consumed by individual A, and so on. The utility function of individual A is $U_A(x_A, y_A) = x_A^{1/2} y_A^{1/2}$, and the utility function of individual B is $U_B(x_B, y_B) - x_B^{1/2} y_B^{1/2}$. Prove that for this economy the **contract curve** is the **diagonal** of the Edgeworth box defined by $\bar{x}$ and $\bar{y}$.

2.22 A total cost function C is subadditive if

$$C(y) < C(\bar{y}) + C(y - y),$$

for all $y \in \Re_{++}$ and any $0 < \bar{y} < y$. Prove that if there are increasing returns to scale in production [$C(y)$ is homogeneous of degree $r < 1$], then the total cost function is subadditive.

2.23 Consider the standard two-good consumer choice problem

$$\max_{\{x\}} U(x_1, x_2)$$

$$\text{Subject to: } p_1 x_1 + p_2 x_2 = M$$

for the particular case of

$$U(x_1, x_2) = (x_1 + 2)(x_2 + 1).$$

(a) Use the substitution technique from Chapter 1 to find the demand functions for the two goods $x_1^* = x_1^*(p_1, p_2, M)$ and $x_2^* = x_2^*(p_1, p_2, M)$.

(b) Are these demand functions homogeneous of any degree? If so what degree? (Show.)

(c) Find expressions for the own-price, cross-price, and income elasticities for both goods (i.e., find ε_{11}, ε_{12}, ε_{1M}, ε_{22}, ε_{21}, and ε_{2M}).

(d) Check the elasticity summation condition [equation (2.57)] for this problem. Does it hold? (Show.)

(e) Derive the indirect utility function (U^*) for this problem, where

$$U^* = U^*(p_1, p_2, M) = U[x_1^*(p_1, p_2, M), x_2^*(p_1, p_2, M)].$$

(f) Roy's identity says

$$x_i^*(p_1, p_2, M) = \frac{-\partial U^*/\partial p_i}{\partial U^*/\partial M} \quad \text{for } i = 1, 2.$$

Demonstrate that Roy's identity holds for this consumer choice problem.

NOTES

1. We will see in Chapter 6 that an additional restriction needs to be imposed on U to guarantee that the transformation from the implicit function (2.20) to the explicit function $x_2 = x_2(x_1)$ is valid. It turns out, not coincidentally, that the additional restriction is $U_2 \neq 0$, the same condition required for the previous total differential approach.

2. This issue probably arises in part because of the way in which economists use the term **linear.** We call a function of the form $f(x) = ax + b$ linear when in fact such a

function is "affine," not linear. Technically a linear function has the form $f(x) = ax$ and always passes through the origin. An **affine function,** however, is a parallel shift of a linear function; in other words, $f(x)$ is affine if $f(x) - f(0)$ is truly linear. Now, of course "truly" linear functions are homogeneous of degree 1, so the term **linearly homogeneous** is not entirely without justification. Nonetheless it is potentially confusing and so it will be avoided.

3. Homothetic functions are sometimes defined as monotonic transformations of functions that are homogeneous of degree 1. This is consistent with our definition, since any homogeneous function can be written as a monotonic transformation of a function homogeneous of degree 1 (see Problem 9).

3

COMPARATIVE STATICS I: ONE
AND TWO VARIABLES WITH AND
WITHOUT OPTIMIZATION

■ ■ ■

This chapter introduces the single most important technique used in modern economic analysis. The technique is called **comparative statics,** and it forms the basis not only of this chapter but also of most of the chapters that follow. You may find it reassuring to know that while this method is extremely important and heavily emphasized in the remainder of the book, it is not an approach to economic analysis that you will find totally new. The particular **way** in which comparative statics results are obtained in this and later chapters may be new, but not the general idea. In fact, comparative statics analysis is presented in almost every economics course. In most elementary economics courses comparative statics analysis is conducted exclusively by means of diagrams, as opposed to the calculus techniques developed here, but the core concept—comparing static positions before and after a change in one or more parameters—is exactly the same, and quite familiar.

As an example of an elementary comparative statics exercise that you will be familiar with from other economics courses, consider the change in the market price of wheat resulting from a severe drought in the primary wheat-growing region of the United States. The standard approach to such a question involves the use of a simple supply and demand diagram like Figure 3.1. Since the drought decreases the supply of wheat, the equilibrium price will increase, as shown by the change from P_W^0 to P_W^1 in Figure 3.2.

Such supply and demand explanations form the basis of most economic analysis of market prices, and such explanations come rather naturally after a brief introduction to economics. Of course many other questions could be answered with this basic analytical framework: What happens to the price and quantity of a particular good when the price of a substitute changes? What happens to the relationship between the quantity supplied and the quantity demanded when an effective price floor is imposed on a particular market? Or, if we convert

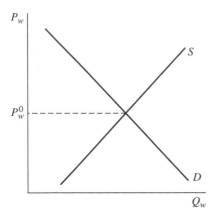

Figure 3.1

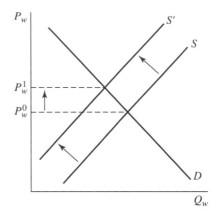

Figure 3.2

the basic supply and demand model into macroeconomic aggregate supply and aggregate demand: What happens to the price level and real output in an entire economy when the money supply is increased? Such comparative statics analysis is the standard approach taken by economists to answer a wide range of different questions. Comparative statics simply means that the phenomenon in question is explained by comparing the properties of two different static (equilibrium) positions. We start with a system in (static) equilibrium; the system is perturbed by a change in one of the parameters; and the system moves to a new (static) equilibrium position. The results are obtained by simply comparing the properties of the first equilibrium with the properties of the second. Hence the name **comparative statics.** A large portion of economic analysis is conducted in precisely this way.

In this chapter (and later chapters), calculus techniques are used to derive comparative statics results for a wide variety of economic models. Calculus offers at least two important advantages over the diagrammatic manipulations used in elementary economics. First, calculus can provide quantitative information, information about magnitude as well as the qualitative information (increases, decreases, or remains the same) available from diagrams. Second, and more importantly, the calculus technique can easily be extended to more complex problems involving more than two dimensions and/or variables.

Thus far we have mentioned only comparative statics results derived from equilibrium positions—like the supply and demand example—but economic analysis often depends on comparative statics results of a related but separate type, those driven by optimization (maximization or minimization). For instance, the indifference curve analysis of the change in consumption of two goods caused by a change in the price of one of them is a type of comparative statics analysis, but it is not based on comparing equilibrium positions. Rather, the two positions compared are the optimum points. In the consumer choice case, the positions are utility-maximizing consumption bundles before and after the change in one of the parameters of the problem. Comparative statics results derived from optimization often differ in important ways from those derived from equilibria. We show in later chapters that the second-order conditions used to derive comparative statics results in the context of optimization often can be replaced by stability conditions in the case of equilibrium. This chapter will examine low- (one- and two-) dimensional examples of comparative statics exercises of both types. For the optimization-based models, second-order conditions and their implications for comparative statics are explicitly discussed. For equilibrium models, comparative statics results are obtained, but the discussion of stability is deferred until Chapter 5. We examine the equilibrium models first.

3.1 Equilibrium Comparative Statics in One and Two Dimensions

Supply and Demand

The simplest way to begin is to elaborate on a simple supply and demand example like the one that introduced this chapter. Since you are already familiar with diagrammatic comparative statics involving supply and demand, this example will allow us to focus exclusively on the technique itself. Our particular case is the change in equilibrium price caused by a shift in the supply function of a simple supply and demand model. We examine this case in three stages, each of increasing generality. First, we consider the case in which both supply and demand are given as linear functions of specific numerical parameters. Second, we examine the case in which both supply and demand are linear, but the parameters in the those linear expressions are given by variables $a, b, c, \ldots$ Third, we examine the general case in which both supply and demand are given by unspecified (and possibly nonlinear) differentiable functions. This general case is the important prototype for the more complex multivariate comparative statics considered later.

For the simplest case, suppose that supply and demand are given by the specific functions

$$Q^D = -P + 100,$$
$$Q^S = P + \alpha, \tag{3.1}$$

where Q^D is the quantity demanded, Q^S is the quantity supplied, P is the price, and $\alpha \in \Re$ is a shift parameter in the supply function (e.g., a parameter representing technological change).

If we are interested in finding the impact of a change in α on the equilibrium price P^*, we set $Q^D = Q^S$ and solve for P^*:

$$P^* = \frac{100 - \alpha}{2}. \tag{3.2}$$

Expression (3.2) gives the equilibrium price P^* as a function of the parameter α. The comparative statics term we are looking for is $\Delta P^*/\Delta \alpha$, the change in the equilibrium value P^* caused by a change in the parameter α.

In general, the desired comparative statics expression can be found by taking the derivative of the expression for the equilibrium value with respect to the parameter in question. For the supply-and-demand example (3.1), taking the derivative of (3.2) gives us $dP^*/d\alpha = -\frac{1}{2}$. Since the right-hand side of (3.2) is linear in α, the comparative statics term $dP^*/d\alpha$ is independent of α and identical to the expression that would be obtained by computing the impact of finite changes in the parameter. For the general case in which the equilibrium expression is non-linear, the derivative is a function of the parameter. Before considering the more general case, we look at a slight generalization of (3.1). Suppose that the supply and demand functions are both linear but the parameters in the linear function are unknowns. That is, consider the system

$$
\begin{aligned}
Q^D &= D(P) = -aP + b, \\
Q^S &= S(P, \alpha) = cP + \alpha,
\end{aligned}
\tag{3.3}
$$

where Q^D, Q^S, P, and α are defined as before and a, b, and c are positive scalars.

Following the approach we used for the numerical case, we set $Q^D = Q^S$ and solve for P^* in terms of α. This gives

$$
P^* = \frac{b - \alpha}{a + c}.
\tag{3.4}
$$

Note that P^* will exist as long as $a \neq -c$, and it will be strictly positive for a fairly wide range of parameter values. Also note that the right-hand side of (3.4) reduces to the right-hand side of (3.2) when $a = c = 1$ and $b = 100$. Taking the derivative of P^* with respect to α gives the desired comparative statics term

$$
\frac{dP^*}{d\alpha} = \frac{-1}{a + c},
\tag{3.5}
$$

which, of course, reduces to $dP^*/d\alpha = -\frac{1}{2}$ under the preceding parameter values.

Not only can expression (3.5) be used to compute the comparative statics impact of a change in α for particular numerical specification of the parameters, but it can also yield more general comparative statics information. When a and c are strictly positive, as in our numerical example, an increase in α will always reduce the equilibrium price; but also note that if demand slopes upward ($a < 0$) or supply slopes downward ($c < 0$), it is possible that an increase in α will increase the equilibrium price. For instance, when demand slopes upward and demand is more price responsive than supply ($|a| > |c|$), an increase in the supply shift parameter will actually increase the price of the good. We shall see in Chapter 5 that such comparative statics results may depend on whether the market is stable (converges to equilibrium). At this point, however, we simply note that the sign of this comparative statics term can be determined by using only the signs and relative magnitudes of the slopes of the linear supply and demand functions.

For the system (3.3) it is quite easy to find an exact expression for the equilibrium price in terms of the parameters, since the exact supply and demand functions are given. But such specific information is not always available: suppose that we were interested in the comparative statics expression $dP^*/d\alpha$ for an unspecified nonlinear case. In particular, let us assume that the only available information is the following: demand depends solely on price, supply depends on both price and the shift parameter α, and both functions are differentiable. What can we say about this general case?

Of course, it is possible that an equilibrium price may not even exist in a general case with so little structure. But suppose it does exist; then it will be given by the equation

$$D(P) - S(P, \alpha) = 0. \tag{3.6}$$

Note that (3.6) characterizes the equilibrium, but it cannot be solved explicitly to determine an expression for P^*. The equation (3.6) simply does not provide enough information about the functions $D(P)$ and $S(p, \alpha)$ to yield an equation like (3.4). What we do know, though, is that whatever the equilibrium price happens to be, it will depend on the value of the parameter α. Thus we write the differentiable function $P^* = P^*(\alpha)$ as the solution to (3.6).[1]

Now if we take the equilibrium price as a function of the parameter α and we substitute it back into (3.6), we obtain the following **identity:**

$$D(P^*(\alpha)) - S(P^*(\alpha), \alpha) \equiv 0. \tag{3.7}$$

The expression is an identity and not merely an equation because we have substituted back into it the exact values that solve the equation.

Given identity (3.7), it is now quite simple to obtain the desired comparative statics term. We simply differentiate both sides of the identity in (3.7) with respect to the variable in question, in this case parameter α. As we argued in Chapter 2, although differentiation of both sides of an equation is not always a valid mathematical operation, differentiation of both sides of an identity certainly is. Performing this differentiation via the chain rule gives us

$$\frac{dD}{dP}\frac{dP^*}{d\alpha} - \frac{\partial S}{\partial P}\frac{dP^*}{d\alpha} - \frac{\partial S}{\partial \alpha} \equiv 0. \tag{3.8}$$

With some rearrangement, we write

$$\frac{dP^*}{d\alpha} = \frac{S_\alpha}{D_p - S_p}, \tag{3.9}$$

where $S_\alpha = \partial S/\partial \alpha$, $S_p = \partial S/\partial P$, and $D_p = dD/dP$. For the case in which $S_\alpha > 0$ and both supply and demand have the "normal" shape (i.e., $D_p < 0$ and $S_p > 0$), an increase in the supply shift parameter will lower the equilibrium price regardless of the exact shapes of the functions involved.

Since (3.9) holds for the general case, it should also hold for the linear system (3.3). It is easy to check that this is true. For the linear system (3.3), $S_\alpha = 1$, $D_p = -a$, and $S_p = c$. Substitution of these values into (3.9) gives us the earlier comparative statics expression (3.5).

This technique is not the only approach that can be used to find comparative statics expressions such as (3.9) for general models. An alternative technique,

THRU TEST #2

called the **total differential approach,** can also be used. Since both approaches are popular in the economics literature, it is useful to briefly discuss this alternative method.

The alternative approach is based on simultaneous variation of all variables and parameters. That is, everything is treated as a variable rather than making the strict distinction between variables (such as P) and parameters (such as α) as we did earlier. If we treat both P and α as variables and restrict ourselves exclusively to values of P and α that equate supply and demand, then the equilibrium equation can be written as one equation in these two variables. Interpreting (3.6) in this way gives

$$E(P, \alpha) = 0, \tag{3.10}$$

where $E(P, \alpha) \doteq D(P) - S(P, \alpha)$. Now taking the total differential of (3.10), we have

$$E_p \, dP + E_\alpha \, d\alpha = 0, \tag{3.11}$$

where $E_p = \partial E / \partial P$ and $E_\alpha = \partial E / \partial \alpha$. A little rearrangement of (3.11) gives us the desired comparative statics term

$$\frac{dP^*}{d\alpha} = \frac{-E_\alpha}{E_p}. \tag{3.12}$$

Notice that since $E_\alpha = -S_\alpha$ and $E_p = D_p - S_p$, expression (3.12) is identical to (3.9). Although economists use both techniques, and the student should be comfortable with both, we emphasize the first approach in most of what follows.

This completes our discussion of one-dimensional, equilibrium-based comparative statics. Later in the chapter we conduct a similar comparative statics analysis for the case of the choice variable that is an optimum (maximum or minimum) rather than an equilibrium value, but for the moment we continue to focus on equilibria. In the next section, which simply provides a two-dimensional extension of the foregoing class of results, we consider a macroeconomic model: the $IS\text{-}LM$ model. This model is Keynesian in orientation—focusing on the demand–expenditure side of the economy—but it should be familiar to the student from intermediate macroeconomics.

The $IS\text{-}LM$ Model

The $IS\text{-}LM$ macroeconomic model has two dependent variables: the level of real national income Y and the rate of interest r. These dependent variables are determined by the interaction of the aggregate goods market and the aggregate money market.

The goods (real output) market is in equilibrium when the aggregate expenditure on goods is equal to the national income. If there is no foreign trade, the aggregate expenditure on goods will be given by

$$C + I + G, \tag{3.13}$$

where C = real consumption expenditure, I = real investment expenditure, and G = real governmental expenditure. The aggregate income generated by the production of these goods is given by

$$C + S + T, \tag{3.14}$$

where S = real savings and T = real taxes. Since the goods market is in equilibrium when (3.13) is equal to (3.14), equilibrium is characterized by

$$I - S + G - T = 0 \quad \text{or} \quad I - S + D = 0, \tag{3.15}$$

where D is the real government deficit $G - T$.

In the most general case, many different factors influence I, S, and D, but we will examine only a relatively simple model; our purpose is only to exhibit the comparative statics technique in two dimensions. In the *IS-LM* model considered here, the savings function depends on both the level of income Y and the rate of interest r. The sign restrictions on the derivative of S with respect to these two variables are the standard assumptions from macroeconomic theory: savings will increase with both real income and the rate of interest. Thus we may write

$$S = S(Y, r) \quad \text{with} \quad S_Y > 0 \quad \text{and} \quad S_r > 0, \tag{3.16}$$

where $S_Y = \partial S / \partial Y$ and $S_r = \partial S / \partial r$. These sign restrictions are all (other than differentiability) that we assume regarding the shape of the savings function; in particular, we do not assume that the function is linear.

The investment function is even simpler to specify. We assume that investment spending depends solely on the rate of interest and that increases in the rate of interest will decrease investment spending. This is the standard assumption regarding investment, and it implies that the function I can be written as

$$I = I(r) \quad \text{with} \quad I_r < 0, \tag{3.17}$$

where $I_r = \partial I / \partial r$. We will assume that the deficit D is simply a policy parameter that is independent of both Y and r.

The IS curve is defined to be the set of all Y and r combinations that clear the goods market. Thus, under our specification of I, S, and D, the IS curve is given by

$$IS(Y, r) = I(r) - S(Y, r) + D = 0. \tag{3.18}$$

Given the relatively weak restrictions we have imposed on I and S, it is certainly not possible to determine the exact shape of the IS curve from (3.18). It is possible, though, to determine the **slope** of the IS curve in (Y, r)-space. Taking the total differential of (3.18) with respect to Y and r gives $dIS = (I_r - S_r)\, dr - S_Y\, dY$. But along the IS curve, both Y and r adjust, so that (3.18) always holds; this means that along the IS curve, $dIS = 0$. Therefore taking the total differential of (3.18) and rearranging, we have

$$\left. \frac{dr}{dY} \right|_{IS} = \frac{S_Y}{I_r - S_r}. \qquad 7 \tag{3.19}$$

The symbolism on the left-hand side of (3.19) simply indicates that the slope dr/dY is restricted to the case of $IS(Y, r) = 0$, that is, along the IS curve. Given the model's sign restrictions, the right-hand side of (3.19) is strictly negative. Thus, the IS curve slopes downward in (Y, r)-space.

Now consider the aggregate money market. The money market is in equilibrium when the demand for real money balances is equal to the supply of real money balances. The demand for real money balances depends on both income and the rate of interest. An increase in the level of income will increase the demand for money, and an increase in the rate of interest will raise the opportunity cost of holding money and thereby lower its demand. Thus the demand for real money balances L is given by

$$L = L(Y, r) \qquad \text{with} \qquad L_Y > 0 \qquad \text{and} \qquad L_r < 0, \qquad (3.20)$$

where $L_Y = \partial L/\partial Y$ and $L_r = \partial L/\partial r$. The real supply of money is easy to specify; it is simply the nominal supply of money M^s, which is a policy parameter of the monetary authority divided by the price level p, which can also be taken as a parameter in this simple IS-LM model.

The LM curve is defined as the set of all Y and r combinations that clear the aggregate money market. Thus, given the foregoing definitions of money demand and money supply, the following expression defines the LM curve:

$$LM(Y, r) = L(Y, r) - \frac{M^s}{p} = 0. \qquad (3.21)$$

Following the same procedure used for finding the slope of the IS curve, we can find the slope of the LM curve by taking the total differential of (3.21). After some rearrangement, this differentiation gives

$$\left. \frac{dr}{dY} \right|_{LM} = \frac{-L_Y}{L_r}. \qquad (3.22)$$

From the sign conditions imposed on the model, the right-hand side of (3.22) is strictly positive; thus the LM curve slopes upward in (Y, r)-space.

The equilibrium level of income (Y^*) and the equilibrium rate of interest (r^*) simultaneously clears both the goods market and the money market; that is, (Y^*, r^*) is given by the intersection of the IS and LM curves. This equilibrium is given by the expressions

$$IS(Y^*, r^*) = I(r^*) - S(Y^*, r^*) + D = 0,$$

$$LM(Y^*, r^*) = L(Y^*, r^*) - \frac{M^s}{p} = 0, \qquad (3.23)$$

and it is shown diagrammatically in Figure 3.3.

Since the equilibrium values of both income and the rate of interest depend on all the parameters of the system, we take the approach used in the one-variable case and write the equilibrium values explicitly as differentiable functions of

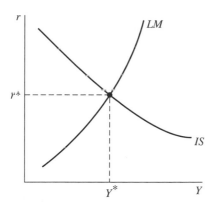

Figure 3.3

the three parameters. This gives the following expressions for the equilibrium values:

$$Y^* = Y^*(D, M^s, p),$$
$$r^* = r^*(D, M^s, p).$$

(3.24)

Substitution of the equilibrium expressions from (3.24) into the equilibrium conditions in (3.23) gives two identities for the equilibrium of the IS-LM system in terms of the three parameters D, M^s, and p. After the substitutions we have

$$I(r^*(D, M^s, p)) - S(Y^*(D, M^s, p), r^*(D, M^s, p)) + D \equiv 0,$$

$$L(Y^*(D, M^s, p), r^*(D, M^s, p)) - \frac{M^s}{p} \equiv 0.$$

(3.25)

The six comparative statics terms $\partial Y^*/\partial D$, $\partial r^*/\partial D$, $\partial Y^*/\partial M^s$, $\partial r^*/\partial M^s$, $\partial Y^*/\partial p$, and $\partial r^*/\partial p$ can now be obtained by differentiation of the identities in (3.25) with respect to each of the three parameters.

First, consider the impact on Y^* and r^* of a change in the amount of government deficit D. Differentiating the identities in (3.25) with respect to D yields

$$I_r\left(\frac{\partial r^*}{\partial D}\right) - S_Y\left(\frac{\partial Y^*}{\partial D}\right) - S_r\left(\frac{\partial r^*}{\partial D}\right) + 1 \equiv 0,$$

$$L_Y\left(\frac{\partial Y^*}{\partial D}\right) + L_r\left(\frac{\partial r^*}{\partial D}\right) \equiv 0.$$

(3.26)

With a little manipulation, this system becomes

$$-S_Y\left(\frac{\partial Y^*}{\partial D}\right) + (I_r - S_r)\left(\frac{\partial r^*}{\partial D}\right) \equiv -1,$$

$$L_Y\left(\frac{\partial Y^*}{\partial D}\right) + L_r\left(\frac{\partial r^*}{\partial D}\right) \equiv 0.$$

(3.27)

System (3.27) is a system of two independent linear equations in two unknowns $\partial Y^*/\partial D$ and $\partial r^*/\partial D$. In Chapter 6 we will develop matrix methods to solve such linear systems, but for now we simply solve the two equations simultaneously. Multiplying the first equation by L_Y, multiplying the second equation by S_Y, and adding, we have

$$[L_Y(I_r - S_r) + S_Y L_r] \left(\frac{\partial r^*}{\partial D} \right) = -L_Y, \tag{3.28}$$

or with some rearrangement

$$\frac{\partial r^*}{\partial D} = \frac{-L_Y}{L_Y(I_r - S_r) + S_Y L_r}. \tag{3.29}$$

Substituting (3.29) into either equation in (3.27) and solving for $\partial Y^*/\partial D$, we get

$$\frac{\partial Y^*}{\partial D} = \frac{L_r}{L_Y(I_r - S_r) + S_Y L_r}. \tag{3.30}$$

The two expressions (3.29) and (3.30) give the comparative statics impact of an increase in the government deficit in our simple IS-LM model. The sign conditions in (3.16), (3.17), and (3.20) ensure that the right-hand sides of both expressions will be positive (the numerator and denominator in both expressions are negative). Thus an increase in the size of the government deficit will increase both the equilibrium level of national income and the equilibrium rate of interest in this model. The impact of $\Delta D > 0$ is shown diagrammatically by the movement from (Y^*, r^*) to (Y^{**}, r^{**}) in Figure 3.4.

To find the impact of a change in the money supply M^s on the equilibrium values of this model, simply repeat the foregoing procedure for M^s rather than D. Differentiating (3.25) with respect to M^s and rearranging, we get

$$-S_Y \left(\frac{\partial Y^*}{\partial M^s} \right) + (I_r - S_r) \left(\frac{\partial r^*}{\partial M^s} \right) \equiv 0,$$

$$L_Y \left(\frac{\partial Y^*}{\partial M^s} \right) + L_r \left(\frac{\partial r^*}{\partial M^s} \right) \equiv \frac{1}{p}. \tag{3.31}$$

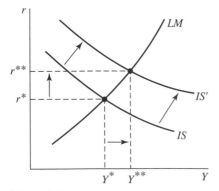

Figure 3.4

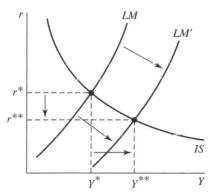

Figure 3.5

Solving this system simultaneously gives the comparative statics expressions

$$\frac{\partial r^*}{\partial M^s} = \frac{S_Y}{p[L_Y(I_r - S_r) + S_Y L_r]} \tag{3.32}$$

and

$$\frac{\partial Y^*}{\partial M^s} = \frac{I_r - S_r}{p[L_Y(I_r - S_r) + S_Y L_r]}. \tag{3.33}$$

Given the sign restrictions of the model, the right-hand side of (3.32) is negative, and the right-hand side of (3.33) is positive. For this model, an expansionary monetary policy will lower the rate of interest and increase the national income. This impact is depicted in Figure 3.5. Similar comparative statics results can be found for a change in the price level p, but this is left as an exercise for the reader.

This completes our discussion of equilibrium comparative statics in one and two variables. Next we shall examine a problem involving optimization rather than equilibrium. In closing this section, we note that our examples were chosen precisely because they demonstrate clearly how the comparative statics technique can be successfully applied. Reasonable economic models do not always provide the kind of nice determinate comparative statics results found here, however. Even for a relatively simple system like the IS-LM model, adding more parameters, weakening the sign conditions, or generally increasing the complexity of the system may completely destroy the nice, clean results we have obtained.

3.2 Comparative Statics with Optimization in One and Two Dimensions

Perfectly Competitive Firm I

In Chapter 1 we briefly discussed the behavior of a profit-maximizing, perfectly competitive firm. We now examine a few comparative statics results for such a competitive firm. The firm's choice variables are the inputs of labor L and capital K rather than output y. To start the analysis, consider a firm with the production function

$$y = f(L, K) = 2L^{1/2}K^{1/2}. \tag{3.34}$$

Since this firm is perfectly competitive with respect to both the product and factor markets, it has no control over either the price of its output or the prices of the two inputs it employs. From the firm's point of view, the price of its output (p), the price of labor (w), and the price of capital (v), are all parameters rather than choice variables.

In the short run, the firm's capital stock $\bar{K}$ is fixed, and the production function is given by

$$y = f(L, \bar{K}) = 2L^{1/2}\bar{K}^{1/2}. \tag{3.35}$$

We examine the case of $\bar{K} = 4$, and so the firm faces the one-variable production function

$$y = f(L) = 4L^{1/2}. \tag{3.36}$$

The firm's objective is to maximize profit, given the market-determined parameter values (prices) and the short-run production function (3.36). Short-run profit is simply total revenue minus total cost, or

$$\pi = py - wL - v\bar{K}. \tag{3.37}$$

Substituting the specific form of the production function from (3.36) into the profit function (3.37), we have

$$\pi(L) = p(4L^{1/2}) - wL - v(4). \tag{3.38}$$

As (3.38) clearly indicates, the only choice variable for this short-run firm is L. Prices p, w, and v are market-determined parameters, and the capital stock is fixed at $\bar{K} = 4$. Thus the firm's problem is to maximize $\pi(L)$ via choice of the level of employment L.

Since this is a one-variable maximization problem, its solution is a straightforward application of the techniques reviewed in Chapter 0. The first-order (necessary) condition for $\pi(L)$ to be maximized at some $L^* > 0$ is[2]

$$\pi'(L^*) = \frac{d\pi(L^*)}{dL} = 0, \tag{3.39}$$

and the second-order condition is

$$\pi''(L^*) = \frac{d^2\pi(L^*)}{dL^2} < 0. \tag{3.40}$$

Remember that the second-order condition, when combined with the first-order condition, is sufficient to ensure a maximum. In other words, if both (3.39) and (3.40) hold for some particular L^*, then that L^* is a local maximum of the profit function $\pi(L)$. If (3.39) holds and the profit function is strictly concave ($\pi'' < 0$ for all L), then by the local–global theorem in Chapter 1, L^* is the unique global maximum of the profit function.

Taking the derivative of (3.38) and setting it equal to zero, we get the following first-order condition for profit maximization:

$$\frac{d\pi}{dL} - 2pL^{-1/2} - w = 0. \tag{3.41}$$

Rearranging this expression and solving explicitly for L^*, we have

$$L^* = L^*(w, p) = \frac{4p^2}{w^2}. \tag{3.42}$$

The expression in (3.42) gives the firm's short-run profit-maximizing quantity of labor employed. For a fixed value of the product price, the expression gives the firm's **labor demand function:** it expresses the relationship between the wage the firm pays (w) and the its profit-maximizing level of employment (L^*). Expressions such as (3.42), which give the optimum value of a particular choice variable explicitly in terms of the parameters of the problem, can be differentiated directly to find the comparative statics impact of a change in one of the parameters. Thus solving the first-order conditions explicitly and differentiating will yield comparative statics results in precisely the same way that solving the equilibrium conditions explicitly and differentiating gave us comparative statics results in the earlier equilibrium models. Direct differentiation of (3.42) with respect to w gives $\partial L^*/\partial w = -8p^2/w^3$, which is the slope of the labor demand function (or the reciprocal of the slope if w is on the vertical axis). Since the right-hand side of this expression is always negative, we know that the labor demand curve for this firm will slope downward.

Fixing w and making p the only variable in (3.42) gives an expression for the profit-maximizing level of employment as a function of the product price. Although this expression does not really have a name in economic theory, it is closely related to the firm's **supply function.** Recall from elementary economic theory that the supply function of a firm relates the price of the good to the firm's profit-maximizing output. To obtain the supply function for this firm, simply substitute (3.42) back into the short-run production function (3.36). Since (3.42) gives the profit-maximizing level of employment L^*, substituting this expression into the production function $y = f(L)$ gives the relationship between the profit-maximizing output and the two parameters. Performing this substitution, we have

$$y^* = y^*(w, p) = \frac{8p}{w}. \tag{3.43}$$

Notice from (3.43) that the supply function slopes upward with respect to the product price (since $\partial y^*/\partial p = 8/w > 0$) and that an increase in the wage will decrease the quantity of output supplied (since $\partial y^*/\partial w = -8p/w^2 < 0$), precisely what we would expect from elementary economic theory. On this same theme, note that (3.42) gives us exactly the expression for the profit-maximizing level of employment that elementary microeconomic theory would lead us to expect. Microeconomic theory tells us that at the profit-maximizing level of employment for a perfectly competitive firm, the wage w is equal to the **marginal revenue product** (MRP_L, where $MRP_L = pMP_L$). For the production function in (3.36), the marginal product of labor is $MP_L = f'(L) = 2L^{-1/2}$, which becomes (3.42) with a little rearrangement.

Now consider the second-order condition in (3.40). For this particular firm we have

$$\pi''(L^*) = -pL^{-3/2} = -p \left(\frac{4p^2}{w^2} \right)^{-3/2} = \frac{-w^3}{8p^2}. \tag{3.44}$$

Since the right-hand side of (3.44) is strictly negative, the second-order condition clearly holds. Note that the second-order condition for short-run profit maximization by a perfectly competitive firm is a very weak condition. By this we mean that not only does it hold for the particular production function we have been considering, but it also holds for a very general class of production functions. To see why this is so, consider the profit function for a perfectly competitive firm when the short-run production function is not given explicitly. This general expression is

$$\pi(L) = pf(L) - wL - v\bar{K}. \tag{3.45}$$

Differentiating this expression gives

$$\pi'(L) = pf'(L) - w \qquad \text{and} \qquad \pi''(L) = pf''(L). \tag{3.46}$$

From the right-hand expression in (3.46), we see that the second-order condition merely requires that $f''(L^*) < 0$. Recall that if a short-run production function exhibits diminishing returns to labor, then $f''(L) < 0$ will hold for all values of L. Thus any production function that exhibits diminishing returns will automatically satisfy the second-order condition for profit maximization by a perfectly competitive firm. In fact, since $f'' < 0$ for all L, any short-run production function with diminishing returns is globally (and strictly) concave, making the L^* for which $\pi'(L^*) = 0$ a unique global maximum of the profit function $\pi(L)$.

This brings us to the comparative statics analysis of the short-run perfectly competitive firm when the production function is **not** known explicitly. Suppose that all we know about the production function $y = f(L) = f(L, \bar{K})$ is that it is at least twice differentiable, it has positive marginal products ($f' > 0$), and it exhibits diminishing marginal returns ($f'' < 0$) for all L. What can we say about comparative statics for the competitive firm in this more general case?

The first-order condition for profit maximization in this general case is obtained by setting the expression on the left-hand side of (3.46) equal to zero:

$$\pi'(L) = pf'(L) - w = 0. \tag{3.47}$$

Now, as in the general function equilibrium models discussed in the first section of this chapter, when the functions are not given exactly, we cannot find an exact solution for L^*. But we do know that the solution will depend on the two parameters

p and w, and so we write the differentiable function $L^* = L^*(w, p)$ as the solution to (3.47).[3] Substituting this expression for L^* back into the first-order condition in (3.47) gives us the identity

$$\pi'(L^*(w, p)) = pf'(L^*(w, p)) - w \equiv 0. \tag{3.48}$$

This identity can now be differentiated with respect to either parameter to find comparative statics expression for the general case.

Differentiating (3.48) with respect to w gives

$$pf''(L^*(w, p))\frac{\partial L^*}{\partial w} - 1 \equiv 0. \tag{3.49}$$

Rearranging and writing $L^*(w, p)$ as simply L^*, we have

$$\frac{\partial L^*}{\partial w} = \frac{1}{pf''(L^*)}. \tag{3.50}$$

Since $f'' < 0$, the expression (3.50) is strictly negative and the demand for labor slopes downward. Now this is a very important result. It says that the demand for labor by a profit-maximizing, perfectly competitive firm in the short run will always be such that lower wages will cause the firm to employ more labor, while higher wages will always cause the firm to employ less labor. This result does not depend on some particular specification of the production function, but rather on the rather weak (and economically quite reasonable) assumption of diminishing marginal returns. Here we see the first of many examples of an economically reasonable assumption such as diminishing returns implying that the second-order condition for the optimization problem is satisfied and also providing important comparative statics information.

Continuing with this exercise, we can also differentiate (3.48) with respect to the parameter p. This gives

$$pf''(L^*)\frac{\partial L^*}{\partial p} + f'(L^*) \equiv 0 \tag{3.51}$$

or

$$\frac{\partial L^*}{\partial p} = \frac{-f'(L^*)}{pf''(L^*)}. \tag{3.52}$$

The economic restrictions on the model ensure that the right-hand side of (3.52) is strictly positive, and so labor employment will increase with the market price of the good. While this result does not seem to be intrinsically interesting, it does lead to another comparative statics result that is important.

Note that if the expression $L^*(w, p)$ is substituted back into the production function, the result will be the supply function for the firm. Thus the supply function is

$$y^* = f(L^*(w, p)). \tag{3.53}$$

Differentiation of (3.53) with respect to price gives

$$\frac{\partial y^*}{\partial p} = f'(L^*)\frac{\partial L^*}{\partial p} > 0. \tag{3.54}$$

This important result tells us that all supply curves for perfectly competitive firms slope upward in the short run. Since this result is almost always assumed in elementary economics, it is very nice to know that it follows automatically from diminishing marginal returns and profit maximization.

These comparative statics results for the short-run perfectly competitive firm are only a sampling of many similar results obtained in the rest of this book. Later in this chapter we obtain comparative statics results for the perfectly competitive firm in the long run when both capital and labor are variables, and in Chapter 7 we examine the n-input case. Before we consider the two-input case, though, it is necessary to discuss some general properties of maximization problems involving two variables. In Chapter 0, we presented the first-order conditions for two-variable (and n-variable) maximization as a straightforward extension of the one-variable case. Unfortunately the second-order conditions are not obtained so easily. In the next section these second-order conditions are discussed informally. This presentation will be enough for us to obtain comparative statics results for the perfectly competitive firm that uses two inputs. A more complete analysis of the second-order conditions is provided in Chapter 7.

First- and Second-Order Conditions for Two-Variable Optimization

Consider the optimization problem of maximizing a differentiable function of two variables. More specifically, consider the problem

$$\underset{x}{\text{Max}} \ z = f(x), \tag{3.55}$$

where $x \in \Re^2$, $f\colon \Re^2 \to \Re$, and f is at least twice differentiable. If $x^* = (x_1^*, x_2^*)$, is a solution to the problem (3.55), then the following first-order conditions must hold:

$$\frac{\partial f(x^*)}{\partial x_1} = f_1(x^*) = 0,$$

$$\frac{\partial f(x^*)}{\partial x_2} = f_2(x^*) = 0. \tag{3.56}$$

If we picture the function $f(x)$ in 3-space with z on the vertical axis, the first equation in (3.56) states that the tangent line through the point $f(x^*)$ and parallel to the $x_1 z$ plane will be horizontal, while the second equation states that a similar condition holds for the tangent parallel to the $x_2 z$ plane. If the maximum is characterized in terms of the total differential dz, then we have $dz = 0$ at the maximum, since $dz = f_1 dx_1 + f_2 dx_2$. This, of course, implies that the tangent plane to $f(x)$ will be horizontal at $f(x^*)$. Figure 3.6 depicts such a maximum.

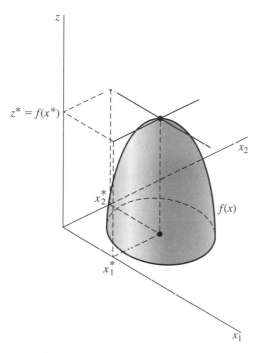

Figure 3.6

So much for first-order conditions. How should the second-order conditions be specified for this two-variable problem? Clearly, the first-order conditions allow for a number of possibilities: $f(x^*)$ could be at the top of a hill (maximum), at the bottom of a bowl (minimum), or even in the saddle between two hills (saddle point). We are interested in the case of a hill. If $f(x^*)$ is at the top of a three-dimensional hill, then for all values of $x = (x_1, x_2)$ within some epsilon neighborhood of x^*, the value of z should be less than $f(x^*)$; in other words, moving away from x^* by small amounts should make $dz < 0$. But $dz = 0$ at x^*, so moving away from x^* by some small increments dx_1 and dx_2 will make $d^2z < 0$. This gives us the desired second-order condition. If $d^2z < 0$ for all dx_1 and dx_2 (not both zero) within some neighborhood of x^* where $f_1(x^*) = f_2(x^*) = 0$, then $z = f(x)$ has a local maximum at x^*. If the first-order conditions hold at x^* and $d^2z < 0$ for all $x \in \Re^2$, then x^* is the unique global maximum of $z = f(x)$. These conditions imply the concavity (local or global) of f, but we do not discuss concavity explicitly until the presentation of the second-order conditions for n-variable maximization (and minimization) problems in Chapter 7.

This second-order condition is quite easy to apply once it has been converted into an expression involving the derivatives of the function $f(x)$ evaluated at x^*. Unfortunately this conversion is not quite as simple as we might hope. For $z = f(x) = f(x_1, x_2)$, the total differential is given by

$$dz = f_1 \, dx_1 + f_2 \, dx_2. \tag{3.57}$$

To obtain the second total differential d^2z, we need to take the total differential of (3.57), remembering that both f_1 and f_2 are functions of the two variables x_1 and x_2. Taking this second total differential, we have,[4]

$$
\begin{aligned}
d^2z &= \frac{\partial(f_1\,dx_1 + f_2\,dx_2)}{\partial x_1}\,dx_1 + \frac{\partial(f_1\,dx_1 + f_2\,dx_2)}{\partial x_2}\,dx_2 \\
&= (f_{11}\,dx_1 + f_{21}\,dx_2)\,dx_1 + (f_{12}\,dx_1 + f_{22}\,dx_2)\,dx_2 \\
&= f_{11}\,dx_1^2 + 2f_{12}\,dx_1\,dx_2 + f_{22}\,dx_2^2,
\end{aligned}
\tag{3.58}
$$

where $f_{ij} = \partial^2 f/\partial x_i \partial x_j$ and $dx_i^2 = (dx_i)^2$.

The second-order condition for a local maximum at x^* requires the right-hand side of (3.58) to be strictly negative for all dx_1 and dx_2 (not both zero) when the second derivatives f_{11}, f_{22}, and f_{12} are all evaluated at x^*. It is obvious from (3.58) that this can be the case only when both f_{11} and f_{22} are negative. Suppose that $f_{11}(x^*) \geq 0$; then $dx_1 > 0$ and $dx_2 = 0$ imply that $d^2z \geq 0$, which violates the second-order condition. Thus the second-order conditions must include $f_{11}(x^*) < 0$ and $f_{22}(x^*) < 0$. The sign restrictions on the cross terms $f_{12} = f_{21}$ are more difficult to obtain.

For the cross terms, let us "complete the square" on the right-hand side of (3.58). We do this by adding and subtracting the term $(f_{12}^2\,dx_2^2)/f_{11}$ to and from the equation. This computation gives

$$
d^2z = f_{11}\,dx_1^2 + 2f_{12}\,dx_1\,dx_2 + \frac{f_{12}^2\,dx_2^2}{f_{11}} + f_{22}\,dx_2^2 - \frac{f_{12}^2\,dx_2^2}{f_{11}}.
$$

Rearranging this expression, we have

$$
\begin{aligned}
d^2z &= f_{11}\left(dx_1^2 + \frac{2f_{12}\,dx_1\,dx_2}{f_{11}} + \frac{f_{12}^2\,dx_2^2}{f_{11}^2}\right) + \left(f_{22} - \frac{f_{12}^2}{f_{11}}\right)dx_2^2, \\
&= f_{11}\left(dx_1 + \frac{f_{12}\,dx_2}{f_{11}}\right)^2 + \left(\frac{f_{22}f_{11} - f_{12}^2}{f_{11}}\right)dx_2^2.
\end{aligned}
\tag{3.59}
$$

Both expressions on the right-hand side of (3.59) involve a squared term. This can be seen more clearly if (3.59) is written as

$$
d^2z = f_{11}a^2 + \left(\frac{f_{11}f_{22} - f_{12}^2}{f_{11}}\right)b^2,
\tag{3.60}
$$

where a represents the first squared term in (3.59) and b the second.

The importance of these squared terms (and the motivation for completing the square in the first place) is that the terms are always positive, regardless of the particular values of a and b. Since these terms are always positive, and since $f_{11} < 0$, the sign of d^2z can be determined by the sign of $f_{11}f_{22} - f_{12}^2$. If this expression is negative, then since $f_{11} < 0$, the term on the right-hand side of (3.60) will be positive, which means that d^2z could be made positive by arbitrarily small changes in x_2, so long as $dx_1 + f_{12}\,dx_2/f_{11} = 0$. However, if $f_{11}f_{22} - f_{12}^2 > 0$, then both terms on the right-hand side of (3.60) will be negative, which certainly guarantees that $d^2z < 0$. Thus we have finally obtained the desired characterization of the **second-order conditions for a two-variable maximization** problem in terms of the derivatives of f:

$$f_{11} < 0, f_{22} < 0 \quad \text{and} \quad f_{11}f_{22} - f_{12}^2 > 0. \tag{3.61}$$

Actually it is not necessary to use both $f_{11} < 0$ and $f_{22} < 0$, since either one, when combined with the expression on the right-hand side of (3.61), implies the other. For instance, $f_{11} < 0$ and $f_{11}f_{22} - f_{12}^2 > 0$ imply that $f_{22} < 0$.

To summarize the results of this subsection, we state that if the first-order conditions (3.56) hold at x^* and the second-order conditions (3.61) hold at x^*, then x^* solves (3.55) and is a local maximum of $f(x)$. If the first-order conditions (3.61) hold at x^* and the second-order conditions (3.61) hold globally (for all x), then x^* solves (3.55) and is the unique global maximum of $f(x)$.

Perfectly Competitive Firm 2

Reconsider the perfectly competitive firm with the production function $y = f(L, K) = 2L^{1/2}K^{1/2}$. We have already derived comparative statics for such a firm for the short-run case of $\bar{K} = 4$. A valuable lesson can be learned by examining the same firm in the long run.

In the long run, the profit function depends on both L and K, and it is given by

$$\pi(L, K) = pf(L, K) - wL - vK. \tag{3.62}$$

For the specific production function considered here,

$$\pi(L, K) = p2L^{1/2}K^{1/2} - wL - vK. \tag{3.63}$$

As in the short run, p, w, and v are parameters to the firm, but now there are two choice variables: L and K.

If a maximum of (3.63) exists, it must satisfy the first-order conditions

$$\pi_L = \frac{\partial \pi}{\partial L} = pK^{1/2}L^{-1/2} - w = 0,$$

$$\pi_K = \frac{\partial \pi}{\partial K} = pL^{1/2}K^{-1/2} - v = 0. \tag{3.64}$$

Manipulation of the two equations in (3.64) gives

$$wL^{1/2}K^{-1/2} = vK^{1/2}L^{-1/2},$$

which reduces to $L = vK/w$. Substituting this into the first equation in (3.64), to eliminate L, gives

$$K^{1/2} = \frac{w^{1/2}v^{1/2}K^{1/2}}{p} \quad \text{or} \quad p = w^{1/2}v^{1/2}. \tag{3.65}$$

Now this seems to be a very strange result. We wanted to find the input demand functions $L^* = L^*(w, v, p)$ and $K^* = K^*(w, v, p)$ that would give the profit-maximizing levels of labor and capital employment as functions of the problem's parameters w, v, and p. What we have in (3.65) is a condition that basically says: "If there exist strictly positive quantities of L and K that maximize profit, then $p = w^{1/2}v^{1/2}$." In other words, if $p \neq w^{1/2}v^{1/2}$, then there does not exist a critical point (L^*, K^*) that satisfies the first-order conditions. This is obviously not a production function that provides a meaningful solution to the long-run profit maximization problem for a perfectly competitive firm.

Let us now consider a long-run profit maximization problem that does have a well-behaved solution. Consider the production function

$$y = f(L, K) = L^{1/2} + K^{1/2}. \tag{3.66}$$

The first-order conditions for long-run profit maximization with this production function are

$$\pi_L = \frac{p}{2L^{1/2}} - w = 0,$$
$$\pi_K = \frac{p}{2K^{1/2}} - v = 0. \tag{3.67}$$

Solving these equations for the input demand functions gives us

$$L^* = \frac{p^2}{4w^2} \quad \text{and} \quad K^* = \frac{p^2}{4v^2}. \tag{3.68}$$

For this production function we have

$$\pi_{LL} = pf_{LL} = \frac{-p}{4L^{3/2}} < 0,$$

$$\pi_{KK} = pf_{KK} = \frac{-p}{4K^{3/2}} < 0, \tag{3.69}$$

$$\pi_{LL}\pi_{KK} - \pi_{LK}^2 = p^2\left(f_{LL}f_{KK} - f_{LK}^2\right) = p^2\left(\frac{-1}{4L^{3/2}}\right)\left(\frac{-1}{4K^{3/2}}\right) > 0.$$

So the second-order conditions clearly hold for this production function.

Comparative statics terms can be obtained by direct differentiation of the factor demand functions in (3.68). For the two choice variables and the three parameters, we have the following six comparative statics terms:

$$\frac{\partial L^*}{\partial w} = \frac{-p^2}{2w^3} < 0, \quad \frac{\partial L^*}{\partial v} = 0, \quad \frac{\partial L^*}{\partial p} = \frac{p}{2w^2} > 0,$$

$$\frac{\partial K^*}{\partial w} = 0, \quad \frac{\partial K^*}{\partial v} = \frac{-p^2}{2v^3} < 0, \quad \frac{\partial K^*}{\partial p} = \frac{p}{2v^2} > 0. \tag{3.70}$$

The demand functions for both inputs decrease with an increase in their own price, are unaffected by the prices of the other input, and increase with output price.

The **supply function** for a competitive firm is defined by

$$y^* = y^*(w, v, p) = f[L^*(w, v, p), K^*(w, v, p)]. \tag{3.71}$$

Substitution of the factor demands from (3.68) into (3.71) gives us the supply function for this particular firm

$$y^* = \left(\frac{p^2}{4w^2}\right)^{1/2} + \left(\frac{p^2}{4v^2}\right)^{1/2} = \frac{p\,(w+v)}{2wv}. \tag{3.72}$$

And by direct differentiation we have the comparative statics expressions

$$\frac{\partial y^*}{\partial p} = \frac{w+v}{2wv} > 0, \qquad \frac{\partial y^*}{\partial w} = \frac{-p}{2w^2} < 0, \qquad \frac{\partial y^*}{\partial v} = \frac{-p}{2v^2} < 0. \tag{3.73}$$

As expected, we find that the profit-maximizing output of the firm will increase with the market price and decrease with higher factor prices.

   While these are only a few of the many results that can be obtained for a competitive firm with this particular production function, we now abandon this specific case and turn to the more general problem in which the exact form of the production function is unknown. Suppose that the only available information is that the production function satisfies the first- and second-order conditions for long-run profit maximization by a perfectly competitive firm. Then what can be said about the comparative statics expressions in this general case? Were our (economically quite reasonable) results a general property of profit-maximizing competitive behavior, or merely a serendipitous quirk of the production function $y = L^{1/2} + K^{1/2}$?

   For the general problem, the first-order conditions are

$$\begin{aligned} \pi_L &= pf_L(L, K) - w = 0, \\ \pi_K &= pf_K(L, K) - v = 0. \end{aligned} \tag{3.74}$$

With a little manipulation these become

$$pf_L(L, K) = w \qquad \text{and} \qquad pf_K(L, K) = v, \tag{3.75}$$

which are the profit-maximizing conditions familiar from elementary economics. These two expressions say that if profit is being maximized, then both inputs should be employed in such a way that the marginal revenue product of each input (pMP) is equal to the price of the input.

   As in the general short-run case discussed earlier, we do not know the exact form of the solutions to (3.74), but we do know that the profit-maximizing employment of the two inputs will depend on the parameters of the problem. Thus under fairly general conditions, we can write the solutions to (3.74) as differentiable functions of the three parameters, so

$$L^* = L^*(w, v, p) \qquad \text{and} \qquad K^* = K^*(w, v, p) \tag{3.76}$$

characterize the general solutions to the first-order conditions in (3.74).

   Now for this type of problem, where the exact form of the production function is unknown, the comparative statics strategy must be different from the approach used in the more specific case, where we "checked" the production function to see whether it satisfied the second-order conditions. When the second-order conditions were satisfied, we obtained the factor demand functions explicitly by solving the first-order conditions and then differentiated these functions to obtain the desired comparative statics results. Such a strategy is not available in the general case. We do not know what the production function is in the general case, so it is impossible to "check" whether it does, or does not, satisfy the second-order conditions. Our strategy in this case—a strategy that will be repeated for more complex models in later chapters—is to **assume** that the production function satisfies the second-order conditions and then explore the comparative statics implications of that assumption. In other words, we want to answer the question: Assuming that first- and second-order conditions for a maximum are satisfied, what can be said regarding the impact of a parameter change on the long-run profit-maximizing input choices of the perfectly competitive firm? This question has been answered for the short run, and now those results are extended to the long-run case of two inputs (the n-input case is discussed in Chapter 7).

Substituting the expressions for $L*$ and $K*$ from (3.76) into the equations in (3.74) yields the following identities:

$$pf_L\left(L^*(w, v, p), K^*(w, v, p)\right) - w \equiv 0,$$
$$pf_K\left(L^*(w, v, p), K^*(w, v, p)\right) - v \equiv 0. \tag{3.77}$$

The comparative statics impact of a parameter change can now be found by differentiating these two identities. We work through the exercise for a change in the price of labor w, but expressions for a change in v or p could easily be found using the same technique.

Differentiating the identities in (3.77) with respect to w, we have

$$pf_{LL}\frac{\partial L^*}{\partial w} + pf_{LK}\frac{\partial K^*}{\partial w} \equiv 1,$$
$$pf_{KL}\frac{\partial L^*}{\partial w} + pf_{KK}\frac{\partial K^*}{\partial w} \equiv 0, \tag{3.78}$$

where all derivatives are evaluated at the point (L^*, K^*). Solving this system simultaneously, we multiply the first expression by $-f_{KL}$, multiply the second expression by f_{LL}, and add the resulting equations:

$$p\left(f_{LL}f_{KK} - f_{LK}^2\right)\frac{\partial K^*}{\partial w} = -f_{KL}$$

or

$$\frac{\partial K^*}{\partial w} = \frac{-f_{KL}}{p\left(f_{LL}f_{KK} - f_{LK}^2\right)}. \tag{3.79}$$

Substituting this expression for $\partial K^*/\partial w$ back into the second identity in (3.78) gives

$$pf_{KL}\left(\frac{\partial L^*}{\partial w}\right) - \frac{pf_{KK}f_{KL}}{p\left(f_{LL}f_{KK} - f_{LK}^2\right)} = 0$$

or

$$\frac{\partial L^*}{\partial w} = \frac{f_{KK}}{p\left(f_{LL}f_{KK} - f_{LK}^2\right)}. \tag{3.80}$$

BOX 3.1
Efficiency Wage Models of Unemployment

It is a well-accepted stylized fact of economic life that firms do not find it in their best interest to cut wages when faced with involuntary unemployment in the labor market. Such behavior is rather paradoxical, since the standard theory of competitive labor markets suggests that wage reductions would be profitable under such conditions. One attempt to give a rational explanation for this observed reluctance to lower wages in the face of unemployment is the theory of **efficiency wages.** According to efficiency wage theory, reducing the wage rate may so adversely affect labor productivity that labor costs actually will increase rather than decrease. Such countervailing productivity changes would, of course, destroy the firm's incentive to make such wage reductions. Many of the seminal papers on the theory of efficiency wages are collected in the Akerlof and Yellen (1986) volume, and the main argument is summarized nicely in Yellen (1984). While criticisms have certainly been raised against the theory by, among others, Barro (1989) and Carmichael (1985), it remains a popular explanation for wage rigidity and involuntary unemployment in the labor market.

The basic efficiency wage argument can be seen from the following simple model. Consider a firm producing output Q from the short-run production function $f(L)$, where labor L is measured in terms of "efficiency units." That is, labor is given by $L = e(w)N$, where N is the number of workers, e is the effort (or efficiency) per worker, and w is the real wage. It is a basic assumption of the efficiency wage model that higher real wages will increase effort, thus $de/dw > 0$. Some of the many explanations offered for this positively sloped effort function include reduced shirking by workers, lower labor turnover rates, improved average quality of job applicants, and improved morale.

From this production function, we have the firm's (real) profit, given by

$$\pi = \pi(w, N) = f(e(w)N) - wN.$$

The firm's objective is to maximize π through choice of the real wage ($w^* > 0$) and the level of employment ($N^* > 0$). First-order conditions for the maximization are given by

$$\frac{\partial \pi}{\partial w} = \left[f' \left(\frac{de}{dw} \right) - 1 \right] N = 0,$$

$$\frac{\partial \pi}{\partial N} = f'e - w = 0.$$

Substituting the second equation into the first, we have the final result of

$$\frac{w}{e}\frac{de}{dw} = 1.$$

This condition, the unitary elasticity of the effort function with respect to the real wage (sometimes called the **Solow condition** from Solow, 1979), defines the **efficiency wage** w^*; it is the wage that minimizes the labor cost per efficiency unit. Of course there is no reason for this efficiency wage w^* to be equal to the market clearing wage. If w^* is greater than the competitive wage, then there will be involuntary unemployment. There is no reason in the context of this model for such unemployment to disappear: that is, there is no reason for the efficiency wage to converge to the equilibrium wage over time. Given the relationship between the real wage and worker effort $e(w)$, it is not in the firm's best interest to lower the wage below w^* even though involuntary unemployment exits.

Sources

Akerlof, G. A., and J. L. Yellen, eds. 1986. *Efficiency wage models of the labor market.* Cambridge: Cambridge University Press.

Barro, R. J. 1989. An efficiency-wage theory of the weather. *Journal of Political Economy* 97: 999–1001.

Carmichael, L. 1985. Can unemployment be involuntary? Comment. *American Economic Review* 75: 1213–17.

Solow, R. M. 1979. Another possible source of wage stickiness. *Journal of Macroeconomics* 1: 79–82. (Reprinted in Akerlof and Yellen, 1986.)

Yellen, J. L. 1984. Efficiency wage models of unemployment. *American Economic Review* 74: 200–5.

The first thing to notice about the comparative statics expressions (3.79) and (3.80) is that the denominators in both are strictly positive by the second-order conditions. In expression (3.80), the own effect of a change in the price of labor, the numerator is negative by the second-order conditions, making the entire expression negative. Thus we see that in the long run, as in the short run, the demand for labor slopes downward for the perfectly competitive firm. This is an important implication of competitive behavior, and it is based on the satisfaction of the first- and second-order conditions for profit maximization; it is not dependent on any particular specification of the underlying production function.

It would be nice if such a definite result were also available for the cross effect $\partial K^*/\partial w$, but unfortunately that is not the case. The second-order conditions do not restrict the sign of the cross derivatives of the production function. These terms can be positive, negative, or zero as long as the condition $f_{LL}f_{KK} - f_{LK}^2 > 0$ holds. Thus first- and second-order conditions alone do not tell us the sign of $\partial K^*/\partial w$. We can say that if the two inputs are complements in production ($f_{KL} > 0$), then it will always be the case that $\partial K^*/\partial w < 0$, whereas if they are substitutes ($f_{KL} < 0$), then $\partial K^*/\partial w > 0$. Finally, if the inputs are unrelated in production ($f_{KL} = 0$), as in the foregoing example $y = L^{1/2} + K^{1/2}$, then $\partial K^*/\partial w = 0$. Even this is a rather impressive result, given how few assumptions we imposed on the model.

In this section we have learned a lot about the general method of finding comparative statics results for maximization-based models. First, we discovered that second-order conditions are extremely important. Second, for problems in which the second order conditions are satisfied and the objective function is known exactly, we saw that it is possible to find both solutions and their comparative statics effects by direct computation. Third, and most important for upcoming chapters, we have learned that it is often possible to obtain qualitative comparative statics information by merely drawing out the implications of the first- and second-order conditions for maximization.

3.3 Comparative Statics with Both Equilibrium and Optimization

The Cournot Duopoly Model

In the preceding sections, we obtained comparative statics results for equilibrium models as well as for models that involve maximization. The final topic of this chapter is the examination of a class of models that explicitly involve both maximization **and** equilibrium. The model to be discussed is one of the oldest models of firm behavior in economics: the **Cournot duopoly** model. This model has been an important part of economic theory for over 150 years, and while its assumptions are quite restrictive, its theoretical approach is extremely general and has been applied successfully to a wide range of different economic phenomena. The general method is called the **Nash equilibria** approach to noncooperative games, and while the Cournot model is only one very special case of this general approach, it remains the single best introduction to this important class of economic models.

In the Cournot duopoly model, two firms produce a single homogeneous good. Since there are only two firms in the market, the amount that one firm will be able to sell, and therefore the amount of profit that it will receive, depends on the behavior of the other firm in the market. This makes the two firms fundamentally interdependent; the behavior of each firm depends on how it expects its rival to respond to its actions. The Cournot model provides one method for analyzing such strategic and fundamentally interdependent behavior.

To introduce the Cournot approach, we consider two firms, firm 1 and firm 2. Both firms produce the same product, which has the demand function $P = P(Q)$, where P is the market price and Q is the quantity demanded. As we stated earlier, this type of demand relation is sometimes called an **inverse demand function** because it expresses the maximum price that consumers are willing to pay as a function of the quantity purchased (rather than expressing the quantity demanded as a function of the market price, as is more commonly done). Since there are only two firms in the market, $Q = q_1 + q_2$, where q_1 is the output of firm 1 and q_2 is the output of firm 2. Each firm has a cost function $C^i(q_i)$ for $i = 1, 2$, which expresses the total cost of producing any particular level of output q_i.

The profit π of each firm is simply total revenue minus total cost. So given our definition of demand and cost, we have

$$\pi^1(q_1, q_2) = P(Q)q_1 - C^1(q_1)$$

and

$$\pi^2(q_1, q_2) = P(Q)q_2 - C^2(q_2)$$

(3.81)

as the profit functions for the two firms. Note the interdependency of the profit functions; since the price depends on the total quantity in the market, both profit functions depend on the output of both firms.

Given the profit functions in (3.81), if each firm considers its own output as a choice variable and maximizes profit, the first-order conditions will be

$$\frac{\partial \pi^1}{\partial q_1} = P(Q) + q_1 \left(\frac{dP}{dQ}\right)\left(\frac{\partial Q}{\partial q_1}\right) - \frac{dC^1(q_1)}{dq_1} = 0,$$

$$\frac{\partial \pi^2}{\partial q_2} = P(Q) + q_2 \left(\frac{dP}{dQ}\right)\left(\frac{\partial Q}{\partial q_2}\right) - \frac{dC^2(q_2)}{dq_2} = 0.$$

Or, rewriting these first-order conditions with $P = P(Q)$, $dP/dQ = P'$, and $MC_i = dC^i(q_i)/dq_i$ for $i = 1, 2$, we have

$$P + P'q_1 \left(\frac{\partial Q}{\partial q_1}\right) - MC_1 = 0,$$

$$P + P'q_2 \left(\frac{\partial Q}{\partial q_2}\right) - MC_2 = 0.$$

(3.82)

The interdependency of the two firms is captured in (3.82) by the term $\partial Q/\partial q_1$ in the first equation and by the term $\partial Q/\partial q_2$ in the second. From the viewpoint of the relevant firm, these expressions are really "conjectural" or "expectational." This is because neither firm really knows how the market output Q will change when it alters its own output because neither knows with certainty how the other will react. Each firm must make a conjecture regarding the response of the other firm to its change in output. This conjecture will be reflected in $\partial Q/\partial q_1$ for firm 1 and $\partial Q/\partial q_2$ for firm 2. Recalling that $Q = q_1 + q_2$, we can expand these two derivatives into

$$\frac{\partial Q}{\partial q_1} = \frac{\partial q_1}{\partial q_1} + \left(\frac{\partial q_2}{\partial q_1}\right)^e = 1 + \left(\frac{\partial q_2}{\partial q_1}\right)^e,$$

$$\frac{\partial Q}{\partial q_2} = \left(\frac{\partial q_1}{\partial q_2}\right)^e + \frac{\partial q_2}{\partial q_2} = \left(\frac{\partial q_1}{\partial q_2}\right)^e + 1,$$

(3.83)

where the $(\cdot)^e$ indicates that anything inside the parentheses is conjectural or expectational, based on what each firm believes the other will do in response to its change in output. The term $(\partial q_i/\partial q_j)^e$ for $i \neq j$ is called the **conjectural variation**.

There are as many different models of duopoly (or oligopoly, since more than two firms could easily be considered) as there are assumptions about the conjectural variation terms. By far the simplest assumption, and yet one that has proven to be quite robust, is the Cournot conjecture. The **Cournot conjecture** is simply zero conjectural variation:

$$\left(\frac{\partial q_i}{\partial q_j}\right)^e = 0 \qquad \text{for } i \neq j. \tag{3.84}$$

That is, firm 1 assumes that firm 2 will not change its output in response to a change in the output of firm 1, and firm 2 assumes that firm 1 will not change its output in response to a change in the output of firm 2. Applying the Cournot conjecture to (3.83), we have $\partial Q/\partial q_1 = 1 = \partial Q/\partial q_2$: each firm assumes that the only change in market output will be its own direct impact. Substituting these derivatives into the first-order conditions (3.82), we have the first-order conditions for the Cournot duopoly model with profit functions given by (3.81):

$$P(q_1, q_2) + P'(q_1, q_2)q_1 - MC_1 = 0,$$
$$P(q_1, q_2) + P'(q_1, q_2)q_2 \quad MC_2 = 0. \tag{3.85}$$

Note that the Cournot assumption that $(\partial q_1/\partial q_2)^e = 0 = (\partial q_2/\partial q_1)^e$ does not imply that the interdependency has disappeared from the first-order conditions. In (3.85) the demand function P (and possibly P' if demand is nonlinear) will involve both q_1 and q_2. Since both first-order conditions for the Cournot model given in (3.85) involve both q_1 and q_2 the Cournot conjecture does not eliminate the interdependency of the two firms—the conjecture only simplifies it. The equations in (3.85) characterize the **reaction functions** of the two firms, since they show the profit-maximizing reaction of each firm as a function of the output of the other firm. The **Cournot equilibrium** is a set of outputs $q^* = (q_1^*, q_2^*)$ that simultaneously satisfies both reaction functions. Only at the Cournot equilibrium can neither firm benefit from a unilateral change in its output.[5]

To make these ideas more concrete, let us examine a very simple Cournot model. Consider the case of a demand curve that is linear with $P = -Q + b, b > 0$, and the only costs are fixed costs: FC_1 for firm 1, and FC_2 for firm 2. Under these assumptions the profit functions for the two firms are given by

$$\pi^1(q_1, q_2) = (-q_1 - q_2 + b)q_1 - FC_1,$$
$$\pi^2(q_1, q_2) = (-q_1 - q_2 + b)q_2 - FC_1. \tag{3.86}$$

For these profit functions, the first-order conditions are

$$\frac{\partial \pi^1}{\partial q_1} = -2q_1 - q_2 + b = 0,$$

$$\frac{\partial \pi^2}{\partial q_2} = -q_1 - 2q_2 + b = 0. \tag{3.87}$$

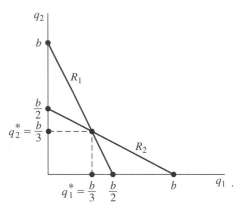

Figure 3.7

Rearranging these first-order conditions, we have the reaction functions R_1 for firm 1 and R_2 for firm 2

$$q_1 = R_1(q_2), \text{ where } R_1(q_2) = \frac{b - q_2}{2}, \tag{3.88a}$$

$$q_2 = R_2(q_1), \text{ where } R_2(q_1) = \frac{b - q_1}{2}. \tag{3.88b}$$

These reaction functions give the profit-maximizing output "reaction" of each firm as a function of its rival's output. For instance, when $q_2 = 0$, firm 1 is the only firm in the market, and the reaction function of firm 1 (3.88a) tells us that the profit-maximizing output for a monopoly firm 1 is $q_1 = b/2$. This is precisely the output we would expect from a profit-maximizing monopolist facing the demand curve $P = -Q + b$ and having zero marginal cost: halfway between the origin and the quantity intercept of the demand function. Thus the Cournot model has the nice property of generating the monopoly model as a special case, the case in which the other firm is producing zero output.

The two reaction functions in (3.88) are shown in Figure 3.7. The Cournot equilibrium is $q^* = (q_1^*, q_2^*) = (b/3, b/3)$, given by the intersection of the two reaction functions. This equilibrium point could be found algebraically by solving the two reaction functions simultaneously. In general the Cournot equilibrium (q_1^*, q_2^*) is given by the simultaneous solution of $q_1^* = R_1(q_2^*)$ and $q_2^* = R_2(q_1^*)$. For the particular Cournot model we are examining here, the equilibrium market output is $Q^* = q_1^* + q_2^* = 2b/3$, and the market price is $P^* = -Q^* + b = b/3$.

This completes our general introduction to the Cournot model and our analysis of this simple linear demand, fixed-cost case. But before moving to the next topic of Cournot comparative statics, we want to examine one additional feature of the model: adjustment to the Cournot equilibrium from any initial nonequilibrium position. Serious discussion of dynamic adjustment will be deferred until Chapter 5, but it is useful to briefly consider the process in our specific Cournot model. To this end, consider Figure 3.8 and suppose that firm 2 is producing at an output

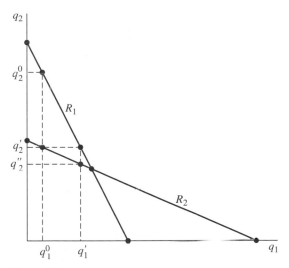

Figure 3.8

other than the Cournot equilibrium: for instance q_2^0. If firm 2 is producing an output of q_2^0, then we can read off R_1 how firm 1 will "react" to that output. The profit-maximizing output for firm 1, given that firm 2 is producing q_2^0, is q_1^0. But now if firm 1 is producing q_1^0, the profit-maximizing output for firm 2 is not q_2^0 but rather q_2', and so on. The only consistent output for both firms is the Cournot equilibrium $q* = (q_1^*, q_2^*) = (b/3, b/3)$. For any other output, the "best reply" or profit-maximizing reaction of each firm involves changing its output. For the Cournot model, unlike the earlier models in this chapter, both equilibrium and maximization are explicitly involved: there is an equilibrium condition that requires the simultaneous satisfaction of two equations, but those equations are themselves derived from the first-order conditions for the maximization of an objective function.

Comparative Statics in the Cournot Model

Consider the slightly more complex Cournot model in which there are two firms with the same demand function used earlier ($P = -Q + b$), but both firms have quadratic cost functions given by $C^i(q_i) = q_i^2 + dq_i + FC_i$ for $i = 1, 2$ and $d > 0$. Since the marginal cost (MC) associated with this quadratic cost function is $MC_i = dC^i(q_i)/dq_i = d + 2q_i$, the parameter d can be thought of as a shift parameter in the marginal cost function; the higher d is, the higher the marginal costs of the two firms. Since d is a shift parameter, a change in its value will change the Cournot equilibrium. This raises the obvious comparative statics question of finding $\partial q_1^*/\partial d$ and $\partial q_2^*/\partial d$. Since b is also a parameter, specifically a shift parameter on the demand function, $\partial q_1^*/\partial b$ and $\partial q_2^*/\partial b$ can also be investigated.

Given these cost and demand conditions, the profit functions for the two firms are

$$\pi^1(q_1, q_2) = (-q_1 - q_2 + b)q_1 - q_1^2 - dq_1 - FC_1,$$
$$\pi^2(q_1, q_2) = (-q_1 - q_2 + b)q_2 - q_2^2 - dq_2 - FC_2.$$

(3.89)

Profit maximization by both firms under the Cournot assumption implies the first-order conditions

$$\pi_1^1 = \frac{\partial \pi^1}{\partial q_1} = -4q_1 - q_2 + b - d = 0,$$

$$\pi_2^2 = \frac{\partial \pi^2}{\partial q_2} = -4q_2 - q_1 + b - d = 0. \tag{3.90}$$

The second-order conditions for this problem are given by

$$\pi_{11}^1 = \frac{\partial^2 \pi^1}{\partial q_1^2} < 0 \quad \text{and} \quad \pi_{22}^2 = \frac{\partial^2 \pi^2}{\partial q_2^2} < 0. \tag{3.91}$$

Taking these second derivatives for this particular example, we have

$$\pi_{11}^1 = -4 \quad \text{and} \quad \pi_{22}^2 = -4, \tag{3.92}$$

so the second-order conditions certainly hold. Note that only two second-order conditions are required for the Cournot duopoly model; in particular, the expression $\pi_{11}^1 \pi_{22}^2 - \pi_{12}^1 \pi_{21}^2$ was not examined. This is because the Cournot duopoly model is not a two-variable maximization problem; it is two maximization problems, each having one variable. While both profit functions depend on both outputs, there are not two choice variables for each firm. Each firm has only one choice variable, its own output, and therefore the second-order conditions are simply those for the maximization of a one-variable function.

Rearranging the expressions in (3.90), we have the two reaction functions

$$q_1 = \frac{(b - d - q_2)}{4},$$

$$q_2 = \frac{(b - d - q_1)}{4}. \tag{3.93}$$

where the first expression is R_1, the reaction function of firm 1, and the second expression is R_2, the reaction function of firm 2. Solving these two reaction functions simultaneously, we have the Cournot equilibrium

$$q^* = (q_1^*, q_2^*) = \left(\frac{b - d}{5}, \frac{b - d}{5} \right). \tag{3.94}$$

This makes the total market output $Q^* = q_1^* + q_2^* = 2(b - d)/5$ in the Cournot equilibrium with a market price of $P^* = 3b/5 + 2d/5$. Notice that $Q^* > 0$ requires the parameter restriction $b > d$.

Since all the functions involved in the maximization were given in exact form, the comparative statics terms we desire can be found by direct differentiation of the Cournot equilibrium values q_1^* and q_2^*. From (3.94) we have the comparative statics expressions

$$\frac{\partial q_i^*}{\partial d} = \frac{-1}{5} \quad \text{and} \quad \frac{\partial q_i^*}{\partial b} = \frac{1}{5} \quad \text{for } i = 1, 2. \tag{3.95}$$

BOX 3.2
International Trade Theory under Imperfect Competition

The theory of international trade has traditionally been based on the assumption of competitive behavior. Under standard competitive conditions, trade occurs only because of differences in tastes, technology, or factor endowments, and there is very little room for welfare-improving governmental policy. In recent years, though, a new approach to international trade theory has been developed, an approach based on the theory of imperfect competition. Often this imperfectly competitive behavior is characterized by the assumptions of the Cournot model (zero conjectural variations).

Because models based on imperfect competition have few economic agents and the possibility of positive economic profits (unlike long-run perfect competition), this new way of characterizing international trade leaves much more room for strategic behavior and governmental policy. In such trade models, often tariffs and/or subsidies can transfer profit from a foreign oligopolist to its domestic competitor and thereby increase the welfare of the home county. Although we cite an example of such pro-interventionist result below, not all imperfectly competitive models have such results. In addition, as emphasized by authors such as Eaton and Grossman (1986), even when such results are obtained for a certain model, they need not continue to hold when the assumptions of the model are changed slightly. As most of the policy applications of this new approach have stressed (e.g., Krugman 1986, 1987), the positive governmental role implied by some of these models is quite interesting, but it is not a reason for the profession to abandon its long-standing preference for free trade. The literature on this topic is vast and growing; our particular example follows Brander and Spencer (1984, 1985) and Dixit (1987). Problem 26 at the end of this chapter and Problem 7 in Chapter 4 are also based on this approach to trade theory.

Consider two firms producing a certain good, one firm producing in the home country (with output x_1) and the other firm producing in the foreign country (with output x_2). Both the firm in the home country (firm 1) and the firm in the other country (firm 2) produce the good under constant marginal (and thus average variable) cost: c_1 for firm 1 and c_2 for firm 2. The fixed costs of the two firms are given by F_1 and F_2, respectively. For simplicity we assume that the good is produced exclusively for export and none of the good (from either firm) is consumed in the home country. These assumptions allow us to avoid discussion of consumer's surplus, a topic discussed in Chapter 4. The total revenue function is $TR_1 = TR_1(x_1, x_2)$ for the domestic firm, and $TR_2 = TR_2(x_1, x_2)$ for the foreign firm. Since this is an oligopoly model, the total revenue of both firms is a function of the output of the other firm. We make the reasonable assumption that $TR_{ij} = \partial TR_i / \partial x_j < 0$ for

$i \neq j$. Finally, let the home country government provide an export subsidy to the domestic firm in the amount of e per unit sold. Under these conditions, we have the following profit functions for the two firms:

$$\pi_1 = TR_1(x_1, x_2) - (c_1 - e)x_1 - F_1,$$
$$\pi_2 = TR_2(x_1, x_2) - c_2 x_2 - F_2.$$

Assuming Cournot behavior on the part of both firms (zero conjectural variation), we have the following first-order conditions for the two firms:

$$TR_{11} - (c_1 - e) = 0 \quad \text{and} \quad TR_{22} - c_2 = 0. \tag{a}$$

Under the Cournot assumption, these first-order conditions also specify the reaction functions of the two firms. Solving these reaction functions simultaneously, we have the Cournot equilibrium outputs of the two firms x_1^* and x_2^*. In general, these Cournot equilibrium outputs are functions of the parameters, specifically, $x_1^* = x_1^*(e)$ and $x_2^* = x_2^*(e)$. Under relatively standard assumptions on the total revenue functions, the comparative statics terms are signed as we would expect: $\partial x_1^*/\partial e > 0$ and $\partial x_2^*/\partial e < 0$. The domestic firm's contribution to the welfare or national income of the home country is given by the amount of its profit π_1 minus the amount that it receives as a subsidy ex_1. Thus firm 1's contribution to the welfare of the home country W_1 is

$$W_1 = \pi_1 - ex_1$$
$$= TR_1 - (c_1 - e)x_1 - F_1 - ex_1$$
$$= TR_1 - ex_1 - F_1.$$

Substituting in the Cournot equilibrium values $x_1^* = x_1^*(e)$ and $x_2^* = x_2^*(e)$, we have

$$W_1(e) = TR_1[x_1^*(e), x_2^*(e)] - c_1 x_1^*(e) - F_1.$$

From this expression, we know that the change in welfare caused by the change in the amount of the export subsidy is given by

$$\frac{\partial W_1}{\partial e} = TR_{11}\left(\frac{\partial x_1^*}{\partial e}\right) - c_1\left(\frac{\partial x_1^*}{\partial e}\right) + TR_{12}\left(\frac{\partial x_2^*}{\partial e}\right).$$

or, substituting $TR_{11} - c_1 = -e$ from the first-order conditions (a), we have

$$\frac{\partial W_1}{\partial e} = TR_{12}\left(\frac{\partial x_2^*}{\partial e}\right) - e\left(\frac{\partial x_1^*}{\partial e}\right).$$

Now suppose that there is no subsidy initially, so that $e = 0$. From the foregoing condition, we have

$$\frac{\partial W_1}{\partial e} = TR_{12}\left(\frac{\partial x_2^*}{\partial e}\right) > 0,$$

since $TR_{12} < 0$ and $\partial x_2^*/\partial e < 0$. Thus we obtain the surprising "interventionist" result that an export subsidy will increase welfare in the home country.

Sources

Brander, J. A., and B. J. Spencer. 1984. Tariff protection and imperfect competition. In *Monopolistic competition and international trade,* edited by H. Kierzkowski. New York: Oxford University Press, 194–206. (Reprinted in Grossman, 1992.)

———. 1985. Export subsidies and international market share rivalry. *Journal of International Economics* 18: 83–100.

Dixit, A. 1987. Strategic aspects of trade policy. In *Advances in economic theory: Fifth World Congress,* edited by T. Bewley. New York: Cambridge University Press, 329–63.

Eaton, J., and G. M. Grossman. 1986. Optimal trade and industrial policy under oligopoly. *Quarterly Journal of Economics* 101: 383–406. (Reprinted in Grossman, 1992.)

Grossman, G. M., ed. 1992. *Imperfect competition and international trade.* Cambridge, MA: MIT Press.

Krugman, P. R., ed. 1986. *Strategic trade policy and the new international economics.* Cambridge, MA: MIT Press.

———. 1987. Is free trade passé? *Journal of Economic Perspectives* 1: 131–44.

The impact on both equilibrium values is precisely the same for both firms because the firms have identical marginal costs. Such cases, in which both firms have identical outputs in the Cournot equilibrium, are called **symmetric.** Both of the examples we examined have been symmetric, but nonsymmetric cases are included in the problems at the end of the chapter.

In closing this discussion of Cournot models, let us briefly address some of the many extensions and modifications that can be made to the basic duopoly model. First and most obvious is to consider more complex demand and cost functions. In both of the examples we examined, the demand function was extremely simple—linear with slope 1. Another obvious extension is to include more firms. The basic structure of the model remains unchanged as the number of firms increases.

Other modifications involve changing the Cournot conjecture itself. For instance, if one firm learns the reaction function of the other firm and takes its reaction explicitly into account, the result is a Stackelberg rather than a Cournot equilibrium. If price rather than quantity is the firms' choice variable, we have instead a Bertrand equilibrium. The model can also be modified to include dynamics.

In our discussion of how the firms reacted to disequilibrium, we implicitly discussed a dynamic adjustment process; this could be made more explicit. Also the Cournot model can be made dynamic in a more substantial sense; it can be modified to include intertemporal decision making. Firms can be modeled as maximizing a discounted future profit stream over a long or possibly infinite horizon, rather than the static profit function considered here. Finally, there has been some work on "rational" or "consistent" conjectures. It is often argued that Cournot models exhibit a type of irrationality because each firm continues to assume that the other firm will not change its output when in fact (outside of equilibrium) it continuously observes the other doing so. Since such irrationality is hard to reconcile with microeconomic theory, alternative models with "consistent" conjectures have been proposed.

PROBLEMS

3.1 For the supply and demand model given by (3.1), how must α be restricted to guarantee that $P^* > 0$ and $Q^* > 0$?

3.2 For the supply and demand model given by (3.3), determine the sign of $dP^*/d\alpha$. Draw simple supply and demand diagrams to demonstrate your results.

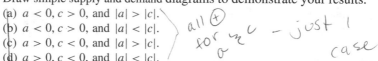

(a) $a < 0, c > 0$, and $|a| > |c|$.
(b) $a < 0, c > 0$, and $|a| < |c|$.
(c) $a > 0, c < 0$, and $|a| > |c|$.
(d) $a > 0, c < 0$, and $|a| < |c|$.

all ⊕
for ⊋ c - just 1
case

3.3 (a) For the *IS-LM* model given by (3.23), find $\partial Y^*/\partial p$ and $\partial r^*/\partial p$ by the method used in the chapter. Then draw an *IS-LM* diagram to depict your results.

(b) The aggregate demand (*AD*) function for such a macroeconomic model is given by the set of (Y, p) combinations that clear both the goods market and the money market. Use your answer from (a) to discuss the shape of *AD*.

3.4 Recall the short-run, perfectly competitive firm characterized by

$$y = f(L) = 4L^{1/2}, \tag{3.36}$$

$$\pi = py - wL - v\bar{K}. \tag{3.37}$$

In the text these equations were used to solve for the firm's profit-maximizing level of employment L^* and the firm's supply function $y^* = f(L^*)$. Solve the same profit maximization problem using y (rather than L) as the choice variable. Show that the output and labor required when y is the choice variable are identical to those found in the text.

3.5 Continuing the example given by (3.36) and (3.37) in Problem 4.

(a) Find the firm's short-run total cost function $TC(y; w, v)$. (*Note:* Total cost is a function of y, not L.)

(b) From (a) find the average total cost (*ATC*), variable cost (*VC*), average variable cost (*AVC*), and marginal cost (*MC*).

(c) The first-order condition for profit maximization by a perfectly competitive firm is $P = MC$. Given the *MC* function from (b), find the profit-maximizing output y^* using $P = MC$, and compare it with the answers found in Problem 4, where y was the choice variable (and in the text, where L was the choice variable).

3.6 Consider the general short-run Cobb–Douglas production function

$$y = f(L, K) = L^a \bar{K}^{1-a},$$

where $0 < a < 1$. Answer the following questions about a perfectly competitive firm with this production function.

(a) Find the short-run total cost function $TC(y; w, v, \bar{K})$.

(b) Find the *ATC* function, the *AVC* function, the average fixed cost function (*AFC*), and the *MC* function.

(c) Find an expression for the firm's profit-maximizing labor demand L^*.

(d) Find an expression for the firm's supply function $y^* = f(L, \bar{K})$.

(e) From elementary microeconomics we know that the supply curve for a perfectly competitive firm should be the MC. Is this true for this firm? (Show that it is true, or explain why it is not true.)

 3.7 Consider a monopoly firm with output y and advertising expenditure A. The monopolist's profit function is

$$\pi = R(y, A) - C(y) - A,$$

where $R(\cdot)$ is the revenue function and $C(\cdot)$ is the cost function.

(a) Assuming that y is the choice variable and A is a parameter in the short run, write down the first- and second-order conditions for profit maximization by this firm.

(b) Assuming that $\partial^2 R/\partial y\, \partial A > 0$, how does an increase in advertising expenditure change the profit-maximizing output? (That is, find $\partial y^*/\partial A$.)

3.8 Do the second-order conditions for long-run profit maximization hold for a perfectly competitive firm with production function $y = f(L, K) = L^{3/2} K^{3/2}$?

3.9 Answer questions (a)–(f) regarding a long-run profit-maximizing, perfectly competitive firm with the following production function

$$y = f(L, K) = \ln(1 + L) + \ln(1 + K).$$

(a) Solve the first-order conditions, and find expressions for the input demand functions $L^* = L^*(w, v, p)$ and $K^* = K^*(w, v, p)$.

(b) Do the second-order conditions hold for this production function?

(c) Are the input demand functions homogeneous of any degree? (Show.)

(d) Find $\partial L^*/\partial w$, $\partial L^*/\partial v$, $\partial L^*/\partial p$, $\partial K^*/\partial w$, $\partial K^*/\partial v$, and $\partial K^*/\partial p$.

(e) Find the profit function $\pi^*(w, v, p) = pf(L^*, K^*) - wL^* - vK^*$.

(f) Do the following conditions hold for the profit function of this problem?

$$\frac{\partial \pi^*}{\partial w} = -L^* \quad \text{and} \quad \frac{\partial \pi^*}{\partial v} = -K^*.$$

3.10 Consider an imperfectly competitive firm that must choose both output y and market research expenditure R to maximize profit. The firm's total revenue TR and total cost TC functions are

$$TR = TR(y, R) = 2yR + 116R,$$

$$TC = TC(y, R) = y^2 + 4y + 5R^2.$$

(a) Solve the first-order conditions for the profit-maximizing level of output y^* and research R^*.

(b) Do the second-order conditions hold for this problem?

3.11 Find the profit-maximizing input demand functions $L^* = L^*(w, v)$ and $K^* = K^*(w, v)$ for the monopolist with the linear demand function $P = -aQ + b, a > 0$, $b > 0$, and the production function

$$Q = f(L, K) = L^{1/2} + K^{1/2}.$$

3.12 For the long-run perfectly competitive firm with first-order conditions given by (3.77), find the impact of a change in the price of capital v (i.e., find $\partial L^*/\partial v$ and $\partial K^*/\partial v$). Can these terms be signed by the second-order conditions? (Show.)

3.13 For the long-run, perfectly competitive firm with first-order conditions given by (3.77), find the comparative statics expression for the change in the supply function y^* with respect to the price of the product p (i.e., find $\partial y^*/\partial p$). Assuming only the problem's first- and second-order conditions, can you prove that this supply function slopes upward?

3.14 Consider the following monopoly firm. The firm's output Q is given by the short-run production function

$$Q = f(L, K) = L^{1/2}K^{1/2},$$

where L is labor input and K is the fixed capital stock. The firm's output is divided into two separate submarkets, each with its own demand curve. These demand curves are

$$P_1 = -(Q_1/2) + 36 \qquad \text{and} \qquad P_2 = -Q_2 + 40,$$

where P_i is the price and Q_i is the quantity in market $i = 1$, 2, and total market output is given by $Q = Q_1 + Q_2$.

(a) Find the firm's total cost TC as a function of output Q when the price of labor is $\$4$ ($w = 4$), the price of capital is $\$20$ ($v = 20$), and the quantity of capital is four units ($K = 4$).

(b) Find the profit-maximizing price and output for both markets (P_1^*, Q_1^*, P_2^*, Q_2^*).

(c) Do the second-order conditions hold for this profit maximization problem? (Show.)

(d) Find the firm's total profit (π^*) at the profit-maximizing outputs.

3.15 Consider the Cournot duopoly model with demand given by $P = -Q + 30$. Firm 1 has the cost function $C^1(q_1) = 5q_1 + 10$, and firm 2 has the cost function $C^2(q_2) = 10q_2 + 10$.

(a) Find the Cournot equilibrium $q^* = (q_1^*, q_2^*)$.

(b) Find the total market output $Q^* = q_1^* + q_2^*$ and price P^* in the Cournot equilibrium.

(c) Find the price and output of the good if the industry were monopolized by firm 1 and if it were monopolized by firm 2.

3.16 Consider the perfectly competitive firm using two inputs L and K to produce output y by means of the production function $y = f(L, K)$. If the profit-maximizing input demand functions are $L^* = L^*(w, v, p)$ and $K^* = K^*(w, v, p)$, then the supply function is $y^* = f(L^*, K^*)$ and the profit function is $\pi^* = py^* - wL^* - vK^*$. Finally **Hotelling's lemma** states that

$$y^* = \frac{\partial \pi^*}{\partial p}, \qquad L^* = \frac{-\partial \pi^*}{\partial w}, \qquad \text{and} \qquad K^* = \frac{-\partial \pi^*}{\partial v}.$$

(a) Prove Hotelling's lemma.

(b) Prove that input demand functions are symmetric (i.e., show that $\partial L^*/\partial v = \partial K^*/\partial w$).

3.17 Consider the Cournot duopoly model with market demand given by $P = -Q + a$, where the cost functions for the two firms are $C^i(q_i) = bq_i + c$ for $i = 1, 2$.

(a) Find the Cournot equilibrium $q^* = (q_1^*, q_2^*)$.

(b) Find the total market output $Q^* = q_1^* + q_2^*$ and price P^* in the Cournot equilibrium.

(c) Find the comparative statics impact of a change in marginal cost on the Cournot equilibrium outputs of the two firms.

3.18 Consider the Cournot equilibrium for an n-firm oligopoly when the market demand is given by $P = -Q + a$ and each of the n firms has the cost function $C^i(q_i) = bq_i + c$ for all $i = 1, 2, \ldots, n$.

(a) Assuming the equilibrium is symmetric ($q_i^* = q_j^*$ for all $i \neq j$), find the Cournot equilibrium output for each firm.

(b) Is the answer in (a) consistent with your answer to part (a) of Problem 17? (Explain.)

(c) Find the output in this market under conditions of monopoly, and show that the monopoly output is a special case of the Cournot equilibrium.

(d) Find the output in this market under conditions of perfect competition (i.e., supply = marginal cost).

(e) Prove that as the number of firms n approaches infinity, the Cournot equilibrium output in the market converges to the perfectly competitive output!

3.19 For the n-firm oligopoly model in Problem 18, show that collusion pays. That is, show that the profit received by each firm in the Cournot equilibrium is less than the profit that each firm would receive if the monopoly profits were evenly divided among the n firms.

3.20 Consider the Cournot duopoly problem with linear demand and cost given in Problem 17. Now suppose that both firms pollute a common water source. This means that an increase in the output of either firm will raise the production cost of the other firm. Thus we write the cost functions of the two firms as

$$C^i(q_i, q_j) = bq_i + dq_j + c \qquad \text{for} \quad i, j = 1, 2, \quad i \neq j, \quad b > 0, \quad d > 0.$$

(a) Find the Cournot equilibrium $q^* = (q_1^*, q_2^*)$ for these two polluting duopolists.

(b) Compare this solution with the solution of Problem 17 and discuss the relationship.

3.21 In a homogeneous duopoly model, the term $(\partial q_i / \partial q_j)^e$, $i \neq j$, expresses the conjectural variation (how firm j expects firm i to respond to a change in q_j), whereas the derivative of the reaction function $\partial R_i(q_j)/\partial q_j$ expresses how firm i will in fact respond to Δq_j. For the model to exhibit "consistent" or "rational" conjectures, actual behavior and expected behavior must be the same, or $(\partial q_i / \partial q_j)^e = \partial R_i(q_j)/\partial q_j$ for all $i \neq j$. Does the Cournot duopoly model given by the profit functions in (3.89) exhibit such consistent or rational conjectures? Discuss in detail.

3.22 One common modification of the *IS-LM* model given by the equilibrium condition (3.23) is to include a so-called real-balance effect in the consumption and savings functions. According to the real-balance effect, real balances $m = M^s/p$ directly influence both consumption and savings. In particular, an increase in real balances will increase consumption and decrease savings. Thus with the real-balance effect included, the savings function in (3.16) should be written as

$$S = S(Y, r, m) \qquad \text{with} \qquad S_Y > 0, \quad S_r > 0, \quad \text{and} \quad S_m < 0,$$

where S_Y and S_r are defined as before but $S_m = \partial S/\partial m = \partial S/\partial(M^s/p)$. Assuming that the other functions in the *IS-LM* model given in the text remain the same, answer the following questions regarding the *IS-LM* model with a real-balance effect included.

(a) Find the impact of an expansionary monetary policy on Y^* and r^* (i.e., find $\partial Y^*/\partial M^s$ and $\partial r^*/\partial M^s$).

(b) Can the expressions derived in (a) be signed from the sign restrictions of the model? If so, what are the signs?

(c) Draw an *IS-LM* diagram to demonstrate the results in (b).

3.23 Consider a classical macroeconomic model described by the market clearing equations for the goods market and the money market in (3.23). In the classical case, the level of income is fixed at the full employment level Y_f, and the price level p is a variable (along with r). Thus the classical model differs from the *IS-LM* case by changing the roles of Y and p. For the *IS-LM* case, p is a parameter and Y is a variable; for the classical case, Y_f is a parameter and p is a variable. Thus for the classical model, the solutions

$$p^* = p^*(D, M^s, Y_f),$$
$$r^* = r^*(D, M^s, Y_f),$$

replace the *IS-LM* solutions in (3.24). Find the comparative statics impact of a change in the money supply M^s on the classical model (i.e., find $\partial r^*/\partial M^s$ and $\partial p^*/\partial M^s$). Interpret your results.

3.24 Consider firm 1 and firm 2, which fish in a common lake. The catch of fish C in any particular time period is a function of the total fishing effort E. In general the catch C is positively related to the effort E, but too much effort (overfishing) will actually reduce the catch. Thus the relationship between catch and total effort will be given by

$$C = E - AE^2,$$

where a is a (very small) positive parameter. The catch C_i of each firm $i = 1, 2$ is proportional to the firm's relative effort. Thus,

$$C_i = \left(\frac{E_i}{E_1 + E_2}\right) C \qquad \text{for } i = 1, 2,$$

with $E = E_1 + E_2$.

(a) Use the information to solve for C_1 and C_2 as a function of E_1 and E_2.

(b) If the price per unit of catch is given by $P > 0$ and the price (opportunity cost) of effort is given by $w > 0$, then the profit of the two firms will be given by,

$$\pi_1 = PC_1 - wE_1 \qquad \text{and} \qquad \pi_2 = PC_2 - wE_2.$$

Find the reaction functions and the Cournot equilibrium values of effort E_1^* and E_2^*. What additional assumption is required to guarantee that the Cournot equilibrium values are strictly positive?

(c) Find the comparative statics impact of a change in each of the three parameters a, P, and w (i.e., find $\partial E_i^*/\partial a$, $\partial E_i^*/\partial P$, and $\partial E_i^*/\partial w$). Sign each of these comparative statics terms (if possible) and interpret each of them. Are these signs what one would expect, given the nature of the problem?

3.25 An alternative model of duopoly behavior is the **Stackelberg** leadership model. In the Stackelberg model, one firm (the leader) "learns" the reaction function of the other firm (the follower) and integrates this knowledge directly into its decision making. For instance, if the Cournot reaction function for firm 2 is $q_2 = R_2(q_1)$ and firm 1 is the Stackelberg leader, then to find its profit-maximizing output q_1^*, firm 1 will substitute $q_2 = R_2(q_1)$ for q_2 wherever it occurs in its profit function and then maximize with respect to q_1. Firm 2 will then "follow" by producing $q_2 = R_2(q_1^*)$. The resulting outputs are called a **Stackelberg equilibrium.** Find the Stackelberg equilibrium with firm 1 as leader for the profit functions given by (3.86).

3.26 Consider a duopoly problem from the theory of international trade. Suppose there are two suppliers of a particular good: one domestic and one foreign. If the demand for the good is given by $P(Q)$, then $Q = q_d + q_f$, where q_d is the quantity sold by the domestic firm and q_f is the quantity sold by the foreign firm. The foreign firm is subject to a tariff of t dollars per unit sold, and the two firms have constant (but different) average total cost: c^d for the domestic firm and c^f for the foreign firm. Thus the profit functions of the two firms are

$$\pi^d = P(Q)q_d - c^d q_d,$$
$$\pi^f = [P(Q) - t]q_f - c^f q_f.$$

Answer the following questions for the case of $P(Q) = -Q + b$.

(a) Find the output of the two firms (q_d^* and q_f^*) as well as the total output Q^* in Cournot equilibrium.

(b) Find the comparative statics impact of a change in costs ($\partial q_d^*/\partial c^d$, $\partial q_d^*/\partial c^f$, $\partial q_f^*/\partial c^f$, and $\partial q_f^*/\partial c^d$), and interpret the signs of these terms.

(c) Find the comparative statics impact of a change in the tariff. How does an increase in the tariff affect the output of the foreign firm ($\partial q_f^*/\partial t$), the domestic firm ($\partial q_d^*/\partial t$), and the total production of the good ($\partial Q^*/\partial t$)? Interpret these results.

3.27 Prove that if a production function $y = f(L, K)$ is homogeneous of degree r **and** satisfies the second-order conditions for profit maximization by a perfectly competitive firm, then $0 < r < 1$.

3.28 Consider a monopoly supplier of a particular input and suppose this monopoly supplier sells the input to two different firms that compete as Cournot duopolists in a market with the demand curve $P = a - bQ$, where $Q = Q_1 + Q_2$. The quantity of the monopoly-supplied input x_i used by firm $i = 1, 2$ is related to the firm's output Q_i by the very simple production function $Q_i = x_i$ (i.e., it takes one unit of input to produce one unit of output). If the price of the monopolized input is w_i to firm $i = 1, 2$ and costs exclusive of the monopolized input are given by $c_i Q_i + FC_i$ for $i = 1, 2$, then the profit functions of the two firms will be:

$$\pi_1 = (a - bQ_1 - bQ_2)Q_1 - w_1 Q_1 - c_1 Q_1 - FC_1,$$
$$\pi_2 = (a - bQ_1 - bQ_2)Q_2 - w_2 Q_2 - c_2 Q_2 - FC_2.$$

(a) Find the output of the two firms in Cournot equilibrium (Q_1^*, Q_2^*).

(b) Given the Cournot behavior on the part of the two firms and assuming the only cost to the monopolist is the fixed cost F, the input supplier has the profit function,

$$\pi(w_1, w_2) = w_1 Q_1^* + w_2 Q_2^* - F.$$

If the monopolist imposes price discrimination, its problem will be to maximize π with respect to the two choice variables (the input prices) w_1 and w_2. Find the profit-maximizing input prices w_1^* and w_2^* under price discrimination.

(c) Suppose that firm 1 has lower marginal cost than firm 2 exclusive of the monopolized input (i.e., suppose that $c_1 < c_2$). What does this imply about the relationship between w_1^* and w_2^*?

(d) Now suppose the monopoly input supplier does **not** impose price discrimination (so that $w_1 = w_2 = w$). This makes the profit function (π) a function of a single variable (w). Find the profit-maximizing input price $w*$ for the non–price discrimination case.

(e) Again (as in c) assuming that $c_1 < c_2$, find the relationship between the input prices under price discrimination (w_1^* and w_2^*) and the non–price discriminating input price ($w*$).

NOTES

1. As in note 1 of Chapter 2, the reader is warned that in Chapter 6 we show that an additional restriction needs to be imposed on functions D and S to ensure that this transformation from implicit to explicit function is possible. For the rest of this chapter, though, we make such transformations without further comment, implicitly assuming that the additional restriction holds for the systems we are considering. Also when **explicit function** is used here, it does not mean a specific function such as $y = x^2 + 10x$. Rather, the explicit functions discussed here are still implicit functions; they are just more explicit forms of these functions.

2. Again we remind the reader that $L* > 0$ is required because the first-order condition is necessary only in the case of an interior optimum. As stated earlier, with the exception of Chapter 9 where noninterior (boundary) optima are explicitly examined, all optima are assumed to be strictly positive and thus in the interior of the (nonnegative) domain.

3. The warning in note 1 applies here as well.

4. The expression (3.58) is a two-dimensional quadratic form. Such expressions will be discussed in detail in Chapter 6.

5. Of course it is possible that a Cournot equilibrium does not exist. The second-order conditions (discussed shortly) ensure that the maximization by each firm is meaningful, but they do not guarantee that the reaction functions have a meaningful simultaneous solution.

C H A P **4** T E R

INTEGRATION, TIME, AND UNCERTAINTY IN ECONOMICS

■ ■ ■

This chapter discusses three separate topics: integration, time, and uncertainty. Integration and a few of its economic applications are examined first. Section 4.2, which discusses the role of time in economic models, covers both analysis in discrete time and analysis in continuous time. The treatment of discrete time will probably be familiar to most readers from other economics courses. The presentation of continuous time is more consistent with the way time is modeled in the natural sciences and draws on the integration techniques discussed in Section 4.1. In Section 4.3, a brief introduction to the economics of uncertainty, we simply introduce the basic concepts of economic decision making under uncertainty and derive one of the most important results, the demand for insurance.

4.1 Integration

The first three chapters contain many economic applications of the derivative, but thus far we have entirely neglected the other fundamental calculus concept, the integral. In this section we partially rectify this neglect. We say "partially" because even after the economic applications in this section have been examined, the integral will not have received (nor will it receive in future chapters) nearly as much attention as the derivative. This is simply because the derivative occurs much more frequently in economics than the integral; most economic analysis is based on optimization and/or comparative statics, and the derivative is **the** fundamental tool for both techniques.

Even though the integral may not be as important as the derivative, it still has an important role in economic analysis. Some of these applications are based on the fact that integration is the reverse of differentiation, while others are based on the integral as the area under a curve. The former case is exemplified by the use of integration to recover "total" functions (cost, product, or whatever) from their respective "marginals"; we illustrate the latter by representing the total as the area under the marginal curve. Our first example of these two interpretations comes from cost theory.

Integration in Cost Theory

Recall that marginal cost MC is the first derivative of the total cost TC function with respect to output: $MC = dTC/dy$, where y is output. Since the marginal cost function is a derivative, integration can be used to "recover" the total cost function from the marginal cost function. When marginal cost is written $MC(y)$, then

$$TC(y) = \int MC(y)\, dy. \tag{4.1}$$

Notice that because the interval of integration is not specified, the right-hand side of (4.1) is an **indefinite integral.** If the interval of integration were specified, the expression would have a specific numerical value and the right-hand side would be a **definite,** rather than indefinite, integral. We discuss the definite integral later; for now let us continue with the more general indefinite form in (4.1). Since indefinite integrals are sometimes called antiderivatives, another way of expressing (4.1) is to say that TC is the (an) **antiderivative** of MC.

Because the derivative of a constant is zero, indefinite integrals such as (4.1) always contain a constant of integration in their solution. If we let C_0 be this constant of integration, then the right-hand side of (4.1) can be written as

$$\int MC(y)\, dy = C(y) + C_0. \tag{4.2}$$

Or, combining this with (4.1), we have

$$TC(y) = \int MC(y)\, dy = C(y) + C_0. \tag{4.3}$$

Expression (4.3) says that if we find total cost by integrating marginal cost, the resulting TC function is composed of two parts, one that is a function of output $C(y)$ and one that is independent of output C_0. Of course, in economics the function $C(y)$ is called **variable cost** while the constant C_0 is called **fixed cost.** By substituting in the standard notation of VC for variable cost and FC for fixed cost, (4.3) becomes

$$TC(y) = \int MC(y)\, dy = VC(y) + FC. \tag{4.4}$$

In the short run, FC will be a positive constant equal to the cost that is incurred even if output is zero; in the long run, all costs are variable and $FC = 0$.

For a particular example of how the marginal cost function can be integrated to obtain the total cost function, let us reexamine the profit-maximizing, perfectly competitive firm discussed in Section 1.2. In that problem we started with a particular *TC* function [given in (1.48)] and then differentiated it to find the *MC* function [given in (1.49)]; this *MC* function was then used (along with information about the price of the product) to compute the firm's profit-maximizing output. Here we reverse the relationship between these cost functions; we start with the particular *MC* function and then recover the *TC* function from which it was derived. The *MC* function in (1.49) is

$$MC(y) = \frac{y^2}{4} - 5y + 30. \tag{4.5}$$

Applying the preceding argument about the relationship between marginal and total costs to this particular example, we have

$$TC(y) = \int MC(y)\, dy = \frac{y^3}{12} - 2.5y^2 + 30y + FC. \tag{4.6}$$

Now the expression on the right-hand side of (4.6) is the general form of the *TC* function associated with the *MC* function in (4.5), but since there are an infinite number of such total cost functions (one for each $FC \in \Re_+$), integration of (4.5) alone does not allow us to recover the particular *TC* function for the firm in question. What we can do, though, is use the information about the profit-maximizing output of the firm to determine the value of *FC* and thus find the exact form of *TC*. We know from the computation in Chapter 1 that when the product price is $p = \$21$, the firm's profit-maximizing output is $y^* = 18$, and its profit is $\pi(y^*) = 62$. Thus since

$$\pi(y^*) = py^* - TC(y^*),$$

we can substitute the relevant values to obtain

$$62 = 378 - \left[\frac{18^3}{12} - 2.5(18^2) + 30(18) + FC \right]. \tag{4.7}$$

Since (4.7) is one equation with one unknown, we can solve it to obtain $FC = 100$. Substituting this into the general form of the *TC* function in (4.6), we have

$$TC(y) = \frac{y^3}{12} - 2.5y^2 + 30y + 100, \tag{4.8}$$

which is precisely the expression initially given in (1.48).

Having explored a particular example, we now return to the more general question of the integral of marginal cost. Instead of taking the indefinite integral of the *MC* function, suppose that we were to compute the **definite integral** of the marginal cost function over a particular interval of output, say, the closed interval $[y_0, y_1]$. How should such a definite integral of marginal cost be interpreted?

Since the definite integral corresponds to the area under the curve, the value of the definite integral

$$\int_{y_0}^{y_1} MC(y)\, dy \tag{4.9}$$

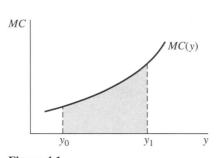

Figure 4.1

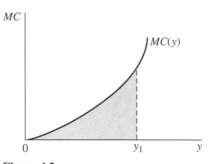

Figure 4.2

is shown by the shaded area in Figure 4.1. The question is: How does this shaded area relate to the total (or any other) cost? Note that the shaded area is not the total cost of y_0, nor the total cost of y_1; rather, it is the **change in the total cost** (and variable cost, since fixed cost does not change) associated with expanding output from y_0 to y_1. The constant of integration does not come into play in the computation of (4.9), since only changes in the value of the function are being considered.

Now consider the case depicted in Figure 4.2 where the initial output is zero. In this case, the definite integral

$$\int_0^{y_1} MC(y)\, dy, \tag{4.10}$$

again measures the change in total cost from the initial output (in this case 0) to the new output y_1, and again it is equal to the area under the curve. But in this case the area has an alternative interpretation. Since the only cost at $y = 0$ is the fixed cost, the change in total cost associated with expanding output from 0 to y_1 is simply the variable cost of producing the output level y_1. Thus an area like the shaded area in Figure 4.2, the area under the MC curve from 0 to any arbitrary output level y_1, is equal to the **variable cost of producing** y_1.

For an example of this relationship between marginal and variable cost, let us reconsider the total cost function in (4.8). The VC function associated with (4.8) is

$$VC(y) = \frac{y^3}{12} - 2.5y^2 + 30y. \tag{4.11}$$

Choosing an arbitrary output level (say, $y = 6$), we have

$$VC(6) = \frac{216}{12} - 2.5(36) + 30(6) = 108. \tag{4.12}$$

Now to demonstrate the foregoing relationship, we need to compute the definite integral of the MC function (4.5) from $y = 0$ to $y = 6$ and compare it with $VC(6)$ in (4.12). The definite integral in question is

$$\int_0^6 MC(y)\, dy = \int_0^6 \left(\frac{y^2}{4} - 5y + 30\right) dy. \tag{4.13}$$

Computing the right-hand side of (4.13) gives

$$\int\limits_{0}^{6} MC(y)\, dy = \left(\frac{y^3}{12} - 2.5y^2 + 30y \right)\Bigg|_{0}^{6} = 108,$$

as expected.

Consumer's and Producer's Surplus

A standard approach to microeconomic policy is to analyze how the change will affect the **total surplus** in the market. This total surplus is composed of two parts, the **consumer's surplus,** which accrues to the buyers of the good, and the **producer's surplus,** which accrues to the sellers of the good. The essence of the argument is that changes that increase the total surplus in the market are, *ceteris paribus,* preferred over those that reduce the surplus or leave it unchanged. Taking the total surplus as a measure of the welfare gains or losses associated with various policy changes is a technique with a long tradition in economics and should be familiar from introductory economics. In this subsection the integral is used to define both the consumer's surplus and the producer's surplus. We consider consumer's surplus first.

The simplest definition of the **consumer's surplus** associated with a particular good is the area under the good's demand curve but above the market price. There are more sophisticated definitions of consumer welfare gains, definitions that eliminate the income effects associated with a price change (discussed in Chapter 8), but only the most basic definition of consumer's surplus is examined here. The motivation behind the "area under the demand curve" definition of consumer's surplus can be seen from Figure 4.3.

In Figure 4.3 the demand curve is drawn as a step function, and each discrete unit of the good is associated with a particular demand price. For instance, the

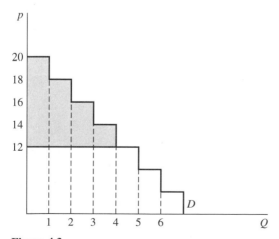

Figure 4.3

maximum price that any buyer would pay for the first unit of the good is $20, while the maximum price any consumer would pay for the third unit is $16. Now suppose that the good's market price is $12; every buyer of the good will pay $12, and 5 units will be sold. Since the buyer of the first unit was willing to pay up to $20 but pays only $12, this consumer receives a "surplus" of $8. That is, there was one buyer who was willing and able to pay $20 for the first unit of the good but who needed to pay only $12, since every buyer pays the same market price. The difference between what the consumer was willing and able to pay and what he or she does pay is the consumer's surplus accruing to the first consumer. By a similar argument, the buyer of the second unit receives a surplus of $6, the buyer of the third unit a surplus of $4, and so on. The final (marginal) buyer of the good, in this case the buyer of the fifth unit, actually pays the full demand price, and thus no surplus is received on the final (marginal) unit. Thus, by summing over all buyers, the total consumer's surplus in this market is given by the shaded area in Figure 4.3: in this case $12.

Now if we extend the argument to the case of an infinitely divisible commodity with a smooth demand curve, the total consumer's surplus is given by the area below the demand curve but above the market price, as shown in Figure 4.4. Based on this argument, if the inverse demand curve is $P = P(Q)$ and the market price is P_0, then the **consumer's surplus** CS in the market is given by

$$CS(Q_0) = \int_0^{Q_0} P(Q)\, dQ - P_0 Q_0, \tag{4.14}$$

where $P_0 = P(Q_0)$.

As an application of this integral definition of consumer's surplus, let us consider the simple case of a linear demand curve. Let the demand for the good be given by $P = -Q + 20$, depicted in Figure 4.5. Examining the shaded area in Figure 4.5, we see that if the market price is $10, then the total consumer's surplus in the market is $50 (the area of the shaded right triangle with sides of 10).

Now we compute this same consumer's surplus using the integral formula in (4.14). Writing (4.14) for the demand function $P = -Q + 20$, with $P_0 = \$10$,

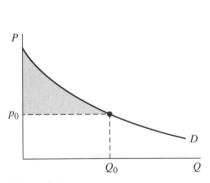

Figure 4.4

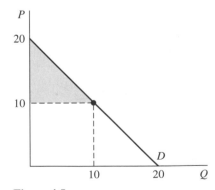

Figure 4.5

and thus $Q_0 = 10$, we have

$$CS(Q_0 = 10) = \int_0^{10} (-Q + 20) \, dQ - (10)(10). \qquad (4.15)$$

Computing the definite integral in (4.15) gives

$$CS(Q_0 = 10) = \left(\frac{-Q^2}{2} + 20Q \right)\Bigg|_0^{10} - 100$$

or

$$CS(Q_0 = 10) = \frac{-100}{2} + 200 - 100 = \$50,$$

precisely the result that was obtained diagrammatically.

The integral formula (4.14) can be used in the same way to compute consumer's surplus along other, possibly more complex, demand functions. But examples of more complex applications are left to the reader as exercises. We now turn to the question of producer's surplus.

The **producer's surplus** is to the supply function as consumer's surplus is to the demand function. The intuitive ideas behind the two surplus notions are exactly the same. For the consumer, the surplus is the amount that buyers would be willing and able to pay but need not because there is only one price in the market; for the producer, the surplus is the amount received in excess of what would be necessary for the producer to supply a particular quantity of the good (again because there is only one price in the market). Consumer's surplus exists because the demand price is above the market price for all but the marginal unit of the good; producer's surplus exists because the market price is above the supply price (marginal cost) for all but the marginal unit of the good. Diagrammatically the producer's surplus is depicted as the area above the supply curve but below the market price. For example, the producer's surplus is shown by the shaded area in Figure 4.6; it is the portion of the total revenue rectangle above the supply curve.

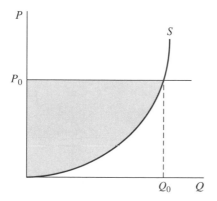

Figure 4.6

Defining the **producer's surplus** PS in terms of a definite integral, we have

$$PS(Q_0) = P_0 Q_0 - \int_0^{Q_0} S(Q) \, dQ, \tag{4.16}$$

where $S(Q)$ is the good's supply function (supply price as a function of output) and P_0 is the market price with $P_0 = S(Q_0)$. If the market is a product (output) market, then the supply function will be the marginal cost, and (4.16) can be written as

$$PS(Q_0) = P_0 Q_0 - \int_0^{Q_0} MC(Q) \, dQ. \tag{4.17}$$

When the market is a product market, the term **producer's surplus** seems to be entirely appropriate; but when the market being considered is a factor (input) market, the area defined by (4.16) is called the rent of the factor, rather than producer's surplus. Verbally, the **rent** is the portion of the factor income that is in excess of what is required to keep the factor in its present level of employment; mathematically, the rent is simply the producer's surplus in a factor market. For example, when the labor supply function is $w = S(L)$ with w the nominal wage and L the labor supplied, then the rent R associated with the market wage w_0 is

$$R(L_0) = w_0 L_0 - \int_0^{L_0} S(L) \, dL, \tag{4.18}$$

where $w_0 = S(L_0)$.

As a numerical example, suppose that the labor supply function in a particular market is $w = S(L) = L^2/200$ and the market wage is $w_0 = \$8$. The rent in this case can be seen diagrammatically in Figure 4.7 as the shaded area below a wage of $\$8$ and above the supply function $w = S(L) = L^2/200$. Applying (4.18)

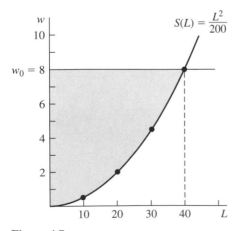

Figure 4.7

to compute the rent, we have

$$R(L_0 = 40) = (8)(40) - \int_0^{40} \frac{L^2}{200}\, dL. \tag{4.19}$$

Computing this definite integral gives

$$R(L_0 = 40) = 320 - \left(\frac{L^3}{600}\right)\Bigg|_0^{40} = 320 - 106.66 = \$213.34. \tag{4.20}$$

This says that of the \$320 of labor income received by workers in this market, \$213.34 is actually rent: that is, a payment in excess of what would be required to have 40 units of this type of labor supplied.

Given the foregoing definitions, we can now define the **total surplus** in the market as the sum of the consumer's surplus and the producer's surplus (or rent). Combining the integral definitions of consumer's surplus CS from (4.14) and of producer's surplus PS from (4.16), we have the following characterization of the total surplus TS at the equilibrium quantity Q_0:

$$TS(Q_0) = CS(Q_0) + PS(Q_0)$$

$$= \int_0^{Q_0} P(Q)\, dQ - P_0 Q_0 + P_0 Q_0 - \int_0^{Q_0} S(Q)\, dQ. \tag{4.21}$$

Simplifying this expression, we can write the total surplus as

$$TS(Q_0) = \int_0^{Q_0} [P(Q) - S(Q)]\, dQ. \tag{4.22}$$

This total surplus is depicted as the shaded area in Figure 4.8.

Surplus and Public Goods

The goods discussed thus far have been **private goods:** the benefit to any individual depends on only the quantity of the good that he or she purchases. With a

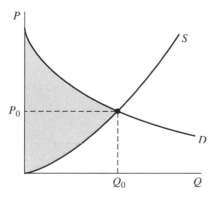

Figure 4.8

public good, the benefit to any individual depends on the aggregate production of the good. The classic example of a public good is national defense: each individual is protected if his or her neighbor is protected; each individual receives benefits from the overall level of national defense, not just from the amount that he or she has "purchased." The previous notion of surplus can be used to analyze the optimal production level of such a public good.

Let x represent the quantity of a particular good and x^h the quantity of the good consumed by individual $h = 1, 2, \ldots, H$; thus

$$x = \sum_{h=1}^{H} x^h.$$

If the good is a private good, then individual h's inverse demand function is given by $p^h(x^h)$; but if x is a **public good,** then the same individual's inverse demand function is given by $p^h(x)$. In both cases the inverse demand function measures the marginal benefits to the individual from a particular quantity of the good. Herein lies the difference: when x is a private good, the relevant quantity is x^h (the individual's own consumption), but when x is a public good, it is the total production of the good that matters to the individual. Let the inverse demand function for the total market be $p(x)$.

We want to discuss the total surplus associated with the two cases of a public and private good, but let us simplify the discussion by considering the case of a producer's surplus that is zero. If the producer's surplus is zero, then the total surplus is exactly equal to the consumer's surplus. To this end, we assume that x is produced under conditions of constant MC. Let the total cost be given by $TC(x) = \bar{c}x$ with $\bar{c} > 0$, and the total surplus in the market will be equal to the consumer's surplus. This case is depicted in Figure 4.9 with the total surplus given by the shaded area. The question we wish to ask about this market is: How should the demand be constructed so that the consumer's surplus (and thus, in this case, total surplus) is a maximum? The answer to this question is different for the cases of private and public goods. Consider the private good first.

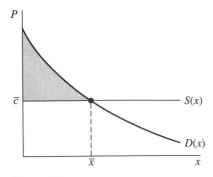

Figure 4.9

Let $\bar{x}^h$ be the consumption of the good by individual h in equilibrium, and thus the market equilibrium output is

$$\bar{x} = \sum_{h=1}^{H} \bar{x}^h.$$

With the perfectly elastic supply at $\bar{c}$, the consumer's surplus received by individual h denoted CS^h, at $\bar{x}^h$ will be

$$CS(\bar{x}^h) = \int_0^{\bar{x}^h} p^h(x^h) \, dx^h - \bar{c}\bar{x}^h. \tag{4.23}$$

The expression in (4.23) is simply the integral definition of consumer's surplus from (4.14) applied to the individual consumer h.

Since the total surplus in the market is equal to the total consumer's surplus, and since the total consumer's surplus is the sum of the consumer's surpluses of all the individuals, we have

$$TS = \sum_{h=1}^{H} CS^h(\bar{x}^h) = \sum_{h=1}^{H} \left[\int_0^{\bar{x}^h} p^h(x^h) \, dx^h - \bar{c}\bar{x}^h \right]. \tag{4.24}$$

Rewriting (4.24) and noting that $TS = TS(\bar{x}^1, \bar{x}^2, \ldots, \bar{x}^H)$ gives

$$TS(\bar{x}^1, \bar{x}^2, \ldots, \bar{x}^H) = \sum_{h=1}^{H} \int_0^{\bar{x}^h} p^h(x^h) \, dx^h - \bar{c}\bar{x}. \tag{4.25}$$

Now the problem of maximizing the total surplus from the good is the problem of maximizing the function in (4.25) with respect to the H variables $(\bar{x}^1, \bar{x}^2, \ldots, \bar{x}^H)$. This problem is substantially more complex than the one- and two-variable maximization problems examined in earlier chapters; this problem involves H choice variables. Although such large-dimensional optimization problems are not formally examined until Chapter 7, the first-order (necessary) conditions for such a problem are relatively simple. No matter how many variables are involved, the first-order conditions for a strictly positive solution to the maximization of a differentiable function require that all the partial derivatives be equal to zero. Thus maximization of the total surplus in (4.25) requires that

$$\frac{\partial TS}{\partial \bar{x}^h} = 0 \qquad \text{for all } h = 1, 2, \ldots, H. \tag{4.26}$$

Taking the derivative of (4.25) with respect to some particular $\bar{x}^h$ looks quite messy until we remember the second fundamental theorem of calculus (reviewed in Chapter 0). Applying the second fundamental theorem to this problem, we have the following first order conditions for maximizing the total surplus in this market:

$$\frac{\partial TS}{\partial \bar{x}^h} = p^h(\bar{x}^h) - \bar{c} = 0 \qquad \text{for all } h = 1, 2, \ldots, H. \tag{4.27}$$

Notice what the H conditions in (4.27) say: they require the price paid by each individual to be equal to the marginal cost of the good. This is exactly the result that would be obtained if the good were produced in a competitive market. If good x is produced in a competitive market, then price $\bar{p}$ will be equal to marginal cost $\bar{c}$ and every consumer of the good will pay the same price, thus satisfying the H conditions in (4.27). This demonstrates that the competitive market will produce a private good in such a way that the total surplus in the market is maximized.

Now let us repeat the exercise for the case of a public good. When x is a public good, each consumer's inverse demand function is $p^h(x)$, and the consumer's surplus received by individual h will be

$$CS^h(\bar{x}) = \int_0^{\bar{x}} p^h(x)\, dx - \bar{c}\bar{x}^h. \tag{4.28}$$

Notice how the public good case in (4.28) differs from the private good case given in (4.23). For the public good, the consumer's surplus received by individual h depends on the total output of the good $\bar{x}$ rather than the individual's own $\bar{x}^h$.

Summing the consumer's surplus of each individual in (4.28) over all H individuals, we have the following expression for the total surplus from the public good:

$$TS(\bar{x}) = \sum_{h=1}^{H} CS^h(\bar{x}) = \sum_{h=1}^{H} \int_0^{\bar{x}} p^h(x)\, dx - \bar{c}\bar{x}. \tag{4.29}$$

In this case, the total surplus from the good is **not** a function of the H variables $(\bar{x}^1, \bar{x}^2, \ldots, \bar{x}^H)$; rather, it is a function of the single variable $\bar{x}$, the total consumption of the good. The maximization of total surplus is thus the maximization of the one-variable function $TS(\bar{x})$ in (4.29).

Again applying the second fundamental theorem of calculus, we have the following first-order condition for maximizing the total surplus from the public good:

$$\frac{dTS}{d\bar{x}} = \sum_{h=1}^{H} p^h(\bar{x}) - \bar{c} = 0. \tag{4.30}$$

This condition is very different from (4.27), the result derived for the private good. Here it is the sum of what each consumer would be willing to pay for the equilibrium total output $\bar{x}$, which must be equated with the marginal cost $\bar{c}$. In other words, for the intersection of supply and demand to yield a quantity of the public good that maximizes the total surplus from the good, the demand curve must be the **vertical sum** of the demand curves of all the individuals in the market. In particular, a competitive market will produce less (possibly far less) than the optimal quantity of a public good.

4.2 Time

Since economic activity takes place in time and over time, economists often include time explicitly in the formal structure of their models. While time may enter in many different ways, the two most common involve dynamic stability and the concept of discounting the future. The issue of dynamic stability will be deferred until Chapter 5, but the next two subsections discuss the notion of discounting (and the related concept of present value). First we consider only **discrete** time, and then **continuous** time. The difference is this: when time is characterized discretely, it consists exclusively of an ordered sequence of points and is indexed by the integers; when time is characterized continuously, it is a continuous variable that takes on real number values (rather than merely integers). Economists, in fact, use both characterizations of time, although continuous time is more popular in models of the types considered in this book, and discrete time is used more in econometric-based models, where the relevant empirical data are given discretely.

Discounting and Present Value in Discrete Time

Consider an individual who deposits an initial amount of A dollars into an account that pays an interest rate of i percent per year. At the end of the first year ($t = 1$), the individual will have the amount V_1, where

$$V_1 = (1 + i)A. \tag{4.31}$$

At the end of the second year ($t = 2$), the individual will have V_2, where

$$V_2 = (1 + i)V_1 = (1 + i)(1 + i)A = (1 + i)^2 A. \tag{4.32}$$

By continuing this line of reasoning, at the end of T years, the amount accumulated will be

$$V_T = (1 + i)^T A. \tag{4.33}$$

In equation (4.33), V_T represents the future value (or compounded value) that will be available at the end of T years when the initial deposit is A and the interest rate is i. Or, if we think in terms of borrowing rather than lending (or depositing), V_T represents the amount to be paid back in T years when amount A is borrowed at the interest rate i.

In the preceding paragraph, equation (4.33) is discussed in terms of future dollars—either dollars that will be received in the future (when A is lent) or the amount that must be repaid in the future (when A is borrowed). Now consider reading expression (4.33) in terms of current (present) dollars rather than future dollars. To this end, we rewrite (4.33) as

$$A = \frac{V_T}{(1 + i)^T}. \tag{4.34}$$

In expression (4.34), amount A tells us the **present value** (or present discounted value) of V_T received at future time T when the interest rate is i. Expression (4.33) told us what today's dollars would be worth in the future; expression (4.34) tells us what future dollars are worth today (i.e., their present value). Present value calculations enable us to compare different streams of income received in the future.

Converting expression (4.34) to standard notation, we see that the present value of V_T received in T years, denoted by PV_T, for interest rate i is

$$PV_T = \frac{V_T}{(1+i)^T}. \tag{4.35}$$

For example, suppose that the amount to be received in the future is only \$1 and we are concerned only with 1 year, so $T = 1$. Applying (4.35) to this case for an interest rate of 8% ($i = 0.08$), we have

$$PV_1 = \frac{1}{1+0.08} = \frac{1}{1.08} = 0.93;$$

the present value of \$1 to be received next year is \$0.93 when the interest rate is 8%. If the interest rate remains at 8% and the future value remains \$1 but the time horizon changes to 5 years ($T = 5$), then the present value will fall to \$0.68, since

$$PV_5 = \frac{1}{(1.08)^5} = 0.68. \tag{4.36}$$

As our first extension of the concept of present value, we apply the foregoing argument to the case in which the future value V is received in each of the T years. In this case, the present value of the first year's payment is $PV_1 = V/(1+i)$, the present value of the second year's payment is $PV_2 = V/(1+i)^2$, and so on. Thus if we sum over all T years, the result is the present value of this T-year future income stream:

$$PV = \frac{V}{1+i} + \frac{V}{(1+i)^2} + \cdots + \frac{V}{(1+i)^T}. \tag{4.37}$$

Or, writing this present value in a more compact form, we have

$$PV = \sum_{t=1}^{T} PV_t = V \sum_{t=1}^{T} \frac{1}{(1+i)^t}. \tag{4.38}$$

After some rather messy algebraic manipulation, (4.38) can be simplified as[1]

$$PV = \frac{V[1 - (1+i)^{-T}]}{i}. \tag{4.39}$$

The expressions in (4.37) through (4.39) assume that the same amount V is received in each of the T years. Now consider what happens when the payments received in each of the future years are different: V_1 is the amount received in the first year, V_2 is the amount received in the second year, and so on. This possibility is easily accommodated by (4.38). If V_t is the amount received in each of the T future years, then the present value of this future income stream is

$$PV = \sum_{t=1}^{T} \frac{V_t}{(1+i)^t}. \tag{4.40}$$

As a simple economic example of the expression in (4.40), consider the question of finding the present value of a firm that will be in business for T years. Since the firm will have a certain amount of profit in each of the T years, the present value of the firm is actually the present value of its future profit stream. If the profit in any year t, denoted π_t, is given by the total revenue minus the total cost in that year ($TR_t - TC_t$), and if the interest rate is i, then (4.40) tells us that

$$PV_\pi = \sum_{t=1}^{T} \frac{\pi_t}{(1+i)^t} = \sum_{t=1}^{T} \frac{TR_t - TC_t}{(1+i)^t}. \tag{4.41}$$

Bond Prices and Interest Rates

Probably the single most important economic application of the present value formula concerns the present value of a financial asset such as a bond. The first type of bond we consider has a "coupon" value that is paid to the owner each year prior to the maturity of the bond and a "face value" that is paid to the owner at maturity. If such a bond matures in T years, has a yearly coupon C, and has a face value F, then its present value PV_B is

$$PV_B = C \sum_{t=1}^{T-1} \frac{1}{(1+i)^t} + \frac{F}{(1+i)^T}, \tag{4.42}$$

when the interest rate is i.

The expression in (4.42) actually gives us more information about the bond than simply its present value; it also tells us the equilibrium price of the bond in a competitive market. If the price of the bond P_B were greater than this present value ($P_B > PV_B$), then no one would want to purchase this bond, since the cost of the asset would be greater than the present value of the income stream it generates. Under competitive conditions, this absence of buyers would cause the price to fall. But if the price of the bond were less than the present value ($P_B < PV_B$), then the income stream from the bond would represent a good financial investment and competition on the demand side would push up the bond's price. Thus the bond market would be in equilibrium when the present value and the price of the bond were equal.

Based on this relationship between bond prices and present values, the expression in (4.42) can be used to analyze the impact of interest rates on bond prices. Note that since the interest rate appears only in the denominator of the right-hand side of the expression, there is an inverse relationship between bond prices and interest rates; higher interest rates will cause lower present values and thus lower bond prices, while lower interest rates will cause higher present values and thus higher bond prices. This inverse relationship between bond prices and interest rates is empirically well established, and it is a result that should be familiar from introductory economics. Expression (4.42) helps us understand why this empirical relationship exists.

As a numerical example of this relationship, consider a bond with a 20-year maturity, a coupon of $1000 per year, and a face value of $10,000. When the interest rate is 5%, this bond will have a price (present value) of

$$P_B = 1000 \sum_{t=1}^{19} \frac{1}{(1.05)^t} + \frac{10,000}{(1.05)^{20}} = \$15,854.21.$$

But if the interest rate falls to 3%, the price of the bond increases to

$$P_B = 1000 \sum_{t=1}^{19} \frac{1}{(1.03)^t} + \frac{10,000}{(1.03)^{20}} = \$19,836.75.$$

The only type of bond we have considered thus far is a bond with a fixed maturity date T years in the future. Often economists are concerned with a different type of bond, one that yields a fixed income in perpetuity (forever). The British consol is such a bond: it pays a fixed yearly return to its owner forever. The basic present value formula from (4.40) can be modified easily to deal with such a perpetual bond. If the consol pays V dollars per year in perpetuity, then given an interest rate of i, the present value of (maximum price a buyer would pay for) the bond is

$$PV = \sum_{t=1}^{\infty} \frac{V}{(1+i)^t}. \qquad (4.43)$$

Although the right-hand side of (4.43) correctly gives the present value of such a perpetual bond, the expression does not seem to be in a very "usable" form. Fortunately, the right-hand side can be simplified. To do this, first factor $1/(1+i)$ out of the sum. This gives

$$PV = \left(\frac{1}{1+i}\right)\left[V + \sum_{t=1}^{\infty} \frac{V}{(1+i)^t}\right]. \qquad (4.44)$$

Now if we substitute PV from (4.43) in (4.44), we have

$$PV = \left(\frac{1}{1+i}\right)(V + PV)$$

or, after some further manipulation,

$$PV = \frac{V}{i}. \qquad (4.45)$$

This is a very easy expression to use in computation. For example, when the interest rate is 5%, the present value of a consol that pays $1 per year in perpetuity is $1/0.05 = \$20$.

There are two important things to note about (4.45) before we move on. First, this expression demonstrates even more clearly the inverse relationship between bond prices and interest rates. This is why bonds are characterized so often as consols in macroeconomics, where the bond price–interest rate relationship is the main concern. Second, expression (4.45) makes obvious sense even without going through the manipulation of infinite sums. Thinking in terms of future value instead of present value, how much would you need to put away at interest rate i to yield V dollars in interest income each year forever? Obviously the required amount is given by x in the expression $xi = V$; this is precisely the present value in (4.45).

Internal-Rate-of-Return Criterion for Investment Decisions

In all our examples so far, the present value formula has been used to solve directly for the present value of a future income steam; that is, given the $V_i's$ we solve for PV. But this is certainly not the only way the relationship between present value and the interest rate is used in economics. Often economists are interested in the reverse relationship: given the present value, solve for the interest rate.

One such case of reversing the relationship between present value and interest rate is the internal-rate-of-return criterion for capital equipment purchased by a firm. Consider a profit-maximizing firm that is deciding whether to purchase a new piece of capital equipment, such as a machine. The machine has a certain fixed cost (FC) today, but it will generate a future profit stream of π_t per year for each of the next T years. Should the firm purchase the machine? According to the internal-rate-of-return criterion for investment decisions, the firm should purchase the machine if the internal rate of return j that solves the equation

$$FC = \sum_{t=1}^{T} \frac{\pi_t}{(1+j)^t} \tag{4.46}$$

is at least as great as the interest rate. But if the internal rate of return is less than the rate of interest, then by the same investment rule the firm should not purchase the machine.

Unless the reader has already encountered the rate-of-return criterion, the logic behind this particular investment rule probably is not obvious. To show why it is an appropriate rule, let us consider a very simple case. Suppose that the machine in question lasts only 1 year ($T = 1$), costs $1000 ($FC = 1000$) initially, has no scrap value at the end of the year, and will generate $1100 in profit next year ($\pi_1 = 1100$). Should this machine be purchased? To answer this question, we need to compute the rate of return that the firm would receive from this machine. The firm invests $1000 and gets $1100 back one year later, so the firm's own (internal) rate of return is found by solving

$$1000(1 + j) = 1100$$

for j. In this case the firm has an internal rate of return of 10% on this particular investment, since $j = 0.10$ in the equation. Now this internal rate of return must be compared with the rate of return available from the next-best alternative use of the $1000. In general, this next-best alternative is given by the rate of interest i. If the rate of interest is 6%, the funds used to purchase the machine will return more (4% more) than they would receive in the next-best alternative, and the machine should be purchased. But if the rate of interest is 12%, then using funds to purchase this particular machine will yield less (2% less) than they would yield in the next-best alternative, and the machine should not be purchased. If this same argument is extended to a machine that lasts T years and yields π_t in each of those years, then the relevant internal rate of return is given by j in (4.46) and the same rule should apply: undertake the project if the internal rate of return is greater than the interest rate; do not undertake the project if the internal rate of return is less than the interest rate.

This internal-rate-of-return criterion for investment decisions is consistent with the standard inverse relationship between the rate of interest and investment spending that is assumed in most macroeconomic models. As the interest rate increases, fewer projects will have an internal rate of return exceeding the higher interest rate, and thus fewer investment projects will be undertaken. As the interest rate falls, more projects will have internal rates of return exceeding the interest rate, and so there will be more investment spending.

Discounting and Present Value in Continuous Time

The preceding subsection treated time exclusively as a discrete variable; time periods were $t, t+1, t+2, \ldots$, and the interest rate was compounded only once a year. We now consider the questions of discounting and present value in the context of continuous time. There are at least two separate motivations for considering continuous time. One is strictly empirical: most of the interest rates encountered in modern economies are compounded continuously rather than discretely. The other motivation concerns the mathematical convenience of continuous time: when time is treated as a continuous variable, many economic problems become amenable to calculus techniques.

To begin, let us return to the situation that opened our treatment of present value in discrete time: an individual has A dollars to deposit in an account that pays an interest rate of i percent per year. If interest is paid only once a year (called a *simple interest rate*), then the individual will have $A(1+i)$ at the end of the first year, $A(1+i)^2$ at the end of the second year, and $A(1+i)^t$ at the end of t years.

Now consider a change in the period of compounding. Suppose the rate is paid semiannually. That is, consider that interest rate $i/2$ is paid at the end of the first 6 months and then $i/2$ is paid again at the end of the year. This is still a yearly interest rate of i, but now it is compounded more frequently (semiannually rather than annually). Under this semiannual compounding, the individual will have

$$V_{6\text{ mo}} = A\left(1+\frac{i}{2}\right) \tag{4.47}$$

at the end of 6 months, and at the end of the year the value will have grown to

$$V_1 = \left(1+\frac{i}{2}\right)V_{6\text{ mo}} = A\left(1+\frac{i}{2}\right)\left(1+\frac{i}{2}\right) = A\left(1+\frac{i}{2}\right)^2. \tag{4.48}$$

Notice how the future value under semiannual compounding in (4.48) compares with the earlier result for annual compounding. If $i=0.05$ and $A=\$100$, the future value at the end of the first year with annual compounding is $(1.05)(\$100) = \$105$. This same initial deposit with semiannual compounding yields $\$105.06$ at the end of the first year; the individual receives $\$0.06$ more during the year when interest is compounded twice rather than once. This is not a particularly large difference, but it is a difference. Now let us extend this argument to more compounding periods.

If we follow this same line of reasoning and compound even more frequently, then during a single year A grows to

$$V_1 = A\left(1 + \frac{i}{3}\right)^3$$

when interest is compounded three times a year; A grows to

$$V_1 = A\left(1 + \frac{i}{4}\right)^4$$

when interest is compounded four times a year; and finally A grows to

$$V_1(n) = A\left(1 + \frac{i}{n}\right)^n \tag{4.49}$$

for the general case of interest that is compounded n times per year. Since the future value will be different for each compounding period, the future value on the left-hand side of (4.49) is written as a function of n, the number of times the rate is compounded per year. As expected, the future value increases with n for any fixed values of A and i. For instance, in our earlier example where $A = \$100$ and $i = 0.05$, the value at the end of the year is $V_1(12) = 100(1 + 0.05/12)^{12} = \$105.12$ when the interest rate is compounded monthly ($n = 12$). The more frequently a fixed i is compounded per year, the greater A will be at the end of the year.

To find the future value under conditions of **continuous compounding,** we simply let $n \to \infty$ in (4.49). This gives

$$V_1 = \lim_{n \to \infty} V_1(n) = \lim_{n \to \infty} A\left(1 + \frac{i}{n}\right)^n \tag{4.50}$$

as the value of the initial A after one year of continuous compounding. The expression on the right-hand side of (4.50) is a bit unwieldy, but it can be simplified. Recall that the exponential function e^x is equal to $\lim_{n \to \infty}(1 + x/n)^n$. Substituting this expression into (4.50) we get

$$V_1 = Ae^r \tag{4.51}$$

for the future dollars continuously compounded at interest rate r. Note that we have changed the interest rate symbol from i to r to indicate the change from discrete to continuous compounding. To convert a simple rate i into a continuously compounded rate r, we simply solve the expression $e^r = 1 + i$ for r. This gives $r = \ln(1 + i)$ as the continuous rate that would accumulate the same value as the simple rate i over any time period.

The expression in (4.51) gives the value at the end of the year under continuous compounding. To find the value at the end of the second year, we simply treat this first-year value V_1 as the initial amount and compound interest again. This second-year value is

$$V_2 = V_1 e^r = (Ae^r) e^r = Ae^{2r}. \tag{4.52}$$

Continuing this argument to an indefinite (but finite) horizon of t years, we have

$$V(t) = Ae^{rt}. \tag{4.53}$$

The most obvious way to read (4.53) is to say that Ae^{rt} gives the amount of value available at the end of t years when an initial amount A is continuously compounded at rate r. But this is not the only way. We can read (4.53) by saying that r represents the **instantaneous rate of growth** in value V. To see why, differentiate expression (4.53) with respect to t. This differentiation gives

$$\dot{V}(t) = rAe^{rt} = rV(t), \tag{4.54}$$

where $\dot{V}(t) = dV(t)/dt$, the time derivative[2] of $V(t)$. Manipulating the expression in (4.54) we have

$$\frac{\dot{V}(t)}{V(t)} = r. \tag{4.55}$$

Since the rate of change in variable V is the change in the variable divided by its initial value $\Delta V/V$, the left-hand side of (4.55) gives the instantaneous rate of change in variable V with respect to time t. Thus the variable r in (4.53) is the **instantaneous rate of growth** in the future value V.

The instantaneous-rate-of-growth interpretation of expressions such as (4.54) is quite common in economics. For example, we will encounter a Solow growth model in Chapter 5 that assumes the labor force L grows at a constant instantaneous growth rate n, so $\dot{L}(t)/L(t) = n$. Equation (4.54) therefore tells us that the total labor force in such a growth model will be given by $L(t) = L_0 e^{nt}$ at any time t, where L_0 is the labor force at $t = 0$.

Thus far our discussion of continuous time and continuous compounding has focused solely on the questions of future values and the instantaneous rate of growth in future value. Now let us turn to the question of **present value** in continuous time. As in equation (4.34) of our earlier discrete time discussion, the present value of an amount V received t years in the future can be obtained by solving for A in the expression for future value. Thus solving for A in (4.53) and letting $A = PV_t$, we have

$$PV_t = V_t e^{-rt} \tag{4.56}$$

as an expression for the present value of V_t dollars received t years in the future when r is the continuously compounded rate of interest. For example, if $\$1$ ($V = 1$) is to be received in 5 years ($t = 5$) and the interest rate is 8% compounded continuously, the present value is

$$PV_5 = (1)e^{-0.08(5)} = 0.67. \tag{4.57}$$

The same computation conducted earlier in (4.36) with a simple interest rate of 8% gave a present value of 0.68. Since continuous compounding generates more future value than a simple interest rate, the present value under continuous compounding will be less than that under the same simple interest rate. When present value rather than future value is being considered, r represents the instantaneous **rate of decay** rather than the instantaneous rate of growth.

In discrete time with simple interest, the present value of V dollars received in each of the next T years was given by (4.38) as

$$PV = \sum_{t=1}^{T} PV_t = V \sum_{t=1}^{T} \frac{1}{(1+i)^t}.$$

In continuous time with continuously compounded interest, this discounted sum becomes a definite integral. More specifically, the present value of V dollars received every year from $t = 0$ to $t = T$ is given by

$$PV = \int_0^T PV_t \, dt = \int_0^T V e^{-rt} \, dt. \tag{4.58}$$

Carrying out the integration in (4.58), we have

$$PV = V \int_0^T e^{-rt} \, dt = V \left(\frac{-e^{-rt}}{r} \Big|_0^T \right) = \frac{V(1 - e^{-rt})}{r}. \tag{4.59}$$

Alternatively, if the amount received in each future period is a variable $V(t)$ rather than the constant V, then the expression for the present value becomes

$$PV = \int_0^T V(t) \, e^{-rt} \, dt. \tag{4.60}$$

Suppose now that the amount received in each period is constant, so $V(t) = V$ for all t, but this amount is received in perpetuity (forever). What will be the present value of V received forever when the interest rate is r and interest in compounded continuously? To answer this question, we need to take the limit of the present value in (4.58) as $T \to \infty$. This limit is

$$PV = \lim_{T \to \infty} \int_0^T V e^{-rt} \, dt. \tag{4.61}$$

By substituting from (4.59), we have

$$PV = \lim_{T \to \infty} \frac{V(1 - e^{-rt})}{r}. \tag{4.62}$$

Now as $T \to \infty$, the expression $e^{-rT} \to 0$, and thus (4.62) further simplifies to

$$PV = \frac{V}{r}. \tag{4.63}$$

This is the same expression obtained earlier for the present value of an income stream received in perpetuity.

The Optimal Time to Cut a Tree

As an economic application of continuous time discounting, consider the problem of finding the optimal time to harvest lumber in a forest. While this may seem to be a relatively narrow application, the tree-cutting problem actually serves as a prototype for a wide class of economic models involving the efficient allocation of renewable resources. The biological framework is that trees in a forest grow quite quickly when the forest is young, but the growth rate slows as the trees mature. Eventually the forest will reach a **stationary state** in which the growth stops; individual trees still grow, but an equal number decay, so that the stock of lumber in the forest remains constant.

If $x(t)$ is the quantity of lumber available from the forest at any time t, then the change in the quantity of lumber with respect to time $\dot{x}$ is itself a function of $x(t)$, and we can write the time derivative of x as

$$\dot{x}(t) = f[x(t)].$$

Assuming that trees grow fast early and more slowly with maturity, the time derivative of x should increase when the forest is small and decrease as it matures. This means that $\dot{x}(t) = f[x(t)] \geq 0$ with $f[x(t)]$ a strictly concave function. If we let $\bar{x}$ represent the **steady-state** forest size where $F(\bar{x}) = \dot{x} = 0$, and $f(x) > 0$ for all $0 < x < \bar{x}$, function f will have the properties exhibited in Figure 4.10.

If the unit price of lumber is constant at $p > 0$, the (present) value of the lumber in the forest at time t is given by

$$V(t) = px(t)e^{-rt}. \tag{4.64}$$

If we assume zero costs, the optimal time to cut the forest t^* is the time that maximizes this present value.

Since V is a function of a single variable t, the first-order (necessary) condition for a maximum at $t^* > 0$ is

$$\dot{V}(t^*) = \frac{dV(t^*)}{dt} = 0. \tag{4.65}$$

The second-order (sufficient) condition for the maximization problem is

$$\ddot{V}(t^*) = \frac{d^2V(t^*)}{dt^2} < 0. \tag{4.66}$$

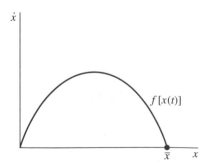

Figure 4.10

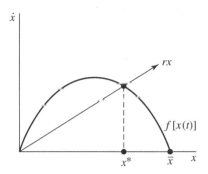

Figure 4.11

Computing the first derivative of the expression in (4.64) and setting it equal to zero, we have

$$\dot{V}(t^*) = p\dot{x}(t^*)e^{-rt^*} - rpx(t^*)e^{-rt^*} = 0. \qquad (4.67)$$

After some rearrangement, this first-order condition can be written as

$$pe^{-rt^*}[\dot{x}(t^*) - rx(t^*)] = 0. \qquad (4.68)$$

Since $p > 0$ and $e^{-rt^*} > 0$ for all $t^* > 0$, equation (4.68) reduces to

$$\dot{x}(t^*) - rx(t^*) = 0 \qquad \text{or} \qquad \frac{\dot{x}(t^*)}{x(t^*)} = r. \qquad (4.69)$$

The optimal $x^* = x(t^*)$ is depicted diagrammatically in Figure 4.11: notice that the slope of ray rx (which is r) is equal to $\dot{x}/x$ at x^* as required by (4.69).

Taking the second derivative of $V(t)$, we have

$$\ddot{V}(t) = p\ddot{x}e^{-rt} - rp\dot{x}e^{-rt} + r^2pxe^{-rt} - rp\dot{x}e^{-rt},$$

or (4.70)

$$\ddot{V}(t) = pe^{-rt}(\ddot{x} - 2r\dot{x} + r^2x).$$

To simplify the expressions in (4.70), x was used in place of $x(t)$. Substituting the first-order condition from (4.69) into (4.70) and evaluating the second derivative at t^*, we have

$$\ddot{V}(t^*) = pe^{-rt^*}[\ddot{x}(t^*) - r\dot{x}(t^*)]. \qquad (4.71)$$

Since $\dot{x}(t) = f[x(t)]$ implies that $\ddot{x}(t) = f'[x(t)]f[x(t)]$, at the optimal $x^* = x(t^*)$ we have $\ddot{x}(t^*) = f'(x^*)f(x^*)$, and the expression (4.71) can be rewritten as

$$\ddot{V}(t^*) = pe^{-rt^*}[f'(x^*)f(x^*) - rf(x^*)] = pe^{-rt^*}[(f'(x^*) - r)f(x^*)]. \qquad (4.72)$$

Since $\dot{x}(t^*) = f(x^*) > 0$ and $pe^{-rt^*} > 0$, the sign of $\ddot{V}(t^*)$ will be determined by the sign of $f'(x^*) - r$. Notice that for any solution $0 < x^* < \bar{x}$ satisfying the first-order conditions, the concavity of $f[x(t)]$ guarantees that $f'(x^*) < r$. Thus the second derivative in (4.72) is strictly negative and the second-order condition is satisfied. In this case, as in the short-run competitive firm in Chapter 3, the economic structure of the problem is sufficient to ensure that the second-order condition is met.

Returning now to the first-order condition, we note that (4.69) lends itself to a rather simple economic interpretation: $\dot{x}/x$ is the rate of growth of the forest, and (4.69) requires that at the optimal cutting time this rate of growth equal the rate of interest. This requirement should make economic sense. Suppose $\dot{x}/x > r$. This says that the rate of growth of the value of the forest is greater than the rate of growth in the value that would be achieved if the forest were cut and the resulting funds invested in the next-best alternative r. But $\dot{x}/x < r$ implies that value held in the forest will return less than it would in the next-best alternative r. Thus $\dot{x}/x > r$ implies that one should continue to leave the forest uncut, while $\dot{x}/x < r$ implies that one should cut and move into the next-best alternative; the optimal time to cut is thus given by the condition that $\dot{x}/x = r$.

4.3 Uncertainty

Many (perhaps most) economic decisions must be made under conditions of uncertainty. When you purchase a particular good, often you are not purchasing a "good" at all; rather, you are purchasing a probability distribution. An apple has one value to the buyer when it is ripe and a different (much lower) value when it is rotten; when you buy an apple, you are actually purchasing a lottery—a high payoff (the utility of a ripe apple) most of the time and a very low payoff (the utility of a rotten apple) the rest of the time. Many of our purchases are like this. They are choices made under uncertainty. One argument for the prevalence of brand names is that consumers are willing to pay extra for them because they feel that brand names reduce uncertainty. Uncertainty of course exists on the supply side as well as the demand side; firms must also make decisions in an uncertain environment. When we discussed the profit-maximizing firm in Chapter 1, we assumed that the firm knew both its demand and its cost with certainty. In fact, most firms try to maximize profit in an environment of uncertainty regarding both demand and cost.

Since the economics of uncertainty is a major area of research, the discussion that follows will be only a brief introduction. The general topic is introduced, and one of the standard results (the theory of insurance) is derived. We assume that the reader is familiar with the basics of (discrete) probability theory and expected value; these topics are reviewed in Chapter 0.

Introduction to the Economics of Uncertainty

Consider an individual playing a relatively simple coin-flipping game. If a head (H) appears, the individual receives a payoff of \$16 ($x_H = 16$); while if a tail (T) appears, the individual receives a payoff of \$4 ($x_T = 4$). The expected value (EV) of this game—the amount the individual would expect to receive on average if the game were played a large number of times—is given by

$$EV = \theta_H x_H + \theta_T x_T = \left(\tfrac{1}{2}\right)(16) + \left(\tfrac{1}{2}\right)(4) = \$10, \tag{4.73}$$

where $\theta_H = \tfrac{1}{2}$ = probability of a head, and $\theta_T = 1 - \theta_H = \tfrac{1}{2}$ = probability of a tail.

Now consider the question of how much an individual would be willing to pay to play this coin-flipping game. Since the expected value (expected payoff) of the game is $10, we say that the game is a fair bet when it costs $10 to play. A bit more formally, the game is a **fair bet** iff $EV - c = 0$, where c is the cost of playing the game. Although this particular coin-flipping game does not sound particularly exciting, it seems reasonable to argue that some individuals would be willing to play such a game if it were a fair bet. Now consider a different coin-flipping game. Let the payoff be zero for a head ($x_H = 0$) and $1 million for a tail ($x_T = 1$ million). Now this game would be a fair bet if it costs $500,000 to play. Even if this game were a fair bet, it seems unlikely that very many people would be willing to play. In fact, few people would agree to play even if the cost were only $499,000, a game clearly in their favor.

The point of this second example, a point made more forcefully by the St. Petersburg paradox (Box 4.1), is that people consider more than the expected value when they are making choices under conditions of uncertainty. What else do they consider? The standard economic answer is that (just as in the case of certainty) they consider the **utility** that they will receive from their choices. In the case of a game like the coin-flipping game, with two possible outcomes (x_1 and x_2) and two probabilities (θ_1 and θ_2), the utility from the game is given by a utility function of the form $U(x_1, x_2, \theta_1, \theta_2)$ or $U(x_1, x_2, \theta_1)$, since $\theta_2 = 1 - \theta_1$. The utility that the individual receives from the game is a function of the probabilities of the occurrence of each event as well as the payoff of each event. In a more general case, with n possible events that can occur with payoffs $x = (x_1, x_2, \ldots, x_n)$ and probabilities $\theta = (\theta_1, \theta_2, \ldots, \theta_n)$ with $\sum_{i=1}^{n} \theta_i = 1$, the utility of the game is given by a utility function $U(x, \theta)$.

At least two background comments are in order before we look at a particular functional form of the utility function $U(x, \theta)$. First, in a game with monetary payoffs (where the x_i's are in terms of money), it is not the amount of money itself that provides utility, but rather the goods and services that can be purchased with the money. While it is true that goods and services are what really matters, not money, the argument is basically the same for both cases; and given that it is much simpler to assume that monetary payoffs enter directly into the utility function, we take that approach throughout. Second, what economists call decision making under **uncertainty** more properly should be called decision making under **risk.** The traditional distinction between risk and uncertainly is that with risk the probability distribution is known (of course the exact outcome is not), whereas with true uncertainty even the relevant probabilities are unknown.[3] Our discussion, and almost everything written about the economics of uncertainty, is really about risk; we assume that the agent does not know which event will actually occur but does know the probability of each possible outcome. Characterizing the agent's uncertain choice in this way makes the payoff a **random variable.**

BOX 4.1
The St. Petersburg Paradox

To the best of our knowledge, the St. Petersburg paradox—a fair game (a fair bet) that no one would play—originated with Daniel Bernoulli in 1738 (English translation, Bernoulli, 1954). Bernoulli's solution amounted to considering the expected utility of the game. When the decision to play is based on expected utility (not expected value) and agents have diminishing marginal utility of income (payoffs), then the reluctance to play Bernoulli's game become explicable. Samuelson (1977) provides a detailed discussion (both historical and mathematical) of the St. Petersburg paradox and the literature that has developed around it.

The St. Petersburg paradox is based on the following game. A fair coin is flipped until a head appears. If a head appears on the first flip, the winner is paid \$2; if a head appears on the second flip, the winner receives \$4; if it appears on the third flip, the winner receives \$8, and so on. Thus if a head does not appear until the nth flip, the winner will receive \$$2^n$ for playing the game. In the language of the chapter, where θ_i is the probability and x_i is the payoff of event i, the expected value (EV) of this game is

$$EV = \sum_{i=1}^{\infty} \theta_i x_i = \sum_{i=1}^{\infty} \left(\tfrac{1}{2}\right)^i 2^i = \sum_{i=1}^{\infty} 1 = \infty.$$

The expected value (expected payoff) is infinite. If individuals considered only the expected value of this game, they would pay any amount to play. In fact, few people will pay very much at all to play such a game. For example, few people would be willing to pay \$1000 to play such a game even though the expected payoff (∞) is substantially greater than \$1000.

Now, of course, if individuals consider expected utility (EU) rather than EV in deciding to play such a game and their utility function exhibits diminishing marginal utility with respect to payoffs, then their unwillingness to play seems quite reasonable. For example, if an individual has the utility function $U(x_i) = \ln x_i$, a utility function with $U' > 0$, and $U'' < 0$, then the expected utility of the game is computed to be 1.39. In other words, an individual with this utility function would pay no more to play the game than the expenditure that would provide 1.39 units of utility if used alternatively.

Sources
Bernoulli, D. 1954. Exposition of a new theory on the measurement of risk. *Econometrica* 22, 23–36 (translated from the 1738 original by L. Summers).

Samuelson, P. A. 1977. St. Petersburg paradoxes: Defanged, dissected, and historically described. *Journal of Economic Literature* 15: 24–55.

Returning now to the utility function $U(x, \theta)$, where x is the payoff vector and θ is the probability vector, first we must address the form of this function. While there is some debate over this issue, the standard approach (and the only one we will discuss) is to assume that the utility function has the special form

$$U(x_1, x_2, \theta_1) = \theta_1 v(x_1) + (1 - \theta_1)v(x_2). \tag{4.74}$$

Or, in the case of n possible outcomes rather than only two, the utility function in (4.74) becomes

$$U(x, \theta) = \sum_{i=1}^{n} \theta_i v(x_i). \tag{4.75}$$

A utility function of the form in (4.75) is called an **expected-utility function** or a **von Neumann–Morgenstern utility function.**[4] It says that utility U may be written as a weighted sum of another function v of each possible payoff, with the weights being given by the relevant probabilities. An alternative way of thinking about this type of utility function is to consider the function v to be the utility function and then to define the weighted sum as the expected utility (EU). Writing $U(\cdot)$ for $v(\cdot)$, and $EU(\cdot)$ for $U(\cdot)$ in (4.75), we have

$$EU(x, 0) = \sum_{i-1}^{n} \theta_i U(x_i) \tag{4.76}$$

as the expected-utility function. Both characterizations, (4.75) and (4.76), appear in the economics literature, but the difference is merely conceptual. Some economists are more comfortable thinking in terms of (4.75) while others prefer (4.76); the mathematical results are fundamentally the same, and both characterizations are called the **expected-utility theory of choice under uncertainty.** In the case of (4.75), we say (without uncertainty) that the agent maximizes **utility;** it is just that the utility function has the particular weighted-sum form given by the right-hand side of (4.75). In the case of (4.76), we say the agent has a utility function $U(\cdot)$ defined over payoffs alone, but chooses so as to maximize the **expected utility** received from playing the game. For heuristic reasons we utilize the latter characterization in the following discussion.

Now it seems obvious in human behavior that some individuals are more prone to take risks than others; some seem to revel in taking chances, while others avoid risk whenever possible. If expected-utility theory is to be used to explain individual behavior under conditions of uncertainty, then it must be able to accommodate these different attitudes toward risk. In fact, this is the case; expected-utility theory provides a very nice way of classifying the risk preference or risk aversion of agents.

To see how expected-utility theory accommodates different attitudes toward risk, recall the simple coin-flipping example that opened our discussion of uncertainty: $\theta_T = \theta_H = \frac{1}{2}$, the payoff for a head was \$16 ($x_H = 16$), and the payoff for a tail was \$4 ($x_T = 4$). The expected value EV of the game was given in (4.73) as

$$EV = \theta_H x_H + \theta_T x_T = \$10. \tag{4.77}$$

This game would be a fair bet if it cost $10 to play ($c = 10$). Following (4.76), the expected utility of this coin-flipping game would be given by the expression

$$EU = \theta_H U(x_H) + \theta_T U(x_T). \tag{4.78}$$

If this coin-flipping game is offered as a fair bet and we rule out hairline cases where the individual is just indifferent, there are only two possible responses that a potential player might have: refuse the bet (keep the $10) or accept the bet (play the game). Let us consider each of these cases.

First, consider the case of the individual who refuses this fair bet. How are we to interpret such a refusal? Refusing a fair bet means that the utility of the expected value of the game, in this case $10, is greater than the expected utility from playing the game. Putting this condition more formally, refusing a fair bet implies that

$$U(EV) = U(\theta_H x_H + \theta_T x_T) > EU = \theta_H U(x_H) + \theta_T U(x_T). \tag{4.79}$$

Such an individual, one who refuses a fair bet, is called **risk averse.** A risk-averse individual always prefers the expected value of a game (which is the cost of a fair bet) to actually playing the game. One example of a utility function that exhibits risk aversion is $U(x) = x^{1/2}$. Applying this particular utility function to the coin-flipping game we have

$$U(EV) = U(10) = (10)^{1/2} \quad \text{and} \quad EU = \left(\tfrac{1}{2}\right) U(16) + \left(\tfrac{1}{2}\right) U(4) = 3,$$

and thus $U(EV) > EU$. This utility function is depicted in Figure 4.12.

Now consider the case of the individual who accepts the fair bet. Acceptance of such a bet means that the utility of the $10, the utility of the EV of the game, is less than the expected utility from playing the game, or

$$U(EV) = U(\theta_H x_H + \theta_T x_T) < EU = \theta_H U(x_H) + \theta_T U(x_T). \tag{4.80}$$

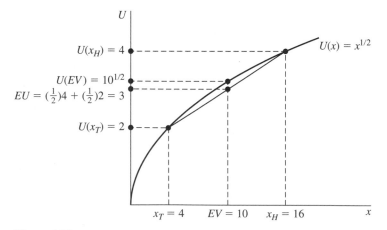

Figure 4.12

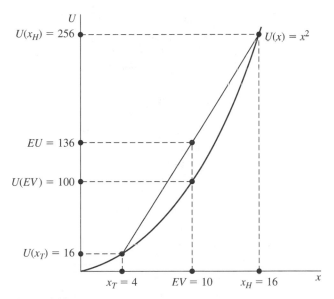

Figure 4.13

Such an individual, one who always accepts a fair bet, is called **risk-loving** (or **risk-preferring**). An example of a utility function with this property is $U(x) = x^2$; applying it to this game, we get

$$U(EV) = U(10) = 100 \qquad \text{and} \qquad EU = \left(\tfrac{1}{2}\right) U(16) + \left(\tfrac{1}{2}\right) U(4) = 136,$$

and thus $U(EV) < EU$. This utility function is depicted in Figure 4.13.

The shapes of the utility functions in Figures 4.12 and 4.13 suggest a more formal characterization of risk-averse and risk-loving behavior. Recall from (1.66) in Chapter 1 the definition of a strictly concave function: a real-valued function of one variable, say $U(x)$, is **strictly concave** if $U(\hat{x}) > \theta U(x_0) + (1 - \theta)U(x_1)$ for all values of x_0 and x_1 in its domain where $x_0 \neq x_1$ and for all $0 < \theta < 1$ where $\hat{x} = \theta x_0 + (1 - \theta)x_1$. Note that this is precisely the same way that risk aversion is characterized. Thus, if an individual's utility function is strictly concave with respect to money income (payoffs), then the individual will exhibit risk-averse behavior. Since a negative second derivative is sufficient for the strict concavity of a differentiable function of one variable, risk aversion is implied by $U''(x) < 0$. Remember, the utility function we are considering here is defined over money income (payoffs); this means that $U'(x)$ is the marginal utility of money, and so the property of $U''(x) < 0$ (risk aversion) should be interpreted as the diminishing marginal utility of money income. By simply reversing the signs of the inequalities, the same type of argument can be applied to the risk-loving case: $U''(x) > 0$, which is the increasing marginal utility of money income, and thus the strict convexity of the utility function implies risk-loving behavior.

In summary, a risk-averse individual will always refuse a fair bet; such an individual prefers the expected value of a fair game to playing the game, so

$U(EV) > EU$. This type of risk-averse behavior is implied by diminishing marginal utility of money income and a strictly concave utility function $U''(x) < 0$. On the other hand, a risk-loving individual will always accept a fair bet; such an individual prefers playing a fair game to receiving the expected value of the game with certainty, so $U(EV) < EU$. Such risk-loving behavior is implied by the increasing marginal utility of money income and a strictly convex utility function, $U''(x) > 0$. There is, of course, a third alternative, which has not been explicitly discussed; it is the case of the individual who is neither risk averse nor risk loving, that is, the case of $U(EV) = EU$. Such individuals are called **risk neutral,** and they are indifferent between playing a fair game and receiving the expected value of the game with certainty. Risk-neutral behavior is implied by a linear utility function where $U''(x) = 0$.

Before we look at the insurance example in the next section, we must emphasize that the categories of risk averse, risk loving, and risk neutral need not be global properties of an individual's behavior. An individual may well exhibit risk-averse behavior for some levels of income (locally) and risk-loving behavior for others. The coin-flipping example was such a case. We argued that for the same probabilities, more people are willing to bet if a very small amount of money is involved than if a very large sum is involved. This also applies to the mathematical properties of concavity, convexity, and the sign of the second derivative. A utility function can exhibit diminishing marginal utility of income and thus strict concavity for some income levels (some values in the domain of the utility function) and increasing marginal utility of income and thus convexity for other income levels. As we mentioned earlier, because of the nature of optimization problems and comparative statics, often economists are concerned with only the local properties of functions.

Insurance

One of the most important economic applications of the theory of risk-averse behavior is the market for insurance. Insurance is protection against risk, and a risk-averse individual will pay a premium to purchase such protection. To introduce this topic, we again rely on the coin-flipping example. After introducing the basic ideas in this simple context, we move on to the more complex and more interesting question of full-coverage insurance against the loss of a currently owned asset.

In the coin-flipping game with $x_H = 16$ and $x_T = 4$, we assume that the (risk-averse) utility function is $U(x) = x^{1/2}$, as shown in Figure 4.12. Notice from Figure 4.12 that the utility of the expected value of the game is $10^{1/2}$ $[U(EV) = 10^{1/2}]$, while the expected utility is 3 ($EU = 3$). As explained earlier, this individual would rather have the expected value (with certainty) than play the game.

Now consider a very simple type of insurance. The individual who pays a certain insurance premium p will receive the expected value of the game ($10) with certainty. Of course, this individual would rather get the $10 without paying the premium, but if this is not an option, the individual has only two choices: play the game or buy the insurance. Given these two choices, how much would the individual be willing to pay as a premium? In other words, how much would the individual be willing to pay to get $10 with certainty rather than play the game?

Assume the premium is $0.50 ($p = 0.50$). The individual who purchased insurance with this premium would receive $9.50 ($FV - p = 10 - 0.50$) with certainty, but what does this mean in terms of utility? Given $U(x) = x^{1/2}$, this payoff with insurance implies a utility level of $(9.50)^{1/2} = 3.08$. This value of 3.08, the utility level when insurance is purchased at $p = 0.50$, is greater than the expected utility of playing the game (3). So the individual would be willing to pay the $0.50 premium to avoid playing the game. How much more than $0.50 would the individual be willing to pay? What is the maximum insurance premium that the individual would pay to avoid playing the game? The answer is that the individual would pay up to $1 as an insurance premium. Why? Because if the premium were $1, the individual would receive $9 ($EV - p = 10 - 1$) with certainty and the utility of this $9 is exactly equal to the expected utility of actually playing the game (3). The individual with this utility function facing these probabilities and payoffs would pay up to $1, but no more than $1, for this type of insurance. This $1 insurance premium is shown diagrammatically in Figure 4.14.

In general, risk-averse individuals will pay some premium to avoid a risky game; the exact amount they are willing to pay depends on the individuals' utility function and the details of the game. Alternatively, and by a similar argument, risk-loving individuals will not purchase insurance. In fact, risk-loving individuals will pay a premium to be allowed to play the game rather than get the expected value of the game with certainty.

Although this coin-flipping example nicely demonstrates the general notion of paying an insurance premium to avoid risk, most insurance is not of the "pay not to

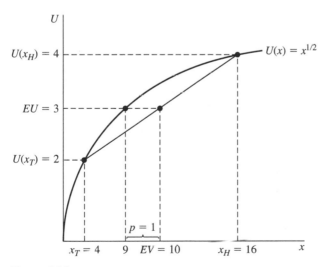

Figure 4.14

play" type. For many insurance problems, the individual in question already owns an asset with a particular value; the premium is paid to insure against the risk of losing the asset and its value. In such cases, if things go well, or the "state of nature" is a good state, the asset will not be lost (the house will not burn down, the car will not be wrecked, etc.). But there is some positive probability that things will not go well, or the "state of nature" will be a bad state, and the asset will be destroyed (the house will burn down, the car will be wrecked, etc.). The question is: How much will the individual be willing to pay as a premium to insure against this loss? Let us consider this question more formally than we did the coin-flipping case.

Let x_0 be the initial income of the individual, and let L be the possible loss. Thus without insurance, the individual will have x_0 in the good state of nature and $x_0 - L$ in the bad state of nature (fire, wreck, etc.). The probability of a loss is given by θ; that is, θ is the probability of a bad state of nature, and thus $1 - \theta$ is the probability of a good state of nature. Thus without insurance, the expected value of this game against nature is $EV = \theta(x_0 - L) + (1 - \theta)x_0 = x_0 - \theta L$, or the initial income minus the expected loss (θL).

Now consider insurance. The individual can purchase a certain amount of insurance coverage C; this coverage is the amount that the insurance provider will reimburse the individual in the event of a loss. Of course, if a good state of nature prevails, there is no loss and the individual receives nothing from the insurance provider. For this coverage the individual must pay a premium p. This premium is given as a certain amount per dollar of coverage. So with a premium of p, the total amount that the individual pays for the coverage is pC; the premium per dollar of coverage times the amount of coverage.

Given this information, we can write the amounts of income that the individual will have (with insurance) in a good state of nature (x_g) and in a bad state of nature (x_b) as

$$x_g = x_0 - pC \tag{4.81a}$$

and

$$x_b = x_0 - L + C - pC. \tag{4.81b}$$

Equation (4.81a) says that if there is no loss, the individual will have the initial income minus the cost of coverage pC. Equation (4.81b) says that if there is a loss, the individual will have the initial income x_0, minus the loss L, plus the amount of coverage C from the insurance provider, minus the cost of coverage pC.

The individual's utility function is $U(x)$, $U: \Re_+ \to \Re_+$. The utility function is at least twice differentiable, with $U'(x) > 0$ and $U''(x) < 0$ for all x, thus exhibiting global risk aversion. Given this utility function, the choice problem for the individual is

$$\underset{C}{\text{Max}}\, EU = \theta U(x_b) + (1 - \theta)U(x_g), \tag{4.82}$$

where x_b and x_g are given by (4.81a) and (4.81b). The individual chooses the amount of insurance coverage C that maximizes the expected utility from this game against nature.

The first-order condition for $C^* > 0$ to solve (4.82) is given by $dEU(C^*)/dC = 0$. Writing out this first-order condition, we have

$$\theta U'(x_b^*)(1 - p) + (1 - \theta)U'(x_g^*)(-p) = 0, \qquad (4.83)$$

where x_b^* and x_g^* are simply the expressions in (4.81) evaluated at C^*. Rewriting this first-order condition, we get

$$\frac{U'(x_b^*)}{U'(x_g^*)} = \frac{p(1 - \theta)}{\theta(1 - p)}. \qquad (4.84)$$

The second-order condition for the problem in (4.82) is that $d^2EU(C^*)/dC^2 < 0$. Taking the second derivative and writing out the inequality, we have

$$\theta(1 - p)^2 U''(x_b^*) + (1 - \theta)p^2 U''(x_g^*) < 0. \qquad (4.85)$$

Notice that no additional restrictions are required to satisfy this second-order condition; the assumption of risk aversion is sufficient for the second-order condition of this problem.

Notice that the first-order condition in (4.84) does not lend itself to a particularly straightforward interpretation. The left-hand side is clearly the marginal rate of substitution *MRS* between consumption in the two possible states of nature, but the right-hand side does not lend itself to any such easy interpretation. To simplify the analysis, let us narrow the discussion a bit and consider only **actuarially fair** insurance.[5] In actuarially fair insurance, the premium paid is equal to the expected value of the insurance: thus $pC = \theta C$ or $p = \theta$.

Given actuarially fair insurance, the right-hand side of (4.84) becomes unity, and the first-order condition reduces to

$$U'(x_b^*) = U'(x_g^*). \qquad (4.86)$$

Since $U''(x) < 0$ for all x, this reduced first-order condition implies that

$$x_b^* = x_g^* \qquad \text{or} \qquad x_0 - L + C^* - pC^* = x_0 - pC^*. \qquad (4.87)$$

This equation reduces to

$$C^* = L. \qquad (4.88)$$

This final result says that a risk-averse individual will always purchase full-coverage insurance at actuarially fair rates; the amount of insurance coverage that maximizes the individual's expected utility is exactly the amount of the potential loss.

The result in (4.88) is very important in the theory of insurance markets and decision making under uncertainty. To increase our understanding of this result, we substitute the solution in (4.88) back into (4.81a) and (4.81b), the expressions for the individual's income in the two states of nature. Making these substitutions and remembering that $p = \theta$, we have

$$x_g^* = x_0 - \theta L \qquad \text{and} \qquad x_b^* = x_0 - \theta L. \qquad (4.89)$$

BOX 4.2
Moral Hazard and Adverse Selection

Moral hazard and adverse selection are both problems that prevent insurance providers from offering the type of actuarially fair insurance considered in the text. Although these two problems were first identified in insurance markets, it is now generally recognized that they can appear in a variety of different economic contexts involving uncertainty.

Moral hazard occurs when the individual has an incentive to engage in more risky behavior because he or she is insured. For example, in the text we demonstrated that a risk-averse individual will purchase full-coverage insurance at actuarially fair rates; with such full-coverage insurance, the individual is no worse off if an accident happens than if it does not happen. Assuming that accident prevention entails some cost, there is no incentive for the fully covered individual to engage in any accident prevention. If the individual really has the same level of utility whether the house burns down or not, why buy a smoke detector? More formally, in the symbolism of the chapter, moral hazard occurs when the probability of a bad state of nature θ is a function of the level of care or safety taken by the individual. In other words,

$$\theta = \theta(\alpha) \qquad \text{with } \frac{d\theta}{d\alpha} < 0,$$

where α is the amount of care (or prevention or caution) taken by the individual. Moral hazard implies that

$$\frac{\partial \alpha}{\partial C^*} < 0,$$

where C^* is the amount of coverage. That is, an increase in the amount of insurance coverage C^* will reduce the amount of care α taken by the insured individual ("It's OK, I'm insured."). Given moral hazard, an insurance provider offering actuarially fair rates would be unable to stay in business. Some responses that insurance companies have made to the problem of moral hazard include (1) deductible policies that provide an incentive for the policyholder to exercise some care, (2) premiums that are systematically above the actuarially fair rate to compensate for moral hazard, and (3) "due-care" clauses that require a certain amount of caution be taken by the policyholder (e.g., automobile insurance policies that do not pay on a car theft when the keys were left in the ignition).

It is now recognized that moral hazard appears in a number of different economic contexts, not simply the insurance market. One example of moral hazard is the "principal–agent problem," the problem of shirking when one person (the agent) does a particular job for another person (the principal). If the quality of the work is a decision variable for the agent and the principal is unable to determine whether the resulting quality is due to the behavior of the agent or to random variation, then there is an incentive for the agent to shirk and an incentive for the principal to attempt to monitor the agent. The literature on the principal–agent problem in economics is quite vast.

Adverse selection occurs when the insured individual has more information about the probability of a loss than the insurance provider does. Adverse selection is different from moral hazard in that moral hazard involves a change in the behavior of the insured party, while adverse selection involves only an asymmetry in information between the insurer and the insured. If someone who applies for health (or life) insurance knowing that he or she has a severe heart condition, and the insurance company is unable to distinguish this individual from the "average" policyholder, then the insurance company is at a disadvantage in terms of adverse selection. Adverse selection, like moral hazard, makes it impossible for insurance to be provided at actuarially fair rates—at such rates, only the most risky will purchase insurance. Group insurance and mandatory physical examinations are two of the ways insurance providers use to protect themselves from adverse selection.

Adverse selection also appears in a number of economic contexts other than the market for insurance. Probably the most famous example is the so-called "market for lemons" discussed in Akerlof (1970). The lemons in Akerlof's example are low-quality used cars. The argument is that in the used-car market the sellers (previous owners) know whether the car is a lemon, but the buyers are unable to differentiate lemons from good used cars. This informational asymmetry leads to an adverse selection problem: since buyers are actually making purchases as if at a lottery, they will be willing to pay only the average (or expected value) for a used car, thus enticing sellers of good used cars to remove them from the market. The result is a used-car market where only lemons are traded (at lemon prices), even though both buyers and sellers of good used cars exist. Such examples often point to a role for government in removing the informational asymmetry.

Source

Akerlof, G. 1970. The market for lemons: Qualitative uncertainty and the market mechanism. *Quarterly Journal of Economics* 84: 488–500.

The expressions in (4.89) say that when the optimal amount of insurance coverage is purchased, the individual has the same level of income (and thus the same level of utility) regardless of the current state of the world; the **insurance simply eliminates risk.** Finally, note that without insurance the expected value of this game against nature was also $x_0 - \theta L$. Thus an alternative way to think about insurance is to say that the optimal coverage provides the expected value of the game against nature with certainty. Insurance, like the earlier coin-flipping example, can therefore be interpreted as paying a premium to avoid playing the game (in the insurance case, the game against nature).

PROBLEMS

4.1 Given the following information, find the total cost functions $TC(y)$.
(a) $MC(y) = 50 + 20y - 9y^2$ and $TC(5) = 700$.
(b) $MC(y) = 75 - 36y + 12y^2$ and $TC(10) = 3000$.

4.2 A perfectly price-discriminating monopolist charges each buyer exactly what he or she is willing and able to pay for each unit of the good. Thus if the monopolist faces the inverse demand function $p(y)$, then the total revenue (TR) associated with an output of $\bar{y}$ units is given by

$$TR(\bar{y}) = \int_0^{\bar{y}} p(y) \, dy.$$

Use the second fundamental theorem of calculus to prove that if such a perfectly price-discriminating monopolist maximizes profit, then the output of the good is the same as under conditions of perfect competition.

4.3 Suppose a consumer solves the particular choice problem

$$\underset{\{x, y\}}{\text{Max}}\, U(x, y) = v(x) + y$$

$$\text{Subject to: } px + y = M,$$

with $v'(x) > 0$, $v''(x) < 0$, and $v(0) = 0$. Show that the following relationship necessarily holds:

$$U(x_0) = M + CS(x_0).$$

4.4 Consider a perfectly competitive firm in the short run with demand and cost conditions given by

$$y = f(L, K) = L^{1/2} K^{1/2}, \quad \bar{K} = 4, \quad w = \$2, \quad v = \$4.50, \quad p = \$6,$$

where y is output, f is the production function, $\bar{K}$ is fixed capital, w is the wage rate, v is the price of capital, and p is the price of the product.
(a) Use the information to derive the variable cost function $VC(y)$, the total cost function $TC(y)$, the marginal cost function $MC(y)$, and the fixed cost FC for this firm.
(b) Find the profit-maximizing output for the firm y^* and the amount of profit at this profit-maximizing output π^*.
(c) Apply equation (4.17) to this firm and check the result with your answers to (a) and (b).

4.5 Consider a utility-maximizing consumer with the utility function $U(x, y) = x^{1/2} + y$ and the budget constraint $px + y = M$ (M = money income, p = price of x, and price of $y = 1$).
(a) Use the substitution technique from Chapter 1 to find expressions for the utility-maximizing quantities of the two goods x^* and y^*.
(b) What level of utility does the consumer have when maximizing utility with $p = 2$ and $M = 10$ [i.e., compute $U(x^*, y^*)$ for these particular parameters].

(c) Compute the consumer's surplus $CS(x^*)$ associated with good x when the prices and money income are as given in (b).

(d) Show $U(x^*, y^*) = M + CS(x^*)$ for this particular problem with these parameters.

4.6 Suppose that the demand for a particular good is given by $x = x(p) = p^{-a}$, with $a > 1$, and the marginal cost is constant at $c > 0$.

(a) Find the perfectly competitive output of the good x_c.

(b) Find the monopoly output of the good x_m.

(c) Find the consumer's surplus in the market at the competitive output $CS(x_c)$. (*Note:* This is also the total surplus, since $MC = c$.)

(d) Find the consumer's surplus in the market at the monopoly output $CS(x_m)$.

(e) Find an expression for the consumer's surplus loss (CSL) from monopoly in this market, where $CSL = CS(x_c) - CS(x_m)$.

4.7 Recall the duopoly international trade problem from Chapter 3 (Problem 26). In that problem the Cournot equilibrium output of the domestic firm q_d^*, that of the foreign firm q_f^*, and thus the total output $Q^* = q_d^* + q_f^*$ depends on the level of the tariff t. Now consider the government's problem of setting the optimal tariff t^* on the good. We can assume that the government acts prior to the Cournot behavior of the two firms and that the government knows how each firm will react to a particular tariff level (i.e., the government knows the answer to Problem 26 in Chapter 3). The government will choose t to maximize the **total welfare** W that the country receives from this good. This welfare (using the symbolism from the earlier problem) is composed of three parts: the consumer's surplus from the good $CS[Q^*(t)]$, the tariff revenue $tq_f^*(t)$, and the total profit of the domestic firm $\pi^d(q_d^*)$. Thus the total welfare $W(t)$ is

$$W(t) = CS(Q^*(t)) + tq_f^*(t) + \pi^d(q_d^*)$$

$$= \int_0^{Q^*(t)} P(Q)\, dQ - P(Q^*)Q^* + tq_f^*(t) + P(Q^*)\, q_d^* - c^d q_d^*.$$

(a) Using the answers from Problem 26 of Chapter 3 and assuming parameter values $b = 300$, $c^f = 10$, and $c^d = 20$, find the level of the tariff t^* that maximizes the welfare $W(t)$.

(b) From the answers to (a), Find q_f^*, q_d^*, Q^*, and P^*.

4.8 Suppose a particular financial asset yields $1000 per year for 20 years. Find the present value of this asset in terms of the simple interest rate of $i = 0.08$.

4.9 Using the discrete time present value formulas, derive the maximum amount that a rational person would pay for a bond that matures in 20 years, has a coupon value $1000 in each year prior to maturity, and has a face value of $10,000 paid at maturity if the interest rate is 6%. How much would be paid if the interest rate were 8%?

4.10 U.S. patents traditionally last 17 years. Suppose that you have an opportunity to purchase a patent right for $1 million. You know that ownership of the patent will give you an extra $100,000 per year during the first 10 years but only $50,000 per year during the remaining 7 years because of the development of a close substitute. After the patent expires, it will cease to yield any additional revenue. Should you purchase the patent if the interest rate is 6%? If the interest rate is 4%? (Use discrete time analysis and show your work.)

4.11 Machine A has a 10-year lifetime, generates \$10,000 additional profit during each of those years, and has no scrap value. Machine B also generates \$10,000 additional profit during each year of its life, but it lasts only 6 years. Machine B, though, has a scrap value at the end of the sixth year. If the rate of interest is 6% ($i = 0.06$) how much must the scrap value of machine B be to make the firm indifferent between the two machines? (Use discrete time.)

4.12 If we extend the model of the two-input, profit-maximizing, perfectly competitive firm from Chapter 3 to an intertemporal environment, the firm will seek to maximize the present value of the future profit stream PV_π rather than merely the single-period profit π. Thus in the infinite-horizon case, the firm's problem is

$$\underset{\{L,K\}}{\text{Max}} PV_\pi = \sum_{t=0}^{\infty} \left(\frac{1}{1+i}\right)^t \pi_t,$$

where i is the interest rate and π_t is the profit in period t. In such an intertemporal context, we should distinguish between the stock of capital in period t, denoted K_t, and the gross investment in period t, denoted I_t, where

$$I_t = K_{t+1} - K_t + \delta K_t \tag{1}$$

and δ is the rate of depreciation on capital. Given the relationship in (1), the firm's intertemporal profit maximization problem is

$$\underset{\{L,K\}}{\text{Max}} PV_\pi = \sum_{t=0}^{\infty} \left(\frac{1}{1+i}\right)^t [pf(L_t, K_t) - wL_t - vI_t], \tag{2}$$

where f is the production function and p, w, and v are the prices of output, labor, and investment goods, respectively.

(a) Substitute (1) into (2) and get a general expression for the present value of profits in terms of the choice variables L_t and K_t.

(b) Using (a), find expressions for the first-order conditions for the firm's problem.

(c) Interpret the first-order conditions from (b) (i.e., provide a microeconomic interpretation of these expressions).

4.13 Consider the costs and benefits of a college education. A college graduate can expect an income of M_c per year in comparison to M_{nc} for someone who is not a college graduate. If this amount is received every year over a working life of T years, the present value of a college education (taken from the year of graduation) is

$$PV = \sum_{t=1}^{\infty} (M_c - M_{nc})(1+i)^{-t}.$$

This present value can be simplified by letting $T \to \infty$ (which is a good estimate for large T) by

$$PV = \frac{M_c - M_{nc}}{i}.$$

Now consider the costs of a college education (also computed in graduation-year dollars). There are both explicit costs (tuition, books, etc.) and implicit costs (forgone income) associated with 4 years of college. Viewed from the graduation year, the implicit cost of college is

$$M_{nc}(1+i)^3 + M_{nc}(1+i)^2 + M_{nc}(1+i) + M_{nc},$$

and the explicit cost is

$$C_x(1+i)^3 + C_x(1+i)^2 + C_x(1+i) + C_x,$$

where C_x is the total explicit cost of college per year.

Using this information, compute how much a student would need to make after graduation M_c^* to break even on college when $i = 8\%$, $M_{nc} = \$40,000$, and $C_x = \$23,000$.

4.14 Find the elasticity of the price of a consol with respect to the interest rate $\varepsilon_{p_B,i}$.

4.15 You are about to make a deposit and you are told that you will receive 7.2% compounded continuously. What simple interest rate would give you the same value at the end of the year?

4.16 Solve the tree problem given by (4.64) for the optimal time to harvest t^* when $x(t) = e^{t^{1/2}}$. Solve for three cases: $r = 5$, 8, and 10%.

4.17 Consider a modified version of the tree-cutting problem in (4.64) where there are initial planting costs C_0 and a flow of maintenance cost of $C(t)$ per year. Under these conditions, the objective is to choose a harvest time T that maximizes the present value of the profit from the forest π, where

$$\pi(T) = px(T)e^{-rt} - C_0 - \int_0^T C(t) \, e^{-rt} \, dt.$$

Find the first-order condition for the optimal harvest time T^* and interpret it.

4.18 The condition for the optimal time t^* to cut a forest that grows at the rate $\dot{x}(t)$ was given in (4.69) as $\dot{x}(t^*)/x(t^*) = r$. Since r is contained in the first-order condition, t^* can be written as $t^* = t^*(r)$. Use the comparative statics technique from Chapter 3 to derive an expression for the change in optimal harvest time with respect to the interest rate (i.e., find $\partial t^*/\partial r$). Can we use the assumptions of the model to sign this comparative statics expression? If so, what is the sign? Draw a diagram to demonstrate your result.

4.19 Consider the problem of a firm that can choose the "durability" of a machine; however, the more durable the machine, the more it costs initially. Thus if we let T be the lifetime of the machine and $C(T)$ its initial cost, we have $C'(T) = dC/dT > 0$. Using continuous time analysis, find a rule for choosing the level of durability T^* that maximizes the present value of the profit π from the machine, under the assumption that it generates $\$R$ in revenue for each year of its lifetime. [Assume there are no operating costs for the machine; the only cost is the initial $C(T)$.]

4.20 Consider the following coin-flipping game: the payoff for a head is $\$25$ ($x_H = 25$), and the payoff for a tail is $\$1$ ($x_T = 1$). If the individual has the utility function $U(x) = 10x^{1/2}$, what is the maximum premium he or she would pay for insurance that gives the expected value of the game (with certainty) rather than playing the game?

4.21 Find an expression for C^* and verify that the result in (4.88) holds for the insurance problem when the individual has the particular utility function $U(x) = \ln(x+1)$.

4.22 Consider a perfectly competitive firm in the short run with production uncertainty. Let the firm's profit π be given by

$$\pi(L) = pf(L) - wL - FC,$$

where $L = $ labor, $FC = $ fixed cost, $w = $ wage, $p = $ price, and $f(L)$ is the production function. This firm is subject to production line breakdown. With a breakdown, the firm has zero output and $\pi = -wL - FC$; without a breakdown, the firm's profit is given by the foregoing expression. If θ is the probability of not having a breakdown, then the firm's expected profit $E\pi$ is given by

$$E\pi = \theta[pf(L) - wL - FC] + (1 - \theta)(-wL - FC).$$

(a) Characterize the first- and second-order conditions for expected profit maximization at $L^* > 0$.

(b) Use comparative statics analysis to find the impact of a change in θ on L^* (i.e., sign $\partial L^*/\partial\theta$).

(c) Interpret your answer in (b).

4.23 Suppose that a particular type of research can be undertaken by a number of different firms at constant cost $c > 0$. Thus if there are n firms conducting this research, the total cost to society is nc. The probability that the research will be successful (a discovery will be made) in at least one firm is $p(n)$, and the more firms the higher the chance that someone will be successful, so $p'(n) > 0$; but this probability increases at a decreasing rate, so $p''(n) < 0$. The benefit to society (no matter who makes the discovery) is given by B. Thus the society's problem is to maximize the (expected) net social benefit $NSB(n)$ by choice of the number of firms doing research, where

$$NSB(n) = Bp(n) - nc.$$

(a) Find an expression for the NSB-maximizing number of firms n^* when $p(n) = 1 - e^{-\alpha n}$.

(b) Find n^* for the case in (a) when $c = 1$, $B = 25$, and $\alpha = 0.2031$.

NOTES

1. To derive (4.39) from (4.38), proceed as follows: multiply both sides of (4.38) by $(1 + i)^{-1}$, subtract this result from both sides of (4.38), and manipulate the result to derive (4.39).

2. This dot notation is often used to indicate differentiation with respect to time, and we will use it in that way throughout the remainder of the text.

3. The classic presentation of this distinction is Knight (1971), a book originally published in 1921.

4. See von Neumann and Morgenstern (1944).

5. We have simply assumed actuarially fair insurance, but this condition also follows from the assumption of a perfectly competitive insurance market. If there is a loss, the insurance company receives $pC - C$; if there is no loss, the insurance company receives pC. Thus the expected profit of the insurance company is $E\pi = \theta(pC - C) - (1 - \theta)pC$. In long-run competitive equilibrium, these expected profits will be driven to zero, which implies that $p = \theta$. This argument of course assumes that the only costs to the insurance company are those paid out in claims.

INTRODUCTION TO
CONTINUOUS TIME DYNAMICS
IN ONE AND TWO DIMENSIONS

■ ■ ■

In this chapter we discuss the continuous time stability of one- and two-dimensional dynamic models. By "stability" we basically mean the question of whether the relevant variables converge to some equilibrium value over time. While stability analysis could be conducted in terms of discrete time (and we will sometimes rely on discrete time when developing the reader's intuition), continuous time dynamics are more consistent with the tools developed elsewhere in this book.

Stability analysis is an extremely important part of mathematical economics because so much of economic theory depends on the comparative statics of equilibrium positions; comparing equilibria makes sense only if the underlying system is stable. As an example of the intimate connection between stability and equilibrium comparative statics, reconsider the elementary supply and demand model from Chapter 3: How are we to explain the change in the price of wheat that might be observed following a severe drought in the midwestern United States? The answer, based on the familiar supply and demand analysis in Figures 5.1 and 5.2, is that the price will increase because the drought decreases the supply of wheat.

It is relatively easy to see that such a comparative statics explanation depends on the stability of the underlying equilibrium. For instance, consider the case depicted in Figure 5.3. In this case, the equilibrium price is still P_w^0, but the market is **unstable:** for any price above P_w^0, there is positive excess demand (a shortage), and thus competition on the demand side will bid the price up, away from P_w^0. Similarly, for prices below P_w^0, competition on the supply side will cause the price to fall, again moving away from P_w^0. For a market like the one depicted in Figure 5.3, a reduction in supply will cause the price to fall (not rise), but more importantly this new lower equilibrium price *will never be reached* after the change in supply. If the supply is reduced in such a market, there will be excess demand at the old equilibrium price P_w^0 and so the price will rise, moving steadily away

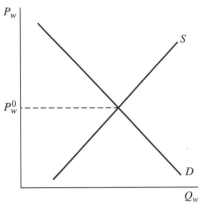

Figure 5.1

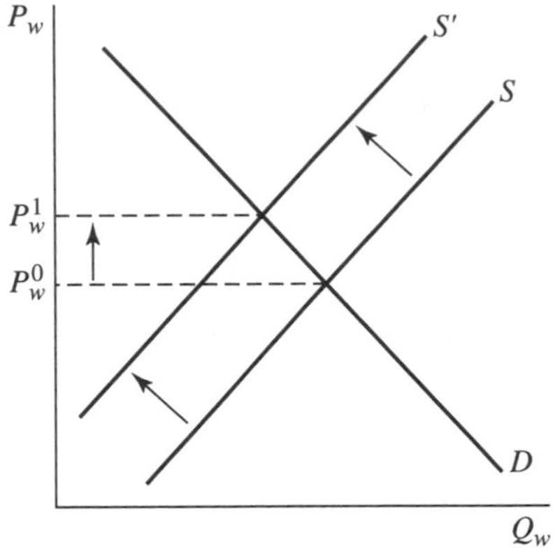

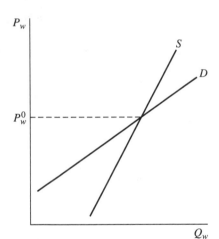

Figure 5.3

Figure 5.2

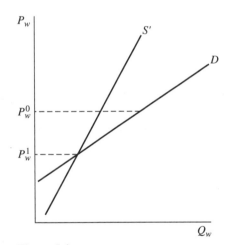

Figure 5.4

from P_w^0 (shown in Figure 5.4). For such an unstable market, comparative statics analysis is inappropriate, even if there is a unique equilibrium both before and after the change.

This example demonstrates that even in very simple economic models, comparative statics is dependent on the stability of the underlying dynamic system. Since comparative statics equilibrium analysis is so fundamental to economic theory, a method for formally analyzing the stability of any arbitrary model is an important tool. This chapter provides the tools for such stability analysis in low- (one- and two-) dimensional models. Our discussion begins with the simple supply and demand model. The stability of this model will be discussed in an intuitive, diagrammatic way in Section 5.1, followed by a bit more formal analysis of the dynamics of supply and demand.

5.1   Single-Market Competitive Equilibrium

A Diagrammatic Approach

Consider the simple supply and demand model in Figure 5.5. The left-hand side of the figure depicts the supply and demand for the good, while the right-hand side depicts the excess demand function $z(p)$, where **excess demand** is simply demand minus supply: $z(p) = D(p) - S(p)$. At the **equilibrium** price p^*, supply is equal to demand, and thus excess demand is equal to zero. Mathematically, the equilibrium price is a **singular point** of the excess demand function; that is, p^* is a price vector such that $z(p^*) = 0$.

Since we are interested in stability, we want to find out whether the price will **converge to** p^* from any initial (disequilibrium) price. The economic argument for convergence is that competitive forces will move the price toward its equilibrium value. Positive excess demand or a shortage of the good will cause the price to rise, while negative excess demand (excess supply) or a surplus of the good will cause the price to fall. For the case depicted in Figure 5.5, such competitive forces will cause the price to converge to p^* from any initial nonequilibrium value. This convergence is indicated by the arrows along the price axis in Figure 5.5.

The following adjustment mechanism characterizes these competitive forces more formally:

$$\Delta p = \delta z(p) \qquad \text{with } \delta > 0. \tag{5.1}$$

This adjustment mechanism simply states that when there is excess demand, that is, when $z(p) > 0$, then $\Delta p > 0$; and when there is excess supply, that is, when $z(p) < 0$, then $\Delta p < 0$. This mechanism captures the standard economic argument regarding the way in which prices adjust in response to competitive market forces. The δ in expression (5.1) is merely a positive scalar that indicates the speed of adjustment.

When the price converges to the equilibrium price from every disequilibrium position, as in Figure 5.5, we say the equilibrium is **stable.** The obvious question is then: Under what circumstances is the adjustment mechanism in (5.1) stable?

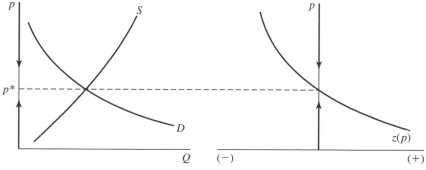

Figure 5.5

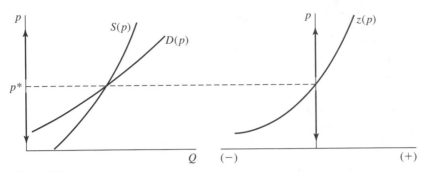

Figure 5.6

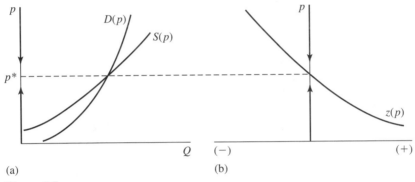

(a)   (b)

Figure 5.7

When is it guaranteed that the competitive process captured in (5.1) will always lead to the equilibrium price?

Figure 5.6 clearly tells us that the stability of the market is related to the shapes of the supply and demand functions. In Figure 5.6 the adjustment mechanism (5.1) is unstable; prices will move away from equilibrium for any initial $p \neq p^*$. This divergence is indicated by the arrows along the price axis in Figure 5.6.

Figure 5.6 might lead us to believe that the instability is a result of the upward-sloping demand. Is it true that an upward-sloping demand (Giffen good) will always cause instability? Figure 5.7 demonstrates that the answer is no. Figure 5.7 shows a market with upward-sloping demand, and the adjustment process (5.1) still converges to the equilibrium price p^*.

What we need is a **stability condition:** a condition that is (at least) sufficient to guarantee that the adjustment process (5.1) will converge to a stable equilibrium. Figures 5.5 to 5.7 suggest that such a stability condition would impose restrictions on the slopes of the model's supply and demand functions. We develop such a stability condition intuitively in this section and then provide a more formal proof of the result.

A close examination of Figures 5.5, 5.6, and 5.7 suggests that the equilibrium is stable whenever the excess demand function slopes downward, that is, whenever

$z'(p) = dz(p)/dp < 0$. If this condition holds, then positive excess demand will force prices upward (toward $p*$), and negative excess demand will force prices downward (toward $p*$). Readers are invited to draw diagrams for other cases where $z'(p) < 0$ [such as both $S(p)$ and $D(p)$ sloping downward with $S(p)$ cutting $D(p)$ from above] and convince themselves that $z'(p) < 0$ is a sufficient condition for the stability of the equilibrium price in the single-market case.

Given the definition of excess demand, the stability condition $z'(p) < 0$ reduces to $D'(p) < S'(p)$. This provides us with a stability condition that lends itself more readily to economic interpretation—that the demand curve has a less steep slope than the supply curve. On first glance, Figures 5.6 and 5.7 might seem to violate this condition, since demand appears to have a less steep slope than supply in Figure 5.6, where the equilibrium is unstable, and to have a steeper slope than supply in Figure 5.7, where the equilibrium is stable. A closer examination of the figures though, reveals that they do not violate the stability condition at all. They merely appear to do so because price is on the vertical, rather than the horizontal, axis.

This stability condition was obtained quite informally, basically by comparing a few diagrams. What we need now is a more formal derivation: a proof that $z'(p) < 0$ is sufficient for the stability of single-market competitive equilibrium. Such a proof requires a short digression into the theory of ordinary differential equations.

A More Formal Approach to Single-Market Stability

Consider the following simple first-order, linear, ordinary differential equation

$$\dot{y}(t) = by(t), \tag{5.2}$$

where $\dot{y}(t) = dy(t)/dt$, $b \in \Re$, and $t \in [0, \infty)$. The equation is first order because the first derivative is the highest-order derivative in the equation; it is linear because the right-hand side is linear; and it is ordinary because y is a function of only one variable, time t. Let the initial condition $y_0 = y(0)$ also be specified: that is, y_0 is the value of the variable y when $t = 0$.

We know from (4.53) through (4.55) in the preceding chapter that $\dot{y}(t)/y(t) = b$ implies that $y(t) = y_0 e^{bt}$, where y_0 is the initial value, but let us derive the same result in an alternative way. The alternative approach is to "solve" the differential equation in (5.2) by integration. To this end, integrating both sides of $\dot{y}(t)/y(t) = b$ gives $\ln y = bt + c$, where c is the constant of integration. From this last equation we have $y = e^{bt}e^{c}$. Since this holds for all values of t, for $t = 0$ we have, $y(0) = e^{c}$, so $y_0 = e^{c}$. Substitution of this constraint back into the expression for y gives us the desired solution

$$y(t) = y_0 e^{bt}. \tag{5.3}$$

We can easily check that (5.3) is a solution to (5.2) by noting that $y(t) = y(0) = y_0$ when $t = 0$, and that differentiation of (5.3) in fact gives $dy(t)/dt = by_0 e^{bt} = by(t)$, as required by (5.2).

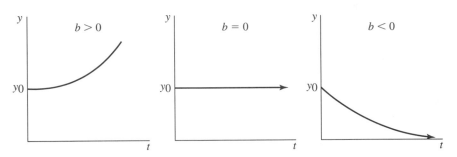

Figure 5.8

For each particular b, the differential equation (5.3) will generate a different path for variable y, but the **qualitative** characteristics of the path can be determined by the **sign of b** alone. Note that if $b > 0$, the value of $y(t)$ will increase without bound as $t \to \infty$; if $b = 0$, the value of $y(t)$ remains at its initial value y_0 for all t; and if $b < 0$, the value of $y(t)$ will decrease asymptotically toward zero as $t \to \infty$. These conditions are depicted diagrammatically in Figure 5.8.

Since the equilibrium value of any dynamic system is the value from which there is no tendency to change, the equilibrium value y^* in the differential equation (5.2) is given by $\dot{y}(t) = 0$. Solving for this equilibrium value, we see that $y^* = 0$ if $b \neq 0$. If $b = 0$, then the system is in equilibrium for any initial position: that is, it stays wherever it starts. For this latter case, the equilibrium is usually called a **trivial** equilibrium because any value is an equilibrium position. We can summarize these results by saying that the path generated by (5.2) **converges** to the nontrivial equilibrium $y^* = 0$ iff $b < 0$. Thus $b < 0$ is a necessary and sufficient condition for the **stability** of the equilibrium value $y^* = 0$, that is, $\lim_{t\to\infty} y(t) = 0$. If $b \geq 0$, the differential equation (5.2) has an equilibrium value that is either trivial or stable.

We can now apply this result from the theory of differential equations to the original question of market stability. We rewrite (5.1) as a first-order differential equation:

$$\dot{p}(t) = \delta z[p(t)] \qquad \text{with } \delta > 0. \tag{5.4}$$

An equilibrium price p^* for the differential equation (5.4) is given by $\dot{p}(t) = 0$. Since $\delta > 0$, $\dot{p}(t) = 0$ implies that $z(p^*) = 0$. Thus the equilibrium for (5.4) preserves all the other properties of the original adjustment mechanism in (5.1).

With respect to stability, the results just obtained cannot be applied immediately, since the right-hand side of (5.4) is, in general, nonlinear. One solution, and the one we will pursue, is to "linearize" the excess demand function by taking its Taylor series expansion around the equilibrium price p^*. Recall that the Taylor series expansion of $z(p)$ around p^* is given by

$$z(p) = z(p^*) + z'(p^*)(p - p^*) + \frac{z''(p^*)(p - p^*)^2}{2} + \cdots . \tag{5.5}$$

Limiting ourselves to prices "close" to p^*, that is, within the ε neighborhood $P_\varepsilon = \{p: |p - p^*| < \varepsilon \text{ for some } \varepsilon > 0\}$, we can truncate the expression at the second term. This truncation and the fact that $z(p^*) = 0$ reduce (5.5) to

$$z(p) = z'(p^*)(p - p^*). \tag{5.6}$$

Equation (5.6) represents a local linear approximation of the excess demand function $z(p)$ in a neighborhood of the equilibrium price p^*. We are now ready to prove the desired result.

THEOREM 5.1: If $z'(p^*) < 0$, the equilibrium p^* of the market adjustment mechanism (5.4) is **stable** for any initial price within some $\varepsilon > 0$ of p^*.

PROOF: Since both δ and $z'(p^*)$ are constants, we can define $b = \delta z'(p^*)$. Also we define $y(t) = p(t) - p^*$, which implies that $\dot{y}(t) = \dot{p}(t)$. Substituting the definition of $y(t)$ into (5.6), we have $z[p(t)] = z'(p^*)y(t)$; and substituting this expression into (5.4) we have $\dot{y}(t) = \delta z'(p^*)y(t)$. Thus, by these substitutions, the differential equation (5.4) is equivalent to $\dot{y}(t) = by(t)$. Thus the stability condition $b < 0$ is sufficient for the stability of (5.4) when b is defined as we have done. Now the theorem supposes that $z'(p^*) < 0$, which implies that $\delta z'(p^*) < 0$ and thus $b < 0$. So system (5.2) converges to the equilibrium value $y = 0$. This implies convergence to p^* because $y = 0$ is equivalent to $p = p^*$ by the definition of y.

Before moving on to the next topic, we note that Theorem 5.1 provides only a sufficient condition for the stability of (5.4), not both a necessary and a sufficient condition. For the linear case in (5.2), the condition $b < 0$ was both necessary and sufficient for stability, but in taking the Taylor series approximation, the necessity is lost. The stability of the linear approximation (5.6) is only sufficient (not necessary) for the stability of the original equation in (5.4).[1] Of course, if $z(p)$ happened to be linear in p, then Theorem 5.1 would provide necessity as well.

We are now in a position to relate the stability of the supply and demand model discussed here to the comparative statics analysis of the same model presented in Chapter 3. Recall from Chapter 3 the general supply and demand model given by the equilibrium condition

$$D(p) - S(p, \alpha) = 0,$$

where α was a shift parameter in the supply function with $S_\alpha = \partial S / \partial \alpha > 0$. In equation (3.9), the comparative statics impact of a change in the shift parameter α was shown to be

$$\frac{dp^*}{d\alpha} = \frac{S_\alpha}{D_p - S_p}.$$

Rewriting this expression in terms of the excess demand functions used in this chapter gives us

$$\frac{dp^*}{d\alpha} = \frac{S_\alpha}{z'(p^*)}.$$

This equation clearly demonstrates the intimate relationship between the stability of the model and the sign of its comparative statics terms. If the sufficient condition (necessary if linear) for stability holds, then an increase in the supply shift parameter will decrease the equilibrium price, since $z'(p^*) < 0$ on the right-hand side of the foregoing equation implies that $dp^*/d\alpha < 0$. This comparative statics result is implied solely by the stability condition; no other information about the shapes of the supply and demand functions is required. This is just one of many examples where knowledge of the stability of the model automatically determines the signs of its comparative statics terms. This important relationship was dubbed the **correspondence principle** in Paul Samuelson's *Foundations of Economic Analysis* (1948), and it holds for a large class of economic models. Unfortunately, "large class" is not "all." While stability often provides comparative statics information, it does not always do so; in more complex models, the correspondence principle may or may not hold.

Local Versus Global Stability

Note that Theorem 5.1 not only formalizes the informal result, it also simplifies it. By Theorem 5.1, for p within some ε neighborhood of p^*, it is not necessary to check that $z'(p) < 0$ for all p; it is only necessary to check the one value of the derivative $z'(p^*)$. If the derivative is negative at the equilibrium, then the price system converges for any p "close" to p^*, regardless of the behavior of $z(p)$ on the rest of the domain.

Theorem 5.1 is a **local stability** result; that is, it gives stability within an ε neighborhood of equilibrium. If the function is nonlinear, there is no necessary reason for such local stability to imply **global stability** (i.e., convergence for **any** initial price within the domain). This is clearly demonstrated in Figure 5.9, which shows stability (convergence to p^*) for any initial price within an ε neighborhood of p^*, but for an initial price above p^{**} the adjustment mechanism (5.1) or (5.4) would drive the price off to infinity.

This seems to be an appropriate time to introduce the standard terminology used in stability analysis. If there exists some $\varepsilon > 0$ such that $\lim_{t \to \infty} p(t) = p^*$ for

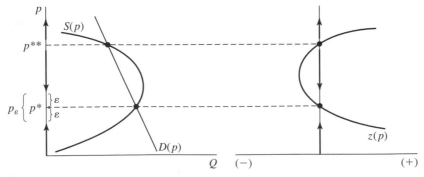

Figure 5.9

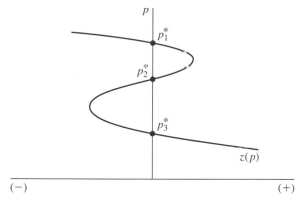

Figure 5.10

any initial price $p(0)$ within ε of p^*, then the **equilibrium** p^* is **locally stable.** Theorem 5.1 provides a sufficient condition for such a locally stable equilibrium in one dimension. If $\lim_{t \to \infty} p(t) = p^*$ for **any** initial price in the domain, then we say the **equilibrium** p^* is **globally stable.** Thus Figure 5.7 depicts a case of a locally stable equilibrium that is also globally stable, while Figure 5.9 depicts an equilibrium p^* that is locally, but not globally stable; and p^{**} is not even locally stable. Finally, we say that a dynamic **system** [such as (5.4)] is **globally stable** if the system converges to **some** equilibrium for every initial value. For example, Figure 5.10 depicts an excess demand function where the dynamic system (5.4) is globally stable. That is, no matter where we start in the domain of the function $\Re_{++}$, the system will always converge to some equilibrium value. Thus the excess demand function in Figure 5.10 generates a globally stable dynamic system, even though none of the three equilibria is globally stable and one (p_2^*) is even locally unstable.

Finding a restriction on the derivative that is sufficient for the global stability of the equilibrium is generally much more difficult than for the local case. In the local case the Taylor series expansion can always be used to provide a local linear approximation of the function, which enables the application of the (relatively simple) theory of linear differential equations. But apart from the somewhat special case in which the function itself is linear, this linearization is not available for global analysis.

It is sometimes possible to obtain global information, or actually to extend local information, if the behavior of the function near the boundary of the domain is known. For instance, in a single market the price domain is simply $\Re_+$, so "boundary" behavior is merely the behavior of the function as $p \to 0$. Suppose we know that as the price goes toward zero, excess demand increases without bound; so $p \to 0$ implies that $z(p) \to \infty$. This boundary condition holds in Figures 5.7, 5.9, and 5.10; it does not hold in Figure 5.6. If an excess demand function with such boundary behavior is differentiable on $\Re_+$, and if $z(p^*) = 0$ implies that $z'(p^*) < 0$, then the equilibrium (if it exists) is unique and globally stable. Basically these conditions ensure that the excess demand function will look like the one in Figure 5.7b.

While global stability results may be available for special cases such as linear systems or systems with boundary restrictions, finding a derivative condition for global stability is very difficult in general. For one- and two-dimensional systems, though, global stability can often be handled diagrammatically. In the next section we find that diagrams are sufficient to discuss stability in a simple neoclassical growth model (although Theorem 5.1 is used as well). The second one-dimensional model we shall discuss is a model of inflationary dynamics. The linear structure of this model makes the local and global stability equivalent. Finally, in the last part of the chapter we turn to two-dimensional systems, and a diagrammatic tool called the phase diagram technique is developed and applied to two important economic models.

5.2 Examples of One-Variable Dynamic Economic Models

The Solow Neoclassical Growth Model

The question of economic growth is as old as economics itself. Certainly Adam Smith's *Wealth of Nations* (1776), the canonical work of classical economics, was concerned with the question of economic growth. And while modern growth theory is quite different from Adam Smith's theory, the subject continues to receive substantial attention from contemporary economic theorists.

During the late 1950s and early 1960s, research on the topic of economic growth was spurred on by a number of different factors. On the empirical side, interest in economic growth was stimulated by attempts to explain the variation in the post–World War II growth rates among developed countries as well as by the more general question of economic underdevelopment. On the theoretical side, there was an impetus from both the prevailing micro- and macroeconomic theories. With respect to macroeconomics, Keynes made certain suggestions regarding the long-run dynamics of market economies in *The General Theory* (1936), and his basic model seemed to lend itself rather naturally to a dynamic reinterpretation. With respect to microeconomics, the 1950s had witnessed so much success in elaborating and formalizing the basic Walrasian general equilibrium model in its atemporal form that an intertemporal extension seemed to be the logical next step.

The earliest models in this modern growth literature, those of Harrod (1939) and Domar (1946, 1947), were based on Keynesian-type assumptions and suggested that market economies were doomed to a "knife-edge" instability. If certain capital/output ratios were not maintained exactly, the economic system would start a cumulative tendency toward collapse. There was, according to the Harrod and Domar models, no intertemporally self-correcting tendency in a dynamic market economy. In contrast to (or in response to) these models, neoclassical models were proposed in which the substitutability of inputs and flexibility of capital/output ratios ensured much more stability and self-correcting capacity. The most significant of these early neoclassical growth models was the contribution of Robert Solow (1956), a model that eventually led to Solow's receiving the

Nobel Prize in economics. In recent years the Solow model has become the standard theoretical framework for discussing not only economic growth, but the supply/real side of macroeconomics in general, as well as the economics of technological change and a number of other subjects. We will examine only a simple version of this multifaceted economic model.

The basic Solow growth model is a one-sector macromodel: the economy produces a single good Q, which is both the capital input and the output of production. While many entertaining names have been suggested for this single good—including schmoos, putty, and leets (steel spelled backward)—it is probably easiest to think of a corn economy. The model economy produces a single output—corn—that can be either consumed or saved. The unconsumed output may be called either investment or savings, since both concepts are equivalent in such an economy (nonmonetary with no borrowing or lending).

Let s be the average propensity to save, or the fraction of total output Q that is not consumed. Thus, since investment I is always equal to savings, at any particular time t, investment is given by

$$I(t) = sQ(t). \tag{5.7}$$

Because investment is simply the change in capital stock K, equation (5.7) can be rewritten as the differential equation

$$\dot{K}(t) = sQ(t). \tag{5.8}$$

The standard Solow model does not embody an economic (endogenous) theory of population growth. The instantaneous rate of growth in population, and thus labor L, is given exogenously by the constant n. This means that n is defined by

$$n = \frac{\dot{L}(t)}{L(t)}.$$

Since $n > 0$ is exogenous, one of the fundamental questions in the model is whether the economy will converge to a capital accumulation path that maintains the continual full employment of this growing population.

The output is produced by using two inputs, capital K and labor L, according to the production function $Q = F(K, L)$. Although both Q and K are actually the same commodity (corn), it helps to use different symbols for corn as an input and corn as an output. Assuming that the production function exhibits constant returns to scale (is homogeneous of degree 1), we can write the output per worker Q/L as a function of the capital/labor ratio k alone. Thus,

$$\frac{Q}{L} = F\left(\frac{K}{L}, 1\right) = f(k). \tag{5.9}$$

We will assume that this function has the standard neoclassical properties of positive marginal products and diminishing marginal returns (discussed in Chapter 2), so: $f(0) = 0$, $f'(k) > 0$, and $f''(k) < 0$ for all $k > 0$.

Remembering that both k and L are functions of t, we can differentiate k to obtain an expression for the change in the capital/labor ratio over time. By application of the quotient rule to the function $k(t) = K(t)/L(t)$ we have

$$\dot{k}(t) = \frac{L(t)\dot{K}(t) - K(t)\dot{L}(t)}{[L(t)]^2}, \tag{5.10}$$

where $\dot{k} = dk/dt$. With some rearrangement (5.10) becomes

$$\dot{k}(t) = \frac{\dot{K}(t)}{L(t)} - k\frac{\dot{L}(t)}{L(t)}. \tag{5.11}$$

By substituting from (5.8), (5.9), and the definition of n, we can convert (5.11) into the relatively simple expression

$$\dot{k} = sf(k) - nk. \tag{5.12}$$

Equation (5.12) is the **fundamental equation of motion** for the basic Solow growth model. It describes the movement of the economy's capital/labor ratio k through time for any given rate of population growth n and average propensity to save s.

Since the equilibrium will be given by $\dot{k} = 0$, equation (5.12) tells us that the equilibrium value of the capital/labor ratio k^* must satisfy the equation

$$sf(k^*) - nk^* = 0. \tag{5.13}$$

At this k^*, the exogenous growth in the labor force is exactly matched by the growth in the capital stock. Once k^* has been reached: output, consumption, and investment all grow continuously at the same percentage rate. This equilibrium is often called the "balanced growth" path of the economy. It is not an equilibrium in the sense that nothing moves; it is an equilibrium in the sense that everything is moving together (growing at the same rate).

There is an obvious question about whether this balanced growth path will be reached. As suggested, the Harrod and Domar precursors to the Solow model exhibited a so-called knife-edge instability. Is this also true in the Solow model, or does the dynamic path generated by (5.12) always converge to k^*? This stability question will be addressed in two ways. First, we prove the local stability of k^* by using Theorem 5.1. Second, we use diagrams to discuss global stability more informally.

To facilitate the application of Theorem 5.1, we rewrite (5.12) as

$$\dot{k} = H(k), \quad \text{where } H(k) = sf(k) - nk. \tag{5.14}$$

From Theorem 5.1, we know that k^*, the equilibrium ratio of capital to labor, will be locally stable if $H'(k^*) = sf'(k^*) - n < 0$ or $sf'(k^*) < n$. Since $f'(k^*) > 0$ and $n > 0$, the stability of k^* will be guaranteed if the ray nk cuts the savings function $sf(k)$ from below at k^*.

Figure 5.11 demonstrates that because of the neoclassical characteristics of the production function, any strictly positive k^* will satisfy this local stability condition. Figure 5.12 shows that without the restriction that $k^* > 0$, $k^* = 0$ may

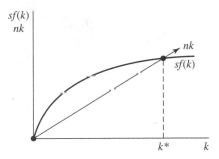

Figure 5.11

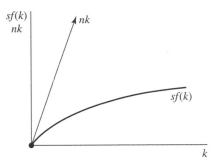

Figure 5.12

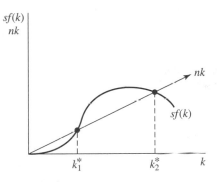

Figure 5.13

be an equilibrium for the model, even under the neoclassical assumptions on the production function. A strictly positive steady-state capital/labor ratio can be guaranteed by the imposition of an additional boundary restriction such as $f'(0) > n$. If the production function does not satisfy the neoclassical strict concavity condition $f''(k) < 0$, there may be more than one equilibrium capital/labor ratio. But as Figure 5.13 demonstrates, those that satisfy the stability condition $sf'(k^*) < n$ will still be locally stable (like k_2^* in Figure 5.13).

Figure 5.11 can be used to informally discuss the global stability of k^* without using the result in Theorem 5.1. Simply note that for any $k < k^*$, we have that $\dot{k} = sf(k) - nk > 0$, and so k increases toward k^*. For any $k > k^*$ we have that $\dot{k} = sf(k) - nk < 0$, and so k falls toward k^*. Thus, for any initial k, no matter how far it is from k^*, the capital/labor ratio converges toward k^*. Under the neoclassical restrictions on the production function, any strictly positive k^* is globally stable.[2] The Solow model thus avoids the knife-edge stability problems of the early models of the Harrod and Domar type. This stability comes as a result of the assumptions on the model's production function.

The analysis of the local stability of k^* completes our discussion of the basic Solow growth model. The question of the comparative statics (actually comparative dynamics) properties of the Solow model is deferred to the problems at the end of the chapter.

BOX 5.1
Optimal Economic Growth in a One-Sector Neoclassical Model

The Solow model in the text focuses on describing how a particular one-sector economy would evolve through time given the technology, the community's savings behavior, and continuous equilibrium in all markets. Suppose that instead of describing the behavior of such an economy, we are interested in the theory of **optimal** economic growth: not merely what would happen under the conditions of the model, but what ought to happen in an economy given some criterion of social welfare. In other words, consider a social planner's problem in which the constraints are given by the Solow growth model, but the capital accumulation and consumption choices are determined on the basis of maximizing some index of the total social welfare. Such optimal growth models were introduced by Ramsey (1928); the field became a major research area in the 1960s and 1970s with Cass (1965), Koopmans (1965), and Dorfman (1969) being a small sample of the many significant contributions. Our discussion follows Intriligator (1971) and Takayama (1985).

First let us formally introduce consumption into the text's Solow growth model. Since per capita savings is given by $sf(k)$ and since all output is either consumed or saved, we have

$$c(t) = f[k(t)] - sf[k(t)] = (1-s)f[k(t)]$$

as the per capita consumption at time t. Rewriting the equation of motion of the Solow model (5.12) in terms of consumption, we have

$$\dot{k} = f[k(t)] - c(t) - nk(t). \tag{a}$$

This differential equation describes the movement of the capital/labor ratio through time in the optimal growth model, just as it did for the simpler Solow model. The difference is that now this equation of motion (a) describes only the "feasible path" for the economy; it is a constraint on the optimization problem of the social planner.

The objective function of the problem is to maximize the societal welfare J, where welfare is given by

$$J = \int_0^T u[c(t)]e^{-rt}\,dt.$$

In this expression $u[c(t)]$ gives the utility as a function of per capita consumption; it is assumed to be monotonic and concave [i.e., $u' > 0$ and $u'' < 0$ for all $c(t) \geq 0$]. The problem has a finite planning horizon starting at $t = 0$ and ending at $t = T$, and the term e^{-rt} discounts the future utility back to present value. Many other objective functions have appeared in the optimal growth literature, but J is a relatively standard way of characterizing social welfare. In addition to the equation of motion (a), the problem will be constrained by an initial and terminal value of the capital/labor ratio k: $k(0) = k_0$ and $k(T) = k_T \geq 0$.

Combining all the pieces, we have the following characterization of the optimal growth problem:

$$\underset{\{c\}}{\text{Max }} J = \int_0^T u[c(t)] e^{-rt} dt$$

$$\text{Subject to}: \quad \dot{k} = f[k(t)] - c(t) - nk(t),$$

$$k(t) \geq 0, c(t) \geq 0,$$

$$k(0) = k_0 > 0,$$

$$k(T) = k_T > 0.$$

The solution to the problem can be characterized either by applying the classical calculus of variations or by using techniques from optimal control theory (maximum principle). Since both techniques are beyond the scope of this text, we simply write down the first-order (necessary) conditions for an interior solution and refer the interested reader to the sources cited for a more detailed discussion. The necessary condition is given by

$$\dot{c}(t) = -\left(\frac{u'}{u''}\right)(f'[k(t)] - n - r). \tag{b}$$

This condition may not seem to have a particularly obvious economic interpretation, but it basically requires the marginal product of capital f' to equal the sum of the rates of time preference r, population growth n, and the change in the marginal utility of savings $-\dot{c}u''/u'$.

The consumption/capital accumulation path $[c(t), k(t)]$ that satisfies both the feasibility condition (a) and the optimality condition (b) as well as the initial and terminal constraints k_0 and k_T is the **solution path,** or the **optimal growth path,** for the economy. Along this path, social welfare J is maximized over the set of all feasible paths available to the economy.

Sources

Cass, D. 1965. Optimal growth in an aggregate model of capital accumulation. *Review of Economic Studies* 32: 233–40.

Dorfman, R. 1969. An economic interpretation of optimal control theory. *American Economic Review* 59: 817–31.

Intriligator, M. D. 1971. *Mathematical optimization and economic theory.* Englewood Cliffs, NJ: Prentice-Hall.

Koopmans, T. C. 1965. On the concept of optimal economic growth. In *The Economic Approach to Development Planning.* Amsterdam: North-Holland, 225–300.

Ramsey, F. P. 1928. A mathematical theory of savings. *Economic Journal* 38: 543–59.

Takayama, A. 1985. *Mathematical economics.* 2nd ed. Cambridge: Cambridge University Press.

Inflationary Dynamics

In this subsection we discuss another topic that has concerned economists for almost as long as the question of economic growth; the quantity theory of money. Specifically, we discuss Phillip Cagan's (1956) classic study of the relationship between the growth of money stock and extremely high inflation rates (hyperinflation). This research has been very important in the development of modern macroeconomics, and it offers a rather nice example of the stability result in Theorem 5.1.

Cagan was concerned with the validity of the quantity theory of money during periods of hyperinflation. Since the simple quantity theory states that inflation can come about only as the result of an increase in the money supply, periods of hyperinflation offer an excellent test of the quantity theory. According to the theory, these periods of rapidly accelerating prices should be accompanied (or preceded) by periods of rapidly accelerating monetary growth, and without this monetary growth, hyperinflation would not be possible.

Cagan recognized that two aspects of monetary behavior interact in a way that presents difficulties for a strict quantity theory of hyperinflation. The first is that expected inflation affects the demand for real money balances. The second source of difficulty is the influence exerted by the level of actual inflation on expected inflation itself. The higher the actual (observed) level of inflation, the higher the expected inflation will be. The interaction of these two factors presents problems for the quantity theory in the following way. Starting from a position of a steady rate of inflation and a steady growth in the money supply, suppose there is (for whatever reason) an increase in the expected rate of inflation. This increase in expected inflation will reduce the demand for real money balances. This reduction in the demand for money will cause an increase in the demand for goods. This increased demand for goods then puts additional upward pressure on prices, producing a higher rate of inflation. But this higher rate of inflation will further reduce the demand for real money balances, and so on. Thus, because of the interaction of these two factors, there is the possibility of a self-generating "flight from money" that results in an explosive hyperinflation even without an acceleration in the growth of the money supply.

Because of such a possibility, the theoretical part of Cagan's paper was concerned with precisely this interaction and the conditions under which such a self-generating inflationary process could develop. After deriving the conditions under which such a process could develop, Cagan presented empirical evidence to demonstrate that such conditions had not existed in actual episodes of hyperinflation. We focus exclusively on the theoretical analysis in Cagan's paper.

The demand for real money balances $(M/p)^D$ is a function of the expected rate of inflation π^e; we assume the following functional form:

$$\ln\left(\frac{M}{p}\right)^D = -\alpha\pi^e, \tag{5.15}$$

with α a positive scalar. If the money market always clears (as Cagan assumed), then (5.15) describes not only the demand for money but also that of the real money supply.

Now consider the expected rate of inflation (π^e), which depends on the actual rate of inflation π. If actual inflation is higher than expected inflation, then expectations will be revised upward. If actual inflation is less than expected inflation, expectations will be revised downward. Thus, this adjustment mechanism can be described by the differential equation

$$\dot{\pi}^e = \beta(\pi - \pi^e), \tag{5.16}$$

where β is a positive scalar. When $0 < \beta < 1$, equation (5.16) describes what is known as an **adaptive expectations** scheme. Such a method of expectation revision implies that expectations are revised by some fraction of the preceding forecasting error. Even though Cagan was a pioneer in the use of such an adaptive scheme, we should note that expectations formed in this way are not "rational"; the expected change in the rate of inflation is not equal to the actual change in the rate of inflation.

Since M, p, and π^e are all functions of time, we can differentiate (5.15) with respect to time to determine the relationship between a change in the money supply and a change in the expected rate of inflation. This differentiation yields

$$\frac{\dot{M}}{M} - \pi = -\alpha\dot{\pi}^e, \tag{5.17}$$

since $\pi = \dot{p}/p$. Substituting the change in expected inflation from (5.16) into (5.17), we have

$$\frac{\dot{M}}{M} - \pi = -\alpha\beta(\pi - \pi^e), \tag{5.18}$$

which after rearrangement gives

$$\pi = \frac{\dot{M}/M}{1 - \alpha\beta} - \frac{\alpha\beta\pi^e}{1 - \alpha\beta}. \tag{5.19}$$

Equation (5.19) describes the rate of inflation as a function of the rate of monetary growth $\dot{M}/M$ and the expected rate of inflation π^e.

We are interested in the behavior of the inflation rate over time $\dot{\pi}$, in particular whether π can increase constantly when the rate of monetary growth is constant. To obtain an expression for this behavior, we simply differentiate (5.19), assuming that $d(\dot{M}/M)/dt = 0$. This differentiation yields

$$\dot{\pi} = -\left(\frac{\alpha\beta}{1 - \alpha\beta}\right)\dot{\pi}^e. \tag{5.20}$$

From (5.20) we see that the equilibrium or steady-state rate of inflation is where $\dot{\pi}^e = 0$. Substituting this condition into (5.17) gives us the equilibrium rate of inflation $\pi^* = \dot{M}/M$.

The question of hyperinflation under constant monetary growth is really a question of the stability of the differential equation (5.20). If π^* is a stable equilibrium, then for any initial π^e, the rate of inflation will eventually converge to π^*; and more importantly, the possibility of hyperinflation is ruled out. Since the right-hand side of (5.20) contains the time derivative of expected inflation, a few more substitutions are required before Theorem 5.1 can be applied to the stability question.

First, we substitute the expectation adjustment equation (5.16) into the right-hand side of (5.20). This gives

$$\dot{\pi} = \frac{-\alpha\beta^2\pi}{1 - \alpha\beta} + \frac{\alpha\beta^2\pi^e}{1 - \alpha\beta}. \tag{5.21}$$

Now we eliminate expected inflation from the right-hand side of (5.21) by substituting from the original money demand equation (5.15). This yields

$$\dot{\pi} = \left(\frac{-\alpha\beta^2}{1 - \alpha\beta}\right)\pi + \frac{\beta^2 \ln(M/p)}{1 - \alpha\beta}. \tag{5.22}$$

The differential equation (5.22) now expresses the change in the rate of inflation $\dot{\pi}$ as a function of the rate of inflation π itself. By Theorem 5.1, the stability of π^* is guaranteed when $-\alpha\beta^2/(1 - \alpha\beta) < 0$. Since α is a positive scalar, this stability condition reduces to

$$\alpha\beta < 1. \tag{5.23}$$

Thus stability is implied by the product $\alpha\beta$, what Cagan called the "reaction index," being less than unity.

Since the right side of (5.22) is **linear** in π, the condition in (5.23) is not only sufficient for the stability of π^* but also **necessary.** Thus, π^* could be unstable **only** if $\alpha\beta \geq 1$; and this is precisely the proposition that Cagan put to an empirical test. If the sensitivity of the demand for money with respect to the expected rate of inflation and the sensitivity of the expected rate of inflation to the actual rate of inflation are both small (as Cagan found empirically), then self-generating hyperinflation is not possible. Finally, since (5.22) is linear in π, these results hold globally as well as locally.

5.3   Multiple-Market Competitive Equilibrium

A Three-Good General Equilibrium Model

In Section 5.1 we discussed the stability of one-dimensional economic models. We are now ready to examine two-dimensional systems, dynamic economic mod-

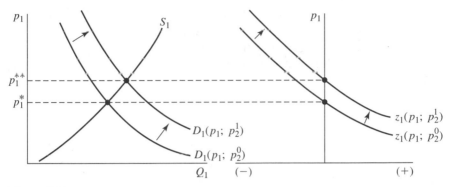

Figure 5.14

els in which two variables are changing simultaneously through time. To analyze the stability of these two-dimensional systems, we will use the **phase diagram technique,** introduced in the next subsection. First it is useful to develop the general equilibrium model that will serve as the technique's first application.

The general equilibrium model is actually more than just an economic model; it serves as the prototype for almost all equilibrium analysis involving more than one market. We shall examine a small Walrasian general equilibrium system having three goods and one market (demand and supply) for each good. Equilibrium is characterized by a price vector (one price for each good) that clears all three markets simultaneously. Each market is fully characterized by its excess-demand function, but unlike the excess demands introduced earlier in this chapter, these are **interdependent.** Thus, the excess demand for good 1 depends not only on the price of good 1 (as in the preceding discussion) but also on the prices of the other goods. These other goods might be substitutes for good 1, complements to good 1, or even factors used to produce good 1 (remember, excess demand includes the supply function); but in any of these cases a change in the price of the other goods will directly affect the excess demand for good 1. In Figure 5.14, for example, the left-hand side depicts the market for good 1, and the right-hand side shows the excess demand for good 1. The figure shows that an increase in the price of good 2 (from p_2^0 to p_2^1) will shift the demand (and excess demand) for good 1 outward, raising its equilibrium price.

Such interrelated markets make stability analysis much more complicated than in the single-market (partial equilibrium) case. A change in the price of one good will, or at least can, change the excess demands, and thus prices, of all other goods. If all markets are initially in equilibrium and the price of one good changes (for whatever reason), the equilibrium in all the other markets will/may be disturbed. These changes in the prices of other goods then feed back into the market for the good that initiated the disturbance, further changing its price. If the system is **stable,** it will eventually settle back down to a new general equilibrium price vector that clears all markets. If the system is not stable, the prices may cycle around forever or blow off to the boundary of the price domain.

Turning now to the three-good case,[3] we let $z_i(p) = z_i(p_1, p_2, p_3)$ be the excess demand function for goods $i = 1, 2, 3$ with $p = (p_1, p_2, p_3) \in \Re^3_{++}$. The general equilibrium price vector $p^* = (p_1^*, p_2^*, p_3^*)$ is a set of prices such that $z_i(p^*) = 0$ for all i. As in the single-market case, the behavior of prices outside equilibrium can be described by an ordinary differential equation. Thus,

$$\dot{p}(t) = \frac{dp_i}{dt} = \delta_i z_i[p(t)] \qquad \text{for all } i = 1, 2, 3 \qquad (5.24)$$

describes the **law of supply and demand** for the three markets (with $\delta_i > 0$ for all i). At the equilibrium price vector p^*, each excess demand function is equal to zero and the price adjustment generated by the system of differential equations in (5.24) terminates, since $\dot{p}_i = \delta_i z_i(p^*) = 0$ for all i.

Before we examine dynamics and the phase diagram technique that will be used to discuss the stability of (5.24), it is useful to discuss some of the standard properties of Walrasian general equilibrium models. The first is known as **Walras' law.** For an n-good general equilibrium model, Walras' law (W) states that

$$\sum_{i=1}^{n} p_i z_i(p) = 0 \qquad \text{for all } p. \qquad (W)$$

It is easiest to see the necessity of Walras' law in the case of a pure exchange (no production) economy. Consider such an economy with n goods and H traders. If each trader h receives a certain initial "endowment" of the n goods given by $\omega^h = (\omega_1^h, \ldots, \omega_n^h)$, then the total income available to trader h when price vector p prevails is given by

$$I^h = \sum_{i=1}^{n} p_i \omega_i^h.$$

If trader h demands quantities $x^h = (x_1^h, \ldots, x_n^h)$ from the market, the budget constraint for trader h is

$$\sum_{i=1}^{n} p_i x_i^h = \sum_{i=1}^{n} p_i \omega_i^h. \qquad (5.25)$$

Rearranging (5.25) and summing over all H traders gives

$$\sum_{h=1}^{H} \sum_{i=1}^{n} p_i \left(x_i^h - \omega_i^h \right) = \sum_{i=1}^{n} p_i \sum_{h=1}^{H} \left(x_i^h - \omega_i^h \right) = 0. \qquad (5.26)$$

Since in this pure exchange economy $\sum_h \omega_i^h$ is the total supply of good i and $\sum_h x_i^h$ is the total demand for good i, (5.26) reduces to Walras' law. For an economy with production, the demonstration is more difficult, but under quite reasonable assumptions on the supply side, (W) will hold for that case as well.

Walras' law has a number of important implications that are used in or discussion of the three-good case as well as in later chapters. First, note that (W) holds for all prices, not just at equilibrium. Thus, (W) is a global restriction on the relationship between prices and excess demands.

Second, if a price vector is found that clears $n - 1$ of the markets in the n-good case, the same price vector will also clear the nth market. For example, let $p' = (p'_1, \ldots, p'_n)$ be a price vector that clears all markets except for the jth. Then by Walras' law we have

$$\sum_{\substack{i=1 \\ i \neq j}}^{n} p'_i z_i(p') = -p'_j z_j(p'). \tag{5.27}$$

Since $z_i(p') = 0$ for all $i \neq j$, the left-hand side of (5.27) sums to zero, and we have $z_j(p') = 0$ as well, thus demonstrating that any price vector that clears $n - 1$ markets is a general equilibrium price vector for the entire system.

Finally, consider the more complex case in which prices are restricted to the nonnegative, rather than strictly positive, orthant. For this case, where $p^* \in \mathfrak{R}_+^n$, then p^* is a general equilibrium price vector if $z_i(p^*) \leq 0$ for all i. Application of Walras' law to such an equilibrium implies that $p_i^* z_i(p^*) = 0$ for each i. This result is obtained by combining $p_i^* \leq 0$ for all i with (W) and the equilibrium condition. Thus, Walras' law implies that in an economy where boundary equilibria are a possibility, the following conditions hold for the equilibrium price vector p^*:

$$p_i^* > 0 \qquad \text{implies that } z_i(p^*) = 0, \tag{5.28a}$$

and

$$z_i(p^*) < 0 \qquad \text{implies that } p_i^* = 0. \tag{5.28b}$$

Condition (5.28a) states that in markets with positive equilibrium prices, excess demand is zero in equilibrium (as is true with strictly positive prices), while (5.28b) states that goods with excess supply (negative excess demand) in equilibrium must have zero prices. The latter case corresponds to the classic definition of a free good. The two conditions (5.28a) and (5.28b) taken together are often called **complementary-slackness conditions** because they say that for each i, only one of the variables p or z can be slack (i.e., nonzero). We will encounter other complementary-slackness conditions in later chapters.

The second general property of Walrasian systems of interest is the **zero-degree homogeneity** (H) of excess demand functions. Recalling the definition of homogeneity from Chapter 2, this condition requires

$$z_i(p) = z_i(\lambda p) \qquad \text{for all } \lambda \in \mathfrak{R}_{++} \text{ and all } p. \tag{H}$$

The zero-degree homogeneity is the economic property of **no money illusion.** As with Walras' law, this condition is most obvious in the pure exchange case [from (5.28)], but it also holds for production economies under rather standard assumptions.

One implication of (H) is that the equilibrium price vector is actually a ray rather than a point in the price domain. This is because λp^* gives exactly the same value for all excess demands as p^*, since $z_i(p^*) = z_i(\lambda p^*) = 0$ for all i and for all $\lambda > 0$. Another implication of (H) is that prices can be "normalized" in any number of ways without destroying the properties of excess demands. For instance, we could redefine all prices so that they sum to unity. This amounts to multiplying all prices by $\lambda = 1/\sum_i p_i$, which of course leaves all excess demands the same under (H). The normalization we shall use involves choosing one good as the "numeraire" and measuring all prices in terms of the price of this good. If good j is the numeraire, this normalization amount to multiplying all prices by $\lambda = 1/p_j$, which also leaves all excess demands unchanged under (H).

Returning now to the three-good case and the adjustment mechanism given in (5.24), we are interested in the equilibrium of the following system:

$$z_1(p) = z_1(p_1, p_2, p_3),$$
$$z_2(p) = z_2(p_1, p_2, p_3),$$
$$z_3(p) = z_3(p_1, p_2, p_3).$$

To reduce the number of variables, let us normalize prices by choosing good 3 as numeraire.[4] Multiplying all prices by $1/p_3$ reduces the system to the following three functions of two variables:

$$z_i(p) = z_i(p_1, p_2) \qquad \text{for all } i = 1, 2, 3.$$

But we can reduce this system still further. Since Walras' law implies that the market for good 3 will automatically clear when the other two markets clear, there is no reason to explicitly consider the market for good 3. If the adjustment mechanism for goods 1 and 2 [given in (5.24)] converges to the equilibrium price vector $p^* = (p_1^*, p_2^*)$, then the market for good 3 will also clear at these prices. Thus judicious application of (W) and (H) has reduced the equilibrium of the three-good Walrasian system to the following two equations in two unknowns:

$$z_1(p^*) = z_1(p_1^*, p_2^*) = 0,$$
$$z_2(p^*) = z_2(p_1^*, p_2^*) = 0. \tag{5.29}$$

The equilibrium price vector for this system is depicted in Figure 5.15, assuming uniqueness (there is only one equilibrium ray). We now turn to the question of stability.

The Phase Diagram Technique

We use the phase diagram technique to analyze the stability of the (now) two-good Walrasian general equilibrium system. This method of analyzing economic dynamics has a long history, dating back at least to Alfred Marshall at the end of the nineteenth century.

Let us write the two equilibrium conditions as

$$z_1(p_1, p_2) = 0, \tag{5.30a}$$

$$z_2(p_1, p_2) = 0. \tag{5.30b}$$

Equation (5.30a) describes the set of all combinations of p_1 and p_2 that clear the market for good 1, and correspondingly equation (5.30b) describes the set of all combinations of p_1 and p_2 that clear the market for good 2. These two equations trace out two curves in (p_1, p_2)-space. The intersection of these two curves

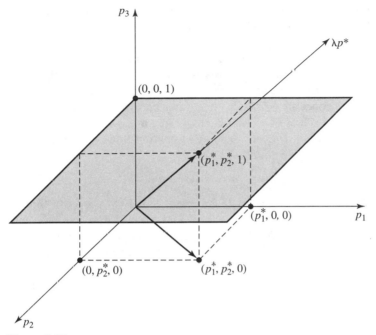

Figure 5.15

corresponds to the general equilibrium price vector p^*. Since the behavior of the system at any point in (p_1, p_2)-space outside of equilibrium is governed by the differential equations in (5.24), p_1 does not change at any point satisfying the equation (5.30a) and p_2 does not change at any point satisfying (5.30b).

If the excess demand functions were known explicitly, we could plot the curves in (p_1, p_2)-space and solve for the equilibrium. In general, though, we do not know the excess demand functions explicitly. What we do know is some general characteristics of the functions (i.e., qualitative information) such as (W) and (H). In the general case, much information can be obtained regarding the disequilibrium behavior of the system by determining the slopes of (5.30a) and (5.30b) in (p_1, p_2)-space. By taking the total differential of these two equations and remembering that $dz_1 = 0$ and $dz_2 = 0$, we have

$$\left.\frac{dp_2}{dp_1}\right|_{z_1=0} = \frac{-z_{11}}{z_{12}}, \tag{5.31a}$$

$$\left.\frac{dp_2}{dp_1}\right|_{z_2=0} = \frac{-z_{21}}{z_{22}}, \tag{5.31b}$$

where $z_{ij} = \partial z_i/\partial p_j$. The expression in (5.31a) describes the slope of the $z_1 = 0$ curve in (p_1, p_2)-space, while (5.31b) describes the slope of the $z_2 = 0$, curve in the same domain. It would be nice if these terms were always signed by some obvious economic condition like (W) and/or (H). Unfortunately that is not the case. As we know from microeconomic theory, utility maximization does not rule out upward-sloping demands. Thus either $z_{ii} > 0$ or $z_{ii} < 0$ is possible, even in the simplest case of pure exchange.

The economic condition that we use to sign these terms is the gross substitute condition. Two goods i and j are called **gross substitutes (GS)** if $z_{ij} > 0$, that is, if an increase in the price of one good increases the excess demand for the other.[5] If we assume that all goods are gross substitutes, then both (5.31a) and (5.31b) will be positive. This is a result of Euler's theorem (Theorem 2.1) and the zero-degree homogeneity of the excess demand functions. Applying Euler's theorem to the excess demand for good 1, we have

$$z_{11}p_1 + z_{12}p_2 + z_{13}p_3 = 0.$$

Since prices are strictly positive, $z_{12} > 0$ and $z_{13} > 0$ imply that $z_{11} < 0$. Similar results hold for good 2. Applying these signs to (5.31a) and (5.31b), we know that both $z_1 = 0$ and $z_2 = 0$ slope upward. If the equilibrium price vector is unique (as implied by *GS*, although we will not prove it), there are only two possibilities for the curves $z_1(p_1, p_2) = 0$ and $z_2(p_1, p_2) = 0$. These are given in Figure 5.16.

To investigate the stability of these two cases, it is necessary to determine the direction of the change in p_1 and p_2 from any point off the curves (5.30a) and (5.30b). In Figure 5.17 these two curves have been separated. Examine

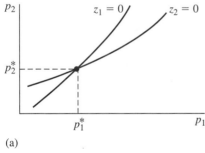

(a)   (b)

Figure 5.16

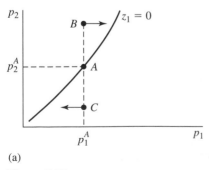

(a)

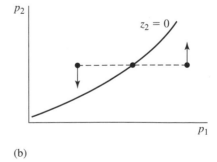

(b)

Figure 5.17

Figure 5.17a first. At point A we have prices (p_1^A, p_2^A), and the market for good 1 is in equilibrium. Now consider moving from point A to an arbitrary disequilibrium point above the curve such as B. In moving from A to B we have increased p_2 without changing p_1. Since these goods are gross substitutes, we have $z_{12} > 0$, and so this increase in p_2 will cause the excess demand for good 1 to increase. Now since the excess demand for good 1 was zero at A, z_1 must be strictly positive at a point like B. By the adjustment mechanism (5.24), this positive excess demand for good 1 will cause an **increase** in the **price of good 1.** Thus from a point like B the price of good 1 will increase, as indicated by the arrow pointing rightward at point B. Since B was chosen arbitrarily, similar increases in the price of good 1 would occur from any other point above the $z_1 = 0$ curve. An identical argument implies that the price of good 1 will decrease from any point below the $z_1 = 0$ curve, and this is shown by the arrow pointing leftward at point C in Figure 5.17a. Thus the gross substitute assumption allows us to completely specify the direction of the dynamic adjustment that will take place from any arbitrary point off (above or below) the $z_1 = 0$ curve.

Figure 5.17b depicts analogous results for good 2. In the case of good 2 we start from an arbitrary point off the curve $z_2 = 0$, which changes p_1 but not p_2 (a point to the right or left of an initial point), and repeat the gross substitute argument we used for good 1. The arrows in Figure 5.17b show that the price of good 2 will increase for disequilibrium prices to the right of the curve $z_2 = 0$ and decrease for prices to the left of it.

By transferring the arrows from Figure 5.17 to the two possible configurations depicted earlier in Figure 5.16, we obtain the two **phase diagrams** given in Figure 5.18. Figure 5.18a shows the behavior of prices outside equilibrium for the case in Figure 5.16a, where the $z_1 = 0$ curve cuts the $z_2 = 0$ curve from below. Figure 5.18b exhibits the price movements for the case in Figure 5.16b, where $z_1 = 0$ cuts $z_2 = 0$ from above. Consider Figure 5.18a first.

In Figure 5.18a the dashed arrows indicate the approximate direction of the price movement in each of the four quadrants defined by the curves $z_1 = 0$ and $z_2 = 0$. We say "approximate" because the exact path from any point is determined by the magnitude of the excess demand (not simply the sign) and the speeds of adjustment, given as δ_1 and δ_2 in (5.24). From a point like D, the price of good 2 will fall and the price of good 1 will rise until the $z_2 = 0$, curve is reached. At that point, the price of good 2 will stop changing, but p_1 will continue to increase. Thus the price path will leave its intersection with $z_2 = 0$, traveling horizontally toward increasing p_1. Upon entering the southwest quadrant, prices are pulled in the direction of increasing both p_1 and p_2. This is indicated by the dashed arrow in the lower left-hand corner of the figure. This movement continues until the general equilibrium price vector p^* is reached. Since similar results would be obtained for any other initial point (such as E), Figure 5.18a depicts the case of a **globally stable** general equilibrium price vector. No matter where the initial price vector lies within the price domain, the system will **converge** to the general equilibrium price vector p^*. Or to state it a bit more formally, for the case depicted in Figure 5.18a

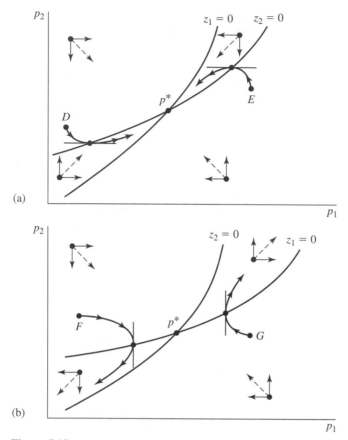

Figure 5.18

we know that

$$\lim_{t \to \infty} p_1(t) = p_1^* \qquad \text{and} \qquad \lim_{t \to \infty} p_2(t) = p_2^*$$

for all $p(0) = [p_1(0), p_2(0)] \in \Re_{++}^2$. This stable case is translated back into three dimensions in Figure 5.19.

Now examining Figure 5.18b, we see a different (in fact, opposite) case: prices **diverge** from p^* for almost all initial positions.[6] Thus Figure 5.18b depicts an **unstable** general equilibrium system; from almost any initial position in the price domain, prices explode away from p^*.

Figure 5.18a can also be used to derive a simpler algebraic stability condition for this model. For the stable case in Figure 5.18a, the slope of $z_1 = 0$ is greater than the slope of $z_2 = 0$. Writing out this condition, we have

$$\frac{-z_{11}}{z_{12}} > \frac{-z_{21}}{z_{22}}. \tag{5.32}$$

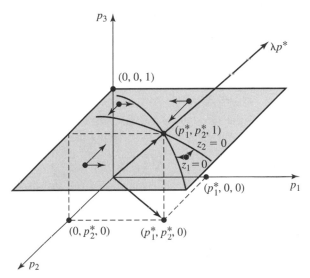

Figure 5.19

Remembering the sign of each term and rearranging, we get

$$z_{11}z_{22} - z_{12}z_{21} > 0. \tag{5.33}$$

The condition (5.33) is clearly sufficient for the stability of this three-good Walrasian model. At this point we have not ruled out the possibility of the unstable case depicted in Figure 5.18b. In the next section we will eliminate the unstable case by showing that it is inconsistent with the restrictions of the gross substitute system. This means that the inequality in (5.33) is implied by the basic assumptions of the gross substitute Walrasian model.

Another way of stating the condition in (5.33) is to say that matrix Z has a positive determinant[7]

$$Z = \begin{bmatrix} z_{11} & z_{12} \\ z_{21} & z_{22} \end{bmatrix}. \tag{5.34}$$

Given that $z_1 = 0$ and $z_2 < 0$ cross but once, condition (5.34) need be checked only at equilibrium prices. This greatly simplifies the analysis of stability. The phase diagram technique often allows us to derive such simplified stability conditions for other dynamic economic models as well.

Since $z_{11} < 0$ and $z_{22} < 0$, the stability condition in (5.33) might seem familiar from the second-order conditions for maximizing a function of two variables (discussed in Chapter 3). For instance, if we intended to maximize a function $z(p_1, p_2)$ and defined z_{ij} as $\partial^2 z / \partial p_i \partial p_j$, then the condition in (5.33) would be one of the second-order conditions for a maximum. This analogy should not be carried too far though. In general, for equilibrium systems there is no function such as $z(p_1, p_2)$; z_{ij} is a first, not a second, derivative; and there is no maximization, only disequilibrium dynamics. Nevertheless, despite these substantial differences, stability conditions for equilibrium systems often (but not always) can be used to sign comparative statics expressions in the same way as second-order conditions are used to sign comparative statics expressions in optimization problems.

Stability in the Three-Good Gross Substitute Case

The principal reason for discussing the three-good Walrasian general equilibrium model is that it provides an excellent vehicle for introducing the phase diagram technique, a technique that is applicable to a large number of dynamic models. Before moving on to other applications, in Section 5.4, let us (in the interest of completeness) derive one final result for the Walrasian gross substitute system.

In this section we show that the two cases illustrated in Figure 5.16 do **not** represent two different possibilities for the three-good gross substitute system. The situation depicted in Figure 5.16b, where $z_1 = 0$ cuts $z_2 = 0$ from above, is inconsistent with the assumptions of the model. For the three-good Walrasian system in which all goods are gross substitutes, the only possible case is depicted in Figure 5.16a. Since Figure 5.16a is the stable case, the gross substitute system is always stable, and it is not necessary to impose any additional restrictions on the model such as (5.33) to ensure that prices will converge to the general equilibrium price vector p^*.

To demonstrate this result, consider Figure 5.20, which reproduces the unstable cases from Figures 5.16b and 5.18b. Consider any point such as p' in the northeast orthant where $p_1' > p_1^*$ and $p_2' > p_2^*$. Thus if we let $dp_1, dp_2,$ and dp_3 represent the change from p^* to p', we have $dp_1 > 0, dp_2 > 0,$ and $dp_3 = 0$, since $p_3 = 1$ for both price vectors. Given the location of p_1', above $z_1 = 0$ and to the right of $z_2 = 0$, we have $z_1(p') > 0$ and $z_2(p') > 0$. This is because moving from p^* to p' increases the excess demand for both goods; but since both excess demands were zero at p^*, they must both be positive at p'.

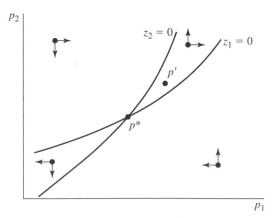

Figure 5.20

BOX 5.2
Counterexamples to Walrasian Stability

The text's discussion of stability in a gross substitute system might lead the reader to assume that stability always prevails in Walrasian general equilibrium models. This is not the case; in fact, stability (particularly global) has been shown for only a small number of special cases, and the gross substitute system is the most economically reasonable of those special cases. In the early work on the stability of the Walrasian system in the 1940s and 1950s, it was suspected that stability could be demonstrated for a wide class of general equilibrium models. By the 1970s this optimistic view had clearly waned.

Two of the causes for this pessimism about Walrasian stability were the influential papers by Herbert Scarf (1960) and David Gale (1963). Both papers demonstrated that unstable equilibria can exist in even relatively simple Walrasian models with only a small number of goods and economically quite reasonable assumptions. In the Scarf counterexample, instability appeared when a particular type of complementarity was introduced into a three-good, three-consumer model. In the Gale counterexample, it was demonstrated that the two-good price adjustment mechanism

$$\dot{p}_1 = \lambda_1 z_1[p(t)]$$
$$\dot{p}_2 = \lambda_2 z_2[p(t)]$$

will always be unstable for some values of the adjustment speeds λ_1 and λ_2 if either good is **Giffen** (i.e., if $\partial z_i / \partial p_i > 0$ for either i). Since neither of these two counterexamples is based on particularly unreasonable economic assumptions, most economists became convinced that global stability was a special case rather than a general property of Walrasian general equilibrium models. This conclusion was further supported by later work, the so-called Debreu–Mantel–Sonnenschein results on aggregate excess demand functions, which demonstrated that the standard assumptions on economic behavior place almost no restrictions on aggregate excess demand functions other than Walras' law (W) and zero-degree homogeneity (H). These results further support those of Gale and Scarf, since the fewer restrictions imposed by economic theory on aggregate excess demands, the more leeway is available to construct unstable counterexamples. The Shafer and Sonnenschein (1982) paper provides a nice survey of this work on aggregate excess demand functions and contains references to the original papers.

Sources
Gale, D. 1963. A note on global instability of competitive equilibrium. *Naval Research Logistics Quarterly* 10: 81–7.

Scarf, H. 1960. Some examples of global instability of the competitive equilibrium. *International Economic Review* 1: 57–72.

Shafer, W., and H. Sonnenschein. 1982. *Market demand and excess demand functions*. In *Handbook of Mathematical Economics,* Vol. 2, edited by K. J. Arrow and M. D. Intriligator. Amsterdam: North-Holland, 671–93.

Now consider the excess demand for good 3. Taking the total differential of $z_3(p)$, we have

$$dz_3 = z_{31}\, dp_1 + z_{32}\, dp_2 + z_{33}\, dp_3. \tag{5.35}$$

Since $z_{31} > 0$, $z_{32} > 0$, $dp_1 > 0$, $dp_2 > 0$, and $dp_3 = 0$, equation (5.35) implies that $dz_3 > 0$. This means that the excess demand for good 3 is positive at p' as well. But $z_3(p') > 0$ is a contradiction of Walras' law, which requires that $\sum_i p_i' z_i(p') = 0$, and so not all three excess demands can be positive at p'. Thus, a point like p' is not possible given the basic assumptions of the model, and the unstable case cannot occur in a consistent gross substitute Walrasian model. An examination of the stable case will reveal no such contradiction, thus demonstrating that the stable case is the only possibility in a three-good Walrasian system in which all goods are gross substitutes.

5.4   A Macroeconomic Example

Dynamics in the *IS-LM* Model

We introduced a simple version of the *IS-LM* macroeconomic model in Chapter 3 and determined some of its comparative statics properties. In this subsection we use the phase diagram technique to discuss the stability of the *IS-LM* model.

Recall that for the *IS-LM* model there are two dependent variables, the level of national income Y and the interest rate r. The level of income is determined by the goods market, where aggregate expenditure is consumption C plus investment I and aggregate income is consumption plus savings S. Thus the excess demand for goods (EG) is given by $I - S$. In the simple model of Chapter 3, investment depends solely on the rate of interest, with $I_r = dI/dr < 0$, while savings depends on both the rate of interest and the level of income with $S_r = \partial S/\partial r > 0$ and $S_Y = \partial S/\partial Y > 0$. The *IS* curve is defined to be the set of all Y and r combinations that clear the goods market, so all (Y, r) that satisfy

$$EG(Y, r) = I(r) - S(Y, r) = 0. \tag{5.36}$$

The rate of interest is determined by the money market, where the demand for real money balances is $L(Y, r)$ with $L_Y = \partial L/\partial Y > 0$ and $L_r = \partial L/\partial r < 0$, while the supply of real money balances is exogenous at the level M^s/p. The *LM* curve is defined to be the set of all Y and r combinations that clear the money market, or all (Y, r) that satisfy

$$EM(Y, r) = L(Y, r) - \frac{M^s}{p} = 0. \tag{5.37}$$

As demonstrated in Chapter 3, the *IS* curve slopes downward in (Y, r)-space, since

$$\left.\frac{dr}{dY}\right|_{EG=0} = \frac{-EG_Y}{EG_r} = \frac{S_Y}{I_r - S_r} < 0,$$

and the *LM* curve slopes upward, since

$$\left.\frac{dr}{dY}\right|_{EM=0} = \frac{-EM_Y}{EM_r} = \frac{-L_Y}{L_r} > 0.$$

The intersection of the *IS* and *LM* curves gives the general equilibrium values of income Y^* and the rate of interest r^*.

In our earlier presentation of the simple *IS-LM* model, the topic of stability or convergence to (Y^*, r^*) was not discussed. We simply examined the equilibrium position and then analyzed the comparative statics impact of a change in the money supply M^s or a change in the fiscal deficit D. We now want to specifically examine the behavior of the system outside equilibrium. Are there automatic forces (as in the gross substitute Walrasian system) that cause income and the interest rate to converge to their general equilibrium values from any initial disequilibrium position?

To examine the behavior of the system outside equilibrium, it is necessary to specify the disequilibrium dynamics of the model. Since the goods market "determines" the level of income and the money market "determines" the rate of interest, we suggest the following characterization of the dynamic adjustment mechanism:

$$\dot{Y} = \delta_Y EG(Y, r) \qquad \text{and} \qquad \dot{r} = \delta_r EM(Y, r), \tag{5.38}$$

with $\delta_Y > 0$ and $\delta_r > 0$. The differential equations in (5.38) have both Y and r adjusting in the "right" direction. Excess demand for goods $(I > S)$ will cause income to rise, and excess supply $(I < S)$ will cause it to fall; excess demand for money $(L > M^s)$ will cause the interest rate to rise, and excess supply $(L < M^s)$ will cause it to fall. The general equilibrium (Y^*, r^*) of course occurs where $\dot{Y} = \dot{r} = 0$. We can now discuss the stability (or instability) of this simple *IS-LM* model.

Stability of the *IS-LM* Model

First consider points off the *IS* curve. In Figure 5.21, the downward-sloping *IS* curve has been drawn, with point A an arbitrarily chosen point on the curve. Now consider any point directly above A, such as B. Notice that in moving from A to B, the interest rate has increased while the level of income has remained the same. What can be said regarding the excess demand for goods, and thus the way in which income will change, at a point such as B?

To answer this question, recall that the impact of a change in the rate of interest on the excess demand for goods is given by

$$EG_r = I_r - S_r < 0.$$

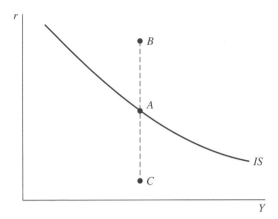

Figure 5.21

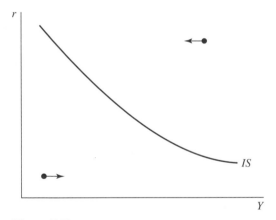

Figure 5.22

Thus, the increase in the rate of interest associated with the movement from A to B will cause the excess demand for goods to be lower at B than it was at A. But since the goods market cleared at A, it must be the case that $EG < 0$ at B. But since $\dot{Y} = EG$ by the adjustment mechanism in (5.38), this means that income will be falling ($\dot{Y} < 0$) at B, or any other point above the IS curve. This decreasing income is indicated by the leftward-pointing arrow above the IS curve in Figure 5.22. The argument is simply reversed for any point below the IS curve, such as C in Figure 5.21, and this is indicated by the rightward-pointing arrow below the IS curve in Figure 5.22.

Now consider the LM curve in Figure 5.23. By increasing income from point D to point F, the excess demand for money is increased since $EM_Y = L_Y > 0$. Given that the money market cleared at D, there must be positive excess demand for money ($EM > 0$) at F, which implies an increasing interest rate ($\dot{r} > 0$) by the adjustment mechanism in (5.38). This is indicated by the upward-pointing arrow

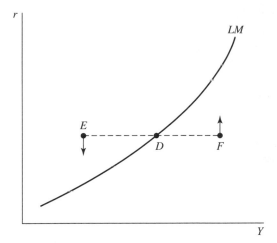

Figure 5.23

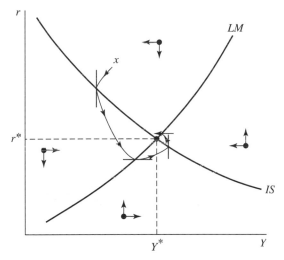

Figure 5.24

at F. Correspondingly, point E represents an excess supply of money ($EM < 0$) and a decreasing rate of interest ($\dot{r} < 0$), as indicated by the downward-pointing arrow at E.

Combining the two curves, we have the IS-LM phase diagram in Figure 5.24. From any arbitrary point such as x, we see that both Y and r will change in a spiral motion, with Y stopping movement when the IS curve is reached and r stopping movement when the LM curve is reached, until both variables are at their general equilibrium levels (Y^*, r^*). Since such a spiraling convergent path exist from any initial combination of Y and r, we have demonstrated that our simple IS-LM model is globally **stable**.

While this proof of the stability of the simple *IS-LM* model is a relatively easy exercise using the phase diagram technique, its importance should not be underestimated. Different, more elaborate, restrictions on the model might give very different stability results; a stability check is always necessary to legitimize the use of comparative statics analysis in such models (whether the analysis is done diagrammatically or more formally). The comparative statics results obtained in Chapter 3 would be meaningless if any parametric disturbance sent income and the rate of interest exploding off to infinity or zero.

Finally, note that the similarities between the *IS-LM* model and the Walrasian general equilibrium model discussed in the preceding section are not just a coincidence. The *IS-LM* model was initially presented by John Hicks (1939), and while it was clearly an attempt to formalize the macroeconomic ideas in Keynes's *General Theory,* Hicks admitted (1980) that he had a three-good Walrasian model squarely in mind during its formulation. Keynes actually had a three-market macroeconomic model; a market for goods, a market for money (liquidity), and a market for bonds. By Walras' law, Hicks eliminated one market—the bond market—leaving the two-market *IS-LM* model we have just discussed.

5.5   An Alternative Notion of Stability

Saddle-Point Stability

Recall the **unstable** case of the three-good Walrasian gross substitute system from Section 5.3. If we momentarily disregard the inconsistencies of this system with the assumptions of the gross substitute Walrasian model, we can use it to introduce an alternative (much weaker) form of stability, so-called saddle-point stability.

For reference, this "unstable" Walrasian gross substitute system has been reproduced in Figure 5.25. Notice that even though this system is unstable and prices do not converge to p^* from most initial values, there is convergence to p^*

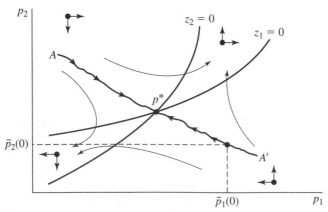

Figure 5.25

for **certain** initial values. For any initial price vector lying along AA', the dynamics of the system will drive prices toward p^*. This type of stability, in which convergence is guaranteed for some "small" subset of initial positions but not "most" initial positions, is called **saddle-point stability.** The curve (such as AA') containing the initial values that guarantee convergence is called the **stable arm** (or **convergent path**) of the dynamic system. In Figure 5.25, this saddle-point stability implies that for any initial value of p_1, say $\tilde{p}_1(0)$, there exists a unique value of p_2 [given by $\tilde{p}_2(0)$] such that $\lim_{t\to\infty} p(t) = p^*$. For any other initial choice of p_2, the system will not converge to the equilibrium from an initial value of $\tilde{p}_1(0)$. Alternatively, we can say that if the system is stable—if it converges to p^*—then the initial price vector must have been somewhere along the stable arm.

Saddle-point stable systems raise some rather interesting questions. Why must the initial values be along the stable arm? What will guarantee this? Are there **economic** reasons for being certain that the initial values of the system will be the right ones? This last question can be answered affirmatively when it can be shown that nonconvergent paths violate (or will eventually violate) the fundamental economic assumptions of the model. If all nonconvergent paths can be eliminated as economically inconsistent, then the only points remaining will lie along the stable arm. This problem, the problem of finding economic reasons for excluding all nonconvergent paths, is sometimes called the **Hahn problem** because it was posed by F. H. Hahn (1966) in the context of a growth model with heterogeneous capital goods. Actually, an argument like this can be used to eliminate the nonconvergent paths from the Walrasian gross substitute system in Figure 5.25. For any initial price vector off AA', it can be demonstrated that prices will eventually enter one of the two regions where the excess demands for both goods are of the same sign—either the northeast corner, where both z_1 and z_2 are positive, or the southwest corner where both z_1 and z_2 are negative. In either case there will be a contradiction with Walras' law (by an argument like the one in Section 5.3). Since Walras' law is fundamental, nonconvergent paths are thus inconsistent with the basic structure of the model, and only the stable arm remains.

A Monetary Growth Model

One class of models that often exhibits the property of saddle-point stability, even in low dimensions, is the class of monetary growth models. The simplest of these models contain only two assets, a capital good that is both an input and an output for the real sector and an exogenously supplied monetary asset (i.e., money). It could be said that such a monetary growth model represents a combination of the one-asset Solow growth model and the real money model from Section 5.2. Since the economic agents must decide how their wealth will be divided between the two assets, such models represent an elementary example of the more general "portfolio choice" problem. To see exactly how saddle-point stability emerges in the context of monetary growth, we examine one such model in detail.

The real side of the economy is only a slight modification of the earlier Solow growth model. Real output per capita y is given by the production function

$$y = \frac{Q}{L} = f\left(\frac{K}{L}, 1\right) = f(k),\qquad(5.39)$$

where k is the capital/output ratio K/L. We assume that this function has the same properties exhibited earlier [$f(0) = 0$, $f'(k) > 0$, and $f''(k) < 0$] as well as the stability condition $sf'(k) - n < 0$.

The monetary side of the economy is characterized by the variable m, which represents per capita real money balances. Thus, $m = M/p$, where M is per capita nominal money balances and p is the price level (price of one unit of real output in terms of money). Variable m will influence the real sector of the economy through a "real-balance" effect. According to this effect, increases in per capita real money balances will increase per capita consumption (and thus reduce per capita savings) at any level of output. Since s represented the average propensity to save in or initial presentation of the Solow growth model, we can integrate the real-balance effect into the model by making

$$s = s(m) \qquad \text{with } s' = \frac{ds}{dm} < 0.\qquad(5.40)$$

Combining (5.40) with the real-sector dynamics initially presented in (5.12), we have the fundamental equation of motion for the real sector of the model given by

$$\dot{k} = F_k(k, m) = s(m)f(k) - nk.\qquad(5.41)$$

Thus, $F_k(k, m) = 0$ describes a set of points in (k, m)-space where the capital/labor ratio is stationary (where $\dot{k} = 0$). As in the models discussed earlier in this chapter, the slope of this curve can be found by taking the total differential of $F_k = 0$. This computation gives

$$\left.\frac{dm}{dk}\right|_{\dot{k}=0} = \frac{-F_{kk}}{F_{km}} = \frac{-(sf' - n)}{s'f} < 0,\qquad(5.42)$$

and so the $\dot{k} = 0$ curve slopes downward in (k, m)-space. Note that the sign of this expression makes economic sense. The higher the real money balances, the lower the average propensity to save, and thus the lower the ratio of steady-state capital to labor.

The behavior of $\dot{k}$ off the $\dot{k} = 0$ curve is shown in Figure 5.26. Since $F_{km} = s'f$ is negative, an increase in m will decrease k, and a decrease in m will increase k. This is precisely the behavior indicated by the arrows in Figure 5.26.

The monetary side of the model is more complex. We assume that the government (or monetary authority) increases the per capita nominal money supply M exogenously at a constant rate θ (so $\dot{M}/M = \theta$). Now defining the rate of inflation $\dot{p}/p$ as π and recalling that $m = M/p$, we have

$$\frac{\dot{m}}{m} = \theta - \pi.\qquad(5.43)$$

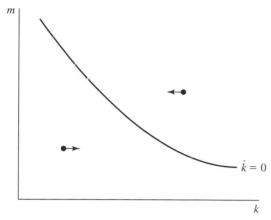

Figure 5.26

Equation (5.43) characterizes the rate of change in real per capita money balances as a function of the rate of inflation π and the exogenous rate of growth in the per capita money supply θ.

The rate of inflation π is also related to the real side of the economy. The connection is the **Fisher equation,** which states (under perfect foresight) that the nominal rate of interest r is equal to the real rate of interest [$f'(k)$ in this model with only one capital good] plus the rate of inflation.[8] Thus,

$$r = f'(k) + \pi. \tag{5.44}$$

Finally, this nominal rate of interest is determined by the flow equilibrium in the money market (i.e., where the real demand for money is equal to the real money supply). This follows the way in which the nominal interest rate was determined in the *IS-LM* model of Section 5.4. From equation (5.37) with a slight modification to account for the per capita nature of the current model, we have

$$L(Y, r) = \frac{M^s}{p}. \tag{5.45}$$

Or rewriting this expression

$$L(k, r) - m = 0, \tag{5.46}$$

since $Y = py$, $y = f(k)$, and $m = M/p$.

Solving (5.46) for the nominal rate of interest, we have

$$r(k, m), \text{ where } L[k, r(k, m)] - m = 0. \tag{5.47}$$

Recalling that $L_r = \partial L / \partial r < 0$ and $L_k = \partial L / \partial k > 0$ (since $L_Y = \partial L / \partial Y > 0$ and $f' > 0$), we see that the change in the nominal rate of interest caused by a change in either k or m can be determined. Differentiating (5.47) with respect to k gives

$$L_k + L_r \frac{\partial r}{\partial k} = 0 \quad \text{or} \quad r_k = \frac{\partial r}{\partial k} = \frac{-L_k}{L_r} > 0. \tag{5.48}$$

Differentiation of the same equation with respect to m gives

$$L_r \frac{\partial r}{\partial m} - 1 = 0 \qquad \text{or} \qquad r_m = \frac{\partial r}{\partial m} = \frac{1}{L_r} < 0. \tag{5.49}$$

Substituting the money market clearing rate of interest $r(k, m)$ from (5.47) back into the Fisher equation (5.44), we have

$$r(k, m) = f'(k) + \pi \qquad \text{or} \qquad -\pi = f'(k) - r(k, m).$$

Substituting this expression into the differential equation for the rate of growth of per capita real money balances (5.43), gives

$$\frac{\dot{m}}{m} = \theta + f'(k) - r(k, m).$$

Or, rewriting this equation for the monetary sector dynamics in a form similar to the equation for the dynamics of the real sector gives us

$$\dot{m} = m F_m(k, m) = m[\theta + f'(k) - r(k, m)]. \tag{5.50}$$

For all $m > 0$, the set of (k, m) combinations such that $\dot{m} = 0$ is given by $F_m(k, m) = 0$. Again we can find the slope of the $\dot{m} = 0$ curve by taking the total differential. This computation and rearrangement gives

$$\left. \frac{dm}{dk} \right|_{\dot{m}=0} = \frac{-F_{mk}}{F_{mm}} = \frac{-(f'' - r_k)}{-r_m} > 0, \tag{5.51}$$

since $r_k > 0$ by (5.48), $r_m < 0$ by (5.49), and $f'' < 0$. Thus the $\dot{m} = 0$ curve slopes upward in (k, m)-space.

The behavior of $\dot{m}$ off the $\dot{m} = 0$ curve is shown in Figure 5.27. Since $F_{mk} = f'' - r_k$ is negative, an increase in k will decrease m and a decease in k will increase m. This behavior is shown by the arrows in Figure 5.27. For any initial

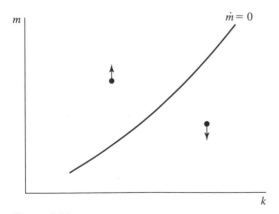

Figure 5.27

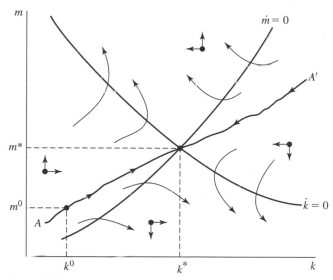

Figure 5.28

point off the $\dot{m} = 0$ curve, the dynamic of the system moves m farther away from $\dot{m} = 0$.

Assuming the equilibrium (steady state) of the system (k^*, m^*) is unique and strictly positive, the dynamic behavior of the model is given by Figure 5.28. This is clearly a case of saddle-point stability. For any initial combination of k and m along AA', the system will converge to (k^*, m^*). For any initial position off AA', the system will diverge, sending m to either zero or infinity. Since the growth rate in nominal money balances θ is given exogenously by the government, the cases of $m \rightarrow 0$ and $m \rightarrow \infty$ imply that $p \rightarrow \infty$ and $p \rightarrow 0$, respectively. Thus for any initial position below AA' the economy will experience hyperinflation, and for any initial position above AA' the economy will experience hyperdeflation.

Since the capital stock and nominal money supply are generally not "chosen" but rather are inherited from the past, the requirement that the initial position of the economy be along AA' is quite severe. For instance, suppose that the initial capital/labor ratio (inherited from the past) is k^0 in Figure 5.28. Now if the economy is to avoid the extremes of both hyperinflation and hyperdeflation, the initial real per capita money supply must be m^0. But the per capita nominal money supply is, like the capital/output ratio, an inherited quantity, say M^0; thus the convergence of the economy from (k^0, M^0) to (k^*, m^*) requires the initial price level to be exactly $p^0 = M^0/m^0$. Alternatively, stability implies that the economy provides some mechanism such that the unique correct price level p^0 is chosen. While there has been quite a bit of literature on this topic, it is not prima facie true that such a mechanism will always exist in a competitive economy.[9]

PROBLEMS

5.1 Derive equation (5.43) from the definition of m, θ, and π.

5.2 Answer the following questions about the equilibrium capital/labor ratio $k*$ in the simple Solow growth model.

(a) Use comparative statics analysis to determine the responsiveness of the equilibrium capital/labor ratio $k*$ to a change in the rate of population growth n (i.e., find $\partial k*/\partial n$).

(b) Use the model's stability condition to sign the comparative statics term in (a). Draw a diagram to demonstrate this result.

(c) Use comparative statics analysis to determine the responsiveness of the equilibrium capital/labor ratio $k*$ to a change in the average propensity to save s (i.e., find $\partial k*/\partial s$).

(d) Use the model's stability condition to sign the comparative statics term in (c). Draw a diagram to demonstrate this result.

5.3 Suppose the production function for the simple Solow growth model is given by the Cobb–Douglas form

$$F(L, K) = L^{1-a} K^a \qquad \text{with } 0 < a < 1.$$

(a) Find $f(k)$ for this particular production function.

(b) Does this production function satisfy the basic neoclassical assumptions of the Solow growth model? (Show.)

(c) Find $k*$ for this case.

(d) Is $k*$ a stable equilibrium? Show why it is or explain why not.

5.4 Consider the supply and demand model given by the following two expressions

$$Q^d = \frac{4}{p} \qquad \text{and} \qquad Q^s = -p + 5,$$

where $Q^d =$ quantity demanded, $Q^s =$ quantity supplied, and $p =$ price.

(a) Find the equilibrium (or equilibria).

(b) Does (do) the equilibrium (equilibria) satisfy the stability condition from Theorem 5.1?

(c) Use a simple supply and demand diagram to support your answer to (b).

5.5 Supply and demand for a particular good are given by

$$Q^d = ap + b \qquad \text{and} \qquad Q^s = cp + d.$$

Suppose the equilibrium is stable: What condition guarantees that $p* > 0$.

5.6 For each of the following market models, determine the equilibrium price $p*$ and the equilibrium quantity $q*$. Also determine whether the sufficient condition for local stability holds. Consider only positive prices.

(a) $D(p) = 20 - 2p$ and $S(p) = 2 + p$.

(b) $D(p) = 2p^2 - p + 1$ and $S(p) = 3p^2 - 2p - 5$.

(c) $D(p) = 2p^2 - 6p + 10$ and $S(p) = p^2 + 2p + 307$.

5.7 Consider a supply and demand model in which demand is given by $Q^d = D(p, t)$ and supply is given by $Q^s = S(p, c)$, where Q^d is the quantity demanded, Q^s is the quantity supplied, p is price, t is a demand shift parameter for "taste," and c is a supply shift parameter for the "cost" of production. Assume the following sign restrictions on these functions:

$$\frac{\partial D}{\partial p} < 0, \qquad \frac{\partial D}{\partial t} > 0, \qquad \frac{\partial S}{\partial p} > 0, \qquad \text{and} \qquad \frac{\partial S}{\partial c} < 0. \qquad (1)$$

(a) Interpret the model's sign restrictions in (1).

(b) Assuming that the equilibrium price–quantity combination (p^*, Q^*) is strictly positive and unique, obtain comparative statics expressions for a change in the parameters t and c (i.e., find $\partial p^*/\partial t$, $\partial p^*/\partial c$, $\partial Q^*/\partial t$, and $\partial Q^*/\partial c$).

(c) Draw simple supply and demand diagrams to demonstrate your results in (b).

(d) Suppose that the last three terms in (1) stay the same, but we alter the assumption on the slope of the demand curve so that $\partial D/\partial p > 0$. Is it still possible to obtain the results in (b)? Explain why or why not.

(e) Suppose the sufficient condition for stability holds for this model. Does this help with the problem in (d)? Explain why or why not.

5.8 Consider the following three-good general equilibrium model, where $z_i(p)$ is the excess demand for good $i = 1, 2, 3$ at price vector $p = (p_1, p_2, p_3)$:

$$z_1(p) = -10 - \frac{p_2}{p_1} + \frac{p_3}{p_1},$$

$$z_2(p) = \frac{-5p_1}{p_2} - 6 + \frac{p_3}{p_2},$$

$$z_3(p) = \frac{15p_1}{p_3} + \frac{7p_2}{p_3} - 2.$$

(a) Do these excess demand functions satisfy Walras' law (W)? Show why or why not.

(b) Are these excess demand functions homogeneous of degree zero (H)? Show why or why not.

(c) Do these excess demand functions satisfy the gross substitute property (GS)? Show why or why not.

(d) Normalize the system by letting $p_3 = 1$, and then solve for the equilibrium values of the other two prices p_1^* and p_2^*.

(e) Use the phase diagram technique to determine whether the system is stable or unstable.

5.9 Repeat Problem 8 for the following general equilibrium system:

$$z_1(p) = -10 + \frac{p_2}{p_1} + \frac{p_3}{p_1},$$

$$z_2(p) = \frac{9p_1}{p_2} - 2 + \frac{p_3}{p_2},$$

$$z_3(p) = \frac{p_1}{p_3} + \frac{p_2}{p_3} - 2.$$

5.10 Alfred Marshall discussed supply and demand dynamics with output y as the independent variable (rather than price). Thus for Marshall the dynamic of the market is given by

$$\dot{y} = P^D(y) - P^S(y), \qquad (M)$$

where P^D is the demand price and P^S is the supply price. Show that if y^* satisfies the sufficient condition for the local stability of (M), then y^* also maximizes the total surplus in the market $TS(y)$ (defined in Chapter 4: see discussion accompanying Figure 4.8).

5.11 Let $z_1(p_1, p_2)$ be the excess demand for good 1 and $z_2(p_1, p_2)$ be the excess demand for good 2 in a three-good Walrasian general equilibrium model normalized with $p_3 = 1$. Assuming that good 2 is a **gross substitute** for good 1 (i.e., $z_{12} = \partial z_1 / \partial p_2 > 0$), but that good 1 is a **gross complement** for good 2 (i.e., $z_{21} = \partial z_2 / \partial p_1 < 0$). Also assume that both excess demand functions slope downward with respect to their own prices (so, $z_{11} = \partial z_1 / \partial p_1 < 0$ and $z_{22} = \partial z_2 / \partial p_2 < 0$).

(a) Determine the slope of the $z_1(p_1, p_2) = 0$ curve.

(b) Determine the slope of the $z_2(p_1, p_2) = 0$ curve.

(c) Assuming the equilibrium $p^* = (p_1^*, p_2^*)$ is unique and strictly positive, use the phase diagram technique to determine the stability of the dynamical system:

$$\dot{p}_1 = z_1(p_1, p_2),$$
$$\dot{p}_2 = z_2(p_1, p_2).$$

(d) Explain, using simple supply and demand diagrams, why the stability or instability found in (c) makes sense.

5.12 For the normalized three-good Walrasian model in Problem 11, let α be a demand shift parameter for good 1 (with $z_{1\alpha} = \partial z_1 / \partial \alpha > 0$) that does not directly affect the market for good 2 (so $z_{2\alpha} = \partial z_2 / \partial \alpha = 0$). Determine the comparative statics impact of a change in the parameter α on the equilibrium prices of the two goods (i.e., find expressions for $dp_1^*/d\alpha$ and $dp_2^*/d\alpha$).

5.13 Assume that the growth rates of national income $\dot{Y}$ and the capital stock $\dot{K}$ in a certain economy are given by the following differential equations:

$$\dot{Y} = K - \frac{Y}{10},$$

$$\dot{K} = Y^{1/2} - K.$$

(a) Find the equilibrium national income Y^* and capital stock K^*.

(b) Draw the diagram for the set of points where $\dot{Y} = 0$ in (Y, K)-space. Discuss the behavior of Y off the curve.

(c) Draw the diagram for the set of points where $\dot{K} = 0$ in (Y, K)-space. Discuss the behavior of K off the curve.

(d) Use a phase diagram to determine the stability or instability of the equilibrium (Y^*, K^*).

5.14 You are given the following neoclassical macroeconomic model

$$\text{money} \longrightarrow \quad EM = L(r) - \frac{M^s}{p},$$

$$\text{goods} \longrightarrow \quad EG = I(r) - S(r),$$

with $L_r = dL/dr < 0$, $I_r = dI/dr < 0$, $S_r = dS/dr > 0$, p is the price level, and r is the real rate of interest. The dynamics of the model are given by

$$\dot{p} = EG(p, r) \quad \text{and} \quad \dot{r} = EM(p, r).$$

(a) Provide an economic interpretation of the differential equations.

(b) Characterize the set of all (p, r) combinations that clear the goods market, and determine the shape of this $EG(p, r) = 0$ curve in (p, r)-space.

(c) Characterize the set of all (p, r) combinations that clear the money market, and determine the shape of this $EM(p, r) = 0$ curve in (p, r)-space.

(d) Use the phase diagram technique to determine the stability or instability of this model.

(e) One way to characterize the strict quantity theory of money is to say that the elasticity of the price level with respect to a change in the money supply is unitary. This is because the elasticity of the price level with respect to the money supply is $\%\Delta p / \%\Delta M$, so $\%\Delta p / \%\Delta M = 1$ implies that $\%\Delta p = \%\Delta M$, which is the quantity theory of money. Use the comparative statics technique to prove that the strict quantity theory holds for the equilibrium values (p^*, r^*) of this model.

5.15 The static Cournot duopoly model was examined in Chapter 3. A continuous time dynamical version of the Cournot model is given by the system

$$\dot{q}_1 = \delta_1[R_1(q_2) - q_1],$$
$$\dot{q}_2 = \delta_2[R_2(q_1) - q_2],$$

where the $\delta_i > 0$ are the speeds of adjustment and $R_i(q_j)$ are the reaction functions for the two firms $i = 1, 2$. Answer the following questions for the specific linear demand and fixed-cost example given in Chapter 3 by the profit functions in (3.86) and the reaction functions in (3.88).

(a) Substitute the reaction functions from (3.88a) and (3.88b) into the dynamical system of this problem.

(b) Demonstrate that the Cournot equilibrium coincides with the equilibrium of the dynamical system.

(c) Use the phase diagram technique to discuss the stability of this dynamic Cournot model.

5.16 Consider a Cournot duopoly model with the following demand and cost conditions:

$$P = -Q + 12,$$
$$TC_1 = 4Q_1 + FC_1,$$
$$TC_2 = \left(12 - Q_1 - \frac{12}{Q_1}\right)Q_2 + FC_2.$$

where $Q = $ total output (with $Q_1 + Q_2 = Q$), TC_i is the total cost, and FC_i the fixed cost for the two firms $i = 1, 2$. Notice that the model involves a production externality; the output of firm 1 affects the cost of producing good 2.

(a) Set up the profit functions for the two firms. Maximize these profit functions to obtain the two reaction functions $R_1(Q_2)$ and $R_2(Q_1)$.

(b) Solve the reaction functions to obtain the Cournot equilibrium (or equilibria).

(c) Use the phase diagram technique to determine the stability of the model's Cournot equilibrium (or equilibria) when the dynamics are defined by the following adjustment mechanism

$$\dot{Q}_1 = R_1(Q_2) - Q_1,$$
$$\dot{Q}_2 = R_2(Q_1) - Q_2.$$

5.17 In Box 5.1 the optimal growth path for the economy was characterized by the two differential equations

$$\dot{k} = f\,[k(t)] - c(t) - nk(t),$$

$$\dot{c}(t) = - \left(\frac{u'}{u''} \right) (f'\,[k(t)] - n - r).$$

Using the definitions and assumptions of the model (from Box 5.1 and the discussion of the Solow growth model in the text) use the phase diagram technique to determine the stability of the steady-state (optimal growth) solution $(\hat{c}, \hat{k})$, where $\dot{k} = \dot{c} = 0$. Assume that $\hat{c} > 0$, $\hat{k} > 0$ and that $\hat{k} < \bar{k}$, where $f(\bar{k}) = n\bar{k}$.

5.18 *Sharks and tuna.* Predator–prey models in biology share many of the properties of dynamic models in economics. Consider the case of one particular predator (sharks $= S$) and one particular prey (tuna $= T$). The dynamics of the sharks and tuna populations are given by the following two differential equations:

$$\dot{T}(t) = a - bT(t) - cS(t),$$

$$\dot{S}(t) = -d + eT(t),$$

where a, b, c, d, and e are all positive parameters. Notice from the first equation that the rate of growth in the tuna population is restricted in two ways: first, the tuna population grows slower the more tuna there are (limitations on food supply, etc.), and second, the tuna are "harvested" by the sharks. The second equation shows that there is a positive relationship between the stock of tuna at any time and the rate of growth in the shark population; the parameter d represents the decay in the shark population in the absence of tuna.

(a) Find an expression for the equilibrium tuna locus $\dot{T} = 0$ in (T, S)-space. Draw this curve in (T, S)-space and analyze the behavior of the tuna population off this curve.

(b) Find an expression for the equilibrium shark locus $\dot{S} = 0$ in (T, S)-space. Draw this curve in (T, S)-space and analyze the behavior of the shark population off this curve.

(c) Find the steady-state (equilibrium) populations of the two species (T^*, S^*). Are T^* and S^* both positive? If an additional restriction is required to guarantee that both species have positive equilibrium populations, find the restriction and interpret it in terms of the diagram.

(d) Use the phase diagram technique to determine the stability of the equilibrium $T^* > 0$ and $S^* > 0$.

NOTES

1. Takayama (1985, p. 316) provides a further discussion of this point.

2. Burmeister and Dobell (1970, p. 28) provide a formal proof of the global stability of the Solow model under the boundary restriction $sf(0) > n$.

3. Excluding zero prices greatly simplifies the analysis; for the case of $p \in \Re_+^3$, boundary behavior must be examined.

4. Normalization actually defines two new prices $q_i = p_i/p_3$ and $q_2 = p_2/p_3$, which represent the relative prices of goods 1 and 2 in terms of good 3. This is possible because

by (H) we have $z_i(q_1, q_2) = z_i(p_1/p_3, p_2/p_3, 1) = z_i(p_1, p_2, p_3)$ for $i = 1, 2, 3$. Rather than introduce a new symbol for these relative prices (such as q), we continue to use the same symbol for prices after normalization as before normalization. Hopefully this will not present any confusion.

5. Gross substitution captures the notion of substitutes used in elementary economics. Goods might also be net substitutes, which refers to the sign of the cross-substitution effect (discussed in Chapter 8).

6. We say "almost all" because there does exist a single one-dimensional path along which the system converges to p^*. Choosing an initial price vector along this path from all possible initial price vectors, would, of course, be an extremely rare occurrence (measure zero). This diagram actually depicts **saddle-point stability,** a topic discussed in the next section.

7. As in the single-variable case, this result can be proved formally for disequilibrium prices "close" to p^* and where (5.33) is evaluated at p^*, but such analysis would take us beyond the scope of the current discussion. The interested reader is invited to consult one of the excellent discussions of continuous time dynamic stability in more advanced texts such as Hirsch and Smale (1974), Luenberger (1979), Murata (1977), or Takayama (1985).

8. The standard expression for the Fisher equation is $r = f'(k) + \pi^e$, where π^e is the expected rate of inflation. We have assumed that $\pi^e = \pi$, which is the restriction of "perfect myopic foresight." This restriction amounts to assuming that expectations adjust infinitely rapidly, or equivalently that $\beta = \infty$ in Cagan's adaptive adjustment scheme [equation (5.16)].

9. See Burmeister (1980, pp. 92–6) and the references there for a discussion of why such a mechanism might or might not exist in a competitive economy.

6

MATRICES AND ECONOMIC THEORY

■ ■ ■

This chapter examines many of the matrix techniques used in modern economic analysis. These methods go beyond the elementary matrix theory reviewed in Chapter 0, and since much of the interest in these mathematical techniques has been motivated by economic problems, they are often neglected in standard linear algebra courses. The techniques to be examined are Cramer's rule, the theory of nonsingular M matrices, and definite quadratic forms. It is also convenient to discuss the inverse and implicit function theorems in this chapter, even though they are technically more multivariate calculus topics than matrix theory per se. We look at many economic applications and include a detailed discussion of the Leontief input–output model.

6.1   Submatrices and Minors

A **submatrix of order k** is the matrix that remains after $n - k$ rows and columns have been deleted from an $n \times n$ matrix.[1] For example, if the original matrix is the generic 3×3

$$A = \begin{bmatrix} a_{11} & a_{12} & a_{13} \\ a_{21} & a_{22} & a_{23} \\ a_{31} & a_{32} & a_{33} \end{bmatrix},$$ (6.1)

then a_{12} is the submatrix of order 1 formed by deleting the second and third rows and the first and third columns, while

$$\begin{bmatrix} a_{11} & a_{12} \\ a_{31} & a_{32} \end{bmatrix}$$

is the submatrix of order 2 formed by deleting only the second row and the third column. Deleting two rows and columns from (6.1) gives a submatrix of order 1 $(n-2)$, while deleting only one row and column leaves a submatrix of order 2 $(n-1)$.

If the **same** $n - k$ rows and columns are deleted, then the submatrix that remains is called a **principal submatrix of order k.** For example, deleting the first and third rows and columns from (6.1) gives the first-order principal submatrix a_{22}, while deleting only the first row and column from (6.1) leaves the second-order principal submatrix

$$\begin{bmatrix} a_{22} & a_{23} \\ a_{32} & a_{33} \end{bmatrix}.$$

For the $n = 3$ case in (6.1), there are a total of three principal submatrices of order 1 (a_{11}, a_{22}, and a_{33}), three principal submatrices of order 2, namely,

$$\begin{bmatrix} a_{11} & a_{12} \\ a_{21} & a_{22} \end{bmatrix}, \quad \begin{bmatrix} a_{11} & a_{13} \\ a_{31} & a_{33} \end{bmatrix}, \quad \text{and} \quad \begin{bmatrix} a_{22} & a_{23} \\ a_{32} & a_{33} \end{bmatrix}, \tag{6.2}$$

and one principal submatrix of order 3, which is A itself.

A **minor** is the determinant of a submatrix; if the submatrix is a principal submatrix, then its determinant is called a **principal minor.** Since the determinant of a scalar is simply the scalar itself, (6.1) has three first-order principal minors (a_{11}, a_{22}, and a_{33}). In addition, the matrix (6.1) has three second-order principal minors, given by the determinants of the three submatrices in (6.2), and one third-order principal minor, given by the determinant of A itself ($|A|$).

It is common to express both the determinant and the inverse of a matrix in terms of cofactors. The **cofactor** C_{ij} of any element a_{ij} is defined as

$$C_{ij} = (-1)^{i+j} |A_{ij}|, \tag{6.3}$$

where A_{ij} is the $(n - 1) \times (n - 1)$ submatrix formed by deleting row i and column j. Given the foregoing definitions, we can see that a cofactor is simply a signed minor. In particular, cofactor C_{ij} is $(-1)^{i+j}$ times the $(n - 1)$st-order minor formed by deleting row i and column j. The diagonal cofactors C_{ij} are simply the $(n - 1)$st-order principal minors of the matrix, since $(-1)^{i+j} = 1$ for $i = j$.

In economics we can often restrict our attention to a particular subset of principal minors, the **leading** (or "naturally ordered" or "successive") principal minors. For the $n \times n$ matrix

$$A = \begin{bmatrix} a_{11} & a_{12} & \cdots & a_{1n} \\ a_{21} & a_{22} & \cdots & a_{2n} \\ \vdots & \vdots & & \vdots \\ a_{n1} & a_{n2} & \cdots & a_{nn} \end{bmatrix},$$

a **leading principal minor of order k** is defined as $|A_k|$, where

$$A_k = \begin{bmatrix} a_{11} & a_{12} & \cdots & a_{1k} \\ a_{21} & a_{22} & \cdots & a_{2k} \\ \vdots & \vdots & & \vdots \\ a_{k1} & a_{k2} & \cdots & a_{kk} \end{bmatrix}, \tag{6.4}$$

for all $k = 1, 2, \ldots, n$. Thus for the $n = 3$ case in (6.1), there are a total of three leading principal minors

$$|A_1| = a_{11}, \qquad |A_2| = \begin{vmatrix} a_{11} & a_{12} \\ a_{21} & a_{22} \end{vmatrix}, \qquad \text{and} \qquad |A_3| = |A|.$$

Similarly, any $n \times n$ matrix has n leading principal minors.

Certain properties of principal minors appear over and over in economic theory. The two most important are the property of being a **P matrix** and the property of being an **NP matrix**. Matrix A is a P matrix if all its principal minors are positive; matrix A is an NP matrix if its principal minors alternate in sign, starting negative. Thus if we let M_i represent an ith-order principal minor of the $n \times n$ matrix A, then we have the following definitions.

A is a **P matrix** iff:

$$M_1 > 0, M_2 > 0, \ldots, M_n = |A| > 0. \tag{6.5}$$

A is an **NP matrix** iff:

$$M_1 < 0, M_2 > 0, M_3 < 0, \ldots, (-1)^n M_n = (-1)^n |A| > 0. \tag{6.6}$$

Notice that (6.5) and (6.6) impose restrictions on all the principal minors of a matrix, not just on its leading principal minors ($|A_1|, |A_2|, \ldots$).

One useful property of P and NP matrices is that if A is a P matrix, then $B = -A$ is an NP matrix (or vice versa). To see why this is the case, consider $|A_i|$, an arbitrary ith-order leading principal minor of matrix A. If A is a P matrix, then we have $|A_i| > 0$ for all $i = 1, 2, \ldots, n$. Now by the rules of determinants, $B = -A$ implies that $|B_i| = (-1)^i |A_i|$, where $|B_i|$ is the corresponding leading principal minor of B. But since $|A_i| > 0$, this implies that $|B_i| < 0$ for $i = 1, 3, 5, \ldots$ and $|B_i| > 0$ for $i = 2, 4, 6, \ldots$. Since the same argument could be made for any principal minor of B, not just the leading principal minors, B is an NP matrix. This somewhat less than intuitive result proves to be useful in a number of different economic models.

6.2   Cramer's Rule in Economics

There is an old joke among journalists and politicians that you can train a parrot to be an economist by simply teaching it to say "supply and demand." Perhaps there is a variation of that same joke among mathematicians that says you can train a parrot to be an economist by simply teaching it to say "Cramer's rule." Mathematicians are often surprised by the number of different uses economists can find for Cramer's rule.

Cramer's rule is a relatively simple technique for solving systems of linear equations; as we will see, it just happens to be particularly well suited for solving equation systems of the types that most interest economists. First, we explain the technique and justify it in terms of the inverse of a matrix. Second, we demonstrate the usefulness of the technique by applying it to a problem that was already solved "the long way" in Chapter 3: comparative statics for the two-input, perfectly competitive firm. Third, we briefly explain why Cramer's rule is so useful in such a wide variety of economic models.

Cramer's Rule

Consider the system of n linear equations in n unknowns characterized by

$$Ax = b, \tag{6.7}$$

where

$$A = \begin{bmatrix} a_{11} & \cdots & a_{1n} \\ \vdots & & \vdots \\ a_{n1} & \cdots & a_{nn} \end{bmatrix}, \qquad x = \begin{bmatrix} x_1 \\ \vdots \\ x_n \end{bmatrix}, \qquad \text{and} \qquad b = \begin{bmatrix} b_1 \\ \vdots \\ b_n \end{bmatrix}.$$

If $|A| \neq 0$, matrix A is nonsingular and system (6.7) has a unique solution vector x for each b.

Cramer's rule states that each x_i in the solution vector x can be written as the ratio of two determinants. The denominator of the ratio is simply the determinant of matrix A, while the numerator is the determinant of the matrix formed by replacing the ith column of A with the column vector b. Thus we have the solution to (6.7)

$$x_1 = \frac{\begin{vmatrix} b_1 & a_{12} & \cdots & a_{1n} \\ b_2 & a_{22} & \cdots & a_{2n} \\ \vdots & \vdots & & \vdots \\ b_n & a_{n2} & \cdots & a_{nn} \end{vmatrix}}{|A|},$$

$$x_2 = \frac{\begin{vmatrix} a_{11} & b_1 & \cdots & a_{1n} \\ a_{21} & b_2 & \cdots & a_{2n} \\ \vdots & \vdots & & \vdots \\ a_{n1} & b_n & \cdots & a_{nn} \end{vmatrix}}{|A|}, \tag{6.8}$$

$$\vdots$$

$$x_n = \frac{\begin{vmatrix} a_{11} & \cdots & a_{1n-1} & b_1 \\ a_{21} & \cdots & a_{2n-1} & b_2 \\ \vdots & & \vdots & \vdots \\ a_{n1} & \cdots & a_{nn-1} & b_n \end{vmatrix}}{|A|}.$$

We do not provide a formal proof of Cramer's rule, but we will motivate the result in terms of A^{-1}, the inverse of matrix A. Since $|A| \neq 0$, the inverse exists, and the solution vector x is given by

$$x = A^{-1}b. \tag{6.9}$$

Recall that the inverse matrix A^{-1} can be expressed as

$$A^{-1} = \frac{\text{adj } A}{|A|},\tag{6.10}$$

where adj A is the adjoint of A. Since the adjoint of A is the transpose of the matrix of cofactors of A, we can write

$$A^{-1} = \frac{C^T}{|A|},\tag{6.11}$$

where each element in the cofactor matrix C is defined as in (6.3). Substituting (6.11) into (6.9) and writing the system out in full, we have

$$\begin{bmatrix} x_1 \\ x_2 \\ \vdots \\ x_n \end{bmatrix} = \frac{1}{|A|} \begin{bmatrix} C_{11} & C_{21} & \cdots & C_{n1} \\ C_{12} & C_{22} & \cdots & C_{n2} \\ \vdots & \vdots & & \vdots \\ C_{1n} & C_{2n} & \cdots & C_{nn} \end{bmatrix} \begin{bmatrix} b_1 \\ b_2 \\ \vdots \\ b_n \end{bmatrix}.\tag{6.12}$$

Now let us choose an arbitrary x_i, say x_1, and write it out as the corresponding sum from the right-hand side of (6.12). For x_1 this expression is

$$x_1 = \frac{\sum_{j=1}^{n} b_j c_{j1}}{|A|}.\tag{6.13}$$

By substituting in the definition of a cofactor from (6.3), we can express the value of x_1 in (6.13) in terms of the minors of A of order $(n-1) \times (n-1)$. This substitution gives

$$x_1 = \frac{\sum_{j=1}^{n} (-1)^{1+j} b_j |A_{j1}|}{|A|},$$

or

$$x_1 = \frac{b_1 |A_{11}| - b_2 |A_{21}| + b_3 |A_{31}| + \cdots + (-1)^{n+1} b_n |A_{n1}|}{|A|}.\tag{6.14}$$

The expression in (6.14) is equivalent to

$$x_1 = \frac{\begin{vmatrix} b_1 & a_{12} & \cdots & a_{1n} \\ b_2 & a_{22} & \cdots & a_{2n} \\ \vdots & \vdots & & \vdots \\ b_n & a_{n2} & \cdots & a_{nn} \end{vmatrix}}{|A|},$$

the result we would obtain by applying Cramer's rule.

An Application: The Perfectly Competitive Firm

Since many economic applications of Cramer's rule appear in later chapters, only one brief example will be given at this point. The example comes directly from

Chapter 3: the comparative statics of the profit-maximizing, perfectly competitive firm using two inputs, labor L and capital K, to produce a single output y. The firm has the production function $y = f(L, K)$ and faces strictly positive parametric prices p, w, and v, so its profit function π is

$$\pi(L, K) = pf(L, K) - wL - vK. \tag{6.15}$$

The solution to the firm's maximization problem is a set of input demand functions

$$L^* = L^*(w, v, p) \qquad \text{and} \qquad K^* = K^*(w, v, p), \tag{6.16}$$

showing the profit-maximizing level of employment of each input as a function of the parameters of the problem.

In Chapter 3, we differentiated the first-order conditions and "solved simultaneously" to find the comparative statics impact of a change in the price of labor ($\partial L^*/\partial w$ and $\partial K^*/\partial w$). We now derive the same comparative statics terms by using Cramer's rule. Substituting the factor demand functions from (6.16) into the first-order conditions and differentiating with respect to w, we have the system (3.78) from Chapter 3:

$$pf_{LL}\frac{\partial L^*}{\partial w} + pf_{LK}\frac{\partial K^*}{\partial w} \equiv 1,$$

$$pf_{KL}\frac{\partial L^*}{\partial w} + pf_{KK}\frac{\partial K^*}{\partial w} \equiv 0, \tag{6.17}$$

where each second derivative is evaluated at the profit-maximizing combination (L^*, K^*). Since (6.17) is a system of two linear equations in two unknowns ($\partial L^*/\partial w$ and $\partial K^*/\partial w$), it can be written in matrix form as

$$\begin{bmatrix} pf_{LL} & pf_{LK} \\ pf_{KL} & pf_{KK} \end{bmatrix} \begin{bmatrix} \dfrac{\partial L^*}{\partial w} \\ \dfrac{\partial K^*}{\partial w} \end{bmatrix} = \begin{bmatrix} 1 \\ 0 \end{bmatrix}. \tag{6.18}$$

Applying Cramer's rule to system (6.18), we derive the comparative statics terms

$$\frac{\partial L^*}{\partial w} = \frac{\begin{vmatrix} 1 & pf_{LK} \\ 0 & pf_{KK} \end{vmatrix}}{\begin{vmatrix} pf_{LL} & pf_{LK} \\ pf_{KL} & pf_{KK} \end{vmatrix}} = \frac{1}{p}\frac{\begin{vmatrix} 1 & f_{LK} \\ 0 & f_{KK} \end{vmatrix}}{\begin{vmatrix} f_{LL} & f_{LK} \\ f_{KL} & f_{KK} \end{vmatrix}} = \frac{f_{KK}}{p\left(f_{LL}f_{KK} - f_{LK}^2\right)}, \tag{6.19a}$$

$$\frac{\partial K^*}{\partial w} = \frac{\begin{vmatrix} pf_{LL} & 1 \\ pf_{KL} & 0 \end{vmatrix}}{\begin{vmatrix} pf_{LL} & pf_{LK} \\ pf_{KL} & pf_{KK} \end{vmatrix}} = \frac{1}{p}\frac{\begin{vmatrix} f_{LL} & 1 \\ f_{KL} & 0 \end{vmatrix}}{\begin{vmatrix} f_{LL} & f_{LK} \\ f_{KL} & f_{KK} \end{vmatrix}} = \frac{-f_{KL}}{p\left(f_{LL}f_{KK} - f_{LK}^2\right)}. \tag{6.19b}$$

The expressions on the far right-hand side of (6.19a) and (6.19b) are precisely the expressions (3.80) and (3.79) found earlier by solving the equations simultaneously. Cramer's rule simplifies the process of finding comparative statics terms, even in a relatively simple two-variable case such as this.

Actually Cramer's rule does more than merely simplify computation; it also helps to clarify the relationship between second-order conditions and comparative statics. Consider the matrix formed from the **second** derivatives of the production function evaluated at the profit-maximizing combination (L^*, K^*). Let us call this matrix Hf:

$$Hf = \begin{bmatrix} f_{LL} & f_{LK} \\ f_{KL} & f_{KK} \end{bmatrix}. \tag{6.20}$$

A matrix of second derivatives such as (6.20) is called a **Hessian matrix.** Thus the matrix Hf is officially the Hessian of the production function $y = f(L, K)$ evaluated at the point (L^*, K^*).

Now recall [from (3.61)] the second-order conditions for this problem. The second-order conditions require the following sign restrictions on the second derivatives of the profit function evaluated at (L^*, K^*):

$$\pi_{LL} < 0, \qquad \pi_{KK} < 0 \qquad \text{and} \qquad \pi_{LL}\pi_{KK} - \pi_{LK}^2 > 0. \tag{6.21}$$

Since $p > 0$, these conditions can be rewritten solely in terms of the second derivatives of the production function f evaluated at (L^*, K^*). So (6.21) becomes

$$f_{LL} < 0, \qquad f_{KK} < 0, \qquad \text{and} \qquad f_{LL}f_{KK} - f_{LK}^2 > 0. \tag{6.22}$$

Notice that the two left-hand terms in (6.22) are the first-order principal minors of matrix Hf, while since $n = 2$, the right-hand term in (6.22) is the second-order principal minor of Hf, namely, $|Hf|$. Thus the second-order conditions for the profit maximization problem impose restrictions on the principal minors of the Hessian Hf; in particular, the second-order conditions require that all first-order principal minors be negative and that all second-order principal minors be positive. In other words, the second-order conditions require that Hf be an **NP matrix.**

Turning back to the comparative statics terms in (6.19), now we can see that the denominator of both expressions is simply $|Hf|$. Since the second-order conditions require that $|Hf| > 0$, the signs of the two comparative statics terms are determined solely by the sign of the numerator of the fraction. For $\partial L^*/\partial w$ the numerator f_{KK} happens to be a principal minor of Hf, a first-order principal minor. Since the second-order conditions require that first-order principal minors be negative, we have $\partial L^*/\partial w < 0$. But the numerator of the expression for $\partial K^*/\partial w$ is not a first-order principal minor of Hf; it is an off-diagonal term that is not signed by the second-order conditions. Thus if the only restrictions on the production function are those imposed by the second-order conditions for profit maximization, then the sign of $\partial K^*/\partial w$ is indeterminate. These results are exactly the same comparative statics results obtained earlier for this model, but the use of Cramer's rule makes it much more clear exactly how the second-order conditions restrict (or fail to restrict) the signs of these terms.

Cramer's rule is useful in economics precisely because there are so many cases like the example just given: that is, cases in which the economic structure of the model imposes only some relatively weak sign restrictions on the relevant matrix or its principal minors. In such cases, and these constitute most of economic theory, we do not know the specific numerical values of the entries of the matrix, and so we cannot find the solution by computing the inverse exactly. We must deduce qualitative (sign) information about comparative statics terms from the limited sign restrictions imposed on the model by second-order conditions, stability conditions, or other economically motivated properties. Cramer's rule is particularly well suited for extracting the maximum information from such minimal restrictions.

6.3   Inverse- and Implicit-Function Theorems

Inverse-Function Theorem and Economics

Consider a particular example of a real-valued function of a single variable, say $y = f(x) = 5x$. Since f is a function, it will associate a unique $y \in \Re$ with each $x \in \Re$; in particular, $f(x) = 5x$ associates $y = 10$ with $x = 2$, $y = -50$ with $x = -10$, and so on. Also $f(x) = 5x$ can be used to relate x and y in the "opposite direction." That is, it can be used to associate a unique x with each y. Looked at in this way, f would be written as $x = y/5$; it would associate $x = 2$ with $y = 10$, $x = -10$ with $y = -50$, and so on. The function $x = g(x) = y/5$ that is derived from f but associates a unique $x \subset \Re$ with each $y \in \Re$ is called the **inverse** of f and is written as $g(x) = f^{-1}(y)$.

More generally, the function $g: \Re \to \Re$ is the **inverse** of the function $f: \Re \to \Re$ if f and g are related by the property that $y = f(x)$ iff $x = g(y)$, that is, that $f(g(y)) = y$ and $g(f(x)) = x$. If the inverse function $g = f^{-1}$ exists for all x in the domain of the function, then we say that f is **globally invertible**; if the inverse exists for all x within some $\varepsilon > 0$ of a particular point $\bar{x}$, then we say that f is **locally invertible** at $\bar{x}$. Thus a function that is locally invertible for all points in its domain is globally invertible. Note that a variety of terms can be used in place of invertible: **one-to-one, univalent,** and **injective.**

If $f: \Re \to \Re$ is a differentiable function, then a sufficient condition for the local univalence of f at a point $\bar{x} \in \Re$ is that $f'(\bar{x}) \neq 0$. If the condition $f'(x) \neq 0$ holds for all $x \in \Re$, then the function is globally invertible. This result is called the **inverse-function theorem** for a function of a single variable. To see why this relationship holds, consider Figure 6.1. The function in Figure 6.1 is obviously univalent for all x between x_0 and x_1 and for all x between x_1 and x_2. The only problems occur at the critical points x_0, x_1, and x_2 where $f' = 0$. No matter how small we make $\varepsilon > 0$, there will always be points within ε of these critical points where the mapping $g = f^{-1}$ is not a function, since each y maps into more than one x.

For an economic application of the inverse-function theorem in one variable, recall the short-run, perfectly competitive firm from Chapter 3. The first-order

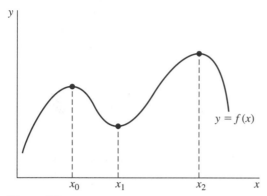

Figure 6.1

condition for profit maximization by such a firm can be written as $h(L) = w/p$, where $w/p =$ wage/price of output $=$ real wage, $L =$ labor, and $h(L) = f'(L) =$ marginal product of labor. If the function h is invertible, we may write $L = g(w/p) = h^{-1}(w/p)$; that is, we may write the firm's profit-maximizing demand for labor L as a unique function of the real wage w/p. The inverse-function theorem tells us that such an inverse exists if $h'(L) \neq 0$. But since $h(L) = f'(L)$ implies that $h'(L) = f''(L)$, the restriction $h'(L) \neq 0$ reduces to the nonvanishing second derivative of the production function $f''(L) \neq 0$. Since the second-order condition for the short-run profit maximization by a perfectly competitive firm implies that $f''(L^*) < 0$ at the profit-maximizing level of employment L^*, this nonvanishing second derivative condition is guaranteed for a profit-maximizing firm. In addition to this local invertibility implied by the second-order condition, the global invertibility of the labor demand function is guaranteed if the short-run production function is strictly concave, or equivalently, if diminishing marginal returns to labor hold throughout.

Now let us extend the discussion of the inverse-function theorem to the case of n variables. For a differentiable function to be univalent, its domain and range must be of the same dimension; so we restrict our attention to $y = f(x)$ where $f: \Re^n \to \Re^n$. In this case we can write the function as $f(x) = (f_1(x), f_2(x), \ldots, f_n(x))$, where $f_i: \Re^n \to \Re$ for each $i = 1, 2, \ldots, n$.

If $f: \Re^n \to \Re^n$ is differentiable, then the n-dimensional analogue of the first derivative is the **Jacobian** matrix Jf:

$$Jf(x) = \begin{bmatrix} f_{11}(x) & \cdots & f_{1n}(x) \\ \vdots & & \vdots \\ f_{n1}(x) & \cdots & f_{nn}(x) \end{bmatrix} = \begin{bmatrix} \dfrac{\partial f_1(x)}{\partial x_1} & \cdots & \dfrac{\partial f_1(x)}{\partial x_n} \\ \vdots & & \vdots \\ \dfrac{\partial f_n(x)}{\partial x_1} & \cdots & \dfrac{\partial f_n(x)}{\partial x_n} \end{bmatrix}. \quad (6.23)$$

Be careful not to confuse the Jacobian matrix Jf with the Hessian matrix Hf defined earlier. The **Jacobian** is an $n \times n$ matrix composed of the **first derivatives** of a function $f: \mathfrak{R}^n \to \mathfrak{R}^n$, while the **Hessian** is an $n \times n$ matrix composed of the **second derivatives** of a function $f: \mathfrak{R}^n \to \mathfrak{R}$. Even though the same symbolism is often used for the elements of these two matrices, in general they have quite different properties. Most importantly, the off-diagonal terms of the Hessian matrix are always symmetric, since $\partial^2 f/\partial x_i \partial x_j = \partial^2 f/\partial x_j \partial x_i$, but since $\partial f_i/\partial x_j$ is not generally equal to $\partial f_j/\partial x_i$, there is no reason for a Jacobian to exhibit such symmetry.

For the n-dimensional case, the univalence question is: What restrictions on f or Jf will guarantee the existence of an inverse function $g = f^{-1}$ such that $y = f(x)$ iff $x = g(y)$? This question is answered by the general **inverse-function theorem,** which we state without proof (the proof is available in most advanced calculus texts).

THEOREM 6.1 (Inverse-Function Theorem): If $|Jf(x^0)| \neq 0$ for $x^0 \subset \mathfrak{R}^n$, then $f: \mathfrak{R}^n \to \mathfrak{R}^n$ is locally one-to-one (univalent), and there exists a unique differentiable inverse function g such that $g(f(x)) = x$ for all x within some ε neighborhood of x^0.

Notice that the inverse-function theorem is exclusively a local result; it guarantees the existence of an inverse function only for values of x within some ε neighborhood of a particular point in $\mathfrak{R}^n$. In the one-variable case just discussed, the local inverse-function theorem could easily be extended to the entire domain; when $f: D \subseteq \mathfrak{R} \to \mathfrak{R}$, then $f' \neq 0$ for all $x \in D$ implies the global univalence of f. It was long conjectured that Theorem 6.1 could be extended globally in the same way. That is, it was suspected that if $|Jf(x)| \neq 0$ for all $x \in D$, then $f: D \subseteq \mathfrak{R}^n \to \mathfrak{R}^n$ would be globally invertible on D for any value of n. A famous counterexample by Lionel McKenzie (1967) demonstrated that this is not the case. A correct sufficient condition for global univalence was provided by Gale and Nikaido (1965). Their result essentially requires that Jf be a P matrix. We will not discuss the Gale–Nikaido result further; it is mentioned only to emphasize the local nature of Theorem 6.1.

One important economic application of the n-dimensional inverse-function theorem is the economic question that initially piqued economists' interest in global univalence: the factor price equalization theorem from international trade theory. The economic issue is as follows. Under conditions of free trade, the international forces of supply and demand will equilibrate the prices of traded goods produced in any one country with the prices of the same goods produced in other countries. The factors of production used to produce these goods, though, are not traded, and their prices are determined solely by domestic supply and demand. The factor price equalization question is: Will the equilibration of product prices in different countries that occurs through international trade also equilibrate the prices of nontraded factors of production used to produce these goods?

Under standard assumptions, the factor price equalization question can be reduced to a question about the invertibility of a particular function. For each output i, we can write the price of output p_i as $p_i = c_i(w)$, where c_i is the average

BOX 6.1
Existence of Competitive Equilibrium

The comparative statics properties of equilibrium positions have been discussed repeatedly in earlier chapters. But throughout these discussions the question of **existence**—the basic question of whether there even is an equilibrium for the model—has been systematically avoided. Obviously the existence question is fundamental; one cannot talk about comparative statics (how equilibrium positions change with a change in the parameters) unless one is certain that an equilibrium exists in the first place. As two parallel lines clearly indicate, simply having the same number of equations and unknowns is not sufficient for the existence of an equilibrium in a system of simultaneous equations; and even if the system does have an equilibrium, mere existence need not guarantee that the equilibrium is economically reasonable (nonnegative prices, for instance).

The existence question, which we will examine, is one of the most important results in post–World War II mathematical economics: the existence of an equilibrium price vector in an n-good Walrasian general equilibrium model. The classic papers on the existence of Walrasian competitive equilibrium are Arrow and Debreu (1954) and McKenzie (1954). Brief surveys of the topic are provided in Quirk and Saposnik (1968) and Takayama (1985), while Weintraub (1983) offers a detailed history of the literature before Arrow, Debreu, and McKenzie. Our presentation is a simplified version of these classic results.

The basic mathematical tool used in economic existence proofs is the **fixed-point theorem.** In general, a fixed point of a function $f(x)$ is a value x^* such that $f(x^*) = x^*$. One familiar example from introductory economics is the equilibrium level of income in the simple Keynesian model in which Y^* is a fixed point of the aggregate demand (AD) function where $Y^* = AD(Y^*)$. The most commonly used mathematical result on fixed points is **Brouwer's fixed-point theorem.** It says that any continuous mapping from a closed, bounded, convex set into itself has a fixed point. The requirement that the domain (and range) be **closed** simply means that any points on the boundary of the domain set are actually in the set (e.g., the set of all x values such that $0 \leq x \leq 1$ is closed, while the set of all x such that $0 < x < 1$ is not closed). The condition that the domain set must be **bounded** means that it is not possible to go off to infinity in any direction and still remain within the set (e.g., the set of all x values such that $0 < x < 1$ is bounded, while the set of all x values such that $x \geq 0$ is not). Finally, the restriction that the domain be a **convex** set means that if a and b are in the set, then $\theta a + (1 - \theta)b$ is in the set for all $0 \leq \theta \leq 1$ (see note 4 in Chapter 1). These domain restrictions are relatively easy to satisfy in the case of the Walrasian general equilibrium model.

Recall the n-good Walrasian model presented in Chapter 5. If zero prices are allowed, the equilibrium is given by an equilibrium price vector $p* = (p_1^*, p_2^*, \ldots, p_n^*)$ such that $z_i(p*) \leq 0$ for all $i = 1, 2, \ldots, n$. To apply Brouwer's fixed-point theorem, we need to restrict the price domain so that it is a closed, bounded, and convex set. This is done by restricting prices to the so-called unit simplex, the set $S = \{p \in \Re_+^n \mid \sum_{i=1}^n p_i = 1\}$. Restricting prices to the set S is not a problem in the Walrasian model, since excess demand functions are homogeneous of degree zero (H) in prices. This domain restriction essentially amounts to multiplying all prices by $\lambda = 1/\sum_{i=1}^n p_i$, and since $z_i(p) = z_i(\lambda p)$ for all i and for all $\lambda \neq 0$, excess demand functions are unaltered by this change.

Now consider the following mapping:

$$h_i(p) = \frac{\max[0, p_i + z_i(p)]}{\sum_{i=1}^n \max[0, p_i + z_i(p)]} \qquad \text{for } i = 1, 2, \ldots, n. \qquad \text{(a)}$$

Notice that if $p \in S$, then $(h_1, h_2, \ldots, h_n)$ is a mapping from S back into S; this is because by the definition of $h_i(p)$ we have $\sum_{i=1}^n h_i(p) = 1$. Also notice that when the excess demand functions are continuous, $h(p)$ will be a continuous mapping. Thus $h(p)$ is a continuous mapping from S (a closed, bounded, and convex set) into itself, and by Brouwer's fixed-point theorem $h(p)$ has a fixed point $p* = (p_1^*, p_2^*, \ldots, p_n^*)$, where

$$p_i^* = h_i(p*) \qquad \text{for all } i = 1, 2, \ldots, n.$$

Thus far we have shown that for a Walrasian general equilibrium model with the standard assumptions (continuity, Walras' law, and zero-degree homogeneity), the mapping $h(p)$ can always be constructed and $h(p)$ has a fixed point $p* = h(p*)$. All that needs to be done now to turn this into an existence proof for equilibrium in the Walrasian model is to demonstrate that the fixed point $p*$ is an equilibrium.

First, we simplify the symbolism and let $H = \sum_{i=1}^n \max[0, p_i^* + z_i(p*)]$. Now suppose $p_i^* = 0$; from (a) we have $p_i^* + z_i(p*) \leq 0$, which implies $z_i(p*) \leq 0$. Alternatively, suppose $p_i^* > 0$. Then we have $p_i^* = [p_i^* + z_i(p*)]/H$ or $p_i^*(H - 1) = z_i(p*)$. Multiplying both sides of the last equation by p_i^* and summing over all i, we have

$$(H - 1) \sum_{i=1}^n (p_i^*)^2 = \sum_{i=1}^n p_i^* z_i(p*).$$

Since the right-hand side of this equation is equal to zero by Walras' law, the equation implies that $H = 1$ and thus $p_i^* > 0$ implies $z_i(p*) = 0$. In summary, we have $z_i(p*) \leq 0$ in the former case and $z_i(p*) = 0$ in the latter case, so $z_i(p*) \leq 0$ for all i in either case and $p*$ is an equilibrium price vector for the Walrasian system. Since such an argument could be made for any

Walrasian model that satisfies the standard assumptions, we have proved that there always exists an equilibrium price vector in such a model.

Sources

Arrow, K. J., and G. Debreu. 1954. Existence of an equilibrium for a competitive economy. *Econometrica* 22: 265–90.

McKenzie, L. 1954. One equilibrium in Graham's model of world trade and other competitive systems. *Econometrica* 22: 147–61.

Quirk, J., and R. Saposnik. 1968. *Introduction to general equilibrium theory and welfare economics.* New York: McGraw-Hill.

Takayama, A. 1985. *Mathematical economics.* 2d ed. Cambridge: Cambridge University Press.

Weintraub, E. R. 1983. On the existence of a competitive equilibrium: 1930–1954. *Journal of Economic Literature* 21: 1–39.

total cost function of good i and w is the vector of domestic factor (input) prices. Assuming that the number of goods is the same as the number of factors, the invertibility of $c(\cdot)$ would imply that $w = c^{-1}(p)$, and a unique domestic input price vector w would correspond to each output price vector p. If all countries have access to the same technology—that is, if all have the same production functions and thus the same $c(\cdot)$s—then world trade that equilibrates p will equilibrate w if $c(\cdot)$ is univalent. The question of local factor price equalization is thus reduced to the question of finding economic conditions that would guarantee that $|Jc| \neq 0$. Although such conditions are known, they are economically quite restrictive.

Another area of economic theory in which the inverse-function theorem has proved to be useful is Walrasian general equilibrium theory. As discussed in Chapter 5, the general equilibrium price vector $p* = (p_1^*, p_2^*, \ldots, p_n^*)$ in an n-good Walrasian model is a price vector that simultaneously clears all n markets. If $z_i(p)$ is the excess demand function for good i and $z(p) = (z_1(p), z_2(p), \ldots, z_n(p))$, then $p*$ must satisfy the system of n nonlinear equations given by $z(p*) = 0$. When $|Jz(p*)| \neq 0$, the inverse-function theorem tells us that $z(\cdot)$ is univalent in some region around $p*$ and thus that the equilibrium price vector is locally unique; there is no other price vector within an ε neighborhood of $p*$ that will simultaneously clear all n markets. Under univalence, the locally unique equilibrium price vector can be written as $p* = z^{-1}(0)$. Since such local unique-ness is a necessary condition for local (i.e., calculus) comparative statics analysis, the univalence of excess demand functions is an important issue in general equilibrium theory. Interest in such questions has led to the development of a whole subfield of general equilibrium theory, the theory of "regular" economics[2] (essentially economies with $|Jz(p*)| \neq 0$).

Implicit-Function Theorem and Economics

While the inverse-function theorem is important in economic theory, a related result—the implicit-function theorem—is perhaps even more important (particularly for comparative statics analysis). Since the implicit-function theory is very similar to the inverse-function theorem, we skip the one-dimensional preliminaries and move directly to the general n-dimensional case. Consider a system of n differentiable equations $f_i(x, \alpha) = 0$ for all $i = 1, 2, \ldots, n$ with $x \in \Re^n$ and $\alpha \in \Re^m$. Thus $f_i \colon \Re^{n+m} \to \Re$, or defining $f = (f_1, f_2, \ldots, f_n)$, we have $f \colon \Re^{n+m} \to \Re^n$. Given such a system of n equations, it is often useful to hold the m variables in α constant as parameters and rewrite the system so that the n variables in x are explicit functions of the m parameters in α, that is, to go from the n **implicit** equations $f_i(x, \alpha) = 0$ for $i = 1, 2, \ldots, n$ to the n **explicit** equations $x_i = x_i(\alpha)$ for $i = 1, 2, \ldots, n$. The question is: Assuming that such a solution exists, when can the n implicit functions be written as n explicit functions? The answer is contained in the **implicit-function theorem** (again the proof can be found in most advanced calculus texts).

THEOREM 6.2 (Implicit-Function Theorem): Consider an $x_0 \in \Re^n$ and $\alpha_0 \in \Re^m$ such that $f(x_0, \alpha_0) = 0$. Then if $|Jf(x_0, \alpha_0)| \neq 0$, there exists a unique differentiable function, h such that $x_0 = h(\alpha_0)$ and $f(h(\alpha), \alpha) = 0$ for every α within some ε neighborhood of α_0.

Before we look at economic applications, we note a number of important facts about the implicit-function theorem. First, like the inverse-function theorem, the implicit-function theorem is entirely a local result. Second, the Jacobian Jf is the $n \times n$ Jacobian with representative term $f_{ij} = \partial f_i / \partial x_j$. In particular, the non-vanishing determinant condition $|Jf| \neq 0$ does not involve any restrictions on the terms $\partial f_i / \partial \alpha_k$. Third, the dimensions of n and m are unrestricted in the implicit-function theorem; it may be that there are more parameters than variables ($m > n$), or more variables than parameters ($n > m$), or an equal number of variables and parameters ($n = m$). Theorem 6.2 holds for all three cases. Finally, as with the inverse-function theorem, $|Jf| \neq 0$ reduces to $f' \neq 0$ when $n = 1$.

The implicit-function theorem has already been needed in a number of the economic models we have examined— for instance, in Chapter 2, where the implicit equation for the indifference curve $U(x_1, x_2) = \bar{U}$ was written explicitly as $x_2 = x_2(x_1)$, and in Chapter 3 where the equations for equilibrium in the *IS-LM* model were solved explicitly for $Y^* = Y^*(D, M^s, p)$ and $r^* = r^*(D, M^s, p)$. Such examples are quite common in economic theory; in fact, almost all comparative statics results depend on the implicit-function theorem. Why? It is because of the way in which comparative statics results are determined. The standard procedure is to start with equations of the form $f(x, \alpha) = 0$—either equilibrium conditions or the first-order conditions for an optimum—and then rewrite these equations as explicit functions of the parameters $x = h(\alpha)$ that are in turn differentiated to find comparative statics terms such as $\partial x_i / \partial \alpha_j$. The nonvanishing determinant condition of the implicit-function theorem is precisely the sufficient condition that will make this transformation from implicit to explicit functions possible. Applying the implicit-function theorem in this context usually amounts to determining whether the economic structure of the model is sufficient to guarantee the nonsingularity of the relevant Jacobian. Often it is.

Recall the two-input perfectly competitive firm whose comparative statics terms were found in (6.19) as an application of Cramer's rule. By using a semicolon to separate the choice variables (L, K) of the problem from the parameters (w, v, p), we can write the first-order conditions as

$$\pi_L(L, K; w, v, p) = pf_L(L, K) - w = 0,$$
$$\pi_K(L, K; w, v, p) = pf_K(L, K) - v = 0.$$
(6.24)

The two equations in (6.24) provide the initial implicit functions that are "solved" for the explicit factor demand functions

$$L^* = L^*(w, v, p) \quad \text{and} \quad K^* = K^*(w, v, p).$$
(6.25)

Now, how do we know that it is possible to go from the implicit system of two equations in five variables in (6.24) to the explicit system of two equations in three variables in (6.25)? How do we know that the profit-maximizing input demands can actually be written as differentiable functions of the three parameters w, v, and p? The answer is, of course, from the implicit-function theorem. We know the transformation is possible because the second-order conditions for profit maximization guarantee that the nonsingularity restriction of the implicit-function theorem is satisfied.

To see how the implicit-function theorem applies to this case, recall from (6.21) the second-order conditions for this problem:

$$\pi_{LL} < 0, \qquad \pi_{KK} < 0, \qquad \text{and} \qquad |H\pi| = \pi_{LL}\pi_{KK} - \pi_{LK}^2 > 0.$$

These conditions require the **Hessian** of the profit function $H\pi$ to have negative first-order principal minors and a positive determinant (to be an *NP* matrix) at the optimum (L^*, K^*). Now consider what would be required to apply the implicit-function theorem to system (6.24). The implicit-function theorem would require that the **Jacobian** of the system (6.24) have a nonvanishing determinant at (L^*, K^*); that is, if we define $\pi' = (\pi_L, \pi_K)$, then the implicit-function theorem requires that $|J\pi'| \neq 0$. What is the relationship between these two conditions? The relationship is that $H\pi = J\pi'$. Since the "system" to which we are applying the implicit-function theorem is a system of functions that are the first derivatives of the profit function π, the Jacobian matrix for this system is the same as the Hessian matrix of the original profit function π. Given this relationship, the second-order conditions for profit maximization clearly guarantee the nonsingularity of the relevant Jacobian.

The close relationship between the second-order conditions and the applicability of the implicit-function theorem is not unique to this particular example of a perfectly competitive firm. In general, if the first- and second-order conditions hold at a certain point, then the first-order conditions can be solved (locally) for the optimal values of the choice variables as explicit functions of the parameters. This makes the implicit-function theorem "implicit" in all optimization-based comparative statics analysis; it also means that it is seldom necessary to actually check for

the nonsingularity of the relevant Jacobian, since the condition is automatically satisfied in any well-behaved problem (i.e., any problem in which second-order conditions hold). A similar result may hold when the initial equations are equilibrium
conditions rather than first-order conditions; but such a result is not guaranteed, as
it is with optimization-based models. Sometimes the economic properties, particularly stability properties, of equilibrium models are sufficient to ensure that the
implicit-function theorem can be applied, but sometimes they are not. For equilibrium models, the question of whether the equilibrium conditions can be solved for
explicit functions of the underlying parameters must be approached on a case-by-
case basis.

6.4   A Special Class of Matrices: M Matrices

This section discusses an important subfield of matrix theory, the theory of **nonsingular M matrices.** Few areas of mathematical research have been as strongly
influenced by problems from economic theory as the theory of M matrices. Economists provided many of the earliest results in the field, and economic problems
have continued to motivate many mathematical researchers. Although we examine only a few of the many properties of M matrices, the "tip of the iceberg" discussed in this section goes a long way in the analysis of many economic models
including the Leontief input–output system, which follows in Section 6.5.

So what is an M matrix? There are a number of slightly different definitions
in the literature, but we use the most standard. An $n \times n$ matrix B with representative element $[b_{ij}]$ is an **M matrix** if it has **both** of the following properties:

$$b_{ij} \leq 0 \qquad \text{for all } i \neq j \tag{6.26a}$$

$$B \text{ is a } P \text{ matrix.} \tag{6.26b}$$

Thus, an M matrix is a matrix with nonpositive off-diagonal terms and all positive
principal minors. Notice that (6.26a) alone does not restrict the elements along the
main diagonal $[b_{ii}]$, but when (6.26b) is added, the diagonal terms must be strictly
positive, since they are the first-order principal minors of the matrix. Also notice
that an M matrix must be nonsingular; the inverse always exists. This is because the
determinant of an $n \times n$ matrix is the nth-order principal of the matrix, and thus
the P matrix condition guarantees that $|B| > 0$ and that B is nonsingular.

It is important to keep the two parts of the definition of an M matrix separate.
This is because if a particular matrix satisfies (6.26a)—that is, if it has nonpositive
off-diagonal elements—then a number of different properties are equivalent to
(6.26b), the property of being a P matrix. This result is shown in Theorem 6.3.
Theorem 6.3 is stated for the general case of an $n \times n$ matrix, but the proof that
follows only proves the $n = 2$ case. The interested reader may consult a more
mathematically detailed source for the general proof.[3]

Before moving on to the next theorem, we want to emphasize a few of the
properties revealed in the proof of Theorem 6.3. First, from the proof of (a)→(b)
it is apparent that $x > 0$. That is, for any matrix B with $b_{ij} \leq 0$ for all $i \neq j$ and

THEOREM 6.3: For any $n \times n$ matrix B with $b_{ij} \leq 0$ for all $i \neq j$, the following three conditions are equivalent:

(a) There exists an $x \in \Re_+^n$, such that $Bx > 0$.
(b) B is a P matrix.
(c) $B^{-1} \geq 0$.

PROOF: We prove the theorem (for $n = 2$) by showing that $(a) \rightarrow (b) \rightarrow (c) \rightarrow (a)$.

For $(a) \rightarrow (b)$: For $n = 2$ with $x^T = (x_1, x_2)$, $Bx > 0$ implies that

$$b_{11}x_1 + b_{12}x_2 > 0,$$
$$b_{21}x_1 + b_{22}x_2 > 0.$$

Since $b_{12} \leq 0$, $b_{21} \leq 0$, and $x_2 \geq 0$, we know that $b_{11} > 0$ and $b_{22} > 0$. Given this sign pattern on the elements of B, the two inequalities reduce to $b_{11}b_{22} > b_{12}b_{21}$, or $|B| > 0$. Thus B is a P matrix.

For (b) $\rightarrow$ (c): Computing B^{-1} directly for the $n = 2$ case, we have

$$B^{-1} = \begin{bmatrix} \dfrac{b_{22}}{|B|} & \dfrac{-b_{12}}{|B|} \\[2mm] \dfrac{-b_{21}}{|B|} & \dfrac{b_{11}}{|B|} \end{bmatrix}.$$

Now when $b_{12} \leq 0$, $b_{21} \leq 0$, and B is a P matrix ($|B| > 0$), clearly each element of B^{-1} is nonnegative, and thus $B^{-1} \geq 0$.

For (c) $\rightarrow$ (a): With $B^{-1} \geq 0$, let $e^T = (1, 1) > 0$ and define $x = B^{-1}e \geq 0$. Then $Bx = BB^{-1}e = e > 0$, and thus there exists an $x \in \Re_+^n$ such that $Bx > 0$.

where there exists $x \in \Re_+^n$ such that $Bx > 0$, then it must be that $x \in \Re_{++}^n$; if any one of the x_i's were equal to zero, the strict inequality $Bx > 0$ could not hold. Second, notice from the proof of (b) $\rightarrow$ (c) that if the off-diagonal terms are strictly negative, then the elements of B^{-1} are strictly positive. That is, for the case of $b_{ij} < 0$ for all $i \neq j$, condition (c) of the theorem can be strengthened to $B^{-1} > 0$. Third, note that the $b_{ij} \leq 0$ condition was not used in the final step of the proof; (c) $\rightarrow$ (a) holds for any matrix. And finally, in the economics literature condition (b) is sometimes called a **Hawkins–Simon condition** in honor of the two authors who first applied it in economic theory (Hawkins and Simon, 1949). The next theorem is a useful result that relates the properties of an M matrix and its transpose.

THEOREM 6.4: If B is an M matrix, then its transpose B^T is also an M matrix.

PROOF: If B is an M matrix, then its transpose B^T will have nonpositive off-diagonal terms as well. Thus to prove the theorem, we need only show that when B is an M matrix, B^T has one of the three properties in Theorem 6.3. Since $(B^{-1})^T = (B^T)^{-1}$ for any matrix, $B^{-1} \geq 0$ implies that $(B^{-1})^T \geq 0$, which implies that $(B^T)^{-1} \geq 0$, and so B^T is a P matrix by Theorem 6.3.

6.5 The Leontief Input–Output System

In this section we examine a particular multisector general equilibrium model, the Leontief input–output system. The model gets its name from W. W. Leontief, the Nobel Prize–winning economist who initially developed it during the 1920s. Since the Leontief system is an n-sector model, in one respect it is more complex than the three-good Walrasian general equilibrium model of Chapter 5. But since its structure is entirely linear and consumer demand is included in only the most rudimentary way, it is in other respects much simpler than the Walrasian model discussed earlier.

The Leontief input–output system is based on the simple notion that it takes goods to make goods. For instance, the production of 1 unit of steel requires the use of various intermediate goods: a certain quantity of iron, a certain quantity of energy, and so on. In fact, often the good itself is used as an intermediate good in its own production (it takes wheat to make wheat). In addition to these intermediate goods, production requires a certain amount of labor, which is called a **primary** factor in a Leontief system because it is "produced" outside the model. We eventually integrate a primary factor into our analysis, but to start, we focus exclusively on the goods-to-make-goods aspect of the model.

Let a_{ij} represent the amount of good i used in the production of 1 unit of good j $(i, j = 1, 2, \ldots, n)$. These a_{ij}'s are called **input coefficients** or **production coefficients.** Each a_{ij} is a nonnegative constant, which implies that no good uses a negative quantity of any input and that production is characterized by fixed coefficients; the amount of good i necessary as an input for the production of 1 unit of good j is the same regardless of the amount of good j being produced.

If x_j is the amount of good j actually produced, then $a_{ij}x_j$ represents the demand for good i as an input into the production of good j. If we sum over all n goods, we have

$$\sum_{j=1}^{n} a_{ij}x_j \tag{6.27}$$

as the total demand for good i as an intermediate good. Since each i is included in the sum from 1 to n, the total demand for i as an input includes the demand for i to be used in its own production.

The "open" Leontief model that we examine includes a final consumption demand for each good in addition to the production demand in (6.27). If we let $d^T = (d_1, d_2, \ldots, d_n) > 0$ represent this exogenously given consumption demand, then the equilibrium of the total supply and the total demand for each good will be given by

$$x_i = \sum_{j=1}^{n} a_{ij}x_j + d_i \qquad \text{for all } i = 1, 2, \ldots, n. \tag{6.28}$$

Or, rewriting this equilibrium condition in terms of the $n \times n$ input–output Leontief matrix A with representative term $[a_{ij}]$ and the output vector $x^T = (x_1, x_2, \ldots, x_n)$, we have

$$x = Ax + d \qquad \text{or} \qquad (I - A)x = d. \tag{6.29}$$

Equation (6.29) is the fundamental equation of the open Leontief system. If $I - A$ is a nonsingular matrix (i.e., if $|I - A| \neq 0$), then the inverse $(I - A)^{-1}$ exists and the output of each good will be given by the solution

$$x^* = (I - A)^{-1}d. \tag{6.30}$$

As a numerical example of a Leontief system, suppose that there are only two sectors ($n = 2$), consumption demand is given by the unit column vector $d^T = (1, 1)$, and the input–output matrix is

$$A = \begin{bmatrix} 0.4 & 0.3 \\ 0.2 & 0.3 \end{bmatrix}, \quad \text{so } I - A = \begin{bmatrix} 0.6 & -0.3 \\ -0.2 & 0.7 \end{bmatrix}. \tag{6.31}$$

For this simple $n = 2$ example, we can compute the inverse $(I - A)^{-1}$ directly:

$$(I - A)^{-1} = \begin{bmatrix} 1.94 & 0.83 \\ 0.55 & 1.66 \end{bmatrix}. \tag{6.32}$$

This inverse tells us that in equilibrium, the output of the two sectors will be given by

$$\begin{bmatrix} x_1^* \\ x_2^* \end{bmatrix} = (I - A)^{-1} \begin{bmatrix} d_1 \\ d_2 \end{bmatrix} = \begin{bmatrix} 1.94 & 0.83 \\ 0.55 & 1.66 \end{bmatrix} \begin{bmatrix} 1 \\ 1 \end{bmatrix} = \begin{bmatrix} 2.77 \\ 2.21 \end{bmatrix}. \tag{6.33}$$

Thus given the input–output matrix (6.31), the economy must produce 2.77 units of x_1 ($x_1^* = 2.77$) and 2.21 units of x_2 ($x_2^* = 2.21$) if 1 unit of each good is to be available for final consumption.

Now the numerical example in (6.31) worked out quite nicely. The inverse matrix $(I - A)^{-1}$ not only existed, but also had positive elements that guaranteed that the solutions would be strictly positive for any final consumption vector $d^T = (d_1, d_2) > 0$. But will such nice properties hold for any arbitrary Leontief matrix? Is the fact that A is a Leontief matrix and thus has $a_{ij} \geq 0$ for all i, j sufficient to guarantee that $|I - A| \neq 0$ and $(I - A)^{-1} \geq 0$, so that $x^* > 0$ for any $d > 0$? Certainly not. For example, if the a_{22} term in (6.31) is changed to 0.9 and the other elements of A are left unchanged, then the inverse $(I - A)^{-1}$ exists but some of its elements are negative. So how can we be certain that a particular Leontief system even has a solution, or, if it has a solution, that it will make economic sense (i.e., have strictly positive outputs for any positive final demand vector)?

The answer is provided by Theorem 6.3. To see how, consider any arbitrary Leontief matrix A. Define the matrix $B = I - A$ so $b_{ii} = 1 - a_{ii}$ for all i, and $b_{ij} - a_{ij}$ for all $i \neq j$. Notice that since $a_{ij} \geq 0$ for all $i \neq j$, matrix B has $b_{ij} \leq 0$ for all $i \neq j$. Thus B satisfies the first condition for the application of Theorem 6.3.

Now suppose that the Leontief matrix A is **productive** in the following (quite specific) sense. Suppose there exists a nonnegative n-dimensional column vector $\bar{x}$ such that

$$\bar{x} > A\bar{x}. \tag{6.34}$$

What does condition (6.34) say? It says that there exists a set of output levels $\bar{x}_i \geq 0$ such that

$$\bar{x}_i > \sum_{j=1}^{n} a_{ij}\bar{x}_j \qquad \text{for all } i = 1, 2, \ldots, n. \tag{6.35}$$

In other words, condition (6.34) says there is at least one way to run the economy "productively," one set of outputs in which the quantity of each good produced is greater than the amount of the good used in the overall production process. Condition (6.34) says there exists some strictly positive final consumption vector $\bar{d} > 0$ that the system can attain. This condition is an additional restriction on the Leontief matrix. It does not follow merely from the fact that $a_{ij} \geq 0$, but it is a very weak restriction, and any system that did not meet such a minimal standard of productivity would not be of any economic interest. For example, any system "observed" to be producing a positive output of all goods automatically satisfies (6.34).

Now when the economy is productive in the sense of (6.34), the matrix $B = I - A$ satisfies condition (a) of Theorem 6.3; there exists an $x \geq 0$ such that $B\bar{x} > 0$. Part (b) of Theorem 6.3 then guarantees that B is nonsingular (since B is a P matrix), and part (c) implies that $B^{-1} = (I - A)^{-1} \geq 0$. Thus the productivity condition (6.34) is sufficient to guarantee that the open Leontief system

$$(I - A)x = d$$

has a strictly positive solution vector $x^* = (I - A)^{-1}d$ for any final consumption demand vector $d > 0$.

The foregoing argument has given us the desired result; as long as the system meets a minimum productivity requirement (6.34), the Leontief model will have an economically reasonable solution. But the discussion is a little weak on intuition. That is, *why* does the productivity condition guarantee the nice results? To help with the intuition, let us look more closely at the $n = 2$ case and draw a two-dimensional diagram.

Consider the $n = 2$ general Leontief system

$$A = \begin{bmatrix} a_{11} & a_{12} \\ a_{21} & a_{22} \end{bmatrix}, \qquad x = \begin{bmatrix} x_1 \\ x_2 \end{bmatrix}, \qquad \text{and} \qquad d = \begin{bmatrix} d_1 \\ d_2 \end{bmatrix}. \tag{6.36}$$

For this case, the fundamental equation $(I - A)x = d$ reduces to

$$(1 - a_{11})x_1 - a_{12}x_2 = d_1, \tag{6.37a}$$

$$-a_{21}x_1 + (1 - a_{22})x_2 = d_2. \tag{6.37b}$$

The solution to the Leontief system is simply the solution to the two linear equations in (6.37). Rather than using matrix methods to solve the system, let us graph the two lines in (6.37) and examine the solution at their intersection. Converting

(6.37a) and (6.37b) into the more familiar slope–intercept form, we have

$$x_2 = \frac{(1 - a_{11})x_1}{a_{12}} + \frac{-d_1}{a_{12}}, \tag{6.38a}$$

$$x_2 = \frac{a_{21}x_1}{1 - a_{22}} + \frac{d_2}{1 - a_{22}}. \tag{6.38b}$$

We know from the foregoing argument that when the system is productive in the sense of (6.34), matrix $B = I - A$ satisfies the conditions of Theorem 6.3. Let us see what this tells us about the shapes of the two lines in (6.38). Since B is a P matrix, Theorem 6.3 tells us that it has all positive principal minors: so $b_{11} > 0$, $b_{22} > 0$, and $b_{11}b_{22} - b_{12}b_{21} > 0$. But $b_{ii} = 1 - a_{ii}$, so $1 - a_{11} > 0$, and $1 - a_{22} > 0$. These inequalities certainly seem reasonable: they say that less than 1 unit of each good is used directly in 1 unit of its own production. From (6.38) the conditions $1 - a_{11} > 0$ and $1 - a_{22} > 0$ tell us that both lines slope upward. Equation (6.38a) has a positive x_1 intercept at $d_1/(1 - a_{11})$, and equation (6.38b) has a positive x_2 intercept at $d_2/(1 - a_{22})$. Now the condition on the second-order principal minor of B, that $|B| = b_{11}b_{22} - b_{12}b_{21} > 0$, implies that

$$(1 - a_{11})(1 - a_{22}) - a_{12}a_{21} > 0, \tag{6.39}$$

or with some rearrangement

$$\frac{1 - a_{11}}{a_{12}} > \frac{a_{21}}{1 - a_{22}}. \tag{6.40}$$

The left-hand side of (6.40) is the slope of (6.38a), while the right-hand side of (6.40) is the slope of (6.38b). Thus condition (6.40) says that under the assumption that the economy is productive, the line (6.38a) is steeper than the line (6.38b). These two lines are drawn in Figure 6.2 with (6.38a) labeled L_1 and (6.38b) labeled L_2. Notice that when the system is productive, when the lines have

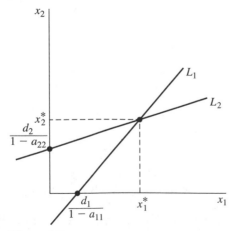

Figure 6.2

the slopes depicted in Figure 6.2, the solution $(x^*)^T = (x_1^*, x_2^*)$ will always exist and be strictly positive for any value of $d^T = (d_1, d_2) > 0$. Increasing or decreasing d_1 simply moves L_1 right or left, respectively, while increasing or decreasing d_2 simply moves L_2 up or down, respectively. Thus we see that the rather unintuitive condition that "B is a P matrix" has a nice graphical interpretation in the $n = 2$ case.

So far, our discussion of the Leontief model has been solely in terms of the quantities produced x^*. We now want to discuss prices in the Leontief system. Let $p = (p_1, p_2, \ldots, p_n) > 0$ be a row vector of prices for the n commodities. Given these prices, $p_i a_{ij}$ is the cost of purchasing the amount of good i required to produce 1 unit of good j. Summing over all n goods, we have

$$\sum_{i=1}^{n} p_i a_{ij} \qquad (6.41)$$

as the total cost of the intermediate goods necessary to produce 1 unit of good j.

Subtracting (6.41), the total cost of the intermediate goods used in the production of 1 unit of good j, from the price of 1 unit of good j (p_j), we have the "value added" by the production of 1 unit of good j, denoted V_j. Thus the **value added** per unit of j is defined as

$$V_j = p_j - \sum_{i=1}^{n} p_i a_{ij}. \qquad (6.42)$$

The condition $V_j > 0$ means that additional revenue is available from each unit of good j produced; in long-run competitive equilibrium with zero economic profits, this value added would be distributed to the primary factors. If $V = (V_1, V_2, \ldots, V_n)$ is the value-added row vector for the whole economy, then in matrix form

$$V = p(I - A). \qquad (6.43)$$

Just as we can ask whether there always exists an economically meaningful solution to $x = (I - A)^{-1}d$ for any $d > 0$, we can ask whether there always exists an economically meaningful price vector $p = V(I - A)^{-1}$ for any value-added vector $V > 0$. Of course, if the system is productive, then $(I - A)^{-1} \geq 0$ and the answer is yes. But suppose we do not know whether the system satisfies the productivity condition (6.34). After all, condition (6.34) is really an output condition. Is there a price analogue to this condition? Is there a pure price condition that will guarantee $(I - A)^{-1} \geq 0$ without any information about the output productivity? The answer is of course yes. If there exists a price vector $\bar{p} = (\bar{p}_1, \bar{p}_2, \ldots, \bar{p}_n) \geq 0$ such that the system is **profitable** (i.e., has a strictly positive value added for each good), then $(I - A)^{-1} \geq 0$, and positive prices exist for any initial value-added vector.

The foregoing argument is based on Theorem 6.4. If the system is **profitable** then there exists $\bar{p} \geq 0$ such that

$$\bar{p} > \bar{p}A. \qquad (6.44)$$

Condition (6.44) implies that $\bar{p}(I - A) > 0$ or $\bar{p}B > 0$, where $B = I - A$ as before. But by the rules of matrix transposition, the condition $\bar{p}B > 0$ is equal to $B^T \bar{p}^T > 0$, where $\bar{p}^T$ is the column vector formed from $\bar{p}$. Now since $\bar{p}^T \geq 0$, Theorem 6.3 proves that B^T is an M matrix and Theorem 6.4 proves that B is an M matrix. Thus $B^{-1} \geq 0$ as well as the other conditions of Theorem 6.3 is guaranteed. This gives a nice **duality** between **productivity** and **profitability.** If there exist nonnegative prices such that the system is profitable, then by Theorems 6.3 and 6.4 there will exist strictly positive outputs for any positive consumption demand vector $d > 0$. Alternatively, if the system is productive, then the same theorems guarantee that there will exist strictly positive prices for any positive value-added vector $V > 0$. This is just one of a number of quite useful duality results that surface at various places in economic theory.

As the final topic of this section, we briefly discuss the inclusion of a primary factor such as labor in the Leontief model. Let $a_L = (a_{L1}, a_{L2}, \ldots, a_{Ln}) > 0$ be a vector of labor coefficients, where a_{Lj} is the amount of labor required to produce 1 unit of good j. If $w > 0$ is the wage per unit of labor, then wa_{Lj} is the labor cost associated with the production of 1 unit of good j. Now with only one primary input, in long-run equilibrium with zero economic profit, the value added in each sector will be paid to labor in that sector, and thus $wa_{Lj} = V_j$ for all j. By using the definition of V_j from (6.42), this long-run equilibrium condition becomes

$$wa_{Lj} = p_j - \sum_{i=1}^{n} p_i a_{ij} \qquad \text{for all } j = 1, 2, \ldots, n \tag{6.45}$$

or, in matrix notation,

$$wa_L = p(I - A). \tag{6.46}$$

Thus the prices of the goods can be expressed in terms of the labor used in production, since

$$p^* = wa_L(I - A)^{-1}. \tag{6.47}$$

Under either the profitability condition (6.44) or the productivity condition (6.34), we always have that p^* always exists and is strictly positive.

6.6 Quadratic Forms and Definiteness

A **form** is a polynomial expression of uniform degree. Thus a **quadratic form** is an expression in which each variable either occurs as a square or is multiplied by another variable. For instance, the expression $3x_1^2 + 12x_1x_2 + 5x_2^2$ is a quadratic form in two variables x_1 and x_2. Quadratic forms have very convenient matrix representations; our example can be written as

$$[x_1 \quad x_2] \begin{bmatrix} 3 & 6 \\ 6 & 5 \end{bmatrix} \begin{bmatrix} x_1 \\ x_2 \end{bmatrix}. \tag{6.48}$$

The general expression for a quadratic form in two variables is

$$Q_A(x_1, x_2) = \sum_{i=1}^{2} \sum_{j=1}^{2} x_i a_{ij} x_j = a_{11}x_1^2 + 2a_{12}x_1 x_2 + a_{22}x_2^2.$$

In matrix form, the two-variable quadratic form is $Q_A(x_1, x_2) = x^T A x$, where $x^T = (x_1, x_2)$ and A is the 2×2 symmetric matrix

$$A = \begin{bmatrix} a_{11} & a_{12} \\ a_{21} & a_{22} \end{bmatrix} \quad \text{with } a_{12} = a_{21}.$$

Quadratic forms of more than two variables are defined analogously. Thus for $n = 3$

$$Q_A(x) = x^T A x = \sum_{i=1}^{3} \sum_{j=1}^{3} x_i a_{ij} x_j \quad \text{with } x^T = (x_1, x_2, x_3),$$

and for the general n-variable case we have

$$Q_A(x) = x^T A x = \sum_{i=1}^{n} \sum_{j=1}^{n} x_i a_{ij} x_j \quad \text{with } x^T = (x_1, x_2, \ldots, x_n).$$

In fact, any $n \times n$ symmetric matrix will define the associated quadratic form $x^T A x$.

Notice that quadratic forms are defined only for symmetric matrices. This is because the quadratic form associated with an asymmetric matrix will always have the same value as the quadratic form generated by only the symmetric part of the matrix. To see why, consider an arbitrary asymmetric matrix C. This matrix (any matrix) can be written as the sum of its symmetric and asymmetric parts. Thus

$$C = \frac{C + C^T}{2} + \frac{C - C^T}{2}. \tag{6.49}$$

Computing the quadratic form $Q_C(x) = x^T C x$ for $x^T = (x_1, x_2, \ldots, x_n)$, we have

$$x^T C x = x^T \left(\frac{C + C^T}{2} \right) x + x^T \left(\frac{C - C^T}{2} \right) x. \tag{6.50}$$

Expansion of the far right-hand term in (6.50) gives

$$x^T \left(\frac{C - C^T}{2} \right) x = \frac{x^T C x - x^T C^T x}{2}. \tag{6.51}$$

But by the rules of matrix transposition, the expression in (6.51) is equal to zero, since $x^T C x = x^T (C x) = (C x)^T x = x^T C^T x$. So we are left with only

$$x^T C x = x^T \left(\frac{C + C^T}{2} \right) x$$

as the quadratic form associated with the asymmetric matrix C. And thus the quadratic form generated from an asymmetric matrix C is identical to the quadratic form generated from its symmetric part alone, $(C + C^T)/2$.

It is often important to know whether a quadratic form is of uniform sign for all values of vector x. Obviously if x is a vector composed entirely of zeros, then the quadratic form is equal to zero; but certain matrices generate quadratic forms that always have the same sign regardless of vector x (other than $x = 0$).

If A is an $n \times n$ symmetric matrix and $x \neq 0$ is an n-vector $x^T = (x_1, x_2, \ldots, x_n)$ with at least one nonzero component, then the following terms are used to classify quadratic forms of uniform sign.

A is **positive definite** if $Q_A(x) = x^T A x > 0$ for all $x \neq 0$.

A is **negative definite** if $Q_A(x) = x^T A x < 0$ for all $x \neq 0$.

A is **positive semidefinite** if $Q_A(x) = x^T A x \geq 0$ for all $x \neq 0$.

A is **negative semidefinite** if $Q_A(x) = x^T A x \leq 0$ for all $x \neq 0$.

To help clarify these definitions, let us consider a few examples.

First, suppose matrix A is given by

$$A = \begin{bmatrix} 1 & 2 \\ 2 & 1 \end{bmatrix} \tag{6.52}$$

so that it generates the quadratic form

$$Q_A(x) = x_1^2 + 4x_1x_2 + x_2^2. \tag{6.53}$$

So is this matrix definite? Does it have any of the four properties just defined? To answer, let us simply examine a few values of $x^T = (x_1, x_2)$ and see what happens to the sign of $Q_A(x)$. Remember, if A has any of the properties listed, then $Q_A(x)$ must be of uniform sign (positive, negative, nonnegative, or nonpositive) for all values of $x^T \neq (0, 0)$. Consider the vector $x^T = (1, 1)$ first. Substituting into (6.53), we have $Q_A(1, 1) = 6$, so matrix A generates a quadratic form that is strictly positive for the vector $x^T = (1, 1)$. Now consider $x^T = (1, -1)$. Substituting this vector into (6.53), we have $Q_A(1, -1) = -2$, and so matrix A generates a quadratic form that is strictly negative for $x^T = (1, -1)$. Since $Q_A(x)$ is positive for some values of x and negative for other values of x, we conclude that (6.52) does not have any of the four listed properties; it is not definite (it is indefinite).

Now consider a different $n = 2$ example. Let A be given by

$$A = \begin{bmatrix} 1 & \frac{1}{2} \\ \frac{1}{2} & 1 \end{bmatrix}, \tag{6.54}$$

which generates the quadratic form

$$Q_A(x) = x_1^2 + x_1x_2 + x_2^2. \tag{6.55}$$

Checking the preceding values of x^T, we have

$$Q_A(1, 1) = 3 \quad \text{and} \quad Q_A(1, -1) = 1. \tag{6.56}$$

Thus the matrix in (6.54) has a strictly positive quadratic form for the two vectors that reversed the sign of the preceding example. This might lead us to suspect that (6.54) is a positive definite matrix; let us try to confirm this suspicion directly.

Expression (6.55) can be written as

$$Q_A(x) = x_1^2 + x_1 x_2 + \frac{x_2^2}{4} + \frac{3x_2^2}{4}. \tag{6.57}$$

With some rearrangement (6.57) becomes

$$Q_A(x) = \left(x_1 + \frac{x_2}{2}\right)^2 + \frac{3x_2^2}{4}. \tag{6.58}$$

Now since both the first and second terms on the right-hand side of (6.58) are squares, $Q_A(x) > 0$ for any $x \neq 0$. Thus the matrix in (6.54) is positive definite.

Since checking for definiteness directly can be quite cumbersome even in the $n = 2$ case and substantially more difficult for $n > 2$, let us develop some relatively "easy to check" necessary and sufficient conditions for the definiteness of a matrix. To this end, let us return to the two-variable general case, where

$$Q_A(x) = a_{11}x_1^2 + 2a_{12}x_1 x_2 + a_{22}x_2^2. \tag{6.59}$$

Remembering the last numerical example, we realize that if we can rewrite $Q_A(x)$ in a form where all the variables appear as squares, then we will have a substantial amount of information about $Q_A(x)$. To write (6.59) in a "squares only" form, we use the trick of "completing the square"; that is, we add/subtract $(a_{12}^2/a_{11})x_2^2$ to/from both sides of the quadratic form in (6.59). Thus $Q_A(x)$ becomes

$$Q_A(x) = a_{11}x_1^2 + 2a_{12}x_1 x_2 + \frac{a_{12}^2 x_2^2}{a_{11}} + a_{22}x_2^2 - \frac{a_{12}^2 x_2^2}{a_{11}}.$$

Rearranging, we have

$$Q_A(x) = a_{11}\left(x_1 + \frac{a_{12}x_2}{a_{11}}\right)^2 + \left(\frac{a_{11}a_{22} - a_{12}^2}{a_{11}}\right)x_2^2. \tag{6.60}$$

If we let $(\cdot)^2$ represent the squared terms in (6.60), the expression is

$$Q_A(x) = a_{11}(\cdot)^2 + \left(\frac{a_{11}a_{22} - a_{12}^2}{a_{11}}\right)(\cdot)^2. \tag{6.61}$$

Notice that the coefficient of the first square in (6.61) is a_{11}, which is a first-order principal minor of A. The coefficient of the second square in (6.61) is the determinant of A divided by a_{11}. Since this is a 2×2 matrix, the determinant is a (the) second-order principal minor, and thus the coefficient on the second square is a second-order principal minor divided by a first-order principal minor. Therefore (6.61) can be written[4]

$$Q_A(x) = M_1(\cdot)^2 + \left(\frac{M_2}{M_1}\right)(\cdot)^2, \tag{6.62}$$

where M_i is an ith-order principal minor of A.

BOX 6.2
Marxian Value Theory

Marxian economics and other heterodox economic theories are often presented as nonmathematical alternatives to the formalization of mainstream economic theory. One exception to this general rule is Marxian mathematical economic theory. This branch of heterodox economics originated with Sraffa's (1960) formalization of the classical Ricardian system and has since provided mathematical formalizations of many Marxian economic concepts such as value and exploitation. Although many radical economists have been quite critical of the mathematical approach to Marxian economics, it remains an important component of a more general program in "analytical Marxism." Significant contributions to the literature include Morishima (1973), Morishima and Catephores (1978), Roemer (1982), and Steedman (1977); our discussion follows the presentation in Murata (1977).

The most basic notion in Marxian economics is the concept of **value;** all goods are measured in terms of the socially necessary labor time or **value** embodied in them. This value comes only from labor, the "living" labor of the workers who actually produce the good and the "dead" labor embodied in the other goods that go into the production of the good. Thus if a_{ij} is the Leontief coefficient measuring the amount of good i necessary to produce 1 unit of good j and λ_i is the value of 1 unit of good i (the socially necessary labor time embodied in each unit of the good), then $\lambda_i a_{ij}$ is the value embodied in good i used to produce 1 unit of good j. Similarly,

$$\sum_{i=1}^{n} \lambda_i a_{ij}$$

is the total value embodied in all the intermediate goods that go into the production of 1 unit of good j.

Now since the total value of any good is the dead labor plus the living labor, we have

$$\lambda_j = \sum_{i=1}^{n} \lambda_i a_{ij} + a_{Lj}$$

as the total value of 1 unit of good j, where a_{Lj} is the amount of direct (living) labor that goes into 1 unit of good j. Because this value equation holds for all goods j, we have the whole economy represented by the system of equations

$$\lambda = \lambda A + a_L \qquad \text{or} \qquad \lambda = a_L(I - A)^{-1},$$

where $\lambda = (\lambda_1, \lambda_2, \ldots, \lambda_n)$, $a_L = (a_{L1}, a_{L2}, \ldots, a_{Ln})$, and A is the $n \times n$ Leontief coefficient matrix. If the Leontief matrix A is productive, then values will be strictly positive.

Prices in the Marxian system are given by a slight modification of equation (6.45) in the text. In (6.45) the price of each good j, p_j, is equal to the cost of intermediate goods used and labor cost; in the Marxian system, profit r_j must also be included, where

$$r_j = p_j - \sum_{i=1}^{n} p_i a_{ij} - wa_{Lj} \qquad \text{for all } j = 1, 2, \ldots, n.$$

If this per unit profit r_j is written as a markup π_j over the cost of production, that is, if

$$r_j = \pi_j \left(\sum_{i=1}^{n} p_i a_{ij} + wa_{Lj} \right),$$

then the preceding expression relating price p_j and profit r_j can be rewritten as the following relation between the price and the rate of profit π_j:

$$p_j = (1 - \pi_j) \left(\sum_{i=1}^{n} p_i a_{ij} + wa_{Lj} \right).$$

If competition equates the rate of profit in all industries so that $\pi = \pi_j$ for all $j = 1, 2, \ldots, n$, then our price equation will have the following matrix form:

$$p = (1 + \pi)[pA + wa_L] \qquad \text{or} \qquad p = (1 + \pi)wa_L[I - (1 + \pi)A]^{-1}.$$

Another basic Marxian notion is the concept of surplus labor or surplus value. **Surplus labor** is the difference between the amount of labor supplied by the worker and the amount of labor embodied in the (subsistence) wage goods the worker receives. If $c_i \geq 0$ is the average quantity of good i necessary to maintain the worker (at subsistence) for 1 unit of labor time, then $\lambda_i c_i$ is the value of good i in the subsistence bundle and

$$\mu = 1 - \sum_{i=1}^{n} \lambda_i c_i$$

is the surplus value associated with 1 unit of labor time. Given this definition of surplus value, the **rate of exploitation** is given by $\mu/(1 - \mu)$.

This basic structure has been used to generate a number of results in mathematical Marxian economics; some of these results are formal proofs of arguments made verbally by Marx, while others are totally new implications of this Marxian model. Probably the most important (and most controversial) is the so-called **fundamental Marxian theorem.** This fundamental theorem asserts that a positive rate of profit is possible if and only if surplus value is positive, that is, $\pi > 0$ iff $\mu > 0$. This and many other results in mathematical Marxian economics are discussed in detail in Morishima (1973) and Morishima and Catephores (1978).

244 ■ Matrices and Economic Theory

Sources

Morishima, M. 1973. *Marx's economics: A dual theory of value and growth.* Cambridge: Cambridge University Press.

Morishima, M., and G. Catephores. 1978. *Value, exploitation and growth: Marx in the light of modern economic theory.* London: McGraw-Hill.

Murata, Y. 1977. *Mathematics for stability and optimization of economic systems.* New York: Academic Press.

Roemer, J. E. 1982. *A general theory of exploitation and class.* Cambridge, MA: Harvard University Press.

Sraffa, P. 1960. *Production of commodities by means of commodities.* Cambridge: Cambridge University Press.

Steedman, I. 1977. *Marx after Sraffa.* London: New Left Books.

If we apply a similar argument to the three-variable case, where A is 3×3 and $x^T = (x_1, x_2, x_3)$, we can write the quadratic form as

$$Q_A(x) = M_1(\cdot)^2 + \left(\frac{M_2}{M_1}\right)(\cdot)^2 + \left(\frac{M_3}{M_2}\right)(\cdot)^2, \tag{6.63}$$

where (again) M_i is an ith-order principal minor of A. For the general case of n variables,

$$Q_A(x) = M_1(\cdot)^2 + \left(\frac{M_2}{M_1}\right)(\cdot)^2 + \cdots + \left(\frac{M_n}{M_{n-1}}\right)(\cdot)^2. \tag{6.64}$$

Given that any quadratic from can be written in the "sum of the ratios of the principal minors" form (6.64), what condition would guarantee that $Q_A(x) > 0$ for all $x \neq 0$? The answer is contained in Theorem 6.5.

THEOREM 6.5: A symmetric matrix A is
   (a) **Positive definite** iff A is a P matrix, and
   (b) **Negative definite** iff A is an NP matrix.

PROOF: (a) If A is a P matrix, then $M_i > 0$ for all $i = 1, 2, \ldots, n$, and so $Q_A(x) > 0$ for all $x \neq 0$ by (6.64). But suppose A is positive definite. Then $M_i > 0$ for all $i = 1, 2, \ldots, n$, because if there existed an $M_j \leq 0$, by choosing the correct vector x, the squared term $(\cdot)^2$ associated with the coefficient M_j could be made sufficiently large that $Q_A(x) \leq 0$.
(b) If A is an NP matrix, then $M_1 < 0$, $M_2 > 0$, $M_3 < 0$, $\ldots$, so an argument similar to the proof of (a) holds for (b) as well.

The results in Theorem 6.5 can be extended to semidefinite matrices in the obvious way. Economic examples are deferred until the next chapter, where Theorem 6.5 is used to characterize the second-order conditions for n-variable optimization problems.

PROBLEMS

6.1 For the following production functions, determine whether their Hessian matrices Hf are P matrices, NP matrices, or neither, for all $L > 0$ and $K > 0$.
(a) $f(L, K) = L^{1/2} + K^{1/2}$.
(b) $f(L, K) = L^3 + K^2$.
(c) $f(L, K) = L^{1/2} K^{1/2}$.
(d) $f(L, K) = L^2 K^2$.

6.2 Let $y = f(x)$ with $x \in \mathfrak{R}_+^5$ be a production function with five inputs. The Hessian of this production function is the 5×5 matrix with representative term $[f_{ij}] = [\partial f_i / \partial x_j]$. Write down all first-, second-, third-, fourth-, and fifth-order principal minors of this Hessian.

6.3 Prove that if the n-input production function $y = f(x)$ with $x \in \mathfrak{R}_+^n$ exhibits constant returns to scale, then its Hessian is a singular matrix.

6.4 Use Cramer's rule to solve for the comparative statics of the *IS-LM* model given by the equation system (3.26) and (3.31).

6.5 In the *IS-LM* model of Chapter 3, functions $I(r)$, $S(Y, r)$, and $L(Y, r)$ were unspecified, so exact values of the equilibrium income level Y^* and the equilibrium interest rate r^* could not be determined. If these functions were linear, though, solutions Y^* and r^* could actually be found, and comparative statics could be obtained by differentiation of these equilibrium values with respect to the parameters in question. Answer questions (a)–(c) on the basis of the following linear *IS-LM* model (you may want to refer to Chapter 3 for definitions).

$$I(r) = ar + I_0 \quad \text{with} \quad a < 0 \quad \text{and} \quad I_0 > 0,$$
$$S(Y, r) = bY + cr \quad \text{with} \quad c > 0 \quad \text{and} \quad 0 < b < 1,$$
$$L(Y, r) = fY + er \quad \text{with} \quad f > 0 \quad \text{and} \quad e < 0.$$

(a) Use Cramer's rule to solve for the equilibrium values Y^* and r^*.
(b) Find $\partial Y^*/\partial D$, $\partial Y^*/\partial M^s$, $\partial r^*/\partial D$, and $\partial r^*/\partial M^s$ by direct differentiation of your answers in (a).
(c) Check for consistency the specific answers in (b) with the comparative statics terms for the general case given by (3.29), (3.30), (3.32), and (3.33).

6.6 Recall the monetary growth model introduced in Chapter 5. The dynamics of the model were given by the two differential equations

$$\dot{k} = s(m)f(k) - nk, \tag{5.41}$$

$$\dot{m} = m[\theta + f'(k) - r(k, m)]. \tag{5.50}$$

The equilibrium of the model (where $\dot{k} = 0$ and $\dot{m} = 0$) is given by $m^* = m^*(\theta, n)$ and $k^* = k^*(\theta, n)$, where θ is the parameter for the exogenous growth rate of the per capita money supply and n is the exogenous rate of population growth.
(a) Given the assumptions imposed on the model in Chapter 5, use Cramer's rule to find the comparative statics (actually comparative dynamics) impact of a change in θ (i.e., find expressions for, and sign, the terms $\partial k^*/\partial \theta$ and $\partial m^*/\partial \theta$).
(b) Repeat (a) for a change in n.

(c) Draw a diagram (like Figure 5.28 without the arrows) demonstrating your results from (a) and provide an economic interpretation.

(d) Repeat (c) for the change in (b).

6.7 Throughout the stability discussion of the three-good gross substitute general equilibrium system of Chapter 5, we assumed that the normalized equilibrium price vector $p* = (p_1^*, p_2^*)$ given in (5.29) was unique. Use the inverse-function theorem to prove that uniqueness is not an additional assumption, but follows from the assumptions of the model.

6.8 In the Cournot duopoly model the first-order conditions for profit maximization were solved so that the profit-maximizing output of each firm was expressed explicitly as a function of the other firm's output (called a **reaction function**).

(a) Do the second-order conditions guarantee, via the implicit-function theorem, that this transformation is possible? Explain why or why not.

(b) To do comparative statics in the Cournot model, the reaction functions are solved for the Cournot equilibrium values as explicit functions of the parameters. Do the second-order conditions for profit maximization by each firm guarantee, via the implicit-function theorem, that this transformation from implicit to explicit function is possible? Explain why or why not.

6.9 It was demonstrated in Chapter 1 that for any demand function, the marginal revenue (MR) and price elasticity of demand (ε) are related by the following equation

$$MR = P\left(1 + \frac{1}{\varepsilon}\right),\tag{1}$$

so $\varepsilon = -1$ iff $MR = 0$. Yet, if we compute MR and ε directly for the particular demand function

$$Q = P^{1/2} + 10,$$

we obtain

$$MR = 3Q^2 - 40Q + 100\tag{2}$$

and

$$\varepsilon = \frac{Q - 10}{2Q}.\tag{3}$$

Now (2) implies that $MR = 0$ at $Q = 10/3$ and $Q = 10$, while (3) implies that $\varepsilon = -1$ only at $Q = 10/3$. Are these numerical results inconsistent with (1)? Explain. (*Hint:* Consider the inverse-function theorem.)

6.10 Consider the utility function $U: \Re_{++}^n \to \Re_+$, which is homogeneous of degree $r > 1$. Prove that if this utility function is monotonic ($U_i = \partial U/\partial x_i > 0$ for all i) and all goods are "substitutes with respect to the utility function" ($U_{ij} = \partial U_i/\partial x_j = \partial^2 U/\partial x_i \partial x_j \leq 0$ for all $i \neq j$), then every good exhibits increasing marginal utility ($U_{ii} = \partial U_i/\partial x_i = \partial^2 U/\partial x_i^2 > 0$ for all i).

6.11 Recall the numerical example of an $n = 2$ Leontief system given by

$$A = \begin{bmatrix} 0.4 & 0.3 \\ 0.2 & 0.3 \end{bmatrix} \quad \text{and} \quad d = \begin{bmatrix} 1 \\ 1 \end{bmatrix}.$$

(a) If the labor coefficients for this system are $a_{L1} = 0.4$ and $a_{L2} = 0.4$, find the amount of labor the system will require to produce the equilibrium outputs x_1^* and x_2^*.

(b) If the wage is \$2 ($w = 2$), find the long-run equilibrium prices when all the value added is paid to labor.

(c) Repeat (a) and (b) for the case in which the labor coefficients are $a_{L1} = 0.5$ and $a_{L2} = 0.3$. Explain the relationship between the equilibrium prices in this case and those in (b).

6.12 Consider the two-good Leontief system with

$$A = \begin{bmatrix} 0.5 & 0.2 \\ 0.1 & 0.4 \end{bmatrix}, \quad d = \begin{bmatrix} 10 \\ 2 \end{bmatrix}, \quad a_L = (0.2, 0.8), \quad \text{and} \quad w = 5.$$

(a) Find (x_1^*, x_2^*).

(b) Find (p_1^*, p_2^*) in long-run equilibrium, where the value added in each sector is paid entirely to labor.

6.13 Suppose we have an n-good Leontief system with $d = (d_1, 0, \ldots, 0)$ and $d_1 > 0$; that is, final consumption demand for good 1 alone is strictly positive. Prove that if A is productive as in (6.34), then the solution to this Leontief system $x^* = (I - A)^{-1}d$ will have $x_1^* > 0$ and $x_i^* \geq 0$ for all $i \neq 1$.

6.14 Show that the following condition holds for any open Leontief system:

$$\sum_{j=1}^{n} V_j x_j = \sum_{i=1}^{n} p_i d_i.$$

Interpret this condition in terms of the national income accounts familiar from introductory macroeconomics.

6.15 Prove that if A is a symmetric matrix that satisfies the productivity condition (6.34), then matrix C is negative definite where $C = A - I$.

6.16 Prove the following. If a utility function is additively separable, that is, $U(x) = \sum_{i=1}^{n} U^i(x_i)$ (the utility received from the consumption of each good is independent of the utility received from the consumption of the other goods), and it exhibits diminishing marginal utility for all goods ($U_{ii} = \partial^2 U / \partial x_i^2 < 0$), then the Hessian of the utility function is negative definite.

6.17 Consider the two-input production function

$$y = f(L, K) = AL^2K^2 - BL^3K^3,$$

with $L > 0$, $K > 0$, $A > 0$, and $B > 0$. Find a restriction on the values of L, K, A, and B that will make the Hessian of this production function negative definite.

6.18 The price adjustment mechanism for the Leontief system with one nonproduced input (labor) is usually given by

$$\dot{p}_j = \sum_{i=1}^{n} p_i a_{ij} + w a_{Lj} - p_j \quad \text{for all } j = 1, 2, \ldots, n.$$

(a) Interpret this adjustment mechanism. That is, what does the mechanism say about the cause of price increases or decreases, and does it make economic sense?

(b) Draw the phase diagram and examine the stability or instability of this system for the $n = 2$ case. Assume the productivity condition (6.34).

NOTES

1. We consider only **square** submatrices, where the same number of rows and columns are deleted.
2. The theory of regular economies is an advanced topic; for a detailed discussion, see Mas-Colell (1985) or Mas-Colell, Whinston, and Green (1995, pp. 589–98).
3. See Berman and Plemmons (1979, p. 134) or Takayama (1985, p. 392), for instance.
4. Notice that completing the square by adding/subtracting $a_{12}^2 x_1^2 / a_{22}$ to/from $Q_A(x)$ yields $Q_A(x) = a_{22}(\cdot)^2 + [(a_{11}a_{22} - a_{12}^2)/a_{22}](\cdot)^2$, which is also of the form (6.62); M_1 is simply a_{22}, the "other" first-order principal minor of A.

7

C   H   A   P   T   E   R

COMPARATIVE STATICS II: n VARIABLES
WITH AND WITHOUT OPTIMIZATION
■ ■ ■

This chapter returns to the comparative statics theme of Chapter 3. As in that chapter, here we examine both equilibrium comparative statics and those explicitly derived from optimization problems; the difference is that in this chapter all the models examined are n-dimensional. Equilibrium comparative statics is considered first: the n-input, n-output Leontief model and the n-good Walrasian general equilibrium model. We then turn our attention to the comparative statics of n-dimensional optimization-based models. The profit-maximizing, perfectly competitive firm using n inputs is the primary focus of this latter discussion.

7.1 Equilibrium Comparative Statics
in n Dimensions

Comparative Statics in the Leontief System

Our first example of n-dimensional comparative statics involves the n-good open Leontief model introduced in Chapter 6. Equilibrium in this Leontief model was characterized by the fundamental equation

$$(I - A)x = d, \tag{7.1}$$

where A is the $n \times n$ coefficient matrix, $x \in \Re^n_+$ is the output vector, and $d \in \Re^n_{++}$ is the final consumption demand vector. When $|I - A| \neq 0$, the open Leontief system can be solved for the equilibrium output vector

$$x = (I - A)^{-1}d. \tag{7.2}$$

Equation (7.2) expresses the solution to the system, the equilibrium output vector, as a function of the elements of the coefficient matrix and the elements of the final demand vector d. Given this, it should be possible to analyze the comparative statics of the Leontief model, just as we have examined the comparative statics properties of other equilibrium systems. In particular, we want to look at the impact of a change in the final demand vector d on the equilibrium output vector x of the model.

For a particular n-good open Leontief model with coefficient matrix A, let $d^0 > 0$ be a column vector of initial final demands and let $d' > 0$ be a different final demand vector for the same model. Thus we have $(d^0)^T = (d_1^0, d_2^0, \ldots, d_n^0)$ and $(d')^T = (d_1', d_2', \ldots, d_n')$, with the change in the final demand of each good given by $\Delta d_i = d_i' - d_i^0$ for all $i = 1, 2, \ldots, n$. If the outputs associated with these two final demand vectors are

$$x^0 = (I - A)^{-1} d^0 \qquad \text{and} \qquad x' = (I - A)^{-1} d', \tag{7.3}$$

then the comparative statics impact of changing final demand from d^0 to d' is given by $\Delta x = x' - x^0$, where the change in each output is $\Delta x_i = x_i' - x_i^0$ for all $i = 1, 2, \ldots, n$. From (7.3) if Δd is the column vector with elements Δd_i for all $i = 1, 2, \ldots, n$, then the comparative statics impact of Δd can be obtained from

$$\Delta x = (I - A)^{-1} \Delta d. \tag{7.4}$$

If, as in Chapter 6, we let $B = I - A$, then (7.4) becomes $\Delta x = B^{-1} \Delta d$, and the total impact of a change in the final demand vector on any particular equilibrium output (say x_i) is

$$\Delta x_i = \sum_{j=1}^{n} B_{ij}^{-1} \Delta d_j, \tag{7.5}$$

where B_{ij}^{-1} is the element in the ith row and the jth column of the inverse matrix B^{-1}. But if we are interested in the direct effect of only one element of Δd on x_i (say Δd_j), or the change in x_i caused by a change in d_j when all other final demands remain unchanged, then the desired comparative statics expression is

$$\frac{\Delta x_i}{\Delta d_j} = B_{ij}^{-1}. \tag{7.6}$$

Do not be confused by the use of discrete changes (Δs) rather than differential changes (ds or ∂s) to characterize the comparative statics of the open Leontief model. The reason for working with discrete changes is only that economists are often confronted with the task of computing the impact of a fairly large change in the final demand vector via (7.5), and such changes are more naturally characterized by Δd_j's than by ∂d_j's. Of course, since the Leontief system is linear with constant coefficients (the a_{ij}'s are not functions of any d_i or x_i), comparative statics expressions like (7.6) would be exactly the same for differential (∂) and discrete (Δ) changes. To see this, let $B = I - A$ in (7.2) and take the derivative of any x_i with respect to any d_j. This differentiation gives us

$$\frac{\partial x_i}{\partial d_j} = B_{ij}^{-1} \qquad \text{for all } i, j = 1, 2, \ldots, n, \tag{7.7}$$

precisely the same result in (7.6).

To simplify our analysis, let us initially assume that a change occurs in **only one component** of the final demand vector, say, d_j. Now from the results in Chapter 6, we know that if the system is **productive** [defined in (6.35)], then

$B^{-1} = (I - A)^{-1} \geq 0$ and each component of the inverse matrix is nonnegative, or $B_{ij}^{-1} \geq 0$ for all $i, j = 1, 2, \ldots, n$. Combining this with (7.6), we find that for a productive system, the comparative statics impact of a change in the final demand for good j is given by $\Delta x_i / \Delta d_j \geq 0$; that is, $\Delta d_j > 0$ implies that $\Delta x_i \geq 0$, and $\Delta d_j < 0$ implies that $\Delta x_i \leq 0$ for all $i = 1, 2, \ldots, n$. This seems to be a rather useful result; for a productive Leontief system, an increase in the final demand for any one good will not decrease the equilibrium output of any good, and a decrease in the final demand for any one good will not increase the output of any good. While this result is helpful, we can actually say something a bit stronger. For a productive system, $\Delta d_j > 0$ implies that $\Delta x_j > 0$ and $\Delta x_i \geq 0$ for all $i \neq j$, while $\Delta d_j < 0$ implies that $\Delta x_j < 0$ and $\Delta x_i \leq 0$ for all $i \neq j$.

To see how the latter result is obtained, recall the basic equilibrium equation for the open Leontief model,

$$Bx = d. \tag{7.8}$$

Without loss of generality, let us assume that there is a change in the final demand for good 1, with no other changes in the final demand vector; thus $\Delta d_1 \neq 0$ and $\Delta d_i = 0$ for all $i \neq 1$. From (7.8) the change in the equilibrium output vector caused by this change in final demand for good 1 is given by

$$B \Delta x = \Delta d, \tag{7.9}$$

where Δx is as before and Δd is a column vector of zeros except for Δd_1 in the first row. Now applying Cramer's rule to the system in (7.9) and solving for Δx_1, we have

$$\Delta x_1 = \frac{\begin{vmatrix} \Delta d_1 & b_{12} & \cdots & b_{1n} \\ 0 & b_{22} & \cdots & b_{2n} \\ \vdots & \vdots & & \vdots \\ 0 & b_{n2} & \cdots & b_{nn} \end{vmatrix}}{|B|}. \tag{7.10}$$

To sign the expression in (7.10), recall from Theorem 6.3 that when the Leontief system is productive, B is a P matrix. This means that the denominator of (7.10) is strictly positive. Now if we expand the determinant in the numerator by the first column, we have Δd_1 times the $(n-1)$st-order principal minor formed by stripping off the first row and column of B. This $(n-1)$st-order principal minor is also positive, since B is a P matrix, and thus the sign of Δx_1 is the same as the sign of Δd_1.

Of course such comparative statics results are not nearly as easy to obtain when more than one component of the final demand vector is altered. If some elements of Δd are positive and others are negative, then the relatively weak productivity assumption is no longer sufficient to guarantee that the elements of Δx will be of uniform sign. For such qualitatively mixed changes in d, the resulting changes in the equilibrium outputs will depend on the actual numerical values of the coefficients in the Leontief matrix A. The only thing we can say is that if the changes in the final demands are all in the same direction (all $\Delta d_i \geq 0$ or $\Delta d_i \leq 0$), then the equilibrium outputs will change in the same way. That is, since the productivity assumption guarantees that $B^{-1} \geq 0$, we know that $\Delta d_i \geq 0$ implies that $\Delta x_i \geq 0$, and $\Delta d_i \leq 0$ implies that $\Delta x_i \leq 0$ for all $i = 1, 2, \ldots, n$.

BOX 7.1
Economic Impact of an Arms Cut

Since empirical input–output data exist for many real-world economies, it is often possible to obtain reasonably accurate quantitative comparative statics information for a particular change in the composition of the final demand vector. One classic example of such quantitative comparative statics is the empirical estimate of the impact of a cut in U.S. military expenditures obtained by Leontief and coworkers in the early 1960s (Leontief and Hoffenberg, 1961; Leontief et al., 1965). The goal of the main (1965) study was to analyze the impact of a 20% across-the-board reduction in military expenditures when the cut was accompanied by a compensating increase in nonmilitary demand. Since the reduction in military demand was compensated by an increase in civilian demand, the model was set up so that total employment would stay the same. The question investigated was not the macroeconomic impact on total employment, but rather the more microeconomic impact on the output mix—which industries and regions of the country would gain and which would lose from such an arms cut.

The basic model used for the empirical estimate was only a slight variation of the Leontief model discussed in the text. The main change was that the final demand vector d was subdivided into three separate components: household final demand h, nonhousehold civilian final demand q, and military final demand m. With the final demand vector so subdivided, the fundamental equation of the Leontief system given by $x = (I - A)^{-1}d$ would be written as

$$x = (I - A)^{-1}[h + q + m].$$

The reduction in military demand is given by substituting αm (with $\alpha = 0.80$) for m on the right-hand side of this equation. The compensating increase in nonmilitary demand is given by substituting $\beta(h + q)$ with $\beta > 1$ in for $h + q$. The relevant β was computed in such a way that the total labor employment remained constant following the changes in final demand; it turned out to be approximately $\beta = 1.02$ for the data used.

The input–output data used in the analysis were from 1958, the latest year for which data were available at the time. Fifty-eight industries were considered, and the regional impact was ascertained by dividing the country into 19 regions. The results were interesting but not too surprising. The industries most hurt by the arms cut were aircraft and ordnance, while those most helped were agriculture and domestic labor. In general, the industries that were hurt were small in number but had relatively large losses, while the industries helped were much larger in number but experienced only a small increase each. Regional impacts were also not too surprising, with California, Colorado, and New Mexico being the big losers and the agricultural Midwest receiving the largest gains.

Sources

Leontief, W. W., and M. Hoffenberg. 1961. The economic effects of disarmament. *Scientific American* 204: 47–65.

Leontief, W. W., A. Morgan, K. Polenske, D. Simpson, and E. Tower. 1965. The economic impact—industrial and regional—of an arms cut. *The Review of Economics and Statistics* 67: 217–40.

Comparative Statics in the n-Good General Equilibrium Model

We now look at the n-good Walrasian general equilibrium model. Although this model was introduced in Chapter 5, it is probably a good idea to review its basic properties before considering comparative statics.

The market for each of the n goods in the Walrasian model is characterized by a differentiable excess demand function z_i, where $z_i = \text{demand}_i - \text{supply}_i$ for all $i = 1, 2, \ldots, n$. The interdependency of the markets is captured by the fact that the excess demand for each good is a function of all the prices in the system. Thus, if the price vector is given by $p = (p_1, p_2, \ldots, p_n)$, the excess demand function of any good i can be written as

$$z_i(p) = z_i(p_1, p_2, \ldots, p_n) \qquad \text{for all } i = 1, 2, \ldots, n. \tag{7.11}$$

We assume, as in our earlier discussion of the Walrasian model, that prices are strictly positive, so $p \in \Re_{++}^n$.

The two most basic restrictions on the excess demands of the Walrasian model are zero-degree homogeneity (H) and Walras' law (W). First consider the **zero-degree homogeneity:** it says that

$$z_i(p) = z_i(\lambda p) \qquad \text{for all } \lambda \in \Re_{++} \qquad \text{and} \qquad \text{for all } p. \tag{H}$$

The economic interpretation of (H) is that individuals and firms in the economy are not subject to "money illusion"; that is, they do not change the quantities they demand or supply when all prices in the economy are scaled up or scaled down by the same amount. The zero-degree homogeneity of excess demand allows us to reduce the number of prices to $n - 1$ by measuring everything in terms of one of the goods (i.e., by making one of the goods the numeraire). Choosing good n as numeraire, we have $\lambda = 1/p_n$ in (H) and each excess demand function is unchanged by the transition to the new price vector[1] $p = (p_1, p_2, \ldots, p_{n-1}, 1)$. The only difference is that now each p_i measures the number of units of good n that can be exchanged for 1 unit of good i, rather than measuring the price of good i in terms of the original unit of account.

The second basic restriction on the excess demand functions of the Walrasian model is **Walras' law:**

$$\sum_{i=1}^{n} p_i z_i(p) = 0 \qquad \text{for all } p. \tag{W}$$

Condition (W) is essentially an expanded version of the consumer's budget constraint. As was argued in Chapter 5, it follows immediately from the budget constraint of the individual traders in a pure exchange model and can be extended to production economies under quite general assumptions.

The Walrasian model is in **general equilibrium** when all n markets clear simultaneously. Thus, assuming the general equilibrium price vector $p*$ exists for the model,[2] it will be characterized by the n market clearing equations:

$$z_i(p*) = 0 \qquad \text{for all } i = 1, 2, \ldots, n. \tag{7.12}$$

Since Walras' law implies that when any $n - 1$ markets clear, the nth market also clears, only $n - 1$ of the excess demand functions in (7.12) are required to characterize equilibrium. Thus (H) and (W) allow us to eliminate one equation as well as one unknown.

So far there are no parameters in the excess demand functions of the model, but let us introduce a parameter in the following way. Let α be a shift parameter in the excess demand function of good 1 that indicates a change in taste away from the numeraire good (good n) toward good 1. Thus we have $z_1(p, \alpha)$ and $z_n(p, \alpha)$ with $z_{1\alpha} = \partial z_1 / \partial \alpha > 0$ and $z_{n\alpha} = \partial z_n / \partial \alpha < 0$. We assume that the parameter does not directly affect the excess demand for any other good. Of course, good 1 was chosen arbitrarily; any other good 2 through $n - 1$ would serve just as well. The important point is that a change in α affects only one of the $n - 1$ markets remaining after the numeraire is chosen. Equilibrium can now be characterized as

$$z_1(p*, \alpha) = 0$$
$$z_i(p*) = 0 \qquad \text{for all } i = 2, 3, \ldots, n - 1 \tag{7.13}$$

with $z_n(p*, \alpha) = 0$ holding by Walras' law.

Assuming the $(n - 1) \times (n - 1)$ Jacobian matrix associated with the system is nonsingular (i.e., that $|Jz(p*)| \neq 0$), we can apply the implicit function theorem and write the solution to these $n - 1$ implicit equations as

$$p*(\alpha) = (p_1^*(\alpha), p_2^*(\alpha), \ldots, p_{n-1}^*(\alpha)). \tag{7.14}$$

Even though parameter α enters explicitly into the excess demand function of only one good, the interdependency of the markets implies that in the most general case a change in α will influence the equilibrium prices of all goods.

To obtain comparative statics terms such as $dp_i^*/d\alpha$, we follow the now familiar technique of substituting the explicit solutions from (7.14) back into the equilibrium conditions in (7.13) and differentiating the resulting identities with respect to α. Then we have the system of $n - 1$ identities

$$z_1(p*(\alpha), \alpha) \equiv 0$$
$$z_i(p*(\alpha)) \equiv 0 \qquad \text{for all } i = 2, 3, \ldots, n - 1. \tag{7.15}$$

Differentiating these identities with respect to α gives the system

$$Jz(p*) \frac{dp*}{d\alpha} = -z_\alpha, \tag{7.16}$$

where

$$
Jz(p^*) - \begin{bmatrix} z_{11}(p^*) & \cdots & z_{1n-1}(p^*) \\ \vdots & & \vdots \\ z_{n-11}(p^*) & \cdots & z_{n-1n-1}(p^*) \end{bmatrix},
$$

$$
\frac{dp^*}{d\alpha} = \begin{bmatrix} \dfrac{dp_1^*}{d\alpha} \\ \dfrac{dp_2^*}{d\alpha} \\ \vdots \\ \dfrac{dp_{n-1}^*}{d\alpha} \end{bmatrix}, \qquad \text{and} \qquad z_\alpha = \begin{bmatrix} z_{1\alpha} \\ 0 \\ \vdots \\ 0 \end{bmatrix},
$$

with $z_{ij} = \partial z_i / \partial p_j$. Since we have assumed that the implicit-function theorem holds ($|Jz(p^*)| \neq 0$), we can write system (7.16) as

$$
\frac{dp^*}{d\alpha} = [-Jz(p^*)]^{-1} z_\alpha. \tag{7.17}
$$

Expression (7.17) is the fundamental comparative statics equation for the Walrasian general equilibrium system.

Now it would be nice if the basic assumptions of the Walrasian model guaranteed that the comparative statics terms $dp_i^*/d\alpha$ were of some definite sign. Unfortunately, this is not the case. Knowing only that the system is a Walrasian general equilibrium model that satisfies (H) and (W) is not sufficient to sign the terms in (7.17), even in the simple case of the parameter affecting only one of the $n - 1$ markets. This should not really come as a surprise, though. The model is very general; not only does it contain n markets, but also the only real restrictions on the model are (H) and (W), certainly not enough mathematical structure to sign the inverse of the Jacobian. To obtain comparative statics terms of definite sign, additional restrictions must be imposed on the model.

The Gross Substitute System

Suppose that an increase in the price of any good will increase the excess demand for any other good. That is, suppose that all goods are **gross substitutes.** The gross substitute (GS) condition was introduced in Chapter 5; formally it says that

$$
z_{ij} = \frac{\partial z_i(p)}{\partial p_j} > 0 \qquad \text{for all } i \neq j \qquad \text{and} \qquad \text{for all } p. \tag{GS}
$$

Now (GS) directly restricts only the signs of the cross-price derivatives of the excess demand functions; it does not directly restrict the sign of the own-price derivatives ($z_{ii} = \partial z_i / \partial p_i$). When (GS) is combined with the zero-degree homogeneity condition (H) though, the signs of the own effects are also restricted. This result is an application of Euler's theorem (Theorem 2.1). By Euler's theorem and because each z_i is h.d. zero, we have

$$\sum_{j=1}^{n} z_{ij} p_j = z_{ii} p_i + \sum_{\substack{j=1 \\ j \neq i}}^{n} z_{ij} p_j = 0 \qquad \text{for all } i = 1, 2, \ldots, n. \qquad (7.18)$$

Since all prices are strictly positive and $z_{ij} > 0$ for all $i \neq j$, (7.18) implies that $z_{ii} < 0$ for all $i = 1, 2, \ldots, n$. Under (H) and (GS) every excess demand function slopes downward with respect to its own price.

Now let us examine the $(n-1) \times (n-1)$ Jacobian $Jz(p^*)$ for the normalized Walrasian model under the gross substitute assumption. The GS condition requires that all nondiagonal terms in the Jacobian matrix have a positive sign and (as argued earlier) when combined with (H), that all diagonal terms be strictly positive. But the matrix involved in the fundamental comparative statics equation (7.17) is the inverse not of $Jz(p^*)$, but rather of $-Jz(p^*)$. Thus if we define a new matrix $S = -Jz(p^*)$, the fundamental comparative statics equation (7.17) can be written as

$$\frac{dp^*}{d\alpha} = S^{-1} z_\alpha, \qquad (7.19)$$

where S is a matrix with strictly negative nondiagonal terms ($S_{ij} < 0$ for all $i \neq j$) and strictly positive diagonal terms ($S_{ii} > 0$).

Recall that Theorem 6.3 in Chapter 6 gave us a number of conditions that guarantee that the inverse of a matrix with negative off-diagonals is nonnegative. If we were able to show that S satisfies one of these conditions, then we would know that $S^{-1} \geq 0$, and our comparative statics terms would be of definite sign. In fact, since the off-diagonal elements of S are strictly negative, satisfaction of one of the conditions in Theorem 6.3 will guarantee the stronger result that $S^{-1} > 0$. But how do we know that Theorem 6.3 can be applied to the matrix S?

Again, we turn to Euler's theorem. Applying Euler's theorem to some arbitrary z_i, we have the expression in (7.18). Rewriting that expression for only the first $n - 1$ goods, we have

$$z_{ii} p_i + \sum_{\substack{j=1 \\ j \neq i}}^{n-1} z_{ij} p_j = -z_{in} p_n \qquad \text{for all } i = 1, 2, \ldots, n - 1. \qquad (7.20)$$

Now since all goods satisfy (GS), the right-hand side of (7.20) is strictly negative. Thus multiplying by -1, we have

$$-z_{ii} p_i - \sum_{\substack{j=1 \\ j \neq i}}^{n-1} z_{ij} p_j > 0 \qquad \text{for all } i = 1, 2, \ldots, n - 1.$$

BOX 7.2
Tobin's q and Asset Market General Equilibrium

In the standard characterization of the Walrasian general equilibrium model, the gross substitute property must surely be considered a rather restrictive assumption; however, when the markets under consideration are asset markets (markets for bonds, money, equities, etc.), then the gross substitute assumption seems to be quite natural. If there are n different types of asset and each one has a real rate of return r_i, then we would expect the demand f_i for any asset $i = 1, 2, \ldots, n$ to satisfy the following conditions:

$$\frac{\partial f_i}{\partial r_i} > 0 \quad \text{and} \quad \frac{\partial f_i}{\partial r_j} < 0 \quad \text{for all } i \neq j. \tag{a}$$

An increase in the rate of return on any asset should naturally increase the demand for that asset and decrease the demand for all others; this is the gross substitute property on asset demands. James Tobin (1969) used this gross substitute property on asset demands to characterize general equilibrium in the market for stocks of assets. In Tobin's model of asset market general equilibrium, the flows in the economy (income, etc.) are assumed to be exogenous, thus making his model an n-asset analogue of the *LM* curve in an *IS-LM* macroeconomic model. In the context of his presentation, Tobin introduced the idea that came to be called **Tobin's q** theory of investment. The concept was introduced because (in the short run) there may be a difference between the market price of existing capital goods and the market price of the newly produced capital goods that might replace them. Since the price of newly produced capital goods p was the numeraire in his model (the units in which "real" values were measured), Tobin used qp as the market price of existing capital goods. Thus if $q = 1$, then $qp = p$ and the price of existing capital goods would be the same as their replacement cost, while $q > 1$ ($qp > p$) indicates a capital value higher than replacement cost, and $q < 1$ ($qp < p$) indicates a capital value lower than replacement cost. Since $q > 1$ should be an incentive to increase current investment and since q seems to be relatively easy to measure empirically, the q theory has evolved into an important theoretical and empirical explanation of aggregate investment activity (Hayashi, 1982; Summers, 1981).

The three-asset version of Tobin's asset market model (the case for which the major comparative statics results were obtained) is specified as follows. Each of the assets (capital K, money M, and government securities S) has a real rate of return given by r_i for $i = K, M, S$. The demand for the real stock of each of the three assets is written as

$$f_i\left(r_K, r_M, r_S, \frac{Y}{W}\right) \quad \text{for } i = M, K, S,$$

with Y representing real income and W real wealth. These demand functions are assumed to satisfy the gross substitute property (a) and be homogeneous of degree 1 (h.d. 1) with respect to income and wealth. If K, M, and S represent the stocks (supply) of the three assets, then given the homogeneity assumption, the general equilibrium is characterized by

$$f_K\left(r_K, r_M, r_S, \frac{Y}{W}\right) W = qK \qquad \text{Capital market}$$

$$f_M\left(r_K, r_M, r_S, \frac{Y}{W}\right) W = \frac{M}{p} \qquad \text{Money market}$$

$$f_S\left(r_K, r_M, r_S, \frac{Y}{W}\right) W = \frac{S}{p} \qquad \text{Securities market}$$

where p is the numeraire, the price of newly produced capital goods (note that $qpK/p = qK$). The wealth constraint for the whole economy is given by

$$W = qK + \frac{M+S}{p}.$$

After introducing some additional restrictions (which may be found in the original paper), Tobin presents a table listing all of the comparative statics results of the model. Some of these results are as follows:

Endogenous variables	Exogenous variables			
	M	S	Y	P
q	+	?	−	−
r_S	−	+	+	?
r_M	−	?	+	+

Many of the results in this table appear to be quite standard, while others ($\partial q/\partial M > 0$ in particular) represent results that are unique to this model. On the basis of these results, Tobin argued that changes in the economy's exogenous variables (including monetary policy) primarily have an impact on aggregate demand through changes in q, that is, through changes in the valuation of physical capital relative to its replacement cost.

Sources

Hayashi, F. 1982. Tobin's marginal q and average q: A neoclassical interpretation. *Econometrica* 50: 213–24.

Summers, L. 1981. Taxation and corporate investment: A q-theory approach. *Brookings Papers on Economic Activity* 1: 67–140.

Tobin, J. 1969. A general equilibrium approach to monetary theory. *Journal of Money, Credit, and Banking* 1: 15–29.

Or at the equilibrium price vector $p*$,

$$S_{ii} p_i^* + \sum_{\substack{j=1 \\ j \neq i}}^{n-1} S_{ij} p_j^* > 0 \qquad \text{for all } i = 1, 2, \ldots, n - 1, \qquad (7.21)$$

since $S = -Jz(p*)$. Because the inequality in (7.21) holds for all $n-1$ goods, we can write it in terms of the matrix S and the equilibrium price vector $p*$. In matrix form (7.21) becomes

$$Sp* > 0, \qquad (7.22)$$

where $(p*)^T = (p_1^*, p_2^*, \ldots, p_{n-1}^*)$. Now since $p* > 0$, we have demonstrated that for a Walrasian system in which all goods are gross substitutes, there exists a vector that will make $S = -Jz(p*)$ satisfy condition (a) of Theorem 6.3. Thus from Theorem 6.3, we know that $S^{-1} > 0$, and from the fundamental comparative statics equation (7.19), we have that

$$\frac{dp_i^*}{d\alpha} > 0 \qquad \text{for all } i = 1, 2, \ldots, n - 1. \qquad (7.23)$$

The result in (7.23) is quite strong. It says that in a Walrasian general equilibrium model where all goods are gross substitutes, a change in taste in favor of good 1 (or any other good) and away from the numeraire good will increase the equilibrium prices of all the goods in the system. Notice that this result was achieved by using only the basic assumptions of the Walrasian model, (H) and (W), and the gross substitute assumption (GS). There are a few other comparative statics implications of the model that will not be examined, but (7.23) seems to be quite a lot of information from an n-dimensional model with so little structure.

7.2 Comparative Statics with Optimization in n Dimensions

First- and Second-Order Conditions for n-Variable Optimization Problems

Consider the optimization problem of maximizing a differentiable function of n variables. More specifically, consider the problem

$$\underset{x}{\text{Max}}\, z = f(x), \qquad (7.24)$$

where $x \in \mathfrak{R}_+^n$, $f \colon \mathfrak{R}_+^n \to \mathfrak{R}$, and f is at least twice differentiable. The first-order conditions for the problem in (7.24) are now familiar. If $x^* = (x_1^*, x_2^*, \ldots, x_n^*) > 0$ is a solution to (7.24),[3] then the following **first-order conditions** must hold:

$$\frac{\partial f(x^*)}{\partial x_i} = f_i(x^*) = 0 \qquad \text{for all } i = 1, 2, \ldots, n. \qquad (7.25)$$

The $n = 2$ version of the unconstrained maximization problem in (7.24) was discussed in Chapter 3. In that discussion, a second-order sufficient condition was presented in addition to the first-order (necessary) conditions in (7.25):

$$d^2z = \sum_{i=1}^{2}\sum_{j=1}^{2} dx_i f_{ij}(x^*)dx_j < 0$$

for all $dx = (dx_1, dx_2) \neq 0$ within some ε neighborhood of x^*. The motivation for this second-order condition was that if z decreases as we move away from x^* infinitesimally in any arbitrary direction, then x^* must be a local maximum of f. The decreasing value of z, combined with the fact that $dz = 0$ at x^*, gives us $d^2z < 0$ as a second-order condition. We demonstrated in Chapter 3 that $d^2z < 0$ is guaranteed by the restrictions

$$f_{11} < 0, \qquad f_{22} < 0, \qquad \text{and} \qquad f_{11}f_{22} - f_{12}^2 > 0 \qquad (7.26)$$

on the second partial derivatives of f evaluated at the critical point x^*. The second-order conditions in (7.26) have been used many times in the preceding chapters to sign the comparative statics terms in economic models.

When the second-order conditions for the $n = 2$ case were introduced in Chapter 3, they were not given a matrix interpretation. Now though, after the discussion of matrix theory in Chapter 6, we know that (7.26) requires the Hessian Hf of f to be an NP matrix at x^*—to have principal minors that alternate in sign, starting negative. This NP matrix condition can also be related to the discussion of quadratic forms in Chapter 6. There, in Theorem 6.5, we proved that if a symmetric matrix is an NP matrix, it generates a negative definite quadratic form. Of course, the foregoing expression for d^2z is a two-variable quadratic form; it is the quadratic form

$$[dx_1 \quad dx_2]\begin{bmatrix} f_{11}(x^*) & f_{12}(x^*) \\ f_{21}(x^*) & f_{22}(x^*) \end{bmatrix}\begin{bmatrix} dx_1 \\ dx_2 \end{bmatrix}, \qquad (7.27)$$

generated by the Hessian of f. Thus Hf, being an NP matrix at x^* is equivalent to the negative definiteness of the quadratic form in (7.27) and guarantees that the second-order condition $d^2z < 0$ is satisfied.

The argument in the preceding paragraph extends immediately to the general case of n variables. The second-order condition in the n-variable case is

$$d^2z = \sum_{i=1}^{n}\sum_{j=1}^{n} dx_i f_{ij}(x^*)dx_j < 0 \qquad \text{for all } dx \neq 0, \qquad (7.28)$$

where $dx = (dx_1, dx_2, \ldots, dx_n)$ are arbitrary changes in the n variables (not all zero) within some $\varepsilon > 0$ of x^*. Since the right-hand side of (7.28) is a quadratic form, we know from Theorem 6.5 that (7.28) will hold if the $n \times n$ Hessian of f evaluated at x^*, that is, $Hf(x^*)$, is an NP matrix. Thus the NP matrix restriction on $Hf(x^*)$ fully characterizes the second-order conditions for the n-variable unconstrained maximization problem in (7.24). If the **first-order conditions** (7.25) hold at some x^* and $Hf(x^*)$ is an **NP matrix,** then **x^* is a local maximum** of function f. In addition to this local result, we can say that if x^* satisfies the first-order conditions and $Hf(x^*)$ is an NP matrix for all x, then x^* is the unique global maximum of f.

These second-order conditions can also be related to the concavity of f. To see this relationship, consider the Taylor series expansion of $f: \mathfrak{R}^n \to \mathfrak{R}$ around x^*

$$f(x) = f(x^*) + \sum_{i=1}^{n} f_i(x^*)(x_i - x_i^*)$$

$$+ \sum_{i=1}^{n} \sum_{j=1}^{n} \frac{(x_i - x_i^*) f_{ij}(x^*)(x_j - x_j^*)}{2} + \cdots$$

for any $x = (x_1, x_2, \ldots, x_n)$ within some ε neighborhood of x^*. If x is sufficiently close to x^*, we can truncate the expression at the second term and write

$$f(x) \approx f(x^*) + \sum_{i=1}^{n} f_i(x^*)(x_i - x_i^*) + \sum_{i=1}^{n} \sum_{j=1}^{n} \frac{(x_i - x_i^*) f_{ij}(x^*)(x_j - x_j^*)}{2}.$$

(7.29)

Rewriting (7.20) in vector and matrix notation, we have,

$$f(x) \approx f(x^*) + \nabla f(x^*)(x - x^*)^T + \frac{(x - x^*) Hf(x^*)(x - x^*)^T}{2}. \qquad (7.30)$$

Now if $Hf(x^*)$ is an NP matrix, then the quadratic form on the far right-hand side of (7.30) is strictly negative and (7.30) implies that

$$\nabla f(x^*)(x - x^*) + f(x^*) > f(x). \qquad (7.31)$$

The inequality in (7.31) is precisely the condition used to characterize a strictly concave function of n variables in (2.61) of Chapter 2. Thus if $Hf(x^*)$ is an NP matrix, f is strictly concave (locally) around x^*. The results of the last few paragraphs can be summarized in Theorem 7.1.

THEOREM 7.1: If $x^* \in \mathfrak{R}^n_{++}$ satisfies the first-order condition that $f_i(x^*) = 0$ for all $i = 1, 2, \ldots, n$ and satisfies the second-order condition that $Hf(x^*)$ is an NP matrix, then x^* is a **local maximum** of f, which solves the problem (7.27), and f is strictly concave locally around x^*.

While Theorem 7.1 is exclusively a local result, it admits a straightforward global extension. If the first-order conditions hold at x^* and $Hf(x^*)$ is an NP matrix **for all** $x \in \mathfrak{R}^n_+$, then x^* is the unique **global maximum** of f and f is strictly concave globally. Although this global extension provides a nice mathematical result, it is seldom needed because so much of economic analysis is concerned exclusively with local comparative statics.

It is possible to weaken the Hessian restriction in Theorem 7.1 to merely a necessary condition for a maximum. In particular, if x^* is a local maximum of f, then, in addition to the first-order conditions, d^2z must be a negative **semidefinite** quadratic form and f must be locally concave (not strictly concave) around x^*. As in the case of the global extension, this weakening to necessary conditions is of less economic interest because of our concern with comparative statics. Notice that $Hf(x^*)$ being an NP matrix (the sufficient condition in Theorem 7.1) guarantees that $|Hf(x^*)| \neq 0$ and thus, by the implicit-function theorem, guarantees that the solutions to the first-order conditions can be written as differentiable functions of the parameters of the problem—precisely what is needed for comparative statics. But if d^2z is merely negative semidefinite, then the implicit-function theorem need not apply, and comparative statics analysis may not be possible.

Theorem 7.1 concerns unconstrained maximization, but what about an unconstrained minimization problem in n variables? How would Theorem 7.1 need to be changed if the problem were

$$\operatorname*{Min}_{x} z = f(x) \qquad (7.32)$$

with $x \in \Re_+^n$ and $f\colon \Re_+^n \to \Re$?

This question is quite easy to answer if we remember that minimizing $f(x)$ is the same thing as maximizing $-f(x)$. Thus for the minimization problem, the second total differential d^2z needs to be a **positive definite** quadratic form, or, by applying Theorem 6.5, the Hessian $Hf(x^*)$ must be a **P matrix.** Since the negation of a concave function is convex, the second-order condition also implies that f will be strictly convex around x^*. These results for the minimization problem are summarized in Theorem 7.2.

THEOREM 7.2: If $x^* \in \Re_{++}^n$ satisfies the first-order condition that $f_i(x^*) = 0$ for all $i = 1, 2, \ldots, n$ and satisfies the second-order condition that $Hf(x^*)$ is a P matrix, then x^* is a **local minimum** of f, which solves the problem (7.32), and f is strictly convex locally around x^*.

This theorem concludes the presentation of the basic mathematical results for unconstrained n-variable optimization problems. We now turn to a particular economic example.

Perfectly Competitive Firm with n Inputs

Comparative Statics of Factor Demands

The comparative statics of factor demands for a perfectly competitive firm that uses only one or two inputs has already been examined. Now let us consider the same problem for the general case of n inputs.

The firm is perfectly competitive in both the product and the factor markets, so it takes prices (both input and output) as parameters. The price of the firm's output is $p > 0$ and the prices of the inputs are given by the factor input price vector $w = (w_1, w_2, \ldots, w_n) > 0$. The firm uses n inputs $x = (x_1, x_2, \ldots, x_n) \geq 0$ to produce output y by means of the production function $y = f(x)$, where $f\colon \Re_+^n \to \Re_+$ and f is at least twice differentiable. For the general case, the exact form of the production function is unknown, but we assume that it has sufficient structure to guarantee that the second-order conditions hold at the optimal point.

The firm's objective function is to maximize profit π, given by

$$\pi(x) = pf(x) - \sum_{i=1}^{n} w_i x_i. \tag{7.33}$$

If the factor demand vector $x^* = (x_1^*, x_2^*, \ldots, x_n^*) > 0$ is the solution to the firm's problem, then the following first-order conditions must hold:

$$\pi_i(x^*) = pf_i(x^*) - w_i = 0 \qquad \text{for all } i = 1, 2, \ldots, n, \tag{7.34}$$

where $\pi_i = \partial \pi / \partial x_i$ and $f_i = \partial f / \partial x_i$ for all i. Notice that these first-order conditions translate into the familiar argument that for a profit-maximizing firm, the prices of each input should be equal to the marginal revenue product of that input. Also these first-order conditions imply that factor demands x^* are **homogeneous of degree zero** with respect to the parameters w and p; if all factor prices and the price of the firm's output are scaled up by the same amount, the first-order conditions in (7.34) and thus the factor demands are unchanged.

The second-order conditions for the firm's problem require that the Hessian of the profit function be an NP matrix at x^*: that is, that the principal minors of $H\pi(x^*)$ alternate in sign starting negative. From (7.34) we have $\partial^2 \pi / \partial x_i \partial x_j = \pi_{ij} = pf_{ij}$ and $\pi_{ij} = pf_{ij} = pf_{ji} = \pi_{ji}$, so the relevant Hessian can be written as the symmetric matrix

$$H\pi(x^*) = \begin{bmatrix} pf_{11}(x^*) & \cdots & pf_{1n}(x^*) \\ \vdots & & \vdots \\ pf_{n1}(x^*) & \cdots & pf_{nn}(x^*) \end{bmatrix}. \tag{7.35}$$

For comparative statics analysis of factor demands, we want to solve the n implicit functions given by the first-order conditions in (7.34) for the n explicit factor demands as functions of the parameters. We want to go from (7.34) to the solutions

$$x_i^* = x_i^*(w, p) \qquad \text{for all } i = 1, 2, \ldots, n. \tag{7.36}$$

But is this transformation from implicit to explicit functions possible?

The implicit-function theorem tells us that the transformation from (7.34) to (7.36) is appropriate and that the resulting explicit functions of the $n + 1$ parameters (the factor demand functions) will be differentiable if the determinant of the Jacobian of the system in (7.34) is nonvanishing. But the Jacobian of the system in (7.34) is simply the Hessian of the original profit function; thus, in the n-variable case, as in the two-variable case discussed earlier, the second-order conditions are sufficient to ensure that the implicit-function theorem holds, and the solutions can be written as differentiable functions of the parameters.

To set up for comparative statics, we use the same technique applied earlier in lower dimensional cases. We substitute the explicit solutions to the profit maximization problem from (7.36) back into the first-order conditions (7.34), thus converting these first-order conditions into identities. This substitution gives us

$$pf_i(x^*(w, p)) - w_i \equiv 0 \qquad \text{for all } i = 1, 2, \ldots, n. \tag{7.37}$$

Now since the expressions in (7.37) are identities, we can differentiate both sides with respect to any of the $n + 1$ parameters that might be of interest.

For the first set of comparative statics results, let us differentiate with respect to one of the input prices, say, w_1. We choose input 1 only because it is relatively easy to keep track of during the analysis; any other input will produce the same comparative statics results. Differentiating the n identities in (7.37) with respect to w_1, we have

$$p \sum_{j=1}^{n} f_{1j}(x^*) \frac{\partial x_j^*}{\partial w_1} - 1 = 0 \qquad \text{for good 1}$$

and (7.38)

$$p \sum_{j=1}^{n} f_{ij}(x^*) \frac{\partial x_j^*}{\partial w_1} = 0 \qquad \text{for all } i \neq 1.$$

Rewriting the n equations from (7.38) in matrix form, we have the system

$$\begin{bmatrix} pf_{11}(x^*) & \cdots & pf_{1n}(x^*) \\ \vdots & & \vdots \\ pf_{n1}(x^*) & \cdots & pf_{nn}(x^*) \end{bmatrix} \begin{bmatrix} \dfrac{\partial x_1^*}{\partial w_1} \\ \vdots \\ \dfrac{\partial x_n^*}{\partial w_1} \end{bmatrix} = \begin{bmatrix} 1 \\ 0 \\ \vdots \\ 0 \end{bmatrix}. \qquad (7.39)$$

The matrix on the left-hand side of (7.39) is simply $H\pi(x^*)$, and if any input price other than w_1 had been chosen initially, the only difference would be the location of the 1 in the right-hand column vector. If we had differentiated with respect to w_i rather than w_1, the 1 on the right-hand side would be in the ith row rather than the first row; but that would be the only difference.

One approach to solving (7.39) for the comparative statics terms $\partial x_i^* / \partial w_1$ would be to sign the elements of the inverse Hessian matrix directly, but that is not the approach we will take. Rather, we are going to solve the system (7.39) by applying Cramer's rule. Since we differentiated with respect to w_1, the n comparative statics terms are of two basic types: one is the **own** effect $\partial x_1^* / \partial w_1$, and the other $n - 1$ terms are the **cross** effects $\partial x_i^* / \partial w_1$ for $i = 2, 3, \ldots, n$. First, consider the own effect.

Applying Cramer's rule to find the own effect, we have

$$\frac{\partial x_1^*}{\partial w_1} = \frac{\begin{vmatrix} 1 & pf_{12}(x^*) & \cdots & pf_{1n}(x^*) \\ 0 & pf_{22}(x^*) & \cdots & pf_{2n}(x^*) \\ \vdots & \vdots & & \vdots \\ 0 & pf_{n2}(x^*) & \cdots & pf_{nn}(x^*) \end{vmatrix}}{|H\pi(x^*)|}. \qquad (7.40)$$

Since the second-order conditions hold, we know that $H\pi(x^*)$ is an *NP* matrix, and so we know the sign of $|H\pi(x^*)|$, right? Well no, not really. Since

$H\pi(x^*)$ is an NP matrix, the determinant $|H\pi(x^*)|$ will be of different sign depending on the number of goods in the model. The NP condition requires the principal minors to alternate in sign starting negative. Thus, if n is odd, the determinant of the Hessian will be negative, and if n is even, the determinant of the Hessian will be positive. Since this is a general n-good model, we do not know whether n is even or odd, and thus we cannot sign the denominator of the fraction in (7.40). But we do not need to sign the denominator in (7.40) to sign the comparative statics term $\partial x_1^*/\partial w_1$. Notice that if we expand the determinant in the numerator by the first row and column, we will have 1 times the $(n-1)$st-order principal minor formed by striking out the first row and column. Now the second-order conditions do not tell us the sign of this $(n-1)$st-order principal minor either, but we can see that $\partial x_1^*/\partial w_1$ is the **ratio** of an $(n-1)$st-order principal minor (the numerator) and an nth-order principal minor (the denominator). Now if $H\pi(x^*)$ is an NP matrix, we do not know what each of these signs will be, but we **do** know that they will be *of* **opposite sign.** The NP condition requires the principal minors to **alternate in sign.** Thus if the numerator of (7.40) is positive, the denominator is negative, and vice versa. In any case, the sign of the fraction will be negative, and we have the comparative statics result that

$$\frac{\partial x_1^*}{\partial w_1} < 0. \tag{7.41}$$

Or, remembering that good 1 was chosen arbitrarily, we have for any own effect that

$$\frac{\partial x_i^*}{\partial w_i} < 0 \qquad \text{for all } i = 1, 2, \ldots, n. \tag{7.42}$$

The comparative statics result in (7.42) is quite important. It says that the factor demand functions of a perfectly competitive firm all slope downward with respect to their own prices. In other words, there are no Giffen inputs. This result had already been derived for the $n = 2$ case, but it is much more powerful to know that it holds regardless of the number of factors employed. It is nice that the result could be found without imposing any additional structure on the model; (7.42) was obtained from only the first- and second-order conditions for profit maximization by a perfectly competitive firm.

Now when the $n = 2$ case was examined earlier, it was found that cross effects could not be signed without adding additional structure to the problem. Unfortunately, but not surprisingly, this result continues to hold in n dimensions. Applying Cramer's rule to (7.40) and solving for any arbitrary cross effect (say, $\partial x_2^*/\partial w_1$), we have

$$\frac{\partial x_2^*}{\partial w_1} = \frac{\begin{vmatrix} pf_{11}(x^*) & 1 & pf_{13}(x^*) & \cdots & pf_{1n}(x^*) \\ pf_{21}(x^*) & 0 & pf_{23}(x^*) & \cdots & pf_{2n}(x^*) \\ \vdots & \vdots & \vdots & & \vdots \\ pf_{n1}(x^*) & 0 & pf_{n3}(x^*) & \cdots & pf_{nn}(x^*) \end{vmatrix}}{|H\pi(x^*)|}. \tag{7.43}$$

Expanding the determinant in the numerator by the second column, we have 1 times an $(n-1)$st-order minor of $H\pi(x^*)$, but **not** a principal minor of $H\pi(x^*)$. Since the second-order conditions sign only principal minors, not all minors, the sign of (7.43), or any other cross effect, is indeterminate. Of course, if more structure were imposed on the model (as in some of the problems at the end of the chapter), it might be possible to sign terms like (7.43). But assuming only the first- and second-order conditions for profit maximization, we are not able to determine the sign of such cross terms; in the general case, we do not know whether the demands for factor inputs are gross substitutes, gross complements, or unrelated.

The demand for any input $x_i^*(w, p)$ is a function of $n+1$ variables, the n factor prices $w = (w_1, w_2, \ldots, w_n)$, and the price of the firm's output p. Thus far we have obtained expressions for the comparative statics impact of a change in any factor price; the own effects are strictly negative, while the $n-1$ cross effects are of indefinite sign. Now let us examine the impact of a change in the price of the product p.

Returning to the first-order identities in (7.37) and differentiating with respect to p, we have

$$p \sum_{j=1}^{n} f_{ij}(x^*)\frac{\partial x_j^*}{\partial p} + f_i(x^*) = 0 \qquad \text{for all } i = 1, 2, \ldots, n. \qquad (7.44)$$

Rewriting this in matrix form gives us

$$\begin{bmatrix} pf_{11}(x^*) & \cdots & pf_{1n}(x^*) \\ \vdots & & \vdots \\ pf_{n1}(x^*) & \cdots & pf_{nn}(x^*) \end{bmatrix} \begin{bmatrix} \dfrac{\partial x_1^*}{\partial p} \\ \vdots \\ \dfrac{\partial x_n^*}{\partial p} \end{bmatrix} = \begin{bmatrix} -f_1 \\ \vdots \\ -f_n \end{bmatrix}. \qquad (7.45)$$

Arbitrarily choosing one input (say, x_1), and solving (7.45) by Cramer's rule, we get

$$\frac{\partial x_1^*}{\partial p} = \frac{\begin{vmatrix} -f_1 & pf_{12}(x^*) & \cdots & pf_{1n}(x^*) \\ -f_2 & pf_{22}(x^*) & \cdots & pf_{2n}(x^*) \\ \vdots & \vdots & & \vdots \\ -f_n & pf_{n2}(x^*) & \cdots & pf_{nn}(x^*) \end{vmatrix}}{|H\pi(x^*)|}. \qquad (7.46)$$

Now it would be nice if (7.46) were signed by the second-order conditions for profit maximization, but as was the case for the cross effects of a change in the price of a factor, no such results are available. In the general case, the expression in (7.46) may be positive, negative, or zero.

In total, then, the results of this section do not seem to be very satisfying. There are $n+1$ comparative statics terms associated with any particular input demand function (1 own effect, $n-1$ cross effects, and 1 price effect), and out of these $n + 1$ expressions, only one, the own-price effect, can be signed in the general case. The paucity of this result might lead one to believe that very little can be said regarding the behavior of a profit-maximizing, perfectly competitive firm.

Actually things are not as bad as the results so far might suggest. While it is true that the first- and second-order conditions sign only one out of the $n + 1$ comparative statics terms associated with any particular factor demand function, they still place a number of additional restrictions on the profit-maximizing behavior of a perfectly competitive firm. To examine these additional restrictions, it is useful to introduce two important concepts: the supply function and the profit function.

The Supply Function and the Profit Function

The supply function for a perfectly competitive firm gives the profit-maximizing output as a function of the parameters of the problem (w and p). Thus when $x^*(w, p) = (x_1^*(w, p), \ldots, x_n^*(w, p))$ is the solution to (7.33), the **supply function** y^* is given by

$$y^* = y^*(w, p) = f(x^*(w, p)). \tag{7.47}$$

Correspondingly, the profit function for the perfectly competitive firm gives the optimal level of the firm's profit as a function of the parameters of the problem. Thus the **profit function** π^* associated with (7.33) is given by

$$\pi^* = \pi^*(w, p) = pf(x^*(w, p)) - \sum_{i=1}^{n} w_i x_i^*(w, p). \tag{7.48}$$

It is standard in elementary microeconomics to draw the supply function as upward-sloping with respect to price (i.e., to assume that $\partial y^*/\partial p > 0$). But do we know that such a condition will always hold for a profit-maximizing perfectly competitive firm, or is it only a property of certain special cases? To find out, let us take the direct approach, differentiating y^* in (7.47) with respect to p. This gives

$$\frac{\partial y^*}{\partial p} = \sum_{i=1}^{n} f_i(x^*) \frac{\partial x_i^*}{\partial p}. \tag{7.49}$$

Now if we knew the sign of the $\partial x_i^*/\partial p$ terms, then it might be possible to sign (7.49); but we do not. We demonstrated earlier that second-order conditions for profit maximization alone are not sufficient to sign these terms. Thus we must conclude that signing (7.49) is hopeless without additional structure being imposed on the model, right? No, actually it is still possible to sign (7.49) without imposing additional structure on the model, even though we do not know the signs of the individual $\partial x_i^*/\partial p$ terms.

To see how $\partial y^*/\partial p$ can be signed, return to (7.44), the expression derived by differentiation of the first-order identities in (7.37) with respect to p. Multiply each of the equations in (7.44) by $\partial x_i^*/\partial p$. This gives

$$f_i(x^*) \frac{\partial x_i^*}{\partial p} + \sum_{j=1}^{n} \frac{\partial x_i^*}{\partial p} p f_{ij}(x^*) \frac{\partial x_j^*}{\partial p} = 0 \qquad \text{for all } i. \tag{7.50}$$

Now since (7.50) holds for all $i = 1, 2, \ldots, n$, we can sum these n equations, which gives us

$$\sum_{i=1}^{n} f_i(x^*)\frac{\partial x_i^*}{\partial p} + \sum_{i=1}^{n}\sum_{j=1}^{n} \frac{\partial x_i^*}{\partial p} pf_{ij}(x^*)\frac{\partial x_j^*}{\partial p} = 0. \tag{7.51}$$

Notice from (7.49) that the far left-hand side of (7.51) is simply $\partial y^*/\partial p$. Thus (7.51) can be written as

$$\frac{\partial y^*}{\partial p} = -\sum_{i=1}^{n}\sum_{j=1}^{n} \frac{\partial x_i^*}{\partial p} pf_{ij}(x^*)\frac{\partial x_j^*}{\partial p}. \tag{7.52}$$

Of course, the signs of the $\partial x_i^*/\partial p$ terms are unknown, but we do not need to know them to sign the right-hand side of (7.52). We know that the second-order conditions require the Hessian of the profit function $H\pi(x^*)$ to generate a **negative definite quadratic form**. Thus, since the right-hand side of (7.52) is a quadratic form of $H\pi(x^*)$, the expression inside the double summation symbols will be negative regardless of the signs of the individual $\partial x_i^*/\partial p$ terms (with the slight caveat that not all can be equal to zero). Given the minus sign in front of the double sum, we have that $\partial y^*/\partial p > 0$. Thus it can be proved that the supply function of a profit-maximizing, perfectly competitive firm slopes upward with respect to the product price even though it is the weighted sum of the $\partial x_i^*/\partial p$ terms that cannot be individually signed.

So much for the supply function. Now let us consider the profit function π^*. The comparative statics expressions for the profit function are so important in economics that they have their own name. Actually they carry the name of one of their discoverers: Harold Hotelling. **Hotelling's lemma** says that

$$\frac{\partial \pi^*}{\partial w_i} = -x_i^* \qquad \text{for all } i = 1, 2, \ldots, n$$

and   (7.53)

$$\frac{\partial \pi^*}{\partial p} = y^*.$$

Before proving Hotelling's lemma, it is important to be clear about what it says. The first part says that the derivative of the profit function with respect to the price of any input is equal to the negative of the demand for that input. Since $x_i^* > 0$, this means that $\partial \pi^*/\partial w_i < 0$ for all i. But Hotelling's lemma really gives much more than just this qualitative (sign) result. It says that when there is an infinitesimal change in the price of an input dw_i, the optimal profit will change in the opposite direction by the direct impact from input i, that is, $d\pi^* = -x_i^* dw_i$; but that is all. In particular, there is no indirect impact through the other inputs used in the production of the good. The use of the other $n - 1$ inputs may change (either up or down, since we do not know the sign of $\partial x_j^*/\partial w_i$ when $i \neq j$), but the optimum level of the firm's profit will not be affected by these indirect effects. The second part of Hotelling's lemma says that when the price of the output changes, the firm's optimal profit will change in the same direction (since $y^* > 0$), but the only effect on profit will be the direct effect $d\pi^* = y^*dp$. As in the case of the wage change, there will be no indirect effect on profits through the variation of the inputs used.

Proving Hotelling's lemma is relatively straightforward. Differentiating the profit function from (7.48) with respect to an arbitrary factor price (say, w_1), we have

$$\frac{\partial \pi^*}{\partial w_1} = \sum_{i=1}^{n} pf_i(x^*) \frac{\partial x_i^*}{\partial w_1} - \sum_{i=1}^{n} w_i \frac{\partial x_i^*}{\partial w_1} - x_1^*. \tag{7.54}$$

Rearranging (7.54), gives us

$$\frac{\partial \pi^*}{\partial w_1} = \sum_{i=1}^{n} (pf_i(x^*) - w_i) \frac{\partial x_i^*}{\partial w_1} - x_i^*. \tag{7.55}$$

But from the first-order conditions for profit maximization, we know that $pf_i(x^*) - w_i = 0$ for all i. Thus since w_1 was arbitrarily chosen, (7.55) reduces to the first part of Hotelling's lemma,

$$\frac{\partial \pi^*}{\partial w_i} = -x_i^* \qquad \text{for all } i = 1, 2, \ldots, n.$$

Since the second part of the lemma is proved in a similar manner, it is left to the reader as an exercise.

One important implication of Hotelling's lemma involves the so-called reciprocity relations on factor demand curves. The **reciprocity relation** says that derivatives of factor demand functions are **symmetric,** that is,

$$\frac{\partial x_i^*}{\partial w_j} = \frac{\partial x_j^*}{\partial w_i} \qquad \text{for all } i \neq j. \tag{7.56}$$

This result can be derived directly from the profit maximization problem of the firm, but since the second derivatives of π^* are symmetric, it follows immediately from the differentiation of the first part of Hotelling's lemma. The reciprocity relation completes our discussion of the comparative statics of the profit-maximizing, perfectly competitive firm. But in closing this section, we point out that even though not every comparative statics term can be signed, overall quite a lot can be said regarding the behavior of such a firm, even in n dimensions and without assuming any additional structure on the model.

The Envelope Theorem

Hotelling's lemma is in fact just a particular application of a more general mathematical result for optimization problems. The mathematical result is called the **envelope theorem,** and it is sufficiently important to warrant a separate discussion.

Consider the general n-variable maximization problem from (7.24)

$$\text{Max}_{x} z = f(x),$$

where $x \in \mathfrak{R}_+^n$, $f: \mathfrak{R}_+^n \to \mathfrak{R}$, and f is at least twice differentiable. Now suppose that a parameter α is included in the objective function so the maximization problem becomes

$$\text{Max}_x \, z = f(x, \alpha), \tag{7.57}$$

where α may be either an individual scalar or an m-dimensional vector $\alpha = (\alpha_1, \alpha_2, \ldots, \alpha_m)$.

The first-order conditions for the problem in (7.57) require that

$$f_i(x^*, \alpha) = 0 \qquad \text{for all } i = 1, 2, \ldots, n, \tag{7.58}$$

where $x^* = (x_1^*, x_2^*, \ldots, x_n^*) > 0$ is the solution vector and $f_i = \partial f / \partial x_i$. Also, as we have argued many times, if the second-order conditions hold, the requirements of the implicit-function theorem are met and so we can write the solution vector to (7.57) as

$$x^*(\alpha) = (x_1^*(\alpha), x_2^*(\alpha), \ldots, x_n^*(\alpha)), \tag{7.59}$$

where each $x_i^*(\alpha)$ is a differentiable function of α.

Now substituting these solutions from (7.59) back into the objective function f determines the **indirect objective function**

$$z^* = f(x^*(\alpha), \alpha). \tag{7.60}$$

This indirect objective function gives the maximum value of z for any value of the parameter α.

To find the change in the indirect objective function with respect to the parameter α, simply differentiate (7.60) with respect to α:

$$\frac{\partial z^*}{\partial \alpha} = \sum_{i=1}^n f_i(x^*) \frac{\partial x_i^*}{\partial \alpha} + \frac{\partial f}{\partial \alpha}. \tag{7.61}$$

From the first-order conditions, though, we know that $f_i(x^*) = 0$ for all i, and thus (7.61) can be written as

$$\frac{\partial z^*}{\partial \alpha} = \frac{\partial f}{\partial \alpha}. \tag{7.62}$$

The result in (7.62) is called the **envelope theorem.** It says that the change in the indirect objective function caused by a change in any parameter is equal to (only equal to) the direct effect of the parameter on the original objective function. In other words, the way in which the optimal value of the objective function changes in response to a parameter change, when all the variables are adjusted to their optimal levels, is precisely the same as the way the objective function changes when all the variables are fixed. The envelope theorem gets its name from cost theory, where the long-run cost curve is the "envelope" of all the short-run cost curves. Hotelling's lemma is just one of many economic applications of this important result. The envelope theorem is extended to constrained optimization problems in the next chapter.

PROBLEMS

7.1 Determine Δx_1 and Δx_2 for the two-good open Leontief model with the coefficient matrix

$$A = \begin{bmatrix} 0.2 & 0.6 \\ 0.5 & 0.2 \end{bmatrix},$$

when $\Delta d_1 = 100$ and $\Delta d_2 = 200$.

7.2 Recall (from Chapter 6) the long-run equilibrium condition for the open Leontief model with one primary factor (labor). The model's equilibrium prices $p^* = (p_1^*, p_2^*, \ldots, p_n^*)$ were given by

$$p^* = wa_L(I - A)^{-1},$$

where $a_L = (a_{L1}, a_{L2}, \ldots, a_{Ln})$ is the vector of labor input coefficients, w is the wage, and A is the Leontief matrix. Use this model to find the elasticity of any long-run equilibrium price (say, p_j^*) with respect to the wage [i.e., find $\varepsilon_{p_j w} = (\Delta p_j^*/p_j^*)/(\Delta w/w)$]. Interpret your result.

7.3 The text considered only the comparative statics impact of a change in the final demand vector d on the open Leontief model. For the $n = 2$ case and under the assumption of productivity (from Chapter 6), find the comparative statics impact of a change in technology (i.e., a change in the elements of the coefficient matrix) on the equilibrium output of good 1. In other words, sign the terms $\partial x_1^*/\partial a_{11}$, $\partial x_1^*/\partial a_{12}$, $\partial x_1^*/\partial a_{21}$, and $\partial x_1^*/\partial a_{22}$.

7.4 Consider the profit-maximizing **monopolist** with the production function

$$Q = f(x_1, x_2) = x_1^{1/2} x_2^{1/2}$$

and the linear demand function given by

$$P = -aQ + b \qquad \text{with } a > 0 \qquad \text{and} \qquad b > 0.$$

(a) Find the factor demand functions $x_1^*(a, b, w_1, w_2)$ and $x_2^*(a, b, w_1, w_2)$ for this monopolist.

(b) Find the comparative statics expressions for x_1^*: $\partial x_1^*/\partial a$, $\partial x_1^*/\partial b$, $\partial x_1^*/\partial w_1$, and $\partial x_1^*/\partial w_2$.

(c) Which of the comparative statics expressions in (b) can be signed? Interpret the signs of those that can be signed.

7.5 In the text, we examined comparative statics for a normalized n-good Walrasian model, that is, one price and one market had been eliminated through zero-degree homogeneity (H) and Walras' law (W). Suppose that we attempted to find comparative statics for the original n-good (nonnormalized) model. What would happen? Explain in detail.

7.6 Prove that the profit function $\pi^*(w, p)$ of a profit-maximizing, perfectly competitive firm is homogeneous of degree 1 and that the supply function y^* is homogeneous of degree 0.

7.7 Prove the second part of Hotelling's lemma (7.53): that $\partial \pi^*/\partial p = y^*$.

7.8 Prove that $\partial y^*/\partial w_i < 0$ for **at least one** $i = 1, 2, \ldots, n$, where y^* is the supply function of a perfectly competitive firm using n inputs.

7.9 Show the following condition holds for the supply function $y^*(w, p)$ and factor demands $x_i^*(w, p)$ for a profit-maximizing, perfectly competitive firm using n inputs:

$$\frac{\partial y^*}{\partial w_i} = \frac{-\partial x_i^*}{\partial p} \qquad \text{for all } i = 1, 2, \ldots, n.$$

7.10 (**Rader, 1968**) In the text we showed that the cross comparative statics terms $\partial x_i^*/\partial w_j$ for $i \neq j$ could not be signed for an n-input perfectly competitive firm when the only assumptions on the model were the first- and second-order conditions for profit maximization. Prove that **if** all inputs were "normal," that is, $f_{ij} \geq 0$ for all $i \neq j$, then the factor inputs will never be gross substitutes (i.e., it will be the case that $\partial x_i^*/\partial w_j \leq 0$ for all $i \neq j$).

7.11 Prove that for the "normal" case in Problem 7.10 (where $f_{ij} \geq 0$ for all $i \neq j$), it must be that $\partial x_i^*/\partial p > 0$ for all $i = 1, 2, \ldots, n$.

7.12 Suppose that a firm producing output y from n inputs $x = (x_1, x_2, \ldots, x_n)$ by means of the production function $y = f(x)$ is perfectly competitive in the product market, but is a monopsonist with respect to its various input markets. That is, suppose that the wage w_i that must be paid for each input x_i is an increasing function of the quantity of the input employed, so that $w_i = w_i(x_i)$ with $dw_i/dx_i > 0$ for all $i = 1, 2, \ldots, n$. Set up the profit maximization problem for such a firm. Find the first-order conditions for the problem and interpret them.

7.13 In the text we showed that for an n-input, profit-maximizing, perfectly competitive firm, the first- and second-order conditions imply that $\partial x_i^*/\partial w_i < 0$, but that the sign of $\partial x_i^*/\partial w_j$ cannot be determined for $i \neq j$. Does this result also hold if the firm is a monopolist? Explain why or why not.

7.14 Consider a three-input, profit-maximizing, perfectly competitive firm with the production function

$$y = f(x_1, x_2, x_3) = x_1^{1/2} + x_2^{1/2} + x_3^{1/2}.$$

(a) Solve the first-order conditions and find expressions for the input demand functions $x_1^*(w_1, w_2, w_3, p)$, $x_2^*(w_1, w_2, w_3, p)$, and $x_3^*(w_1, w_2, w_3, p)$.
(b) Do the second-order conditions hold for this production function? (Show.)
(c) Are the input demand functions homogeneous of any degree? (Show.)
(d) Find the four comparative statics expressions associated with input x_1.
(e) Find an expression for the firm's supply function $y^*(w_1, w_2, w_3, p)$.
(f) Is the supply function from (e) homogeneous of any degree? (Show.)
(g) Find an expression for the firm's profit function $\pi^*(w_1, w_2, w_3, p)$.
(h) Verify that Hotelling's lemma holds for this particular firm.

7.15 In the econometric technique of least-squares regression, the difference between the actual value of a variable y_i and its predicted value $a + bx_i$ is called the **residual** or **error term** e_i. Thus we have

$$e_i = y_i - [a + bx_i] \qquad \text{for all } i = 1, 2, \ldots, n.$$

The values of the regression coefficients a and b are chosen so that they **minimize the sum of the squared residuals.** Thus the least-squares regression coefficients a and b are the solution to the problem

$$\underset{(a,b)}{\text{Min}} \sum_{i=1}^{n} e_i^2.$$

(a) Determine the first-order conditions (the so-called normal equations) for the problem.

(b) Do the second-order conditions hold? (Show.)

(c) Show that the solution to the problem (a^*, b^*) is given by

$$a^* = y - b\bar{x} \quad \text{and} \quad b^* = \frac{\sum_{i=1}^{n} x_i y_i - n\bar{x}\bar{y}}{\sum_{i=1}^{n} x_i^2 - n\bar{x}^2},$$

where

$$\bar{x} = \sum_{i=1}^{n} \frac{x_i}{n} \quad \text{and} \quad \bar{y} = \sum_{i=1}^{n} \frac{y_i}{n}.$$

7.16 Suppose that the government taxes the output of two firms in Cournot equilibrium. If the market demand for the output of the two firms is $P = -Q + b$ (with $b > 0$) and each firm has the cost function $c_i(q_i) = cq_i$ (with $c > 0$) for $i = 1, 2$, then the profit functions of the two firms will be given by

$$\pi^1(q_1, q_2) = (-q_1 - q_2 + b) q_1 - cq_1 - t_1 q_1,$$
$$\pi^2(q_1, q_2) = (-q_1 - q_2 + b) q_2 - cq_2 - t_2 q_2,$$

where t_1 is the tax rate on firm 1 and t_2 is the tax rate on firm 2. In such a case, the Cournot equilibrium outputs (q_1^*, q_2^*) are functions of the tax rates t_1 and t_2 as well as the parameters b and c. In Cournot equilibrium, the tax revenue TR received by the government will be

$$TR(t_1, t_2) = t_1 q_1^* + t_2 q_2^*.$$

Find the tax rates t_1^* and t_2^* that maximize tax revenue under these assumptions.

7.17 Consider a perfectly competitive firm that produces pollution in addition to output y, which sells at price p. The cost of production is given by the cost function $c(y, a)$, where a is the quantity of pollution abatement. The partial derivatives of the cost function are restricted in the following way:

$$c_y > 0, \qquad c_{yy} > 0, \qquad c_a > 0, \qquad c_{aa} > 0. \tag{1}$$

The firm produces pollution in addition to output y. This pollution output (e for emissions) is determined by the pollution production function $e(y, a)$. The partial derivatives of the pollution production function are restricted in the following way:

$$e_y > 0, \qquad e_{yy} > 0, \qquad e_a < 0, \qquad e_{aa} > 0. \tag{2}$$

Assume that the cross effects on both the cost and pollution functions are strictly positive, so:

$$c_{ya} = c_{ay} > 0 \quad \text{and} \quad e_{ya} = e_{ay} > 0.$$

The firm's short-run profit π will thus be given by

$$\pi(y, a) = py - c(y, a) - te(y, a),$$

where t is the tax rate paid by the firm per unit of emission.

(a) Interpret the sign restrictions in (1) and (2).

(b) Determine the first-order conditions for profit maximization with respect to output y and abatement a.

(c) Assuming that the second-order conditions for the problem hold, find the comparative statics impact on the optimal levels of output and abatement caused by an increase in the price p of the firm's product (i.e., find $\partial y^*/\partial p$ and $\partial a^*/\partial p$).

(d) Again assuming that the second-order conditions for the problem hold, find the comparative statics impact on the optimal levels of output and abatement caused by an increase in the pollution tax t (i.e., find $\partial y^*/\partial t$ and $\partial a^*/\partial t$).

(e) Interpret your answers to (c) and (d). Do they make economic sense?

(f) Find an expression for the firm's profit function $\pi^* = \pi^*(p, t) = \pi(y^*(p, t), a^*(p, t))$. Use the envelope theorem to find the change in π^* caused by a change in p and t (i.e., find $\partial \pi^*/\partial p$ and $\partial \pi^*/\partial t$).

7.18 An alternative (unconstrained) way of characterizing the standard (constrained) consumer choice problem is:

$$\text{Max}_{\{x\}} V(x), \text{ where } V(x) = rU(x) - \sum_{i=1}^{n} p_i x_i,$$

with $x = (x_1, x_2, \ldots, x_n) \geq 0$, $p_i > 0$ for all $i = 1, 2, \ldots, n$, $U(x)$ is the consumer's utility function, and the parameter $r > 0$ is the "price" of utility. The solutions to this problem are called **Frisch demands** and are given by

$$x_i^F = x_i^F(r, p_1, p_2, \ldots, p_n) \qquad \text{for all } i = 1, 2, \ldots, n.$$

(a) Show that Frisch demand curves slope downward with respect to their own price (i.e., show $\partial x_i^F/\partial p_i < 0$ for all $i = 1, 2, \ldots, n$).

(b) Show that cross effects on Frisch demand curves are symmetric (i.e., show $\partial x_i^F/\partial p_j = \partial x_j^F/\partial p_i$ for all $i \neq j$).

NOTES

1. The same warning given in note 4 of Chapter 5 applies here as well.
2. See Box 6.1.
3. As in earlier discussions, we consider only interior optima.

C H A P T E R 8

COMPARATIVE STATICS III:
OPTIMIZATION UNDER CONSTRAINT

■ ■ ■

This chapter discusses the Lagrange multiplier technique for solving constrained optimization problems. This technique is one of the most important tools of modern economic theory. The reason for its importance is that it allows us to solve **constrained** optimization problems. What could be more fundamental to economic theory than the idea of constrained optimization? Even the most elementary definitions of economics involve problems of scarcity and choice, on satisfying unlimited wants with limited resources. The Lagrange technique provides a useful tool for analyzing just such problems.

8.1 The Lagrange Technique:
First- and Second-Order Conditions

First-Order Conditions

Consider the general n-variable constrained maximization problem

$$\text{Max } f(x)$$
$$x$$
$$\text{Subject to } g(x) = 0. \tag{8.1}$$

In (8.1) $x \in \Re_+^n$, and we assume that both f and g are at least twice differentiable.

The constraint in (8.1) prevents a direct application of the results of Chapter 7. But if we could convert the constrained problem (8.1) into an unconstrained problem, then the results obtained earlier could be applied. Such a conversion is exactly what the Lagrangian multiplier technique enables us to do.

We define the following **Lagrangian function** (or simply **Lagrangian**) in $n + 1$ variables

$$L(x, \lambda) = f(x) + \lambda g(x). \tag{8.2}$$

Notice that the Lagrangian (8.2) introduces a new variable λ. This variable is called the (undetermined) **Lagrange multiplier.** Functions g and f are the constraint function and the objective function from (8.1), respectively. The Lagrangian is a function in $n + 1$ variables, the n variables $x_1, x_2, \ldots, x_n$, and the new variable λ.

Now consider the problem of finding a critical point of the unconstrained Lagrangian function

$$L(x, \lambda). \tag{8.3}$$

From Chapter 7 we know that if (x^*, λ^*) is a critical point of (8.3) in the interior of the domain, then the following necessary conditions must hold:

$$L_i(x^*, \lambda^*) = f_i(x^*) + \lambda^* g_i(x^*) = 0 \qquad \text{for all } i = 1, 2, \ldots, n$$

and

$$L_\lambda(x^*, \lambda^*) = g(x^*) = 0. \tag{8.4}$$

The fundamental result of the Lagrangian multiplier technique is that a solution to (8.1) also satisfies the conditions in (8.4). That is, the necessary conditions for a solution to the constrained problem (8.1) are also the necessary conditions for a solution to the unconstrained problem (8.3). Geometrically, this is because the gradient of the objective function is parallel to the gradient of the constraint at the optimum, and λ^* is the factor of proportionality between these two gradient vectors.

The following theorem proves this result for the case of $n = 2$. The interested reader may consult more mathematically detailed sources for the general proof.[1]

THEOREM 8.1: If $x^* \in \Re^2_{++}$ is a local maximum for (8.1), then there exists a λ^* such that the conditions in (8.4) hold.

PROOF: Let x^* solve (8.1) for the case of $n = 2$. For all $x \in \Re^2$ in a neighborhood of x^* that satisfy the constraint $g(x) = 0$, the condition $dg = g_1 dx_1 + g_2 dx_2 = 0$ must hold. This condition can be rewritten as

$$\frac{dx_2}{dx_1} = -\frac{g_1}{g_2}.$$

From this condition it is possible to solve for x_1 as a function of x_2. By writing this as $x_2 = h(x_1)$, the preceding condition becomes

$$\frac{dh}{dx_1} = -\frac{g_1}{g_2}.$$

Given that $x_2 = h(x_1)$ for x in a neighborhood of x^* and satisfying the constraint, the problem in (8.1) can be expressed as Max $f(x_1, h(x_1))$. Since x^* solves (8.1), we know that

$$f_1(x^*) + f_2(x^*)\frac{dh(x^*)}{dx_1} = f_1(x^*) - \frac{f_2(x^*)}{g_2(x^*)}g_1(x^*) = 0. \tag{8.5}$$

Thus defining $\lambda^* = -f_2(x^*)/g_2(x^*)$, we have from (8.5)

$$f_1(x^*) + \lambda^* g_1(x^*) = 0. \tag{8.6}$$

A similar argument for x_2 gives

$$f_2(x^*) + \lambda^* g_2(x^*) = 0,$$

and since $g(x^*) = 0$, the theorem is proved.

This Lagrangian result is extremely useful, as the many examples later in this chapter will demonstrate. The result provides first-order (necessary) conditions for a local constrained maximum of the objective function. Formally, the result states that if $f(x^*) \geq f(x)$ for all x within an ε neighborhood of x^* satisfying $g(x^*) = 0$, then there exists a λ^* such that conditions (8.4) hold. As in the case of unconstrained problems, these first-order conditions also hold for a constrained **minimization** problem. The differences between maximization and minimization are contained in the second-order conditions (discussed shortly); the necessary conditions are exactly the same for both problems.

This result can easily be extended to the case of m independent equality constraints (where $n > m$). For instance, the first-order (necessary) condition for x^* to solve

$$\text{Max } f(x)$$
$$\text{Subject to: } g^1(x) - 0$$
$$\vdots$$
$$g^m(x) = 0$$

(8.7)

is that there exist a $\lambda^* \in \mathfrak{R}^m$ such that

$$f_i(x^*) + \sum_{j=1}^{m} \lambda_j^* g_i^j(x^*) = 0 \qquad \text{for all } i = 1, 2, \ldots, n$$

and

$$g^i(x^*) = 0 \qquad \text{for all } j = 1, 2, \ldots, m.$$

Interpretation of Lagrangian Multipliers

The introduction of the Lagrange multiplier (or multipliers) not only allows us to reduce the constrained problem to an unconstrained problem, it often provides additional information about the problem that can be extremely useful. In economic problems the optimal value of the Lagrange multiplier λ^* often has an important economic interpretation.

To see how Lagrange multipliers can be interpreted, first consider the general problem in (8.1) in the specific case of the constraint that can be written in the form $g(x) = b - h(x)$, where b is a scalar. The Lagrangian for the problem is thus

$$L(x, \lambda) = f(x) + \lambda(b - h(x)).$$

At the optimal (x^*, λ^*), the first-order conditions $f_i(x^*) - \lambda^* h_i(x^*) = 0$ for all $i = 1, 2, \ldots, n$ and $h(x^*) = b$ must hold. Under the conditions of the implicit-function theorem given in Chapter 6 (conditions guaranteed by the second-order conditions discussed later), these $n + 1$ equations can be solved for the $n + 1$ optimal values in terms of parameter b. By writing these parameterized optimal values as $x^*(b) = (x_1^*(b), \ldots, x_n^*(b))$ and $\lambda^*(b)$, the **indirect objective function** (optimal value of the objective function) is $f(x^*(b))$.

Consider the change in the indirect objective function caused by a change in the parameter b. Differentiating and writing out this change, we have

$$\frac{df(x^*)}{db} = \sum_{i=1}^{n} f_i(x^*)\frac{dx_i^*}{db}. \tag{8.8}$$

Recalling the n first-order conditions, we can rewrite (8.8) as

$$\frac{df(x^*)}{db} = \lambda^* \sum_{i=1}^{n} h_i(x^*)\frac{dx_i^*}{db}. \tag{8.9}$$

The remaining first-order condition is $h(x^*) = b$. Differentiation of this condition gives $\sum_{i=1}^{n} h_i(x^*)(dx_i^*/db) = 1$. Substituting this into (8.9) gives the following simple expression for the change in the indirect objective function caused by a change in the parameter:

$$\frac{df(x^*)}{db} = \lambda^*. \tag{8.10}$$

The result in (8.10) says that the optimal value of the Lagrange multiplier measures the "sensitivity" of the indirect objective function with respect to a change in the value of the parameter b. It thus constitutes an extension of the **envelope theorem** from Chapter 7 to the case of constrained optimization problems. The envelope theorem will be examined more closely in the next section.

As an economic example, consider the long-run cost minimization problem of a firm employing n factor inputs to produce a specific level of output $\bar{y} > 0$:

$$\operatorname*{Min}_{x}\ \sum_{i=1}^{n} w_i x_i \tag{8.11}$$

$$\text{Subject to: } \bar{y} = f(x),$$

where $x_i \geq 0$ is the quantity and $w_i > 0$ is the wage of input i for all $i = 1, 2, \ldots, n$ and $y = f(x)$ is the firm's production function, with $x = (x_1, x_2, \ldots, x_n)$. The Lagrangian for the problem is

$$L(x, \lambda) = \sum_{i=1}^{n} w_i x_i + \lambda(\bar{y} - f(x)), \tag{8.12}$$

with first-order conditions

$$w_i - \lambda^* f_i(x^*) = 0 \qquad \text{for all } i = 1, 2, \ldots, n$$

and

$$\bar{y} = f(x^*).$$

Solving these first-order conditions gives us the optimal employment of the n inputs as functions of the wage vector $w = (w_1, w_2, \ldots, w_n)$ and the fixed output level $\bar{y}$. These cost-minimizing input demand functions can be written as $x_i^*(w, \bar{y})$ for all i. Substituting these input demands into the original objective function gives us the firm's **total cost** function $TC(w, \bar{y})$:

$$TC(w, \bar{y}) = \sum_{i=1}^{n} w_i x_i^*(w, \bar{y}).$$

Differentiation of $TC(w, \bar{y})$ with respect to $\bar{y}$ gives the change in total cost with respect to output, or marginal cost MC. Applying (8.10) to this problem, we have

$$MC(w, \bar{y}) = \frac{\partial TC(w, \bar{y})}{\partial \bar{y}} = \lambda^*(w, \bar{y}); \tag{8.13}$$

that is, the optimal value of the Lagrange multiplier for the cost minimization problem is equal to the marginal cost. Given the importance of marginal cost in economic analysis, this is a very important result. This is only one of many examples where the Lagrange multiplier has an important economic interpretation.

The Envelope Theorem for Constrained Optimization Problems

The foregoing result is based on the envelope theorem for constrained optimization problems; let us examine that theorem more directly. To that end, consider the n-variable constrained maximization problem

$$\operatorname*{Max}_{x} z = f(x, \alpha)$$

$$\text{Subject to } g(x, \alpha) = 0, \tag{8.14}$$

where α is an arbitrary parameter. The Lagrangian for this problem is $L(x, \lambda) = f(x) + \lambda g(x)$, and the first-order conditions are

$$L_i(x^*, \lambda^*) = f_i(x^*) + \lambda^* g_i(x^*) = 0 \qquad \text{for all } i = 1, 2, \ldots, n,$$
$$L_\lambda(x^*, \lambda^*) = g(x^*) = 0. \tag{8.15}$$

Writing $x^*(\alpha) = (x_1^*(\alpha), x_2^*(\alpha), \ldots, x_n^*(\alpha))$ and remembering that $g(x^*) = 0$, we have the indirect objective function

$$z^*(\alpha) = f(x^*(\alpha), \alpha) = L(x^*(\alpha), \lambda^*(\alpha), \alpha).$$

Differentiation of the far left-hand side and the far right-hand side of this expression gives

$$\frac{\partial z^*}{\partial \alpha} = \sum_{i=1}^{n} L_i \frac{\partial x_i^*}{\partial \alpha} + L_\lambda \frac{\partial \lambda^*}{\partial \alpha} + L_\alpha,$$

where $L_\alpha = \partial L / \partial \alpha = \partial f / \partial \alpha + \lambda^* \partial g / \partial \alpha$. By substituting from (8.15) this reduces to

$$\frac{\partial z^*}{\partial \alpha} = \frac{\partial f}{\partial \alpha} + \lambda^* \frac{\partial g}{\partial \alpha}. \tag{8.16}$$

This is the **envelope theorem** for constrained optimization problems. Since only first-order conditions were used, the result would be exactly the same if the initial problem had been a minimization instead of a maximization in (8.14).

BOX 8.1
The General Theory of Second Best

The seminal paper on the general theory of second best was Lipsey and Lancaster (1956). Their paper, like most that have followed, presented the second-best problem in the context of welfare economics. The issue is basically this. Suppose that all the necessary conditions for a Pareto-optimal allocation of resources have been met (the so-called first-best conditions), and then another constraint is added that violates one of these Pareto conditions. One might suspect that even though the new constraint violates one of the necessary conditions, the others would continue to hold for the newly constrained (second-best) optimum.

The general theory of second best demonstrates that this is **not** the case. In general, the new second-best optimum requires departure from all of the original Pareto-optimal conditions. Or, presented alternatively, when some of the optimality conditions are violated, moving to a situation in which fewer but still some are violated will not necessarily be an improvement.

The general theory of second best has rather negative implications for "piecemeal" welfare policies (e.g., eliminating one monopoly in an economy with other imperfectly competitive firms). The theory of second best implies that such a piecemeal social welfare policy may make the society worse off. This basic argument has been applied to a number of specific policy issues including the theory of tariffs, customs unions, regulated utilities, and nationalized industries. Since Lipsey and Lancaster's original presentation of the argument involved a direct application of the Lagrangian technique developed in this chapter, we follow their original approach even though there are now more mathematically sophisticated and more general approaches to the second-best argument available in the literature (see, e.g., Allingham and Archibald, 1975). Our only departure from the original presentation is that we include a correction made by Rapanos (1980).

Suppose that the objective function is to be maximized (or minimized) is $F(x)$ and there is one constraint, given by $\phi(x) = 0$. Let F and ϕ be differentiable functions from $\Re_+^n$ into $\Re$ that have sufficient structure to guarantee an interior solution. The Lagrangian for the problem is given by

$$L(x, \lambda) = F(x) + \lambda\phi(x).$$

Letting the subscript i indicate the partial derivative with respect to x_i, we have the following first-order conditions:

$$L_i = F_i + \lambda\phi_i = 0 \qquad \text{for all } i = 1, 2, \ldots, n.$$

By eliminating λ and writing all of the equations in terms of the nth, these first-order conditions become

$$\frac{F_i}{F_n} = \frac{\phi_i}{\phi_n} \qquad \text{for all } i = 1, 2, \ldots, n-1. \tag{a}$$

Now suppose we introduce another constraint into the problem, in particular, an additional constraint that prevents the fulfillment of one of the necessary conditions. Let the constraint by given by

$$\frac{F_1}{F_n} = \frac{k\phi_1}{\phi_n} \qquad \text{with } k \neq 1.$$

Given this new constraint, as well as the original one, the Lagrangian for the problem becomes

$$L'(x, \lambda', \mu) = F(x) + \lambda'\phi(x) + \mu \left[\frac{F_1}{F_n} - k\left(\frac{\phi_1}{\phi_n}\right) \right].$$

The first-order conditions for this problem are substantially messier, but after some algebraic manipulation they reduce to

$$\frac{F_i}{F_j} = \frac{\phi_i + (\mu/\lambda')(Q_i - kR_i)}{\phi_j + (\mu/\lambda')(Q_j - kR_j)}, \tag{b}$$

for all $i, j = 1, 2, \ldots, n$ with $i \neq j$. The R's and the Q's in this expression are defined as

$$R_i = \frac{F_{1i} F_n - F_{ni} F_1}{F_n^2},$$

$$Q_i = \frac{\phi_{1i} \phi_n - \phi_{ni} \phi_1}{\phi_n^2},$$

with double subscripts indicating second derivatives.

The optimality conditions for the original (first-best) problem are given by (a) and the optimality conditions for the second (second-best) problem are given by (b); there is no reason for these conditions to be the same. They would be the same only if one of the following conditions were satisfied:

1. $\mu = 0$.
2. $\mu \neq 0$ but $Q_i - kR_i = Q_j - kR_j$ for all $i \neq j \neq 1$.
3. $\mu \neq 0$ but $F_i/F_j = \phi_i/\phi_j = (Q_i - kR_i)/(Q_j - kR_j)$ for all $i \neq j \neq 1$.

Condition 1 cannot hold because it would violate the additional constraint. The other two conditions could hold, of course; but given that almost no restrictions have been placed on the terms defining the R's and the Q's, there is in general no reason for them to be satisfied. Thus we must conclude, as Lipsey and Lancaster did in their original paper, that in general all the conditions for the second-best optimum will differ from the conditions for the attainment of the original (first-best) optimum.

Sources

Allingham, M. G., and G. C. Archibald. 1975. Second best and decentralization. *Journal of Economic Theory* 10: 157–73.

Lipsey, R. G., and K. Lancaster. 1956. The general theory of second best. *Review of Economic Studies* 24: 11–36.

Rapanos, V. T. 1980. A comment on the theory of second best. *Review of Economic Studies* 47: 817–19.

To apply the envelope result (8.16) to the cost minimization problem in (8.11), notice that for the parameter $\alpha = \bar{y}$ we have from the Lagrangian (8.12) that

$$\frac{\partial f}{\partial \alpha} = \frac{\partial TC}{\partial \bar{y}} = 0 \quad \text{and} \quad \frac{\partial g}{\partial \alpha} = \frac{\partial g}{\partial \bar{y}} = 1. \tag{8.17}$$

Thus substituting the particular values from (8.17) into the envelope result in (8.16) we have

$$\frac{\partial TC(w, \bar{y})}{\partial \bar{y}} = \lambda^*(w, \bar{y}), \tag{8.18}$$

the result already obtained in (8.13).

The envelope theorem can be applied with equal ease to a variety of different parameter changes in wide array of different economic models. Some of these are discussed in this chapter, while others are left to the reader as exercises.

Second-Order Conditions

So far we have discussed only the first-order conditions for a solution to (8.1): conditions that would be exactly the same whether the problem involved maximization or a minimization. We now turn to the second-order conditions. Throughout our discussion of second-order conditions for the constrained optimization problem, we assume that x^* satisfies the first-order conditions (8.4). In specifying second-order conditions, remember that we are specifying conditions which, together with the first-order conditions, imply that x^* is a solution to (8.1). For reference we reproduce the general n-variable constrained maximization problem

$$\underset{x}{\text{Max }} f(x)$$

$$\text{Subject to } g(x) = 0.$$

From the argument in Chapter 7 we know that if $f(x)$ were **unconstrained,** then the desired second-order condition would be that $d^2 f(x^*) < 0$. Writing this out more formally, we have

$$d^2 f(x^*) = \sum_{i=1}^{n} \sum_{j=1}^{n} dx_i f_{ij}(x^*) \, dx_j < 0 \qquad (8.19)$$

for all dx_i and dx_j (not all equal to zero).

This second-order condition means roughly that the slope decreases as we move away from the optimal point in any direction. Now for the **constrained** case, this condition is actually "too strong." We do not require that $d^2 f(x^*) < 0$ for every direction, only for directions that satisfy the constraint $g(x) = 0$. To put it a bit differently, we can no longer say that the "directions" $dx_1, dx_2, \dots, dx_n$ are entirely arbitrary. The relevant directions are now interdependent; the change in one direction, say dx_i, depends on the change in the other directions. For this reason condition (8.19) is inappropriate for the constrained problem (8.1). The second-order condition for the constrained problem is given by

$$d^2 f(x^*) < 0 \qquad \text{for all } dx_1, dx_2, \dots, dx_n \text{ (not all zero)}$$

such that the constraint $g(x) = 0$ is satisfied. $\qquad (8.20)$

While condition (8.20) is sufficient to guarantee that an x^* satisfying the first-order conditions is a local maximum, it does not seem to be in a particularly "usable" form. It would be nice to convert (8.20) into a matrix condition, as we did for the unconstrained case. Such a matrix condition not only simplifies the verification of the second-order condition in specific problems, but it also proves invaluable in obtaining comparative static results. Such a matrix condition is provided in Theorem 8.2 for the $n = 2$. Since the proof of Theorem 8.2 is rather messy—even in two dimensions—the reader is referred to the more technical literature for a proof.[2]

THEOREM 8.2: For the case of $n = 2$, x^* satisfies the second-order condition for a constrained maximum given in (8.20) iff $|\bar{H}| > 0$ where $\bar{H}$ is the bordered matrix

$$\bar{H} = \begin{bmatrix} L_{\lambda\lambda}(x^*) & L_{\lambda 1}(x^*) & L_{\lambda 2}(x^*) \\ L_{1\lambda}(x^*) & L_{11}(x^*) & L_{12}(x^*) \\ L_{2\lambda}(x^*) & L_{21}(x^*) & L_{22}(x^*) \end{bmatrix}, \qquad (8.21)$$

with $L_{ij} = \partial^2 L / \partial x_i \partial x_j$, $L_{i\lambda} = \partial^2 L / \partial x_i \partial \lambda$, and $L(x, \lambda)$ is the Lagrangian $L(x, \lambda) = f(x_1, x_2) + \lambda g(x_1, x_2)$.

The matrix in Theorem 8.2 is written in terms of the second derivatives of the Lagrangian function evaluated at the optimal point x^*. When this matrix is written in terms of $f(x^*)$ and $g(x^*)$ instead, then $\bar{H}$ becomes

$$\bar{H} = \begin{bmatrix} 0 & g_1(x^*) & g_2(x^*) \\ g_1(x^*) & f_{11}(x^*) + \lambda^* g_{11}(x^*) & f_{12}(x^*) + \lambda^* g_{12}(x^*) \\ g_2(x^*) & f_{21}(x^*) + \lambda^* g_{21}(x^*) & f_{22}(x^*) + \lambda^* g_{22}(x^*) \end{bmatrix}. \qquad (8.22)$$

Matrix $\bar{H}$ is a **bordered** matrix; the Hessian of the Lagrangian in variables x_1 and x_2 is "bordered" by the derivatives of the constraint $g(x) = 0$. For this reason the matrix $\bar{H}$ is called a **bordered Hessian.**

The minors used in the second-order conditions for constrained optimization problems are exclusively **border-preserving** principal minors. For instance, the first-order border-preserving principal minor $|\bar{H}_1|$ of $\bar{H}$ is the 2×2 determinant

$$\bar{H}_1 = \begin{vmatrix} 0 & g_1(x^*) \\ g_1(x^*) & f_{11}(x^*) + \lambda^* g_{11}(x^*) \end{vmatrix}. \tag{8.23}$$

Correspondingly, the second-order border-preserving leading principal minor $|\bar{H}_2|$ of $\bar{H}$ is the 3×3 determinant $|\bar{H}|$ itself. Notice that $|\bar{H}_1| < 0$ regardless of the values of f and g. This latter fact allows us to characterize the second-order condition for the two-variable case as follows: The border-preserving leading principal minors of the Hessian evaluated at the optimal point alternate in sign, starting negative. Notice that this condition does not imply that $\bar{H}$ is an *NP* matrix, since it is not the principal minors of $\bar{H}$ that alternate in sign, but rather the border-preserving principal minors.

Before we state the second-order conditions for the n-variable case, a few facts should be noted about the $n = 2$ case. First, for a **minimization** problem, the second-order condition is $d^2 f(x^*) > 0$ for all directions satisfying $g(x) = 0$; in two dimensions this reduces to $|\bar{H}_2| = |\bar{H}| < 0$. Thus for the two-variable constrained minimization problem, all the border-preserving leading principal minors of the Hessian evaluated at the optimum point should be **negative.**

Second, the value of the minors are the same whether the border is placed in the northwest (NW) corner—as in (8.22)—or in the southeast (SE) corner. The value of the following two determinants is always the same:

$$\begin{vmatrix} 0 & g_1 & g_2 \\ g_1 & L_{11} & L_{12} \\ g_2 & L_{21} & L_{22} \end{vmatrix} = \begin{vmatrix} L_{11} & L_{12} & g_1 \\ L_{21} & L_{22} & g_2 \\ g_1 & g_2 & 0 \end{vmatrix}. \tag{8.24}$$

As will be apparent from the examples to be discussed, sometimes the form on the right-hand side of (8.24) follows more naturally from the structure of the economic problem, and sometimes just the opposite is the case. The restrictions on the signs of the minors required for the second-order conditions are identical for the NW and SE versions of $\bar{H}$ (even in n variables).

Finally, a word should be said regarding "leading" principal minors. The conditions given shortly for the n-variable case are specified as restrictions on the signs of the leading (or "naturally ordered" or "successive") border-preserving principal minors of $\bar{H}$. In many applications, we will be interested in the signs of all border-preserving principal minors, not just the leading ones. Since matrix $\bar{H}$ is **symmetric,** the **sign conditions on the leading principal minors imply that the same sign conditions hold for all principal minors of the same order.** Thus, if the border-preserving leading principal minors of order i have sign $(-1)^i$, then all border-preserving minors of order i have sign $(-1)^i$.

We now turn to the n-variable case. For the n-variable case with one constraint, the border-preserving leading principal minors of the Hessian are

$$|\bar{H}_2| - \begin{vmatrix} 0 & g_1 & g_2 \\ g_1 & L_{11} & L_{12} \\ g_2 & L_{21} & L_{22} \end{vmatrix}, \ |\bar{H}_3| = \begin{vmatrix} 0 & g_1 & g_2 & g_3 \\ g_1 & L_{11} & L_{12} & L_{13} \\ g_2 & L_{21} & L_{22} & L_{23} \\ g_3 & L_{31} & L_{32} & L_{33} \end{vmatrix}, \ldots, |\bar{H}_n| = |\bar{H}|.$$

In terms of these principal minors, the second-order conditions for the n-variable constrained **maximization** problem (8.1) are

$$|\bar{H}_2| > 0, \ |\bar{H}_3| < 0, \ldots, (-1)^n |\bar{H}_n| = (-1)^i |\bar{H}| > 0.$$

For the **minimization** of $f(x)$ subject to $g(x) = 0$, the second-order conditions are

$$|\bar{H}_2| < 0, |\bar{H}_3| < 0, \ldots, |\bar{H}_n| = |\bar{H}| < 0.$$

Of course, these principal minors are to be evaluated at the optimal value for both cases. It is easy to see that the two-variable case discussed earlier is simply an application of these general second-order conditions to the case of $n = 2$. These conditions can be written more compactly as $(-1)^r |\bar{H}_r| > 0$ for all $r = 2, 3, \ldots, n$ in the case of a **maximum** and $|\bar{H}_r| < 0$ for all $r = 2, 3, \ldots, n$ in the case of a **minimum.**

Similar results can be obtained for the case of m independent constraints (with $n > m$) by adding the appropriate number of borders to $\bar{H}$. If there are m constraints, the leading principal minors of the $m \times n$ bordered matrix $\bar{H}$ that determine the second-order conditions are the $n - m$ minors $|\bar{H}_{m+1}|, |\bar{H}_{m+2}|, \ldots, |\bar{H}_n|$. For a maximum, these should alternate in sign, starting with the sign of $(-1)^{m+1}$; for a minimum they should all have the sign $(-1)^m$. Although these relatively simple rules exist for the case of m constraints, most of the economic examples we consider will have only a single constraint.

These second-order conditions on the leading principal minors of the bordered Hessian are related to the local quasi-concavity and quasi-convexity of the objective function around the optimal point x^*. In fact, for the special case in which the constraint function is linear in variables $x_1, x_2, \ldots, x_n$ with $x_i \geq 0$ for all i, the second-order conditions for a constrained **maximum** at x^* imply the **quasi-concavity** of the objective function around x^*, and the second-order conditions for a constrained **minimum** at x^* imply the **quasi-convexity** of the objective function around x^*. While this relationship does not hold for more general constraint functions, it does hold in many important economic problems, including the standard consumer choice problem. We now turn to some specific economic examples, beginning with a consumer choice problem in which this relationship does hold.

8.2 A Specific Utility Function

Consider the standard two-good consumer choice problem where the consumer purchases two commodities x_1 and x_2 at competitive prices p_1 and p_2, respectively, with fixed money income M. The first utility function we examine is the one discussed briefly in Chapter 1, $U(x_1, x_2) = x_1x_2$. For this particular utility function, the consumer choice problem becomes

$$\text{Max}_x U(x_1, x_2) = x_1x_2$$

$$\text{Subject to: } M = p_1x_1 + p_2x_2.$$

(8.25)

We can solve the problem (8.25) directly to find the utility-maximizing consumption of the two goods in terms of the three parameters p_1, p_2, and M. In general these utility-maximizing consumption levels (demand functions) will be written as $x_1^* = x_1^*(p_1, p_2, M)$ and $x_2^* = x_2^*(p_1, p_2, M)$. Any comparative statics information we might desire, such as $\partial x_1^*/\partial p_1$, $\partial x_1^*/\partial p_2$, or $\partial x_1^*/\partial M$, can be obtained by direct differentiation of the demand functions.

The Lagrangian for the problem in (8.25) is

$$L(x_1, x_2, \lambda) = x_1x_2 + \lambda(M - p_1x_1 - p_2x_2).$$

(8.26)

From (8.26) we have the following first-order conditions for $x^* = (x_1^*, x_2^*)$ and λ^*:

$$L_1(x^*, \lambda^*) = x_2^* - \lambda^*p_1 = 0,$$

(8.27a)

$$L_2(x^*, \lambda^*) = x_1^* - \lambda^*p_2 = 0,$$

(8.27b)

$$L_\lambda(x^*, \lambda^*) = M - p_1x_2^* - p_2x_2^* = 0.$$

(8.27c)

Upon eliminating λ^* from (8.27a) and (8.27b) and then substituting into (8.27c), we have the two demand functions

$$x_1^* = \frac{M}{2p_1} \quad \text{and} \quad x_2^* = \frac{M}{2p_2}.$$

(8.28)

The second-order conditions for (8.25) restrict the sign of the following determinant:

$$|\bar{H}| = \begin{vmatrix} L_{11}(x^*) & L_{12}(x^*) & g_1(x^*) \\ L_{21}(x^*) & L_{22}(x^*) & g_2(x^*) \\ g_1(x^*) & g_2(x^*) & 0 \end{vmatrix} = \begin{vmatrix} 0 & 1 & -p_1 \\ 1 & 0 & -p_2 \\ -p_1 & -p_2 & 0 \end{vmatrix}.$$

(8.29)

Direct computation reveals that $|\bar{H}| = 2p_1p_2 > 0$, as required by the second-order conditions for a constrained maximum. Thus the conditions (8.27a) through (8.27c) are both sufficient and necessary for the solution to (8.25).

There are a number of important things to notice about the demand functions in (8.28). First, consider the own-price effects. Differentiation of the two demand functions with respect to their own prices demonstrates that both demand functions slope downward. That is, the goods are non-Giffen, since

$$\frac{\partial x_1^*}{\partial p_1} = \frac{-M}{2p_1^2} < 0 \quad \text{and} \quad \frac{\partial x_2^*}{\partial p_2} = \frac{-M}{2p_2^2} < 0.$$

Similarly, differentiation of these demand functions with respect to the price of the other goods yields zero cross-price effects, since

$$\frac{\partial x_1^*}{\partial p_2} = 0 \quad \text{and} \quad \frac{\partial x_2^*}{\partial p_1} = 0.$$

These zero cross-price effects tell us that the goods are neither gross substitutes nor gross complements. The demands for the goods are "unrelated" even though the quantity of either good consumed influences the marginal utility of the other. This demonstrates that the complement/substitute relation with respect to the utility function is independent of the complement/substitute relation with respect to the demand functions.

Probably the most interesting results for this utility function are obtained by differentiating the demand functions with respect to money income:

$$\frac{\partial x_1^*}{\partial M} = \frac{1}{2p_1} \quad \text{and} \quad \frac{\partial x_2^*}{\partial M} = \frac{1}{2p_2}. \tag{8.30}$$

The derivatives in (8.30) prove that both goods are "normal" (i.e., that consumption increases as income increases), but they tell about more than the normality of the goods. They also provide information about the shape of the Engel curves for the two goods. Since the change in consumption of either good caused by a change in money income is independent of income, both goods have linear Engel curves through the origin. This condition of linear Engel curves follows from the fact that the utility function $U(x_1, x_2) = x_1 x_2$ is **homothetic**; the indifference curves are radial blowups of each other (Theorem 2.3).

The homotheticity of the utility function also implies that both goods have **unitary income elasticities** of demand. Recall the definition of income elasticity given in Chapter 1:

$$\varepsilon_{iM} = \frac{M}{x_i^*} \frac{\partial x_i^*}{\partial M}.$$

Applying this definition to the demand function for either commodity (given in 8.28), we have by direct computation

$$\varepsilon_{iM} = \left(\frac{2p_i}{1}\right)\left(\frac{1}{2p_i}\right) = 1. \tag{8.31}$$

This unitary income elasticity implies that the own elasticity of demand is also unitary. While the fact of unitary own elasticity can be computed directly, as for income elasticity, it is useful to approach the question from the perspective of homogeneity.

The demand functions in (8.28), like all demand functions, are homogeneous of degree 0 in prices and money income. Thus for x_1,

$$x_1^*(\alpha p_1, \alpha p_2, \alpha M) = x_1^*(p_1, p_2, M) \quad \text{for all } \alpha > 0.$$

As noted earlier, this homogeneity can be interpreted as the economically reasonable assumption of no money illusion. As we argued in Chapter 2, this zero-degree homogeneity and Euler's theorem imply that

$$\frac{\partial x_1^*}{\partial p_1} p_1 + \frac{\partial x_1^*}{\partial p_2} p_2 + \frac{\partial x_1^*}{\partial M} M = 0,$$

or

$$\frac{\partial x_1^*}{\partial p_1} \frac{p_1}{x_1^*} + \frac{\partial x_1^*}{\partial p_2} \frac{p_2}{x_1^*} + \frac{\partial x_1^*}{\partial M} \frac{M}{x_1^*} = 0. \tag{8.32}$$

Condition (8.32) simply says that the sum of all demand elasticities must equal zero. For the utility function $U(x_1, x_2) = x_1 x_2$, we know that $\partial x_1^*/\partial p_2 = 0$, so the center term in (8.32) vanishes. We also know from (8.31) that the far right-hand term is equal to 1. Thus, equation (8.32) implies that $\varepsilon_{11} = -1$. This unitary own-price elasticity of demand is exactly what would be obtained by direct computation from the demand function $x_1^* = M/2p_1$.

The utility function $U(x_1, x_2) = x_1 x_2$ also provides interesting insights into the relationship between second-order conditions and the concavity of the objective function. Recall the definition of a concave function from Chapter 1. The function $U(x)$ is **concave** if for any x^0 and x^1 in the domain of U, the condition $U(\hat{x}) \geq \theta U(x^0) + (1 - \theta)U(x^1)$ holds for all $0 \leq \theta \leq 1$, where $\hat{x} = \theta x^0 + (1 - \theta)x^1$. Since the domain of $U(x)$ is simply $\mathfrak{R}_+^2$, we can show that $U(x_1, x_2) = x_1 x_2$ is not concave by finding any θ and two points x^0 and x^1 in $\mathfrak{R}_+^2$ such that $U(\hat{x}) - [\theta U(x^0) + (1 - \theta)U(x^1)] < 0$. Such values can indeed be found. For instance, $\theta = 1/2$ and $x^1 = 4x^0$ is quite easy to compute and will demonstrate the nonconcavity of $U(x) = x_1 x_2$. But even though this utility function is not concave, it is quasi-concave (in fact, it is strictly quasi-concave globally).

The quasi-concavity of this particular utility function can be seen from the second-order conditions to the maximization problem. As stated in the last paragraph of Section 8.1, for a nonnegative domain and for the case of a linear constraint (which the budget constraint clearly is), the satisfaction of the second-order conditions for a constrained maximum implies the local quasi-concavity of the objective function. For this problem the second-order conditions do hold, and so the utility function is **quasi-concave** in a neighborhood around x^*. In fact, since the bordered Hessian for the problem is

$$|\bar{H}| = \begin{vmatrix} 0 & 1 & -p_1 \\ 1 & 0 & -p_2 \\ -p_1 & -p_2 & 0 \end{vmatrix} = 2p_1 p_2,$$

the sign is positive everywhere in the domain of the objective function, and so $U(x_1, x_2) = x_1 x_2$ is globally quasi-concave.

This example has provided a number of interesting insights into the problem of consumer choice. Constrained maximization of this homothetic utility function generates demands that have linear Engel curves. These linear Engel curves imply unitary income elasticity as well as unitary own elasticity of demand. This utility function generates convex indifference curves that yield unique strictly positive demands for both goods for all prices, and yet $U(x)$ is not concave. In fact, $U(x_1, x_2) = x_1 x_2$ does not even exhibit the traditional property of diminishing marginal utility, since both U_{11} and U_{22} are identically zero for all $x \in \Re_+^2$. Because the budget constraint is linear, the second-order conditions imply that the utility function is quasi-concave even though it is not concave. This clearly demonstrates how much "weaker" the second-order conditions (quasi-concavity) are for the constrained maximization problem than for the unconstrained problem. These second-order conditions guarantee that the maximization is meaningful and the indifference curves have the appropriate shape, even in the absence of the traditional assumptions of concavity and diminishing marginal utility.

8.3 Choice between Labor and Leisure

We now turn to an example of a utility function that is not explicitly specified. In this case we will be able to get some information about the general characteristics of the consumer's choice, but less than in the preceding example, where the exact utility function was known. We look at the problem of **labor supply** (or correspondingly, the problem of leisure demand).

Since labor L gives disutility, it is much easier to model the problem of labor supply as a problem of leisure demand. Leisure l is a commodity that provides utility, as any other commodity, and thus finding the utility-maximizing consumption of leisure should be no more difficult than finding the utility-maximizing consumption of any other good. Once the utility-maximizing level of leisure consumption (leisure demand) has been chosen, the optimal amount of labor supplied L is also determined, since an hour working is necessarily an hour not consuming leisure. With this in mind, we can model the general labor supply problem in the following way:

$$\underset{\{C,l\}}{\text{Max}}\, U(C, l)$$

$$\text{Subject to: } w(\bar{T} - l) + \bar{N} = C. \tag{8.33}$$

In (8.33), C is the consumption level of some composite commodity, l is leisure, and w is the real wage (in terms of C). The objective (utility) function $U(C, l)$ assigns utility levels to bundles of C and l. We assume that U is at least twice differentiable and satisfies the second-order conditions for a constrained maximum. Parameters $\bar{T}$ and $\bar{N}$ specify the time constraint and real nonlabor income available, respectively.

The budget constraint in (8.33) is actually constructed from two separate constraints, the income and the time constraint. The (real) income constraint is

$$C = wL + \bar{N}. \tag{8.34}$$

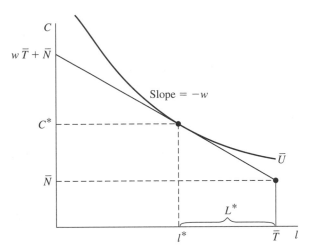

Figure 8.1

This income constraint simply states that real consumption must come from either real nonlabor income $\bar{N}$ or real wages wL. The time constraint is

$$\bar{T} = l + L. \tag{8.35}$$

The time constraint states that the total time available $\bar{T}$ must be split (mutually exclusively and exhaustively) between leisure and labor. Together, (8.34) and (8.35) imply the budget constraint in (8.33). In Figure 8.1 this budget constraint is drawn along with the optimal levels of consumption C^*, leisure l^*, and labor L^*.

The Lagrangian $\mathscr{L}$ for problem (8.33) is[3]

$$\mathscr{L}(C, l, \lambda) = U(C, l) + \lambda[w(\bar{T} - l) + \bar{N} - C]. \tag{8.36}$$

First-order conditions for a maximum at (C^*, l^*) are

$$\mathscr{L}_C(C^*, l^*, \lambda^*) = U_C(C^*, l^*) - \lambda^* = 0, \tag{8.37a}$$

$$\mathscr{L}_l(C^*, l^*, \lambda^*) = U_l(C^*, l^*) - w\lambda^* = 0, \tag{8.37b}$$

$$\mathscr{L}_\lambda(C^*, l^*, \lambda^*) = w(\bar{T} - l^*) + \bar{N} - C^* = 0. \tag{8.37c}$$

Elimination of λ^* from (8.37a) and (8.37b) and rearranging gives

$$w = \frac{U_l(C^*, l^*)}{U_C(C^*, l^*)}. \tag{8.38}$$

This condition states that at the optimal level of consumption C^* and leisure l^*, the slope of the budget constraint w should be equal to the marginal rate of substitution (*MRS*) between the two goods C and l. This result is depicted in Figure 8.1. The remaining first-order condition (8.37c) simply states that the optimal bundle is on the budget constraint. This is also shown in Figure 8.1.

We assume in the initial specification of the problem that the utility function satisfies the second-order conditions. This requires that

$$|\bar{H}| = \begin{vmatrix} U_{CC} & U_{Cl} & -1 \\ U_{lC} & U_{ll} & -w \\ -1 & -w & 0 \end{vmatrix} > 0 \qquad (8.39)$$

for $|\bar{H}|$ evaluated at (C^*, l^*). Condition (8.39) implies (through the implicit-function theorem) that the three equations representing the first-order conditions can be solved for the optimal values as functions of parameters w, $\bar{T}$, and $\bar{N}$. Thus from (8.37a) to (8.37c) we write

$$C^* = C^*(w, \bar{T}, \bar{N}),$$
$$l^* = l^*(w, \bar{T}, \bar{N}), \qquad (8.40)$$
$$\lambda^* = \lambda^*(w, \bar{T}, \bar{N}).$$

Since we are ultimately interested in labor supply, we are interested in how the optimal quantity of l^* responds to a change in the real wage w. By finding how leisure responds to a change in w, we will be able to get information about the responsiveness of labor supply, since

$$L^* = \bar{T} - l^* \qquad \text{implies} \qquad \frac{\partial L^*}{\partial w} = -\frac{\partial l^*}{\partial w}. \qquad (8.41)$$

We will follow a general methodology used repeatedly in this chapter; it is the same method we used to derive general comparative statics results for the unconstrained problems in Chapters 3 and 7. What we do is substitute the parameterized optimal solutions from (8.40) back into the first-order conditions (8.37a) to (8.37c) and then differentiate with respect to the parameter of interest (in this case w). This differentiation is valid because the substitution of the expressions from (8.40) into the first-order conditions converts these conditions into identities. This substitution amounts to the assertion that only consumers who **always** satisfy the first-order conditions will be considered.

Since we are interested primarily in w, for notational convenience we drop parameters $\bar{T}$ and $\bar{N}$ and write $C^* = C^*(w)$, $l^* = l^*(w)$, and $\lambda^* = \lambda^*(w)$. Of course, if we were interested in the impact of additional nonlabor income or available time on the consumer's optimal choices, we could drop w and differentiate with respect to $\bar{T}$ or $\bar{N}$. The methodology is the same regardless of which parameter interests us. Completing this substitution gives the following first-order identities as functions of w:

$$U_C(C^*(w), l^*(w)) - \lambda^*(w) \equiv 0, \qquad (8.42a)$$

$$U_l(C^*(w), l^*(w)) - w\lambda^*(w) \equiv 0, \qquad (8.42b)$$

$$w(\bar{T} - l^*(w)) + \bar{N} - C^*(w) \equiv 0. \qquad (8.42c)$$

Differentiation of these three identities with respect to the real wage gives

$$U_{CC}\frac{\partial C^*}{\partial w} + U_{Cl}\frac{\partial l^*}{\partial w} - \frac{\partial \lambda^*}{\partial w} \equiv 0,$$

$$U_{lC}\frac{\partial C^*}{\partial w} + U_{ll}\frac{\partial l^*}{\partial w} - \left(w\frac{\partial \lambda^*}{\partial w} + \lambda^*\right) \equiv 0, \qquad (8.43)$$

$$-\frac{\partial C^*}{\partial w} - w\frac{\partial l^*}{\partial w} + \bar{T} - l^* \equiv 0.$$

The second derivatives in (8.43) are evaluated at the optimal choice (C^*, l^*). Rearranging (8.43) into matrix form and remembering that $L^* = \bar{T} - l^*$, we have

$$\begin{bmatrix} U_{CC} & U_{Cl} & -1 \\ U_{lC} & U_{ll} & -w \\ -1 & -w & 0 \end{bmatrix} \begin{bmatrix} \dfrac{\partial C^*}{\partial w} \\ \dfrac{\partial l^*}{\partial w} \\ \dfrac{\partial \lambda^*}{\partial w} \end{bmatrix} \equiv \begin{bmatrix} 0 \\ \lambda^* \\ -L^* \end{bmatrix}. \qquad (8.44)$$

Since the matrix on the left-hand side is simply $\bar{H}$ defined in (8.39), we have $|\bar{H}| > 0$ from the second-order conditions. By applying Cramer's rule to (8.44), the responsiveness of leisure to a change in the real wage is given by

$$\frac{\partial l^*}{\partial w} = \frac{\begin{vmatrix} U_{CC} & 0 & -1 \\ U_{lC} & \lambda^* & -w \\ -1 & -L^* & 0 \end{vmatrix}}{|\bar{H}|} = \frac{-\lambda^* + (U_{lC} - U_{CC}w)L^*}{|\bar{H}|}.$$

Combining this expression for the leisure demand response with (8.41) gives the following for the labor supply response:

$$\frac{\partial L^*}{\partial w} = \frac{\lambda^* + (U_{CC}w - U_{lC})L^*}{|\bar{H}|}. \qquad (8.45)$$

As demonstrated in earlier chapters, often we can determine qualitative (sign only) comparative statics information just from the assumption that the second-order conditions hold. This does not seem to be the case for the labor supply problem currently under consideration. An examination of (8.45) reveals that it is not possible to determine the response of labor supply to a change in the real wage on the basis of second-order conditions alone. We know that $|\bar{H}| > 0$, so the denominator in (8.45) is positive, but the second-order conditions do not provide sufficient information to allow us to sign the numerator.

Actually this indeterminacy is expected. The labor supply function may slope either upward or downward with respect to the real wage. For instance, Figure 8.2 depicts an upward-sloping labor supply curve. The increase in the real wage rotates the budget constraint upward as shown. The optimal choice moves from a point such as A to a point such as C. As the indifference curves are drawn in

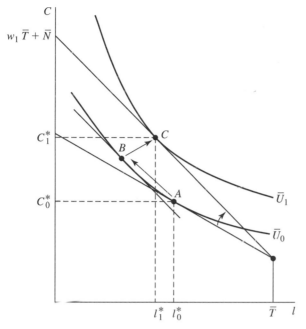

Figure 8.2

Figure 8.2, the optimal consumption of leisure at C is less than at A, and therefore the higher wage has caused more labor to be supplied. This result, though, is only one possibility. The picture could easily be drawn so that point C was to the right of point A, without violating the convexity of the indifference curves as required by the second-order conditions.

Even though it is not possible to sign $\partial L^*/\partial w$ with merely the second-order conditions, expression (8.45) does provide some valuable information about labor supply. First, notice that $\lambda^* > 0$. This condition does not follow strictly from the second-order conditions, but it does make economic sense, since $\lambda^* = U_C$ from (8.37a) and the marginal utility of consumption should be positive. With $\lambda^* > 0$, it is possible to sign the first term on the right-hand side of (8.45) as positive. So for an increase in the real wage, "one part" of the total effect always tends to increase the labor supplied. In this way we can interpret $\lambda^*/|\bar{H}|$ as the **substitution effect**, since the substitution effect always causes the consumption of leisure to decrease (and thus labor to increase) when the price of leisure increases (the wage increases). The expression on the far right-hand side of (8.45), which may be either negative or positive, must then be the **income effect** associated with a change in the real wage. The substitution effect is shown by the movement from point A to point B in Figure 8.2, while the income effect is shown by the movement from B to C. Substitution and income effects will be discussed in more detail in Section 8.5.

Second, expression (8.45) allows us to interpret the labor supply response for various more restrictive special cases. For example, when $U_{CC} < 0$ (again this is not required by the second-order conditions, but it is economically reasonable), the only way in which the income effect can reinforce the substitution effect is for U_{lC} to be negative and relatively large. This should make economic sense. Higher wages always increase C and decrease l through the substitution effect; this effect could be reinforced if additional C lowers the desirability of l (i.e., if $U_{lC} < 0$), thus making the optimal consumption of leisure fall still further.

8.4 Comparative Statics from Constrained Optimization: Two Approaches

The preceding discussion of labor supply (as well as all the other examples in this chapter) utilized only one approach to the general comparative statics problem. As we demonstrated in Chapter 3, though, an alternative technique is available for obtaining comparative statics information when the specific objective function is unknown. Since this alternative technique (the total differential approach) is used in many economic models, it is useful to be comfortable with both approaches. The equivalence of the two techniques is guaranteed mathematically by the uniqueness of the total differential, but we demonstrate it only informally by applying both approaches to a particular (very important) economic example. We shall compare the techniques by applying both to the simple two-good consumer choice problem. This example will demonstrate the desired equivalence and also set the stage for the more detailed discussion of n-good consumer choice in Section 8.5.

The standard two-good consumer choice problem is given by

$$\operatorname*{Max}_{x} U(x_1, x_2)$$

$$\text{Subject to: } M = p_1 x_1 + p_2 x_2. \tag{8.46}$$

where all variables have the now familiar definitions. The Lagrangian associated with (8.46) is

$$L(x_1, x_2, \lambda) = U(x_1, x_2) + \lambda(M - p_1 x_1 - p_2 x_2).$$

At the optimal $(x_1^*, x_2^*, \lambda^*)$, the first-order conditions are

$$L_1(x_1^*, x_2^*, \lambda^*) = U_1(x_1^*, x_2^*) - \lambda^* p_1 = 0,$$
$$L_2(x_1^*, x_2^*, \lambda^*) = U_2(x_1^*, x_2^*) - \lambda^* p_2 = 0, \tag{8.47}$$
$$L_\lambda(x_1^*, x_2^*, \lambda^*) = M - p_1 x_1^* - p_2 x_2^* = 0.$$

To demonstrate the equivalency of the two approaches, we find the change in optimal consumption of x_1 caused by a change in p_2 by both methods and compare the results. We first employ the approach used in the preceding examples, and then consider the alternative (total differential) approach.

In the first approach, the optimal values $x_1^*(p_1, p_2, M)$, $x_2^*(p_1, p_2, M)$, and $\lambda^*(p_1, p_2, M)$ are substituted back into the first-order conditions (8.47), and these identities are differentiated with respect to the parameter in question (in this case p_2). So we have

$$U_1(x_1^*(p_1, p_2, M), x_2^*(p_1, p_2, M)) - \lambda^*(p_1, p_2, M)p_1 = 0,$$
$$U_2(x_1^*(p_1, p_2, M), x_2^*(p_1, p_2, M)) - \lambda^*(p_1, p_2, M)p_2 \equiv 0,$$
$$M - p_1 x_1^*(p_1, p_2, M) - p_2 x_2^*(p_1, p_2, M) \equiv 0.$$

Differentiating with respect to p_2, gives us

$$U_{11}\frac{\partial x_1^*}{\partial p_2} + U_{12}\frac{\partial x_2^*}{\partial p_2} - p_1\frac{\partial \lambda^*}{\partial p_2} \equiv 0,$$
$$U_{21}\frac{\partial x_1^*}{\partial p_2} + U_{22}\frac{\partial x_2^*}{\partial p_2} - p_2\frac{\partial \lambda^*}{\partial p_2} \equiv \lambda^*, \tag{8.48}$$
$$-p_1\frac{\partial x_1^*}{\partial p_2} - p_2\frac{\partial x_2^*}{\partial p_2} \equiv x_2^*.$$

Writing the system (8.48) in matrix form gives us

$$\begin{bmatrix} U_{11} & U_{12} & -p_1 \\ U_{21} & U_{22} & -p_2 \\ -p_1 & -p_2 & 0 \end{bmatrix} \begin{bmatrix} \dfrac{\partial x_1^*}{\partial p_2} \\ \dfrac{\partial x_2^*}{\partial p_2} \\ \dfrac{\partial \lambda^*}{\partial p_2} \end{bmatrix} \equiv \begin{bmatrix} 0 \\ \lambda^* \\ x_2^* \end{bmatrix}. \tag{8.49}$$

Finally, solving (8.49) for the relevant comparative statics term by Cramer's rule, we have

$$\frac{\partial x_1^*}{\partial p_2} = \frac{\begin{vmatrix} 0 & U_{12} & -p_1 \\ \lambda^* & U_{22} & -p_2 \\ x_2^* & -p_2 & 0 \end{vmatrix}}{\begin{vmatrix} U_{11} & U_{12} & -p_1 \\ U_{21} & U_{22} & -p_2 \\ -p_1 & -p_2 & 0 \end{vmatrix}} = \frac{\lambda^* p_1 p_2 + x_2^*(p_1 U_{22} - p_2 U_{12})}{|H|}. \tag{8.50}$$

In the second approach, the first-order conditions are treated as three identities in six variables $(x_1, x_2, p_1, p_2, \lambda, M)$. By taking the total differential of these identities and assuming $dp_1 = dM = 0$, we can also obtain the desired expression.

Rewriting the first-order conditions as identities in six variables gives

$$L_1(x_1, x_2, p_1, p_2, \lambda, M) \equiv 0,$$
$$L_2(x_1, x_2, p_1, p_2, \lambda, M) \equiv 0, \tag{8.51}$$
$$L_\lambda(x_1, x_2, p_1, p_2, \lambda, M) \equiv 0.$$

Total differentiation of (8.51) produces

$$\frac{\partial L_1}{\partial x_1}dx_1 + \frac{\partial L_1}{\partial x_2}dx_2 + \frac{\partial L_1}{\partial p_1}dp_1 + \frac{\partial L_1}{\partial p_2}dp_2 + \frac{\partial L_1}{\partial \lambda}d\lambda + \frac{\partial L_1}{\partial M}dM \equiv 0,$$

$$\frac{\partial L_2}{\partial x_1}dx_1 + \frac{\partial L_2}{\partial x_2}dx_2 + \frac{\partial L_2}{\partial p_1}dp_1 + \frac{\partial L_2}{\partial p_2}dp_2 + \frac{\partial L_2}{\partial \lambda}d\lambda + \frac{\partial L_2}{\partial M}dM \equiv 0, \qquad (8.52)$$

$$\frac{\partial L_\lambda}{\partial x_1}dx_1 + \frac{\partial L_\lambda}{\partial x_2}dx_2 + \frac{\partial L_\lambda}{\partial p_1}dp_1 + \frac{\partial L_\lambda}{\partial p_2}dp_2 + \frac{\partial L_\lambda}{\partial \lambda}d\lambda + \frac{\partial L_\lambda}{\partial M}dM \equiv 0.$$

Given the definition of $L_1(\cdot)$, $L_2(\cdot)$, and $L_\lambda(\cdot)$, the expression in (8.52) reduces to

$$U_{11}\,dx_1 + U_{12}\,dx_2 - \lambda\,dp_1 - p_1\,d\lambda \equiv 0,$$
$$U_{21}\,dx_1 + U_{22}\,dx_2 - \lambda\,dp_2 - p_2\,d\lambda \equiv 0, \qquad (8.53)$$
$$dM - p_1\,dx_1 - x_1\,dp_1 - p_2\,dx_2 - x_2\,dp_2 \equiv 0.$$

Writing (8.53) in matrix form, we have

$$\begin{bmatrix} U_{11} & U_{12} & -p_1 \\ U_{21} & U_{22} & -p_2 \\ -p_1 & -p_2 & 0 \end{bmatrix} \begin{bmatrix} dx_1 \\ dx_2 \\ d\lambda \end{bmatrix} \equiv \begin{bmatrix} \lambda\,dp_1 \\ \lambda\,dp_2 \\ x_1\,dp_1 + x_2\,dp_2 - dM \end{bmatrix}. \qquad (8.54)$$

For our particular case of interest we let $dp_1 = dM = 0$ and solve (8.54) via Cramer's rule. This gives

$$dx_1 = \frac{\begin{vmatrix} 0 & U_{12} & -p_1 \\ \lambda\,dp_2 & U_{22} & -p_2 \\ x_2\,dp_2 & -p_2 & 0 \end{vmatrix}}{\begin{vmatrix} U_{11} & U_{12} & -p_1 \\ U_{21} & U_{22} & -p_2 \\ -p_1 & -p_2 & 0 \end{vmatrix}} = dp_2\frac{\begin{vmatrix} 0 & U_{12} & -p_1 \\ \lambda & U_{22} & -p_2 \\ x_2 & -p_2 & 0 \end{vmatrix}}{\begin{vmatrix} U_{11} & U_{12} & -p_1 \\ U_{21} & U_{22} & -p_2 \\ -p_1 & -p_2 & 0 \end{vmatrix}}. \qquad (8.55)$$

Notice that dx_1/dp_2 from (8.55) is identical to the solution $\partial x_1^*/\partial p_2$ from (8.50). Thus the two approaches yield exactly the same result. We simply state without proof that this equivalence is not dependent on the specific nature of the problem, nor on the fact that we restricted ourselves to two variables.

Given the equivalence, why choose one approach over the other? One answer is simply the consideration of relative convenience. If the system is of relatively low dimension, the second approach is often easier. This is because we can go from (8.54) to compute changes with respect to any of the other parameters (p_1 or M) without going back to the first-order conditions. For changes with respect to p_1 simply let $dp_2 = dM = 0$ in (8.54). For changes with respect to M, simply let $dp_1 = dp_2 = 0$ in (8.54), and so on. The problem with the second approach in higher dimensions is that since we must vary everything, the expression (8.52) can quickly become unwieldy.

The first approach is both more tractable in higher dimensions and more consistent with the underlying economic process. In most economic problems, everything is not variable. In the consumer choice case, for instance, consumers treat prices and income as constants when making consumption decisions; x_1 and x_2 are naturally choice variables, while p_1, p_2, and M are naturally parameters. Of course, parameters change, but finding the impact on the optimal choices as a result of a variation in the parameters is what the comparative statics method is all about. For this reason, only the first approach is used in the following presentation of consumer choice theory, although by now it is clear how one might proceed with the alternative method.

8.5 Consumer Choice: The *n*-Good Case

This discussion is not intended to be a complete examination of consumer choice theory. Since we are concerned with the interaction of mathematics and economic theory rather than economic theory per se, the focus is on consumer theory as an application (albeit an extremely important application) of the Lagrangian approach to constrained optimization. This said, consumer choice theory is so basic and so fundamental to all of modern economic theory that not every temptation to examine the theory itself has been avoided.

There is always the question of "where to start" the theory of consumer choice. The traditional starting point assumes the consumer has a real-valued utility function $U(x)$ that assigns a real number to each commodity bundle $x \in \Re_+^n$. The alternative is to assume that the consumer has an ordinal preference ordering over all the commodity bundles in $\Re_+^n$. With the preference approach, the primitive concept is preference—the binary relation "is preferred to"—rather than utility. For the preference approach, rationality means choosing the most preferred bundle from all the attainable choices; for the utility approach, rationality means choosing to maximize the utility received from the attainable bundles. Since we would like to employ the Lagrangian technique, and since well-ordered preferences can always be "represented" by an ordinal utility function, we will restrict our discussion to the traditional approach. We will assume that the consumer has a real-valued differentiable utility function defined over all commodity bundles; we will also restrict our discussion to the case in which all prices p_i and money income M are strictly positive.

The General Utility Maximization Problem: Consumer Demands

The general *n*-good consumer choice problem is

$$\operatorname*{Max}_{x} U(x)$$

$$\text{Subject to: } M = \sum_{i=1}^{n} p_i x_i. \tag{8.56}$$

In (8.56), $x = (x_1, x_2, \dots, x_n) \in \Re_+^n$ and $U \colon \Re_+^n \to \Re_+$. We assume that $U(x)$ is monotonic increasing, so $U_i(x) = \partial U(x)/\partial x_i > 0$ for all i and for all x. The general approach will be to assume that the utility function satisfies the second-order conditions for some $x^* \in \Re_+^n$ satisfying the first-order conditions, and then draw out a number of implications of this maximization assumption. Since the budget constraint is linear, the second-order conditions amount to the assumption that $U(x)$ is quasi-concave in a neighborhood of x^*. For certain problems we make the even stronger assumption that $U(x)$ is globally quasi-concave. The global quasi-concavity implies that all indifference curves [level sets of $U(x)$] have the standard convex shape, although the more restrictive assumption of strict quasi-concavity would need to be made to rule out linear segments in the indifference curves.

The Lagrangian for the general consumer choice problems (8.56) is given by

$$L(x, \lambda) = U(x) + \lambda \left(M - \sum_{i=1}^{n} p_i x_i \right). \tag{8.57}$$

The first-order conditions require

$$L_i(x^*, \lambda^*) = U_i(x^*) - \lambda^* p_i = 0 \qquad \text{for all } i = 1, 2, \ldots, n$$

and $\tag{8.58}$

$$L_\lambda(x^*, \lambda^*) = M - \sum_{i=1}^{n} p_i x_i^* = 0,$$

at the maximum (x^*, λ^*).

The second-order conditions are that the leading principal minors of the bordered Hessian of L [evaluated at (x^*, λ^*)] alternate in sign starting negative. Given the definition of L in (8.57) this sufficient condition requires

$$|\bar{H}_1| = \begin{vmatrix} 0 & -p_1 \\ -p_1 & U_{11} \end{vmatrix} < 0,$$

$$|\bar{H}_2| = \begin{vmatrix} 0 & -p_1 & -p_2 \\ -p_1 & U_{11} & U_{12} \\ -p_2 & U_{21} & U_{22} \end{vmatrix} > 0,$$

$$|\bar{H}_3| = \begin{vmatrix} 0 & -p_1 & -p_2 & -p_3 \\ -p_1 & U_{11} & U_{12} & U_{13} \\ -p_2 & U_{21} & U_{22} & U_{23} \\ -p_3 & U_{31} & U_{32} & U_{33} \end{vmatrix} < 0, \tag{8.59}$$

$$\vdots$$

$$(-1)^n |\bar{H}_n| = (-1)^n |\bar{H}| > 0,$$

where all U_{ij} are evaluated at x^*.

The first-order conditions (8.58) form a system of $n + 1$ equations ($L_1 = 0, \ldots, L_n = 0, L_\lambda = 0$) in the $n + 1$ variables (x^*, λ^*) and the $n + 1$ parameters $p = (p_1, p_2, \ldots, p_n)$ and M. From the implicit-function theorem, we know that it is possible to solve for the $n + 1$ variables in terms of the $n + 1$ parameters if the $(n + 1) \times (n + 1)$ Jacobian determinant formed by the derivatives of the L_i functions does not vanish at (x^*, λ^*). But this Jacobian is simply $|\bar{H}|$, and thus the second-order conditions guarantee that such explicit functions exist. Therefore we can write the solution to the general consumer choice problem as

$$x_i^* = x_i^*(p, M) \qquad \text{for all } i = 1, 2, \ldots, n$$

and   (8.60)

$$\lambda^* = \lambda^*(p, M).$$

The n functions x_i^* in (8.60) are the **consumer demand functions.** They depend on the prices of all goods and the consumer's money income. These demand functions are sometimes called **Marshallian** demands or **money-income-held-constant** demands. These names are used to distinguish these demands, obtained by maximizing utility subject to a linear budget constraint, from the "compensated" demands that will be discussed in the next section. Actually both these terms are to some extent misnomers. These demands are not really Marshallian because Alfred Marshall discussed the inverse of these functions; for Marshall, the demand price of the good p_i was a function of the quantity consumed x_i, so x_i rather than p_i was the independent variable. These functions are not really money-income-held-constant demands either, since income is no more held constant than prices are held constant: there are $n + 1$ parameters, and income is only one. These demands are really Walrasian demands, or simply **ordinary demand functions.** By "ordinary" we mean they are the demands one first encounters in economics; they are the demands in every supply and demand example from elementary economics.

By eliminating λ^* from the first-order conditions, we can write the first n of these conditions in the more familiar form

$$\frac{p_i}{p_j} = \frac{U_i(x^*)}{U_j(x^*)} \qquad \text{for all } i, j = 1, 2, \ldots, n, i \neq j. \qquad (8.61)$$

The conditions in (8.61) simply state that at the maximizing choices, the *MRS* between any two goods must be equal to the ratio of the prices. This condition should be familiar from the two-good case.

Writing the first-order conditions in the form of (8.61) makes it clear that demands are **homogeneous of degree zero** in prices and money income. If all prices and money income are increased (or decreased) by some scalar $\alpha > 0$, we can see from (8.61) that the first n of the necessary conditions remain unchanged. The remaining necessary condition is simply the budget constraint, which also remains unchanged by a scale change in all prices and money income. Thus we have

$$x_i^*(\alpha p, \alpha M) = x_i^*(p, M) \quad \text{for all } i = 1, 2, \ldots, n \qquad \text{and} \qquad \alpha > 0. \quad (8.62)$$

The way in which the problem was set up created an "extra" optimal value, the Lagrange multiplier λ^*. What can be said about this term? Does it have an economic interpretation? In Section 8.1 we demonstrated that λ^* always measures the change in the optimal value of the objective function with respect to a particular parameter. To see how this should be interpreted in the context of consumer choice, let us define the **indirect utility function** V. Since the indirect utility function is simply the value of utility at the utility maximizing choices, we have

$$V(p, M) = U(x^*(p, M)) = U(x_1^*(p, M), \ldots, x_n^*(p, M)). \qquad (8.63)$$

Differentiating V with respect to M gives us

$$\frac{\partial V}{\partial M} = \sum_{i=1}^{n} U_i(x^*) \frac{\partial x_i^*}{\partial M}. \qquad (8.64)$$

The expression in (8.64) does not have an obvious interpretation. It could be simplified by substituting from the first-order conditions (8.58), but rather than take this approach, let us directly apply the **envelope theorem** from (8.16). For this particular problem, $\partial f / \partial M = 0$ and $\partial g / \partial M = 1$, so the envelope theorem implies that

$$\frac{\partial V}{\partial M} = \lambda^*(p, M). \qquad (8.65)$$

Expression (8.65) says that the optimal value of the Lagrange multiplier measures the additional utility (assuming optimal choices are made) from an increase in the available money income. Thus the optimal value of the Lagrange multiplier is the **marginal utility of money income.**

The properties of the marginal utility of money income were long debated in economics. Certain early neoclassical economists (particularly Alfred Marshall) argued there were good economic reasons for assuming that marginal utility should be constant. Economic theorists have been unable to decide whether this constancy should mean that $\partial \lambda^* / \partial M = 0$ or that $\partial \lambda^* / \partial p_i = 0$ for all i, that is, constant with respect to what variable![4] It can be proved from the specific example given in Section 8.6 that only one of these interpretations is consistent with the structure of the utility functions assumed by early neoclassical economists such as Marshall (Problem 8.7). In general, we know that $\lambda^* > 0$ from the first-order conditions and the assumption of monotonicity (that $U_i > 0$ for all i), but little else. For instance, in the two-good homothetic preference example discussed in Section 8.2, we can compute $\lambda^* = M/2p_1 p_2$. Thus, for this specific utility function, we have the following comparative statics results for λ^*:

$$\frac{\partial \lambda^*}{\partial M} = \frac{1}{2p_1 p_2} > 0 \qquad \text{and} \qquad \frac{\partial \lambda^*}{\partial p_i} = \frac{-M}{p_i^2 p_j} < 0 \qquad (8.66)$$

$$\text{for all } i, j = 1, 2.$$

The most important properties of consumer demand functions are given by the comparative statics terms

$$\frac{\partial x_i^*}{\partial p_i}, \frac{\partial x_i^*}{\partial p_j} \qquad \text{for } i \neq j \qquad \text{and} \qquad \frac{\partial x_i^*}{\partial M}. \qquad (8.67)$$

It would be extremely useful to know whether the signs of these terms could be determined by assuming only the first- and second-order conditions for the consumer's maximization problem. The own-price effect $\partial x_i^*/\partial p_i$ measures the **slope of the demand function** with respect to its own price. We suspect that $\partial x_i^*/\partial p_i < 0$ for most goods, but it would be nice to demonstrate that such "downward-sloping" demand functions follow necessarily from the maximization hypothesis alone. The terms $\partial x_i^*/\partial p_j$ for $i \neq j$ determine whether the goods are **gross substitutes** (if > 0) or **gross complements** (if < 0). Again, it would be nice to know that maximizing utility necessarily guaranteed one case or the other. Finally, there is the term $\partial x_i^*/\partial M$. This measures the responsiveness of the quantity demanded to changes in money income. If $\partial x_i^*/\partial M > 0$, then x_i is a **normal good:** consumption increases with income. If $\partial x_i^*/\partial M < 0$, then x_i is an **inferior good:** consumption decreases with income. As with the other comparative terms, it would certainly be desirable to know whether maximization necessarily implies one of these cases. Unfortunately, we will discover that such general results are not available. Simply assuming that utility is maximized (that first- and second-order conditions are satisfied) is **not** sufficient to sign any of the $n + 1$ terms in (8.67).

One way to demonstrate this is to substitute the expressions in (8.60) into the first-order conditions (8.58) and then differentiate with respect to the parameter of interest. This method was used earlier in Section 8.4. Applying it to the simplest two-good case we have [from (8.49) and Cramer's rule] the following conditions for a change in the price of good 2:

$$\frac{\partial x_1^*}{\partial p_2} = \frac{\begin{vmatrix} 0 & U_{12} & -p_1 \\ \lambda^* & U_{22} & -p_2 \\ x_2^* & -p_2 & 0 \end{vmatrix}}{\begin{vmatrix} U_{11} & U_{12} & -p_1 \\ U_{21} & U_{22} & -p_2 \\ -p_1 & -p_2 & 0 \end{vmatrix}}$$

and (8.68)

$$\frac{\partial x_2^*}{\partial p_2} = \frac{\begin{vmatrix} U_{11} & 0 & -p_1 \\ U_{21} & \lambda^* & -p_2 \\ -p_1 & x_2^* & 0 \end{vmatrix}}{\begin{vmatrix} U_{11} & U_{12} & -p_1 \\ U_{21} & U_{22} & -p_2 \\ -p_1 & -p_2 & 0 \end{vmatrix}}.$$

From the second-order conditions, we know that the denominators of both expressions in (8.68) are positive.[5] But without adding more restrictions, we do not have any information about the sign of the numerator of either expression. The second-order condition tells us the sign of the bordered principal minors of the denominator and nothing more.

In our homothetic example (Section 8.2), we demonstrated that diminishing marginal utility ($U_{11} < 0$ and $U_{22} < 0$) is not implied by the second-order

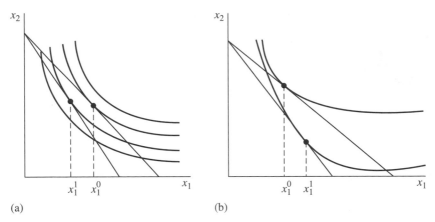

(a)   (b)

Figure 8.3

conditions for the constrained maximization problem. It is now interesting to note that even if we add the assumption of diminishing marginal utility, we are still unable to unequivocally sign either expression in (8.68). Neither the second-order conditions for a constrained maximum (quasi-concavity) nor the traditional assumption of diminishing marginal utility guarantees that demand curves slope downward or that the cross-price effects are of any particular sign. This is similar indeterminacy vis-à-vis the effect of a change in income on the demand for any good.

This indeterminacy should not be surprising. It is well known from elementary microeconomic theory that Giffen goods are possible even if consumers have convex indifference curves. Examples are shown in Figure 8.3. Figure 8.3a depicts the case of an increase in the price of good x_1 that causes the consumption of good x_1 to decrease (the demand curve slopes downward), while Figure 8.3b depicts the Giffen case of upward-sloping demand. In both cases the indifference curves are convex, and utility is being maximized.

This result (or perhaps absence of results) is not actually as disturbing as it first appears. Even though comparative statics information is not available from the first- and second-order conditions alone, we can deduce a number of interesting results from the basic consumer choice problem (even with n goods). The most important of these relationships is the so-called Slutsky relation discussed later. Before considering this relation though, it is useful to first look at the expenditure minimization problem.

The Expenditure Minimization Problem: Compensated Demands

An alternative way of formulating the consumer choice problem is to characterize it as an expenditure minimization problem. The desired level of utility (rather than income) is given as a parameter, and the consumer's problem is to minimize the expenditure necessary to achieve the given level of utility. For the n-commodity case, we can write the expenditure minimization problem as

$$\operatorname*{Min}_{x} \sum_{i=1}^{n} p_i x_i \tag{8.69}$$

$$\text{Subject to: } \bar{U} = U(x).$$

The Lagrangian for this expenditure minimization problem is

$$L(x, \delta) = \sum_{i=1}^{n} p_i x_i + \delta(\bar{U} - U(x)). \tag{8.70}$$

We use δ as the Lagrange multiplier for this problem to prevent confusion with λ from the utility maximization problem. We also write $x^u = (x_1^u, x_2^u, \ldots, x_n^u)$ as the optimal values for this minimization problem to distinguish them from the utility-maximizing values x^*. Our reason for choosing u as opposed to some other symbol will be apparent from the discussion. First-order conditions require the following conditions at the minimum (x^u, δ^u) that

$$L_i(x^u, \delta^u) = p_i - \delta^u U_i(x^u) = 0 \qquad \text{for all } i = 1, 2, \ldots, n$$

and

$$\tag{8.71}$$

$$L_\delta(x^u, \delta^u) = \bar{U} - U(x^u) = 0.$$

Second-order conditions for the constrained minimization are that all leading principal minors of the bordered Hessian of L [evaluated at (x^u, δ^u)] must be negative. Given the definition of L in (8.70), this requires that

$$|\bar{H}_1| = \begin{vmatrix} 0 & -U_1 \\ -U_1 & -\delta^u U_{11} \end{vmatrix} < 0,$$

$$|\bar{H}_2| = \begin{vmatrix} 0 & -U_1 & -U_2 \\ -U_1 & -\delta^u U_{11} & -\delta^u U_{12} \\ -U_2 & -\delta^u U_{21} & -\delta^u U_{22} \end{vmatrix} < 0, \tag{8.72}$$

$$\vdots$$

$$|\bar{H}_n| = |\bar{H}| < 0.$$

As in earlier examples, the first-order conditions form a system of $n + 1$ equations in the $n + 1$ variables (x^u, δ^u) and the $n + 1$ parameters $(p, \bar{U})$, and the second-order conditions guarantee (by the implicit-function theorem) that it is possible to solve for the $n + 1$ variables in terms of the parameters. Thus we can write the solution to the expenditure minimization problem as

$$x_i^u = x_i^u(p, \bar{U}) \qquad \text{for all } i = 1, 2, \ldots, n$$

and

$$\tag{8.73}$$

$$\delta^u = \delta^u(p, \bar{U}).$$

These x_i^u functions are the **compensated demand functions:** they show the amount of each good purchased when the utility level $\bar{U}$ is obtained at minimum expenditure (or cost). These demands are also called **Hicksian demands** or **utility-held-constant demands.** As with the regular demand from the preceding sections, these names are to some extent misnomers. The reasons for calling them **compensated** will be clear in the next section, when we compare these demands with their "regular" counterparts from the utility maximization problem. Our choice of the symbolism x^u is to indicate that utility is a parameter in the optimization problem that generates these demands.

The comparative statics terms for the expenditure minimization problem (particularly the price effects)

$$\frac{\partial x_i^u}{\partial p_i} \quad \text{and} \quad \frac{\partial x_i^u}{\partial p_j} \quad \text{for } i \neq j \tag{8.74}$$

are extremely important. The own effect $(\partial x_i^u / \partial p_i)$ determines the slope of the compensated demand curve. This demand curve for good 1 is depicted in the lower half of Figure 8.4. In the top half of Figure 8.4, when the consumer faces prices $(p_1^o, \bar{p}_2)$ and solves the expenditure minimization problem (8.69) for $n = 2$ and utility level $\bar{U}$, the optimal choice for good 1 is x_1^o. When the price of good 1 changes to p_1' (with $\bar{p}_2$ and $\bar{U}$ fixed), the expenditure-minimizing consumption of good 1 changes to x_1'. Changing the price of x_1 and solving the expenditure minimization problem for these different prices, with the price of the other good and the utility level held constant, produce the compensated demand curve $x_1^u(p_1; \bar{p}_2, \bar{U})$, which is given in the bottom diagram. From Figure 8.4 we see that changes in the compensated demand caused by changes in the price of the good actually measure the **substitution effect** of the price change. Thus, the compensated demand curve is really a demand curve composed exclusively of substitution effects.

The cross effects $\partial x_2^u / \partial p_1$, however, determine the relationship between a change in the price of one good and the corresponding change in the compensated demand for the other. If $\partial x_i^u / \partial p_j > 0$ for $i \neq j$, we say that the goods are **net substitutes;** if $\partial x_i^u / \partial p_j < 0$ for $i \neq j$, we say that the goods are **net complements.** These definitions should not be confused with the cross effects on the regular demand curves, where $\partial x_i^* / \partial p_j > 0$ implies that the goods are **gross substitutes** and $\partial x_i^* / \partial p_j < 0$ implies that the goods are **gross complements.**

As with regular demand curves, it would be nice to know that expenditure minimization (first- and second-order conditions) necessarily implies certain signs on these own- and cross-price effects. Do we know that an expenditure-minimizing consumer always generates downward-sloping compensated demand that exhibits the net substitute property as in Figure 8.4, or is such a situation just one possibility? Unlike for the case of regular demands, we can answer this question affirmatively, at least with respect to the slope of the compensated demand curve (own effects). The first- and second-order conditions for expenditure minimization are sufficient to guarantee that $\partial x_i^u / \partial p_i < 0$ for all i.

To prove this, plug the $n + 1$ solutions to the expenditure minimization problem given in (8.73) back into the first-order conditions given in (8.71) and differentiate these identities with respect to an arbitrary price (say p_1). This is the same

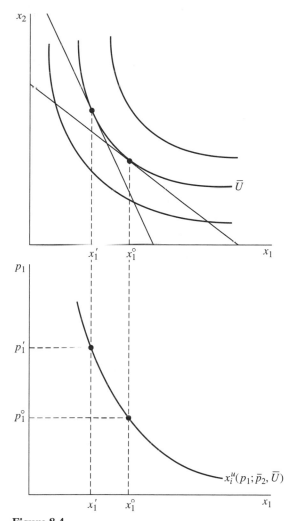

Figure 8.4

procedure we followed (unsuccessfully) in the utility maximization case. This differentiation yields (in matrix form):

$$
\begin{bmatrix}
-\delta^u U_{11} & \cdots & -\delta^u U_{1n} & -U_1 \\
\vdots & & \vdots & \vdots \\
-\delta^u U_{n1} & \cdots & -\delta^u U_{nn} & -U_n \\
-U_1 & \cdots & -U_n & 0
\end{bmatrix}
\begin{bmatrix}
\dfrac{\partial x_1^u}{\partial p_1} \\
\vdots \\
\dfrac{\partial x_n^u}{\partial p_1} \\
\dfrac{\partial \delta^u}{\partial p_1}
\end{bmatrix}
\equiv
\begin{bmatrix}
-1 \\
0 \\
\vdots \\
0
\end{bmatrix}.
\tag{8.75}
$$

Calling the matrix on the left-hand side D, we can solve for the own effect by using Cramer's rule,

$$\frac{\partial x_1^u}{\partial p_1} = \frac{\begin{vmatrix} -1 & -\delta^u U_{12} & \cdots & -\delta^u U_{1n} & -U_1 \\ 0 & -\delta^u U_{22} & \cdots & -\delta^u U_{2n} & -U_2 \\ \vdots & \vdots & & \vdots & \vdots \\ 0 & -\delta^u U_{n2} & \cdots & -\delta^u U_{nn} & -U_n \\ 0 & -U_1 & \cdots & -U_n & 0 \end{vmatrix}}{|D|}. \tag{8.76}$$

From the second-order conditions for the constrained minimization given in (8.72), we know that $|D| < 0$. Expanding the determinant in the numerator by the first column gives -1 times an $(n-1)$st-order bordered principal minor of D. Since this $(n-1)$st-order minor is also negative by the second-order conditions, the numerator is positive. The positive numerator with the negative denominator implies that $\partial x_1^u / \partial p_1 < 0$. Since p_1 was chosen arbitrarily, the result will be the same for any other good, and thus we have proven that $\partial x_i^u / \partial p_i < 0$ for all i. Compensated demand curves, unlike regular demand curves, do indeed slope downward. We can obtain comparative statics information from the expenditure minimization problem because **substitution effects are always negative.**

Regarding the net substitute or net complement relation, the comparative static results are less definite. For $n = 2$, both goods are net substitutes, as depicted in Figure 8.4. Readers may prove this to themselves by following the approach used earlier to determine the own effects. Even without going through the proof, Figure 8.4 and the fact that the own effect is always negative clearly indicate that the goods must be net substitutes for the $n = 2$ case. If an increase in p_1 causes x_1^u to decrease, and indifference curves are convex, then x_2^u must increase. Regrettably, this net substitute condition is not guaranteed for $n > 2$.

While the downward slope of the compensated demand curve is an important result, even more important is the relationship between the change in the compensated demand and the change in the regular demand. This relation is called the Slutsky relation, and we now turn to its derivation.

The Slutsky Relation

We now consider the relationship between the utility maximization problem that generates regular demands and the expenditure minimization problem that generates compensated demands. For convenience, both problems are reproduced for the $n = 2$ case. We have labeled the utility maximization problem (P) for the **primary** (or primal) problem, and the expenditure minimization problem (D) for the **dual** problem.

$$\underset{x}{\text{Max}} \; U(x_1, x_2)$$

$$\text{Subject to: } \bar{M} = p_1 x_1 + p_2 x_2 \tag{P}$$

$$\operatorname*{Min}_{x} p_1 x_1 + p_2 x_2 \tag{D}$$

$$\text{Subject to: } \bar{U} = U(x_1, x_2)$$

The solutions to (P) are, of course, the **regular demands** $x_1^*(p, \bar{M})$ and $x_2^*(p, \bar{M})$, while the solutions to (D) are the **compensated demands** $x_1^u(p, \bar{U})$ and $x_2^u(p, \bar{U})$.

We defined the **indirect utility function** $V(p, \bar{M})$ as the optimal value of the objective function for the utility maximization problem. Thus, for (P) we have

$$V(p, \bar{M}) = U(x_1^*(p, \bar{M}), x_2^*(p, \bar{M})).$$

We now define the **expenditure function** $E^u(p, \bar{U})$ as the optimal value of the objective function in the (dual) expenditure minimization problem. Thus for (D) we have

$$E^u(p, \bar{U}) = p_1 x_1^u(p, \bar{U}) + p_2 x_2^u(p, \bar{U}). \tag{8.77}$$

Because of the structure of these two problems, the following relations hold between the two solutions for any commodity i:

$$\begin{aligned} x_i^*(p, E^u(p, \bar{U})) &\equiv x_i^u(p, \bar{U}), \\ x_i^u(p, V(p, \bar{M})) &\equiv x_i^*(p, \bar{M}). \end{aligned} \tag{8.78}$$

In other words, if the optimal value of (D) is the constraint in (P), or if the optimal value of (P) is the constraint in (D), then the two solutions are identical.

Even though these two problems have the same solution, they do not necessarily have the same comparative statics results. The conditions in (8.78) do not necessarily imply that $\partial x_i^*/\partial p_i = \partial x_i^u/\partial p_i$, or that $\partial x_i^*/\partial p_j = \partial x_i^u/\partial p_j$ for $i \neq j$. It is easy to see that the two problems do not have the same comparative statics by examining Figures 8.3 and 8.4. In both figures p_1 has increased, but the consumption of x_1 is different in the two cases. In the utility maximization problem (Figure 8.3), the money income remains the same and the maximum level of utility changes. In the expenditure minimization problem (Figure 8.4), the level of utility remains the same and the minimum expenditure changes. The latter case considers only the substitution effect of a change in the price of the good, while the former considers both the substitution effect and the income effect associated with the higher price. This income effect exists because the real income available is decreased by the increase in the price of one of the goods. Solutions to (D) are called **compensated** because they represent the case of the consumer who is compensated for this loss in real income.

To determine the exact comparative statics relationship between these two problems, first we establish an important property of the cross effects for the expenditure minimization problem. For the rest of the discussion we focus on the general *n*-variable case. Consider the expenditure function

$$E^u(p, \bar{U}) = \sum_{i=1}^{n} p_i x_i^u(p, \bar{U}). \tag{8.79}$$

Substituting from the first-order conditions of the expenditure minimization problem (8.71), we have

$$\frac{\partial E^u(p, \bar{U})}{\partial p_j} = \delta^u \sum_{i=1}^{n} U_i \frac{\partial x_i^u(p, \bar{U})}{\partial p_j} + x_j^u(p, \bar{U}). \tag{8.80}$$

Also from the same first-order conditions (8.71),

$$\bar{U} = U(x^u(p, \bar{U})) \qquad \text{which implies } 0 = \sum_{i=1}^{n} U_i \frac{\partial x_i^u}{\partial p_j}. \tag{8.81}$$

Substitution of (8.81) into (8.80) yields

$$\frac{\partial E^u}{\partial p_j} = x_j^u(p, \bar{U}). \tag{8.82}$$

This result could also have been obtained as a direct application of the envelope theorem (8.16).

Thus we have shown that the change in the expenditure function caused by a change in the price of any good is exactly equal to the compensated demand for that good. Since second derivatives are independent of the order of differentiation, (8.82) implies that

$$\frac{\partial x_i^u}{\partial p_j} = \frac{\partial x_j^u}{\partial p_i} \qquad \text{for all } i \text{ and } j. \tag{8.83}$$

The cross effects of compensated demand functions are thus **symmetric.** The change in compensated demand for good i caused by a change in the price of good j is identical to the change in the compensated demand for good j caused by a change in the price of good i. While this symmetry does not generally hold for regular demand functions, it is a very important result in the theory of consumer choice.

Now we are (finally) ready to address the general question of the comparative statics relationships between the two problems. Recall the first expression from (8.78):

$$x_i^*(p, E^u(p, \bar{U})) \equiv x_i^u(p, \bar{U}).$$

Differentiation of both sides of this identity with respect to an arbitrary price p_j produces

$$\frac{\partial x_i^*}{\partial p_j} + \frac{\partial x_i^*}{\partial E^u} \left(\frac{\partial E^u}{\partial p_j} \right) = \frac{\partial x_i^u}{\partial p_j}. \tag{8.84}$$

Recalling the results in (8.82) and by substitution of M for E^u, we have

$$\frac{\partial x_i^*}{\partial p_j} + x_j^u \frac{\partial x_i^*}{\partial M} = \frac{\partial x_i^u}{\partial p_j}. \tag{8.85}$$

But $x_i^* = x_i^u$, so (8.85) reduces to the following expression relating the **cross effects** of the two problems:

$$\frac{\partial x_i^*}{\partial p_j} = \frac{\partial x_i^u}{\partial p_j} - x_j^* \frac{\partial x_i^*}{\partial M}. \tag{8.86}$$

Similarly for the **own effects:**

$$\frac{\partial x_i^*}{\partial p_i} = \frac{\partial x_i^u}{\partial p_i} - x_i^* \frac{\partial x_i^*}{\partial M}. \tag{8.87}$$

Expressions (8.86) and (8.87) are the **Slutsky equations,**[6] and they are generally considered to be the single most important result in demand theory. These expressions break the total demand effect of a price change into two parts: the **substitution effect** (the first term on the right-hand side), which measures the change in compensated demand, and the **income effect** (the second term on the right-hand side), which measures the change in consumption of the good caused by the change in available real income.

The Slutsky equation (8.87) allows us to demonstrate that the results regarding substitution and income effects obtained from two-dimensional diagrams in elementary microeconomic theory also hold in the general *n*-commodity case. In elementary theory, it is argued that a good is **Giffen** (i.e., it has an upward-sloping demand curve) only if it is inferior and the income effect outweighs the substitution effect. The Slutsky expression (8.87) demonstrates that this result also holds when the consumer is choosing *n* commodities. Since the own-substitution effect is always negative (already proved), the only way in which the regular demand curve could slope upward is for the income effect to be positive and larger than the substitution effect. Since the income effect is given by $-x_i^*(\partial x_i^*/\partial M)$, it could be positive only if the good is inferior ($\partial x_i^*/\partial M < 0$). This result, which is easily demonstrated diagrammatically for the two-dimensional case, can thus be shown to hold for the general *n*-commodity problem by use of the Slutsky equation.

The results for the cross effect are less definitive, but some information is available from the cross-Slutsky expression (8.86), as well. For instance, suppose the utility function is homothetic; as in the example presented in Section 8.2. The homotheticity of the utility function implies that each demand curve is unit elastic, so

$$\frac{\partial x_i^*}{\partial M}\frac{M}{x_i^*} = 1 \qquad \text{or} \qquad \frac{\partial x_i^*}{\partial M} = \frac{x_i^*}{M} \qquad \text{for all } i. \tag{8.88}$$

From the Slutsky expression for cross effects (8.86), for any two goods x_i and x_j we have

$$\frac{\partial x_i^*}{\partial p_j} = \frac{\partial x_i^u}{\partial p_j} - x_j^* \frac{\partial x_i^*}{\partial M} \qquad \text{and} \qquad \frac{\partial x_j^*}{\partial p_i} = \frac{\partial x_j^u}{\partial p_i} - x_i^* \frac{\partial x_j^*}{\partial M}. \tag{8.89}$$

BOX 8.2

The Household Production Approach to Consumption

The text presents the traditional approach to consumer choice theory: an individual chooses goods to maximize utility subject to a fixed budget constraint. While this traditional approach is standard in the economics literature, there is another approach to questions of consumer choice. The alternative is the household production approach developed by Becker (1965), Lancaster (1966), and Michael and Becker (1973); this alternative approach has been applied to a number of different economic and social questions, including issues of family formation (marriage and divorce), travel time, educational attainment, health care, illegal activities, and the sexual division of labor.

According to the household production approach, the household receives utility from commodities, but these commodities are not simply goods purchased in the market. The commodities consumed by the household are "purchased" in the household by using purchased goods as well as the time of the members of the household. For example, the household receives utility from "the evening meal," but this commodity is actually produced in the household by combining various products purchased in the market with the preparation and cleanup time of various family members. Advantages attributed to the household production approach include the emphasis on the household as the decision-making unit, explicit consideration of the role of time in consumption decisions, and the ability of the theory to explain changes in consumption behavior on the basis of changes in the household production relations and their implicit prices, rather than relying on a change in "tastes." We will present the basic argument of this alternative approach to consumption decisions and suggest some of the many results that have been obtained by applying it to the economics of the family. Our discussion follows Becker (1981, 1993); a more general approach to household production theory is given by Gronau (1986).

Let the commodities consumed by the household be given by Z_1, $Z_2, \ldots, Z_m$. These commodities are the arguments of the household utility function

$$U = U(Z_1, Z_2, \ldots, Z_m). \tag{a}$$

This utility function is assumed to have all the standard properties of utility functions in the traditional theory. Each commodity Z_i is produced by using a vector of market goods x_i, a vector of quantities of time t_i, and a vector of other variables (education, talent, human capital, etc.) given by E_i. Simplifying a bit and treating x_i, t_i, and E_i as scalars, we have the following production function for each commodity Z_i:

$$Z_i = f_i(x_i, t_i, E_i).$$

The household budget constraint is given by

$$\sum_{i=1}^{m} p_i x_i = w t_w + V,$$

where the p_i are the prices of the market goods, w is the wage, t_w is the time spent working in the labor market, and V is nonlabor income. The total time available T is divided between working in the labor market and engaging in household production. Thus,

$$T = \sum_{i=1}^{m} t_i + t_w.$$

Combining these two budget constraints (income and time) and rearranging, we have

$$\sum_{i=1}^{m} (p_i x_i + w t_i) = w T + V. \tag{b}$$

The right-hand side of the expression in (b) is usually called **full income,** since it represents the income that would be available if all time were devoted to market labor.

Now commodities do not have market prices, since they are not actually purchased, but they do have shadow prices (implicit valuations). The shadow price of commodity Z_i is given by π_i, where

$$\pi_i Z_i = p_i x_i + w t_i.$$

Thus π_i depends on the price of market goods p_i and the price (opportunity cost) of time w as well as the production relationship among x_i, t_i, and Z_i. As the shadow prices are defined, they depend on the average cost of goods and time used in the production of Z_i.

The Lagrangian for the problem of maximizing the household utility function (a) subject to the budget constraint (b) is given by

$$L = U(Z_1, Z_2, \ldots, Z_m) + \lambda \left[\sum_{i=1}^{m} (p_i x_i + w t_i) - w T - V \right].$$

At this level of generality, the solution does not lend itself to a particularly easy interpretation, but with the addition of a little more mathematical structure (such as equal average and marginal costs: $\partial t_i / \partial Z_i = t_i / Z_i$ and $\partial x_i / \partial Z_i = x_i / Z_i$), the first-order conditions can be written as

$$\frac{\partial U / \partial Z_i}{\partial U / \partial Z_j} = \frac{MU_i}{MU_j} = \frac{\pi_i}{\pi_j} \qquad \text{for all } i \text{ and } j.$$

The first-order conditions give us the optimal consumption of the goods just as they would in the traditional model. The difference is that now these demands depend on not only the prices of the goods but also the wage rate (value of time) and the efficiency of household production (the production function for each commodity and the other variables in E). A change in education, for example (one of the things influencing E), will change the household's demand for certain goods because (unlike in the traditional theory) it changes the efficiency of household production; a family with more education may be better able to convert goods to commodities. It is similar for a change in the wage rate; an increase in the wage rate will increase the (shadow) price of all commodities, but it will increase the price of those that are relatively time intensive more than the price of those requiring less time to produce. An increase in the market wage will thus discourage the consumption of some goods and encourage the consumption of others. Economists applying the household production approach have used such results to suggest explanations for many of the changes that have taken place in family life during the last few hundred years.

Sources

Becker, G. S. 1965. A theory of the allocation of time. *The Economic Journal* 75: 493–517.

———. 1981. *A treatise on the family.* Cambridge, MA: Harvard University Press.

———. 1993. *A treatise on the family.* 2d ed. Cambridge, MA.

Gronau, R. 1986. Home production—A survey. In *Handbook of labor economics,* Vol. 2, edited by O. Ashenfelter and R. Layard. Amsterdam: North-Holland, 273–304.

Lancaster, K. 1966. A new approach to consumer theory. *Journal of Political Economy* 74: 132–57.

Michael, R. T., and G. S. Becker. 1973. On the new theory of consumer behavior. *Swedish Journal of Economics* 75: 378–96.

Substituting (8.88) into (8.89) we have that for the homothetic case

$$\frac{\partial x_i^*}{\partial p_j} = \frac{\partial x_i^u}{\partial p_j} - \frac{x_j^* x_i^*}{M} \quad \text{and} \quad \frac{\partial x_j^*}{\partial p_i} = \frac{\partial x_j^u}{\partial p_i} - \frac{x_i^* x_j^*}{M}. \tag{8.90}$$

Since we know that the cross-substitution effects are always symmetric (8.83), the equations in (8.90) imply that for the **special case of homothetic preferences**

$$\frac{\partial x_i^*}{\partial p_j} = \frac{\partial x_j^*}{\partial p_i} \quad \text{for all } i \text{ and } j. \tag{8.91}$$

This demonstrates that cross-price effects on regular demands generated from homothetic preferences are symmetric. Of course, this homothetic case is just one example of the way in which comparative statics information can be obtained from the Slutsky equation for cross-price effects.

   With the derivation of the Slutsky expressions, we have completed our discussion of the principal results of consumer demand theory. Throughout this discussion we have utilized the mathematical results of the Lagrangian multiplier technique developed at the beginning of the chapter. We close with a specific example that provides a more concrete presentation of the ideas we have developed.

8.6 Additively Separable Utility Functions

As the final topic in this chapter, we consider a particular form of the utility function: the **additively separable utility function.** "Additive separability" means that the utility received from a particular good x_i is independent of the utility received from the consumption of any of the other goods. We already encountered such a utility function when we examined expected utility in Chapter 4. Mathematically, the additively separable utility function is written as

$$U(x) = \sum_{i=1}^{n} U^i(x_i). \tag{8.92}$$

Notice that additive separability implies that $U_{ij} = 0$ for all $i \neq j$.

There are at least two reasons for analyzing the additively separable case. One concerns its historical interest. This is the form of the utility function assumed (at least implicitly) by the founders of modern economics. Second, the assumption of separability is often made in econometric work. In econometric analysis of consumption, it is often assumed that the commodities can be divided into various groups for household decision making (housing, recreation, transportation, etc.)—this "separation" is a weak form of the additive separability examined here.

For the additively separable case, the general n-good consumer choice problem is given by

$$\underset{x}{\text{Max}} \sum_{i=1}^{n} U^i(x_i)$$
$$\text{Subject to: } M = \sum_{i=1}^{n} p_i x_i \tag{8.93}$$

The Lagrangian for the problem is

$$L(x, \lambda) = \sum_{i=1}^{n} U^i(x_i) + \lambda \left(M - \sum_{i=1}^{n} p_i x_i \right).$$

The first-order conditions for an optimum at (x^*, λ^*) are

$$U_i(x_i^*) - \lambda^* p_i = 0 \qquad \text{for all } i \tag{8.94a}$$

and

$$M - \sum_{i=1}^{n} p_i x_i^* = 0. \tag{8.94b}$$

The term $U_i(x_i^*)$ it the marginal utility of good i, and it is a function of the consumption of x_i alone. For notational convenience, the superscript i of (8.93) has been dropped from (8.94a). Regarding second-order conditions, it is sufficient to make the traditional assumption of diminishing marginal utility, that is, $U_{ii} < 0$ for all i.

Let us now turn to the comparative statics results for this problem. In particular, let us examine the own-price effects $\partial x_i^*/\partial p_i$. We know from the discussion in Section 8.5 that the sign of the own-price effect is indeterminate for the general consumer choice problem in which no assumptions are made other than the first- and second-order conditions. Does the additional assumption of additive separability change this? Do demand curves generated from additively separable utility functions slope downward?

Before we try to find the sign of $\partial x_i^*/\partial p_i$ for the additively separable case directly, it is useful to recall the Slutsky relation. From the Slutsky relation (8.87), we know that the demand curve will slope downward with respect to its own price as long as the good is normal, that is, $\partial x_i^*/\partial M > 0$. Since this term is usually simpler than the complete effect $\partial x_i^*/\partial p_i$, it seems to be a good place to start our investigation of the slope of the demand curve.

We determine the sign of $\partial x_i^*/\partial M$ in two separate ways. First, we take the "long" way, using Cramer's rule. This method was used to obtain comparative statics results in Sections 8.4 and 8.5. Second, we use a simple method to obtain the same results. The second method avoids the use of Cramer's rule by taking advantage of the absence of cross effects in the utility function.

For both approaches we start by substituting the optimal values $x_i^*(p, M)$ into the first-order conditions (8.94a) and (8.94b) and differentiating these identities with respect to M. This yields

$$U_{ii}\frac{\partial x_i^*}{\partial M} - p_i\frac{\partial \lambda^*}{\partial M} \equiv 0 \qquad \text{for all } i \tag{8.95a}$$

and

$$1 - \sum_{j=1}^{n} p_j\frac{\partial x_j^*}{\partial M} \equiv 0. \tag{8.95b}$$

Writing the $n + 1$ equations from (8.95) in matrix form, we have

$$
\begin{bmatrix}
U_{11} & 0 & \cdots & 0 & -p_1 \\
0 & U_{22} & \cdots & 0 & -p_2 \\
\vdots & \vdots & & \vdots & \vdots \\
0 & 0 & \cdots & U_{nn} & -p_n \\
-p_1 & -p_2 & \cdots & -p_n & 0
\end{bmatrix}
\begin{bmatrix}
\dfrac{\partial x_1^*}{\partial M} \\[2mm]
\dfrac{\partial x_2^*}{\partial M} \\[2mm]
\vdots \\[2mm]
\dfrac{\partial x_n^*}{\partial M} \\[2mm]
\dfrac{\partial \lambda^*}{\partial M}
\end{bmatrix}
\equiv
\begin{bmatrix}
0 \\
0 \\
\vdots \\
0 \\
-1
\end{bmatrix}. \tag{8.96}
$$

Calling the matrix on the left-hand side H, we can solve for the impact of a change in money income on any good (say x_1^*) by using Cramer's rule:

$$\frac{\partial x_1^*}{\partial M} = \frac{\begin{vmatrix} 0 & 0 & \cdots & 0 & -p_1 \\ 0 & U_{22} & \cdots & 0 & -p_2 \\ \vdots & \vdots & & \vdots & \vdots \\ 0 & 0 & \cdots & U_{nn} & -p_n \\ -1 & -p_2 & \cdots & -p_n & 0 \end{vmatrix}}{|H|}. \tag{8.97}$$

From the second-order conditions for a maximum, we know that $(-1)^n|H| > 0$, and so the sign of the denominator is $(-1)^n$. By expanding the determinant in the numerator by the first column, we change the numerator to

$$(-1)^{n+1} \begin{vmatrix} 0 & \cdots & 0 & -p_1 \\ U_{22} & \cdots & 0 & -p_2 \\ \vdots & \cdots & \vdots & \vdots \\ 0 & \cdots & U_{nn} & -p_n \end{vmatrix}. \tag{8.98}$$

Expanding this new determinant by the first row reduces the numerator to

$$(-1)^{n+1}(-1)^n p_1 \begin{vmatrix} U_{11} & \cdots & 0 \\ \vdots & & \vdots \\ 0 & \cdots & U_{nn} \end{vmatrix} = (-1)^{2n+1} p_1 \prod_{i=2}^{n} U_{ii}. \tag{8.99}$$

Since the sign of $\prod_{i=2}^{n} U_{ii}$ is $(-1)^{n-1}$ when $U_{ii} < 0$ for all i, the sign of the numerator is $(-1)^{3n}$. Given that the sign of the denominator is $(-1)^n$, the sign of the entire expression is $(-1)^{2n}$, and so $\partial x_i^*/\partial M > 0$. Thus we can see from this rather laborious manipulation that for the case of additively separable utility functions exhibiting diminishing marginal utility, there are no Giffen goods: that is, $\partial x_i^*/\partial p_i < 0$ for all i.

For the second approach to this question, notice from (8.95a) that we can write each term $\partial x_i^*/\partial M$ as a function of $\partial \lambda^*/\partial M$. Thus if we can find an exact expression for $\partial \lambda^*/\partial M$, we will be able to determine $\partial x_i^*/\partial M$. Substituting each of the $\partial x_i^*/\partial M$ terms from (8.95a) into (8.95b), we obtain

$$\frac{\partial \lambda^*}{\partial M} = \frac{1}{\sum_{j=1}^{n} p_j^2 / U_{jj}}. \tag{8.100}$$

Substituting this expression for $\partial \lambda^*/\partial M$ back into (8.95a), we have the desired expression:

$$\frac{\partial x_i^*}{\partial M} = \frac{p_i}{U_{ii} \sum_{j=1}^{n} p_j^2 / U_{jj}}. \tag{8.101}$$

From (8.101) clearly the second approach is simpler, and it seems to be more informative: it provides an exact expression for $\partial x_i^*/\partial M$ and determines its sign. Actually an identical expression could have been obtained by multiplying the determinants from the first approach (8.97), but this second approach provides a much simpler and more direct path to the desired expression. Similar expressions can be obtained for the other comparative statics terms, but these are left to the reader as exercises.

PROBLEMS

8.1 The elasticity of substitution between any two goods i and j is given by

$$\varepsilon_j = \frac{-x_j^*}{MRS_{ij}} \frac{\partial(MRS_{ij})}{\partial x_j^*},$$

where x_j^* is the regular (money-income-held-constant) demand for good j and $MRS_{ij} = (\partial U/\partial x_j)/(\partial U/\partial x_i) = U_j/U_i$. Prove that if the utility function is additively separable, the following proposition holds for all i and j:

$$\frac{\partial x_i^*}{\partial p_j} = -(\varepsilon_j - 1)\frac{\partial x_i^u}{\partial p_j},$$

where x_i^u is the compensated (utility-held-constant) demand for good i.

8.2 Prove that if the utility function is additively separable and $U_{ii} < 0$ for all i, then the following conditions hold for the elasticity of substitution ε_j defined in Problem 8.1.
(a) All goods are gross substitutes if $0 < \varepsilon_j < 1$ for all j.
(b) All goods are gross complements if $\varepsilon_j > 1$ for all j.

8.3 Prove that the following condition holds on the optimal value of the Lagrange multiplier $\lambda^* = \lambda^*(p, M)$ for the standard n-good consumer choice problem:

$$-\lambda^* = \sum_{i=1}^{n} p_i \frac{\partial\lambda^*}{\partial p_i} + M\frac{\partial\lambda^*}{\partial M}.$$

8.4 Answer the following questions for the two-good consumer choice problem where the utility function is given by

$$U(x_1, x_2) = a_1 \ln x_1 + a_2 \ln x_2.$$

(a) Set up the Lagrangian and solve the first-order conditions to find the regular demand functions x_1^* and x_2^* for the case of $a_1 + a_2 = 1$.
(b) Compare your answers for this utility function with those obtained for $U(x_1, x_2) = x_1 x_2$ in Section 8.2. Explain the relationship.

8.5 Answer the following questions regarding the three-good consumer choice problem with the utility function

$$U(x_1, x_2, x_3) = a_1 \ln x_1 + a_2 \ln x_2 + a_3 \ln x_3$$

$$\text{and} \quad a_1 + a_2 + a_3 = 1.$$

(a) Set up the Lagrangian and solve the first-order conditions for the regular demand functions.

(b) Does this utility function satisfy the second-order conditions for a constrained maximum? (Show why or why not.)

(c) Find all the comparative statics terms $\partial x_i^*/\partial p_i$, $\partial x_i^*/\partial p_j$ for $i \neq j$, and $\partial x_i^*/\partial M$ for $i = 1, 2, 3$.

(d) Find the comparative statics terms for λ^*: $\partial\lambda^*/\partial p_i$ for $i = 1, 2, 3$ and $\partial\lambda^*/\partial M$. Interpret these expressions.

8.6 Prove that for the standard two-good consumer choice problem, the constancy of the marginal utility of income with respect to price (i.e., $\partial\lambda^*/\partial p_1 = \partial\lambda^*/\partial p_2 = 0$) implies that the regular demand curves are symmetric: $\partial x_1^*/\partial p_2 = \partial x_2^*/\partial p_1$. Make the standard assumptions including monotonicity: $U_1 > 0$ and $U_2 > 0$.

8.7 Prove that $\partial\lambda^*/\partial M = 0$ is inconsistent with utility maximization when the utility function is additively separable and $U_{ii} < 0$ for all i.

8.8 Consider the labor/leisure choice problem given in Section 8.3 for the case of the particular utility function $U(C, l) = Cl$:

$$\underset{\{C,l\}}{\text{Max }} U(C, l) = Cl$$

$$\text{Subject to: } w(\bar{T} - l) + \bar{N} - C.$$

(a) Set up the Lagrangian and solve this problem for the optimal consumption level $C^* = C^*(w; \bar{T}, \bar{N})$ and the optimal supply of labor $L^* = L^*(w; \bar{T}, \bar{N})$.

(b) Does this utility function satisfy the second-order conditions? (Show why or why not.)

(c) Suppose that nonlabor income is positive ($\bar{N} > 0$). Does an increase in the real wage increase the labor supply (i.e., does the labor supply function slope upward?)?

(d) Suppose nonlabor income is zero ($\bar{N} = 0$). Does an increase in the real wage increase the labor supply in this case?

(e) What do your answers to (c) and (d) say about the "incentive" impact of a tax cut designed to increase the real wage of "workers" (those with labor as the sole source of income)? Discuss the economic implications of your result.

8.9 Consider an economy that produces only two goods, x and y. These goods are produced using labor L input according to the production functions

$$x = 2(L_x)^{1/2} \quad \text{and} \quad y = 2(L_y)^{1/2},$$

where L_i is the amount of labor used in the production of good i.

(a) Do the production functions in this economy exhibit diminishing marginal returns? (Demonstrate.)

(b) Find an expression for the production possibilities curve for this economy (in xy-space) when the economy has only 1 unit of labor in total ($L_x + L_y = 1$).

(c) Does the production possibilities curve from (b) have the standard concave shape?

(d) Suppose the social welfare function for the society is given by $W(x, y) = xy$. If the central planning authority desires to maximize the social welfare subject to the economy's technology constraint (given by the production possibilities curve), how much of each of the two goods x^* and y^* should be produced?

8.10 A firm can spend its fixed advertising budget B on two forms of advertising: television advertising t, which has a price of p_t per minute, and newspaper advertising N, which has a price of p_N per line. The firm wishes to purchase t and N in amounts that will maximize sales S subject to the constraint of the advertising budget B. The firm's sales S are related to the expenditure on each type of advertising by a sales function $S = f(t, N) = kt^3 N$, where $k > 0$.

(a) Set up the Lagrangian for this sales maximization problem for $p_t = \$1000$, $p_N = \$10$, and $B = \$10,000$.

(b) Solve the first-order conditions and find t^* and N^*.

(c) Do the second-order conditions hold for this problem? (Show why or why not.)

8.11 Consider the following intertemporal choice problem. An individual lives only two periods: $t = 0$ (youth) and $t = 1$ (old age). The individual receives utility from the consumption of an aggregate commodity c during the two periods. The individual therefore seeks to maximize $U(c_0, c_1)$, where c_0 is youth consumption and c_1 is old-age consumption. Assume that U is at least twice differentiable, has positive marginal utilities, and satisfies the second-order conditions for a maximum. The individual is certain to receive an endowment of the aggregate commodity of e_0 during youth and e_1 during old age. Any of the youth endowment that is not consumed during youth ($e_0 - c_0$) can be saved at an interest rate factor of r for old-age consumption. The interest factor is $r = 1 +$ the interest rate.

(a) Find the individual's intertemporal budget constraint.

(b) Set up the Lagrangian and write out the first-order conditions for utility maximization subject to the intertemporal budget constraint.

(c) Find expressions for the comparative statics terms $\partial c_0/\partial r$ and $\partial c_1/\partial r$.

(d) Now consider the special case in which the optimum choice $c_0^*(r)$, $c_1^*(r)$ is a "no intertemporal transfer" optimum, that is, $c_0^*(r) = e_0$ and $c_1^*(r) = e_1$. Sign the comparative statics results from (c) under this special assumption and interpret your results.

8.12 Answer the following questions about an individual with the constant-elasticity-of-substitution utility function

$$U(x_1, x_2) = \left(x_1^\gamma + x_2^\gamma\right)^{1/\gamma} \qquad \text{with } 0 < \gamma < 1,$$

who maximizes utility subject to the standard budget constraint:

$$p_1 x_1 + p_2 x_2 = M.$$

(a) Find the regular demands $x_1^*(p_1, p_2, M)$ and $x_2^*(p_1, p_2, M)$.

(b) Are these demand functions homogeneous of degree zero? (Show why or why not.)

(c) Find an expression for the optimal value of the Lagrange multiplier $\lambda^* = \lambda^*(p_1, p_2, M)$.

(d) Find an expression for the indirect utility function $V(p_1, p_2, M) = U(x_1^*(p_1, p_2, M), x_2^*(p_1, p_2, M))$ associated with this particular utility function.

(e) Is the indirect utility function $V(p_1, p_2, M)$ homogeneous of any degree? If so, what degree? (Demonstrate.)

8.13 In Problem 2.10 of Chapter 2 we showed that the elasticity of technical substitution σ could be written as

$$\sigma = \frac{f_1^2 x_1 + f_1 f_2 x_2}{f_2 x_1 x_2 \left[f_1 \frac{\partial MRTS}{\partial x_2} + f_2 \frac{\partial MRTS}{\partial x_1} \right]}$$

where $y = f(x_1, x_2)$ is a production function, $f_i = \partial f/\partial x_i$, and $MRTS = f_1/f_2$. Now prove that if the second-order conditions for the following cost minimization problem are satisfied, then $\sigma > 0$:

$$\underset{\{r_1, r_2\}}{\text{Min}} \sum_{i=1}^{2} w_i x_i$$

Subject to: $\bar{y} = f(x_1, x_2)$.

8.14 Prove that if the utility function in the standard n-good consumer choice problem is additively separable and $U_{ii} < 0$ for all i, then the second-order conditions for a constrained maximum are satisfied.

8.15 The regular demands $x_1^*(p_1, p_2, M)$ and $x_2^*(p_1, p_2, M)$ were derived from the utility function $U(x_1, x_2) = x_1 x_2$ in Section 8.2.

(a) Set up the dual problem for this particular utility function and solve the first-order conditions to obtain the compensated demands $[x_1^u(p_1, p_2, \bar{U}), x_2^u(p_1, p_2, \bar{U})]$.

(b) Are these compensated demand functions symmetric? (Show why or why not.)

(c) Find the expenditure function $[E^u(p_1, p_2, \bar{U})]$ for this problem.

(d) Is it true that $x_i^*(p_1, p_2, E^u(p_1, p_2, \bar{U})) = x_i^u(p_1, p_2, \bar{U})$ for $i = 1, 2$? (Show why or why not.)

(e) Does the Slutsky equation (own and cross) hold for the demand function of good 1 of this problem? (Show why or why not.)

8.16 Social security. Consider the following overlapping-generations model. Each individual in the economy lives in two periods, youth and old age. During youth, each individual works and receives a real income of unity (1). During old age, the individual retires and lives on the income that was not consumed during youth. Thus, if C_1 is the first-period (youth) consumption and C_2 is the second period (old-age) consumption, each individual has the lifetime income constraint $C_1 + C_2 = 1$ (assuming that real income is perfectly storable at zero cost).

(a) Find the utility-maximizing consumption during youth C_1^* and old age C_2^* for the individual with the utility function $U(C_1, C_2) = C_1 C_2$.

(b) Now suppose the population in the economy is growing exogenously at rate n. That is, for each generation, $(N_y - N_o)/N_o = n$ where N_y is the number of young individuals, N_o is the number of old individuals, and $0 < n < 1$. Let the government of this growing economy introduce a social security system. The government borrows the savings of the young in each period and transfers this savings to the old in that period. For this borrowing the government promises to pay each young person a real rate of interest n on what is borrowed. Thus, an individual who consumes C_1 during youth can lend the remainder of his or her income $(1 - C_1)$ to the government and receive $(1 + n)(1 - C_1)$ back from the government when old. This means that each individual has a total income of $1 + n(1 - C_1)$ for the two periods of life, giving an intertemporal budget constraint of

$$C_1 + C_2 = 1 + n(1 - C_1).$$

Again, assuming that each individual has the utility function $U(C_1, C_2) = C_1 C_2$, compute the optimal consumption of goods C_1^{**} and C_2^{**} under this new budget constraint.

(c) Are individuals better off with this social security system or in the initial situation, where each individual saves for retirement? [Compare $U(C_1^*, C_2^*)$ with $U(C_1^{**}, C_2^{**})$.]

(d) Will the government be able to finance this "pay as you go" social security system without subsidizing the system from other sources of revenue? (Show why or why not.)

8.17 Consider a pure exchange economy with two goods (x_1, x_2) and two traders ($s =$ Sally and $f =$ Fred). Both traders have the same Cobb–Douglas utility function

$$U(x_1, x_2) = x_1^{\alpha_1} x_2^{\alpha_2} \qquad \text{with } \alpha_1 > 0, \alpha_2 > 0, \alpha_1 + \alpha_2 = 1.$$

If we let $\bar{x}_i^j$ be the initial endowment of good $i = 1, 2$ held by individual $j = s, f$, then the endowment vector for individual j is $\bar{x}^j(\bar{x}_1^j, x_2^j)$ and the economy's total endowment (supply) of good i is $\bar{x}_i = \bar{x}_i^s + \bar{x}_i^f$. Assume that the initial endowment vectors are $\bar{x}^s = (0, 100)$ and $\bar{x}^f = (100, 0)$.

(a) Set up the Lagrangian and solve the first-order conditions to find each individual's demand function for the two goods (i.e., find $x_1^{*s}, x_2^{*s}, x_1^{*f}, x_2^{*f}$).

(b) Sum the two individual's demands [from (a)] to get an expression for the market demand for each good (i.e., find $x_1^* = x_1^{*s} + x_1^{*f}$ and $x_2^* = x_2^{*s} + x_2^{*f}$).

(c) Find the market excess demand functions for the two goods (i.e., find $z_1 = x_1^* - \bar{x}_1$ and $z_2 = x_2^* - \bar{x}_2$).

(d) Do these excess demand functions satisfy Walras' law (W) and the zero-degree homogeneity condition (H)? (Show why or why not.)

(e) Find the equilibrium price ratio $p^* = p_1^*/p_2^*$ for this pure exchange economy. (*Note:* Only the price ratio can be determined, not the absolute prices.)

8.18 Consider the cost-minimizing firm using two inputs K and L to produce a positive fixed level of output $\bar{y}$ by means of the production function $y = f(K, L)$. This firm thus solves the problem:

$$\underset{\{K,L\}}{\text{Min}} \ vK + wL$$

$$\text{Subject to: } \bar{y} = f(K, L),$$

where $v > 0$ is the price of capital K and $w > 0$ is the price of labor L. Assume the firm's production function satisfies the following conditions:

$$f_K = \partial f/\partial K > 0, \ f_L = \partial f/\partial L > 0,$$
$$f_{KK} = \partial^2 f/\partial K^2 < 0, \ f_{LL} = \partial^2 f/\partial L^2 < 0,$$
$$f_{KL} = f_{LK} = \partial^2 f/\partial K \, \partial L > 0.$$

(a) Show that the second-order conditions for a constrained minimization problem hold for the production function of this firm.

(b) Prove that the firm's marginal cost MC increases with an increase in the price of labor w.

8.19 Consider a consumer with fixed money income M, who purchases goods x_1 and x_2 so as to maximize the utility function $U(x_1, x_2) = b + a \ln x_1^{1/2} x_2^{1/2}$, where a and b are positive constants.

(a) Solve the consumer choice problem to find the regular demands for the two goods [$x_1^*(p_1, p_2, M)$ and $x_2^*(p_1, p_2, M)$].

(b) Does this utility function satisfy the second-order conditions for a constrained maximization? (Show why or why not.)

(c) Many exercises in welfare economics require the marginal utility of money income to be constant with respect to either prices or money income. Does either of these two properties hold for this particular utility function? (Show why or why not.)

8.20 A profit-maximizing bank receives rate r_L on loans L and pays out the regulated rate r_D on its demand deposits D. Since both loans L and deposits D are costly to administer, the bank's profit π is given by

$$\pi(L, D) = r_L L - r_D D - C(L, D),$$

where $C(L, D)$ is the cost function of the bank with $\partial C/\partial D = C_D > 0$, $\partial C/\partial L = C_L > 0$, $\partial^2 C/\partial D^2 = C_{DD} > 0$, $\partial^2 C/\partial L^2 = C_{LL} > 0$, and $\partial^2 C/\partial L \partial D = C_{LD} = C_{DL} = 0$.

The constraint the bank faces is its balance sheet, which requires that total assets be equal to total liabilities (assuming zero net worth). The assets of the bank are its loans L and reserves R, while its only liability is the amount of outstanding demand deposits D. Thus the balance sheet imposes the following constraint on the bank:

$$L + R = D.$$

The monetary authority imposes a reserve ratio q on the bank, where $q = R/D$ with $0 < q < 1$. Rewriting the balance sheet constraint in terms of q gives

$$L = (1 - q)D.$$

(a) Set up the Lagrangian and write out the first-order conditions for the bank's constrained maximization problem.
(b) Do the second-order conditions hold for this problem? (Show why or why not.)
(c) Suppose the monetary authority increases the regulated rate that the bank pays on demand deposits. Use Cramer's rule to determine how this will affect the π-maximizing amount of loans L^* and deposits D^*.
(d) Do your answers in (c) make economic sense? (Explain in detail.)

8.21 Consider (as in Problem 8.18) a cost-minimizing firm using two inputs L and capital K to produce a positive fixed level of output $\bar{y}$. In this case let the production function be given explicitly by $y = 2L^{1/2}K^{1/2}$, so the firm has the problem

$$\min_{\{K,L\}} wL + vK$$

$$\text{Subject to: } \bar{y} = 2L^{1/2}K^{1/2}.$$

(a) Solve the firm's problem to find expressions for the cost-minimizing levels of labor and capital employed: $L^* = L^*(w, v, \bar{y})$ and $K^* = K^*(w, v, \bar{y})$.
(b) Use your answers from (a) to find the long-run total cost function $TC^* = TC(w, v, \bar{y}) = wL^*(v, w, \bar{y}) + vK^*(v, w, \bar{y})$.
(c) From the long-run total cost function in (b), find the long-run average total cost (ATC) and the long-run marginal cost (MC).
(d) Explain your answers to (c) on the basis of the properties of the production function $y = 2L^{1/2}K^{1/2}$.

8.22 In Chapter 1 the problem of maximizing $U(x_1, x_2)$ subject to $p_1x_1 + p_2x_2 = M$ was solved by substitution of $x_2 = -p_1x_1/p_2 + M/p_2$ into $U(x_1, x_2)$ and reducing it to a one-variable problem: maximizing $U(x_1, g(x_1))$, where $g(x_1) = -p_1x_1/p_2 + M/p_2$. Show that the first- and second-order conditions for this one-variable problem are the same as those from the Lagrangian approach developed in this chapter.

8.23 Show that for the standard n-good consumer choice problem, the assumptions of additive separability ($U_{ii} < 0, U_i > 0$, for all i and $U_{ij} = 0$ for all $i \neq j$) **and** the constancy of the marginal utility of money income with respect to price ($\partial\lambda^*/\partial p_i = 0$ for all i) implies that both the following conditions hold:
(a) All goods are (gross) independent ($\partial x_i^*/\partial p_j = 0$ for all $i \neq j$).
(b) All goods have unit own-price elasticity [$\varepsilon_{ii} = (\partial x_i^*/\partial p_i)/(p_i/x_i^*) = -1$ for all i].

8.24 Consider the three-input cost minimization problem

$$\underset{\{x\}}{\text{Min}}\, TC = \sum_{i=1}^{3} w_i x_i$$

$$\text{Subject to: } y = f(x),$$

where $x = (x_1, x_2, x_3)$ is the input vector (with $x_i > 0$ for all i), $w = (w_1, w_2, w_3)$ is the input price (wage) vector (with $w_i > 0$ for all i), and $y = $ output (with $y > 0$), where the production function is given by

$$f(x) = x_1 x_2 x_3.$$

(a) Set up the Lagrangian and write out the first-order conditions for this minimization problem.
(b) Are the second-order conditions satisfied by this production function? (Show why or why not.)
(c) Solve the first-order conditions for the cost-minimizing factor demand functions $x_1^*(w, y), x_2^*(w, y)$, and $x_3^*(w, y)$.
(d) Find an expression for the total cost function

$$TC^* = \sum_{i=1}^{3} w_i x_i^*(w, y).$$

(e) Find an expression for the marginal cost function $MC = \partial TC^*/\partial y$.
(f) Do the cost functions in (d) and (e) make economic sense given this particular production function? (*Hint:* Consider returns to scale.)

8.25 For the standard n-good consumer choice problem, show that having a utility function that is homogeneous of degree 1 implies the unitary income elasticity of the indirect utility function.

8.26 For the standard n-good consumer choice problem, **Roy's identity** says that

$$\frac{\partial V}{\partial p_j} + x_j^* \frac{\partial V}{\partial M} = 0 \qquad \text{for all } j = 1, 2, \ldots, n,$$

where V is the indirect utility function. Prove Roy's identity.

8.27 For the n-input cost minimization problem in (8.11) **Shephard's lemma** says that

$$\frac{\partial TC(w, y)}{\partial w_j} = x_j^* \qquad \text{for all } j = 1, 2, \ldots, n,$$

where

$$TC(w, y) = \sum_{i=1}^{n} w_i x_i^*(w, y).$$

Prove Shephard's lemma.

8.28 For the standard n-good consumer choice problem, show that if preferences are monotonic (i.e., $U_i = \partial U/\partial x_i > 0$ for all i), then there must be at least one pair of goods that are net substitutes.

8.29 One measure of the welfare effect of a change in the price of a good is called the **compensating variation** (CV). For the case in which the price vector changes from p^0 to p' with $p_i^0 > p_i'$ for some $i = 1, 2, \ldots, n$ and $p_j^0 = p_j'$ for all $j \neq i$, the compensating variation CV_i is the amount of income that would need to be taken away (at the new prices) to return the consumer to the original level of utility U_0. Thus

$$CV_i = E^u(p^0, U_0) - E^u(p', U_0).$$

(a) Explain why the expression for CV_i measures the compensating variation.
(b) Show that

$$CV_i = \int_{p_i'}^{p_i^0} x_i^u(p, U_0)\, dp_i.$$

8.30 Given the expression for the compensating variation in (b) of Problem 8.29, show that when $n = 2$ and the utility function has the form

$$U(x_1, x_2) = x_1 + g(x_2),$$

with $g' > 0$ and $g'' < 0$, then the compensating variation associated with a change from p^0 to p' with $p_1^0 = p_1'$ and $p_2^0 > p_2'$ is given by the area under the ordinary demand curve x_2^* between p_2^0 and p_2'. In other words, show that the following relation holds for the foregoing utility function:

$$CV_2 = \int_{p_2'}^{p_2^0} x_2^*(p, M)\, dp_2.$$

8.31 Consider the problem of extracting an exhaustible resource such as coal or oil. The time horizon for the owner of the resource is T years, and the initial stock of the resource is $\bar{y}$. This makes the resource constraint

$$\bar{y} = \sum_{t=1}^{T} y_t,$$

where y_t is the amount extracted at time t. If future prices p_t and the cost function $c(y_t)$ are known with certainty, then the objective function will be to maximize the present value of the profit stream from the resource (π)

$$\pi = \sum_{t=1}^{T} [p_t y_t - c(y_t)](1+i)^{-t}$$

subject to the resource constraint.
(a) Set up the Lagrangian for this problem and find the first-order conditions for the optimal extraction y_t^* in each period.
(b) Interpret your first-order conditions.
(c) Find a restriction that guarantees that the second-order conditions hold and interpret it.

8.32 Would an individual with the utility function $U(x_1, x_2) = x_1 x_2$ (from Section 8.2) rather play (balanced) coin-flipping game A, where a head pays \$6 and a tail pays \$4, or coin-flipping game B, where a head pays \$8 and a tail pays \$2? Explain your answer.

NOTES

1. See Panik (1976) or Takayama (1985), for instance. The general result also follows as a special case to the Kuhn–Tucker conditions, which are presented in Chapter 9. The theorem actually requires an additional constraint restriction—that there exist at least one partial derivative of the constraint that does not vanish at x^*. We have implicitly assumed this additional restriction in the proof.

2. Early and elegant proofs for the n-dimensional case are contained in Debreu (1952); for one of the many textbook presentations, see Panik (1976).

3. In general, we use L as the symbol for the Lagrangian; $\mathscr{L}$ is substituted here to avoid possible confusion with the labor supply L.

4. For instance, Paul Samuelson (1942) argued that Marshall meant that $\partial \lambda^*/\partial p_i = 0$ for all i, while Milton Friedman (1953) argued that Marshall meant that $\partial \lambda^*/\partial M = 0$. The important issue in this discussion is the homogeneity of λ^* (see Problem 8.3).

5. Remember [from (8.24)] that the determinant is the same whether the border is in the northwest (NW) or the southeast (SE) corner. The second-order conditions in (8.59) are written with NW borders and the denominator of the expression in (8.68) is written with SE borders, but the signs are identical.

6. The equations are named after the Russian mathematician–economist Eugene Slutsky, who originally published the result in 1915; the paper has been translated and reprinted in a number of places (e.g., Slutsky, 1952).

CHAPTER

9

C H A P T E R

INEQUALITY CONSTRAINTS
IN OPTIMIZATION THEORY

■ ■ ■

A variety of different optimization problems have been examined in the preceding chapters. Because of the economic structure of these problems, the domain of the choice variable has almost always been restricted to the nonnegative orthant. For example, in both the consumer choice problem and the profit maximization problem for the competitive firm, the choice variables were restricted to the nonnegative values $x_i \geq 0$ for all $i = 1, 2, \ldots, n$. In all such problems that had nonnegativity restrictions imposed on the domain of the choice variables, it was possible for the problem to exhibit **boundary optima,** that is, to have solution vectors with $x_i^* = 0$ for some i. Now while such boundary optima were often a possibility, we never actually examined them. In fact, we have been quite careful to explicitly rule out such boundary optima; in all the optimization problems thus far we have assumed that all elements of the solution vector were **strictly positive** (we considered only interior optima).

Certainly a complete discussion of optimization theory in economics would need to examine boundary optima, both for mathematical completeness and because of the economic relevance of such "corner" solutions. Most consumers do not buy a positive amount of every good in their choice space, and most firms do not purchase a positive amount of every input they could use in the production process; $x_i^* = 0$ is frequently an optimal choice of economic interest.

This chapter modifies the optimization techniques from earlier chapters to accommodate boundary optima. The general approach is called the theory of **nonlinear programming,** but this label is actually a bit of a misnomer, since the technique includes **linear** programming as a special case. Our discussion of the topic starts with a simple one-variable unconstrained problem, but the main result will apply the theory of nonlinear programming to n-variable problems with multiple constraints. This main result is called **Kuhn–Tucker theory** after two of the early contributors to the field (Kuhn and Tucker 1951).

9.1 A Simple Inequality Constraint

Consider the general one-variable maximization problem

$$\text{Max}_{x} z = f(x),$$

where $x \in \Re_+$ and f is a differentiable function with $f: \Re_+ \to \Re$. Since we are specifically concerned with the domain restriction, let us rewrite the problem as

$$\text{Max}_{x} z = f(x)$$
$$x \geq 0. \tag{9.1}$$

If x^* is a solution to (9.1), then only three relations can hold between x^* and the derivative of f at x^*. If $x^* > 0$, then x^* is an interior optimum, and we have the familiar result that the derivative of f must vanish at x^*; thus $x^* > 0$ implies that $f'(x^*) = 0$. But if x^* solves (9.1) and $x^* = 0$, then x^* is a **boundary optimum** and there are two possibilities for $f'(x^*)$: it might be that $f'(x^*) = 0$ as in the interior case, or it might be that $f'(x^*) < 0$. These three cases are depicted in Figure 9.1.

Figure 9.1a depicts the familiar case of an interior maximum with $x^* > 0$ and $f'(x^*) = 0$. The other two diagrams in the figure depict cases of boundary maxima in which $x^* = 0$. In Figure 9.1b, $x^* = 0$, but the derivative vanishes just as in the interior case. In Figure 9.1c, though, $x^* = 0$ is the maximum of f on $\Re_+$ (at least locally), but the derivative does not vanish at x^*. Instead, Figure 9.1c depicts the case in which $x^* = 0$ and $f'(x^*) < 0$. These examples clearly demonstrate that when we allow for (or do not assume away) boundary optima, $f'(x^*) = 0$ is no longer a necessary condition for x^* to be a solution of the maximization problem in (9.1).

If $f'(x^*) = 0$ is no longer necessary for x^* to solve (9.1), then how should such a necessary condition be characterized? How can the first-order conditions for the maximization of a one-variable function be modified to account for the possibility of boundary maxima? Actually, the answer is revealed in Figure 9.1. First, notice from Figure 9.1 that the derivative of f evaluated at x^* must be **nonpositive:** $f'(x^*) \leq 0$. Second, if the maximum is strictly positive, then the derivative must vanish; and if the derivative is strictly negative, then the optimal value must be

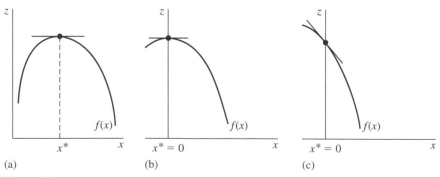

(a)　　　　　　　　　(b)　　　　　　　　　(c)

Figure 9.1

zero. These conditions can be summarized in the following way:

If $x^* \in \mathfrak{R}_+$ is a local maximum then $f'(x^*) \leq 0$,

but if $x^* > 0$ then $f'(x^*) = 0$, $\qquad$ (9.2)

and if $f'(x^*) < 0$ then $x^* = 0$.

Or, these conditions can be written more simply as

$$f'(x^*) \leq 0 \qquad \text{and} \qquad x^* f(x^*) = 0. \qquad (9.3)$$

The conditions in (9.3) are the **first-order** (necessary) conditions for $x^* \geq 0$ to solve the one-variable maximization problem in (9.1). Notice that the one condition on the right-hand side of (9.3) implies both the last two conditions in (9.2). Conditions like those on the right-hand side of (9.3) are called **complementary-slackness conditions** because they say that both variables [in this case x^* and $f'(x^*)$] cannot be simultaneously "slack" (i.e., nonzero).

Since minimizing $f(x)$ is the same operation as maximizing $-f(x)$, the result from (9.3) can easily be extended to the **minimization** problem

$$\operatorname*{Min}_{x} z = f(x) \qquad (9.4)$$
$$x \geq 0,$$

with $f: \mathfrak{R}_+ \to \mathfrak{R}$. The first-order conditions for x^* to be a solution to (9.4) are

$$f'(x^*) \geq 0 \qquad \text{and} \qquad x^* f(x^*) = 0. \qquad (9.5)$$

For the minimization problem (9.4), the derivative must be nonnegative at the optimum, but the same complementary-slackness condition holds as for the maximization problem. If the result in (9.5) is not obvious to the reader, it can be obtained by reproducing the three diagrams in Figure 9.1 for the case of minimization.

These results generalize immediately to a problem with n choice variables. If the **maximization** problem is

$$\operatorname*{Max}_{x} z = f(x) \qquad (9.6)$$
$$x \geq 0,$$

with $x \in \mathfrak{R}_+^n$ and $f: \mathfrak{R}_+^n \to \mathfrak{R}$, then the **first-order conditions** for a solution at $x^* \in \mathfrak{R}_+^n$ are given by

$$\frac{\partial f(x^*)}{\partial x_i} = f_i(x^*) \leq 0 \qquad \text{and} \qquad x_i^* f_i(x^*) = 0 \qquad \text{for all } i = 1, 2, \ldots, n.$$
$$(9.7)$$

Since $x_i^* \geq 0$ and $f_i(x^*) \leq 0$ for all i, the n separate conditions on the right-hand side of (9.7) can be aggregated into a single complementary-slackness condition. After this aggregation, the first-order conditions for the problem (9.6) can be written as

$$f_i(x^*) \leq 0 \qquad \text{for all } i = 1, 2, \ldots, n \qquad \text{and} \qquad \sum_{i=1}^{n} x_i^* f_i(x^*) = 0, \qquad (9.8a)$$

or, in vector notation,

$$\nabla f(x^*) \leq 0 \qquad \text{and} \qquad \nabla f(x^*)(x^*)^T = 0, \tag{9.8b}$$

where $\nabla f(x^*) = (f_1(x^*), f_2(x^*), \ldots, f_n(x^*))$ is the gradient (row) vector and $(x^*)^T$ is the transpose of $x^* = (x_1^*, x_2^*, \ldots, x_n^*)$. If (9.6) were a **minimization** problem, the inequalities on the left-hand side of the first-order conditions would simply be reversed.

The conditions in (9.8) are only **necessary** conditions; sufficient conditions for problems with inequality constraints are usually written in terms of the concavity or convexity of the objective function. Theorem 9.1 provides necessary and sufficient conditions for x^* to solve the **maximization** problem in (9.6).

THEOREM 9.1: If the objective function f is **concave,** then the conditions in (9.8) are necessary and sufficient for $x^* \in \mathfrak{R}_+^n$ to be a **global maximum** of f that solves the problem (9.6). If f is **strictly concave,** then the global maximum is also **unique.**

PROOF: The necessity of the condition in (9.8) has been demonstrated; let us consider their sufficiency when f is concave. By (2.61) in Chapter 2, the concavity of f implies that

$$\nabla f(x^*)(x - x^*)^T + f(x^*) \geq f(x) \qquad \text{for all } x \in \mathfrak{R}_+^n.$$

Now from (9.8) we have $\nabla f(x^*)(x^*)^T = 0$, and so the foregoing inequality reduces to

$$\nabla f(x^*)x^T + f(x^*) \geq f(x) \qquad \text{for all } x \in \mathfrak{R}_+^n.$$

But also from (9.8) we have $\nabla f(x^*)x^T \leq 0$ since $\nabla f(x^*) \leq 0$ and $x \geq 0$; thus,

$$f(x^*) \geq f(x) \qquad \text{for all } x \in \mathfrak{R}_+^n,$$

which proves that x^* maximizes f on $\mathfrak{R}_+^n$. If f were strictly concave, the inequality would be strict and x^* would be the unique maximizer of f on $\mathfrak{R}_+^n$.

If (9.6) were a **minimization** problem, then in addition to reversing the inequalities on the left-hand side of (9.8), we would need to replace the word **concave** in Theorem 9.1 with **convex.** Theorem 9.1 completes our discussion of inequality-constrained problems without functional constraints. Let us now turn to the more general case of problems constrained not only by the nonnegativity of the choice variables, but also by functional constraints.

9.2 The General Kuhn–Tucker Theorem

Consider the following functionally constrained maximization problem:

$$\begin{aligned} &\text{Max } z = f(x) \\ &\quad x \\ &\text{Subject to: } g(x) \geq 0, \\ &\qquad\qquad x \geq 0, \end{aligned} \tag{9.9}$$

where g is a differentiable function $g: \mathfrak{R}_+^n \to \mathfrak{R}$ and the other terms are defined as before.

Let us convert the problem in (9.9) to a more familiar form by introducing a "slack" variable $s \geq 0$ such that the constraint function becomes the equality

$$g(x) - s = 0.$$

Given this equality constraint, we can apply the familiar Lagrangian results from Chapter 8. In particular, the problem

$$\text{Max } z = f(x)$$
$$\underset{x,s}{}$$
$$\text{Subject to: } g(x) - s = 0, \tag{9.10}$$
$$x \geq 0 \quad \text{and} \quad s \geq 0,$$

has the Lagrangian function

$$\mathscr{L}(x, s, \lambda) = f(x) + \lambda [g(x) - s], \tag{9.11}$$

where λ is the Lagrange multiplier and $\mathscr{L}$ is used to distinguish the problem from the main Kuhn–Tucker results in the next section.

Since the Lagrangian (9.11) is without functional constraint, we can combine the results from the problem in (9.6) with the familiar results from Chapter 8. Thus a necessary condition for (x^*, s^*) to solve problem (9.10) is that there exists a λ^* such that:

$$\mathscr{L}_i(x^*, s^*, \lambda^*) = f_i(x^*) + \lambda^* g_i(x^*) \leq 0 \quad \text{for all } i = 1, 2, \ldots, n,$$
$$\sum_{i=1}^{n} x_i^* \mathscr{L}_i(x^*, s^*, \lambda^*) = \sum_{i=1}^{n} x_i^* [f_i(x^*) + \lambda^* g_i(x^*)] = 0,$$
$$\mathscr{L}_s(x^*, s^*, \lambda^*) = -\lambda^* \leq 0, \tag{9.12}$$
$$s^* \mathscr{L}_s(x^*, s^*, \lambda^*) = -s^* \lambda^* = 0,$$
$$\mathscr{L}_\lambda(x^*, s^*, \lambda^*) = g(x^*) - s^* = 0,$$
$$s^* \geq 0 \quad \text{and} \quad x_i^* \geq 0 \quad \text{for all } i = 1, 2, \ldots, n.$$

The conditions in (9.12) allow us to eliminate the slack variable s^*. From the third expression in (9.12) we have $\lambda^* \geq 0$, and from the fifth expression we have that $g(x^*) = s^* \geq 0$. Combining these two results with the fourth expression in (9.12) gives us $\lambda^* g(x^*) = 0$. Replacing the expressions in (9.12) with the ones we just derived (which excludes s^*) and using L for the Lagrangian, provides the following necessary conditions[1] for $x^* \in \mathfrak{R}_+^n$ to solve the functionally constrained problem (9.9):

$$L_i(x^*, \lambda^*) = f_i(x^*) + \lambda^* g_i(x^*) \leq 0 \quad \text{for all } i = 1, 2, \ldots, n,$$
$$\sum_{i=1}^{n} x_i^* L_i(x^*, \lambda^*) = \sum_{i=1}^{n} x_i^* [f_i(x^*) + \lambda^* g_i(x^*)] = 0,$$
$$L_\lambda(x^*, \lambda^*) = g(x^*) \geq 0, \tag{9.13}$$
$$\lambda^* L_\lambda(x^*, \lambda^*) = \lambda^* g(x^*) = 0,$$
$$\lambda^* \geq 0 \quad \text{and} \quad x_i^* \geq 0 \quad \text{for all } i = 1, 2, \ldots, n,$$

where $L(x, \lambda) = f(x) + \lambda g(x)$.

Several things should be said regarding the conditions in (9.13), but first let us extend the argument to the more general case of m constraints. We honor the necessary conditions for this general case with the title of **Kuhn–Tucker conditions.** In the general m-constraint problem, given as (9.14), there are n variables and m functional constraints with no necessary relationship between n and m. The general problem is

$$\text{Max } z = f(x) \atop x,s$$
$$\text{Subject to: } g^1(x) \geq 0,$$
$$g^2(x) \geq 0,$$
$$\vdots$$
$$g^m(x) \geq 0,$$
$$x \geq 0,$$

(9.14)

where each g^i is restricted as g in (9.9). The Lagrangian function L for the general problem (9.14) is

$$L(x, \lambda) = f(x) + \sum_{j=1}^{m} \lambda_j g^j(x) = f(x) + \lambda^T g(x),$$

(9.15)

where $\lambda^T = (\lambda_1, \lambda_2, \ldots, \lambda_m)$ is the m-dimensional row vector of Lagrange multipliers (one for each constraint function) and $g(x)$ is the m-dimensional column vector of constraint functions with $[g(x)]^T = (g^1(x), g^2(x), \ldots, g^m(x))$.

The **main result of the theory of nonlinear programming** is that if x^* is a solution to (9.14), then there must exist a $\lambda^* \in \Re_+^m$ such that the following **Kuhn–Tucker conditions** hold[2]:

$$L_i(x^*, \lambda^*) = f_i(x^*) + \sum_{j=1}^{m} \lambda_j^* g_i^j(x^*) \leq 0 \qquad \text{for all } i = 1, 2, \ldots, n, \quad (9.16a)$$

$$x_i^* L_i(x^*, \lambda^*) = x_i^* \left[f_i(x^*) + \sum_{j=1}^{m} \lambda_j^* g_i^j(x^*) \right] = 0 \qquad \text{for all } i = 1, 2, \ldots, n,$$

(9.16b)

$$L_{\lambda_j}(x^*, \lambda^*) = g^j(x^*) \geq 0 \qquad \text{for all } j = 1, 2, \ldots, m, \quad (9.16c)$$

$$\lambda_j^* L_{\lambda_j}(x^*, \lambda^*) = \lambda_j^* g^j(x^*) = 0 \qquad \text{for all } j = 1, 2, \ldots, m, \quad (9.16d)$$

$$\lambda_j^* \geq 0 \quad \text{for all } j = 1, 2, \ldots, m \qquad \text{and} \qquad x_i^* \geq 0 \quad \text{for all } i = 1, 2, \ldots, n.$$

(9.16e)

As before, the number of these conditions can be reduced by $n-1$ if the n equations in (9.16b) are replaced by the single condition $\sum_i x_i^* L_i(x^*, \lambda^*) = 0$. Given the other Kuhn–Tucker conditions, these two ways of characterizing the

BOX 9.1
Monetary Overlapping-Generations Models

Economic theorists have not (yet) found completely satisfactory answers for two closely related questions: Why do rational agents hold money? and Why does money have value in equilibrium? The student may feel that such questions have obvious answers, but those "obvious" answers have proved very difficult to reconcile with the standard characterization of rational choice that most economists find acceptable. The general field of inquiry for such questions is called the microfoundations of monetary theory, and it is a field populated by a number of different theoretical approaches. One approach that has received a lot of attention is the **overlapping-generations** approach to monetary theory. Most contemporary overlapping-generations (OG) monetary models are based on the earlier work of Samuelson (1958) and Cass and Yaari (1966). Defenders of the OG approach include Cass and Shell (1980) and Wallace (1980), among others. Although this class of models has received some serious criticism (e.g., Hahn, 1983, and McCallum, 1983, 1989)—primarily because it emphasizes the store-of-value, rather than means-of-exchange, function of money—it continues to be one of the main approaches to questions of monetary microfoundations. Our approach follows McCallum (1983) and utilizes the Kuhn–Tucker conditions presented in the chapter.

As one might suspect, the basic notion in an OG model is that generations "overlap." Each agent lives two periods (youth and old age), and old agents from the preceding generation overlap with the youth of the current generation. The simplest version of a monetary OG model includes money and one other commodity (Problem 8.16 in Chapter 8 presented a simple nonmonetary OG model). Let each member of the younger generation receive an endowment e_0 of the single commodity. This endowment can be consumed during youth (c_t^0), "stored" for consumption in old age (k_t), or sold for money (M_t). Thus if the price of the commodity is given by P_t, the first-period (youth) budget constraint is

$$e_0 - c_t^0 - k_t - \frac{M_t}{P_t} = 0. \tag{a}$$

Agents receive no endowment in the second period (old age); consumption c_{t+1}^1 is limited to that which has been stored and that which can be purchased with the money holdings from the preceding period. The commodity, while it can be stored, is somewhat perishable; it depreciates at the rate δ, thus $k_t - k_{t+1} = \delta k_{t+1}$. It is convenient to write this relationship as $k_{t+1} = \gamma k_t$, where $\gamma = 1/(1 + \delta)$. Thus the second-period (old-age) budget constraint is

$$\gamma k_t + \frac{M_t}{P_{t+1}} - c_{t+1}^1 = 0. \tag{b}$$

Assuming that the agent has a utility function $U(c_t^0, c_{t+1}^1)$ defined over consumption in the two periods and satisfying standard assumptions on utility functions, the agent's intertemporal choice problem has four choice variables c_t^0, c_t^1, k_t, and M_t, and two constraints (a) and (b). The Lagrangian for the problem can be written

$$L\left(c_t^0, c_t^1, k_t, M_t, \lambda_1, \lambda_2\right) = U\left(c_t^0, c_{t+1}^1\right) + \lambda_1\left(e_0 - c_t^0 - k_t - \frac{M_t}{P_t}\right)$$

$$+ \lambda_2\left(\gamma k_t + \frac{M_t}{P_{t+1}} - c_{t+1}^1\right).$$

If we restrict ourselves to the case of strictly positive consumption in both periods, and the two constraints hold with strict equality, we have the following eight Kuhn–Tucker conditions:

$$\frac{\partial U}{\partial c_t^0} - \lambda_1 = 0, \tag{1}$$

$$\frac{\partial U}{\partial c_{t+1}^1} - \lambda_2 = 0, \tag{2}$$

$$-\lambda_1 + \lambda_2\gamma \le 0 \quad \text{or} \quad \lambda_2 - \lambda_1(1 + \delta) \le 0, \tag{3}$$

$$k_t(-\lambda_1 + \lambda_2\gamma) = 0, \tag{4}$$

$$\frac{-\lambda_1}{P_t} + \frac{\lambda_2}{P_{t+1}} \le 0 \quad \text{or} \quad \lambda_2 - \lambda_1(1 + \mu) \le 0, \tag{5}$$

$$M_t\left(\frac{-\lambda_1}{P_t} + \frac{\lambda_2}{P_{t+1}}\right) = 0, \tag{6}$$

$$e_0 - c_t^0 - k_t - \frac{M_t}{P_t} = 0, \tag{7}$$

$$\gamma k_t + \frac{M_t}{P_{t+1}} - c_{t+1}^1 = 0. \tag{8}$$

These eight conditions characterize the solutions to the intertemporal choice problem of a typical agent in the economy. One issue that can be examined in such a model is the impact of monetary growth. To this end, assume a continuously clearing money market and a monetary growth rate of μ, thus $M_{t+1} = (1 + \mu)M_t$. Also assume that agents have complete knowledge (perfect foresight) of the impact of monetary growth on prices, so $(P_{t+1} - P_t)/P_t = \mu$ or $P_{t+1} - P_t = \mu + 1$. Notice that this definition of μ has already been substituted into equation (5) of the Kuhn–Tucker conditions.

First, consider the case of $\mu > \delta$: the rate of growth of the money supply is greater than the rate of depreciation of the storable commodity. Since both μ and δ are nonnegative, $\mu > \delta$ implies that $\lambda_2 - \lambda_1(1 + \mu) < \lambda_2 - \lambda_1(1 + \delta)$; which, by expression (3) in the Kuhn–Tucker conditions, implies that $\lambda_2 - \lambda_1(1 + \mu) < 0$. This strict inequality, combined with (6), implies that $M_t = 0$. Thus if money grows faster (thus depreciates in value faster) than the storable commodity, no money is held by rational agents. Correspondingly, if the commodity does not depreciate at all ($\delta = 0$), then $\mu > 0$ (positive monetary growth) implies that money will not be held in equilibrium.

Second, suppose $\mu < \delta$: the rate of growth of the money supply is less than the rate of depreciation of the storable commodity. In this case $\mu < \delta$ implies $\lambda_2 - \lambda_1(1 + \delta) < \lambda_2 - \lambda_1(1 + \mu)$, which by (5) implies that $\lambda_2 - \lambda_1(1 + \delta) < 0$. This strict inequality, combined with (4), implies that $k_t = 0$. Now if no storage takes place and second-period consumption is strictly positive, then by (8) we must have $M_t > 0$. Thus when the storable good depreciates more quickly than the rate at which the money supply grows, we have a monetary equilibrium in which money is valued by rational agents. Such results, though based on a relatively simple OG framework, are fairly representative of the type of results available from monetary OG models.

Sources

Cass, D., and K. Shell. 1980. In defense of a basic approach. In *Models of monetary economies,* edited by J. H. Kareken and N. Wallace. Minneapolis, MN: Federal Reserve Bank of Minneapolis, 251–60.

Cass, D., and M. Yaari. 1966. A re-examination of the pure consumption loan model. *Journal of Political Economy* 74: 353–67.

Hahn, F. 1983. *Money and inflation.* Cambridge, MA: MIT Press.

Kareken, J. H., and N. Wallace, eds. 1980. *Models of monetary economies.* Minneapolis, MN: Federal Reserve Bank of Minneapolis.

McCallum, B. T. 1983. The role of overlapping-generations models in monetary economics. *Carnegie–Rochester Conference Series on Public Policy* 18: 9–44.

_____. 1989. *Monetary economics: Theory and policy.* New York: Macmillan.

Samuelson, P. A. 1958. An exact consumption–loan model of interest with or without the social contrivance of money. *Journal of Political Economy* 66: 467–82.

Wallace, N. 1980. The overlapping generations model of fiat money. In *Models of monetary economies,* edited by J. H. Kareken and N. Wallace. Minneapolis, MN: Federal Reserve Bank of Minneapolis, 49–82.

complementary slackness of the choice variables and the first derivatives of the Lagrangian function are mathematically equivalent. By a similar argument, we could replace the m conditions in (9.16d) with the single complementary-slackness condition $\sum_j \lambda_j^* g^j(x^*) = 0$. Since these alternative characterizations are mathematically equivalent, the choice is simply a matter of convenience within the context of the particular economic problem.

A number of things should be noted regarding the Kuhn–Tucker conditions in (9.16). First, when $x_i^* > 0$ for all i and $\lambda_j^* > 0$ for all j, the Kuhn–Tucker conditions reduce to the familiar Lagrangian results from Chapter 8. Second, unlike in the earlier case with equality constraints, it **does** matter how the Lagrangian function is defined; subtracting λ_j times a constraint function does not produce the same problem obtained from adding λ_j times a constraint function. In the earlier case of strict equality constraints, it did not matter whether the Lagrangian was formed by adding or subtracting the constraints. But when the constraints are inequalities, how the Lagrangian is formed becomes very important. Third, since the Kuhn–Tucker conditions are necessary, they provide a screening device for rejecting certain vectors as possible solutions. This is particularly important because numerical nonlinear programming problems are often solved by computational algorithms that search for the optimum among various candidate vectors. In such a computational context, the Kuhn–Tucker conditions provide a rejection criterion for candidates; if the Kuhn–Tucker conditions do not hold at a particular vector, then it cannot be a solution. In a similar way, the Kuhn–Tucker conditions serve as an existence theorem for nonlinear programming problems. Since the existence of an optimal value implies that the Kuhn–Tucker conditions must hold at that value, the impossibility of simultaneous satisfaction of all the conditions implies that the problem has no solution. For example, if the Kuhn–Tucker conditions imply a contradiction for all values of the choice variables, then the problem has no solution. Finally, if the problem is to **minimize** $f(x)$ subject to m constraints of the form $g^j(x) \leq 0$, the inequalities in the Kuhn–Tucker conditions (9.16) will **all be reversed.**

As in the absence of functional constraints, the Kuhn–Tucker conditions in (9.16) can be strengthened to necessary and sufficient conditions when all the functions involved are concave. This result is contained in Theorem 9.2.

THEOREM 9.2: If the objective function and all constraint functions are differentiable and **concave,** then the Kuhn–Tucker conditions in (9.16) are necessary and sufficient for $x^* \in \Re_+^n$ to be the **global maximum** of f, which solves the problem (9.14). If f is **strictly concave,** then the global maximum is **unique.**

PROOF: The necessity of the Kuhn–Tucker conditions has been established; let us consider the sufficiency when all the functions involved are concave. For fixed λ^*, the Lagrangian in (9.15) will be concave in x, since it is the sum of concave functions. Thus from (2.60) in Chapter 2, the concavity of the Lagrangian implies that

$$\sum_{i=1}^{n} L_i(x^*, \lambda^*)(x_i - x_i^*) + L(x^*, \lambda^*) \geq L(x, \lambda^*) \qquad \text{for all } x \in \Re_+^n. \quad (9.17)$$

Now writing out the left-hand term of the inequality, we have

$$\sum_{i=1}^{n} L_i(x^*, \lambda^*)(x_i - x_i^*) = \sum_{i=1}^{n} x_i L_i(x^*, \lambda^*) - \sum_{i=1}^{n} x_i^* L_i(x^*, \lambda^*).$$

Applying (9.16a) and (9.16b) from the Kuhn–Tucker conditions to this expression, we have

$$\sum_{i=1}^{n} L_i(x^*, \lambda^*)(x_i - x_i^*) = \sum_{i=1}^{n} x_i L_i(x^*, \lambda^*) \leq 0, \qquad (9.18)$$

since $x_i \geq 0$, $L_i(x^*, \lambda^*) \leq 0$, and $x_i^* L_i(x^*, \lambda^*) = 0$ for all $i = 1, 2, \ldots, n$. Combining (9.17) and (9.18), we have $L(x^*, \lambda^*) \geq L(x, \lambda^*)$ for all $x \in \Re_+^n$. Written out in full, this inequality is

$$f(x^*) + \sum_{j=1}^{m} \lambda_j^* g^j(x^*) \geq f(x) + \sum_{j=1}^{m} \lambda_j^* g^j(x) \qquad \text{for all } x \in \Re_+^n. \qquad (9.19)$$

Now from (9.16d) the second term on the left-hand side of (9.19) is zero, while the second term on the right-hand side is nonnegative, by the nonnegativity of the constraint functions and (9.16e). Thus (9.19) implies that

$$f(x^*) \geq f(x) \qquad \text{for all } x \in \Re_+^n,$$

proving that x^* maximizes f on $\Re_+^n$. If f were strictly concave, the inequality would be strict and x^* would be the unique global maximizer of f on $\Re_+^n$.

As in Theorem 9.1, the result in Theorem 9.2 can be extended to **minimization** problems by changing the Kuhn–Tucker conditions appropriately and changing concave to **convex**.

The last topic to be discussed before we turn to economic applications of nonlinear programming is the so-called saddle-point characterization of the Kuhn–Tucker conditions. Notice that conditions (9.16a) and (9.16b) seem to suggest that the Lagrangian function is maximized with respect to the variables in vector x, while conditions (9.16c) and (9.16d) seems to suggest that the Lagrangian function is minimized with respect to the variables in vector λ. If these suggestions are correct, then the Lagrangian will satisfy the following condition:

$$L(x, \lambda^*) \leq L(x^*, \lambda^*) \leq L(x^*, \lambda) \qquad \text{for all } x \in \Re_+^n \qquad \text{and} \qquad \lambda \in \Re_+^m.$$
$$(9.20)$$

The condition in (9.20) says that (x^*, λ^*) is a **saddle point** of the Lagrangian; the optimal value of the Lagrangian can be written as

$$L(x^*, \lambda^*) = \max_{x \geq 0}[\min_{\lambda \geq 0} L(x, \lambda)]. \qquad (9.21)$$

Thus on the basis of the Kuhn–Tucker conditions, one might conjecture that solving (9.14) and finding a saddle point for the Lagrangian are equivalent problems. The following Kuhn–Tucker equivalency theorem proves such a conjecture to be correct.

THEOREM 9.3: When the objective function and all constraint functions are concave, the existence of an $\lambda^* \in \Re_+^m$ that satisfies the **saddle-point** condition (9.20) is necessary and sufficient for $x^* \in \Re_+^n$ to solve (9.14).

PROOF: The reader is directed to a more mathematically detailed source for the proof of the necessity part of the theorem.[3] For sufficiency, consider (9.20). From the center and right-hand terms of (9.20), we have

$$\sum_{j=1}^{m} (\lambda_j - \lambda_j^*) g^j(x^*) \geq 0 \qquad \text{for all } \lambda \in \Re_+^m. \qquad (9.22)$$

Suppose there exists an index j such that $g^j(x^*) < 0$; then since (9.22) must hold for all λ, the value of λ_j could be chosen sufficiently large that the inequality in (9.22) is violated. Thus $g^j(x^*) \geq 0$ for all j, and x^* satisfies the constraints in (9.14). Also since (9.22) holds for all $\lambda \in \Re_+^m$, it must hold for $\lambda = 0$, which implies that $\sum_j \lambda_j^* g^j(x^*) \leq 0$. But since $\lambda_j^* \geq 0$ and $g^j(x^*) \geq 0$ for all j, this latter condition could only be satisfied by $\sum_j \lambda_j^* g^j(x^*) = 0$. Applying this result to the center and left-hand terms of (9.20), we have

$$f(x^*) \geq f(x) + \sum_{j=1}^m \lambda_j^* g^j(x). \tag{9.23}$$

Now for problem (9.14), we have $g^j(x) \geq 0$, and thus $\sum_j \lambda_j^* g^j(x) \geq 0$ since $\lambda^* \geq 0$. Combining this with (9.23) implies that $f(x^*) \geq f(x)$ for all $x^* \in \Re_+^n$, which proves the sufficiency part of the theorem.

9.3 Economic Examples of Kuhn–Tucker Theory

Consumer Choice with Inequality Constraints

Our first economic application of Kuhn–Tucker theory involves a very familiar model: the two-good consumer choice problem. Since this problem has been thoroughly examined in earlier chapters, it is a useful vehicle for comparing the Kuhn–Tucker results with those from the standard Lagrangian technique.

Consider the consumer who maximizes the utility function $U(x_1, x_2)$ by the choice of the two goods x_1 and x_2. Assume that the marginal utility of both goods is positive ($U_i > 0$), that the consumer has fixed positive money income M, and that both prices p_1 and p_2 are strictly positive. When we explicitly consider inequality constraints, this consumer choice problem can be written

$$\text{Max } U(x_1, x_2)$$
$$\text{Subject to: } M \geq p_1 x_1 + p_2 x_2, \tag{9.24}$$
$$x_1 \geq 0 \quad \text{and} \quad x_2 \geq 0.$$

The Lagrangian for the problem is given by

$$L(x_1, x_2, \lambda) = U(x_1, x_2) + \lambda(M - p_1 x_1 - p_2 x_2). \tag{9.25}$$

Applying (9.16) to this version of the consumer choice problem gives us the following Kuhn–Tucker conditions:

$$L_1(x^*, \lambda^*) = U_1(x_1^*, x_2^*) - p_1 \lambda^* \leq 0, \tag{9.26a}$$

$$x_1^* L_1(x^*, \lambda^*) = x_1^*[U_1(x_1^*, x_2^*) - p_1 \lambda^*] = 0, \tag{9.26b}$$

$$L_2(x^*, \lambda^*) = U_2(x_1^*, x_2^*) - p_2 \lambda^* \leq 0, \tag{9.26c}$$

$$x_2^* L_2(x^*, \lambda^*) = x_2^*[U_2(x_1^*, x_2^*) - p_2 \lambda^*] = 0, \tag{9.26d}$$

$$L_\lambda(x^*, \lambda^*) = M - p_1 x_1^* - p_2 x_2^* \geq 0, \tag{9.26e}$$

$$\lambda^* L_\lambda(x^*, \lambda^*) = \lambda^*(M - p_1 x_1^* - p_2 x_2^*) = 0, \tag{9.26f}$$

$$\lambda^* \geq 0 \quad \text{and} \quad x^* = (x_1^*, x_2^*) \geq 0. \tag{9.26g}$$

First, consider the case of $x_1^* > 0$ and $x_2^* > 0$. From (9.26b) and (9.26d) we have that $x_1^* > 0$ and $x_2^* > 0$ imply that the inequalities in (9.26a) and (9.26c) are actually equalities. Since $U_1 > 0$, $U_2 > 0$, $p_1 > 0$, and $p_2 > 0$, equalities in (9.26a) and (9.26c) imply that $\lambda^* > 0$, which means that (9.26e) is also an equality because of (9.26f). Thus when $x_1^* > 0$ and $x_2^* > 0$, the Kuhn–Tucker conditions in (9.26) reduce to the standard first-order conditions for the two-good consumer choice problem

$$U_1(x_1^*, x_2^*) - p_1 \lambda^* = 0,$$
$$U_2(x_1^*, x_2^*) - p_2 \lambda^* = 0, \tag{9.27}$$
$$M - p_1 x_1^* - p_2 x_2^* = 0.$$

Second, it is not possible for both $x_1^* = 0$ and $x_2^* = 0$ to be optimal values. From (9.26f) we have that $x_1^* = 0$ and $x_2^* = 0$ imply that $\lambda^* M = 0$, but since M is strictly positive, this would imply that $\lambda^* = 0$. Substituting $\lambda^* = 0$ into either (9.26a) or (9.26c) generates a contradiction, since $U_1 > 0$ and $U_2 > 0$.

Finally, either $x_1^* > 0$ and $x_2^* = 0$, or $x_1^* = 0$ and $x_2^* > 0$ are possible, and their interpretations are similar. We examine the case of $x_1^* > 0$ and $x_2^* = 0$, leaving the other case to the reader. From (9.26b), $x_1^* > 0$ implies that $U_1(x_1^*, x_2^*) = p_1 \lambda^*$. Since $U_1 > 0$ and $p_1 > 0$, we have that $\lambda^* > 0$, and the budget constraint must hold with equality from (9.26f). Thus when $x_1^* > 0$ and $x_2^* = 0$, the optimum consumption bundle occurs on the boundary of the budget constraint. This optimum is shown diagrammatically in Figure 9.2. From (9.26d) the condition $x_2^* = 0$ does not allow us to say anything about the inequality in

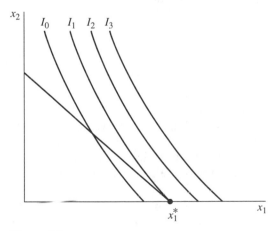

Figure 9.2

(9.26c); so the Kuhn–Tucker conditions for the $x_1^* > 0$ and $x_2^* = 0$ case reduce to the following

$$U_1(x_1^*, x_2^*) - p_1\lambda^* = 0, \tag{9.28a}$$

$$U_2(x_1^*, x_2^*) - p_2\lambda^* \leq 0, \tag{9.28b}$$

$$M - p_1 x_1^* - p_2 x_2^* = 0. \tag{9.28c}$$

To interpret these conditions, first rearrange (9.28a) and (9.28b) as

$$\lambda^* = \frac{U_1}{p_1} \geq \frac{U_2}{p_2}. \tag{9.29}$$

Eliminating λ^* from (9.29) and rearranging again, we have

$$\frac{U_1}{U_1} \geq \frac{p_1}{p_2}. \tag{9.30}$$

The right-hand side of (9.30) is the absolute value of the slope of the budget line, and the left-hand side of (9.30) is the *MRS* between x_1 and x_2. Thus the inequality in (9.30) says that at an optimal bundle where $x_1^* > 0$ and $x_2^* = 0$, the *MRS* is greater than or equal to the price ratio. This property can be seen in Figure 9.2.

Thus the two-good consumer choice problem clearly demonstrates that the Kuhn–Tucker conditions are much more general than the first-order conditions discussed in earlier chapters. The Kuhn–Tucker conditions subsume the standard Lagrangian conditions as a special case, where the optimal values are strictly positive, and yet allow for the possibility of boundary optima. Now while this generality is appreciated, it does not come without cost. The greatest cost is that the derivative comparative statics results obtained so often in the preceding chapters will generally be lost with the Kuhn–Tucker conditions. The differentiation of first-order conditions is valid only when first-order conditions can be specified as identities; such differentiation is not valid across the Kuhn–Tucker inequalities. We leave it to the reader's own judgment to decide how to weigh this loss against the gain of increased generality.

Monopoly Behavior under Rate-of-Return Regulation

Our second economic application of the Kuhn–Tucker theory concerns the so-called **A-J effect** in the theory of regulated monopoly.[4] The problem arises because fair-rate-of-return pricing is often used to regulate natural monopolies. Under the fair-rate-of-return pricing strategy, the regulatory agency limits the profit of the regulated monopoly to a certain fixed proportion of the capital employed. This additional constraint causes the regulated firm to distort its use of inputs in a way that has come to be called the A-J effect. To examine this effect, consider the following model of a regulated monopoly.

The firm's (inverse) demand function is given by $p = p(y)$, where p is the price of output y. The firm uses two inputs, labor L and capital K, to produce output by means of the production function $y = f(L, K)$ and thus total revenue R

can be written as a function of the two inputs L and K:

$$R = R(L, K) = R(f(L, K)) = p[f(L, K)] f(L, K). \tag{9.31}$$

We assume that this revenue function has positive first derivatives and is strictly concave, so $R_L > 0$, $R_K > 0$, $R_{LL} < 0$, $R_{KK} < 0$, and $R_{LL}R_{KK} - R_{LK}^2 > 0$ for all L and K. These assumptions are consistent with the standard restrictions on a monopolist's marginal revenue function and the production function $y = f(L, K)$. If the price of labor is w and the price of capital is v, then the firm's profit π is given by

$$\pi(L, K) = R(L, K) - wL - vK. \tag{9.32}$$

The regulatory constraint imposed on the firm limits its rate of return on capital to some maximum rate s. Since this permitted rate of return is at least as large as the firm's cost of capital v, the regulated firm faces the following two constraints:

$$R(L, K) - wL \leq sK, \tag{9.33a}$$

$$s - v \geq 0. \tag{9.33b}$$

Thus under rate-of-return regulation, the monopolist solves the following nonlinear programming problem:

$$\begin{aligned}
&\underset{L,K}{\text{Max }} \pi(L, K) = R(L, K) - wL - vK \\
&\text{Subject to: } R(L, K) - wL \leq sK, \\
&\qquad\quad L \geq 0, \qquad K \geq 0.
\end{aligned} \tag{9.34}$$

The inequality (9.33b) is not written as a second constraint in (9.34), since it does not include any of the choice variables.

The Lagrangian function for the regulated monopoly is then

$$\mathcal{L}(L, K, \lambda) = R(L, K) - wL - vK + \lambda[sK + wL - R(L, K)], \tag{9.35}$$

where $\mathcal{L}$ has been used for the Lagrangian function to avoid confusion with labor L.

Writing out the Kuhn–Tucker conditions in full, we have at the optimal choice (L^*, K^*, λ^*),

$$\begin{aligned}
\mathcal{L}_L &= R_L - w + \lambda^* w - \lambda^* R_L \leq 0, \\
L^* \mathcal{L}_L &= L^*(R_L - w + \lambda^* w - \lambda^* R_L) = 0, \\
\mathcal{L}_K &= R_K - v + \lambda^* s - \lambda^* R_K \leq 0, \\
K^* \mathcal{L}_K &= K^*(R_K - v + \lambda^* s - \lambda^* R_K) = 0, \\
\mathcal{L}_\lambda &= sK^* + wL^* - R(L^*, K^*) \geq 0, \\
\lambda^* \mathcal{L}_\lambda &= \lambda^*[sK^* + wL^* - R(L^*, K^*)] = 0, \\
\lambda^* &\geq 0, \qquad L^* \geq 0, \qquad K^* \geq 0.
\end{aligned} \tag{9.36}$$

While the Kuhn–Tucker conditions in (9.36) may appear to be quite forbidding, the economic structure of the problem allows us to simplify some of the expressions immediately. For instance, restricting ourselves to strictly positive values of both choice variables ($L^* > 0$ and $K^* > 0$) reduces the system by two expressions. Also we impose the assumption (standard in the regulatory literature) that the permitted rate of return s is strictly greater than the price of capital: thus $s > v$. After the elimination of these expressions and some algebraic rearrangement, system (9.36) reduces to

$$(1 - \lambda^*)(R_L - w) = 0, \tag{9.37a}$$

$$(1 - \lambda^*)(R_K - v) + \lambda^*(s - v) = 0, \tag{9.37b}$$

$$sK^* + wL^* - R(L^*, K^*) \geq 0, \tag{9.37c}$$

$$\lambda^* [sK^* + wL^* - R(L^*, K^*)] = 0, \tag{9.37d}$$

$$\lambda^* \geq 0, \qquad s - v > 0, \qquad L^* > 0, \qquad K^* > 0. \tag{9.37e}$$

Now if $\lambda^* = 1$, then equation (9.37b) would imply that $s - v = 0$, which contradicts the assumption that $s > v$. Thus, it must be the case that $\lambda^* \neq 1$. But if $\lambda^* \neq 1$, then $R_L = w$ from (9.37a) and $R_K = v - \lambda^*(s - v)/(1 - \lambda^*)$ from (9.37b). Combining these two expressions, we have

$$\frac{R_K}{R_L} = \frac{v}{w} - \frac{\lambda^*(s - v)}{(1 - \lambda^*)w}. \tag{9.38}$$

The expression in (9.38) will play a fundamental role in our discussion of the A-J effect.

If rate-of-return regulation causes a firm to alter its behavior from unregulated profit maximization, the A-J effect will be observed; that is, the firm will produce at a **higher capital/labor ratio** than the cost-minimizing value. To see how (9.38) demonstrates this effect, first consider the case of $\lambda^* = 0$. Notice that the condition $\lambda^* = 0$ reduces the Lagrangian in (9.36) to the unregulated profit maximization problem. Thus, if regulation is to alter the behavior of the firm, then it must be that $\lambda^* \neq 0$. Now from (9.38), $\lambda^* \neq 0$ implies that the far right-hand term is not equal to zero, and thus that $R_K/R_L \neq v/w$. This inequality implies that

$$\frac{f_K}{f_L} \neq \frac{v}{w}. \tag{9.39}$$

That is, the ratio of the marginal products is not equal to the ratio of the input prices. The left-hand side of (9.39) follows from the definition of the revenue function in (9.31). Differentiating (9.31) with respect to L and K gives $R_L = (p + fp')f_L$ and $R_K = (p + fp')f_K$, so $R_K/R_L = f_K/f_L$. Now **if** the firm were producing its current (regulated) output in a cost-minimizing way, it would be hiring capital and labor so that $f_K/f_L = v/w$. If this is not obvious, return to

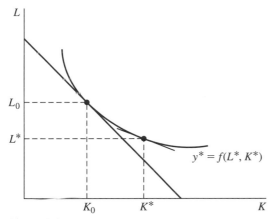

Figure 9.3

the first-order conditions for minimizing the cost of producing a fixed output from (8.13) in Chapter 8.

So far we have demonstrated that the monopoly firm subjected to fair-rate-of-return regulation will fail to produce in a cost-minimizing way. While this is an important result, it is not quite the A-J effect. The A-J effect says that (1) the regulated monopoly will have a capital/labor ratio different from the cost-minimizing capital/labor ratio, and (2) the bias will be in one particular direction—toward higher capital intensity.

To demonstrate this stronger result, we first suppose that the A-J effect holds. If a regulated firm does produce at a capital/labor ratio higher than the cost-minimizing capital/labor ratio, then the *MRTS* at the regulated solution L^* and K^* must be less than v/w. To see why, look at Figure 9.3. The cost-minimizing levels of labor and capital are given by L_0 and K_0, respectively, in Figure 9.3 where the isocost line is tangent to the y^* isoquant. At (K_0, L_0), the slope of the isocost line v/w is equal to the *MRTS*. Now if the regulated monopolist employs a higher capital/labor ratio than K_0/L_0, then the optimal choice (K^*, L^*) must be farther down the y^* isoquant, as shown in Figure 9.3. This implies that $MRTS = f_K(L^*, K^*)/f_L(L^*, K^*) < v/w$.

Now return to expression (9.38). The left-hand side is the *MRTS* at (L^*, K^*), since $R_K/R_L = f_K/f_L = MRTS$. Thus from the argument in the preceding paragraph, the A-J effect will occur if the far right-hand term in (9.38) $[\lambda^*(s - v)/(1 - \lambda^*)w]$ is **positive.** But we already know that $\lambda^* > 0, w > 0$, and $s - v > 0$; so the issue is simply that the A-J effect will hold if $\lambda^* < 1$. In the preceding analysis, we showed that $\lambda^* \neq 0$ and $\lambda^* \neq 1$, but (thus far) we have not demonstrated that $\lambda^* < 1$. To do so requires returning to the technique of Chapter 8, that is, using second-order conditions to sign the term in question. We can return to the technique of an earlier chapter at this point because we have systematically eliminated the inequalities from the problem's first-order (Kuhn–Tucker) conditions.

Since we now know that $\lambda^* \neq 0$, the Kuhn–Tucker conditions in (9.37) can be simplified still further to:

$$(1 - \lambda^*)(R_L - w) = 0,$$
$$(1 - \lambda^*)R_K - v + \lambda^* s = 0,$$
$$sK^* + wL^* - R(L^*, K^*) = 0,$$
$$L^* > 0, \qquad K^* > 0, \qquad \lambda^* > 0.$$

(9.40)

But the equations in (9.40) are simply the first-order conditions for the standard Lagrangian problem

$$\underset{L,K}{\text{Max}} \; \pi(L, K) = R(L, K) - wL - vK$$

Subject to: $R(L, K) - wL = sK,$

(9.41)

without inequality constraints.

The second-order conditions for the problem (9.41) require the bordered Hessian

$$\bar{H} = \begin{bmatrix} (1 - \lambda^*)R_{LL} & (1 - \lambda^*)R_{LK} & 0 \\ (1 - \lambda^*)R_{KL} & (1 - \lambda^*)R_{KK} & s - R_K \\ 0 & s - R_K & 0 \end{bmatrix}$$

(9.42)

to have a positive determinant. Expanding $|\bar{H}|$ by the term in the second row and third column, we have

$$|\bar{H}| = -(s - R_K)^2 (1 - \lambda^*)R_{LL}.$$

For this expression to be positive, as the second-order conditions require, we need

$$(1 - \lambda^*)R_{LL} < 0.$$

(9.43)

Recall that when the revenue function $R(L, K)$ was introduced, we assumed that it was strictly concave, which requires $R_{LL} < 0$. Thus from (9.43) we have that,

$$\lambda^* < 1,$$

and thus the A-J effect has been demonstrated. Let us briefly review the result.

What has been demonstrated is that if rate-of-return regulation alters the profit-maximizing behavior of the monopolist (and it certainly seems unlikely that such regulation would be imposed otherwise), then the regulation causes the firm to use more capital and less labor than it would have used if its chosen output were being produced in a cost-minimizing way. This results in inefficiency and has important policy implications for the regulation of natural monopolies.

9.4 Linear Programming

Introduction

Suppose the general n-variable, m-constraint problem in (9.14) is such that the objective function $f(x)$ as well as the constraint functions $g^1(x), g^2(x), \ldots, g^m(x)$

are all **linear.** In this case the problem is called a **linear programming problem.**
The general form of the linear programming problem with n variables and m
constraints is

$$\text{Max}_{x} \ f(x) = \sum_{i=1}^{n} c_i x_i$$

$$\text{Subject to: } \sum_{i=1}^{n} a_{1i} x_i \leq b_1,$$

$$\sum_{i=1}^{n} a_{2i} x_i \leq b_2, \tag{9.44}$$

$$\vdots$$

$$\sum_{i=1}^{n} a_{mi} x_i \leq b_m,$$

$$x_i \geq 0 \qquad \text{for all } i = 1, 2, \ldots, n,$$

where all c_i, b_j, and a_{ji} are constants. If we let A be the $m \times n$ matrix with repre-
sentative term $[a_{ji}]$, $c^T = (c_1, c_2, \ldots, c_n)$, $x^T = (x_1, x_2, \ldots, x_n)$, and $b^T = (b_1, b_2, \ldots, b_m)$, we can write the general linear programming problem in (9.44)
in the more convenient matrix form

$$\text{Max}_{x} \ f(x) = c^T x$$

$$\text{Subject to: } Ax \leq b, \tag{9.45}$$

$$x \geq 0.$$

Eventually we will examine the solution of the general linear programming problem (9.45), but first let us orient the discussion with a two-dimensional economic
example. An economy produces only two goods x and y, by means of three
primary inputs: land T, labor L, and capital K. The economy has a fixed, strictly
positive, supply of the three inputs $(\bar{T}, \bar{L}, \bar{K})$ and wants to maximize the value
of its gross domestic product GDP given the fixed resources. When the price
of good x is $p_x > 0$ and the price of good y is $p_y > 0$, the economy has
$GDP = p_x x + p_y y$. Thus if the production coefficient $a_{ji} > 0$ represents the
amount of primary resource $j = T, L, K$ required to produce 1 unit of output
$i = 1, 2$ (so $a_{Lx} = $ the amount of L required for 1 unit of x, and so on), then the
problem for the economy is

$$\text{Max}_{(x,y)} \ GDP = p_x x + p_y y$$

$$\text{Subject to: } a_{Tx} x + a_{Ty} y \leq \bar{T},$$

$$a_{Lx} x + a_{Ly} y \leq \bar{L}, \tag{9.46}$$

$$a_{Kx} x + a_{Ky} y \leq \bar{K},$$

$$x \geq 0, \qquad y \geq 0.$$

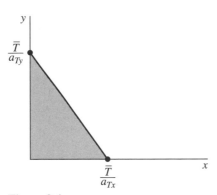

Figure 9.4

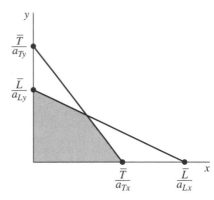

Figure 9.5

Any combination of x and y that satisfies all three resource constraints in (9.46) is called a **feasible output,** and the set of all feasible outputs is called the **feasible set** for the economy. This feasible set corresponds to the production possibilities set discussed in elementary economics, since it shows all possible output combinations available to the economy given its fixed resources. For example, if land were the only resource constraint the economy faced, then the feasible outputs would be given by the intersection of $a_{Tx}x + a_{Ty}y \leq \bar{T}$, $x \geq 0$, and $y \geq 0$. This feasible set is depicted in Figure 9.4. But if land and labor were the only two resource constraints the economy faced, then the feasible set might look like Figure 9.5. Of course, the shape of Figure 9.5 is only one possibility, since the relative slopes or intercept values have not been specified in (9.46).

So that we may actually draw the feasible set and find the solution diagrammatically, let us consider a particular numerical example of problem (9.46). The parameters are given by

$$\begin{bmatrix} a_{Tx} & a_{Ty} \\ a_{Lx} & a_{Ly} \\ a_{Kx} & a_{Ky} \end{bmatrix} = \begin{bmatrix} 1 & 2 \\ \frac{3}{2} & 2 \\ 2 & 1 \end{bmatrix} \qquad \begin{aligned} (p_x, p_y) &= (1, 1), \\ (\bar{T}, \bar{L}, \bar{K}) &= (100, 120, 140). \end{aligned}$$

Given these parameters, the *GDP* maximization problem (9.46) can be written:

$$\underset{(x,y)}{\text{Max}}\ GDP = x + y$$

Subject to: $x + 2y \leq 100,$

$$\frac{3x}{2} + 2y \leq 120, \qquad (9.47)$$

$$2x + y \leq 140,$$

$$x \geq 0, \qquad y \geq 0.$$

Finding the feasible set for the problem (9.47) is merely a matter of graphing the relevant inequalities. This feasible set is depicted in Figure 9.6, where T is the land constraint, L is the labor constraint, and K is the capital constraint. The

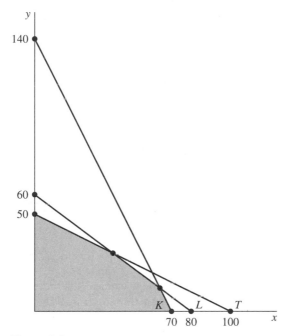

Figure 9.6

objective function $GDP = x + y$ is equally easy to graph. Since the prices of the two outputs are $p_x = 1$ and $p_y = 1$, the GDP line (or iso-GDP line) has slope = -1; higher levels of GDP are simply associated with higher x and y intercepts for $y = -x + GDP$.

Combining this linear objective function with the feasible set from Figure 9.6 allows us to diagrammatically determine the solution to the problem (9.47). By shifting $y = -x + GDP$ out as far as possible while still having both x and y within the feasible set, we arrive at the solution $x^* = 64$ and $y^* = 12$. This solution is shown in Figure 9.7. Thus, given the three resource constraints in (9.47) and unit output prices, the highest level of GDP that the economy can achieve is $GDP^* = 64 + 12 = 76$. Going back to Figure 9.6, we can see that this optimal output combination is actually within, rather than on, the boundary of the land constraint. Thus while the economy faces three resource constraints, only two are actually binding at the optimal combination $(x^*, y^*) = (64, 12)$.

This simple numerical example has given us an introduction to linear programming in economic theory and has shown how solutions of two-variable problems can be found diagrammatically. If a particular numerical problem involves more than two variables or cannot be reduced to only two variables, then such diagrammatic solutions are not available and other computational techniques must be used. The most popular of these techniques (and the one used in most computer software packages for solving linear programming problems) is the **simplex method.** Since it is primarily a computational algorithm for solving large-dimension numerical problems, we refer the reader to more computationally

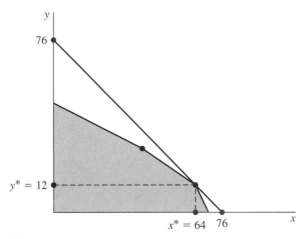

Figure 9.7

oriented sources for a discussion of the simplex method and its kindred techniques.[5] Rather than considering more complex numerical problems—a job best left to the appropriate software—we return to the general characterization of the linear programming problems in (9.44) and (9.45) and examine some of its important properties.

The Dual Problem

Now we return to the matrix form of the general n-variable, m-constraint linear programming problem from (9.45):

$$\underset{x}{\text{Max }} f(x) = c^T x$$
$$\text{Subject to: } Ax \le b,$$
$$x \ge 0.$$

Since this linear programming problem is simply a special case of the general nonlinear programming problem from (9.14), the Kuhn–Tucker conditions (9.16) must hold at the problem's solution. Actually, since linear functions are concave (although not strictly concave), Theorem 9.2 holds and the Kuhn–Tucker conditions are both necessary and sufficient for a solution to (9.45). The Lagrangian for problem (9.45) is:

$$L(x, \lambda) = \sum_{i=1}^{n} c_i x_i + \sum_{j=1}^{m} \lambda_j \left(b_j - \sum_{i=1}^{n} a_{ji} x_i \right). \tag{9.48}$$

Or, writing this Lagrangian in more convenient matrix form, we have

$$L(x, \lambda) = c^T x + \lambda^T (b - Ax),$$

where $\lambda^T = (\lambda_1, \lambda_2, \ldots, \lambda_m)$ is the m-dimensional row vector of Lagrange multipliers.

Now applying the Kuhn–Tucker conditions (9.16) to this problem, we know that if $x^* \in \Re_+^n$ is a solution to (9.45), then there exists an $\lambda^* \in \Re_+^m$ such that

$$c_i - \sum_{j=1}^{m} \lambda_j^* a_{ji} \leq 0 \qquad \text{for all } i = 1, 2, \ldots, n,$$

$$\sum_{i=1}^{n} \left(c_i - \sum_{j=1}^{m} \lambda_j^* a_{ji} \right) x_i^* = 0,$$

$$b_j - \sum_{i=1}^{n} a_{ji} x_i^* \geq 0 \qquad \text{for all } j = 1, 2, \ldots, m,$$

$$\sum_{j=1}^{m} \lambda_j^* \left(b_j - \sum_{i=1}^{n} a_{ji} x_i^* \right) = 0,$$

$$\lambda_j^* \geq 0 \qquad \text{for all } j = 1, 2, \ldots, m,$$
$$x_i^* \geq 0 \qquad \text{for all } i = 1, 2, \ldots, n.$$

Rewriting these Kuhn–Tucker conditions in matrix form yields

$$c^T - (\lambda^*)^T A \leq 0, \tag{9.49a}$$

$$[c^T - (\lambda^*)^T A] x^* = 0, \tag{9.49b}$$

$$b - A x^* \geq 0, \tag{9.49c}$$

$$(\lambda^*)^T (b - A x^*) = 0, \tag{9.49d}$$

$$\lambda^* \geq 0, \qquad x^* \geq 0, \tag{9.49e}$$

where $(\lambda^*)^T = (\lambda_1^*, \lambda_2^*, \ldots, \lambda_m^*)$ and $(x^*)^T = (x_1^*, x_2^*, \ldots, x_n^*)$. We will return to these Kuhn–Tucker conditions, but first we introduce the notion of **duality** in linear programming.

Associated with any particular linear programming problem involving maximization there is a related linear programming problem involving minimization (and vice versa). It is standard to call the original problem (in our case the maximization problem) the **primal problem** and its associated problem (in our case the minimization problem) the **dual problem.** If the maximization problem in (9.45) is the primal problem, then its associated dual problem is

$$\underset{\lambda}{\text{Max }} h(\lambda) = \lambda^T b$$
$$\text{Subject to: } \lambda^T A \geq c^T, \tag{9.50}$$
$$\lambda^T \geq 0,$$

where b, c, and A are the same as in (9.45) and $\lambda^T = (\lambda_1, \lambda_2, \ldots, \lambda_m)$ is the m-dimensional row vector of choice variables for the dual minimization problem. It is not a coincidence that we have chosen the symbol λ for these choice variables; but temporarily disregard any other use of this symbol and simply consider λ to be a vector of new choice variables for the minimization problem (9.50).

The dual problem in (9.50) was formed from the primal problem (9.45) by (1) making the constants in the constraints of (9.45) the constants in the objective function of (9.50), (2) making the constants in the objective function of (9.45) the constants in the constraints of (9.50), (3) reversing the inequality in the linear constraints, and (4) changing the maximization to a minimization. The primal problem has n choice variables given by x, while the dual problem has m choice variables given by λ; but both problems have the same number $(n + m)$ of inequality constraints. Given one of these problems, it is always possible to form the other; and in this sense neither problem can really be considered "primal." The two problems also have the property that the dual of the dual is always the primal.

We present two theorems relating the solution of the primal problem (9.45) to the solution of its dual (9.50). The first, Theorem 9.4, is probably the single most important result in the theory of linear programming. It is usually called the **duality theorem** of linear programming. The second, Theorem 9.5, is usually called the **complementary-slackness theorem** of linear programming. Both have important economic applications.

THEOREM 9.4:   If one of the problems, the primal (9.45) or the dual (9.50) has a solution, then both problems have solutions, and the **optimal value of the objective function is the same for both.**

PROOF: Suppose the primal problem (9.45) has a solution x^*. Then there exists a $\lambda^* \in \Re_+^m$ such that the Kuhn–Tucker conditions (9.49) hold. Now from (9.49a) we have $(\lambda^*)^T A \geq c^T$, and from (9.49e) we have $\lambda^* \geq 0$; thus the vector λ^*, which exists as a result of the primal problem having a solution, is feasible for (satisfies the constraints of) the dual problem (9.50). From the equality $c^T x^* = (\lambda^*)^T A x^*$ in (9.49b) and the equality $(\lambda^*)^T b = (\lambda^*)^T A x^*$ in (9.49d), we know that $f(x^*) = c^T x^* = (\lambda^*)^T b = h(\lambda^*)$. To prove the theorem, we need only show that $h(\lambda^*) \leq h(\lambda)$ for any other feasible vector λ. To this end, consider any $x \geq 0$ feasible for the primal and any $\lambda \geq 0$ feasible for the dual. This feasibility implies that $Ax \leq b$ and $\lambda^T A \geq c^T$. Premultiplying the first inequality by λ^T and postmultiplying the second by x, we have $h(\lambda) = \lambda^T b \geq c^T x = f(x)$ for any feasible x and λ. In particular, for x^* we have $h(\lambda) \geq f(x^*)$; but this implies that $h(\lambda) \geq h(\lambda^*)$ for any feasible λ. Since a similar argument can be constructed starting from the existence of a solution to the dual problem, the theorem is proved.

THEOREM 9.5:   If one of the problems, the primal (9.45) or the dual (9.50), has a solution, then the following **complementary-slackness** conditions hold:

$$[c^T - (\lambda^*)^T A]x^* = 0 \qquad \text{and} \qquad (\lambda^*)^T (b - Ax^*) = 0.$$

PROOF: The theorem follows immediately from the Kuhn–Tucker conditions (9.49).

BOX 9.2
The Diet Problem

The diet problem is one of the oldest (perhaps the oldest) economic problems solved by linear programming. The diet problem is the problem of finding the least expensive combination of foods (the optimal diet) that satisfies a set of minimum nutritional requirements. It is a problem that is probably more suited to determining livestock "diets" than human "diets," but an important early application of linear programming in any case. The problem was first solved by Stigler (1945) without the aid of linear programming theory; the best discussion of the diet problem using linear programming is DOSSO (1958).

Suppose there are n different types of food available, and let x_j for $j = 1, 2, \ldots, n$ represent the quantity of each of these foods in the diet (in common units, say, ounces per day). Let there be m different nutritional requirements (calories, vitamin A, etc.), and let $a_{ij} \geq 0$ for $i = 1, 2, \ldots, m$ and $j = 1, 2, \ldots, n$ represent the amount of nutrient i supplied by 1 unit of food j (normally $n > m$). If the minimum amount of nutrient i is given by c_i, then the nutritional constraint associated with nutrient i is simply

$$\sum_{j=1}^{n} a_{ij} x_j \geq c_i \qquad \text{for all } i = 1, 2, \ldots, m. \tag{a}$$

When prices of each food is given by p_j, the total cost of the diet is

$$\sum_{j=1}^{n} p_j x_j, \tag{b}$$

and the "diet problem" is to **minimize** (b) subject to the nutritional constraints in (a). In vector notation with $p^T = (p_1, p_2, \ldots, p_n)$, $x^T = (x_1, x_2, \ldots, x_n)$, $c^T = (c_1, c_2, \ldots, c_m)$, and A is the $m \times n$ matrix with representative element a_{ij}, the diet problem can be written

$$\text{Min}_{\{x\}} \, p^T x$$

$$\text{Subject to: } Ax \geq c,$$

$$x \geq 0.$$

In Stigler's original characterization of this problem, the diet comprised 80 different foods ($n = 80$) and there were nine basic dietary requirements ($m = 9$), this latter number being all that the U.S. government listed as minimum daily requirements in 1944. Solving this problem, Stigler found that the optimal diet cost less than \$0.17 per day, surprisingly little, even at 1944 prices.

Since the primal for the diet problem is a minimization, we can immediately write the dual of the diet problem as

$$\text{Max } \lambda^T c$$
$$_{\{\lambda\}}$$
$$\text{Subject to: } \lambda^T A \leq p^T,$$
$$\lambda^T \geq 0.$$

where $\lambda^T = (\lambda_1, \lambda_2, \ldots, \lambda_m)$ is the m-dimensional vector of dual variables. These dual variables should be interpreted as "shadow prices" or imputed values of the various nutrients. The dual problem can then be interpreted as maximizing the imputed value of an adequate diet subject to the constraint that the actual price of each food be at least as great as the imputed value of the nutrients it contains.

Sources

Dorfman, R., P. A. Samuelson, and R. M. Solow. 1958. *Linear programming and economic analysis.* New York: McGraw-Hill.

Stigler, G. J. 1945. The cost of subsistence. *Journal of Farm Economics* 27: 303–14.

The complementary-slackness conditions in Theorem 9.5 are easier to interpret and apply when they are written out in full. The condition $[c^T - (\lambda*)^T A]x* = 0$ says:

$$c_i - \sum_{j=1}^{m} \lambda_j^* a_{ji} < 0 \qquad \text{for some } i = 1, 2, \ldots, n \Rightarrow x_i^* = 0 \qquad \text{for that } i$$

and (9.51)

$$x_i^* > 0 \qquad \text{for some } i = 1, 2, \ldots, n \Rightarrow c_i - \sum_{j=1}^{m} \lambda_j^* a_{ji} = 0 \qquad \text{for that } i.$$

Moreover, the condition $(\lambda*)^T (b - Ax*) = 0$ says

$$b_j - \sum_{i=1}^{n} a_{ji} x_i^* > 0 \qquad \text{for some } j = 1, 2, \ldots, m \Rightarrow \lambda_j^* = 0 \qquad \text{for that } j$$

and (9.52)

$$\lambda_j^* > 0 \qquad \text{for some } j = 1, 2, \ldots, m \Rightarrow b_j - \sum_{i=1}^{n} a_{ji} x_i^* = 0 \qquad \text{for that } j.$$

To interpret these complementary-slackness conditions verbally, Theorem 9.5 implies that (1) if a primal constraint is a strict inequality, then the corresponding dual variable is zero, and (2) if a primal variable is strictly positive, then the corresponding dual constraint holds with equality.

The Ricardian Model of International Trade

We use the Ricardian model of international trade to demonstrate the usefulness of the duality theorems from linear programming. Although the model initially appeared in nonmathematical form in Ricardo's *Principles* in 1817, it is a model that continues to be a cornerstone of international trade theory.

The model has two countries (1 and 2), two goods (x and y), and one factor input (labor). The amounts of the two goods produced in each country are denoted x_i and y_i for $i = 1, 2$. The amount of labor input required to produce one unit of good $j = x, y$ in country $i = 1, 2$ is given by the positive scalar a_{ji} (so a_{x1} is the amount of labor required to produce one unit of output x in country 1, etc.). Notice that the notation used for the labor coefficients differs from that used in the *GDP* maximization problem (9.46). This change is only to avoid the notational inconvenience of having subscripts on subscripts. The change should not create any difficulty, since the model has only one input (labor).

Given these fixed production coefficients, if the total supply of labor in countries 1 and 2 is given by $L_1 > 0$ and $L_2 > 0$, respectively, then the two countries will face the following labor constraints:

$$a_{x1}x_1 + a_{y1}y_1 \leq L_1,$$
$$a_{x2}x_2 + a_{y2}y_2 \leq L_2. \tag{9.53}$$

The objective function of each country is to maximize the value of the goods it produces (*GDP*), where

$$GDP_1 = p_x x_1 + p_y y_1,$$
$$GDP_2 = p_x x_2 + p_y y_2. \tag{9.54}$$

The prices of the two goods in (9.54) are strictly positive "world" prices, measured in a common unit of account. In a more sophisticated model, demand conditions could be used to determine these prices, but in the simple Ricardian model the two countries merely take these prices as given parameters.

Combining (9.53) and (9.54), we have the following linear programming problem for each country $i = 1, 2$:

$$\begin{align} \underset{(x_i, y_i)}{\text{Max}}\ GDP_i &= p_x x_i + p_y y_i \\ \text{Subject to: } a_{xi}x_i + a_{yi}y_i &\leq L_i, \\ x_i \geq 0, \qquad y_i &\geq 0. \end{align} \tag{9.55}$$

Since the problems in (9.55) are linear programming problems in standard form, we can immediately write down their duals. The dual linear programming problems associated with (9.55) are given by:

$$\begin{align} \underset{\lambda_i}{\text{Min}}\ NI_i &= \lambda_i L_i \\ \text{Subject to: } \lambda_i a_{xi} &\geq p_x, \\ \lambda_i a_{yi} &\geq p_y, \\ \lambda_i &\geq 0, \end{align} \tag{9.56}$$

where λ_i is the dual choice variable for each country $i = 1, 2$ and NI stands for national income.

Although these dual problems follow automatically from the structure of the primal problems in (9.55), let us give them a separate economic interpretation. We interpret the dual choice variable λ_i to be the price of labor (wage) in country i. Since labor is the only factor of production, this interpretation of λ_i makes the objective function $\lambda_i L$ the national income of country i (thus the motivation for our choice of NI). The constraints $\lambda_i a_{xi} \geq p_x$ and $\lambda_i a_{yi} \geq p_y$ restrict wage λ_i so that the (per unit) profit in each industry is nonpositive. Thus under the wage interpretation, the dual problem for each country is to minimize its factor cost (national income) subject to the constraint that no strictly positive profits occur in either industry when the goods are sold at world prices p_x and p_y. Now given this wage interpretation of the dual choice variables, let us apply the duality Theorems 9.4 and 9.5 to the primal and dual problems in (9.55) and (9.56).

Suppose x_1^*, x_2^*, y_1^*, and y_2^* are the solutions to the primal problems in (9.55). The duality theorem then tells us that the dual solutions λ_1^* and λ_2^* exist and that the **optimum values of the two objective functions are equal.** Since the objective function for the primal problem is *GDP*, and the objective function for the dual problem is *NI*, the duality theorem gives us the familiar result from introductory macroeconomic theory that **national product is equal to national income.**

Now consider Theorem 9.5. Applying the first set of complementary-slackness conditions from (9.55) to good x, we know that $p_x - \lambda_i^* a_{xi} < 0$ implies $x_i^* = 0$, and that $x_i^* > 0$ implies $p_x - \lambda_i^* a_{xi} = 0$ for $i = 1, 2$. Applying the same conditions to good y, we have that $p_y - \lambda_i^* a_{yi} < 0$ implies $y_i^* = 0$, while $y_i^* > 0$ implies $p_y - \lambda_i^* a_{yi} = 0$ for $i = 1, 2$. These conditions say that any good actually produced in either country is produced at zero profit.

The second set of complementary-slackness conditions from (9.56) says that if $L_i > a_{xi} x_i^* + a_{yi} y_i^*$ then $\lambda_i^* = 0$, and if $\lambda_i^* > 0$ then $L_i = a_{xi} x_i^* + a_{yi} y_i^*$ for $i = 1, 2$. These conditions can easily be interpreted in terms of the labor market in each country. Notice that L_i is the supply of labor in country i, while $a_{xi} x_i^* + a_{yi} y_i^*$ is the demand for labor in country i. Thus the first complementary-slackness condition says that if there is an excess supply of labor in a particular country, then the wage in that country will be zero ($\lambda_i^* = 0$). This is precisely what we would expect; if there is a positive excess supply of any good in equilibrium, we expect it to have a zero price. The second complementary-slackness condition says that if the wage is positive ($\lambda_i^* > 0$) in either country, then that country's supply of labor will equal its demand for labor. Again, this result seems to be economically quite reasonable.

These implications of the duality theorem and the complementary-slackness theorem are quite interesting and useful, but they are not exactly Ricardo's results. They are important implications of the Ricardian model, but they are not the implications that Ricardo obtained in 1817. Ricardo was specifically concerned with the case of two countries that had different climates and/or soil fertility, so that the labor coefficients in the two countries were different. Without loss of generality, we assume that the ratio of the amount of labor required to produce one unit of good x to the labor required to produce one unit of good y is lower in country 1 than in country 2. Thus in terms of our simple Ricardian model, we consider the special case of $a_{x1}/a_{y1} < a_{x2}/a_{y2}$. Under such circumstances, we say that country 1 has a **comparative advantage** in the production of good x and (therefore) country 2 has a **comparative advantage** in the production of good y. Ricardo's examples were England and Portugal, with the two goods being cloth and wine; Portugal had a comparative advantage in wine, and England a comparative advantage in cloth.

In addition to these assumptions regarding comparative advantage, Ricardo restricted the prices of the goods. He assumed that the price ratio p_x/p_y was strictly between the two labor coefficient ratios of the two countries. Thus given our assumption that country 1 has the comparative advantage in x, the Ricardian price ratio assumption is given by

$$\frac{a_{x1}}{a_{y1}} < \frac{p_x}{p_y} < \frac{a_{x2}}{a_{y2}}. \tag{9.57}$$

Ricardo's main result is called the **Ricardian theory of comparative advantage;** it says that each country will **completely specialize** in the production of the good in which it enjoys a comparative advantage. Thus in his example of England and Portugal, Ricardo argued that England would completely specialize in (produce only) cloth, while Portugal would completely specialize in (produce only) wine.

To obtain Ricardo's result from our model, first note that complementary slackness implies that zero outputs of both goods cannot be optimal for either country. This is because $x_i^* = 0$ and $y_i^* = 0$ imply that $\lambda_i^* = 0$ by the complementary-slackness conditions. This is a contradiction to the feasibility of λ_i^* for the dual problem, since $p_x > 0$ and $p_y > 0$. Thus both countries must produce a positive amount of at least one good. Now consider the inequality on the left-hand side of Ricardo's restriction (9.57),

$$\frac{p_y}{a_{y1}} < \frac{p_x}{a_{x1}}. \tag{9.58}$$

But we know from the feasibility of λ_1^* that $p_x/a_{x1} \le \lambda_1^*$; thus $p_y/a_{y1} < \lambda_1^*$. By the complementary-slackness conditions, the latter inequality implies that $y_1^* = 0$. Since both outputs cannot be zero, we have that $y_1^* = 0$ and $x_1^* > 0$. A similar argument shows that $y_2^* > 0$ and $x_2^* = 0$ under the Ricardian assumption (9.57). Thus, as Ricardo argued, each country will completely specialize in the production of the good in which it has a comparative advantage.

PROBLEMS

9.1 For the two-good consumer choice problem in (9.24), analyze the case of $x_1^* = 0$ and $x_2^* > 0$. What must be true regarding the relationship between the *MRS* and the price ratio if $x_1^* = 0$ and $x_2^* > 0$ is the solution?

9.2 For the two-good consumer choice problem in (9.24), analyze the case of $U_1 < 0$ and $U_2 > 0$ (good 2 is a "good," but good 1 is a "bad"). Use Kuhn–Tucker theory to discuss the optimal consumption of these two goods. Does your answer make economic sense?

9.3 For the two-good consumer choice problem in (9.24), analyze the case of $U_1 = U_2$ and $U_i > 0$ for $i = 1, 2$. Use Kuhn–Tucker theory to prove that in this case $p_2 > p_1$ implies $x_1^* > 0$ and $x_2^* = 0$. Draw a diagram to demonstrate your result.

9.4 The inequality form of the cost minimization problem for a firm that uses two inputs x_1 and x_2 to produce output $\bar{y} > 0$ is

$$\underset{(x_1, x_2)}{\text{Min}} \ TC = w_1 x_1 + w_2 x_2$$

$$\text{Subject to: } \bar{y} \leq f(x_1, x_2),$$

$$x_1 \geq 0,$$

$$x_2 \geq 0,$$

where $w = (w_1, w_2) > 0$ is the wage vector and f is the production function. For the particular production function $y = f(x_1, x_2) = x_1 + x_2$, use Kuhn–Tucker theory to find x_1^* and x_2^* for $w_1 > w_2$ and $w_2 > w_1$. Draw diagrams demonstrating your answers.

9.5 Consider the following monopolist:

$$P = -Q + 8 \qquad \text{Demand}$$

$$Q = L^{1/2} K^{1/2} \qquad \text{Production function}$$

Verify that this firm **exhibits the A-J effect** when $v = 1$, $w = 1$, and $s = 2$. [Solve the problem in (9.34) for L^* and K^*, compute y^*, solve the cost minimization problem for $y = y^*$ to find the cost-minimizing solutions L_0 and K_0, and show that $K^*/L^* > K_0/L_0$.]

9.6 For the monopoly firm under rate-of-return regulation (9.34), show that an increase in the allowable rate of return will **reduce** the capital stock employed (i.e., show that $\partial K^*/\partial s < 0$).

9.7 It is sometimes argued that monopolists maximize revenue (sales) instead of profit. A revenue-maximizing firm using two inputs labor L and capital K would maximize $R(L, K)$ in (9.31) instead of profit $\pi(L, K)$ in (9.32). Repeat the Kuhn–Tucker analysis of the behavior of a monopoly under fair-rate-of-return regulation for the case of a revenue-maximizing firm. Does the A-J effect hold in this case as well? Discuss the economic implications of your result.

9.8 Often a time constraint is associated with the consumption of certain goods as well as a budget constraint. Consider the consumer purchasing two goods x_1 and x_2 with utility function $U(x_1, x_2) = x_1 x_2$ that faces **both** a time constraint and a budget constraint. The time constraint is

$$T \geq t_1 x_1 + t_2 x_2,$$

where t_1 and t_2 are the amounts of time necessary to consume one unit of each good and T is the total time available. The second constraint is the standard budget constraint,

$$M \geq p_1 x_1 + p_2 x_2,$$

where p_1 and p_2 are the prices and M is money income.

Assuming the optimal consumption of the two goods is strictly positive ($x_1^* > 0$ and $x_2^* > 0$) use Kuhn–Tucker theory to derive x_1^* and x_2^* for $p_1 = 1$, $p_2 = 2$, $M = 40$, $t_1 = 1$, $t_2 = 1$, and $T = 24$. After you have found the solution, draw a diagram to demonstrate your result. Are both constraints binding?

9.9 An economy produces only two goods, x and y, by means of production functions

$$x = f(L_x, K_x) \quad \text{and} \quad y = g(L_y, K_y),$$

where L_i is the amount of labor used in the production of good i and K_i is the amount of capital used in the production of good i. Let the total labor be constrained by $\bar{L} \geq L_x + L_y$ and the total capital be constrained by $\bar{K} \geq K_x + K_y$. In such an economy, **efficiency in production** would require that the output of any one good be as large as possible without decreasing the output of the other good. Thus if $\bar{y}$ is the initial output of good y, then the efficiency problem is given by:

$$\underset{(L_x, K_x)}{\text{Max}} \ x = f(L_x, K_x)$$

$$\text{Subject to: } g(L_y, K_y) \geq \bar{y},$$

$$L_x + L_y \leq \bar{L},$$

$$K_x + K_y \leq \bar{K},$$

$$L_x \geq 0, \qquad L_y \geq 0,$$

$$K_x \geq 0, \qquad K_y \geq 0.$$

Set up the Lagrangian and use the Kuhn–Tucker conditions to demonstrate that when all inputs have positive marginal products and positive amounts of both inputs are used in the production of both goods, efficiency in production requires the marginal rate of technical substitution (*MRTS*) of L for K to be the same in the production of x as it is in the production of y.

9.10 An economy has two individuals, a and b. Each individual has a certain positive income, M_a for individual a and M_b for individual b, that is allocated between consumption of a private good x and donation to the public as g. Thus the budget constraints for the two individuals are

$$M_a \geq x_a + g_a,$$

$$M_b \geq x_b + g_b. \tag{1}$$

Let the utility functions of the two individuals be given by

$$U_a(x_a, G) = x_a + \ln G,$$

$$U_b(x_b, G) = x_b + \beta \ln G, \tag{2}$$

where $G = g_a + g_b = $ total amount of the public good and $\beta < 1$. Notice that G is a "public good"; each individual gets utility not from what is donated, but rather from the total amount available.

Let both individuals behave in a Cournot–Nash way with respect to each other's contribution to the public good; a assumes that b will not change his or her public good contribution in response to a change in a's own contribution, and vice versa. Thus in the language of the Cournot model, $\partial G / \partial g_i = 1$ for $i = a, b$. A Cournot–Nash equilibrium for this economy is a set of private good consumption levels $x_a^* > 0$ and $x_b^* > 0$, as well as a set of public good contribution levels $g_a^* \geq 0$ and $g_b^* \geq 0$, such that each individual is simultaneously maximizing the utility function in (2) subject to the budget constraint in (1).

Use Kuhn–Tucker theory to prove that individual b is a **free rider** in **Cournot–Nash equilibrium.**

9.11 Consider the problem faced by a macroeconomic policy maker (e.g., a country's central bank) who can control the level of real national income Y and the rate of inflation π via various policy instruments. Since higher real output is a "good" and higher inflation is a "bad," we can model the behavior of such a policy maker as maximizing a utility function $U(Y, \pi)$ with $\partial U/\partial Y = U_Y > 0$ and $\partial U/\partial \pi = U_\pi < 0$. The constraint for such a policy maker is the trade-off between inflation and unemployment: the short-run Phillips curve. If $\bar{Y} > 0$ is the full-employment (or natural) level of real income, then the short-run Phillips curve can be written as

$$\pi = \gamma(Y - \bar{Y}) + \pi^e,$$

where π^e is the expected rate of inflation and γ is the responsiveness of the inflation rate to levels of output higher than the natural rate (i.e., γ is the slope of the short-run Phillips curve). Given this constraint, the policy maker's choice problem can be written as:

$$\text{Max}_{(Y,\pi)} U(Y, \pi)$$

$$\text{Subject to: } \pi = \gamma(Y - \bar{Y}) + \pi^e,$$

$$Y \geq 0, \qquad \pi \geq 0.$$

(a) Provide an economic interpretation of the short-run Phillips curve. What does it look like in (Y, π)-space? What does it say about full employment $(Y = \bar{Y})$ and correct expectations $(\pi = \pi^e)$?

(b) Set up the Lagrangian and write out the Kuhn–Tucker conditions for the policy maker's problem.

(c) Solve the Kuhn–Tucker conditions to find $Y^* > 0$ and $\pi^* > 0$ for the particular case of $U(Y, \pi) = Y - \pi^2$.

(d) Sign the comparative statics terms $(\partial Y^*/\partial \gamma, \partial \pi^*/\partial \pi^e, \text{etc.})$ for the case in (c).

(e) Interpret each of the terms in (d). Do they make macroeconomic sense?

(f) Sketch a few indifference curves for the case in (c) and verify your answers in (e) for some arbitrary parameter values.

9.12 Suppose that the problem in (9.46) has only two constraints, one for land T and one for labor L. So it can be written

$$\text{Max}_{(x,y)} GDP = p_x x + p_y y$$

$$\text{Subject to: } a_{Tx} x + a_{Ty} y \leq \bar{T},$$

$$a_{Lx} x + a_{Ly} y \leq \bar{L},$$

$$x \geq 0, \qquad y \geq 0.$$

For such an economy, the **Rybczynski theorem** says that if the supply of some resource increases, then the industry using that resource most intensively will increase its output while the other industry will decrease its output.

Use Kuhn–Tucker theory to **prove** the Rybczynski theorem under the assumption that

$$\frac{a_{Tx}}{a_{Ty}} < \frac{p_x}{p_y} < \frac{a_{Lx}}{a_{Ly}},$$

and draw a diagram to demonstrate your result.

9.13 Consider the following variant of the *GDP* maximization problem in (9.47):

$$\underset{(x,y,z)}{\text{Max }} GDP = 3x + 4y + 3z$$

$$\text{Subject to: } x + y + 3z \le 12,$$

$$2x + 4y + z \le 42,$$

$$x \ge 0, \qquad y \ge 0, \qquad z \ge 0.$$

The economy produces three goods (x, y, and z), and there are only two resource constraints. Solve this problem for the optimal outputs of the three goods (x^*, y^*, z^*).

9.14 The **Stolper–Samuelson theorem** says that if the price of the good that is most labor-intensive increases, then the price of labor will increase, and it will increase proportionately more than the initial rise in the price of the output.

Prove the Stolper–Samuelson theorem for the model in Problem 9.12. [Set up the dual to the *GDP* maximization in Problem 9.12 with λ_L and λ_T as the dual variables. Show that under the assumptions in Problem 9.12, $\partial\lambda_L^*/\partial p_x > 0$ and $(p_x/\lambda_L^*)(\partial\lambda_L^*/\partial p_x) > 1$.]

9.15 Recall the particular *GDP* maximization problem in (9.47). Set up the dual to this problem and use the duality theorems of linear programming to find the solution to the dual $\lambda^* = (\lambda_1^*, \lambda_2^*, \lambda_3^*)$.

9.16 Consider the following world welfare maximization problem for the Ricardian international trade model given in the chapter:

$$\underset{(x_1,x_2,y_1,y_2)}{\text{Max }} p_x(x_1 + x_2) + p_y(y_1 + y_2)$$

$$\text{Subject to: } a_{x1}x_1 + a_{y1}y_1 \le L_1,$$

$$a_{x2}x_2 + a_{y2}y_2 \le L_2,$$

$$x_1 \ge 0, \qquad x_2 \ge 0, \qquad y_1 \ge 0, \qquad y_2 \ge 0.$$

Show that the solution to this world welfare maximization problem is the same as the solution to the maximization problems of the two countries (9.55) behaving independently.

9.17 Consider the two-good consumer choice problem (9.24) for the case where

$$U(x_1, x_2) = (x_1 + 1)(x_2 + 1).$$

Use Kuhn–Tucker theory to find the demand functions x_1^* and x_2^* for all three cases: (a) $x_1^* > 0$ and $x_2^* = 0$; (b) $x_1^* = 0$ and $x_2^* > 0$; and (c) $x_1^* > 0$ and $x_2^* > 0$. Find restrictions on the parameters that would generate cases (a) and (b).

9.18 **Peak load pricing.** Let there be n outputs $x = (x_1, x_2, \ldots, x_n) \in \mathfrak{R}_+^n$, where each output has the demand function $p^i(x_i)$ with $dp^i/dx_i < 0$ and constant marginal cost $c_i > 0$ for all $i = 1, 2, \ldots, n$. Let the capacity output for each good be given by $y = (y_1, y_2, \ldots, y_n) \in \mathfrak{R}_{++}^n$ so that each output is constrained by $x_i \le y_i$ for all $i = 1, 2, \ldots, n$ with

$$x_i = y_i \text{ at full capacity (peak period)}$$

and

$$x_i < y_i \text{ at less than full capacity (off-peak period)}.$$

The welfare (W_i) or consumer's surplus for each good i is given by

$$W_i(x_i) = \int_0^{x_i} p^i(\tau_i) \, d\tau_i - c_i x_i,$$

so the total welfare is given by $W(x)$:

$$W(x) = \sum_{i=1}^{n} W_i(x_i) = \sum_{i=1}^{n} \left[\int_0^{x_i} p^i(\tau_i) \, d\tau_i - c_i x_i \right].$$

Thus the peak load pricing problem is given by:

$$\underset{\{x\}}{\text{Max}}\, W(x) = \sum_{i=1}^{n} \left[\int_0^{x_i} p^i(\tau_i) \, d\tau_i - c_i x_i \right]$$

Subject to: $x_i \leq y_i$

and $x_i \geq 0$ for all $i = 1, 2, \ldots, n$.

(a) Write out the Lagrangian for this problem.
(b) Write out the Kuhn–Tucker conditions for a solution at $x^* = (x_1^*, x_2^*, \ldots, x_n^*)$.
(c) Find the **peak load pricing rule** (i.e., find the optimal p^i for x_i in the peak period, and find the optimal p^i for x_i in an off-peak period). You may assume that $x_i^* > 0$ for all $i = 1, 2, \ldots, n$.
(d) Discuss your answers from (c) in terms of marginal cost pricing (i.e., the relationship between the optimal p^i and c_i).

NOTES

1. Actually these conditions are necessary for the constrained case only if an additional restriction is imposed on the problem. The additional restriction is a "constraint qualification" that rules out problematic boundary irregularities in the constraint. Since this additional restriction can be mathematically quite complex, and since the economic structure of many problems guarantees that it is satisfied, we do not explicitly discuss the constraint qualification. The interested reader is referred to Takayama (1985, pp. 90–104) for a more formal presentation of the topic.

2. The comment in note 1 regarding the constraint qualification applies here as well. For this reason, when we use the term **Kuhn–Tucker conditions,** or refer to the conditions in (9.16), we are always assuming that the appropriate constraint qualification is met for the problem being considered.

3. See Takayama (1985, pp. 72–3), for instance.

4. The effect is named after the authors of the original paper in which it was presented: Averch and Johnson (1962). Our analysis borrows heavily from Baumol and Klevorick (1970).

5. The classic text Luenberger (1973) contains a detailed discussion of such computational techniques.

REFERENCES

Averech, H., and L. L. Johnson. 1962. Behavior of the firm under regulatory constraint. *American Economic Review* 52: 1053–69.

Baumol, W. J., and A. K. Klevorick. 1970. Input choices and rate-of-return regulation: An overview of the discussion. *The Bell Journal of Economics and Management Science* 1: 162–90.

Berman, A., and R. J. Plemmons. 1979. *Non-negative matrices in the mathematical sciences.* New York: Academic Press.

Burmeister, E. 1980. *Capital theory and dynamics.* Cambridge: Cambridge University Press.

Burmeister, E., and A. R. Dobell. 1970. *Mathematical theories of economic growth.* New York: Macmillan.

Cagan, P. 1956. The monetary dynamics of hyperinflation. In *Studies in the Quantity Theory of Money,* edited by M. Friedman. Chicago: University of Chicago Press.

Debreu, G. 1952. Definite and semidefinite quadratic forms. *Econometrica* 20: 295–300.

Domar, E. D. 1946. Capital expansion, rate of growth and employment. *Econometrica* 14: 137–47.

———. 1947. Expansion and employment. *American Economic Review* 37: 34–55.

Dorfman, R., P. A. Samuelson, and R. M. Solow. 1958. *Linear programming and economic analysis.* New York: McGraw-Hill.

Friedman, M. 1953. The Marshallian demand curve. In *Essays in positive economics.* Chicago: University of Chicago Press, 47–99.

Gale, D., and H. Nikaido. 1965. The Jacobian matrix and global univalence of mappings. *Mathematische Annalen* 159: 81–93.

Hahn, F. H. 1966. Equilibrium dynamics with heterogeneous capital goods. *Quarterly Journal of Economics* 89: 633–46.

Harrod, R. F. 1939. An essay in dynamic theory. *Economic Journal* 49: 14–33.

Hawkins, D., and H. A. Simon. 1949. Note: Some conditions of macroeconomic stability. *Econometrica* 17: 245–48.

Hicks, J. R. 1939. Mr. Keynes and the "classics": A suggested interpretation. *Econometrica* 5: 147–59.

———. 1980. IS-LM: An explanation. *Journal of Post-Keynesian Economics* 3: 139–54.

Hirsch, M. W., and S. Smale. 1974. *Differential equations, dynamical systems, and linear algebra.* New York: Academic Press.

Knight, F. H. 1971. *Risk, uncertainty and profit.* Chicago: University of Chicago Press.

Kuhn, H. W., and A. W. Tucker. 1951. Nonlinear programming. In *Proceedings of the Second Berkeley Symposium on Mathematical Statistics and Probability,* edited by J. Neyman. Berkeley: University of California Press, 481–92.

Luenberger, D. G. 1973. *Introduction to linear and nonlinear programming.* Reading, MA: Addison-Wesley.

———. 1979. *Introduction to dynamic systems.* New York: Wiley.

Mas-Colell, A. 1985. *The theory of general economic equilibrium: A differentiable approach.* Cambridge: Cambridge University Press.

Mas-Colell, A., M. D. Whinston, and J. R. Green. 1995. *Microeconomic theory.* New York: Oxford University Press.

McKenzie, L. W. 1967. The inversion of cost functions: A counterexample. *International Economic Review* 8: 271–78.

Murata, Y. 1977. *Mathematics for stability and optimization of economic systems.* New York: Academic Press.

Panik, M. J. 1976. *Classical optimization: Foundations and extensions.* Amsterdam: North-Holland.

Rader, T. 1968. Normally, factor inputs are never gross substitutes. *Journal of Political Economy* 76: 38–43.

Samuelson, P. A. 1942. Constancy of the marginal utility of income. In *Studies in mathematical economics and econometrics,* edited by O. Lange, F. McIntyre, and O. T. Yntema. Chicago: University of Chicago Press, 75–91.

———. 1948. *Foundations of economic analysis.* Cambridge, MA: Harvard University Press.

Slutsky, E. 1952. On the theory of the budget of the consumer. In *Readings in price theory,* edited by G. Stigler and K. E. Boulding. Chicago: Irwin, 27–57.

Solow, R. M. 1956. A contribution to the theory of economic growth. *Quarterly Journal of Economics* 70: 65–94.

Takayama, A. 1985. *Mathematical economics.* 2d ed. Cambridge: Cambridge University Press.

Varian, H. R. 1992. *Microeconomic analysis.* 3d ed. New York: Norton.

Von Neumann, J., and O. Morgenstern. 1944. *Theory of games and economic behavior.* Princeton, NJ: Princeton University Press.

ANSWERS TO
SELECTED PROBLEMS

■ ■ ■

Chapter 1

1. (a) $MR = 0$.

   (b) The function is undefined for $Q = 0$.

3. (a) $MR = [(1 + a)/a](Q/A)^{1/a}$.

   (b) $a = 1$ implies $MR = 0$,

   $a < 1$ implies $MR > 0$,

   $a > 1$ implies $MR < 0$.

5. (a) $\varepsilon_{M,\pi} = -\alpha\pi$.

   (b) $\pi = 1/\alpha$.

7. $\varepsilon_{x,p_x} = -1, \varepsilon_{x,M} = 1$.

9. $dAVC/dy > 0$ implies $a > 0$ ($dMC/dy > 0$ implies $a > 0$ also).

   $dMC/dy = 0$ implies $y = -b/3a$.

   $dAVC/dy = 0$ implies $y = -b/2a$.

   $MC > 0$ at $y = -b/3a$ implies $c > b^2/3a$.

   $AC > 0$ at $y = -b/2a$ implies $c > b^2/4a$.

11. (a) $-m/(1 - m)$.

    (b) 1.

13. $P = 56$.

15. $Q^* = (c - a)/2b, P^* = (c + a)/2$.

17. $L^* = 3$.

19. (a) $x^* = (M/p_x) - 1$, $y^* = p_x/p_y$.

    (b) $\varepsilon_{x, p_x} = -M/(M - p_x)$, $\varepsilon_{x, p_y} = 0$, $\varepsilon_{x, M} = M/(M - p_x)$.

       $\varepsilon_{y, p_y} = -1$, $\varepsilon_{y, p_x} = 1$, $\varepsilon_{y, M} = 0$.

    (c) $p_x = 0$.

23. Elasticity of labor supply must be positive and greater than $(1 - t)/t$.

Chapter 2

1. (a) $U_1 = x_2$, $U_2 = x_1$, $U_{11} = U_{22} = 0$, $U_{12} = U_{21} = 1$, $MRS = x_2/x_1$,

      no diminishing MU, and goods are complements.

    (b) $U_1 = \frac{1}{2}x_1^{1/2}$, $U_2 = \frac{1}{2}x_2^{1/2}$, $U_{11} = -\frac{1}{4}x_1^{3/2}$, $U_{22} = -\frac{1}{4}x_2^{3/2}$,

      $U_{12} = U_{21} = 0$, $MRS = x_1^{1/2}/x_2^{1/2}$, diminishing MU,

      unrelated with respect to the utility function.

    (c) $U_1 = x_2^{2/3}/3x_1^{2/3}$, $U_2 = x_1^{1/3}/3x_2^{1/3}$,

      $U_{11} = -2x_2^{2/3}/9x_1^{5/3}$, $U_{22} = -2x_1^{1/3}/9x_2^{4/3}$,

      $U_{12}U_{21} = 2/9x_1^{2/3}x_2^{1/3}$, $MRS = x_2/x_1$,

      diminishing MU and complements with respect to the utility function.

5. Yes.

7. (a) Yes, $r = a + b$.

    (b) No.

    (c) Yes, $r = 1 + a + b$.

9. (a) $f(\lambda x) = \lambda^r f(x) \Rightarrow [f(\lambda x)]^{1/r} = \lambda [f(x)]^{1/r} \Rightarrow \psi(\lambda x) = \lambda \psi(x)$.

    (b) Let $f(\lambda x) = \lambda^r f(x)$ for some r and for all $\lambda > 0$ and for all x. Suppose $f(0) = a$ when $a \neq 0$. Now choose $a \neq 0$ and $\lambda \neq 1$; then we have $f(\lambda x) = \lambda^r f(x)$ so $f(0) = \lambda^r f(0)$ or $a = \lambda^r a$. Thus if $a \neq 0$, we have $\lambda^r = 1$ or $\lambda = 1$, which is a contradiction.

11. (a) 1.

    (b) $1/(1 - p)$.

13. $\varepsilon_{x_i, p_i} = -1$.

15. (a) h.d. $r = 2$.

    (b) h.d. $r = \frac{1}{4}$.

    (c) h.d. $r = -1$.

17. (a) Linear through the origin.

    (b) $\varepsilon_{1M} = \varepsilon_{2M} = 1$.

19. (a) $x_i = L_i^{1/(1-a_i)} = L_i^{b_i}$, where $b_i = 1/(1 - a_i)$.

    (b) $f'(L_i) = b_i L_i^{b_i - 1}$.

    (c) $f''(L_i) = b_i(b_i - 1)L_i^{b_i - 2} < 0$ when $0 < b_i < 1$.

(d) $x_2 = \left(\bar{L} - x_1^{1/b_1}\right)^{b_2}$.

(e) $dx_2/dx_1 = -(b_2/b_1)x_1^{(1-b_1)/b_1}\left(\bar{L} - x_1^{1/b_1}\right)^{b_2-1}$.

21. $MRS^A = MU_x^A/MU_y^A = y_A/x_A$.

$MRS^B = MU_x^B/MU_y^B = y_B/x_B = (\bar{y} - y_A)/(\bar{x} - x_A)$.

Contract curve is where

$MRS^A = MRS^B = y_A/x_A = (\bar{y} - y_A)/(\bar{x} - x_A)$ or $y_A = (\bar{y}/\bar{x})x_A$.

Chapter 3

1. $-100 < \alpha < 100$.

3. (a) $\partial Y^*/\partial p < 0$ and $\partial r^*/\partial p > 0$.

   (b) AD slopes downward in (Y, p)-space.

5. (a) $TC(y; w, v) = (wy^2/16) + v\bar{K}$.

   (b) $ATC = (wy/16) + v\bar{K}/y$, $VC = wy^2/16$,

   $AVC = wy/16$, $MC = wy/8$.

   (c) $P = MC$ implies $y^* = 8\,p/w$ (same answer as other approaches).

7. (a) $dR/dy - dC/dy = 0$ and $d^2R/dy^2 - d^2C/dy^2 < 0$.

   (b) $\partial y^*/\partial A > 0$.

9. (a) $L^* = (p/w) - 1$, $K^* - (p/v)$ 1.

   (b) Yes.

   (c) Yes, homogeneous of degree 0.

   (d) $\partial L^*/\partial w = -p/w^2$, $\partial L^*/\partial v = 0$, $\partial L^*/\partial p = 1/w$,

   $\partial K^*/\partial v = -p/v^2$, $\partial K^*/\partial w = 0$, $\partial K^*/\partial p = 1/v$.

   (e) $\pi^* = p\left[\ln(p/w) + \ln(p/v)\right] - 2p + w + v$.

   (f) Yes.

11. (a) $L^* = b^2v^2/4(aw + av + wv)^2$, $K^* = b^2w^2/4(aw + av + wv)^2$.

13. $\partial y^*/\partial p = \left(-f_{KK}f_L^2 + 2f_{LK}f_Lf_K - f_{LL}f_K^2\right)/p\left(f_{LL}f_{KK} - f_{LK}^2\right)$.

    yes it can be signed $(\partial y/\partial p > 0)$.

15. (a) $q_1^* = 10$ and $q_2^* = 5$.

    (b) $Q^* = 15$ and $p^* = 15$.

    (c) $q_1^m = 12.5$ and $q_2^m = 10$.

17. (a) $q_1^* = (a - b)/3$ and $q_2^* = (a - b)/3$.

    (b) $Q^* = 2(a - b)/3$ and $P^* = (2b + a)/3$.

    (c) $\partial q_1^*/\partial b - \partial q_2^*/\partial b = -1/3$.

19. Profit of each firm in Cournot equilibrium is $\pi_i = (a - b)^2/(n + 1)^2 - c$, and the monopoly profit is $\pi_m = (a - b)^2/4 - c$, thus $\pi_i > \pi_m/n$.

21. No, the Cournot model does not exhibit rational or consistent conjectures. Each firm continues to assume that the other firm will not change its output when in fact each observes the other firm doing so.

23. $\partial r^*/\partial M^s = 0$ and $\partial p^*/\partial M^s = p/M^s$; the responsiveness of the price level to a change in the money supply is unit elastic, so an x percent change in M^s causes an x percent change in p.

25. $q_1^* = b/4$ and $q_2^* = b/2$.

Chapter 4

1. (a) $TC = 50y + 10y^2 - 3y^3 + 575$.

   (b) $TC = 75y - 18y^2 + 4y^3 + 50$.

3. $U(x) = v(x) + M - px$,

   $U'(x) = v'(x) - p = 0$ implies $p(x) = v'(x)$,

   $$CS(x_0) = \int_0^{x_0} p(x)\,dx - p(x_0)x_0 = \int_0^{x_0} v'(x)\,dx - p(x_0)x_0$$

   $$= v(x_0) - p(x_0)x_0 = U(x_0) - M.$$

5. (a) $x^* = 1/4p^2$ and $y^* = M - 1/4p$.

   (b) $U(x^*, y^*) = \frac{81}{8}$.

   (c) $CS(x^*) = \frac{1}{8}$.

   (d) $CS(x^*) = \frac{1}{8}$, $M = 10$, and $U(x^*, y^*) = \frac{81}{8}$.

7. (a) $t^* = \$96.67$.

   (b) $q_f^* = 35.56$, $q_d^* = 122.22$, $Q^* = 157.78$, $P^* = 142.22$.

9. $\$14,281.92$ at $r = 0.06$,

   $\$11,645.92$ at $r = 0.08$.

11. $\$34,651$.

13. $\$42,730.40$.

15. 7.46%.

17. $[p\dot{x} - C(Y^*)]/px(t^*) = r$; the rate of growth in the value of the forest net of maintenance cost is equal to the interest rate.

19. $Re^{-rT^*} = C'(T^*)$; the optimal life of the machine is the point at which the present value of increased durability is equal to the marginal cost of durability.

Chapter 5

1. $\dot{m} = (p\dot{M} - M\dot{p})/p^2 = (M/p)(\dot{m}/m - \dot{p}/p) = (M/p)(\theta - \pi)$, so $\dot{m}/m = \theta - \pi$.

3. $dk^*/dn = k^*/[sf'(k^*) - n] < 0$,

   $dk^*/ds = -f(k^*)/[sf'(k^*) - n] > 0$.

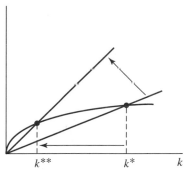 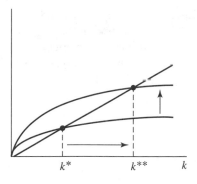

5. $p^* > 0$ requires $d - b < 0$.

7. (b) $\partial p^*/\partial t = -D_t/(D_p - S_p) > 0,$
   $\partial p^*/\partial c = S_c/(D_p - S_p) > 0,$
   $\partial Q^*/\partial t = -D_t S_p/(D_p - S_p) > 0,$
   $\partial Q^*/\partial c = D_p S_c/(D_p - S_p) < 0.$

   (d) No.

   (e) Yes, all the comparative statics are the same except for $\partial Q^*/\partial c$, which is now positive.

9. (a) Yes.

   (b) Yes.

   (c) Yes.

   (d) $p_1^* = \frac{3}{11},\ p_2^* = \frac{19}{11}.$

   (e) The system is stable.

11. (a) Slopes upward.

    (b) Slopes downward.

    (c)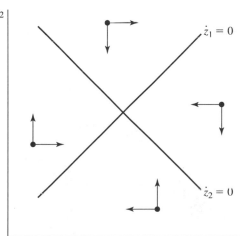

(d) Since good 2 is a substitute for good 1 and good 1 is a complement to good 2, a reduction in the price of good 1 will increase the demand for good 2, thus raising the price of good 2; this in turn increases the demand for good 1, moving its price back upward.

13. (a) $Y* = 100$, $K* = 10$.

(b)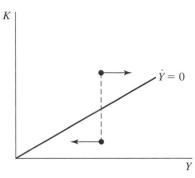

(c)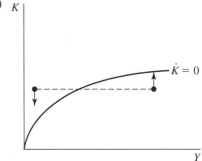

(d) It is stable.

Chapter 6

1. (a) NP matrix.

(b) P matrix.

(c) Neither.

(d) Neither.

3. If f is homogeneous of degree 1, then the f_i are all homogeneous of degree 0, so $[Hf]x = 0$; thus $|Hf| = 0$.

5. (a) $Y* = \dfrac{e(I_0 + D) + M^s(a - c)/p}{be + f(a - c)}.$

$r* = \dfrac{bM^s/p - f(I_0 + D)}{be + f(a - c)}.$

(b) $\dfrac{\partial Y^*}{\partial D} = \dfrac{e}{de + f(a - c)}$.

$\dfrac{\partial Y^*}{\partial M^s} = \dfrac{a - c}{p[de + f(a - c)]}$.

$\dfrac{\partial r^*}{\partial D} = \dfrac{-f}{de + f(a - c)}$.

$\dfrac{\partial r^*}{\partial M^s} = \dfrac{b}{p[de + f(a - c)]}$.

(c) They are consistent.

7. Since both $z_1 = 0$ and $z_2 = 0$ slope upward in the *GS* case, local uniqueness (at p^*) implies global uniqueness. Since *GS* implies that the Jacobian of the system is positive (5.34), the excess demand function is locally invertible and so local uniqueness is guaranteed.

9. Relationship (1) depends on $dP/dQ = 1/(dQ/dP)$, which requires the invertibility of $Q = f(P)$. But since $dP/dQ = -2(10 - Q)$, we have $dP/dQ = 0$ at $Q = 10$. Thus the function is not invertible at $Q = 10$.

11. (a) 2.

(b) $(p_1^*, p_2^*) = (2, 2)$.

(c) $(p_1^*, p_2^*) = (2.26, 1.80)$. The price of the more labor-intensive good has increased.

13. By Cramer's rule, x_1^* is the ratio of two P matrices.

15. If A is productive, then $B = I - A$ is a P matrix, but then $-B$ is an NP matrix. Since $C = A - I = -B$, matrix C is an NP matrix, and since it is symmetric, it is negative definite.

17. $3 < 2ALK/B < 5$.

Chapter 7

1. $\Delta x_1 = 587$, $\Delta x_2 = 617$.

3. All four comparative statics terms are positive.

5. Since the excess demand functions are h.d. 0, by Euler's theorem $|Jz(p^*)| = 0$, and the fundamental comparative statics equation (7.18) does not have a solution.

7. $\partial \pi^*/\partial p = \sum_{i=1}^{n} (pf_i - w_i)\partial x_i^*/\partial p + f(x^*) = y^*$, since $pf_i - w_i = 0$ for all i by the first-order conditions.

9. Direct implication of Hotelling's lemma.

11. This result follows immediately from the answer to Problem 7.10 and the fact that input demand functions $x_i^*(w, p)$ are h.d. 0.

13. Yes, the same conditions hold.

15. (a) $\sum_{i=1}^{n} y_i = na + b \sum_{i=1}^{n} x_i$ and $\sum_{i=1}^{n} x_i y_i = a \sum_{i=1}^{n} x_i + b \sum_{i=1}^{n} x_i^2$.

   (b) Yes.

   (c) From algebraic manipulation of the expression in (a).

Chapter 8

1. Since $\lambda^*(p, M) = U_i[x^*(p, M)]/p_i$ by the first-order conditions and since $x_i^*(p, M)$ is h.d. 0, for all i we have $\lambda^*(\alpha p, \alpha M) = \alpha^{-1}\lambda^*(p, M)$ so λ^* is h.d. -1. The result thus follows from Euler's theorem.

5. (a) $x_i^* = Ma_i/p_i$ for $i = 1, 2, 3$.

   (b) Yes.

   (c) $\partial x_i^*/\partial p_i = -Ma_i/p_i^2 < 0$, $\partial x_i^*/\partial p_j = 0$ for $i \neq j$, and $\partial x_i^*/\partial M = a_i/p_i > 0$.

   (d) $\partial \lambda^*/\partial p_i = 0$, $\partial \lambda^*/\partial M = -1/M^2 < 0$; diminishing marginal utility of money income.

7. Follows immediately from (8.100).

9. (a) Yes.

   (b) $x^2 + y^2 = 4$.

   (c) Yes.

   (d) $x^* = y^* = \sqrt{2}$.

11. (a) $rc_0 + c_1 = re_0 + e_1$.

   (b) $U_0/U_1 = r$.

   (c) $\partial c_0^*/\partial r = -[U_1 - (c_0 - e_0)(U_{01} - rU_{11})]/|D|$,
$\partial c_1^*/\partial r = [rU_1 - (c_0 - e_0)(U_{10} - U_{00})]/|D|$.

   (d) $\partial c_0^*/\partial r < 0$, $\partial c_1^*/\partial r > 0$.

15. (a) $x_1^u = (\bar{U}p_2/p_1)^{1/2}$ and $x_2^u = (\bar{U}p_1/p_2)^{1/2}$.

   (c) $E^u = 2(p_1 p_2 \bar{U})^{1/2}$.

17. (a) $x_1^{*f} = 100\alpha_1$, $x_2^{*f} = 100p_1\alpha_2/p_2$,
$x_1^{*s} = 100p_2\alpha_1/p_1$, $x_2^{*s} = 100\alpha_2$.

   (b) $x_1^* = 100\alpha_1(1 + p_2/p_1)$, $x_2^* = 100\alpha_2(1 + p_1/p_2)$.

   (c) $z_i^* = x_i^* - 100$.

   (d) Yes.

   (e) $p_1^*/p_2^* = \alpha_1/\alpha_2$.

19. (a) $x_1^* = M/2p_1$ and $x_2^* = M/2p_2$.

   (b) Yes.

   (c) $\partial \lambda^*/\partial p_i = 0$ and $\partial \lambda^*/\partial M = -a/M^2$.

21. (a) $K^* = \bar{y}w^{1/2}/2v^{1/2}$ and $L^* = \bar{y}v^{1/2}/2w^{1/2}$.

   (b) $TC + \bar{y}w^{1/2}v^{1/2}$.

(c) $ATC = MC = w^{1/2}v^{1/2}$.

(d) Horizontal ATC and MC, since the production function is h.d. 1.

27. $\partial TC/\partial w_j = \sum_{i=1}^{n} w_i \partial x_i^*/\partial w_j + x_j^* = -\lambda^* \sum_{i=1}^{n} \partial x_i^*/\partial w_j + x_j^*$, but $\sum_{i=1}^{n} f_i \partial x_i^*/\partial w_j = 0$ from the first-order conditions, so $\partial TC/\partial w_j = x_j^*$ for all j.

29. (a) The expression measures the change in expenditure necessary to maintain the same level of utility U_0.

(b) Notice $E^u(p^0, U_0) - E^u(p', U_0) = \int_{p'}^{p^0} [\partial E^u(p, U_0)/\partial p_i] dp_i$. But we also know that $\partial E^u/\partial p_i = x_i^u$, which gives the desired result.

Chapter 9

1. MRS must be less than the price ratio.

3. Proof by manipulation of Kuhn–Tucker conditions.

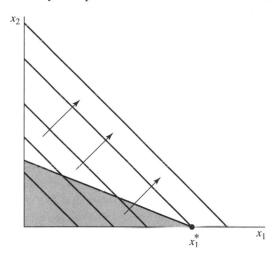

5. $L_0 = K_0 = 3.5$, $K^* = 7$, and $L^* = 1.75$.

7. No, you get the opposite effect for the sales-maximizing case.

11. (c) $Y^* = \bar{Y} + (1 - 2\gamma\pi^e)/(2\gamma^2)$ and $\pi^* = \frac{1}{2}\gamma$.

13. $x^* = 3$, $y^* = 9$, and $z^* = 0$.

15. $\lambda_1^* = 0$, $\lambda_2^* = \frac{2}{5}$, and $\lambda_3^* = \frac{1}{5}$.

INDEX

■ ■ ■